Additional Acclaim for Dominic Streatfeild's *Cocaine*

"A sweeping and highly readable investigation."

—The Boston Phoenix

"A worthy primer to a global problem."

—Miami Herald

"It is a sane and sober review of a vast body of accumulated knowledge dislodged from forgotten archives, obscure texts, government records, definitive histories, and human sources with impeccable credentials."

—The Baltimore Sun

"Well presented . . . Brisk and well researched, *Cocaine* is informed by obscure archives and lost books as well as dynamic first-hand reporting."

—San Diego Union-Tribune

"Thorough, engrossing, balanced, and entertaining, it is important social history in palatable form."

—Booklist

"A definitive history."

—The Sunday Times (London)

"A happy combination of page-turning pace and thought-provoking substance."

—The Independent (London)

"It's a wonderful piece of work! Compelling, complex, clear. The way [Streatfeild] involves [himself] is brilliant. A pacifist, radical, robust fop of a guy without a gun enters into the dark world of Colombia to have tea with the Ochoas while the DEA boys are cleaning their Glocks. A preservation of innocence. Congratulations. Fuck it!"

—George Jung, the real-life subject of the movie and book *Blow*

DOMINIC STREATFEILD

Cocaine

[An Unauthorized Biography]

Picador
New York

www.picadorusa.com

Picador® is a U.S. registered trademark and is used by St. Martin's Press under license from Pan Books Limited.

For information on Picador Reading Group Guides, as well as ordering, please contact the Trade Marketing department at St. Martin's Press.
Phone: 1-800-221-7945 extension 763
Fax: 212-677-7456
E-mail: trademarketing@stmartins.com

Book design by Michael Collica

Library of Congress Cataloging-in-Publication Data

Streatfeild, Dominic.
    Cocaine : an unauthorized biography / Dominic Streatfeild.
        p. cm.
    Originally published: London : Virgin, c2001.
    Includes bibliographical references and index.
    ISBN 0-312-28624-4 (hc)
    ISBN 0-312-42226-1 (pbk)
    1. Cocaine—History. I. Title.
QP801.C68S77 2003
362.29'8'09—dc21   2003041332

First published in Great Britain by Virgin Publishing, Ltd.

First published in the United States by St. Martin's Press

10 9 8 7 6 5

Contents

Acknowledgements

This book relies heavily on personal testimony. Writing it would have been impossible without the assistance of the 150-or-so people who agreed to be interviewed. Due to the nature of the subject matter many interviewees wish to remain anonymous but of those who might appreciate a mention, I would like to thank:

The traffickers: George Jung, Ricky Ross, Allen Long, Magic Eddie, RL, Martin, Meco Dominguez, Luis and the Ochoa family

The scientists: Nora Volkow, Hans Breiter, Fernando Cabieses, David Paly, Sandy Knapp, Brian Humblestone and Nelson Clarke

The academics: Paul Gootenberg, David Musto, Peter Swales, the Freud Museum, Bruce Johnson and Elouise Dunlap at NDRI, Ron Siegel, Baldomero Caceres, Milton Friedman, Warwick Bray, Enrique Tandeter, Albrecht Hirschmuller, Han Israels. Also Kew Gardens, the British Library, Drugscope, the Natural History Museum, UNDCP, the Home Office and the Public Record Office at Kew

The journalists: Gary Webb, Fabio Castillo, Robert Sabbag, Bruce Porter, Clare Hargreaves, Tim Ross, Elizabeth Thornton, Nick Bostock and Naomi Westland

The US Customs Service: Zach Mann, Van Brown, Roger Maier and Lisa Fairchild

The DEA: John Phillips, Harry Fullett, John Coleman, Gene Francar, Aaron Graham, Joe Toft, Jim Nims, Richard Hahner, James Borden, Charles Gutensohn, Robert Nieves, Mike Fredericks, Jerry Strickler, Mike McManus, Richard Meyers, Mark Eissler and James McGiveney. And *Goodfellows.*

USA: Tony Estrada, Floyd Thayer, Jack Blum, Donna Warren, Bill Simpich, ONDCP and the Lindesmith Center

Bolivia: UMOPAR, General Tarifa and FELCN, Evo Morales, General Cespedes and Marcio Alejandro

Colombia: Hugo Martinez, Juan Mayr, Simon Trinidad and the FARC, Maria Ines and Lelo

Peru: ENACO, CORAH, CADA, Fox Sanchez and the Peruvian National Police, Contradrogas, Antonio Brack Egg, Emma Martinez, Moises Saldana Lozano and the villagers of San Jorge

For assistance above and beyond the call of duty I would like to thank: Marcela (I owe you!), Pip Clarke, Justyn Comer, Virginia Martinez, Helen and Liezel. And Rol—who put up with more cocaine-based paranoia than any man ought to. Nothing would have happened without Humphrey, Kirstie and their team. Or Julian Alexander. Or my parents. Thank you.

NOTE: *This is supposed to be a true story. If it's not, it's my fault. Where possible, true names of interviewees and sources are given. In some cases, however, names have been deleted or altered so as to conceal identities and/or locations. Unless attributed, views expressed in the book are my own.*

Introduction

It's going on 4.30 p.m. and the alkaloid has just begun to bite. I am swinging gently from side to side in a hammock, watching a livid orange sun sink into the hills of La Bella Durmiente, headphones on, plugged into a bit of music, thinking about nothing in particular. And suddenly I know—it's working.

Now, I know what you're thinking: 'cocaine' because this is a book about cocaine, right? You're not wrong: it is a book about cocaine. And, if you were to take a sample of my blood, it would test positive. But the thing is, I don't use cocaine. So what's going on?

The first thing you have to understand is that here in the Andes people don't shove cocaine up their noses like smug advertising executives before dabbing up the excess with a finger and rubbing it onto their gums. They don't do it in the toilet. In fact, they don't use cocaine at all. Not really. If you want to get to the cocaine in the Andes, you chew it. And that's what I am doing—or trying to do.

After the best part of a month tooling about South America on the cocaine trail I am in Tingo Maria, Peru, looking for quality product, and I've come to the conclusion that either I am doing something seriously wrong or there is nothing in this chewing thing at all. Could 40 centuries of South American Indians really be wrong? It's possible. All these thoughts go around in my mind as I lie in my hammock, listening to this bit of music, swinging gently from left to right, watching the sun go down.

Then I realise that the tip of my tongue has gone numb. Not numb like after an injection at the dentist (although this would be entirely appropriate) but numb like I've eaten too many peppermints. Tingly. Although I haven't eaten, I'm not hungry. I haven't drunk anything and it's hot, but I'm not thirsty either.

It suddenly occurs to me that sitting here in my hammock is an extremely pleasant way to spend the afternoon. Despite the fact that a dust storm of mosquitoes has mangled my legs and that the *palmito* salad I ate for dinner last passed through my system like an Exocet, compelling me to spend a large percentage of the day perched on the lavatory, I actually feel pretty good. I don't laugh until I feel sick, or talk as if there's no tomorrow, or get up and dance, or fall asleep, or get the urge to reveal to my mates that the real meaning of life is the colour green. None of that. I just lie here.

So here I am lying in my hammock, swinging gently from side to side, and it hits me that this piece of music I'm listening to has exactly the same harmonies as *Rain*, which happens to be the Beatles' greatest-ever B-side. And I'm swinging and swinging and my tongue is feeling numb and my throat is beginning to head that way too and it hits me: I feel all right. Now I *know* that it's the cocaine coming through. Because the thing is this: hammocks are great. But not that great.

It is wholly appropriate that I should finally get the hang of chewing coca here in the Upper Huallaga Valley just north of Huánuco, Peru. Because it was here, tens of thousands of years ago, that cocaine was invented—not by man but by nature. It was here that the pre-Incan tribes discovered it and where it has been grown ever since. It was here that Peru's plantations fuelled the cocaine industry in the late nineteenth century, and then the illicit resurgent industry in the late twentieth century. Huánuco is the heart of Peru's cocaine identity. And thus it's here that I have come, after two years in libraries and prison cells and army bases and more libraries and doctors' surgeries and politicians' offices—and still more libraries—on a hare-brained pilgrimage to seek out the cause of cocaine. And it is here that in my dumb gringo way I have finally got the message.

Cocaine is a sensational drug. There is no more efficient product for delivering pleasure for your cash than cocaine: not fast cars, not expensive clothes, not speedboats. Nothing will make you feel as good. The moment you shove it up your nose it races into your bloodstream, heads directly into the pleasure centre of your brain, kicks down the door, jams your Fun Throttle forwards into 'way too fast' and dumps the clutch. Cocaine doesn't bother about looking, smelling or tasting good. It doesn't have flashy packaging. It doesn't need to.

Real cocaine—by which I mean pure cocaine, not the crap you pick up on the street from a friend of a friend called Malcolm, that's seen more cuts than a budget Japanese feature and leaves you squatting on the lavatory for a week because, ha-ha, one of the cuts was *manitol—real* cocaine is in a different league. Put it this way: this is the drug that, when offered to animals, they will take—to the exclusion of all else including sex, water and food—until they drop dead. No other drug on earth has this effect. It is not possible to buy more fun than cocaine. It is just not possible. William Burroughs called it 'the most exhilarating drug I have ever taken', and, bearing in mind that he spent his entire life taking exhilarating drugs, we should perhaps take his word for it. Cocaine is at the top of the fun pyramid; science has not yet bettered it, and probably never will. And that's the problem: because cocaine is so much fun that users are willing to pay preposterous prices for it. One way or another, most of them do.

While the price of cocaine is high for consumers, it is considerably higher for producers. Here in South America the dangers of the drug are a lot more scary than the occasional perforated nasal septum. The unfeasible amounts of hard currency generated by the drug ricochet around this continent creating casualties wherever they go. In the last 25 years alone, cocaine-generated cash has been responsible for coups d'etat in Bolivia and Honduras; has infiltrated the governments of the Bahamas, Turks and Caicos, Haiti, Cuba, and every single Latin American country without exception; has helped to fund a guerrilla war in Nicaragua (creating one of the most embarrassing scandals in the CIA's history); and has prompted the US invasion of Panama. In the late 1980s, traffickers in Peru and Bolivia were so wealthy that they offered to pay off their countries' national debts; meanwhile Colombia's traffickers were so powerful that they declared war on their own country—and brought it to its knees. At the time of writing, the cocaine industry is creating riots in Peru, policemen are being kidnapped and tortured to death because of it in Bolivia and, if I was a betting man, I would put money on the cocaine industry cranking Colombia's ongoing civil war to its highest levels for the last thirty-six years within the next six months. At this very moment the governments of Peru, Ecuador and Venezuela are stationing troops on their Colombian borders to handle the expected influx of refugees.

All this trouble, just because of cocaine? The drug you take on special occasions, in the lavatory with your mates, when out clubbing? The drug you take because it's a laugh? Crazy, isn't it?

As I lie in my hammock I wonder, what's going on? How can it possibly have come to this? As luck would have it, these are the exact same questions I *didn't* ask myself that day nearly two years earlier when my agent called me out of the blue and asked if I was serious about writing a book on cocaine—and if so, how serious? I had thought about it. The story had obvious appeal: guns, violence, coups, criminals, tons of money, and the glamour and mystique of cocaine itself.

'Pretty serious,' I told him. And I was. I was about to become unemployed again. A couple of weeks later the publisher had insisted we have a glass of champagne to celebrate. We chinked glasses and grinned at each other: it was going to be a great book. He was excited. I was excited. We were both excited. Despite the fact that the sum total of my knowledge of cocaine was a Channel 4 documentary I had researched two years previously, which had never actually got filmed, and a single reading of Charles Nichol's *The Fruit Palace*, which had succeeded in scaring the pants off me, everything had seemed straightforward. No problem.

And so, as I had headed into the British Library on that first day with a fresh publishing contract, a virgin A4 notepad, a pile of pencils and eighteen months ahead of me to excavate everything there was to know about cocaine, I had no clue what I was getting into. When I figured I would have a quick dig into the history before getting to the guns, the money and the false-bottomed suitcases, I was kidding myself. And as I sat in seat 2308, ploughing my way through every book I could find on the subject, the minutes groaning by on the British Library clock (a clock slower than any other in the known universe), it gradually dawned on me that I might just have bitten off more than I could chew. Because the story of cocaine telescopes horribly.

The more I dug, the deeper the problem became and the more digging was required. Because, I discovered, if you want to know about cocaine and where it all started—I mean, if you *really* want to know—you have to go back a long way. Way back before the drug lords and the cartels, before Bush and Panama and the War on Drugs, Noriega, Reagan and the Contra scandal, crack and John Belushi. Before meaningless surveys told you that 99 per cent of all banknotes in circulation carried traces of cocaine, before the yuppie coke boom of the early 1980s, before the wild freebasing of the 1970s. Way back. Before everything. You have to go back to where it all began. You have to go back to one innocuous-looking plant. To coca.

Cocaine

1 Introducing Coca

Erythroxylum coca is a peculiarly ordinary-looking shrub native to South America. Textbooks say that it grows to a height of two to three metres and that once a year it produces small, bright-red, dupe-type seeds, but in fact it is usually no more than a metre or so tall and you are unlikely ever to see it fruit. If you were a gardening expert you might comment that it rather resembles a camellia; that its leaves are elliptical with two distinctive lines running parallel to the midrib on the underside; or that its creamy white flowers look like tiny apple blossoms. If you get close to the leaves you might even notice their aroma: famously described as a cross between freshly mown hay and chocolate. You might—but, then again, you might not.

Experts who have studied it describe *Erythroxylum coca* as 'beautiful', but then experts who study cockroaches describe them as 'beautiful' too, so it probably doesn't count for much. To the layman coca is beautiful only in hindsight. Once you learn about it, what it represents, it acquires a kind of terrible fascination, like things we wish we could uninvent: atom bombs, perhaps, or boy bands.

It's not that coca is ugly. Just unremarkable to look at. To be honest, a less distinctive-looking plant would be hard to find. Imagine a small shrubby bush. If you're imagining something with roughly oval-shaped leaves and a stalk, you've got it. That's coca. It's so anonymous that when you mention it to people they assume you are talking about cocoa, or coconuts, perhaps. You're not. And yet coca has started wars, prompted invasions, embarrassed politicians, toppled governments, filled prisons, created billionaires and bankrupted countries, and both taken and possibly saved thousands of lives. And all this for one simple reason: because *Erythroxylum coca,* a shrub of peculiar ordinariness, is the Earth's leading source of cocaine.

The genus *Erythroxylum* contains some 250 species, most native to

South America and Madagascar. Only two botanists have ever studied the genus in detail; both are dead. What we do know, however, is that many of the members of the 250 species produce cocaine. A 1974 paper analysed 29 *Erythroxylum* species, of which 13 turned out cocaine-positive. Only a handful, however, produce enough cocaine to make it worthwhile to cultivate them commercially, and those all grow in South America. First there's *Erythroxylum coca* variety *coca*. This, the original—and until recently the market leader—is traditionally known as 'Bolivian coca', and it certainly grows well there: in fact last year, some 23,000 tons grew well there.

Then there's *Erythroxylum coca* variety *ipadu*, which grows in the Amazon Basin, where it has been harvested by local tribes for thousands of years. No one used to grow this commercially: its cocaine content is relatively low. In the 1980s, however, as coca plantations spread further afield to counter drug raids, growers hit the Amazon. Since then, *ipadu* has been a player.

Erythroxylum novogranatense variety *novogranatense* was named after Nueva Granada (New Granada, the Spanish colonial name for Colombia), because that's where it grows. This was the first coca ever seen by a white man, and samples were shipped all over the world. Once cocaine was eventually isolated, it became the cornerstone in the world drug industry, when the Dutch East India Company took it to Indonesia. Never really used in the illicit cocaine industry, *novogranatense* also made a big comeback in the mid-1980s when the Colombian cartels decided to stop buying leaves from Bolivia and Peru and to grow them at home. Home growing has turned into a right little earner for them: *novogranatense* currently accounts for some 85 per cent of the world's illicit cocaine.

Finally, there is the most elusive and highly prized of all: *Erythroxylum novogranatense* variety *truxillense*. In its own way, this is the most widespread of all of the cocas—but not for reasons you might think. Commonly known as 'trujillo', it grows only in the remote and dry reaches of desert coasts, usually on the western slopes of the Andes around the town of that name. Thanks to the arid conditions there, trujillo is entirely reliant on man for survival (coca seeds must remain moist if they are to germinate—one reason why most coca grows in wet, humid regions). Its leaves are small, dark, and renowned for their strong flavour and high cocaine yield—the Incas thought *truxillense* was so good that they called it 'Royal Coca'. Unfortunately—or fortunately, depending on your point of view—although there is a lot of cocaine in the leaves, it is hard to extract, so trujillo has never really played a big role in the cocaine industry. Not the illegal cocaine industry, anyway: even today a few big-name companies—companies that might benefit from the fact that trujillo is found only in very remote, out-of-the-way areas—are willing to spirit its leaves away for processing, including the biggest of all: trujillo leaves are still used to give Coca-Cola its flavour. But don't tell anyone.

It's a bizarre situation: one of the world's most lucrative illegal industries apparently supporting one of the world's most lucrative legal ones. Of course, Coca-Cola buys coca leaves only with a license—all above board, and all that. Yet the problem of coca production for legitimate industrial use versus coca production for illegal processing is a tricky one: you can't just stop people from growing this plant—and, since the plant is the raw material for cocaine, this leads to problems. But we're getting ahead of ourselves. That's the thing about coca: once you start digging for facts, the stories cobweb out from the centre in all directions at once, every little piece of information leading simultaneously everywhere and yet nowhere. And it's such a bizarre story that it's important to get the facts straight.

Erythroxylum species are not especially choosy: they grow all over the place. But (with the exception of trujillo and *ipadu*) there's nowhere the cocaine-rich varieties like to grow more than the eastern slopes of the Andes. If there's heat, no risk of frost, lots of water and little alkalinity in the soil, coca should be your crop of choice. This means that cultivation usually takes place in a fairly remote—if large—region along the western edge of South America from Colombia in the north, stretching down through Peru to Bolivia in the south, reaching as far east as the first stages of the Amazon Basin; but it can grow much further afield. Although you are unlikely to get rich growing it at home under strip lights in Brixton, there's no reason why this wouldn't work. Equally, a number of Caribbean islands have been used for coca cultivation at one time or another, as have Taiwan, Hawaii, Thailand, India, Sri Lanka, North Africa and Indonesia.

Although most coca grows faster the closer to sea level it is planted, its cocaine content increases the higher it is, so it is usually grown on steep Andean mountainsides at an elevation of between 1,500 and 6,000 feet (457 and 1,830 metres), in plantations carved into terraces like contour lines on a map. Here in the Andes, coca has been cultivated in exactly the same way for longer than anyone can remember. Today it is so widespread across South America that there is no such thing as a 'wild' coca plant any more and botanists are unable to pinpoint what country it was indigenous to in the first place.

Scientists suspect that the 'original' coca was Bolivian, if only from its distribution across the continent, but the details are academic. The main thing is this: that this peculiarly ordinary-looking shrub, by a quirk of evolution, is essentially a little living chemistry laboratory which sucks up the nutrients from the dark Andean soil, juggles them around, and combines them to produce a series of natural stimulants, one of which just happens to be the world's most exclusive illegal drug. In doing so, it fuels an industry worth $92 billion a year.

For thousands—possibly tens of thousands—of years, South American Indians have grown coca in order to utilise its stimulants and throughout that time they have been almost, but not entirely, successful. Because, while coca does contain cocaine, it doesn't contain very much. In fact somewhere between 99.3 and 100 per cent of each leaf is *not* cocaine. A recent assay rated one sample of trujillo as containing a 'massive' 1.02 per cent cocaine, but this was regarded as exceptional: its mean rate was 0.72 per cent. At this rate if you wanted to coke up for a night out you'd have to stuff some 40–50 grams of dried leaves up your nose: about a jam jar full. However, thousands of years ago some astute Indian tribe discovered that chewing small amounts of coca over time caused the slow release of all the natural stimulants (called alkaloids: cocaine is only one of those present), so coca chewers, known as *coqueros*, received a slow, constant buzz as they chewed.

Coca chewing is an acquired art. The procedure, unchanged over thousands of years, usually goes like this: take a small handful of leaves from your coca pouch (or *chuspa*), fold them neatly into a wad and place it in the corner of your mouth between the teeth and the cheek. Now take out your *iscupuru*, the gourd in which you keep a strong alkaline powder called *llipta*. This may be made from burned roots, crushed seashells or anything else with a suitably high pH. Caution is advised here: *llipta* can be extremely caustic and cause a painful burn if placed in direct contact with your mouth. Thus you should remove a tiny amount from your *iscupuru* with the end of a small stick or wire and carefully poke it into the centre of the wad of leaves in your cheek. There the alkali, safely diluted by your saliva, will be slowly released, raising the pH of the inside of the mouth and thus increasing the rate at which the body can absorb the cocaine in it. (It's only GCSE chemistry really, but the addition of the alkali to the leaf has yet to be bettered as a means of rendering its alkaloids available to the chewer—pretty impressive considering someone thought this up thousands of years ago.) To chew coca you don't actually have to chew at all: simply move the quid of leaves around from time to time with your tongue to keep it moist, and let the flavour seep out. The most immediate result is that your saliva turns a shocking green but if you stick with it you will begin to notice subtler effects: tingling in the mouth, mild anaesthesia of the throat, suppression of hunger and a noticeable energy boost.

Deep in the Amazon basin, in the wet, shady hollows where only *ipadu* coca grows, the Indians have a slightly different take on coca chewing. Instead of drying the leaves and chewing them whole, they toast them in a large dish over an open fire, pound them until they form a fine green powder, and then add the alkaline ash of either *imbauba* or *yarumo* trees. This dusty mixture, which may be treated with smoke to give it a more pleasant taste, is either made into small balls to be chewed later or placed directly into the mouth. It may also be mixed with tobacco. Having been pounded into dust, the natural alkaloids are more easily soluble, leading to better absorption through the gums and the insides of the cheeks—important, since *ipadu* coca has a naturally low cocaine content. There are numerous other variations on the coca chewing theme: snuff tubes have been found in burial mounds, indicating ingestion by snorting, and the uses of coca among *mestizos* today are legion. In the 1980s the Peruvian government spent a fortune plugging everything from coca creams to coca toothpaste in a desperate attempt to legitimise what appeared to the outside world to be government-sponsored drug production.

None of these products really caught on but the old favourites are still going strong: visitors to growing regions invariably encounter coca as *mate de coca*, or coca tea—the traditional remedy for stomach complaints and altitude sickness. In 1986 health-food stores in North America were found to have been selling coca tea off the shelf as 'Health Inca Tea'. It was pointed out that, while these teabags were pretty harmless, they were actually Class-A controlled substances and could lead to problems in exceptional circumstances (one advocate admitted to feeling agitated after drinking an infusion of 80 tea bags), whereupon the product was swiftly withdrawn. In the Andes coca is also used to treat snow blindness, headaches, open wounds—you name it: whatever is wrong with you in South America, there's a fair chance that coca will make it better. And, if it doesn't make it better, it will sure make you feel better about being ill.

Only a few of these coca applications have been adopted in the West—no doubt because coca and its derivative, cocaine, are illegal. Prior to legislation against them, however, it was common knowledge that coca and cocaine cured various ailments: Ernest Shackleton took Forced March cocaine tablets to Antarctica in 1909 for the energy boost they gave, and Captain Scott took cocaine and zinc tablets with him on his ill-fated 1910 expedition to the South Pole as a cure for snow blindness. The pills acquitted themselves extremely well.

One of the earliest Spanish commentators, Padre Blas Valera, a colleague of the great Incan historian, Garcilaso de la Vega, was an early believer in its medicinal properties:

> Coca protects the body from many ailments, and our doctors use it in powdered form to reduce the swelling of wounds, to strengthen broken bones, to expel cold from the body or prevent it from entering, and to cure rotten wounds or sores that are full of maggots. And if it does so much for outward ailments, will not its singular virtue have even greater effect in the entrails of those who eat it?
>
> Padre Blas Valera, *cit. Royal Commentaries of Peru*, de la Vega, 1609

The majority of coca use is not medicinal but recreational. Coca chewing keeps the Andes on the go the way coffee keeps the rest of the world on the go, and the simple equation of coca-plus-saliva-plus-alkali is responsible. Admittedly, the idea of putting dried leaves in your mouth and adding caustic compounds to break them down is kind of left-field, but then the Indians who came up with it are cousins of the jokers who decided it would be a neat idea to put dried leaves in their mouths and set fire to them. They have a history of slightly off-the-wall uses for plants.

Experts pontificate endlessly about how much cocaine the average *coquero* absorbs during a day's or a lifetime's chewing but no one has yet managed to agree on a figure. Estimates vary from 13 milligrams per day—about equivalent to the caffeine in an espresso—to half a gram a day, representing a sizable coke habit (equivalent to somewhere between a full gram and a gram and a half of adulterated street cocaine). Thus one scientist concludes that the *coqueros'* activity is a harmless, refreshing pastime, while another labels them all inveterate addicts. Anti-coca polemic is bitter and evangelical because its proponents believe that the salvation of a continent is at stake:

> Coca claims more addicts, per capita, than any other narcotic yielding plant; 15m South Americans, mostly Indians and *cholos*...are addicted to the cocaine-yielding leaf. Half of Bolivia's heaven-high population are *coqueros*, 3,000,000 Peruvians are enslaved by it, and in Colombia whole populations are addicted to it and the process of slow degeneration from its cumulative effects.
>
> Carlos Gutierrez-Noriega, *cit. Economic Botany*, 1951

Pro-coca proponents are equally dramatic but more realistic:

> Without coca there would be no Peru.
>
> Juan Matiezo de Peralta, 1566, *cit. Economic Botany*, 1951

From time to time the two groups come to blows and every now and again some fool gringo ships up to South America and suggests that coca chewing should be banned. Clearly, they say, this is in everyone's interest. But it's not. Not really. Coca growers are about as welcoming to these people as the English would be to some bloody foreigner who rocked up and suggested that it would be a great idea if everyone stopped drinking tea. Frequently they are openly hostile. All suggestions to discontinue the habit (and the industry) are met with disbelief, anger or general amusement on the part of the *coqueros*, who shake their heads, curse under their breath and continue chewing, exactly as before. It doesn't stop anyone trying again, however, because the one thing the West refuses to understand about coca is that it will never, ever, go away. Bolivian and Peruvian peasants chewed coca here long before the gringos arrived. They will continue to chew coca long after they have gone.

And with good reason. A small energy boost is not the only benefit of chewing coca. In June 1974 a scientist called Tim Plowman (legendary among botanists today) decided he had had just about enough of the 'coca is dangerous/coca is not dangerous' argument, and took a step so ridiculously obvious that no one had ever thought of it before: he sent a kilogram of leaves from the Chapare in Bolivia for a nutritional assay in the US, telling them to give him a call when they had a full list of ingredients. The results were surprising. It seemed that our innocuous-looking *Erythroxylum coca* not only made cocaine, but also a number of other goodies. So rich were the leaves in nutrients that he concluded that 100 grams of the leaf more than satisfied the recommended daily allowance for calcium, iron, phosphorus and vitamins A, B_2 and E. Two ounces of coca chewed daily provided the chewer with all the vitamins he needed—important, since there's a scarcity of fresh fruit and vegetables on the sierra.

No other South American vegetable even came close to coca's calcium content. This was important because there's not a great deal of milk knocking around on the sierra, either: for nursing mothers, it seemed, coca was a Good Thing (Plowman's figures are still contested: since coca leaves are discarded rather than swallowed after chewing, it has been pointed out that their nutritional value is not so high). It has since been suggested that coca is helpful in regulating the metabolism at elevation, which would explain why it has been used for thousands of years to combat altitude sickness; Dr Carlos Monge, South America's leading expert in altitude biology, reinforced this view by noting a direct relationship between the amount of coca chewed and the altitude at which the chewers lived. It has since been argued that coca both restricts blood flow to the skin and increases core body temperature—again important for those who live at high altitude where it's cold. These facts, like almost all others about coca, are still hotly disputed. Anyway, *mestizos* didn't need a bunch of fancy tests to tell them coca was good for them: they'd known it for centuries. That was why they had used it in the first place.

Archaeological evidence of coca use dates back at least to 2500 BC—pretty much as far back as the first discoveries on the continent—in the form of paintings and statuettes of human figures with cheeks bulging on one side: a dead giveaway for coca chewing. Graves are found all over South America containing items left to prepare the bodies for the afterlife. Coca leaves are invariably included. The very word 'coca' is thought to be derived from Aymara, the language of the pre-Incan Tiwanaku tribes, in which '*khoka*' means 'plant', or 'tree'. There is an emphasis not carried across in the translation here, however, in that '*khoka*' denotes not just any old plant, but the quintessential, the original, *the* plant. Before language, it seems, there was coca. To this day in Peru, coca is used as the standard measurement of both distance and time. Walks are described in terms of a number of *cocada*: the number of coca wads one will get through when walking at a comfortable pace (one *cocada* equals around 45 minutes, totalling about 3 kilometres on level ground or 2 kilometres on steep climbs). There's a certain beauty in the fact that people have been planning their day around coca for centuries: what a *cocada* equals today is exactly what a *cocada* equalled yesterday. And what it will equal tomorrow or the next day. It is not possible to decimalise it, nor will it ever be. This is just one reason why North America, with a total history of five hundred years behind it, will never succeed in stopping South America from using coca—with a history of 4,000 years. Because, in its heart, South America runs on Coca Time.

No one really knows why coca evolved to produce cocaine. It has been suggested that its cocaine content proved evolutionarily advantageous as an insecticide, rendering plants containing the drug immune to attack from parasites. This may be true. Perhaps cocaine was just an accident of nature. Historical commentators, however, report all sorts of other tales to account for its origins. Although these vary widely from culture to culture, there is common ground: coca is always seen as a gift from the gods to man, usually to enable him to bear some hardship, and often following a terrible tragedy. In one myth a mourning mother, wandering heartbroken on the sierra, is so distraught that she plucks a leaf from the nearest bush and puts it into her mouth. The gods take pity on her and feed her through the leaf to enable her to bear her grief. In another, the fault is placed on man. A beautiful woman, loved by all, is found to have loose morals. As a punishment she is cut into two and buried. From her two graves grow beautiful bushes: the first coca. And this is why young men are not allowed to taste coca until they have had relations with their first woman—until they have 'become men'.

Often there are similarities to Christian myths: stories tell of some terrible earthly indiscretion near the beginning of time which causes man to be banished from his state of perpetual happiness to a life of work and suffering. Perhaps the most famous of these relates to the Indians of the Antiplano, who journeyed a great distance to find their first home. After crossing many mountains they eventually came to the perfect place, with beautiful deep valleys (*yungas*). The land was rich and fertile—so fertile, in fact, that before they could build their homes they had to make a clearing. Despite having been specifically forbidden from doing so, they made a fire to burn off the underbrush. The fire spread until they could no longer control it. As the flames grew higher and higher the smoke rose into the mountains, blacking out the sun and throwing the world into darkness.

As it rose, the smoke blackened the snow-white peaks of Illimani and Illampu—the icy home of Khunu, god of thunder and lightning. When Khunu saw what man had done he was angry and sent forth a terrible storm. In the great flood that ensued many were drowned and the farms and homes of man were carried away. When the rain finally stopped, a few bedraggled survivors emerged from caves in the cliff where they had been hiding and surveyed the damage. Everything was gone. There was no shelter. No food. Worse, the path they had followed to get to the yungas was washed away, so they could never get back. They wandered over the mountains like nomads looking for something to eat, but there was nothing. Just when they thought they would die, they came upon a luxuriant green bush. Taking the leaves from the bush, they placed them in their mouths. Magically, the leaves restored them and gave them the strength to rebuild the village.

In this case the similarities between Indian and Christian myths are so close that one must have influenced the other: there is the original Eden-like state, the fundamental breaking of a law, and the terrible revenge wreaked from above for breaking it. There is a terrible flood and many die—yet at the end there is a gift to make life more bearable. Like the first rainbow in the Christian myth, the gift of coca affirms the relationship between man and god: each knows his domain, and will not transgress it.

The truth is that we don't know how coca was first used, where it was first domesticated, or when. We can guess, however, that it didn't take long before the early Indians, recognising its stimulating properties, would have attributed divine characteristics to it. Its earliest use was probably shamanic: coca produced a different state of mind for those who chewed it, and so would have been used as a means of communicating with ancestors or spirits (tobacco would later serve the same purpose). It would also have been used by the shaman for ritual purposes: divination, warding off evil spirits, exorcisms and various propitiatory rituals to secure everything from plentiful harvests to plain old good luck. Equally, because primitive religion was the only source of medical knowledge, coca was used both symbolically and literally as a medicine.

Since archaeology indicates that coca chewing was widespread by 2500 BC its origins must lie further back than that. How far, exactly, is anyone's guess. Of the first South American crops (maize, squash, beans and coca), coca was the only one that was not a foodstuff. At the Culebras site in Peru two human bodies were found, accompanied by a coca vessel and shell containers in which was powdered lime: the earliest recorded discovery of *llipta*—the alkali still used to assist the absorption of alkaloids in the leaf when chewing. The bodies at the Asia I site (1300 BC) were likewise accompanied by *llipta* and, in common with most bodies found from this period, mummified. It has been suggested that coca played a part in the mysterious—and still largely unexplained—embalming process.

The most impressive of coca's early uses, however, was also the most misguided: trepanning. Essentially the idea behind trepanning is that if your head feels a bit too tight, it probably is, and the best way to remedy this is to drill a hole in it. This may relieve the pressure. It may also kill you—and it will certainly hurt a great deal. Unfortunately for native South Americans, a couple of thousand years ago their continent had the dubious distinction of being the world leader in trepanning technology.

Skulls from the pre-Christian era attest to the practice of drilling into the head, and examination of these indicates that this was usually done with flints or sharp stones—not so much drilling, then, as scraping. One chronicler reports that the survival rate for these operations could be 'as high as' 60 per cent—successful enough for it to be used for cosmetic purposes, in which the skull was deformed to make its owner more attractive.

It has been suggested that trepanning was in fact a surgical procedure way ahead of its time. Apparently head wounds inflicted in battle by the weapons in common use 3,000 years ago (such as clubs) are such that the relief of pressure within the skull—by creating a fissure—might actually save someone's life. This seems slightly optimistic: frankly, if someone hit me over the head with a club I would want sympathy from my mates, not some idiot in a loincloth sitting on me and scraping his way into my head with a rock. If it was absolutely necessary for some idiot in a loincloth to sit on me and scrape his way into my head with a rock, however, I would insist on an anaesthetic. Luckily, in pre-Incan times, there was one to hand. Medicine men used coca—chewed, mixed with saliva and decanted—to numb the pain of the trepanning process. Without meaning to they had invented local anaesthesia, predating the civilised world by over a thousand years. Bizarrely, the drug they were using as an anaesthetic was the very same one that was first discovered (in reality rediscovered) in Europe all that time later: cocaine.

Chewing, embalming, trepanning. So far so good. Things seemed to be going OK but I didn't appear to be much closer to the coke mules and the crack houses. And what about the Contras? Nothing. At this point in my research, however, I got my first real break—when I ran into a chap with the unlikely name of William Golden Mortimer MD. I never discovered whether 'Golden' was part of a double-barrelled surname, a proto-hippie Christian name or some bizarre fraternity handle from college, but it didn't really matter. Mortimer was my man. His arrival proved a major turning point in my research and marked the start of a bizarre relationship—with a man who had been dead for the best part of a century.

In every research project there is one book that holds the key to wherever it is that you want to go. However long you slave over other, less relevant texts is a matter of choice or chance or perhaps how diligent you are, or how good a journalist you are, or possibly divine providence—I'm not sure. But eventually, if you stick with it long enough and read everything that comes your way, you bump into a book and you realise that *this* is the book you should have read in the first place. That if you had read it in the first place you could have saved yourself endless hours of toil and pain. The one that everyone who has written anything about your subject has read—but no one thought of letting you know about it. The one that for some inexplicable reason was omitted from the library catalogue altogether until you go back and try it again and find that—hey, that's strange—it has mysteriously appeared right at the top of the list. And look: there are stars all around it and a large neon sign saying 'forget about the others: I'm the book you need'. The moment you start to read this book it seems uncannily familiar: not because you're grateful to have found it or because it's an 'old friend' or anything flaky like that, but because every thieving bastard ever to have written on your subject has lifted all his quotes and stories from it. For most stories you will ever handle there is one inalienable truth: there's a text. There's always a text. The question is: where is it? If you are lucky, you'll bump into it early on in your research.

I was lucky. I did bump into it early on in my research. Where I wasn't so lucky was that my magical, missing text was: *Peru—History of Coca:*

'the Divine Plant' of the Incas, by William Golden Mortimer. A century ago Mortimer had dedicated four whole years of his life to this book. It showed. In some 600 pages the book covers every conceivable aspect of coca history in the most preposterous detail, featuring sections on such cocaine essentials as 'the Drama of Ollaway, a Worthy Plot for a Comic Opera', 'the science of harmonics' and 'the similarity of Incan songs to the poetry of the Hebrews'.

Clearly of the opinion that the number of his readers would be directly proportional to the amount of detail he put into his book, Mortimer quoted references the way lost navigators read out street names from maps: in the hope that something might ring a bell with someone. He also appeared to have taken the bold step of deciding not to tell the story of coca by beginning at the beginning, going on to the end and then stopping, but by starting somewhere in the middle and proceeding towards both beginning and end simultaneously. As I discovered over the course of many hours, there was nothing he liked more than to tease the reader with a story by distributing it at random over three or four differ-ent chapters. I picked up the book for the first time and, at that moment, started a relationship with William Golden Mortimer MD that was to last nigh on two years. Which was about two years too long for me.

From the prehistory of coca, Mortimer led me pretty much directly to the Incas. And, if there was one thing he loved, it was Incas. Because it was the Incas who, although they had no idea what they were doing, taught the West about coca—a crucial step in its simultaneously sluggish yet headlong rush towards cocaine. Shrouded in mystery, hearsay and myth, the roots of this introduction lie further back in time.

The original Incas were three brothers, children of the Sun, who came out of a cave in the cliffs at Paqari-Tambu, 20 miles south of Cuzco. The oldest of the three, Manco Capac, emerged with his bride, Mama Occlo, daughter of the Moon—who also happened to be his own sister (the Incas had *seriously* close families); his two brothers, Ayar Cachi Asauca and Ayar Uchu, came just a short time after him with theirs. Together, the six of them set off in search of a place to settle. It was a hazardous quest: at one point things went seriously wrong and brother Ayar Uchu turned to stone, which just goes to show how careful you had to be in those days. Nevertheless, they pressed on. On their journey they carried a great staff of gold and when they came to Cuzco they put it to the ground, whereupon it drove itself into the depths of the earth, never to re-emerge. This was the sign they had been waiting for. This was the place. As children of the Sun they claimed the land for their own, and from here they set out to conquer the earth.

Well, that's the story, anyway. The truth is more mundane. In fact many of the early Incas are legendary, including Manco Capac himself. Admittedly they did emerge from the Cuzco Valley in the twelfth century but that's about as much as we know. All evidence points to the fourth Inca, Mayta Capac (late twelfth century), as the one who really started the process of expansion and to his son, Capac Yupanqui, as the first to start taking land outside the valley itself.

By the time of the eighth Inca, Viracocha (early fifteenth century), however, they were seriously shifting. In his lifetime Viracocha took enough territory—and was sufficiently enlightened to realise that he had taken enough territory—for it to be necessary for him to settle garrisons of soldiers in conquered regions to maintain order. This was to prove a crucial step in securing the future of the empire. By 1438, when Pacha-cuti ('reformer of the world') took the throne and led his troops south into the Titicaca Basin, the Incas were unstoppable. He took the entire central Andes and marched on Quito.

The Incas were pretty smart. Five hundred years before anyone had even heard of the Cold War they mastered the notion of Credible Strate-gic Deterrence: the idea that it is not actually necessary to annihilate your opponent to win—it is necessary only to have the *ability* to annihi-late your opponent. Not that they were averse to annihilating their oppo-nents if they absolutely had to—it was just less hassle to steer clear of annihilation generally. Thus they offered rival tribes a choice: surrender and live, or fight and die. Faced with the greatest empire the Americas had ever known, most opponents found the decision fairly simple, and tribes fell before them in droves.

The conditions of becoming part of the Incan empire were straightfor-ward: learn the language, follow the Incan religion, donate young men to the Incan army. Hand over one-third of your land's produce and pay tithes in the form of labour (*mita*) for a certain number of weeks per year, and the Incas would pretty much leave you alone. It was a small price to pay for your lives. Well, that was the way the Incas saw it, any-way. Today, it seems fairly clear that what the Incas had actually pio-neered was more than simply the notion of credible strategic deterrence: they had invented the protection racket.

Protection racket notwithstanding, the inevitable result was that, as the Incas made more conquests, their armies grew and they found themselves having to fight fewer and fewer battles. Civil peace was upheld by a smart technique of displacing the dangerous elements of conquered tribes, moving them to new regions so as to disperse potential troublemakers; the young men (most likely to start any serious problems) were taken care of by being shipped off into the Inca army, anyway. Inca rule was totalitarian: everything belonged to the state and everybody worked for the state—and, as long as you went along with that, everything was fine and dandy. Socialism, but with one key difference: it worked. In just one hundred years they succeeded in uniting over a hundred tribes and taking all of Bolivia, Peru, Chile, the lion's share of Ecuador and a fair whack of Argentina—an area encompassing some 907,000 square kilometres. And still they expanded. At their peak the Incas held 75 per cent of the Pacific coast of South America, from the northern border of Ecuador all the way through to central Chile—a distance of some 4,830 kilometres: roughly five times the entire length of the United Kingdom, or the distance between New York and Colombia. They had 12 million subjects.

The logistics must have been staggering but the Incas were assisted by an important discovery: they had realised early on that communication was the key to successful empire management and set about building roads. By the time they had finished, South America was traversed by over 24,000 kilometres of paved highways, linked with tunnels carved through the mountains and suspension bridges made of vines. (Admittedly the Romans had built roads 1,500 years before, but then the Romans didn't have the Andes to deal with.) For safety and ease of communication, Incan roads featured journey-posts at distances of a day's walk from one another. These posts contained huge storehouses of food for official travellers and were manned by garrisons of soldiers to guard both the road and the region. They also contained the finest runners in the empire, called *chasquis*, so that, by running colossal *chasqui* relays along their exceptional highways, Incan chiefs were able to send messages at a rate of over 240 kilometres a day. It is said that when the Inca demanded fish at Cuzco it could be fetched from the Pacific and still be fresh by the time it arrived—over 320 kilometres away.

They were also master craftsmen. Major construction efforts had started when Pachacuti took the throne in 1438, ordering the construction of a capital city at Cuzco and at the heart of this, the famous Temple of the

Sun. Surviving masonry shows that their stonework was probably further advanced than most medieval European efforts. Machu Picchu, the 'lost city of the Incas' in Peru, is a testament to their skill: a perfect walled city, on the top of a precipice, every single stone fitting its neighbours so perfectly that no mortar is necessary. Crops in the fields were watered by means of vast, ingenious irrigation systems to support the empire's huge agricultural economy. Meanwhile, their gold work—virtually all of which would be looted and melted down by the Spanish—was unsurpassed in the world at the time. Ruled by a well-run, central, stable government beneath the ruler himself, South America was as close to being united and peaceful as it would ever be. And at the heart of the operation was coca.

Nothing was held in higher regard by the Incas than coca. The fate of the empire depended on it, and without it nothing could prosper. Coca, with its magical powers of rejuvenation and stimulation, was divine, and as such it merited special treatment. In sacrifices, special priests offered up perfect coca leaves to the heavens at the Temple of the Sun—themselves chewing the divine leaf as they approached the altar. The high priest mumbled cryptic incantations while chewing the leaf to ensure spiritual cleanliness; in special rituals coca was burned so that the gods might smell its heavenly aroma—and the smoke be read for signs of portent.

Coca was also reduced to ashes to propitiate the earth goddess, Pachamama, to ensure plentiful harvests and good fortunes for the army in war; it was offered to the dead, the spirits and supernatural powers so that they would rest peacefully and stay away from the living. Divination with coca was crucial to wartime manoeuvres: leaves were placed in a pot filled with liquid and read to determine the likely outcomes of various strategies. Fire, also, was read for the future—pumped to a tremendous heat with huge bellows by priests chewing coca to ensure spiritual purity and perfect communion with the spirit world. Not only the gods merited this treatment: coca was also chewed in the presence of the Inca himself. And the Inca was invariably a fan. Living a charmed life, he carried only one object in his life: his *chuspa*, or coca pouch. Two of the Incas enjoyed the leaf so much that they named their wives after it, giving them the most sacred title that could be bestowed on a woman: *Mama Coca*. Only three objects merited the prefix 'Mama' and all were essential to the survival of the empire: coca, cinchona (from which quinine is derived) and maize.

Coca was easily the drug of choice for Inca GPs and, as a means of diagnosis, it took a lot of beating. Coca juice, spat on to the hand with the first two fingers extended was read according to the way it flowed across the skin and on to the ground. This diagnostic technique told the informed observer everything he needed to know, and was a sure indicator of physical or spiritual imbalance.

Once diagnosed, of course, problems had to be treated and, here again, coca came into play. Poultices of chewed leaves were ideal for wounds, broken bones, infections, sores and all minor ailments. Internally coca was the prescription par excellence: stomach problems, pains, difficult pregnancies—there was nothing to which its medicinal properties could not be applied.

Ultimately, if the worst came to the worst and topical application failed, Incan patients could rest assured that they were in good hands: their doctors were terrific surgeons. Trepanning had by now been honed to such an art that a morning's drilling hardly merited taking the afternoon off. Medical science, meanwhile, had advanced to the stage where doctors were willing to try much more ambitious procedures, including amputations, internal extractions and the kind of organ and limb transplants that would make Jeffrey Dahmer curl his toes. Here again, surgeons made use of coca's anaesthetic properties. Its numbing effect was also used in other terminal procedures: while pro-Inca chroniclers later did their best to stifle reports of it, human sacrifice was practised throughout the period. Coca would almost certainly have been administered to victims in order to render them more compliant. Women unlucky enough to be married to warriors killed in battle were sometimes buried alive with their husbands, and it is hard to imagine that they would accompany their spouse's corpses into the grave without some sort of chemical persuasion. They weren't the only ones to be accompanied by coca on their journey into the beyond. Buried Incas are invariably found accompanied by their *chuspa* of leaves and their *iscupuru* of *llipta*. Legend relates that he who appreciates the flavour of coca at the moment of death is propelled directly into paradise.

While coca marked the exit from this world, it also marked the entrance. For young Inca nobles the transition from boy to man was truly an event worthy of celebration, and they underwent elaborate rites of passage. Coca was the key. Accounts of the ceremonies vary, some relating gruelling ordeals involving sparring competitions which ended with the death of the loser (the first stage, says one commentator, was to be 'fitted for endurance by a severe flogging'), or races in which the loser had more to be concerned about than just losing face. Others make the event out to be more fun and the standard image, related by almost everyone, is of the initiates running races before the elders, ending up passing through ranks of young women offering them *chicha* (weakly fermented beer) and coca, taunting them coquettishly: 'Come quickly, youths, for we are waiting!' At the end of the ceremony, to mark the arrival of their manhood, survivors were awarded the gifts of a ceremonial sling and a *chuspa* filled with coca leaves. To this day, native Amerindians are awarded their *iscupuru* on reaching manhood. Members of the Kogi tribe in Colombia go one stage further and undergo an elaborate ritual involving symbolic marriage to the leaf.

The Inca chronicler Garcilaso de la Vega reports that the gods gave coca to the children of the Sun 'to satisfy the hungry, provide the weary and the fainting with new vigour, and cause the unhappy to forget their miseries'. Vega's mother was an Incan princess, so he probably knew what he was talking about, yet he has been credited with starting a misconception about coca and the Incas that lingers to this day: that its use was restricted to nobles or to those with special royal consent.

Ever since Vega's *Royal Commentaries of Peru* (1609), historians have speculated as to just who those important enough to have access to coca actually were. Obviously the Inca himself was allowed it, as were his courtiers, who were always to chew in his presence. The Inca also retained the right to award coca to anyone who particularly pleased him. Priests chewed coca because this was necessary if the gods were not to be offended, as did doctors and magicians, who were allowed to use the leaf—but only for medicinal or divining purposes.

Senior cadres were allowed coca, as were the leaders of conquered tribes—provided they kept their minions in order and paid their *mita* taxes. Elsewhere, however, whether you were allowed to chew or not depended on your job. The military had access to coca because it rendered men capable of travelling further and fighting harder on fewer rations. The imperial runners, *chasquis*, likewise were allowed it, as they had to run great distances extremely fast to maintain the empire's lines of communication. Those engaged in public works—road building, for example—also received coca rations: the Incan empire was, in a very real sense, built on coca.

The need for coca was not restricted to those with arduous physical roles, however. With an empire the size of the Incas' it was important that administration be kept up to scratch, but this was a tricky business owing to the fact that the Incas were illiterate: this magnificent empire never discovered writing. They did, however, have their own special bookkeeping system. They employed memory men, known as *yaravecs*, whose job it was to memorise everything about everything. *Yaravecs* held the archives of the Inca kingdom, and their role was passed down through families. On ceremonial occasions they were called upon to demonstrate their knowledge, reciting the history of battles, crop yields or Inca lineage.

To assist them in these prodigious feats of memory they employed elaborate knotted llama-wool strings, known as *quipus*. From these strings, somewhere between sixty centimetres and a metre long, hung further knotted strings of various colours and lengths, and, by examining these, *yaravecs* would be able to access vast quantities of information (to this day no one is quite sure how this worked; many of the surviving *quipus* remain undeciphered). Thus, with recourse to a series of knotted llama wool strings, the entire logistical records of an empire twelve million strong were learned by rote. It was an extraordinary feat of memory but the *yaravecs* did have help. They had coca. Its stimulant properties kept them awake for the long process of memorising and reciting to which they had dedicated their lives.

While commentators are correct that these important figures in the empire's hierarchy had special access to coca, it is unlikely that its use was banned among the rank-and-file Inca. Archaeological evidence of coca use is so common that it seems impossible that only a minority of the empire was allowed it.

Also, as we shall see, many of the early Spanish arrivals commented on coca use—so it must have been pretty widespread by the time they arrived. In addition, when one recalls that coca use had been embedded in South American culture for at least three thousand years before the Incas even arrived, it is surely unlikely that one empire, even an empire as great as theirs, could have suppressed it. Why would they want to, anyway? It's not as if there was a shortage: early on in the Inca period great coca plantations had been established in the Yungas in Bolivia (still the centre of Bolivian coca production today) and the Peruvian montana. The Huánuco Valley was little short of an industrial supply operation, churning out tons of the leaves that produced the stimulant that kept the Incan empire running. Conditions in the hotter lowland plantations were nigh on intolerable for the farmers. What with tropical diseases to which they had no immunity, the inevitable infections that got into cuts and sores, and the possibility of attack by outlying tribes, no one wanted to go there.

Ultimately the only people who could be relied upon to tend these all-important plantations were criminals, who by so doing earned themselves remission from their sentences. If they got back alive, that was: coca growing has never been—and is still not today—a life-enhancing occupation. (It is worth noting at this point that this was one of only two periods in South American history when coca growers were actually criminals. It was far from the last, however, when they would be treated like them.)

It has been suggested that having created a monopoly on coca the Incas used the leaf as a means of political control, simply withholding supplies from any tribe that caused trouble. This smacks of historical revisionism. The truth is that we don't really know about Incan control of coca, but the notion that access to this divine, lifesaving crop was restricted lingers on. That this leaf—presented to the parents of the bride to ensure permission for her hand in marriage, thrown into the air before journeys to ensure a safe return, buried in the ground by farmers to ensure plentiful harvests, burned at the cornerstones of new houses to ensure good luck within them, laid on piles of stones dedicated to Pacha-camac to ensure safe passage through the mountains, and so on and so on—could have been banned beggars belief.

Coca has always been used throughout South America by manual workers (and at this period there was no other kind) to help them to get through their day. The very first thing they did in the morning, and the very first thing that farmers in Peru still do when they get up in the morning, is to reach for the coca and start the day's chewing.

Coca rituals are not observed only by priests: everyone has their own little procedure to ensure good luck, or a good day, or an early finish, or good weather, or rain or whatever. Five hundred years on no one has resolved the question of coca use among the Incan lower classes and, bearing in mind that the majority of the information we have about them is the same information we had about them a hundred years ago, it seems unlikely that, excepting some amazing archaeological find (and it is hard to imagine what it would take to prove it conclusively), anyone is going to prove the case one way or another. The fact is, we don't really know who was and was not allowed coca in the Incan empire, only that it was widespread.

Regardless of how much or how little coca the Incan hoi polloi were allowed, things were about to change, as at the end of the fifteenth century something occurred that was to sever the life of this great South American empire right in its prime. Because, while the Incas were busying themselves building cities, uniting tribes, winning wars and worshipping the sun, 8,000 miles away an ambitious young Italian was hatching a plan that was ultimately to reduce all their efforts to nothing.

Christopher Columbus had never heard of coca. But, then, he hadn't heard of America, either. No one had. His mind was elsewhere. An inveterate armchair traveller, as a child he had read and reread Marco Polo's *Travels* and become obsessed with the idea of visiting China. He wasn't the only one. The East held a powerful allure—there was all the glamour and spice and exotica of the Orient, and of course glamour and spice and exotica meant Money. There was also the likelihood of coming into contact with throngs of heathens who could be converted to Christianity, so the bonuses were twofold: gaining huge credibility with the Pope (and unlimited credit in the hereafter) while simultaneously rendering yourself utterly, disgustingly, filthy-rich. No doubt about it: China was the place for an up-and-coming young navigator looking to make his fortune.

Columbus was no fool. He knew that the world was round. Thus he figured that if he sailed west for long enough he would eventually arrive in the east. He had heard the rumours: it was said that on a clear day it was possible to see the Orient from the Azores, or, if not the Orient, certainly islands on the way there. Doubtless they would have gold and non-Christians, too. The idea of heading west to head east was not in fact new: Aristotle had suggested it in the fourth century BC—the difference now was that here was someone dumb enough to try it. Columbus prepared meticulously, studying every available map and rereading his Marco Polo. He calculated the exact distance to the Orient, telling potential sponsors that if he sailed due west he stood to hit Chipangu (Japan) after a total of just 4,450 kilometres (2,760 miles). China was just next door. He even employed the services of an Arabic translator—because the Chinese were known to speak Arabic. It was so close: how hard could it be? Eventually the Spanish fell for the plan, Columbus got his money and his ships and proceeded to write himself into the history books. Although his scheme was hare-brained, his navigation completely half-baked (even as late as his third voyage, he thought the Earth was the shape of a pear and that the north star kept changing its position relative to his because he was sailing uphill) and he had no real clue what he was doing, on Friday, 12 October 1492, he struck land: the Dominican Republic! The trouble was, the Dominican Republic hadn't been invented yet. This was to create some confusion.

It never occurred to Columbus that he was lost. When Kublai Khan proved not to be in attendance, however, he realised he had made a silly error: the Dominican Republic wasn't China—it was Japan. Still, there was land and there was money to be made and gold to dig. There were certainly locals to convert. It was a triumph. When news of his discovery hit the street back home, there were serious celebrations—he was a national hero.

But what was this new land good for, exactly? Clearly there would have to be further investigation. Columbus had his work cut out for him, and young explorers signed up in droves to visit the New World. The countdown had begun for the Incas. The next year, the treaty of Tordesillas resolved that the new land was to be split equally between Spain and Portugal. The demarcation was a north–south line 370 leagues west of Cape Verde, everything to the east going to Portugal, all to the west going to Spain. The spoils were to be divided and that was that. The question was—how big was this new island?

Even as Columbus was making these discoveries, events were afoot that were to rob him of the glory of naming his new land. Because, while he was busy discovering America back in 1492, a banker's clerk named Amerigo Vespucci had been sent to Cadiz to handle his employer's shipping interests. In Cadiz Vespucci had caught the travel bug and dropped out. A talented astronomer, within three years he had arranged passage to the New World, travelling as navigator to a flotilla of three ships.

It was Vespucci, of course, whose name was to be given to the new continent, America, as a result of an error on the Waldseemuller Map of 1507. And it was Vespucci who was to discover coca.

Vespucci's second voyage, under the command of Alonso de Hojeda, set off on 16 May 1499, arriving in Brazil 42 days later. The flotilla then headed northwest along the coastline, looking for gold. They discovered the Gulf of Paria, then quickly skirted Trinidad and Tobago, which they named 'Yslas de los Canibles' after rescuing four young boys, recently kidnapped and castrated in preparation for eating. Following the coastline of Venezuela to the northwest, in mid-August they unexpectedly sighted land to starboard and went to investigate, landing on an island 'about 15 leagues out to sea from the mainland'. This was Santa Margarita. And here, says Vespucci, they encountered the most disgusting, repulsive, brutish and loathsome race that man had ever set eyes upon. Not only were their manners and appearances execrable but they practised a truly revolting habit:

> They all had their cheeks swollen out with a green herb inside, which they were constantly chewing like beasts, so they could scarcely utter speech: and each one had upon his neck two dried gourds, one of which was full of that herb which they kept in their mouths, and the other full of a white flour, which looked like powdered chalk, and from time to time, with a small stick which they kept moistening in their mouths, they dipped it into the flour and then put it into their mouths in both cheeks, thus mixing with flour the herb which they had in their mouths: and this they did very frequently. And marvelling at such a thing, we were unable to comprehend their secret, nor with what object they acted thus.
>
> Vespucci: letter to Pier Soderini, pub. 1504, trans. London, 1913[1]

Meanwhile the Incas had problems of their own: in 1493, the very same year that the Pope, without consulting them, had given their entire empire to the Spanish, Topa Inca Yupanqui had died. He was replaced by Huayna Capac, who proceeded to invade Ecuador. Things had never looked better but in reality they were living on borrowed time. Reports started to come in of strange-looking foreigners in huge wooden boats, skirting the mainland like sharks around a shipwreck. The Incas were not concerned: an empire the size of theirs had little to fear from these occasional visitors. What could so few men do in the face of so many? Unfortunately, quite a lot. This land belonged to Spain, and everywhere they went, they claimed it as such. Looking for gold and silver, they navigated their way around the coastlines, taking stock of their weird and

---

[1] In fact, this is the first *published* incidence of coca chewing. In the records of Columbus's fourth voyage (published later) there is an earlier account:

> The lieutenant went into the country with 40 men, a boat following with 14 more. The next day they came to the river Urisa, seven leagues west from Belem. The cacique [head man] came a league out of the town to meet him with some 20 men and presented him with such things as they feed on, and some gold plates were exchanged here. This cacique and his chief man never ceased putting dry herb into their mouths, which they chewed, and sometimes they took sort of powder, which they carried along with that herb, which singular custom astonished our people very much.

wonderful new possessions. Everywhere they went, they reported that the Indians were savages, hardly human, who indulged in barbarous practices and habits. Chronicles of their utter unspeakableness are reported in the breathless, repetitive manner of a young child asked to describe the contents of a sweet shop:

> The Indians eat human flesh and are sodomites and shoot arrows poisoned with herbs...and...live from the said Gulf of Uraba or point called Caribana westwards, and it is also a coast with cliffs and they eat human flesh, and they are abominable sodomites...
>
> de Ovieda, 1526

It is hard to think of anything more likely to appal the Spanish than cannibalism and sodomy, and, however these were exaggerated (or simply invented), this kind of coverage was not an auspicious start to the Indians' relationship with their new landlords. The image of them as subhuman, flesh-eating barbarians was to persist among the Spanish, who regarded these reports as a pretty good reason either to hunt them down actively, or at least not to be too worried when they all started dying out.

Moreover, the early explorers had another reason to be angry with the Indians. Sodomy was a sin that no Catholic god worth his salt would leave unpunished. And, sure enough, early travellers discovered that the Indians had been punished for it, with a disease hitherto unknown in Europe. It was one they lost no time in passing on to the Spanish explorers wherever they landed: syphilis. The Spanish were not happy recipients of an easily communicable disease to which they had no immunity, but they very quickly had their revenge. Which, as it turned out, was considerably more communicable than anything the Indians had managed to come up with.

The bacteria could have arrived with Columbus and taken time to spread across the northern coast of South America, where tribes were still quite disparate. Perhaps they came later. No one knows, but early reports say that some Incas, fighting a rebellion in the mangrove swamps of Colombia, had run into some Spanish. Both groups had beaten a hasty retreat but the damage was done. By the time news of the new plague reached Huayna Capac in Quito, 200,000 Incas were dead.

Capac had been experiencing strange dreams of portent for nearly two years. His magicians and doctors could not explain them. The only thing anyone knew was that they were signs that something important was about to happen. In outlying reaches of the kingdom astrologers had reported strange comets and lights; the Inca's palace was rumoured to have been struck by a thunderbolt. Holy men were too scared to tell Huayna Capac but they read these as omens of his looming death—and, worse, the destruction of his royal bloodline. But, when he emerged from a swim feeling unwell, they knew it was only a matter of time. He caught a chill, which rapidly turned into a fever, and he knew that he was in trouble.

Smallpox? Measles? To this day no one is quite sure. Whatever the diseases there was no natural immunity among the Indians and the results were catastrophic. Quite apart from the terrible casualties of the waves of plagues that were to sweep the continent for the next hundred years, there was another crisis: Huayna Capac had left a dispute concerning which of his sons, Huascar or Atahualpa, should succeed him and, as soon as he was dead, the two fell out. They formed opposing camps and postured at each other. Finally Huascar sent an emissary to Atahualpa to discuss peace terms. Atahualpa had the man skinned, made into a drum and delivered back to Huascar by return of post. Then things began to get really nasty.

Five years of bloodshed later, just as Atahualpa was gaining the upper hand, who was to show up but Francisco Pizarro—an illiterate, illegitimate megalomaniac looking for a mountain of gold that did not even exist. Pizarro had received special permission from Charles I of Spain to invade Peru on the condition that the king receive one-fifth of all profits. This financial transaction agreed, he had set sail from Panama in 1530 with his own little army. The Incas were about to experience Spanish diplomacy.

Pizarro arranged to meet Atahualpa on 15 November 1532. The Incas, a diplomatic lot, were not expecting trickery—especially not from this small band of ragged travellers—but had come in force just in case. There were nearly five thousand of them. When they got to the rendezvous they were surprised to be greeted not by Pizarro but by a lone priest, who presented Atahualpa with a bible, asking if he would accept Christ as his saviour and Charles as his king. Atahualpa was not impressed: unable to read the bible, he flung it to the ground. At this point the priest ran for cover, shouting to the concealed Spaniards around him, 'Fall on: I absolve you.'

The moment the Spanish riflemen opened fire, the Incas, who had never heard gunfire before, were paralysed with fear. They were also terrified of the horses that Pizarro's men proceeded to charge among them and huddled to the ground in a desperate attempt to save themselves from being cut down. In the turkey-shoot that followed, 168 ragged Spanish adventurers wiped out 3,000 Incas. They also managed to kidnap Atahualpa. In return they suffered one casualty: Pizarro himself, accidentally stabbed in the hand by one of his own men. The whole episode lasted just half an hour.

Pizarro was now in a position of some power. Not only were the majority of the Incan population terrified of him but he held their king hostage. He took up residence in the Imperial Palace and considered his options. As long as he held Atahualpa, he reckoned, he was safe: no one would try anything for fear that he might kill him. But then Atahualpa surprised him with an offer. It was perfectly clear to the Incas that what the Spanish were looking for was gold and Atahualpa offered them plenty of it, suggesting that he pay his own ransom, in the form of enough gold and silver to fill the room he was imprisoned in. This was more like it. Pizarro accepted; he had always known there was a mountain of gold around here somewhere. The Spanish watched very closely to determine where, exactly, the silver and gold were coming from, then followed it all up and stole whatever else they could find.

By July the next year, however, when the room was nearly full, Pizarro realised he was going to have to do something about Atahualpa, and that releasing him was probably not a smart move. Instead of letting him go he had him publicly garrotted in the square at Cajamarca. The room full of priceless Inca jewellery Atahualpa had assembled to buy his freedom was melted down and shifted straight back to Spain. It was a great result for Pizarro, and he was so pleased with himself that he ordered the construction of a new capital city, Ciudad de Los Reyes. Today it is known by a bastardised form of the name of the river upon which it stands: Lima.

The Conquest was under way. Soldiers led by priests made full use of the comprehensive Incan road system, which rendered the process of moving an invading army around such a huge empire comparatively simple. Wherever they went, there was carnage. Pablo Jose de Arriega later wrote of the standard opening move for missionaries converting locals: 'Everything that is inflammable is burned at once and the rest broken into pieces.' The Incas, meanwhile, having lost their leader, shocked by the sheer quantity of pestilence and death around them, put up little resistance. But the invaders faced a problem—what was to be done with the survivors? Pizarro, busy carving up their empire and giving it to his mates, didn't really care. His priests *were* concerned, however: should they all be killed? The question was put to the Vatican. On 9 June 1537, Pope Paul III ruled that these savages were actually human beings and that they must not be killed in cold blood: they must be converted. They were also not to be treated as slaves.

This created a bit of a problem for the Spanish. There was a lot of manual work to be done by someone and who was to do it if the Indians refused? And the Indians weren't looking too keen. They found ways around this, hiring Indians as helpers and not paying them enough. Or just not paying them at all. Of course, if the Indians were really intransigent, special measures had to be taken. Hernando Pizarro, Francisco's little brother, was one of many willing to take such measures. He made a number of expeditions into the jungle, taking with him hundreds of 'voluntary' porters, all so keen to work for him that they had to be chained together by their necks. If one fell ill or died along the way (and many of them, carrying huge weights with little or no rations, did) the only way to continue without breaking up the chain was to cut his head off. Admittedly, such porters were unchained at nights when the walking was over but rules were rules: they slept in the stocks. It was only a precaution.

The conquest of the Incas was achieved in 6 years with a total of just 183 men, 27 horses and 100 firearms. It was an astonishing feat—but this had little to do with military prowess and a lot to do with chance. Huge swathes of the native population had been laid to waste by Spanish diseases from the north before Pizarro had even arrived. And the Incas had just ended a bloody five-year civil war—a war that had started in the first place because Manco Capac had died of the Spanish plague.

Numbers were so depleted that, by the time the soldiers got to many of the villages, there were few people left alive. In uncontaminated regions the results were even more impressive: missionaries and priests arrived just in time to see the Indians mysteriously sicken and die before their very eyes. Here was evidence, as if it were needed, that God was on the Spanish side. And of course if God is on your side you can do no wrong. In the villages, soldiers oversaw the massacres and rapes of thousands, confident that the lives they were taking were worthless. Faced with such appalling casualties, the Incas initially assumed that the Spanish were killing them by magic, boiling their bodies down and shipping the remains back to Spain for some sort of unholy medicine. Eventually the numbers were too great even for that: to the Incas, plagues of such ferocity were evidence that the gods were on the Spanish side, because only the gods could mete out death on such a preposterous scale.

And it *was* a preposterous scale: an early census in Peru established that the population dropped from over eight million in 1548 to one million in 1561. Across South America the story was the same.

But the Spanish were faced with a problem. Where was all the money? The gold? The Indians were subservient, all right, but what was there for them to do? Pizarro's mates, receiving large chunks of land for services rendered, didn't know what to do with it. The Spanish had come to Peru looking for *things*—things they could buy, sell, exploit. But when they actually got there they couldn't find anything worth exploiting. The only thing that had any real market value was coca. And so they seized the opportunity and began growing it—and peddling the leaves to the Indians—as fast as they could go. Here was something the Indians really cared about, and could be made to work (and pay) for. To this day commentators still argue about the amount of coca used in Peru before the Conquest but everyone agrees on one thing: once the Spanish arrived coca production went ballistic. It was the only profitable industry, and everyone wanted a slice of the pie. And so the Spanish helped to spread the habit of coca chewing across the continent.

When Pizarro returned to Spain to report to the king, he loaded up with all the goodies he could carry, including coca. But the king wasn't interested in coca. He was interested in gold—and, specifically, his fifth share of it. It is perhaps surprising that, although there were already written chronicles attesting to the miraculous invigorating properties of coca, no one back home seems to have paid any attention to it at all. Coca was to prove the slowest of all the South American plants to catch on in the Old World for a number of reasons. Firstly, its leaves travelled very badly: any hint of moisture and the entire shipment discoloured and rotted immediately. Secondly, there was the fact that coca chewing was a rather unseemly habit—masticating leaves with lime could hardly be described as a dignified activity. Thirdly, there was a natural prejudice against any custom invented by a bunch of savages halfway around the world. And it wasn't as if coca chewing was an easy habit to pick up: 150 years on, a Spaniard reports the effect of his first taste of coca:

> As soon as I placed two leaves in my mouth, my tongue seemed to grow so
> thick that there was no room for it in my mouth, and it burned and prick-

led so much that...I could not bear it, owing to the effects of the coca. He laughed at me and gave me a small piece of a doughy substance resembling a black lozenge, saying that it was called 'sugar' and that if I took it along with the coca the bad effects that it had would disappear...I swear that I have never tasted anything so bitter in my life, so much so that I spat out the so-called sugar with the herb I had in my mouth and would have vomited up my entrails after them had not the symptoms passed off. I was then told that the Indians call that little lozenge *'llipta'*.

Historia de la villa imperial de Potosi, Arzan, 1674

There was also a general suspicion of new products: just five years before Pizarro brought coca to Spain the Church had come very close to banning potatoes because they did not feature in the Bible. Perhaps it is not surprising that the Spanish did not pay more attention to coca. Ironic, really, because if they had really wanted to make an investment they should have forgotten about El Dorado, whacked a patent on coca, set their chemists to work on it, isolated cocaine and flogged it around the royal houses of Europe. This didn't occur to them and so, in the absence of gold, they made do with the next best thing.

As it turned out, the next best thing was silver. Bolivia was full of it. A hundred years before the Spanish arrived, the Incas had discovered rich deposits in the mountains at Potosi but had stopped extracting them when the mountain rumbled at them in a voice that told them that this place was not theirs. However, shortly after the conquest the mountain's silver reserves were rediscovered and the Spanish started digging. They had hit the big time: Potosi was the largest silver reserve in the world, and it was right there for the Spanish picking. Within a year a city had sprung up and 7,000 Indians were working the mines, chiselling some 3 tons of silver ore out of the earth every week. Another sad chapter in the tragedy of the Indians was about to start, along with the first truly tragic chapter in the history of coca.

Initially the Indians were happy. Silver was so abundant that the work was easy, they were paid modestly and allowed to keep a certain amount of ore for themselves. This was far more profitable than any other work around. They also had the expertise: the Incas had worked out a much better way of smelting their native silver than the Spanish method, resulting in higher yields. Everyone at Potosi got rich fast: from the time of Columbus to 1550, 70 tons of silver poured out of the mine each year.

The chronicler Pedro Cieza de Leon actually saw the king's fifth in 1549, estimating it to be worth thirty or forty thousand pesos per *week*; German explorer von Humboldt estimated that Potosi produced over one hundred and twenty-seven million pesos in its first eleven years. But, as the seams were exploited, the mines grew deeper and more dangerous and Indians became less keen to work there. Potosi itself is inhospitable and cold and conditions in the mines were dark, dank and dangerous. They also refused to work without coca.

Coca was still rather a mystery to the Spanish but they had cottoned on to the fact that there was money to be made by selling it to the Indians. It was a serious growth industry. As long as there was arduous manual work to be done—especially in the mines—there would be a market for it. There was also every chance that as the mines were exploited, silver would become harder to come by—requiring more effort to extract, and thus more coca. By 1548 the miners were getting through 100,000 cestas of coca (over a million kilograms) per year, the economy was booming and everyone was getting rich. La Paz was founded in 1549 as a stopping point for Potosi's silver on its way to the coast, but in fact much of the city's wealth was made in coca, a trade that operated in the opposite direction to fuel the process of shipping silver to Spain. As Potosi's silver grew scarcer so the Indians needed more and more coca to get it and the city flourished. Meanwhile, the Indians, who had never experienced hard currency and distrusted Spanish coins, demanded to be paid in coca (a tradition that continued until the start of the Cold War four hundred years later). Thus, in addition to being its own, extremely lucrative, business, coca was now supporting both the silver mines and the city of La Paz. It wasn't long before it was supporting the Spanish treasury, too.

At this point the Church conveniently decided to ban it. To the Catholics coca represented the worst kind of threat after cannibalism and sodomy: it was used in pagan ceremonies, it was chewed before communion and it was associated with all sorts of popular folklore. Worse, it appeared to have some sort of magical property that gave the Indians energy—and plants that did this were no less than cuttings from the window box of Satan. More to the point, any indigenous belief that appeared to stand in the way of the Indians' wholehearted acceptance of Christianity was dangerous and must be eradicated.

The Church decided to make a stand and, in doing so, started a controversy over coca that rages to this day. Initial opposition emerged at the First Council of Lima in 1552, accompanied by accounts of shamanic rituals and sacrifices, frenzies, orgies and worse. The king was petitioned and some serious polemic changed hands:

> The plant is idolatry and the work of the Devil, and appears to give strength only by a deception of the Evil One; it possesses no virtue but shortens the life of many Indians who at most escape from the forests with ruined health... [it is] a useless object liable to promote the practices and superstitions of the Indians... asserted by every competent judge to possess no true virtues...

It was the world's first antidrug campaign and, as with every antidrug campaign since, everyone fell over one another in the rush to jump on the bandwagon. There was even a royal proclamation attesting to the fact that in the king's opinion coca was 'un ilusion del demonio'. When, however, it was brought to his attention that coca was the number-one industry in Peru and that without it no one would work in the mines, he turned down the Church's request to ban it.

This did not stop them trying again. Fifteen years on, the Second Council of Lima called for a ban on coca production. Again were cited the dangers: intoxication, demonic influences, paganism. It was said that women working in the cocales either became barren or, when they gave birth, delivered deformed monsters. Clearly, this would not do. Spanish nobleman Diego de Robles called coca 'a plant that the Devil invented for the total destruction of the natives'. It was quite some coincidence that the Devil had provided the natives with this plant some five and a half millennia before the Spanish arrival, yet the process of their total destruction had only just begun when they arrived to witness it. This did not occur to de Robles.

And yet, in their own simple way, the Spanish clergy were actually thinking of the Indians' welfare. By now even they had noticed that the Indians were dying out in alarming numbers and in some cases coca really was the cause. Coca plantations were just as dangerous under the Spanish as they had been under the Incas: the risk of illness for those living in the lowland plantations was high. Chronicles quote various common diseases among planters, usually leishmaniasis, 'El mal de los Andes', which led to horrendous facial deformation and ultimately death.

Such was the risk that, by the mid-sixteenth century, Indians were permitted to work in the *cocales* for only five months at a time. It was estimated that 40 per cent of the Indians sent there died before even this short stint was up. Antonio de Zúñiga wrote to the King: 'Every year among the natives who go to this plant a great number of Your Majesty's vassals perish.'

Because of the high mortality rate in the *cocales* Philip had previously ordered that no Indians be forced to work there—but this had fallen on deaf ears. Many thousands were forced there, and there they died. He knew this. So would coca be banned this time? It looked likely, until administrator Juan de Matienzo informed him that without coca the Indians would refuse to work in the mines, and silver production would stop. Specifically, his one-fifth share. Not for the first time, the issue of coca production came down to its real essence: money. Phillip declined to ban it but ordered further reforms, and in charge of these reforms he put his new viceroy, Francisco de Toledo.

Toledo, in an attempt to stop this exploitation, restricted the time that Indian workers were allowed to spend in the *cocales*. It was the right sort of gesture but he followed it up with one that was to have terrible consequences. In 1573 he reorganised Peruvian industry. Toledo figured that increased productivity on the part of the Indians would increase the king's fifth of the profits, and thus boost his own chances of imperial favour. But how to get more work out of the Indians? He decided to reintroduce the *mita*—the traditional Incan tax in the form of labour. Despite the fact that the Indians were not allowed to be used as slaves, this was justified on the basis that it was 'in the public interest' (no prizes for guessing whose).

In 1573 he announced that all males between the ages of eighteen and fifty must work for the Spanish government every sixth year. According to a census he had ordered in 1570, 1,677,697 Indian males were available. He ordered them to step to. Toledo's *mita* was not really that similar to the Incan notion of it—it was simply a means of organising cheap labour for the benefit of the Spanish Empire. Referring to it as a '*mita*', however, lent it an air of continuity with the Incan empire: the idea was that the Incan leaders had fallen and the Spanish had taken over more or less seamlessly. In this way the Spanish were indeed the rightful heirs of the Incas: they, too, appreciated the power of the protection racket.

Toledo was not inhuman. To ensure that the Indians were not overexploited, he instituted special clauses: they were to work only one week on, two weeks off; they were to be paid proper salaries; they were to be guaranteed land on which to grow their own food; their working and living conditions were to be acceptable. They were to receive a payment for travelling to work from their villages, and only to work certain hours.

Unfortunately, it didn't quite work out this way. The *mita* system, applied much more ruthlessly by the Spanish than it had ever been by the Incas, soon became a form of institutionalised slavery. Workers were given impossible quotas for which they received paltry salaries—and the quotas increased so much that by the eighteenth century they would have to draft in their families to help. Meanwhile, the land they were given to grow crops was stolen and they were forced to pay extortionate rates for food and lodging so that all they accumulated was debt.

While the fact that the Indians had to work only one year in six was meant to ensure that their workload was not too severe, it simply encouraged their bosses to work them even harder. They knew that they could exhaust their men because another batch of fresh workers would be arriving at the end of the year. Although Toledo had instituted the *mita* as a temporary measure, it was to remain in effect until the time of Simon Bolívar 250 years later. In that time it was to cause the demise of countless thousands—possibly millions—of Indians, worked to death in the cause of an empire too far away for them to be able to imagine. Even the everyday Spaniard recognised the injustice of it:

> This manner of payment is worse than if they had paid them nothing but kept them as branded slaves in their houses; for a master gives his slave food and clothing and cures him when he is ill. But they make an Indian work like a slave and give him no food or clothing or medical attention; for the maize is insufficient to feed him and the salary not enough to clothe him.
>
> Felipe Guamam Poma de Ayala, *cit.*
> *The Conquest of the Incas*, John Hemming, 1970

Although the Indians were not to appreciate it, however, the *mita* got results, and Potosi silver production went through the roof. By 1577 there were two thousand Spaniards in the city, overseeing the work of over twenty thousand Indian miners, and by the early seventeenth century Potosi would be the largest city in the Americas—and quite possibly the richest city in the world. From 1556 to 1780 over 21,500 tons of silver were gouged out of the ground by Indian workers and sent home to Spain. By the start of the eighteenth century the French were in on the act, too, sending galleons of luxury European goods to the New World to exchange for the famous Potosi silver. Coca now began to support the French treasury, too.

The *mita* was a great economic success but it would never have worked without coca. Indians chewing coca worked harder and needed less food, which meant more money for the mine owners—and more money for the king. In many cases Indians simply refused point-blank to work without it. This didn't stop the Third Council of Lima from trying to ban it yet again. It did stop the king from agreeing to let them do so. Again. Although openly hostile, the Church eventually managed to reconcile itself to its repeated failure to stop the trade in this unspeakable leaf by placing itself on the payroll: a 10 per cent tax was levied on coca—which, paid by the Indians on purchase, promptly ended up in the bishops' pockets. Now the Church had a finger in the pie, it was willing to look the other way, and busied itself worrying instead about such pressing issues as whether it was a mortal sin for the Indians to chew coca to suppress their hunger during the fast days of Easter (no, not 'mortal' but 'venial'), and what—crucially—about those who indulged in chocolate before Mass? When the financial details were ironed out it was business as usual: the mine owners were happy with their increased production rate and the Church was happy with its 10 per cent—a point noted eloquently in 1609:

> The great usefulness and effect of coca for labourers is shown by the fact that the Indians who eat it are stronger and fitter for their work; they are often so satisfied by it they can work all day without eating...It has another great value, which is [that] the income of the bishops, canons and other priests of the cathedral church of Cuzco is derived from the tithe on the coca leaf, and many Spaniards have grown rich, and still do, on the traffic in this herb.
>
> Valera, 1609

Around the time Toledo reimposed the *mita*, another discovery was further to increase silver production, simultaneously cranking even higher both the need for coca and the Indian death toll: the discovery of mercury at Huancavelica in Peru. In 1571 a new, more efficient, technique for silver refining had been discovered, using mercury—a technique that ensured richer silver yields from the same amount of ore.

Thus the discovery of huge mercury reserves was great news for the Spanish. It was less than ideal for the Indians. In fact the Incas had discovered the mercury here hundreds of years before and gone to some effort to mine it. However, while the lustre and mobility of the metal was appreciated by all, no one could find any particular use for it. And, when men who had worked in the mines had begun to die off (mercury is carcinogenic), the Inca ordered the mine shafts to be sealed, and banned any references to mercury in public. Within a hundred years, mercury had been obliterated from the Indians' consciousness—there was not even a word for it any more.

Until the Spanish found it, that is. Toledo was beside himself with excitement when he heard about Huancavelica, and the *mita* was swiftly applied to this mining complex, too.

As the mining process continued the Spanish began to notice that their miners were all dying off. It was not surprising: at Potosi, conditions were atrocious. Within fifty years of its discovery, the mine shaft was so deep that miners had to descend 300 metres vertically in order to get to the seams. There were no lights, no ventilation, and cave-ins were common. Miners fumbled their way underground, guided by the light of a single candle tied to their thumbs (they were forced to pay for the candles themselves). Frequently miners would descend to the seam at the start of the week knowing they would not be allowed out until their shift was finished—at the end of the week.

Not only the mining was dangerous. Once the ore was up at the surface it had to be broken up and ground into dust so the silver could be extracted, a process that was responsible for crippling many of the workers. As the dust filled their lungs they contracted silicosis, a condition that, when combined with malnutrition, often proved fatal. At Huancavelica this problem was hampered by the fact that the dust itself—and the very mineral they were extracting—was toxic. Mercury ore was so dangerous that mules and lamas carrying the ore on the surface lasted less than a year. It soon became obvious that a *mita* service at the mercury mines was tantamount to a death penalty—the hardy few who emerged at the end of the their mining period alive were no use for any other kind of work and never recovered. As miners began to die out, more were needed. The catchment areas for *mita* drafts were expanded and the age of initial *mita* service was dropped. The length of service was increased as more work had to be done by fewer and fewer people.

Coca made this possible. Miners, malnourished and uncared for, bought coca because it supported them better underground than did the expensive, low-nutrient food they were peddled by the mine owners, and because it numbed them to the pain and misery of their condition. The Spanish, now well versed in the capabilities of coca, sold wads of over-priced leaves to their workers and had them work 48-hour shifts on the trot. De Leon appreciated the value of the trade:

> Coca was so highly valued in Peru in the years 1548, 1549, 1550 and 1551 that there was not a root nor anything gathered from a tree, except spice, which was held in such estimation. In those years they valued the *repartimentos* of Cuzco, La Paz and Plata at eighty thousand dollars, more or less, all arising from this coca. Coca was taken to the mines of Potosi for sale, and the planting of the leaves and picking of the leaves was carried on to such an extent that coca is not now worth so much, but it will never cease to be valuable. There are some persons in Spain who are rich from the produce of this coca, having traded with it, sold and resold it in the Indian markets
>
> *The Seventeen-Year Travel of Pedro Cieza de Leon*
> *Throughout the Mighty Kingdom of Peru XCVI, 1553*

Coca facilitated the enslavement of the nation. Estimates of the death rate vary. One source says that, at Potosi, mining and silver refining with mercury was to kill 10,000 Indians every year from 1560 to 1620. Many say this is too high but it seems to be borne out by the statistics: in 1683 a census established that the Indian population eligible for work had dropped by 45 per cent in just ten years. *Mita* catchment areas were expanded and periods between *mita* service were dropped, from six years often to as low as one.

Father Jose de Acosta, who accompanied Viceroy Toledo across the continent to visit Potosi, wrote to the King in person: 'many believe what remains of the Indians will cease before long.' Dominican chronicler Rodrigo de Loaisa wrote: 'I must advise Your Catholic Majesty that the wretched Indians are being consumed and are dying out. Half have disappeared, and all will come to an end within eight years unless the situation is remedied.'

It didn't do much good. The *mita* was to continue at Potosi for another 250 years.

2 De Jussieu Loses His Marbles

You know sometimes when you meet someone, and somehow, before they even open their mouth to speak, you know that you are going to be friends? It's the same with books. With some books, you see someone reading them on the bus or in the bookshop or the library and you know that that one—that one there—is the book you should be reading right at this very moment. Not a book you *ought* to read, but a book you *have to* read. These books tap you on the shoulder as you go past them in a shop and you glance at them and you just find yourself thinking, Well, isn't that interesting? And before you know it you've just had to buy them and take them home to see what they are trying so hard to tell you, and the second you start reading them they grab you by the lapels and won't let go. Books you reread from the start the moment you have finished them. Books you wish you could read more slowly but no matter how hard you try you just can't. Books you buy up in bulk at Christmas to give to everyone you have ever known, or that you lend to an old college friend even though you know he reads books only after running them over with a motorcycle and giving them to the dog to chew for a couple of months so that if you do ever get them back the backs will have fallen off, the covers will be ripped and pages 38 through 46 will be missing. Books that put you in touch with something real. Books that you get. Books that get you.

Peru—History of Coca: 'the Divine Plant' of the Incas, by William Golden Mortimer MD, is not one of these books.

On the contrary, Mortimer does the opposite. Initially you pick him up and he sucks you in, but after just a short period you begin to feel unwell and wish you hadn't started—like the moment in a horror film when you realise that this is actually quite scary stuff, or the feeling when you reach the top of the hill on a roller coaster and it tips forward with a clunk and, despite the fact that there's absolutely nothing you can do about it, you realise that you've made a terrible mistake and that actually you'd quite like to get off now.

Mortimer does strange things to you. One minute he's telling you about vocal harmonics in *Aida* and their improvement with coca lozenges; the next you find yourself slumped face down on your desk in the British Library completely disorientated—no idea where you are, where you've been, or for how long. Although you eventually recover after lumbering off for a cup of tea and a piece of cake, it sets you thinking. Do other people have this problem? Yes. A good 50 per cent of the readers in the library spend a good 50 per cent of their time talking to themselves: you can see them in the cafeteria, solitary figures, mouths clamped tight shut, eyebrows leaping and crashing as they argue their way through some medieval philosophical treatise or other. Barking mad, every last one of them. Once you've been in that library for long enough, weird things began to happen to your mind. Perhaps spending too long inside makes everyone go a bit loopy. Perhaps the British Library was built on an old Indian burial ground (this might explain the clock running so slowly). I told myself this but I didn't really buy it. Secretly, I knew. I sipped my tea and I knew. Mortimer was messing with my head.

And so I sat in the library, staring around the room at all the lucky readers who didn't have to read Mortimer, eventually settling my attention on the young woman with the hazel eyes in seat 2242. I wondered who she was. I wondered what she was reading. I wondered about my ex-girlfriend, who had told me the week before that, well, she thought I ought to know that she had started seeing someone else: some computer-programming buffoon who supported Stoke City, played the guitar, bought her flowers, earned a zillion times my salary and didn't wander around in public muttering to himself. What an arsehole. She had wanted to know whether I had met anyone. I'd tried to think of a suitably nonchalant reply but nothing came: not only had I not met anyone, I had hardly spoken to another human being in five months. I nearly told her about the girl in seat 2242 but I figured that might be a bit tragic even for me. But how was the book going? she wanted to know. When was I off to Colombia to interview drug barons? I looked at my feet and mumbled something about trepanning.

I had already been through this routine once, with my publisher. I had felt like an idiot then, too. But the thing was this: I was five months into my cocaine story and I appeared to be no closer to either the cartels or the Contras. Where was the glamour? Where were the drugs? Incas, archaeologists, Columbus—it was all a bit more long-winded than I had anticipated. So, with my complete lack of any idea about anything at all, I oafed my way back to my seat, waited for the girl in seat 2242 to come back from her coffee break and gazed at her for the rest of the afternoon. That's what reading Mortimer does for you. It makes you wonder about things. Most of all, your mortality.

It wasn't long, however, before obscure conquistadors and chroniclers began to emerge from the book stacks and fall open to reveal their secrets. These texts constituted my escape route from coca into cocaine, for only when coca was well documented would someone actually take note and look at it closely.

Pedro Cieza de Leon was a Spaniard born in the early sixteenth century who had set out for the New World to make his fortune at the age of just fourteen. Once there, he had served under the notorious Sebastian de Belalcazar, a man so brutal in his treatment of the Indians that his own men had lynched him and given his body to them to eat because 'he had caused many Indians to be killed with crossbows and dogs. And God permitted that he should be sentenced to death in the same place, and have for his tomb the bellies of Indians.' De Leon had started writing in 1541 and the first volume of his great work, *The Seventeen-Year Travel of Pedro Cieza de Leon Throughout the Mighty Kingdom of Peru*, emerged twelve years later. It contained news of all sorts of wonderful produce including potatoes and, more importantly, coca.

> In all parts of the Indies through which I have travelled, I have observed that the Indians take great delight in having herbs or roots in their mouths...In most of the villages subject to the cities of Cali and Popayan they go about with small coca leaves in their mouths, to which they apply a mixture, which they carry in a calabash, made from a certain earth-like lime. Throughout Peru the Indians carry this coca in their mouths, and from the morning until they lie down to sleep they never take it out. When I asked some of these Indians why they carried these leaves in their mouths (which they do not eat but merely hold between their teeth) they replied that it prevents them from feeling hungry, and gives them great vigour and strength. I do believe that it does have some such effect although, perhaps, it is a custom only suited for people like these Indians.

> *The Seventeen-Year Travel of Pedro Cieza de Leon XCVI*, 1553

Next up was Augustin de Zarate, the royal comptroller under the first
Peruvian viceroy, who, in his 1555 classic, *Strange and Delectable History of the Discovery of Peru*, mentioned that coca was esteemed more
than gold or silver, but had no really new information to offer me. His
colleague, Santillan, however, marked a turnaround: writing just eight
years after Zarate, he was obviously right in there with the ecclesiastical
authorities—who were just getting ready to ban coca—and as such
launched the first printed broadside on the herb:

> There is in that kingdom (Peru) another type of gain which is the worst of
> all and the most harmful to the Indians, that is the coca, which is a herb
> like zuzamal. The Indians have it in their mouths while they work or walk
> or do any other job, and this is the oldest habit amongst them, from even
> before the Incas subjugated them... And as it was a precious thing among
> them, due to that imagination, all of them began to use it after the Spanish
> entered in the land... which has costed and costs now an infinite number
> of Indian lives.
>
>   Santillan, 1563

Most reports of early coca use, whether pro or con, are pretty similar,
describing the leaves and how the Indians look like cattle with them in
their mouths; giving various names for the lime compound used to aid
the chewing process and relating the Indian belief that coca gives energy
to those who use it. But Mortimer alerted me to one account in particular: that of Nicolas Monardes. Monardes, a Spanish physician, had taken
it upon himself to report the arrivals of products from the New World
that were either fantastical (armadillos, for instance) or might be of use
as medicines. Living in Seville, he made sure he received word of all new
arrivals, and in 1577 published his compilation under the title *Joyfulle
News out of the New Founde Worlde*. Monardes gave the first really
accurate account of coca cultivation and this version is generally cited as
the first real botanical reference to coca. Luckily there was a copy of the
1596 translation in the library. I found coca in the third book, snappily
titled: *The Third Parte of the Medicinall Historie Whiche Doth Treate of
the Thinges that are Brought from our Occidental Indias, which Doeth
Serve for the Use of Medicine—Where is Put Many Thinges Medicinall,
That Hath Greate Secretes and Vertues.* Clearly coca had acquired some
reputation by this point because Monardes opens by commenting that he

had long wanted to get his hands on some, having heard so much about it. But what else did he have to say?

Thei take Cokles or Oisters, in their shelles, and they doe burne them and grinde them, and after they are burned they remaine like Lime, verie small grounde, and they take the leves of the Coca, and they chawe them in their Mouthes, and as they goe champing, they goe mingling with it of that pouder made of the shelles in suche sorte, that they make it like to a Paste, taking lesse of the pouder than of the Hearbe, and of this Paste they make certaine smalle Bawles rounde, and they put them to drie, and when they will use of them, they take a little Ball in their mouthe, and they chawe hym: passing hym from one parte to an other, procuring to conserve hym all that they can, and that beyng doen, they doe retourne to take an other, and so they goe, using of it all the tyme that they have neede, whiche is when they travaill by the waie and especially if it be by waies where is no meate, or lacke of water. For the use of these Bawles dooe tke the hunger and thurste from them, and they say that they do receive substaunce, as though that they did eate.

Joyfulle News..., Monardes, 1577

I couldn't really see why everyone quoted this as a classic text when it just seemed to reiterate what other people had been saying for eighty-odd years. His spelling was also atrocious: how could he spell the word 'receive' and not manage 'they'? My spellchecker nearly exploded. Like some cutesy-retro hotel chain, he used the word 'ye' a lot and virtually every word he wrote he ended in 'e'. It all felt rather twee. I reminded myself that it probably could not qualify as 'twee' if it was genuine and pressed on. Generally, the later the writings were the more interesting they became, as they began to ask not simply what coca was, but what its effects were and whether they were real. Argument over whether coca's invigorating effects were illusory were to rage for the next three hundred years. Was there perhaps something in this bizarre habit after all? Acosta (1590) clearly thought there was:

They say it gives them courage and is very pleasing to them. Many grave men hold this as a superstition and a mere imagination. For my part, and to speak the truth, I persuade not myself that it is an imagination, but contrawise I think it works and gives force and courage to the Indians, so

as to go some days without meat, but only a handful of coca, and other
like effects.

Natural and Moral History of the Indies, 1590

What is interesting about Acosta is not simply that he was a high-
ranking official willing to go on the record stating that coca's effects
were real but that he was willing to do it as a Jesuit. At this point, according to the clergy, coca was an '*ilusion del demonio*'. Twenty-six years
later the Inquisition, which narrowly missed Peru but passed through
Mexico, became so concerned about the native Indians' practice of drug
taking that a proclamation was issued against it. Yet Acosta quite clearly
approved of coca; perhaps his visits to the mines at Potosi had convinced
him. He wasn't infallible, however. In the same volume he writes of a
despicable Peruvian drink adored by the locals but which was 'loathsome...having a scum or froth that is very unpleasant to taste...' This
loathsome drink was none other than hot chocolate.

Despite a number of advocates, old superstitions about coca lingered
on, and nowhere more so than in the Church. Over a century after coca
was taxed by the clergy, we still find reports of its satanic influences, and
it is just such reports that, blindly cited by later commentators, would
help to propagate the myth of coca chewing as a dangerous, addictive
habit—a myth that survives to this day.

> I wish to declare the unhappiness and great evil that, among so many felic-
> ities, this kingdom of Peru experiences in possessing the coca herb (which
> is taken by those ministers of the Devil for their abominable vices and exe-
> crable evil-doing)...Would that our lord the King had ordered this nox-
> ious herb pulled up by the roots wherever it is found, not permitting even
> the memory of it to remain; Great good would follow were it to be extir-
> pated from this realm: the Devil would be bereft of the great harvest of
> souls he reaps, God would be done a great service, and vast numbers of
> men and women would not perish.
>
> Arzan, 1674

While Spanish commentators and priests debated the relative merits
of coca, another school of thinkers concerned itself with a more pressing issue: what *was* coca? Botany was taking great leaps forward and
plant classification in the modern sense was just about to start. Where

did coca fit into all this? Mortimer told me that the first attempt at classification was in Plukenetius. While I had no idea what 'in Plukenetius' meant, I found out soon enough: Leonard Plukenet, compiler of the great seventeenth-century botanical work, *Phytographia*. On the off chance that there might be a recent translation or reissue, I typed 'Plukenetius' into the library's computer search and it came up immediately: a first edition, dated 1692. You had to hand it to the British Library: it may have cost too much and taken too long to build and their bloody clock ran slow—but it certainly had a lot of obscure books. When *Phytographia* actually arrived, I found the page, and there it was:

> Coca Peruiana Hernandez apud Recc.302. Arbusta pro Numinibus habita, Mamacocae vocata (hoc est) Matres Coca 1 Deae Cocae Nieremberg fol 304—tab 339.
>
> *Phytographia*, 1692

What on earth was Plukenet going on about? I reread it a couple of times but was still none the wiser. The text, later deciphered for me by someone who actually knew what they were talking about, said that the plant was known in Peru as 'mama coca', and it had taken its name from that: coca. I had half the name. I had 'coca'. If Mortimer was to be believed, the first botanical classification as *Erythroxylum* came sixty years later, in *Natural History of Jamaica*, a botanical anthology compiled by Dr Patrick Browne in 1756. What was coca doing in Jamaica in 1756? I had no idea but, once again, there it was on the screen: 'shelfmark X219 4765, Rare Books and Manuscripts. Press "F4" to order'. Back to the Rare Books Reading Room I went.

Browne's *Natural History of Jamaica*, when it eventually arrived, was so dilapidated that it came in a box. But that doesn't quite do it justice: *Natural History of Jamaica* came in a box the same way a corpse comes in a coffin. It was large—about twice the size of an encyclopedia—and deceptively heavy, and the librarian had dropped it on to himself when he took it down for me. 'I've just dropped your box on to myself,' he told me, deadpan, as he slid it over the Issues counter. I apologised, cradled it in my arms and carried it back to my desk. Opening the box, I found that it might as well have been a coffin: inside, the book was in pieces, with a broken spine and a powdery cover that left red smudges on my fingers when I touched it. There was a strong reek of old people's homes about it.

Natural History of Jamaica was 500-odd pages long, a foot and a half tall, and completely shredded. Inside were a lot of pictures of Jamaican plants and a large dead spider, which rather took me by surprise. Unlike Plukenetius—which was considerably older but had been restored—*Natural History* really looked its age. And it was old: George II had been king when it was published and the American Revolution was still twenty years in the future. *Natural History of Jamaica* had been lodged in the vaults of the British Library for nearly sixty years by the time Napoleon invaded Russia.

There was an index but it was in neither numerical nor alphabetical order. Eventually, when I located my page (page 278—but this didn't help much, as the pages weren't numbered), I found the right bit:

ERYTHROXYLUM 1: RED-WOOD, OR IRON-WOOD, WITH OVAL LEAVES

This is a small, but beautiful tree: the leaves are of an oval form, and marked with two slender longitudinal lines upon the back, which were the utmost limits, of the part of the leaf that was exposed, while it lay in a folded state. The flowers grow in little clusters, and are very thick upon the branches. The inward bark is of a fleshy colour; and the wood is a reddish-brown. It is reckoned an excellent timber-wood, for the size of the tree, which seldom exceeds sixteen or eighteen feet in height, or five or size inches in diameter.

The Civil and Natural History of Jamaica, Browne, 1756

This didn't sound much like coca to me, particularly the 'height of sixteen to eighteen feet' bit. A footnote referred me to plate 38, fig. 2, which did look a bit like a coca leaf but it was pretty obvious that something was wrong. In fact this wasn't coca at all: it was the first classification of any plant as belonging to the genus *Erythroxylum*. Admittedly, it gave a hint as to the derivation of the name *Erythroxylum* (literally 'red root'), but, apart from this, there was nothing for me here. Mortimer had tricked me. Meanwhile, the librarian was mad at me, my hands were covered with red stains, and I stank of old people's homes. As I closed the book, I wondered how many other people had read it. Probably none. Well, maybe *one*...I liked to think that Mortimer, on a research trip to London, had been the last to take it out. Perhaps he had been as careful with it as I was—it would have been 150 years old by the time he got to it. It had probably required careful handling even then. Perhaps it was already in a box. Perhaps it already smelled of old people's homes. Perhaps he had put the spider in. Perhaps it was Mortimer who broke the spine. The bastard.

The fact that *Erythroxylum coca* had not actually been classified botanically by the eighteenth century indicated that, while the Old World was aware of it and of its effects, it had very little actual knowledge at all. This was because the Spanish, having claimed South America, had declared it off limits to non-Spanish nationals. The wonders of the New World were accessible to other Europeans only in print; and many of the more groundbreaking books were classified. Yet Spain had not bothered to send any scientific expeditions into the New World. And having decided not to bother exploring themselves, it was to be two hundred years before they would allow any other scientists on to the continent, and then only under close observation. The expedition that they allowed—the expedition that was to bring coca to the Old World—was not botanical. It had higher goals than simply collecting a few plants. It was a voyage to measure the shape of the earth.

For some time, everyone had known that the earth was round but there remained a controversy: was it perfectly round? It was a question that had important repercussions on practical matters such as navigation, for if the earth was not perfectly round a distance of one degree of latitude would vary according to where on the globe you were. This kind of uncertainty made navigators edgy: one degree might mean the difference between discovering a new island or not—or perhaps the difference between driving your ship through a nice calm ocean as opposed to stoving it head first into a mountain.

In December 1734 the French Academie decided to resolve the matter. Two expeditions were to be sent to different regions of the globe— one to the equator, one to Lapland (as close as possible to the North Pole)—to measure one degree of latitude. When they both got back and their measurements were compared the dispute would be over. There were a couple of problems, however. The first was that the French didn't hold any territory on the equator. Where could the first expedition go to that was flat, reasonably straightforward to get to, and safe? The ideal spot was Quito in Ecuador but it had been closed to foreigners since its discovery. The Academie petitioned the Spanish crown and—to everyone's surprise—promptly received permission to stay in Peru for as long as their measurements would take. The second problem, now much more pressing, was who was capable of leading such an expedition?

There was no shortage of volunteers. When it became public knowledge that French scientists were to visit South America for the first time, everyone wanted to go. At the head of the queue, however, was a precocious young mathematician by the name of Charles-Marie de la Condamine. Admitted to the Académie Française at the age of just 29, he was a prodigy. Voltaire, who knew him well, described him as being possessed of a *'curiosité ardent'*. The two men had met when they found themselves seated next to each other at a dinner party held by the comptroller of France, who was attempting to raise money by holding a lottery. Condamine, a talented statistician, had scribbled a few quick calculations on his napkin and realised that the lottery organisers had not printed enough tickets. He shared this information with Voltaire, explaining that anyone who bought up all the tickets would be guaranteed a healthy profit. Voltaire—fortified by a couple of large shandies—decided to try it, and ended the dinner 500,000 francs richer. This exchange cemented their friendship, and whenever Condamine needed assistance, Voltaire could be relied upon to pull a few strings for him. It was thus not entirely coincidental that when a really plum job came up (leading an expedition to the equator to measure a degree of latitude), Voltaire arranged an audience with the king and mentioned that he knew the ideal man for the job. This move, together with the fact that the independently wealthy Condamine offered to pitch in 100,000 livres of his own money for the expedition, succeeded in getting him the job.

While the northern expedition had to wait till summer to leave, the equatorial group departed in the spring of 1734. To assist him, Condamine had assembled a crack team of scientists including an astronomer, a mathematician, a botanist and a watchmaker. They were to be accompanied on their journey by two young Spanish naval officers, who were to ensure that they were not in fact French spies assembling intelligence for a future invasion. The team arrived in South America in November 1734, the first scientific expedition ever to set foot in the New World.

It was a portentous moment: the start of a mission that was to last some 45 years and would truly be over only when all of its participants were dead. It was a mission that was to bring coca to science. The history of this mission is recounted by Condamine in a book entitled *A Succinct Abridgement of a Voyage Made within the Inland Parts of South America*, a first edition of which is lodged safely in the British Library. It's quite good. You should read it. Really. 978.K.31, if you're interested.

No sooner than they had arrived, they split up. Condamine headed off on his own to reach Quito by foot; the others preferred to travel by boat. They should perhaps have rethought, as it was on Condamine's epic walk that the greatest discovery of the whole trip was made: an elastic, gummy substance that came from the cahout-chou tree and appeared to have almost unlimited uses. He lost no time in making himself a set of waterproof covers for his scientific apparatus out of it and was so impressed with their performance that he took a sample of cahout-chou resin home, sparking an interest in this magical, elastic substance.

Some years later, Joseph Priestly, noticing that lumps of Condamine's gum could be used to rub out pencil-lead writing, named the substance 'rubber'. Although the resin of cahout-chou ('the weeping tree') had been noted before, it was Condamine's account of it that was to spark popular interest—and that is credited with opening up the world rubber market. He was also, by the bye, to pick up some rocks rich in an ore the locals called 'platino'. Out of curiosity, he took them back to France and was surprised to find himself the discoverer of platinum.

The real measurements started in mid-1735, and were to go on for another eight years. However in 1739 the team received devastating news: the Lapland trip—which had a considerably shorter distance to travel—had completed their measurements and were already safe back in France. Their measurements were sufficient, without those of the equatorial team, to prove the shape of the earth. The team was devastated: they had been away from home, living in the jungle for four years, and their results were obsolete. To cap it all, one of the members of the team was dead of malaria and, just after the news of the results arrived, the team's doctor was beaten to death by an angry mob.

They went into hiding in a monastery. Then, just when things looked as if they could not possibly get worse, they did. The team's botanist, Joseph de Jussieu—a member of France's most distinguished botanical family—having spent his time collecting and preserving indigenous plant species to take back home and classify, had entrusted them to a servant to keep. In five years he had amassed a huge collection of new species, all of which he would have the honour of naming. There was every chance that he would go down as the greatest botanist of all time. While the team were in hiding, however, the servant lost the entire collection. On receiving this news Jussieu went insane.

When their work was finally complete in 1743, things continued to go wrong. The mathematician decided he didn't want to go home to France after all and took a job at Lima University. His cousin married a local thirteen-year-old girl. Another of the crew went insane. The draughtsman was killed when some scaffolding he was working on collapsed. The doctor, of course, was already dead and Jussieu was still somewhere orbiting the planet Zanussi.

In March, nine years after leaving France, Condamine decided it was time to call it a day and, being the last survivor who had not gone either mad or native, he had to travel alone, navigating the entire length of the Amazon on the way. He arrived home in February 1745, a tired and broken man. Various tropical diseases and the rigours of the trip had left him partially deaf and lame in one leg. Although he was elected to the Académie Française as one of the forty Immortals, he never recovered his vitality, writing: 'As for me, M la Condamine, you can consider me only half a man.'

It's a sad story. But not as sad as that of Joseph de Jussieu. History relates that he never recovered from the shock of having his specimen collection lost. That none of the collection survived. But history only relates that because it's what Condamine wrote when he got back. The truth is more bizarre.

After the measurements were taken, Jussieu had wanted to accompany Condamine to Paris but Condamine had insisted on taking the long and expensive route home via the Amazon. Jussieu could not afford this so Condamine, either unwilling or unable to lend him the money, left for home alone. Jussieu headed off to Lima to sort out his financial situation. This done, he was unable to resist conducting a few botanical researches of his own. He retraced the journey Condamine had taken without him, making observations and taking samples along the way. On his trek he conducted ground-breaking research into rubber. Jussieu was understandably wary of collecting too many of his specimens in the same place and thus throughout this period, he dispatched them, along with his notes, home. Unfortunately, most of them never made it. Worse, by the end of his trip, he was flat broke again and was forced to take a position as a doctor in Quito.

Just when he had got the money together, however, smallpox broke out and, being one of only a handful of Western doctors in the city, he was forbidden to leave. As a sign of their gratitude for his assistance, his hosts kept him under house arrest and imposed strict penalties on anyone who assisted his escape. He whiled away his time studying infectious diseases.

Jussieu was finally given permission to leave Quito in 1747 and left for Lima to catch a boat for home. On the way he conducted work on the canella tree (from whose bark cinnamon is derived). Once again, he dispatched all his specimens back home—and, once again, most were lost along the way.

Arriving in Lima in 1748, he met up with another member of the original expedition called Godin. For some reason the two men then set off on an arduous journey across the Andes so that they could spend the winter in Buenos Aires. On the way they travelled to Potosi and inspected the silver mines and then the mercury mines at Huancavelica. Stopping off in La Paz, Jussieu was excited to discover completely new flora and decided to leave Godin to go on alone while he stayed to study it. By 1749 he was studying coca in the Yungas valleys. Once again, however, he ran out of money and in 1750 he was forced to return to doctoring in La Paz, where the governor was so impressed with him that he insisted he stay with him in his own house—and then refused to let him leave.

Jussieu was then employed in various scientific pursuits—notably building bridges. Four years later, exhausted, broke and incarcerated, he managed to persuade the governor to allow him to leave. At this point, however, disaster struck again: he learned that the vast majority of his botanical specimens and notes had been lost en route for Paris. He was devastated. He was also informed by post of the death of his mother and his brothers. Perhaps not unnaturally, he fell into a deep depression. He took a position as a doctor again—writing to a relative in Paris that botany and medicine had together wrecked his life and that he had decided to give both disciplines up—to become a mathematician. This time Jussieu had lost his mind for keeps.

Destitute, he took a small house in Lima, where he was to stay for another ten years, a broken man. Finally a group of French travellers, hearing of his plight, gave him the money he needed to get home and forcibly put him on the right ship. He arrived home in Paris in July 1771—having been away for 36 years. He was met by his two remaining brothers, Antoine-Laurent and Bernard, both of whom he was unable to recognise.

Even back in Paris, luck was not going his way. Not willing to dispatch his new specimen collection ahead of him before he left Lima, he had left it with a trusted servant, promising to send someone reliable back to safeguard it home after he had gone. In the meantime the servant died and the collection, including all the academic papers he ever wrote, was burned. This single tragedy would perhaps have broken Jussieu completely had it not been for the fact that he was already broken completely. He established himself at the Sorbonne and, despite being elected to the Académie, never once visited it. He never recovered his sanity. Joseph de Jussieu died, as his biographer succinctly says, 'after a short agony' eight years later. The last image we have of him is a fitting one: old, senile, embittered, alone in his flat, '*cloué dans son fauteuil*'—literally 'nailed into his armchair'. But perhaps I translated that bit wrong.

What does all this have to do with coca? Quite a lot. Of all of the specimens that Jussieu collected, the vast majority never made it back to Europe. One did. It was coca, and the same plant remains today in the Natural History Museum in Paris, together with Jussieu's original drawing of it. It was this very plant that was analysed and named by various botanists, until, in 1786, French biologist Jean Chevalier de Lamarck classified it *Erythroxylum coca*. The name stuck. Now that scientists knew what they were looking for, further reports of coca's amazing properties came in thick and fast.

From 1777–88 Don Hipolito Ruiz travelled through Peru and Chile, reporting that:

> For a long time I was convinced that coca is, like tobacco, a habit-forming plant used to keep the Indian happy but experience has made me change that groundless belief. I have seen positive proof of the wonderful effects of these leaves that appear to be tasteless, odourless and inert. Moreover, coca is a remedy with proven medicinal properties. As a decoction or infusion it cures dysentery, checks diarrhoea and stimulates delayed menstruation after childbirth; as a powder, mixed with sugar, it corrects acidity and strengthens the teeth
>
> Journals of D H Ruiz; trans R E Schultes, 1998

Unfortunately Ruiz's perceptive remarks went unnoticed: his journals were lost for two hundred years and, by the time they were rediscovered in the bomb-damaged archives of the Natural History Museum in London during the Second World War, his work had been superseded by other, less well-informed travellers.

German explorer Alexander von Humboldt arrived in Peru in 1801 and immediately set about trying to work out what it was about this leaf that gave the Indians such energy. But asking about the active constituent was quite a new thing to do: science was just now coming to terms with cause and effect in biology, and the fact that things just don't happen by magic. Humboldt wanted to know what caused coca's energy boost. Clearly, there were only two possible answers: some kind of invigorating natural property in the leaves, or some kind of invigorating property in the alkali. With a possible choice of two elements, he chose the wrong one, concluding that it was the alkali. It was reports of coca's use, such as Humboldt's, however, that led to a more widespread appreciation of the debate surrounding this bizarre herb, and the recognition that here might be something of general interest to science. Even the popular press picked up on this strange habit, and wanted to know—what was the South American Indians' secret?

> We are certain of this very extraordinary fact: that they have that secret, and put it in practice for weeks together; and undergo the greatest fatigue, without any injury to their health or bodily vigour—they want neither butcher, nor baker, nor brewer, nor distiller, nor fuel, nor culinary utensils... now if Professor Davy, when he returns from his travels, will apply his thoughts to this subject, I have here given him some important materials for his experiments. There are thousands, even in this happy land, who will pour their blessings on him, if he will but discover a temporary Anti-Famine, or substitute for food, free from all inconvenience of weight or bulk, and expense; and by which any person might be enabled, like a Peruvian Indian, to live and labour in health and spirits, for a month now and then, without eating.
>
> *Gentleman's Magazine*, September 1814

Humphrey Davy obviously didn't read *Gentleman's Magazine*. Instead of investigating coca, he had discovered electrolysis and was busy using it to discover potassium, sodium, barium, strontium, calcium and magnesium; on the side he was also investigating the anaesthetic properties of laughing gas.

As the Incas could have told him, he should have been looking at coca. He never did. Meanwhile, reports were still flooding in commending coca's use to one and all. Instead of being academic texts for travellers or scientists, these new books were aimed at a general readership—a readership that was fascinated by the mystery of the New World and the mystery of coca. Not everyone was enthusiastic. A natural prejudice against such an unseemly habit (and one invented by a group of savages half the way around the world) surfaced periodically, especially when reported by those who had little tolerance for Indian customs anyway. The most famous of these, and the first real anti-coca campaigner, was the German naturalist Poeppig, who revealed his natural inclinations against both Indians and coca pretty early on when he wrote of the problems beset by coca chewers:

> Weakness in the digestive organs... increasing continually in greater or less degree first attacks the unfortunate coquero. This complaint, which is called OPILACION, may be trifling in the beginning but soon attains an alarming height. Then come bilious obstructions, attended with all those thousand painful symptoms which are so much aggravated by tropical climate. Jaundice and derangement of the nervous system follow, along with pains in the head, such prostration of strength that the patient speedily loses all appetite; the hue of the whites assumes a leaden colour, and a total inability to sleep ensues, which aggravates the mental depression of the unhappy individual, who, in spite of all his ills, cannot relinquish the use of the herb but craves brandy in addition. The appetite becomes quite irregular, sometimes failing altogether, and sometimes assuming a wolfish voracity, especially for animal food. Thus do years of misery drag on, succeeded at length by a painful death.
>
> *Reise in Chile, Peru und auf dem Amazon Strom*, 1827–32

Where Poeppig got this information from is anyone's guess: no one else reports these symptoms. It certainly doesn't seem accurate, as millions of chewers in Bolivia and Peru would attest today. However, his personal prejudices (he admitted that he had little time for either the Indians or their customs) were to influence the public perception of coca chewing. Later on, when cocaine was isolated and had been revealed to be dangerous, the anti-coca brigade immediately referred to Poeppig who, long dead, emerged from the archive crooning 'I told you so'.

Even with reports such as Poeppig's, readers were intrigued. And, now that South America was finally opening up, botanists were dispatched there to see what was going on. Just six years after Poeppig, the greatest botanist of them all, Englishman Richard Spruce, headed into the Amazon. When he eventually emerged from the forest 15 years later he brought with him a collection of over 20,000 specimens, all of which he shipped back to the Royal Botanical Gardens at Kew.

Like most travellers, Spruce had been impressed by the Indians' ability to travel for days on end without either food or sleep after chewing coca and he was to offer a unique insight into the leaf, describing for the first time its use in the Amazon. His collection was eventually to lead to controversy, however, because one of the things that Kew inherited was a coca plant, which was hastily classified—incorrectly—and put on display. Because this was the first living coca plant in Europe, the Kew Plant (as it became known) became the source of the cuttings sent to other herbaria around the continent, which were all likewise incorrectly classified. This was to lead to some head scratching among botanists when it later emerged that the plant they called 'Bolivian coca' did not actually grow in Bolivia but Colombia, while the species *novogranatense*—named after Colombia—tended to reside in Bolivia. (This dispute was finally cleared up in 1982 by Tim Plowman.)

For no particular reason I decided to give Kew Gardens a call. Perhaps a cutting of the original plant was on display. Perhaps I could photograph it, or touch a leaf or just look at it. Even if they didn't have the plant, they were bound to know a lot about coca, so I stood to gain something. Most importantly, it would be a day out of the library without the guilt of taking a sickie. It didn't work out quite like this. My conversation with Kew was short, to the point, and peppered with phrases such as 'no comment'.

The problem, as I should perhaps have anticipated, was that family tourist attractions are not keen to advertise the fact that they have narcotic-producing flora on the premises. Not keen at all. In fact, the reaction I got on the phone was pretty much the one I would have expected had I rung the White House, told the press office I was doing a feature for *Cigar Aficionado* magazine and asked if President Clinton had a couple of minutes for a chat.

I spoke to a guy named Elvis (not his real name), who was immediately wary of any questions. When I asked why, he said that he was concerned about who he was talking to. I couldn't think of a neat way of proving my identity over the phone, so I pressed on: did they have coca? Elvis thought for a moment. No. They didn't. Well, actually, yes, they did. But it wasn't labelled. They didn't want it advertised. In fact, the plant was sick at the moment. Very sick. Elvis was unsure what was wrong with it but seemed fairly convinced that, when he went back to see it that afternoon, it would be dead. He had planted it himself but he was not sure when, or where he had got the seeds from. He had had to obtain a special licence from the Ministry of Agriculture in order to grow the plant but was unsure when or how he had applied for it. When I asked where exactly the coca was on display so I could come and see it, he refused to tell me. What Elvis did tell me, however, was that, if I were to ask any of his staff to point it out to me when he wasn't around, he would be 'very angry'.

I tried a different tack: what had happened to the old plant, the original? No one seemed to know. There was a large coca bush on display here, I was told, until 1984 but its growth had been erratic. Each year it had flourished until spring when, mysteriously coinciding with the increase in visitors, the leaves all went missing and it went into decline. By the time it had recovered over the winter, the tourist season had come back around and the leaves started vanishing again.

No wonder they were worried. If the average Kew visitor was desperate enough to defoliate the exhibits in order to get their hands on drugs, what wouldn't some nutcase on the phone do to get a whole plant for himself? Perhaps they thought I was about to leap into my car and ram-raid the herbarium. Or sneak in quietly after dark and asset-strip one of their prize possessions. Either way, I was bad news and they didn't want to show me their coca. I did consider showing up unannounced, under-cover, with a coca leaf recognition chart so I could work out which plant it was on my own, but I didn't want to incur Elvis's ire.

Who knows what kind of strange things happen to people who ask too many questions in these tropical plant houses? I imagined myself tied to a chair in some back room in the Palm House, wrists bound with those green plastic ties gardeners use to hold back climbing creepers, heavy-duty gardening tape over my mouth. Elvis standing back while some meathead from Cirencester with a teapot complexion in wellingtons approached with a pair of pruning shears and a manic, gap-toothed country grin: 'Shall oi do 'im loike we done the larst wun?' Meathead would ask. Elvis would nod and say, 'Yes, Jethro, show Mr Streatfeild how we prune the *thunbergia*'. I would turn my head left and right and try to speak through the tape: 'No. Please. Not the *thunbergia*.'

I had nightmares for a week. My housemate told me that, if I was afraid already, I was going to have serious problems when I got to Colombia. I couldn't believe that Mortimer had had to put up with this sort of thing.

3 From Coca to Coca-*ine*

In 1859, Dr Clements Markham travelled to South America to procure cinchona seeds (cinchona is the source of quinine). Once there, he could not help but notice coca. Like everyone else, he was amazed by the quantity of it that the Indians were getting through, estimating that the continent's annual coca yield was some 13,700,000 kilograms. Faced with such a huge crop, he became convinced that there must be something in it after all, and tried it himself.

> I chewed coca, not constantly, but very frequently... and beside the agreeable soothing feeling it produced, I found that I could endure long abstinence from food with less inconvenience than I should otherwise have felt, and it enabled me to ascend precipitous mountain-sides with a feeling of lightness and elasticity, and without losing breath. This latter quality ought to recommend it to members of the Alpine Club and to walking tourists in general.
>
> *Travels in Peru and India*, 1862

History does not relate whether the Alpine Club took up Markham's suggestion but it is pretty obvious that, by the time European travellers were recommending it to walking groups for recreational use, the time had come for some serious investigation. Clearly coca was more than simply a leaf chewed by a bunch of savages for the sake of it: by now there were enough reports testifying to its energising qualities to suggest that its effects were real. Little did anyone realise that just such an investigation was already under way.

For some time scientists had been isolating natural chemicals from plants and applying them to medicine. In 1803 FWA Sertürner had isolated morphine from opium. Strychnine was discovered in 1817, quinine and caffeine in 1820. In 1821 science gave these products—nitrogen-based organic compounds produced by plants with diverse effects on the body—the umbrella term 'alkaloids'. Nicotine was isolated in 1828, and atropine in 1833. More were on the way. After centuries of guessing, it was finally clear that these bizarre plants did not function by magic but contained active constituents which, when administered, caused specific effects on the body. It was also clear that, if these active constituents could be chemically isolated, they would be powerful drugs.

In 1708 Hermann Boerhaave, the founder of organic chemistry, had included coca in his classic text *Institutiones Medicae* because, he said, there was some sort of chemical inside the juice of the plant that led to all these miraculous qualities. While he did not have the knowledge of chemistry to work out what it was at the time, his comments helped to launch the search for the active principles of all narcotic-producing plants. Ironically, coca, the one that had first piqued his imagination, was the last to have its alkaloid isolated.

There were a number of theories about the chemistry of coca. Von Humboldt had said that the energising properties came not from the coca but from the alkali chewed with it. The French botanist Weddell thought that coca contained some kind of mild stimulant such as theine, or perhaps even caffeine. Meanwhile a German chemist, Friedrich Gaedcke, had claimed to have isolated this ingredient by distilling the dry residue of coca and then refining the result. He had managed to produce some needlelike crystals that he had named Erythroxyline but no one had ever managed to duplicate his experiments so no one paid much attention.

Swiss expert JJ von Tschudi, who spent four years travelling in Bolivia, commissioned a repeat trial at La Paz University. Chemists there managed to repeat Gaedcke's experiments with fresh leaves and told him that they had succeeded in isolating Erythroxyline, giving him a sample to take back to Europe. When he got home, however, he took this sample to a chemist, who pronounced that it was simply powdered gypsum. He had been duped.

Whatever was in the leaves, it seemed, was extremely hard to extract. In fact this was not the case. The real problem with trying to isolate the active constituent of coca was not the chemistry but the lack of coca itself. Coca did not grow well in Europe, and degraded on the journey from South America, so there was a great shortage of leaves with which to experiment. The few leaves that were available were invariably old and contained little or no cocaine. Scientists needed a reliable supply of good-quality coca. In a bizarre twist of fate, they were about to get one—courtesy of the Austrian military.

In 1856 Emperor Franz Joseph I sent a frigate, the *Novara*, right around the globe to demonstrate to the world the prowess of the Austrian navy. On its trip the *Novara* was to carry 352 men, including 7 scientists. One of these scientists, Dr Carl Scherzer, would end up publishing the definitive account of the voyage, a bore-fest so preposterously verbose that everything I had read so far seemed positively interesting by comparison.

Voyage of the Novara, conveniently condensed into three monstrous tomes, tells the story of the ship's circumnavigation of the world in such excruciating, buttock-clenching detail that even Mortimer had steered clear of it. A random dig revealed some truly fascinating facts: that the *Novara* had started her journey with 1,500 litres of vinegar, which ran out after 95 days, and that their 16,000 rations of sauerkraut lasted only till day 299. Just at the point where I was preparing to extract my own fingernails out of sheer boredom, however, Scherzer did something extraordinary: he said something interesting. Just before departure, he said, he had been contacted by a German scientist who asked a favour. The scientist was none other than Friedrich Wöhler, one of the most celebrated chemists of the century. Wöhler had succeeded in isolating aluminium and beryllium, invented acetylene and been the first to synthesise urea—the first time anyone had managed to create an organic compound in the laboratory. It was Wöhler who had tested Tschudi's Bolivian sample and discovered that it was, in fact, gypsum. Far from putting him off, this had piqued his interest and he had a request for Scherzer. He wanted coca. Lots of it. Faced with a request from such an illustrious figure—a man of science like himself—Scherzer agreed.

Scherzer knew nothing about coca but bumped into a Scotsman in Peru named Campbell, who reported that he had seen an Indian walk 90 miles in a single day, never resting and eating nothing but coca and a few grains of maize. At the end of the journey the Indian had proceeded to stand on his head for half an hour (apparently a common custom to rest the feet and redistribute the blood) before drinking a glass of brandy and setting off on foot for home, 90 miles away. Scherzer was fascinated and, when the *Novara* arrived home after her massive two-and-a-half-year voyage, among the other 23,700 scientific specimens in the hold was a trunk, marked as belonging to Scherzer, containing a 30-pound bale of coca.

At the University of Göttingen, Wöhler gave the leaves to his most promising PhD student, Albert Niemann. Niemann's account of his analysis, a slim, palm-sized work that won him his PhD in March 1860, rests in the British Library. It is entitled *On a New Organic Base in the Coca Leaves*, and describes every step he took in the summer of 1859 to isolate the active constituent of coca. His first step was to wash the leaves in 85 per cent alcohol with a trace of sulphuric acid, then distil off the alcohol to leave a sticky substance. From this was separated a resin that was repeatedly shaken up with bicarbonate of soda. The resulting mixture was then distilled to yield a small quantity of white rod-shaped crystals. Here, finally, was the active constituent of coca. Following the names of other alkaloids—morphine, nicotine, strychnine and so on—he named his new compound coca-ine, or cocaine.

Niemann's great work in providing the answer to this age-old riddle was met with a thundering silence. Although it did win him his PhD, he was never to appreciate the full value of what he had done, and died just a year later, aged only 26.

However, in the same year that Niemann was isolating cocaine, an Italian doctor had written a paper that was to create a sensation. In 1859, the year Wöhler's leaves arrived from Peru, Paolo Mantegazza returned to Milan after a sojourn there himself. His paper, written from the perspective of a man of science, carried a great deal of weight, and was to alert the scientific world to the potential of cocaine. Of course, he was writing about coca, not cocaine, but the moment the alkaloid was isolated from the leaf they were assumed to be one and the same.

Mantegazza, in the tradition of the great early doctors, had conducted experiments on himself in order to determine the effects of various drugs, and this was the case with coca. The results were impressive. Medicinally, he declared that coca was useful in the treatment of 'a furred tongue in the morning, flatulence, [and] whitening the teeth'. Coca's ability to invigorate and excite showed through not only in his medical analysis but also in his prose—as he tried to describe what increasing doses did to him he often lost track of grammar, and sometimes even of what he was saying altogether. Mantegazza's paper, published in 1859, is enthusiastic, disorientated and over the top, illustrating one key fact: he had fallen in love with coca.

From 2–4 drachms [6–12g] one starts to become more and more isolated from the exterior world, and one is plunged into a consciousness of blissful pleasure, feeling oneself animated with overabundant life ... I am by nature extremely unsuited to any sort of gymnastic exercise but having reached a dose of 4 drachms [12g] of coca, I felt myself to be extraordinarily agile, and one time I leapt with both feet together on to a high writing desk with so much confidence that I did not even upset the lamp on the table. Other times I felt myself capable of jumping on my neighbours' heads.

Coca Experiences, Mantegazza, 1859

Then Mantegazza went too far.

The strongest dose of coca I ever chewed in one day was 18 drachms [54g], absorbing the last ten during the evening, an hour apart from each other. That was the only occasion I experienced coca drunkenness to its very limits and I must confess to having found that pleasure superior to all other pleasures known in the physical order ... I sneered at all the poor mortals condemned to live in the valley of tears while I, carried on the wings of two leaves of coca, went flying through the spaces of 77,438 worlds, each more splendid than the one before. An hour later I was sufficiently calm to write these words with a steady hand: God is unjust because he made man incapable of sustaining the effects of coca all life long. I would rather live a life of ten years with coca than one of 100,000 (and here I inserted a line of zeros) without it.

Mantegazza, 1859

One man who paid particular attention to Mantegazza's paper was a Corsican chemist called Angelo Mariani. Mariani, who had moved to Paris in 1860 to make his fortune, immediately saw coca's potential and realised that there was serious money to be made out of it. From that moment on he dedicated himself to learning all there was to know about coca: clearly there was a market for it, but where? It was fairly obvious that Europeans were unlikely ever to chew coca, so it was up to him to find another way of feeding it to them.

He decided to put it into a drink, and soon came up with the perfect medium: wine. Wine had a strong natural flavour that disguised the taste of the coca, was acceptable in all classes of society and was cheaply available in Paris. It also contained alcohol, which was a good cocaine solvent. When mixed together, wine leached the alkaloids from the coca leaves, which were then discarded, leaving a pleasant-tasting alcoholic brew with a real edge. In 1863 he named this new product Vin Mariani.

To launch his wine Mariani conceived a publicity campaign way ahead of its time. In addition to regular advertisements in the press he sent out free cases of wine to leading celebrities of the day, asking what they thought of it. Cannily, he also requested a signed photograph in return.

It is difficult to know whether the celebrities who responded were simply acknowledging the receipt of a gift, or whether they were genuinely impressed with the product, but the result was the same: a huge pile of letters from the most impressive men and women of the age, all apparently advocating the use of Vin Mariani. Mariani had the letters reprinted and inserted into leading French newspapers as free collectors' supplements. Over 50 million leaflets would be published and distributed like this. Pretty soon, everyone had heard of Vin Mariani.

From 1894 to 1913 he published these letters in a series of thirteen volumes of albums called *Portraits*, a complete set of which rests in the British Library. Each page featured an outline of the celebrity, followed by their picture, their signature and their comments on Vin Mariani.

Celebrities featuring in Mariani's great coca plug include Louis Blériot (first to fly across the Channel in 1909), who wrote, 'I took the precaution of bringing a small flask of Mariani Wine along with me, and it was a great help. Its energetic action sustained me during the crossing.' Thomas Edison, inventor of the lightbulb and the gramophone, was likewise impressed, as was the Norwegian writer Henrik Ibsen. Back in France the Lumière brothers, Antoine, Auguste and Louis (who had just invented cinema), commended the wine, as did the mathematician Henri Poincaré, who wrote cryptically, '20 Mariani = 100T'. Rodin signed his letter 'Your Friend', and Auguste Bartholdi, recently back from building the Statue of Liberty, commented that if he had known about Vin Mariani earlier, it 'would have attained a height of several hundred metres'.

In England, Jules Verne joked: 'Since a single bottle of Mariani's extraordinary coca wine guarantees a lifetime of 100 years, I shall be obliged to live until the year 2700! Well, I have no objections!' HG Wells was even more amenable: instead of writing he penned two caricatures of himself, one sad and one happy, labelling them 'before' and 'after' Vin Mariani.

Mariani then went further upmarket, sending a case of wine to the president of the United States, William McKinley, whose secretary wrote to say that the president was already well acquainted with it. He then posted a case to Pope Leo XIII, from whom he received a special papal gold medal honouring his creation. Meanwhile it was reported that Ulysses S Grant, the great American Civil War general, took a teaspoon of Vin Mariani every night before going to bed for the last five months of his life, and that this had been enough to sustain him through the process of writing his memoirs.[2]

Quite by chance, the Princess of Batenburg, having been presented with a set of the *Portraits*, commented how much her mother would enjoy them. A set was promptly dispatched, whereupon Mariani received a personal letter of thanks, saying that Queen Victoria considered them 'among the finest volumes in her collection'. (By a weird coincidence I bumped into Queen Victoria's original volumes in Los Angeles while searching for the inventor of crack.) Readers were impressed. Clearly, many of the world's leading minds were drinking Vin Mariani. Sales went through the roof.

As the first to see the marketing potential of coca, Mariani had opened the floodgates—and they were never to shut. Such was the success of Vin Mariani that it was shortly followed by a host of other coca products, including Pâte Mariani (throat lozenges), Pastilles Mariani (throat lozenges with added cocaine), Elixir Mariani (more alcoholic than Vin Mariani) and Mariani tea (a nonalcoholic version).

In conservative Britain, however, coca was more controversial and slower to catch on. In 1870 an amateurish trial into its stimulating effects was conducted by a Scottish doctor called Christison, who sent two of his students on a sixteen-mile walk with neither food nor water. When they returned home, exhausted, he fed them an infusion of coca, noting that 'presently hunger left them entirely, all sense of fatigue soon vanished, and they proceeded to promenade Prince's Street for an hour, which they did with ease and pleasure'.

He then tried coca himself—hiking 24 kilometres without food or water and noting how tired he was at the end of the day, before duplicat-

---

[2] Grant's appreciation of coca gave him something in common with his publisher, Mark Twain, who had read a book in his youth describing the wonders of the leaf. In *The Turning Point of My Life*, 1910 (*cit.* Strausbaugh and Blaise, 1991), he recalled: 'I was fired up with a longing to ascend the Amazon, also with a longing to open up a trade in coca in the world. During months I dreamed that dream, and tried to get to Para and spring that splendid enterprise upon an unsuspecting planet.' When he actually got around to leaving, however, things did not go according to plan. There were no boats to Para and he found himself stuck in New Orleans. 'After a few days I was out of money. Then Circumstance arrived, with another turning point of my life—a new link. On my way down, I had made the acquaintance of a pilot. I begged him to teach me the river, and he consented. I became a pilot.' Coca was forgotten—and the rest, as they say—is history.

ing the walk chewing coca. The results, he told the *British Medical Journal*, were impressive:

> I was surprised to find that all sense of weariness had vanished, and that I
> could proceed not only with ease but with elasticity. I got over the six miles
> in an hour and a half without difficulty, found it easy when done to get up
> to a four and a half mile pace, and to ascend quickly two stairs at a time to
> my dressing room, two floors upstairs.
>
> *BMJ*, 29 April 1876

In 1876 Christison took a group of his students to the top of Ben Vorlich (980 metres/3,224 feet), chewing coca when he arrived at the top. 'I at once felt that all fatigue was gone, and I went down the long descent with an ease that felt like that which I used to enjoy in the mountainous rambles in my youth.' Repeating the climb eight days later with the same result, Christison concluded that 'the chewing of coca not only removes extreme fatigue, but prevents it. Hunger and thirst are suspended; but eventually appetite and digestion are unaffected. No injury is sustained at the time or subsequently in occasional trials.'

These feats were noteworthy not simply because Christison was president of the British Medical Association but also because he happened to be 78 years old at the time.

Such enthusiasm was not highly regarded in all quarters. The *British Medical Journal*'s rival, the *Lancet*, wrote bluntly:

> One of our contemporaries has got coca leaf on the brain, and really seems
> to be in a very bad way. The marvellous plant has obliterated that ordinary
> politeness which gives a person credit for speaking the truth...There is
> nothing in Sir Robert Christison's experience of the coca leaf, or in that of
> anybody else to explain...the weekly essays which appear in our contemporary
> in place of actual information. The explanation of these essays is
> simple—coca leaf on the brain.
>
> *Lancet*, 1 April 1876

Across the pond in America, the verdict was the same.

I have been conversant with coca for the past eight years and would say that the great encomiums lavished upon its use are all 'bosh'. Coca will relieve and in a measure prevent thirst but so will chewing a bullet. I do not think it will prevent hunger as well as tobacco. In the meantime I would only advise my professional brethren not to consider that the elixir of life has been found in the leaves of *E coca*.

—GA Ward, *Medical Record* 17, 1880; 497

Christison's experiments may have invited ridicule from some of his peers but others were intrigued and sought to duplicate them. Soon reports began to appear citing similar cases of enhanced physical abilities. One group of climbers repeated Christison's experiment on Mont Blanc and reported that they had managed both ascent and descent with little difficulty, despite having taken no food all day. A Canadian doctor gave coca leaves to the Toronto Lacrosse Club before a tough match, noting that the leaves sustained them beautifully throughout the game. Christison's experiments were also to inspire perhaps the most famous cocaine addict of all time—as we shall see.

Coca was not only of interest to the medical world. It was speculated behind closed doors that coca, since it enabled men to perform more efficiently on less food, would be an ideal addition to military rations. This idea was not new: a variety of chroniclers had pointed out the possible military applications of the leaf. In 1599 Vargas Machuca had commented that the fierce warrior tribes of the Magdalena Valley could fight for three whole days without sleep or food after chewing coca and that they found it to be essential for nightwatchmen who had to stay awake when on duty.

In 1793 Dr Don Pedro Nolasco Crespo had suggested coca as an addition to normal naval rations (given our present knowledge of its nutritious value, this seems an eminently sensible suggestion), and a common feature in writings on coca was that it enabled the Peruvian military to endure terrible hardships. Both Tschudi and Peruvian doctor Hipolito Unanue had related that the Bolivian army used coca to travel on the 'coldest plateaux', relating that it had performed a great service during the siege of La Paz in 1771, when inhabitants were reduced to eating 'all types of things, even leather and revolting animals'.

Meanwhile General Miller—a British soldier—fought with the Peruvian army for nine years until 1826 and immediately noticed the superior physical abilities of his men when they chewed coca:

Their every day pedestrian feats are truly astonishing. Guides perform a
long journey at the rate of twenty or twenty-five leagues a day...They go
up and down mountain-sides quicker than a mule, and horsemen, whom
they accompany as guides, have frequently occasion to call after them, to
request them to slacken their pace. A battalion, eight hundred strong, has
been known to march thirteen or fourteen leagues in one day, without
leaving more than ten or a dozen stragglers on the road.

Memoirs of General Miller in the Service of the Republic of Peru, 1828

But if coca helped Bolivian and Peruvian soldiers, what would it do
for the British infantry? One doctor suggested that, had coca been available to the military, the wholesale slaughter of 16,000 men, women and
children during the great retreat from Afghanistan in 1842 might have
been avoided altogether. In 1893 Field Marshal Sir Henry Evelyn Wood
tested the effectiveness of coca on operational soldiers in the British
army. Results were reported in a document entitled 'Reports on army
Manoeuvres in Berkshire and Wiltshire':

The experiment was made of the use of coca leaves to allay thirst. About
1/8th ounce of leaves was issued at a time to each of those making the
experiment, and they were chewed with a small quantity of slaked lime.
The men, except for a few who objected to the taste, declared that they
found great benefit from the leaves, the feeling of thirst at once being
allayed.

cit. Coca and Cocaine, Martindale, 1892

These tests were never properly written up and were, we may assume,
abandoned fairly swiftly. This was not the case with a group of tests carried out on the Bavarian army in the summer of 1883 by a doctor called
Theodore Aschenbrandt. Aschenbrandt went one stage further than
having his boys chew coca. Because he was German, he was familiar
with the work of Wöhler and Niemann at Göttingen and knew all about
their escapades in alkaloid isolation. Instead of the inferior coca leaf,
he decided to give his troops the real thing: cocaine. The results were
promising:

Case LT, volunteer of one year, collapsed of exhaustion directly upon leaving W on the second day of the march; the weather was extremely hot. I

gave him approximately one tablespoon of water with 20 drops of a cocaine solution (0.5/10). A few minutes later (approximately five), he stood up of his own accord and travelled the distance to H, several kilometres, easily and cheerfully and with a pack on his back.

—Aschenbrandt, 1883, *cit. Coca Exotica*, Kennedy, 1985

He concluded:

I hope that with this study, which certainly is not complete nor entirely exact as to dosage and which certainly does not claim to be final proof of the properties of cocaine, I have drawn the attention of the military and inspired them to further research. I believe I have given sufficient evidence of its eminent usefulness.

Aschenbrandt, 1883, *cit. Coca Exotica*, Kennedy, 1985

It was this report that was to start the cocaine bandwagon rolling. Because—unknown to Aschenbrandt—a young medical student in Vienna, looking for a new research project, had set his sights on cocaine. It was his research that was to lead to the first cocaine addicts and the huge ensuing wave of recreational cocaine use, and was to unleash what one of his contemporaries called 'the third scourge of humanity'. His contribution was to change the course of the history of coca and cocaine irreversibly. Indeed, if there is one figure who can be credited with the introduction of cocaine into modern society—both medical and illicit—it is this one 29-year-old medical student.

He was Sigmund Freud.

4 The Third Scourge of Humanity

Peru—history of coca: 'the Divine Plant' of the Incas, by William Golden Mortimer MD, is one of the most powerful sedatives known to man. I know this now; I didn't then. After eight months in the library, however, I began to get the impression that something was seriously wrong.

Mortimer made me suspicious: a combination of such excruciatingly boring yet methodical writing and intricate cross-referencing, done in such a random manner, with such enthusiasm? It didn't add up. Try this, for example. Page 3, paragraph 5:

> Even though others may point the way, everyone must fight his own battles. To each of us the world may appear as we shape it for ourselves—a thought poetically expressed by the composer Wagner, who said: 'the world exists only in our heart and conception'. This shaping, if done by weakly hands or influenced by a troubled brain, may not always prove symmetrical. A sensitive imagination, sharply attuned, jars discordantly amidst inharmonious surroundings, which will be all the more harshly apparent if made possible through a known impotence.
>
> *Peru—History of Coca: 'the Divine Plant' of the Incas,*
> William Golden Mortimer MD

What drug was this guy on? I was willing to hazard a guess. As I ploughed through the book it became clear that Mortimer's enthusiasm for coca and cocaine was not based on scientific fact. Well, it *was* based on scientific fact, but it was tempered by something else. This first really hit me when I examined the frontispiece and noticed that Mortimer had dedicated the book to Angelo Mariani, inventor of Vin Mariani. Why? Was Mortimer a fan of coca wine? Or was he a stooge, some second or third cousin planted by Mariani to write a glowing account of the wine and its constituents? One thing was sure: Mortimer was a coca aficionado—probably cocaine as well—and, perhaps because of this, he fostered an intense craving for mind-numbing detail, leading to that kind of boredom so excruciating that it causes paint to creak off walls and Roman arches that have stood for thousands of years to groan, give up the ghost and just collapse.

In the early 1980s freebase cocaine users would become used to this: it was a trait associated with excessive use of the drug known as stereotypy—expressing inordinate interest in details, pointless repetitions, minutiae. Mortimer's writing betrayed all the symptoms of the habitual cocaine user. But was he a coke fiend? Or simply a Victorian writer?

Mortimer didn't go into the Freud story in any detail. Perhaps he didn't know about it. He should have, because, if there is one person who can be held responsible for the emergence of cocaine as a recreational pharmaceutical, it was Freud. Of course, this angle would have been less appealing back in 1897 when Mortimer was writing, for the simple reason that Freud was still relatively unknown. Also, there was the fact that the story was genuinely interesting—a feature that would pretty much have precluded his writing about it.

Mortimer was uninterested but I was intrigued: how could Freud—doctor, founder of psychoanalysis and general all-round dour nineteenth-century bloke—have been behind the emergence of the hippest drug of the twentieth century? I turned to Ernest Jones's massive 1953 biography. Jones seemed to think that the source of what he coyly termed 'the cocaine episode' dated back to Freud's early career as a researcher at university. I didn't know anything about all this. It had never really occurred to me that Freud had even been to university. I mean, obviously he had been to university—I had just never given the matter of Freud's education much thought. Come to think of it, I didn't know much about Freud at all.

I flicked back a couple of chapters to try to gain an insight into the life of the guy whose early work was to provide Keith Richards with more than a few good nights out.

The Freuds, Jakob and Amalia, moved to Vienna in 1860. Sigmund, the eldest child, was very bright at school and there was every hope that he would go on to achieve great things. As the eldest son he was the favourite, and the only member of the family to have his own bedroom, which he quickly filled to the ceiling with his one overriding passion: books. Such was his thirst for knowledge that often he would even eat his meals in his room, leaving more time available for reading. In 1873 he decided to become a doctor and went up to the University of Vienna, where, working as a research student in the laboratory of Professor Ernst Brucke, he fell in love with medical research. He became involved in the study of the new science of neurology and spent long hours examining the nerve cells of crayfish and other molluscs, eventually gaining the dubious distinction of becoming the first scientist ever to locate eels' genitals (a pressing scientific quest if ever there was one). There was no doubt that he was a brilliant young student and it seemed only a matter of time until he made his mark. Until, that is, something extraordinary and unplanned happened.

One evening in April 1882, Freud returned home and was on the verge of disappearing to his room to continue his studies when he heard voices from the dining room: his sisters had invited some friends to tea. Among them were two girls he did not know, Martha and Minnie Bernay. On his way upstairs Freud glanced through the open door and caught sight of Martha, who, peeling an apple, happened to look up at that very moment. Five years younger than he, short, petite and extremely intelligent, she caught his eye. One glimpse was all it took. Much to the consternation of his family he walked into the room, sat down and introduced himself. As far as Freud the bachelor was concerned, it was all over. Two months later they were engaged.

Martha's family did not approve of the match. The Freuds had neither money nor name, and although they themselves were not especially wealthy they came from a well-respected family. In the interests of decency—and perhaps in the hope that Martha might find someone more eligible—she was dispatched to live with her mother at Wandsbek, near Hamburg, until Freud could afford to support her so they could marry. This move was to place him under considerable pressure. He lived a long way away from her and was unable either to take the time, or to afford the necessary train tickets, to visit her regularly.

Also painfully insecure, he had visions of her backing out of the engagement. The only solution was to make some money so that they could afford to get married as soon as possible. But how? Freud figured that his best bet was to discover something tremendous in medicine, making both his name and a fortune simultaneously: eel genitals were one thing, marrying Martha quite another. To this end he spent more and more time at the laboratory.

His first real discovery, a new technique for staining nerve tissues with gold chloride, was simply not lucrative enough—although reported enthusiastically in the two new neurological journals, *Brain* and the *Journal of Nervous and Mental Diseases*—and it was clear he would never make any money with it. Then he had an idea. He wrote to tell Martha about it in April.

> I have been reading about cocaine, the essential constituent of coca leaves which some Indian tribes chew to enable them to resist privations and hardships. A German [Aschenbrandt] has been employing it with soldiers and has in fact reported that it increases their energy and capacity to endure. I am procuring some myself and will try it with cases of heart disease and also of nervous exhaustion...Perhaps others are working at it; perhaps nothing will come of it. But I shall certainly try it, and you know that when one perseveres sooner or later one succeeds. We do not need more than one such lucky hit for us to be able to think of setting up house.
>
> 21 April 1884, *cit. The Life and Work of Sigmund Freud,*
> Ernest Jones, 1953

Freud ordered a gram of cocaine from a local pharmacy called Angel's and received it the week of 24 April. Although concerned about the cost of the drug (he had miscalculated the quantity and it ended up costing him a tenth of his month's salary), the first thing he did was to take one-twentieth of a gram himself. The results were immediate: he felt much better about the money, the research project and life in general. He wondered if it might be useful in the treatment of melancholia. Moreover, since it had removed his hunger, he figured that it might be of use as a gastric anaesthetic.

Freud took some more. Clearly, he had made a big find and he was extremely enthusiastic—perhaps not entirely surprising, bearing in mind he was as high as a kite. Adhering to his theory that it might be useful for ailments of the stomach, he fed some to a patient suffering from gastric catarrh and the results were so successful that he began to farm samples out to his friends and colleagues to try. He ordered some more and sent half a gram to Martha to 'make her strong and give her cheeks a red colour', advising her to 'make yourself 8 small (or 5 large) doses from it'.

His tendency to farm out cocaine to friends could be seen today as reckless. As his biographer later noted, 'He pressed it on his friends and colleagues, both for themselves and their patients, he gave it to his sisters. In short, looked at from the vantage point of our present knowledge, he was rapidly becoming a public menace.'

Freud's appreciation of cocaine was heightened by the fact that when he was not taking it he was miserable. He had not seen Martha for over a year and her prolonged absence was exacerbating his natural tendency towards depression. Cocaine provided the perfect antidote, and he fell for it immediately. He planned his next visit to Wandsbek for the late summer of 1884, writing to her excitedly:

> Woe to you, my princess, when I come. I will kiss you quite red and feed you till you are plump. And if you are forward you shall see who is the stronger, a little girl who doesn't eat enough or a big strong man with cocaine in his body. In my last serious depression I took cocaine again and a small dose lifted me to the heights in a wonderful fashion. I am just now collecting the literature for a song of praise to this magical substance.
>
> 2 June 1884, *cit. The Life and Work of Sigmund Freud*, Ernest Jones, 1953

The resulting paper, *Über Coca* (About Coca), was eventually printed in the journal *Archiv Für Der Gesämmte Therapie* in June 1884. He would never write anything quite like it again. A recent chronicler comments that: 'Untypical for Freud, he makes a lot of slips, miswrites names, confuses places and dates, gives titles of works imprecisely and even has a mistake in the cocaine formula.' Reading the paper today, one must agree with his biographer in his analysis that it is an unusual piece of work:

> There is...in this essay a tone that never recurred in Freud's writings, a remarkable combination of objectivity with a personal warmth, as if he were in love with the content itself. He used expressions uncommon in a scientific paper, such as 'the most gorgeous excitement' that animals display after an injection of cocaine, and administering an 'offering' of cocaine rather than a 'dose'.
>
> *The Life and Work of Sigmund Freud*, Ernest Jones, 1953

The fact that he referred to the paper, in advance, as a 'song of praise' gives a fair indication of his opinions regarding cocaine at this stage. With the benefit of hindsight it is obvious that his enthusiasm for the drug, while partly derived from its medical potential, also comes to some extent from the exhilaration that he himself was experiencing with it— Freud was on a different planet.

Having dispatched the paper to the printers, he headed off to Wands-bek to see Martha, expecting to come back to moderately favourable reviews and a possible future for his new drug. In fact, by the time he got back in late September, cocaine was more famous than he could possibly have imagined—but not for the reasons he had expected. Because, while he was away on holiday with Martha, something truly momentous hap-pened, and everything changed.

While following up his research into cocaine, Freud had conducted some experiments with a colleague called Carl Koller. Koller, an ophthal-mology intern eighteen months younger than Freud, had the reputation of being so preoccupied with medicine that he was actually quite tiresome on the subject. His particular interest, which had become an obsession of late, was pain relief. Owing to a complete lack of local anaesthetics he had been taught to conduct eye operations with no analgesia at all, a pro-cedure that involved strapping down and gagging the patient, forcing their eyes open and simply hacking away. It was torture for the patient—and hardly a picnic for the surgeon. Moreover, some ophthalmic proce-dures required the active participation of the patients, who might have to rotate their eyeballs, blink their eyelids, or tell the surgeon what they could see. But getting a patient to do anything after cutting their eyeball with a scalpel without anaesthetic was quite impossible.

In really serious procedures ether could be administered to knock the patient out altogether but this was far from ideal: it was dangerous for those with weak constitutions and often made people violently sick when they came round. If they were sick, the retching tended to tear out stitches around the operation site, making another procedure necessary. Hence it was preferable to conduct optical surgery without anaesthesia, and the most important quality of eye procedures was how fast the sur-geon could get them done.

Koller was determined to change this. For some time he had been experimenting with various chemicals, including morphine and chloral bromine, looking for the magic combination that would remove pain but leave his patients conscious. By a bizarre coincidence, his collaboration with Freud was to provide him with just such a drug. Because what nei-ther he nor Freud realised was that the drug that they were experimenting with was the very substance that he had been looking for all this time.

The pair spent a number of afternoons together, dosing each other up with cocaine, using a dynamometer to test their muscular strength before and after it was administered. In the course of their experiments they injected and ate a fair quantity of the drug and at one point, according to Freud, Koller touched some to his lips and commented that it made them feel numb. Freud agreed but clearly he himself missed the significance of this effect altogether. Koller didn't. While Freud was on holiday with Martha in Wandsbek, Koller continued to test cocaine and it was then that the importance of the numbness hit him. Some years later he recounted the moment of realisation.

> upon one occasion another colleague of mine, Dr Engel, partook of some [cocaine] with me from the point of his penknife and remarked 'How that numbs the tongue.' I said, 'yes, that has been noticed by everyone that has eaten it'. And in that moment it flashed upon me that I was carrying in my pocket the local anaesthetic for which I had searched some years earlier.
>
> *Coca Erythroxylon*, 1885, Parke, Davis

Koller ran out of the room, across the quad and straight into the laboratory of Professor Stricker's Institute of Pathological Anatomy, telling the duty laboratory assistant, a Dr Gaertner, that he needed to conduct an important experiment. Thirty-five years later Gaertner recounted the event:

> Dr Koller ... drew a small flask in which there was a trace of white powder from his pocket, and addressed me, Professor Stricker's assistant, in approximately the following words: 'I hope, indeed I expect, that this powder will anaesthetise the eye.' 'We'll find out about that right away,' I replied. A few grains of the substance were thereupon dissolved in a small quantity of distilled water, a large, lively frog was selected from the aquarium and held immobile in a cloth and now a drop of the solution was trickled into one of the protruding eyes ... after about a minute came the historic moment—I do not hesitate to designate it as such. The frog permitted his cornea to be touched and even injured without a trace of reflex action or attempt to protect himself—whereas the other eye responded with the usual reflex action to the slightest touch ... the same tests were performed on a rabbit and a dog with equally good results. Now it was necessary to go one step further and to repeat the experiment on a human being. We trickled the solution under the upraised lids of each other's eyes. Then we put a mirror before us, took a pin in hand, and tried to touch the cornea with its head. Almost simultaneously we could assure ourselves, 'I

can't feel a thing.' We could make a dent in the cornea without the slight-
est awareness of the touch, let alone any unpleasant sensation or reaction.
With that the discovery of local anaesthesia was completed. I rejoice that I
was the first to congratulate Dr Koller as a benefactor of mankind.

cit. Coca Exotica, Kennedy, 1985

Koller might indeed have been a benefactor of mankind but he was
still an unpaid and unknown intern and there was a question of how he
was to alert the world to his discovery. Unable to afford to travel to the
next convention of the Heidelberg Ophthalmological Society to announce
his breakthrough, he wrote up a preliminary communication announcing
his discovery of the world's first local anaesthetic and gave it to a friend
who was going, Dr Joseph Brettauer.

When Brettauer read the paper and demonstrated cocaine's anaesthetic properties in front of the congress on 15 September 1884, the
result was a stupefied silence: Koller, a 27-year-old intern from Vienna,
had solved one of the most important problems in medicine. By the time
Freud got back from Wandsbek, his friend was an international celebrity.

The Incas—had there been any left—would not have been surprised by
any of this: they had been using coca for its analgesic qualities for centuries.
Koller had not been the first to notice the anaesthetising properties of
cocaine itself, either: he was just the first to appreciate their significance.
No sooner had he published his paper than doctors came out of the wood-
work claiming to have known all along that cocaine was a local anaesthetic.
The list of others who had mentioned the numbing effect but not appreciated its significance was long and distinguished: even Freud himself had
suggested its application as an analgesic in *Über Coca*. After submitting his
paper he had specifically told a colleague, Leopold Königstein, that cocaine
might be useful as a painkiller in eye conditions such as trachoma. Königstein had tried an aqueous solution on a patient suffering from this disorder, only to find that it made the condition worse. It later emerged that he
had used a solution of cocaine ten times too strong, hence the irritation.

Meanwhile, in Paris, a French doctor called Gazeau had been pre-
scribing Vin Mariani for years as a topical painkiller for opera singers
with sore throats, trying to persuade anyone who would listen that coca
had anaesthetic qualities. Angelo Mariani later attempted to gain Gazeau
some recognition for this but his motives were not so much altruistic as
nepotistic: he was Gazeau's cousin.

In 1880 a young Russian surgeon called Vassily von Anrepp had even suggested explicitly that cocaine might be a useful local anaesthetic, publishing his ideas as to how it might be used in *Pfluger's Archiv*. Why this was never picked up on is anyone's guess. By a curious coincidence, however, Anrepp's successor in his research post was none other than Theodore Aschenbrandt—whose work was, of course, to inspire Freud and thus lead indirectly to local anaesthesia. The fact that no one had listened to Anrepp in the first place leaves him in the file of unrecognised pioneers of medicine. Koller was a hero; Anrepp was no one. He died, a complete unknown, in Paris in 1925.

Freud saw his condition as rather unfortunate. He had done all the work; Koller had just followed up a hunch. Here was the drug that he had brought to the attention of the medical community and someone else was taking all the credit. It must have been galling, as this was exactly the kind of discovery that would have enabled him to marry Martha and settle in Vienna immediately.

Freud had no excuse for not recognising the potential of cocaine: he had been studying it for months and had even suggested to Königstein that it might be useful for pain relief in certain eye conditions. Yet he had not made the leap from cocaine as a numbing agent to cocaine as an anaesthetic. He was later—uncharitably—to blame this failure on his fiancée, Martha.

I may go back a little and explain how it was the fault of my fiancée that I was not already famous at an early age. A side interest, though it was a deep one, had led me in 1884 to obtain from Merck what was then a little known alkaloid, cocaine, and to study its physiological action. While I was in the middle of this work, an opportunity arose for making a journey to visit my fiancée, from whom I had been parted for two years. I hastily wound up my investigation of cocaine and contented myself in my book on the subject with prophesying that further uses for it would soon be found...Koller is therefore rightly regarded as the discoverer of local anaesthesia by cocaine, which has become so important in minor surgery; but I bore my fiancée no grudge for the interruption of my works.

cit. The Life and Work of Sigmund Freud, Ernest Jones, 1953

This must surely go down as one of the most slope-shouldered attempts to shift blame on to someone else ever to appear in print. It isn't even true. Freud had not been away from Martha for 'two years', only one. The opportunity to go to Wandsbek did not arise suddenly, as he implies, but had been planned for some time. And he did not 'hastily' wind up his research at all: in fact he dispatched *Über Coca* to the printers in mid-June and then didn't get around to visiting Martha until September. Freud's wall of excuses disguises how disappointed he was not to have discovered local anaesthesia himself; he later admitted, in private, that he had not followed up his research thoroughly out of 'laziness'.

He does not seem to have been too despondent at the time, however. So convinced was he of the numerous applications of this new drug that he presumed there would be more glory on the way. This was not to be: other than as a local anaesthetic, there was no legitimate use for cocaine. Koller had indeed stolen Freud's thunder but, in a bizarre turn of events, Freud soon had a reason to thank him for it.

Six months after the discovery, Freud received a visit from his father, who told him that one of his eyes hurt. Koller happened to be at Freud's house that afternoon and examined him, immediately diagnosing glaucoma. The very next day Freud, Koller and Königstein operated on Freud's father, saving his eyesight. Cocaine was used as an anaesthetic.[3]

Freud's father was not the only one who was pleased. The medical community, alerted to the anaesthetic qualities of cocaine, became obsessed with the drug: OK, so it anaesthetised—but what else did it do? Just about everything, it seemed. Freud was working on cocaine cures for neurasthenia and melancholia; others thought it might relieve diabetes, asthma or syphilis. Reports of its uses in surgery were everywhere, relieving pain in procedures ranging from tonsillectomies and labour pains to tooth extraction and haemorrhoid operations. The *British Medical Journal*, which had previously reported the antics of Sir Robert Christison in the Scottish Highlands, was delighted:

HYDROCHLORATE OF COCAINE, THE NEW LOCAL ANAESTHETIC
Hydrochlorate of cocaine is at the present moment attracting an amount of attention rarely accorded to any therapeutic agent not of the very first

---

[3] How jealous was Freud of Koller's discovery? Academics still dispute this point today. A recent work on the subject suggests that Freud hated Koller, writing of him fifty years later as 'a pathological personality, [and] a self-tormenting quarreller'. Possibly. It does not explain, however, why Freud would have presented him with a copy of *Über Coca*, inscribing it—with rare humour—'to my friend, Carl "Coca" Koller'.

rank. It may be fairly said that the news of the introduction of a new local anaesthetic has been hailed with universal satisfaction...Obviously we have here a new agent of great value in aiding the physician or the surgeon to fulfil that first and most important of tasks—the relief of pain. Not only do the whole range of surgical neuralgias appear to be amenable to its use, but as a local anaesthetic in the operations, especially, of the ophthalmic and laryngeal surgeon, and of the gynaecologist, a wide field of useful application appears at once to have been opened to this last addition to our therapeutic armoury.

BMJ, 2 November 1884

Suddenly the medical papers were filled with a glut of young doctors testing the drug on themselves and reporting its effects. How else could cocaine be applied? What else might it be useful for? A typical example was the American ophthalmologist Hermann Knapp who ordered up some cocaine and, when it arrived, proceeded to paint it all over his tongue and into his ears, eyes and mouth. He then sprayed it into his lungs, up his nose and then (perhaps beyond the call of duty) injected a syringe full of the stuff into his own penis. He noted paleness and insensitivity. In a well-meaning but rather masochistic experiment, he then proceeded to insert a series of catheters and 'other instruments' (one has horrific images of clarinets or perhaps trombones) into his penis to find out how much it would hurt. 'For the sake of completeness', he repeated this experiment on his own rectum. These experiments, he cites proudly as 'the first ever to have been conducted'. Hopefully they were the last.

Meanwhile the American medical press was reporting cocaine's successful use in urethral operations, removal of ingrowing toenails, dental procedures, gynaecological excisions and even the removal of 'superfluous hairs from the upper lip of a lady by electrolysis'. Somewhat implausibly, among its nonsurgical uses were cited the relief of impotence in men and the cure of both masturbation and nymphomania in women. A physician in Cleveland claimed to have cured two cases of tinnitus with it. The *New York Times* reported: 'The new uses to which cocaine has been applied with success in New York...include hayfever, catarrh and toothache and it is now being experimented with in cases of seasickness...All will be given to understand that cocaine will cure the worst cold in the head ever heard of.'

Other papers were likewise enthusiastic, especially regarding an idea that was floating around at the time that cocaine might be useful in weaning alcoholics and morphine addicts off their addictions.

The *Boston Medical Journal* reported that 'the moderate use of coca is not only wholesome but beneficial'. The *Therapeutic Gazette* commented that 'one feels like trying coca, with or without the opium habit. A harmless remedy for the blues is essential.' Pharmaceutical companies began marketing cocaine cures for all sorts of ailments and discomforts, from seasickness to hay fever—in lozenges, cigarettes, cough medicines, cold cures; there was no limit to what cocaine could do.

As medical reports indicate, by late 1884 no one was in any doubt as to the miraculous tonic effect of cocaine on the body. *Why* the drug had this effect, however, was a different matter altogether. Knowing that this kind of explanation was way beyond their comprehension, most of the original experimenters didn't bother to speculate what the drug was actually doing, or how it was doing it. Even such pioneers as Freud and Mantegazza were at a complete loss as to what was going on. Perhaps this was not surprising: it was to be over a century before science even began to prise open the secrets of cocaine's mysterious allure.

At Brookhaven, New Jersey, I was introduced to one of their modern counterparts. Dr Nora Volkow, a petite American with a Spanish accent and a hundred-mile-per-hour delivery, is one of an exclusive group of scientists around the world examining the effects of cocaine on the human brain. Her research has allowed her a unique insight into the drug's modus operandi, and she has now reached the position where she can actually explain why cocaine was making everyone feel so good in the late nineteenth century. Or, in other words, Why Cocaine is Fun.

Fifty miles east of New York City, Volkow has been feeding cocaine to volunteers for the best part of twenty years. As we sat down in her office she told me how she got into cocaine, way back in 1984 when she was studying at the University of Texas at Houston: 'I was seeing a lot of patients coming up with cocaine intoxication and we were seeing several patients in the emergency room—and that was intriguing. So I started to work with them and, from the time I did my first study, I was surprised to see that the brains of the cocaine abusers had very severe changes. They were very disrupted.'

At this point Volkow was not looking for cocaine's mechanism in the brain but, instead, for proof that the drug caused permanent damage in the brains of habitual abusers. She discovered that serious addicts often manifested symptoms similar to those presented by stroke victims, including paralysis of certain regions of the face. Volkow concluded that because cocaine caused blood vessels to constrict—one of the factors that had made it an effective local anaesthetic, owing to a reduction in bleeding at the site of operation—it was reducing blood flow in the brain.

'Blood-vessel diameter is very important in regulating the amount of blood you get in your brain—which is crucial, because the brain is very sensitive to oxygen,' she said, 'so what happens is cocaine produces vasoconstriction. It makes your blood vessels constrict and then no blood can get through them, and that's when you start having the symptoms.'

It was an interesting discovery but it was only a start. More important than her actual conclusion was the technique she was using in her research. In her quest to prove that cocaine produced stroke-like episodes in users, Volkow did something that no one before her had tried: she took pictures of the human brain under the influence of cocaine. Photographing people's brains in Freud's day involved lopping the tops of their heads off, so we can hardly blame him for not considering it. To take pictures of the brain without disturbing it, you need a very special—and expensive—camera called a PET (Positron Emission Tomography) scanner.

PET is a bit like that police operation where they place a locator beacon in a stolen car to monitor where it goes. Specific molecules are tagged with a radioactive emitter (a positron source, hence the name) before being injected into the body. As they travel through the bloodstream into the brain the tagged molecules emit a homing signal and the scanner logs their emissions, providing a series of pictures that show where these specific molecules are at any given time. You can tag almost anything and watch it flow through the brain like this.

Volkow began by tagging water, changing the oxygen molecule to ^{15}O. Then she began toying with other molecules that might be involved in the process of cocaine use: glucose and, later, cocaine itself. Her work has produced the first concrete demonstration of the way cocaine operates inside the human brain. And the key to the whole operation, says Volkow, is a chemical neurotransmitter called dopamine.

Electrical circuits make connections physically by mechanical switches, like points on a railway track. The brain, however, has no moving parts. Instead, for its electrical connections, it relies on interlocking circuits that communicate with one another chemically: when cell A wants to make a connection with cell B, instead of physically touching it, it releases neurotransmitters. These chemicals, picked up almost simultaneously by cell B, trigger a new signal and the message is relayed down the line. One of these neurotransmitters is dopamine.

Dopamine is found in the limbic areas of the brain—regions that deal with emotion. From an evolutionary point of view, these regions evolved because it was important for an animal such as man to be programmed to pursue certain species-propagating actions (having sex, eating) as opposed to certain other, non-species-propagating, actions (leaping off cliffs, thrusting body parts into threshing machines and so on). Dopamine is the chemical that lets your body know when something is species-propagating, and the response that it generates in the body is what we call 'pleasure'. Dopamine creates this by firing up the pleasure circuitry to make you feel good. Better: to make you feel great. Thus dopamine is responsible for the way that cocaine makes you feel.

The fact is that more dopamine in the right places means more pleasure. While people have very individual tastes, certain things seem to be pretty effective at increasing the human dopamine count. Chocolate, a cold beer on a hot day, or perhaps a hot bath, will all increase your dopamine count. However, the pleasure created by these stimuli is always short-lived because no sooner has the dopamine been released than it is swept up and recycled again for use next time. This is the reason that a bar of chocolate, while it does taste exquisite for a while, does not make you feel great for the rest of the afternoon. The brain provides just enough dopamine to let you know that this is pleasurable, and then starts clearing it away again.

However, there are certain ways of boosting your dopamine count artificially: drugs. The reason that chocolate tastes so great after a few joints is that marijuana increases dopamine production so there is more of it around when the chocolate hits. Stronger drugs, such as the opiates, force the release of vast amounts of dopamine, flooding the pleasure centres in the brain—leading to intense euphoria.

Cocaine is a bit smarter than this. Instead of simply cranking up dopamine production in the brain, what cocaine does is to block its re-uptake. It does this by hitting a molecule called the dopamine transporter, bonding to, and thus disabling, it. As more cocaine is taken, the more dopamine transporters are kept busy, the less dopamine is reabsorbed, thus the more dopamine there is floating around—and the better you feel.

Volkow has been the first to see this in action, on the screen of her PET scanner, and has shown that the peak of cocaine-induced dopamine correlates perfectly with what users refer to as the 'rush' and the 'high'. She has shown that cocaine at doses commonly used by the drug taker binds between 60 and 77 per cent of all dopamine re-uptake sites. And guess what? *That's* why cocaine makes you feel good.

Freud and his colleagues, of course, had no idea about any of this. By now they were busying themselves elsewhere.

After its anaesthetic qualities, the most exciting of cocaine's potential uses was as a cure for opium and morphine addiction. The idea of a simple cure for addiction had created great excitement in America as, following the Civil War, numerous soldiers had returned home addicted to the opiates (a fact that had led morphine addiction to become known euphemistically as 'the army disease'). The only treatment for such addiction at the time was either to do violent cold turkey or to remain an addict for the rest of your life. Thus, when, initiated by a letter from a Dr WH Bentley in the *Therapeutic Gazette* in May 1878, a series of reports appeared in American medical journals suggesting that cocaine could be used to cure morphine addiction, physicians had taken note—Freud being one of them. Was this true? Bentley quoted four cases of removal from opium habits with cocaine, adding that he had also cured three 'drunks', too. From all over the US, reports came in agreeing with him.

In Atlanta one man had an especially good reason for wanting to test cocaine's efficacy at prising addicts away from morphine. A middle-aged pharmacist by the name of John Styth Pemberton, he was a Confederate soldier who had fought in the Civil War and then set up as a pharmacist in 1869. Like thousands of others of his generation he was a morphine addict. Pemberton had spent a number of years cooking up patent cures for all kind of ailments. As the proud inventor of BBB ('Botanic Blood Balm'), Triplex Liver Pills, Globe Flower Cough Syrup and Indian Queen Hair Dye, he also had a reputation to uphold.

In 1880 he, too, read the accounts of miracle morphine cures with cocaine. He read the accounts of Sir Robert Christison's mountaineering exploits in the *British Medical Journal*. He also noticed how well Vin Mariani was selling. Pemberton began conducting research into coca, eventually cooking up his own Vin Mariani copy, 'French Wine Coca' ('an ideal tonic and stimulant'), later that year. It hit the market in 1881 and Pemberton was soon to boast to a journalist that 'I believe that I am now producing a far better preparation than that of Mariani'.

Pemberton even copied Mariani's advertising campaign, his advertisements telling punters that French Wine Coca was drunk by '20,000' of the world's greatest scientists. Still seeking a cure for morphine addiction, he used the plug that 'to the unfortunates who are addicted to the morphine or opium habit, or the excessive use of alcoholic stimulants, the French Wine Coca has proven a great blessing'. However, it wasn't long before French Wine Coca ran into trouble.

On 25 November 1885 Atlanta voted to ban the sale of alcohol, leaving Pemberton high and dry. No longer allowed to manufacture French Wine Coca, he removed the alcohol and began searching for new ingredients to add to the flavour of the drink. He also decided to rename it. But what was a suitable name for a coca wine that had no wine in it? His accountant, Frank M Robinson, suggested that it should be named after its two main stimulating ingredients: coca leaves and kola nuts. In a creative moment it was decided to misspell kola to make the name more attractive on the label, and Coca-Cola was born.

Advertised as 'a remarkable therapeutic agent' and an 'ideal nerve and tonic stimulant', Coca-Cola was sold to pharmacists in a syrup form and dispensed in six-ounce glasses, mixed with water. Soon it was discovered that Coca-Cola syrup tasted better mixed with soda water, a fact that helped to enhance its reputation as a curative (fizzy drinks were trendy and the bubbles seemed reminiscent of health spas). Gradually the drink caught on, but not fast enough for Pemberton. In 1891 he sold out to Asa Griggs Candler, a former medical student who had noticed that pharmacists made considerably more money than doctors. In one of the most astute financial investments ever made, Candler acquired the rights and recipes of Coca-Cola for the princely sum of $2,300. When he died 38 years later, the medical student who had always wanted to be richer than a doctor was worth $50 million.

The success of Coca-Cola was an inspiration for quack cure peddlers everywhere and it soon spawned a ridiculous number of imitations: Velo Cola, Metcalf's Coca Wine, Inca Cola, Café Coca, Dr Don's Coca, Kola Ade, Kos Kola, Celery Cola, Nicol's Compound Kola Cordial, Kumfort's Cola Extract, Pillsbury's Coke Extract, Vani Cola, Rococola, Quina-Coca,

Vin de Coca de Perou, Dr Sampson's Coca Spirits, Sutcliff and Case Company's Beef, Wine and Coca, Lambert Company's Wine of Coca with Peptonate Iron, Maltine's Coca Wine, Liebig's Coca Beef Tonic, Cola-Coca and so on, and so on, and so on. A company in Birmingham, Alabama, called a spade a spade and released a version called simply Dope Cola. All claimed marvellous efficiency as general tonics or cures for everything from depression and fatigue to 'those nervous conditions peculiar to females'.

Since one of cocaine's first actions was to dry up the nasal passages it was deemed to be of particular use for sinus problems such as hayfever and asthma. Many of these preparations were snuffs—leading to the trend for taking cocaine nasally. Dr Tucker's Specific, Az-ma-syde, Ryno's Hay Fever 'n' Catarrh Remedy, Nyall's Compound Extract of Damiana and Paine's Celery Compound were just a few of the bogus nasal powders whose active constituent consisted entirely of cocaine.

But cocaine was not only bought in patent medicines: all around the world it could be bought over the counter in aqueous preparations of varying strengths and as pure cocaine hydrochloride itself. The first commercial cocaine production operation was run by Merck of Darmstadt, Germany, who produced a total of 50 grams in 1879. Following Koller's discovery, the price of the drug rocketed from 6 marks per gram to 23 marks per gram in just 3 months. In the US, where cocaine was manufactured only by Parke, Davis of Detroit, it was even more expensive, leaping from $2.50 to $13 per gram.

No sooner had these companies realised that there was a market for this innocuous alkaloid than they cranked up production. From 1881 to 1884, Merck had made a total of 1.4 kilograms of cocaine. In 1885 they churned out 30 kilograms. Soon more drug companies began production and the price began to drop. And drop. From February to October 1885, Merck's prices plummeted from 23 marks per gram to 1 mark per gram. As the 1880s drew on the price dropped to such an extent that it became increasingly common to buy pure cocaine directly over the counter; in some US states barmen even offered drinkers a shot of whiskey with cocaine in it.

Cocaine looked to be the saviour of doctors the world over. But, apart from its use as an anaesthetic in surgical procedures, it was not really curing anything: it was just making people feel great for a while. And there was another, far more worrying, problem. Because, at the heart of the cocaine community, things were going wrong.

As early as January 1885 reports had begun to surface of cocaine's side effects—a shock, since the drug was initially regarded as entirely safe. The first reports mentioned patients losing their facial colour, going into cold sweats and passing out. There followed more serious symptoms: complete blackouts and convulsions. It seemed that certain applications of cocaine were likely to cause toxic reactions, and that these could be serious. A Russian doctor administered 23 grains of cocaine to a girl prior to a minor operation and she died right there on the operating table. He committed suicide afterwards. All drugs had side effects, and cocaine was liable to fluctuations in strength, making dosage calculations haphazard, so this was not too surprising, but there was a much more serious problem—as Freud was soon to realise when he watched the drug take over the life of a great friend of his, Ernst von Fleischl-Marxow.

Fleischl-Marxow was one of Professor Ernst Brücke's laboratory assistants, a brilliant, handsome, charismatic doctor, renowned for his charm and eloquence. Everybody liked Fleischl-Marxow and Freud was no exception, becoming something of a disciple. He described him as:

A most distinguished man, for whom both nature and upbringing have done their best. Rich, trained in all physical exercises, with the stamp of genius in his energetic features, handsome, with fine feelings, gifted with all the talents, and able to form an original judgement on all that matters, he has always been my ideal and I could not rest till we became friends and I could experience pure joy in his ability and reputation.

cit. The Life and Work of Sigmund Freud, Ernest Jones, 1953

Freud's admiration of this remarkable man reached new heights when he discovered his stoicism: Fleischl-Marxow had had an accident in an experiment a few years before, resulting in an infection. This had led to the amputation of a part of his right thumb, and a condition that caused the growth of neuromata—abnormal proliferations of nerve endings— which were exquisitely painful. Despite repeated operations to remove them, these neuromata kept multiplying, each more agonising than the last. Fleischl-Marxow's situation deteriorated each time.

Although he never complained, the pain was soon so bad that he was unable to sleep. At night, while the world slept, Fleischl-Marxow sat up through the small hours studying mathematics to keep his mind off the pain. When he ran out of mathematical problems he couldn't solve, he moved to physics and, when this was too easy, he taught himself Sanskrit. Freud described Fleischl-Marxow's life as 'an unending torture of pain and of slowly approaching death'. But, as he was to learn, Fleischl-Marxow's quiet suffering was not his only secret.

In order to numb the pain Fleischl-Marxow had begun to administer himself injections of morphine and soon found himself unable to regulate his intake. By the time Freud arrived on the scene, he was a confirmed addict. Freud discovered this in October 1883, recording in a series of letters to Martha:

> I asked him quite disconsolately where all this was going to lead to. He said that his parents regarded him as a great savant and he would try to keep at his work for as long as they lived. Once they were dead, he would shoot himself, for he thought it was quite impossible to hold out for long...[two weeks later] he is not the sort of man you can approach with empty words of consolation. His state is precisely as desperate as he says and one cannot contradict him. 'I can't bear,' he says, 'to have to do everything with three times the effort others use, when I was accustomed to doing things more easily than they. No one else would endure what I do,' he added, and I know him well enough to believe him.
>
> *cit. The Life and Work of Sigmund Freud*, Ernest Jones, 1953

In April 1884 Freud had sat up through the night caring for Fleischl-Marxow, who was in a warm bath, in desperate pain. He wrote later that he was unable to describe that night because it was unlike anything he had ever experienced before, but that 'every note of the profoundest despair was sounded'. That terrible night, however, he had an idea.

One of the reasons that Freud had become interested cocaine in the first place was that he, too, had read Dr Bentley's accounts of cocaine cures for morphine addicts. He became convinced that cocaine was the only solution for Fleischl-Marxow when, two weeks later, he went to visit his digs only to find the door locked from the inside but no reply from within. Together with two colleagues Freud broke the door down to find his friend 'almost senseless with pain'. Freud suggested cocaine to Fleischl-Marxow who, driven to desperation, was willing to try anything and 'clutched at it like a drowning man'. The results seemed miraculous: with repeated doses, Fleischl-Marxow's morphine intake dropped away.

Freud now became an advocate of cocaine to cure morphine withdrawal and mentioned in papers and lectures that it had near magical effects in such cases, speculating that it might one day eliminate the need for 'inebriate asylums'. In a paper read to the Psychiatric Society the next year he referred to Fleischl-Marxow's cocaine cure, saying that the whole process had taken only twenty days and that 'no cocaine habituation set in; on the contrary, an increasing antipathy to the drug was unmistakenly evident'.

But it wasn't long before things started to go wrong. By April 1885, a year after Fleischl-Marxow had first tried cocaine, he was in a serious decline. Freud later learned that he was using 1,800 marks' worth of cocaine every three months—equivalent to a full gram of pure cocaine every day—intravenously. He began to experience symptoms of cocaine poisoning. First there were bouts of fainting and convulsions, then increasingly eccentric behaviour. This soon led to a peculiar delusion: Fleischl-Marxow became obsessed with the idea that there were insects and snakes crawling beneath his skin and spent long periods locked in intense concentration trying to pick them out (these tactile hallucinations, one of the classic symptoms of cocaine toxosis, are known today—as they were fairly swiftly after their discovery in the late 1880s—as 'coke bugs').

Things reached a head on 4 June, when Freud again spent the night with Fleischl-Marxow, later describing the experience as 'the most frightful night of my life'. He immediately wrote to Martha, warning her that he thought Fleischl-Marxow may have become addicted to cocaine and that she should be very careful when taking the sample he had sent her lest she did the same.

Under such heavy doses of cocaine Fleischl-Marxow's side effects—effects more severe than he had ever experienced with morphine—convinced him that he had to stop taking the drug, but he found himself strangely unable to. Unwittingly, Freud had created the world's first cocaine addict. What even he did not realise was that Fleischl-Marxow was not only taking cocaine now: he was back on the morphine as well, injecting colossal doses of both drugs simultaneously. He had discovered, as many would rediscover after him, that opiates and cocaine mix extremely well, the 'up' of one drug counterbalancing the 'down' of the other. Fleischl-Marxow, chemically stomping on the gas while holding the brake pedal firmly to the floor, had invented the 'speedball', the peculiarly dangerous cocktail of cocaine and morphine (or heroin) that would go in and out of fashion for the next century—and the same concoction that was to kill the comedian John Belushi in March 1982.

When Freud finally grasped the gravity of the situation he was despondent. Later that year he wrote that Fleischl-Marxow's body would not be able to tolerate this kind of punishment much longer and that he would die—hopefully—within six months. In fact he was to endure another six years. Freud was to keep a photograph of his tragic friend hanging above his desk for the rest of his life.

Fleischl-Marxow may have been the first to experience cocaine addiction but there were soon others. Rumours began to circulate of cocaine addicts, made insane by their craving for the drug. These circulated fast inside the medical community because the addicts were usually doctors themselves (pharmacists and dentists were also hit hard). Correspondents swapped cocaine horror stories in medical journals. In one case a doctor was arrested in the street, 'mad' under the influence of cocaine. In another, even more worrying, case—cited by JB Mattison of Brooklyn—'a physician attempted to write a prescription for a patient but, instead, wrote for the sheriff to come and take him to jail'. Cocaine, it seemed, could do strange things to you. News of the dangers was broken in England by the *British Medical Journal*, which had its own cautionary tale:

From the US correspondent:

Cucaine is being used in this country for nearly everything; but we have already found that this sweet rose of our therapeutic bouquet has its bitter thorn. A poor fellow (a physician) out in Chicago, in his earnest desire to investigate its wonderful properties, has become a habitué, and has drugged himself and his family down to the lowest depths of degradation. Taking cucaine himself, and giving it to his wife and little children, he mercilessly hacked their flesh to test its anaesthetic properties. He is now in an asylum, where he will probably soon end his career.

BMJ, 2 January 1886

As morphine addicts across the United States succumbed to cocaine addiction their doctors, through self-testing with the drug, did the same. A wave of addiction swept through the American upper middle class. Often those addicted turned out to be not only doctors and dentists but their wives, too.

Just as the scientists and doctors of the nineteenth century had not understood why cocaine made them feel good, so they had no idea why it now appeared to be enslaving them. At the time there was a serious debate as to whether cocaine even had the potential to be addictive. It was an argument that would rage on for nearly a century—as late as the 1980s a few die-hard scientists were still holding that it didn't. On the face of it their argument seemed quite reasonable because cocaine, unlike heroin, does not induce obvious physical symptoms when it is withdrawn from a user; cocaine users do not do cold turkey the way opiate addicts do. Equally, only a small percentage of people who try the drug go on to experience problems with it. This may be a result of its price: cocaine is expensive and tends to be used only on special occasions, with bouts of abstinence in between, making it difficult to become habituated. Among those who can afford substantial quantities, however, the results can be rather different (which is why we read about so many celebrities having coke problems when no one we know has one.) And when the price drops enough to make it easily affordable to everyone, as it did with crack in America in the mid-1980s, the story changes. In the late 1970s cocaine was so rare—and expensive— as to make addiction a real rarity. Thus, concluded some of the hipper members of the medical community, cocaine was not physically addictive. Perhaps, they conceded, it may be psychologically addictive. But then, so was chocolate—to someone who was weak-willed. It was the same argument Freud would use to exonerate himself from blame for the arrival of this new addictive substance. And it was rubbish.

Cocaine *is* an addictive drug. And the key to its sinister grasp is the very same molecule that holds its allure. Dopamine. At Brookhaven in New Jersey, Dr Volkow explained why.

Cocaine blocks transporters in the brain, increasing dopamine concentration in regions associated with pleasure and the result is an intense wave of euphoria. This is the rush. However, when the cocaine is eventually flushed from the system and transporter molecules begin mopping up the excess dopamine, pleasure circuits stop firing and the euphoria rapidly subsides. This is the crash. The fact that the rush is so intense immediately prior to the crash makes the change in mood all the more profound. Moreover, because your natural dopamine levels have been depleted, you now feel worse than you did before you took the drug in the first place and you experience a strong urge to pep yourself up again.

You enter a state that scientists refer to as 'craving'. Of course, the only thing capable of boosting your dopamine to its previous level, and thus making you feel better, is more cocaine.

If you have more cocaine, you now find yourself in a binge pattern: taking cocaine, waiting for it to wear off, craving cocaine and then taking more. It's like a feedback loop: cocaine makes you feel great so you take more; when it wears off there is less dopamine so you feel bad; so you take cocaine to make you feel great again. On top of all this, the fact that the drug is a stimulant means that people on cocaine tend to do most things faster than usual, from talking to smoking cigarettes. Unfortunately, one of the things they also do faster than usual is take cocaine. And so the problem escalates.

Animal studies demonstrate how this binge pattern operates. A famous experiment in the late 1960s gave two sets of laboratory rats unlimited access to cocaine for one group or heroin for the other, and left them to take as much as they wanted. It didn't take either group long to discover the drugs. The difference was that heroin, a sedative, made the rats sleepy and thus put a brake on its own consumption. Cocaine, a stimulant, did exactly the opposite. Within a couple of days, the heroin rats had settled into a routine: taking heroin, sleeping, wandering around, eating, taking more heroin and going back to sleep. The cocaine rats, meanwhile, took cocaine. And that was *all* they did. Cocaine didn't make them feel like sleeping or eating. It made them feel like taking more cocaine. When they finally collapsed of exhaustion their intake of the drug stopped temporarily, but the moment they woke up they started taking it again. The experiment lasted a month, at the end of which all of the heroin rats had developed serious drug habits but were, otherwise, relatively healthy: they were eating, grooming and drinking normally. All of the cocaine rats were dead.

Unfortunately we have not yet invented a scientific test capable of determining how addictive a particular drug is. One common experiment to determine the addictive *potential* of a drug, however, involves putting animals into a cage and training them to hit a bar in order to deliver themselves a small dose of it. Once the animals have learned that hitting the bar gives them a shot of the drug and makes them feel good, the number of times the bar must be hit to administer the drug is increased. The animals learn to hit the bar more frequently, and the number of hits is again increased. This continues until the animals figure that hitting the bar is no longer worth the effort—giving experimenters an idea of how hard animals are willing to work for that particular drug.

In such tests of addictive potential, cocaine always wins. One recent source cites an experiment that was eventually abandoned after a chimp hit the cocaine bar just under thirteen thousand times for a single shot. Admittedly, stimulants usually produce the most impressive results in this test, so we might expect cocaine to do well. But not that well: thirteen thousand hits was between 100 per cent and 1,600 per cent more than had been logged for any other drug known to man.

Another experiment, at the University of Michigan, where chimps were given free access to cocaine, demonstrated just how keen they were to take the drug once they had got the hang of it. Having learned to administer themselves doses of the drug, the chimps immediately proceeded to ignore each other and everything else, including food and water, and take cocaine in one long binge for five days without sleeping. By the end of this period they were so agitated that some of them had gnawed their own fingers off. Yet they continued to hit the cocaine bar. The experiment was stopped when it became clear that they would starve themselves to death rather than forgo the cocaine.

At Brookhaven, Nora Volkow has discovered another factor that may account for the binge-like behaviour induced by cocaine. Her PET scans of addicts have revealed strange abnormalities in a region of the brain just behind the eyes—known as the orbito-frontal cortex. This is thought to be the area of the brain that decides the salience of a stimulus: how important it is at any given point. When you are starving, food is a top priority. When you are not, it will be ignored. Somewhere in the brain a decision must be made as to the value of all stimuli like this. As you eat your dinner this evening, your orbito-frontal cortex will be constantly re-evaluating the food in front of you in terms of priorities, and, when you are full, it will alter your priority from 'eating' to something else altogether. Thus you will stop. But, if your orbito-frontal cortex were damaged in some way, the result would be different. 'If you destroy that area of the brain,' says Volkow, 'what would happen is you would continue eating. You would not be able to notice that the salience of food has changed. And that is what happens in animals who have had that area of the brain destroyed: they basically eat and eat.'

Dysfunctions of the orbito-frontal cortex have long been associated with such conditions as obsessive-compulsive disorder—people who get into physical routines that they cannot stop. Volkow's work indicating that this region is damaged by cocaine abuse may indicate another method that this drug uses to exert a hold on users. 'If you disrupt this area you can see how you could get into processes like the inability to refrain from taking a drug even when it is no longer pleasurable. And that's what cocaine abusers tell you: "It's no longer for pleasure." ... You see how dangerous this could become.'

Volkow's research has recently unearthed an even more alarming trend in cocaine abusers. By tagging a chemical, methylphenidate, that binds to the dopamine transporter—just like cocaine—and imaging it in her scanner, she has managed to measure the dopamine potential of cocaine users versus non-cocaine users. The results are worrying. Not only do cocaine users have a lower dopamine count shortly after taking the drug (which, as we have seen, leads to their repeating the dose), but they have abnormally low dopamine counts even as late as three months after their last dose. Cocaine, by artificially boosting their dopamine levels, has caused their bodies to downgrade the pleasure system through overuse. Now other stimuli that produce dopamine (such as chocolate) no longer cause them to release as much dopamine as before. For cocaine users, it seems their enjoyment of everything is reduced. Everything, that is, except for more cocaine.[4]

A few days after my meeting with Volkow I bumped into another neurologist, Dr Hans Breiter, at Harvard University. Like Volkow, Breiter had been feeding cocaine to addicts and scanning their brains while it hit. Unlike Volkow, however, he was using a much bigger scanner, called a Magnetic Resonance Imager, capable of taking moving pictures of the activity within the brain rather than simply snapshots of points in time. But then he wasn't interested in cocaine per se: he had a much bigger target. Breiter, at the Motivational Emotional Neuro-Science Centre, was (and still is) searching for the holy grail of neurology: the source of human motivation itself. Cocaine was just the starting point.

At the heart of all human decisions lies a complex system ranking everything we encounter in terms of simple priorities. For seven years

---

[4] An interesting result of Volkow's work with PET and methylphenidate is the revelation that people with naturally low dopamine counts tend to enjoy stimulants such as cocaine, while those with naturally high dopamine counts don't—perhaps indicating why some people are more likely to become addicted to it than others.

Breiter has been trying to figure out how this system works: attempting to decipher what it is that makes people want to do what they want to do. To do this he puts volunteers into his scanner, hits them with stimuli that he thinks will promote strong motivational responses, and then monitors how specific areas of their brains react. As the starting point of this quest, in 1993, Breiter decided to look for the neural circuits involved with learning and reward. 'We're mapping out the circuitry of human motivation,' he told me. 'That's our overall goal, and to get there we had to go the quick and dirty route, which was to see what was involved in pleasure itself... so we said "What is the most likely drug to hit this system? What is the biggest sledgehammer we can use?" Cocaine. It's the most addictive substance known.'

Breiter recruited a clutch of addicts, put them into his scanner and fed them intravenous shots of cocaine, telling them to rate their high, low, rush and craving every minute as the drug took effect. Initially I was excited by the possibility that he might put me into his scanner and give me some, too, but I changed my mind when I heard about the dosage: 'We were giving them a good party dose,' he said, grinning. 'I mean, you and I... getting a dose like this would probably have a coronary attack.' I didn't particularly fancy a coronary attack and thus was not altogether disappointed when he told me that he was allowed to give cocaine only to registered addicts anyway.

From previous experiments with reward circuitry on animals, Breiter knew that he was looking for various areas in the brain's limbic system to fire up once the cocaine hit. His predictions turned out to be bang on. Not only that, but he also recorded the brain's reaction as the cocaine euphoria wore off—noting that some of the areas that accounted for the rush were also implicated in the crash. For the first time, Breiter had succeeded in imaging the reward structures of the human brain in action. The next step was to repeat the experiment with different stimuli and see if what he had seen with cocaine was the same for other rewards. By the time I met him, he had tried gambling, morphine and sexual attraction, and, in all of these cases the same areas of the brain lit up.

What Breiter had hit upon was the mechanism by which the brain takes a sensory experience and decides whether it is good or bad. What cocaine does is to tamper with that mechanism. 'This is a system of the brain that is involved with learning that can say, basically, "Look, this was a very aversive stimulus; *learn* that it was aversive," or "This was a very rewarding one; *learn* that it was rewarding,"' says Breiter. 'Cocaine happens to hit that learning signal . . . so it forces us to learn a new signal—and a very powerful one—around reward.'

In this way, he explains, cocaine hijacks the brain's motivational system. The entire hierarchy of the decision-making process is reordered, downplaying conventional rewards such as sex and food, and placing cocaine at the top. This is not easily unlearned. In fact it appears to operate at a completely unconscious level, as has been demonstrated by a number of experiments.

If you take cocaine addicts and repeatedly give them cocaine, all the while monitoring their dopamine levels, as Breiter has, you soon begin to notice something strange: that their dopamine counts actually begin to leap *before* the cocaine has been administered. Because of the way the drug works on the motivational system, the brain logs not only the pleasurable experience of the cocaine but also all the sensory information around the experience. Like Pavlov's dogs, addicts subconsciously learn the indicators that cocaine is imminent and react—even in the absence of the drug. To them, cocaine has been prioritised as so important that their dopamine systems fire up in expectation at any of the numerous stimuli that normally accompany it. If the drug is then not administered, their brains trigger a terrible craving for it—in effect, telling them that this very important thing is absent and that they had better do something about it.

Any number of cues that remind the brain of cocaine—from the street corner where they used to buy it to piles of sugar or flour that look a bit like coke—trigger this craving. Other rewards don't do this. Not like cocaine.

'Chocolate doesn't do that,' says Breiter. 'Chocolate in itself may be a rewarding stimulus; sex the same way, having a good conversation with someone is the same way. These are rewards. But they aren't rewards that change the neurochemistry of the brain.'

Volkow had said something similar about dopamine: that each time you take the drug, as it forces more and more dopamine into the system, the brain learns again and again that *this* is what pleasure feels like. Everything else is downgraded. And so the brain continually resets itself, throwing off normal responses to other pleasurable stimuli—and downplaying them. The entire brain is reorganised.

If Breiter and Volkow are right, and cocaine does really alter the brain at this fundamental level—a level beyond the conscious will—then the traditional 'moral' tone of authority—telling people to stop using the drug and threatening them if they don't—is pretty much pointless. The argument that 'it's illegal' is unlikely to have any effect: telling a cocaine addict not to take cocaine is like trying to train a dog that has been badly beaten not to flinch when you raise your arm. Taking cocaine is not a conscious decision like this. Doubtless, over time, these reactions *can* be unlearned. Just not easily.

Breiter is scathing about people who equate addiction with lack of drive. 'To come out with these arguments saying, "This has to do with moral backbone" and things like that is completely ridiculous without the evidence... people who talk about this in terms of "moral fibre" and "just being able to say no", I think are fucking wrong. I will come as close to saying they are idiots as possible. They have no idea what's going on.'

So much for the 'cocaine is not addictive' argument.

Of course, the science that led to these explanations of addiction was a million miles away from the pioneering surgeons of the late nineteenth century, many of whom became addicted to cocaine through their experiments with the drug. Besides, addiction was an embarrassing thing to admit to, and many of these addictions were swiftly hushed up anyway. In fact, so effectively were they hushed up that news of the most famous case was only to emerge a century later when the personal diary of one of the world's most eminent surgeons, Sir William Osler, was leaked to the press.

Osler, senior professor of medicine at Oxford University at the time of his death in 1919, bequeathed his entire library of rare medical textbooks to McGill University in Canada. Among his collection was a small, leather-bound volume, locked with a tiny silver key, which appeared to have no title. Osler had referred to this book as 'The Secret History' and instructed his librarian, a Dr William Francis, that its contents were not to be released to the public until 1989. Handwritten by Osler himself, it was an inside account of the foundation of Johns Hopkins Hospital, Baltimore, and it contained a startling account of the life of one of its four founders, Dr William Halsted, the 'father of modern surgery'.

Halsted, perhaps the most gifted surgeon of his generation, was an all-American hero. Captain of the football team at Yale, he had started practising medicine in 1870, making such a name for himself that when a group of benefactors decided to form Johns Hopkins in 1889 he was recruited, along with Osler, to head up the surgical team. Together these two surgeons were to practise at the forefront of their fields for the next thirty years, and Halsted is today remembered for pioneering the use of rubber gloves in surgery.

He had made his name in December 1884 when, at the age of 33, he had invented nerve-block anaesthesia, a technique in which cocaine is injected into the region around a nerve cell in such a way as to induce localised analgesia all along that nerve. Carl Koller had discovered that cocaine could be used as a local anaesthetic but only on mucous membranes such as the eyes, the mouth or the inside of the nose; with nerve-block, Halsted enabled it to be used anywhere in the body. However, in the course of perfecting the nerve-block technique he had himself become addicted (he has been cited as America's first cocaine addict). By 1886 he had a two-gram-per-day habit, and was in such a state that he had to abandon his medical practice altogether. Mysteriously, he then vanished.

In fact, a friend, William Welch, had abducted him, hired a schooner and a crew, put him aboard it and taken him on an enforced cruise to the Windward Isles in an attempt to cure him of his dependency. When he reappeared six months later he suffered from terrible panic attacks and, as one of his pupils later recollected, 'the brilliant and gay extrovert seemed brilliant and gay no longer'. He checked into Butler Hospital, Rhode Island, in an attempt to complete his withdrawal from cocaine and emerged clean. However, by the time of his move to Johns Hopkins in 1889, everyone knew that he was 'strangely altered'. No one really understood why.

The little leather-covered book with the silver key, however, revealed the truth. Although the librarian had been instructed not to release it until 1989, he had decided to publish it in 1958, since everyone mentioned in it was already dead. However, he himself died the next year. The book was eventually released in 1969, in the *Journal of the American Medical Association (JAMA)*. In it Osler, writing sometime around 1893, revealed that Halsted had managed to cure himself of his cocaine addiction only by substituting it for addiction to another drug: morphine. Just as Freud's friend, Fleischl-Marxow, had turned from morphine to cocaine, so Halsted had gone the opposite way. It was this combination of morphine and cocaine that had transformed his personality.

But Osler revealed something further: that sometime around 1890 he had noticed Halsted with a severe chill and realised that in fact he was still a morphine addict. He confronted Halsted, who admitted everything. Such was the difficulty of coming off the cocaine, he said, that he had found it quite impossible to shake his morphine habit, never getting it below three grains per day. William Halsted, perhaps the most brilliant surgeon of his generation, was to remain a drug addict for the rest of his life. One of his letters reports that he was not the only one: 'Poor Hall and two other assistants of mine acquired the cocaine habit in the course of our experiments on ourselves—injecting nerves. They all died without recovering...'

The rumour that cocaine was effective as a cure for morphine addiction was to blame for many of the cases of addiction across the United States. As had been the case with Fleischl-Marxow, however, treating morphine addiction with cocaine simply temporarily substituted one addiction for another, frequently leaving victims with sizable appetites for both drugs.

But where did this rumour originate? In fact the idea was not as ludicrous as it sounds today. In the late nineteenth century little was understood about the action of drugs on the body. It was known, however, that morphine was a powerful sedative and cocaine an equally powerful stimulant. It was simply surmised that the stimulating action of the latter might counterbalance the narcotic effect of the former (in the 1960s, similarly misguided theories were to lead to the administration of shots of amphetamines for heroin addiction—kick-starting the international taste for illicit 'speed'). An easy mistake to make, you might think. But was it really a mistake?

In 1995 at the University of Tuebingen in Germany, Dr Albrecht Hirschmuller revealed a more sinister angle to this story. Reports of cocaine's efficacy at weaning morphine addicts from the drug had originated in the *Therapeutic Gazette*, a journal that, Hirschmuller discovered, had been entirely owned by the Parke, Davis pharmaceutical company of Detroit. In fact the *Therapeutic Gazette* was not so much a medical journal as a free newsletter for physicians across the US—a newsletter with the sole purpose of advertising Parke, Davis's products. And guess what? Parke, Davis was the only American drug company manufacturing and distributing cocaine. As with virtually every significant event in the history of cocaine since, the story was not so much about cocaine itself but something far more insidious: money. The whole story of cocaine's ability to cure opiate addicts was, from beginning to end, no more than a series of rumours, hyped into a smart sales campaign. As a piece of advertising, it was astonishingly effective; as a piece of medical reporting, however, it was bogus.

Freud, when he had first started his research into cocaine, had begun by looking up 'cocaine' in the index catalogue of the Surgeon General's Office—a comprehensive list of published American papers on any subject. Here he had discovered a number of papers in the *Therapeutic Gazette* and, having no idea of its illegitimacy, ordered them up and swallowed the story hook, line and sinker. In *Über Coca* he cited seven papers testifying to cocaine's ability to cure opiate addiction. All had appeared in the *Therapeutic Gazette*. He was not even suspicious when Parke, Davis approached him in April 1885 and asked him to endorse their cocaine in print, offering him $24 for his trouble. He took the money, tested some of their product, concluded that it was quite as good as Merck's and, in doing so, lent his name to the Parke, Davis campaign bandwagon. His acceptance of their recommendations was to land him in deep water.

In July 1885 one of Freud's colleagues, Albrecht Erlenmeyer, voiced his concerns in a German medical journal, warning that the risk of cocaine addiction was a very real one. Freud denied this but by the start of 1886, after his experiences with Fleischl-Marxow, even he had to admit that there was some pretty conclusive evidence that cocaine could be dangerous. However, he argued, it was addictive only when injected, and he had never suggested that anyone do this. This was not true: in 1885 he had specifically advised 'cocaine being administered in subcutaneous injections of 0.03g–0.05g per dose and without minding an accumulation of the drug'. This was quietly glossed over. Friends and cocaine devotees rallied around him: his old colleague Obersteiner put up a valiant defence at a conference in Copenhagen and the former Surgeon General of the army, William Hammond (himself a staunch fan of cocaine), wrote a piece in the *New York Medical Journal* saying that the drug was no more harmful than tea or coffee and that he had never heard of a single case of genuine addiction. At a conference of the New York Neurological Society he made light of the rumours of addiction and the aggressive behaviour it caused:

> On four different days, I gave myself an injection. And, gentlemen, I experienced none of the horrible effects, no disposition to acts of violence whatsoever; why, I didn't even want to commit a murder!
>
> cit. *Coca Exotica*, Kennedy, 1985

Other physicians found less to laugh about. As more and more addicts sprang up, a strong anticocaine lobby emerged who saw cocaine abuse as a more pernicious habit than morphine use. Unlike morphine, cocaine required no syringes and thus was easily applicable—leading to more rapid addiction. Meanwhile morphine addicts were known to be able to live fairly normal lives on the drug while cocaine users just appeared to go crazy. In May 1886 Erlenmeyer launched his most vicious attack on cocaine yet, in which he specifically pointed his finger at Freud for releasing 'the third scourge of humanity' after opium and alcohol. By now the medical press was up in arms over cocaine addiction, the *New York Medical Record* citing a Dr Charles H Hughes of St Louis to the effect that 'the cocaine habit, more pernicious than the morphine neurosis, is the certain entailment of its frequent administration, and its thraldom is far more tyrannical than the slavery of opium'. Even Freud now wished that he had never heard of cocaine.

Koller had won the glory of local anaesthesia but, when it all went wrong, Freud took the blame. His judgement was seriously in question: either he had been reckless in his research or he was incompetent for having recommended a dangerous drug so unreservedly. His mood was further lowered when he administered a large dose of cocaine to a patient who promptly died as a result—an incident, he later wrote, that led to 'grave reproaches'. In 1887 he made his final report on the drug in the journal *Wiener Medizinsche Wochenschrift*, in which he quoted Hammond heavily. He agreed that cocaine could be toxic, but only when injected into the body—and again neglected to quote in the bibliography the papers in which he had specifically recommended this. He stood by his assertion that cocaine could be useful in the process of weaning opium addicts from their addiction, justifiying this statement by asserting that cocaine would be addictive only to a certain type of weak personality. Other than these unfortunate former morphine addicts, however, 'cocaine has claimed no other victim, no victim on its own'. He was well aware of the truth, however, later writing of 1887 as 'the least successful and darkest year of my life'. The March 1885 paper in which he had advised cocaine administration by injection 'without hesitation' was never listed among his published papers and he destroyed his own copy of it. After this Freud stopped publishing on the subject of cocaine and appeared to have dropped the subject. In fact this is not quite the case—as we shall see.

Bizarrely, Freud's cocaine use was to create a stir over a hundred years later when, in honour of the centenary of his founding of psychoanalysis, the Library of Congress in Washington decided to mount a special exhibition to celebrate his life's work. Included was a display on the 'cocaine episode', with exhibits partly culled from a pile of old manuscripts that had once belonged to Carl Koller. These items had been discovered in a cardboard box tied up with ribbons by Koller's daughter in 1969, and had prompted her to write an article for the *Psychoanalytic Quarterly* about her father's discovery of local anaesthesia. In 1995 she had bequeathed them to the library.

What the library curators did not know, however, was that the contents of the box were not limited to paperwork: Koller had also included a small souvenir of his discovery for posterity. Thus in March the following year, the division chief of the Manuscript Reading Room was surprised to be approached by a researcher with a small envelope, bearing a German inscription in Koller's hand. The researcher translated the inscription: 'remainder of the first dose, with which I made my initial cocaine experiment in August 1884'. Inside the first envelope was a smaller one inscribed in another hand: 'to be taken in two doses'. And inside that was a slip of paper which, when unfolded, revealed . . . a small stash of coke.

The discovery of cocaine in the Library of Congress Reading Room was probably the most exciting thing to have happened in any library anywhere, ever. The division chief summoned the library's inspector-general, who took one look, realised he was looking at a pile of trouble and promptly summoned the FBI, who sped over and took the envelope into custody. Upon analysis, it emerged that the cocaine was, after all this time, inert and the Feds thoughtfully returned it to the library, where it rests in a vault in the manuscript division to this day. Perhaps somewhere up there, Freud was watching this fiasco, laughing.

While cocaine was gaining itself a dangerous reputation, however, its open sale continued. Such was the excitement surrounding the drug that its use was not only advocated by pharmaceutical companies and travelling salesmen, but in Britain its use was advertised by the lay community—most notably the greatest detective of all time, Sherlock Holmes.

Holmes's drug use is first reported in *A Scandal in Bohemia* (1886), in which Watson describes him as 'alternating between cocaine and ambition', referring confusingly to 'the drowsiness of the drug'. Presumably Holmes's creator, Sir Arthur Conan Doyle, had yet to try cocaine himself but, knowing of its recent discovery as an anaesthetic, assumed it would have a depressing effect like morphine. He was not to make this mistake again. In later stories, we discover that Holmes takes cocaine out of boredom. As he himself says,

> 'I suppose that its influence is physically a bad one. I find it, however, so transcendently stimulating and clarifying to the mind that its secondary action is a matter of small moment...my mind,' he said, 'rebels at stagnation. Give me problems, give me work, give me the most abstruse cryptogram, or the most intricate analysis, and I am in my own proper atmosphere. I can dispense then with artificial stimulants. But I abhor the dull routine of existence. I crave for mental exaltation'.
>
> *The Sign of Four*, 1890

It has always been assumed that Conan Doyle, being an ophthalmologist, first heard of cocaine from the furore in the medical press following Koller's original paper, but this is not the case. In fact he had probably been aware of the drug for some time. Doyle had studied medicine at Edinburgh University under one of the great toxicologists of the century, Sir Robert Christison—the very same Christison who had spent the mid-1870s experimenting with coca by climbing mountains, publishing his results in the *British Medical Journal*. There is no doubt that Conan Doyle knew him.

To Conan Doyle, writing just before the first wave of addiction hit, Holmes's hobby was a harmless if eccentric one. Holmes was bored and cocaine seemed to be a pretty effective cure for boredom. News of the deleterious effects of the drug over time were not widely published; nor would they be for a year or so yet. Until then, the world's greatest detective continued to use cocaine.

Sherlock Holmes was not the only literary figure to find inspiration in cocaine. In 1971 an article in the *Journal of the American Medical Association* shed new light on another—perhaps even more famous—case of cocaine abuse in literature, one that was to scare the bejesus out of readers around the world and yet one that, at the same time, presents an impressive account of the stimulating and inspirational effects of the drug. It centres on another British author, Robert Louis Stevenson.

Having contracted tuberculosis from his mother at an early age, Stevenson had been sick all his life, but by 1884 he was even sicker than usual. So sick, in fact, that on doctor's orders he took his family to Bournemouth because the fresh sea air would be good for his lungs. His new doctor, Thomas Scott, was so shocked by his condition that he ordered him to lie absolutely motionless, not even speaking, to avoid 'pulmonary haemorrhages'. However, Stevenson needed money and his publisher was waiting for the next book. By the autumn of 1885 things were pretty dire.

For some time, Stevenson had wanted to write a novel about the duality of human nature—the struggle between good and evil within man—but he had never managed to find a suitable way of telling it. Now, unable even to talk, he lay in bed, becoming more frustrated by the day. One night however, his wife, Fanny, was woken up by the sound of him whimpering in his sleep: he was having a nightmare. She woke him, whereupon he turned on her angrily: 'Why did you wake me? I was having a fine bogey tale!' The dream clearly had a great impact on Stevenson because the next morning he woke up and started to write. And write. He did not sleep, or move away from the desk. He wrote. In fact, he wrote so fast that he completed an entire 85-page novella in just 3 days—an average of nearly 30 pages a day. It was an astonishing achievement—especially for a man in his condition.

After the three days were up, Stevenson gave Fanny the manuscript and asked her to tell him what she thought. She gave it back to him that afternoon and told him that she thought it should be more allegorical. Coming back up the stairs half an hour later, she was shocked to find him sitting on the bed, staring at a pile of ashes in the fireplace. He had burned the entire manuscript. Ignoring her protests he set back to work. Once again, he was done within three days. Fanny commented:

> The amount of work this involved was appalling; that an invalid in my husband's condition of health should have been able to perform the manual labour alone of putting 60,000 words to paper in six days seems incredible.
>
> 'The Strange Case of Robert Louis Stevenson',
> *Journal of the American Medical Association*, 5 April 1971

The book went to the publishers and into print straight from the second draft. By the time Dr Scott arrived the next week for Stevenson's regular check-up, he found the man he had left so ill that he could not even speak sitting up in bed smirking: 'I've got my shilling shocker,' said Stevenson. The book? *The Strange Case of Dr Jekyll and Mr Hyde.*

How did Stevenson, an invalid so weak he was not supposed even to speak, write so much, so fast? How did he stay awake for six days and nights? Why is *Dr Jekyll and Mr Hyde* written in a different style from that of his other works? Perhaps because he was taking cocaine when he wrote it. Cocaine would have given him the energy, the drive, and the necessary mania to sit up every night for six days. Above all, consider the subject of the book: Dr Jekyll, a physician, discovers an elixir that transforms him into a completely different, and evil, person—Mr Hyde. While Jekyll is a clean-living man, Hyde is pure evil, uninhibited enough to indulge every base vice that Jekyll can never attempt. Hyde eventually beats an old man to death, all the time hiding out in the respectable body of Dr Jekyll.

Oscar Wilde was later to write, 'The transformation of Dr Jekyll reads dangerously like an experiment out of the *Lancet*.' He was only partly right: rather than simply an experiment out of the *Lancet*, doesn't it sound, more specifically, like an experiment with cocaine?

Certainly Stevenson had tried morphine, because Dr Scott had given it to him, but there are no records of his taking cocaine. The author of the *JAMA* article suggested that circumstantial evidence was strong enough to be able to suggest, with some confidence, that it was cocaine that had given him the energy necessary to write the story. But there was more. When she was researching the *JAMA* article, the author had written to Fanny Stevenson's son and asked if this was in fact possible. Did he know of his stepfather's use of any drugs? The reply came back just before publication, too late to include in the article, but just in time for a footnote. No, he didn't know whether his stepfather had taken cocaine when he was writing *Dr Jekyll* but he did recall one thing: that his mother had been so obsessed with Stevenson's health that she always read the *Lancet* to see whether there were any new therapies in it that might be of use to him. 'My mother glued herself to it,' he wrote, 'it was the worst reading in the world for her, as it is for any layman who foolishly tries to trespass on a highly technical domain' but she did it 'with a view of keeping up with the advance of medicine and getting some hints that might help RLS'.

The Strange Case of Dr Jekyll and Mr Hyde was written in October

1885. That whole year the medical papers in England were inundated with reports of the wonderful new drug 'cocaine'. That winter the *Lancet* alone carried 22 pieces about cocaine. Did cocaine really provide the inspiration and the motivation behind *Dr Jekyll and Mr Hyde*? Perhaps we will never know. But doesn't it seem rather likely?

Just as Jekyll's mysterious elixir took its toll on him in the end, so his contemporary Sherlock Holmes soon found himself in trouble with cocaine. Watson tells us at one point that Holmes injected cocaine three times a day for three whole months, so that his arm and wrist were 'all dotted and scarred with innumerable puncture marks'. He clearly disapproves of Holmes's cocaine habit and warns him off it but gives no very good reason for stopping other than that he might incur 'a permanent weakness'. The fact that Watson here, in 1888, does not warn Holmes of the risk of cocaine addiction or of its toxicity is a fairly reasonable indicator that Conan Doyle himself was not aware of, or did not take seriously, the risks of cocaine abuse. If he had known much about the drug, he would have recognised that anyone taking cocaine intravenously three times a day for three months would already have acquired a sizable habit.

Although Conan Doyle does not say so, many Holmes commentators have concluded from the numerous hints in his adventures that the world's greatest detective soon did. After such a prolonged use of the drug and Watson's departure (he got married), Holmes apparently fell into a slough of despair and—more dangerously—boredom. His use, it is said, increased to the point where paranoia set in. Just as Freud's friend, Fleischl-Marxow, had begun to sense bugs beneath his skin, so Holmes began to sense criminal enterprises in everything. Cocaine convinced him—as it convinces most people, if they take enough of it—that there was a vast, intricate conspiracy around him but that he was the only one to see it. According to these commentators the last Holmes adventure before his disappearance at the Reichenbach Falls in 1890, *The Final Problem*, is an example of the extent of his paranoia.

The Final Problem revolves around a criminal of such cunning that even Holmes is unable to track him. Watson, of course, is blissfully unaware. Until, that is, the afternoon of 24 April is disturbed by an unexpected visit from his frantic, agitated—and underweight—former colleague. Holmes bursts into the room and immediately demands that the shutters be closed, running around the room to make sure they are securely fastened. When asked why he has done this he admits that he is afraid of 'air-guns' and, without explaining, tells Watson that he must leave not by the front door, but scrambling over the back garden wall. And then the paranoia tumbles out:

'You have probably never heard of Professor Moriarty?' said he
'Never.'

'Ay, there's the genius and the wonder of the thing!' he cried. 'The man pervades London, and no one has heard of him...'

Holmes's delusion, like all paranoid conspiracy theories, features two main qualities: it is both fearsomely intricate and important; and the world at large is blissfully ignorant of it. Holmes reinforces the notion that he is paranoid by going into some detail about this elusive, phantom figure, Moriarty:

'For years past I have been conscious of some power behind the malefactor, some deep organising power which forever stands in the way of the law, and throws its shield over the wrongdoer...He is the Napoleon of crime, Watson. He is the author of half that is evil and nearly all that is undetected in this great city. He is a genius, a philosopher, an abstract thinker. He has a brain of the first order. He sits motionless, like a spider in the centre of its web, but that web has a thousand radiations, and he knows well every quiver of each of them.'

The Final Problem, Conan Doyle

It is worthy of note that no one other than Holmes ever gets a good look at Moriarty. On the basis of this, together with Holmes's known cocaine habit before the incident—and of his return later, clean of the drug—it has been suggested that Moriarty is not in fact a real figure but a fantasy existing only in the mind of the drug-crazed detective. Like an addict picking imaginary bugs from his skin, Holmes is plucking imaginary villains out of his imagination.

Alternatively the story can be seen as allegorical: Holmes, the addict, pursued by his shadowy nemesis, Moriarty, who represents either cocaine, or addiction itself. When Holmes returns, two and a half years later, he is much healthier and no longer uses cocaine, leading to the assertion that Watson's account of his disappearance at the Reichenbach Falls is misinformation, disguised to conceal the truth from the public: namely that that Holmes left England to attend an addiction cure somewhere in Switzerland. No specific sanatorium has never been located (although in one neo-Holmesian novel, *The Seven Percent Solution*, it is suggested that Holmes was personally treated by the world expert on cocaine at the time: Sigmund Freud). Even after this absence, however, Watson fears for Holmes's safety with the drug:

> I had learned to dread such periods of inaction, for I knew by experience that my companion's brain was so abnormally active that it was dangerous to leave it without material upon which to work. For years I had gradually weaned him from that drug mania which had threatened once to check his remarkable career. Now I knew that under ordinary conditions he no longer craved for this artificial stimulus, but I was well aware that the fiend was not dead but sleeping...
>
> *The Adventure of the Missing Three-Quarter*

It has been speculated that Holmes did go back to cocaine, leading to another enforced absence from criminal work—the famous 'missing year' from November 1895 to winter 1896, and that he then relapsed yet again, causing still another unexplained absence from March 1897 until summer 1898, when Watson says that he took him away to Cornwall for a 'rest cure' but goes into no more detail. Holmes eventually takes early retirement, settling in Sussex where, free of the drug at last, he takes up swimming and photography. There is no evidence of any further relapse; perhaps the world's greatest detective had finally learned his lesson.

Sherlock Holmes was not the only one who should have known better than to have put himself at risk with cocaine. Because, as the first wave of cocaine addiction swept the West, taking morphine addicts, physicians and professionals in its wake, another man—one who was fully conversant with the dangers of the drug—was still meddling with it. One who had already had a close shave with cocaine but whose early career seems to have been strangely intertwined with it.

Ironically, while cocaine was to create innumerable problems with most doctors, in the case of this particular one, it was perhaps ultimately to be responsible for his most important discovery, the most significant movement in twentieth-century science. The science was psychoanalysis and the scientist—once again—was Sigmund Freud.

5 Craving for, and Fear of, Sigmund Freud

It is generally assumed that, following Fleischl-Marxow's addiction, Freud stopped taking cocaine. This is not the case. In fact his use of the drug went on well beyond the point where he knew it was dangerous and even continued after Fleischl-Marxow's tragic death in October 1891.

In mid-1885 he was awarded a scholarship to travel to Paris to study under the celebrated neurologist, Jean-Martin Charcot. Having arrived in October, he swiftly worked his way into Charcot's inner circle by offering to translate medical papers into German for him. This gained him access to the great doctor's famous soirées, at which the leading intellectual lights of the city gathered to socialise, exchange ideas and demonstrate their erudition in public. Freud was intimidated—writing to Martha that he took cocaine on these occasions to help him relax. Thus we find that his preparations before going out to dine include 'white tie and white gloves, even a fresh shirt, a careful brush of my last remaining hair, and so on. A little cocaine, to untie my tongue...'

But Freud was not using cocaine only on such occasions. He used it when he was down generally, and particularly when he was lonely, thinking of Martha. The drug had the capacity to make him loquacious, a symptom he seems to have enjoyed, telling her just a fortnight later:

> The bit of cocaine I have just taken is making me very talkative, my little woman... [two pages later]... here I am making silly confessions to you, my sweet darling, really without any reason whatever unless it is the cocaine that makes me talk so much...
>
> *The Complete Letters, Freud–Fleiss*,
> 2 February 1886, *cit.* Masson (ed.), 1985

On formal occasions cocaine was the only thing that kept him awake. The letter goes on to describe another night out with the doyennes of

Parisian society, an evening, he says, 'dull to bursting, only that bit of cocaine kept me from it'. His cocaine use declined in September the next year, however, when he returned to Vienna and married Martha: now his future was secure, it would seem that he no longer had any use for the drug. But was that the end of it? Biographers would have us believe so. Far from it. In fact the truth about Freud's continued use of cocaine is much more bizarre—and elusive.

The true extent of Freud's use of cocaine was not to emerge until fifty years after his marriage when a collection of his personal letters appeared for sale in an antique-book shop in Berlin. These letters, written to a young physician in Berlin called Wilhelm Fliess, offer a startling insight into his thought processes at the time. They centre on a strange friendship between the two men from 1887 to 1904. It was this relationship, say some, that led to the advent of Freud's theories concerning sexuality, and that would ultimately bring about the advent of the discipline of psychoanalysis itself. And yet these letters should have been destroyed on Freud's request. The fact that they survive today is the result of a series of incredible coincidences.

In 1936 the Freud–Fliess correspondence was given by Fliess's widow to a German book dealer to sell. He took them to Paris and showed them to a Greek and Danish princess named Marie Bonaparte. Bonaparte, who happened to be one of Freud's disciples, immediately recognised the value of the letters and bought the entire collection for £100. She then wrote to Freud to alert him to their existence. He replied that he was grateful to her for having taken them off the market and asked her to destroy them on the basis that they contained material of an embarrassing nature: 'our correspondence was the most intimate you can imagine. It would have been highly embarrassing to have it fall into the hands of strangers...I do not want any of them to become known to so-called posterity.'

Bonaparte refused to burn the letters, instead lodging them in the Rothschild bank in Vienna in 1937 for safekeeping. No sooner had she done this than Germany invaded. Rothschild was a Jewish bank and it was clear that not much inside its walls was likely to remain safe with the Nazis in town, so she reclaimed the letters and smuggled them to Paris, which was itself invaded three years later.

Bonaparte made a quick getaway to Greece, leaving the letters in the Danish legation. They were then smuggled again—in a mine-sweeper this time—to Britain. In case the ship was torpedoed they were wrapped in a waterproof covering, attached to a 'buoyant' substance. Luckily, they made it over safely. And in England they remained, unpublished, for more than ten years.

The Freud family, when it finally managed to gain custody of the letters, was in a quandary: what was to be done with them? Clearly Freud himself had not wanted them released, but wouldn't it be a crime to destroy this unique record of his thoughts in the immensely fertile period leading up to his most famous works? They eventually bit the bullet and published the letters in 1954, in a book called *The Origins of Psycho-Analysis*.

Freud scholars were terribly excited: here were his innermost thoughts, right around the time when he released his seminal work—*The Interpretation of Dreams*. One expert described it as 'like coming upon the earliest and roughest drafts of a great poem'. However, the more they studied the letters, the more it became clear that there were bits missing. They had been censored. In fact, of the 284 letters, only 168 were included. It was quickly assumed that this censorship had been done to protect some dark secret. Since a number of the missing passages apparently contained references to cocaine it was speculated that the Freud family was attempting to hide the true extent of his drug use. But was this true? What had really been going on between Freud and Fliess?

Wilhelm Fliess was an ear, nose and throat specialist just two years younger than Freud. He had visited Vienna in 1887 and the two men had hit it off immediately: both were young, Jewish medical researchers with rapidly expanding families to take care of. Each was fiercely ambitious. They began to correspond in November and quickly became best friends. Fliess's wife, Ida, was soon to become jealous of the intimacies that her husband shared with Freud, and Freud, for his part, was so captivated by his new friend that he resolved to name his last two children after him (this proved inappropriate: they were both girls).

Crucially, Freud and Fliess had one key attribute in common: they shared a dream of revolutionising medicine through new, unconventional theories. Thus they spent their time writing reams of material to each other, positing all sorts of implausible theories. Far from criticising each other's efforts, however, each heaped the most lavish praise on the other, and they soon became a two-man support group for each other's wacky theories. This society, it turns out, was based not only on their incessant ravings about each other's work but on their shared use of cocaine.

Fliess had a theory—a syndrome he had 'discovered' in the early 1890s—which held that the origin of all physical ailments could be traced to a certain region inside the nose. The nasal recess, he said, was a microcosm of the body itself, and as such both reflected and was responsible for a patient's wellbeing. He termed this discovery the 'nasal reflex neurosis'. From now on, he insisted, instead of treating physical symptoms locally, doctors should treat noses. And what better medicine was there for noses than that discovered by his new friend Freud, cocaine? He was soon to claim that he had cured over a hundred patients of problems ranging from depression and chest pains to dizziness, headaches, heartburn and backache—all by analysing which exact region of the nose was at fault, and then painting it with cocaine. It was a breakthrough.

Fliess's theory was not regarded highly by the medical community. His key work on the nasal reflex neurosis—*The Relationship Between the Nose and the Female Sexual Organs*—received short shrift in the medical press:

> the book...has nothing to do with medicine or natural science...in not a few places the reader of this book has the impression that the author is making fun of him...In view of the fact that the publisher's extensive list also contains good scientific products, it should not be difficult for them to wipe out this disgrace.
>
> Wiener Klinische Rundschau, 1897,
> *cit. Complete Letters, Freud–Fleiss*, Masson (ed.)

Freud begged to differ: he was convinced not only that the nasal reflex neurosis was a real condition but that he himself was suffering from it. At the time he was enduring bouts of depression accompanied by heart pains and migraines. Various doctors were called in to examine him but none was able to pinpoint the cause. It was suggested that his smoking was the problem, then that he had a congenital heart condition. No one was quite sure. Nasal reflex neurosis, however, seemed to provide the answer. Carefully, Freud painted the inside of his nose with cocaine and shortly he felt much better. This was all the proof he needed: Fliess was a genius! From this point on, the correspondence between the two men revolves uncannily around their relative states of health and—more particularly—the state of each other's nose. The details are graphic:

> ...something strange but not unpleasant has happened to me. I put a noticeable end to the last horrible attack with cocaine; since then things have been fine and a great amount of pus is coming out...[and the very next day]...Since the last cocainisation three circumstances have continued to coincide: 1) I feel well; 2) I am discharging ample amounts of pus; 3) I am feeling *very* well...
>
> *Complete Letters, Freud–Fliess,*
> 26 and 27 April 1897, *cit.* Masson (ed.), 1985

In serious cases of nasal reflex neurosis, simple applications of cocaine were not enough: lumps and swellings had to be excised. Hence when Freud's symptoms grew intolerable, Fliess would visit him in Vienna and cut pieces out of the inside of his nose. Fliess likewise had his own nose operated on. Both reported feeling better afterwards. Naturally cocaine was used as the anaesthetic, and afterwards to numb the pain at the operation site. In between such operations, outbreaks of minor discomfort and depression were self-treated by both, again by painting the insides of their noses with cocaine.

What Fliess did not realise was that cocaine is readily transferred across mucous membranes, including those of the nose (which is why it is snorted today). By painting the inside of his patients' noses with the drug, he was ensuring that their bodies would absorb it. Consequently, although cocaine had no effect on their symptoms, they would report that they felt a lot better. Fliess might not have been expected to understand this but Freud should have known better. He had had enough experience with the drug to understand the two key points here, namely that cocaine induces feelings of euphoria and wellbeing (remember Freud's letter: 'I feel well...I am feeling *very* well'), and that it is absorbed through the nose perfectly easily. Perhaps the reason that he did not recognise this was that in his prior adventures he had eaten the drug, whereas now he was painting it into his nose. Another, less charitable, explanation may be that he was too wrecked to be able to think straight.

Freud and Fliess were led by their repeated applications of cocaine into a circle of abuse. Cocaine did genuinely appear to clear up their nasal problems for a while. However, it extracted a price for this. Cocaine is a vasoconstrictor and bronchodilator—it reduces blood flow to vessels near the surface of the skin and opens up the breathing passages. Consequently, someone with a stuffed-up nose, like Freud, will breathe more easily after taking it. However, as soon as the cocaine wears off the blood returns to the surface of the skin, causing the capillaries to swell and itch. They become inflamed, and the congestion returns—worse than before. Thus cocaine applications for these symptoms tend to become repetitive, as users have to keep their noses continually painted with the drug to prevent a relapse. But repeated applications of cocaine lead to damage to the nasal passages, which, in turn, manifests itself in the form of catarrh and stuffiness.

Far from being the cure for Freud's catarrh problem, cocaine was in fact the source of it. Freud and Fliess were not curing each other with the drug: it just *felt* as if they were. This never occurred to either of them.

Freud's cocaine use and his association with Fliess, while uncomfortable for his friends and later a source of embarrassment for him, were to provide him with just the environment he needed to create the legacy we know today. Cocaine tends to fill the user with unlimited confidence and, as noted by Mantegazza when he tried writing under its effects, all kinds of new and original ideas. Most of these are self-indulgent flights of fancy but in some cases they can actually lead somewhere new and exciting. At this point in his career, Freud was on the verge of replacing nineteenth-century psychological theory with something completely new. He was coming up with bold, unconventional ideas that no other doctor at the time could have produced. His friend Fliess, although totally misguided, was to provide him with encouragement that he was on the right track. Cocaine, meanwhile, was to give him both the depth of vision necessary to jettison conventional thought, and the arrogance to believe that he was right and everyone else was wrong. Thus the combination of Fliess and cocaine was to act as a catalyst for Freud's development in this crucial period of his life.

Well, that's the argument, anyway. But is there any truth in it?

My starting point in the library had been a book by EM Thornton called *The Freudian Fallacy: Freud and Cocaine*. Thornton believed that cocaine not only provided Freud with the impetus to come up with his theories but that without it he wouldn't have come up with anything at all. On the face of it, this seemed a bit rash: it was one thing to say that

Freud plus cocaine led to psychoanalysis but quite another to say that Freud minus cocaine led to nothing. Was it true? I decided to find out.

My first stop was the Freud Museum in Hampstead. Freud had actually lived and died there so I figured they ought to know a thing or two. I had reservations, however: I had been told that these were the guys who had censored the original Freud–Fliess correspondence and that they would never help me if they found out I was going to publicise Freud's cocaine abuse. This, it turned out, was not true. Not only were these not the people who had censored the letters, but they were terribly helpful. I popped by for a chat about drugs, they invited me in, sat me at a desk with a pile of books—on top of which was a copy of Thornton (so much for their fear of my writing about drugs). They did warn me, however, that it had been pretty much discredited by serious Freud scholars. 'Ye-es,' I said knowingly, stroking my chin. I wanted them to understand that I, too, was a serious Freud scholar. They seemed to believe me and offered me a cup of herbal tea.

I stayed in Freud's house for two days, ploughing through their library. Before I left I asked who else I should speak to about Freud, gathering myself a little stash of telephone numbers of experts around the world— just in case I got stuck. Of course, I got stuck almost immediately.

From what I could gather, Freud had been convinced of the veracity of the nasal reflex neurosis until a young lady called Emma Eckstein came to him in March 1895 suffering from hysteria. It was a tricky case—one in which a diagnosis of nasal reflex neurosis seemed appropriate. Knowing of Fliess's expertise in this field, he called him in for a consultation and the pair decided that Emma should undergo an operation to remove a swelling inside her nose. Fliess returned home to Berlin after the procedure and both men assumed that this was the end of the case.

Two weeks later a rancid smell emanated from Emma's nose. Clearly something had gone wrong. Freud called in another specialist, who cleaned the area around the operation site and discovered a length of thread lodged in her nose. He pulled this, only to find that it was attached to half a metre of surgical gauze. He then pulled out the entire length of gauze, with unexpected results. Freud recounts the events that followed:

> The next moment came a flood of blood. The patient turned white, her eyes bulged and she had no pulse...at the moment the foreign body came

out and everything became clear to me—and I immediately afterward was confronted by the patient—I felt sick. After she had been packed, I fled to the next room, drank a bottle of water and felt rather miserable...

Complete Letters, Freud–Fleiss, 8 March 1895, *cit*. Masson (ed.)

Emma was patched up but was to remain in danger for some time. Six weeks later Freud wrote to Fliess that she had been bleeding again, so seriously this time that, had the wound not been repacked swiftly, she would have died within thirty seconds. The pair had messed up big time and they knew it. The shock that Freud received, wrote one contemporary expert, was so serious that it forced him to confront his belief in the nasal reflex neurosis. Freud had been convinced all this time that the source of Emma's illness was physical—in her nose. In fact, he now realised, it was psychological. This was the first step in his move towards the discovery of the unconscious.

It seemed pretty reasonable: the cocaine in Freud's brain, the mistaken search for physical causes of ailments and the terrible cocaine-caused error with Emma. It could have led to some sort of realisation. But did it? It was time to use my list of experts.

My first call was to Peter Swales. Now, Swales is a bit of a legend in the Freud world. The *enfant terrible* of Freud research and former personal assistant to the Rolling Stones, he is known as a maverick with no patience for fools, who on occasion launches huge attacks of vitriol on people who don't know what they are talking about. He has no scientific degree and is not a psychoanalyst but manages continually to infuriate the Freudian community by unearthing 'lost' Freud material that often shows Freud in a bad light (he has further muddied the Freud–Fliess waters by digging up an assertion from Fliess that Freud had plotted to kill him, and unearthed evidence of a sexual relationship between Freud and Martha's sister, Minnie). Perhaps because of these controversial theories and his low tolerance of people who don't share them, he has had a number of falling-outs with other experts. *In the Freud Archives*, Janet Malcolm's account of the in-fighting in the Freudian community in the 1980s, said that Swales had been known to write 45-page diatribes to people he did not like. The Freud Museum had told me in hushed tones that he had once sent someone a letter written in blood. I dialled his number, and prepared for fireworks.

There were none. Swales turned out to be a quiet, helpful guy who, although he admitted that there were a lot of 'somnambulists' in the field of Freudian scholarship, was not especially terrifying. He was more than happy to give me the names of some people I should speak to about Freud and cocaine. I had heard about an article in the *Sunday Times* in 1981, which had used his research, and asked whether it was worth reading. What did he think of it? Not much, it seemed—'a fucking abortion', he said. Clearly some of the old charm remained.

We chatted for half an hour and he explained some of the basics about Freud to me, suggesting I call some other academics and get back to him a week later in case he had forgotten to give me any relevant numbers. In the meantime, I tracked down the *Sunday Times* article. Here things got really convoluted. Because, according to the *Sunday Times*, Emma didn't even come into the equation. Instead they cited the case of another patient of Freud's, called Irma.

Irma was the subject of a dream Freud had—a dream that apparently marked the real birth of psychoanalysis. Freud records and analyses the dream in his first great work, *The Interpretation of Dreams*. According to the *Sunday Times* the dream was all about cocaine, and, more importantly, showed how the drug had led Freud directly to the discovery of psychoanalysis.

In his dream, Freud is approached by Irma at a party. He examines her, noticing some nasty-looking scabs on the inside of her throat. Yet in his interpretation he indicates that it's not really her throat he is looking into, but her nose. And there is no doubt why she has scabs there: 'The scabs on her turbinal bones recalled a worry about my own state of health. I was making frequent use of cocaine at the time to reduce some troublesome nasal swellings...' An infection is diagnosed—apparently the result of a prior treatment when she was injected with a series of chemicals including trimethylamine (Freud is very specific about this chemical, recounting, 'I see its formula before me printed in bold type'). According to the *Sunday Times* the real significance of the dream lies not in the scabs but in the chemical he named. Trimethylamine.

Eleven years earlier, he had remarked in *Über Coca* that one of the chemicals yielded by coca leaves in the extraction of cocaine had a very distinctive scent: the scent of trimethylamine. Here was the connection. This was what tied it all together. This was the realisation that led to Freud's discovery of psychoanalysis. Trimethylamine. QED.

Eh? What did trimethylamine have to do with anything? Now I was totally confused. I rang a Freudian analyst who Swales told me had done some work on cocaine in the 1970s. What on earth did all this mean? What was Irma getting at? And suddenly, before I knew it, I was up to my neck in psychoanalytical gunk a whole lot weirder than the weirdest stuff I'd ever encountered. Even on my weirder days.

When he picked up the phone I began to introduce myself but he cut me short. 'I know who you are,' he said. 'I've heard all about you. I'll call you back.' I gave him my number and began to apologise for ringing at an inconvenient time but suddenly I realised that he had already hung up. Half an hour later the phone rang and there he was. 'You should speak to Peter Swales about this.' I explained that Peter Swales had suggested that I call him but he wasn't having any of it. 'I can't help you,' he said. But then he came up with an idea. 'Tell you what,' he said: 'the best thing is for you to write your chapter and then send it to me and I'll tell you what I think.' I said that my problem was not one of proofreading a text but that I didn't have a clue what to write in the first place. Nothing made sense to me. Perhaps I could just ask him a couple of questions about the Dream of Irma's Injection? But it was no good. He had already hung up. Hmm.

I rang another expert, in Holland this time, who promptly refused to speak to me altogether unless I sent him a full CV, together with a letter explaining why I wanted to contact him. I asked if this was strictly necessary. 'Yes,' he said. He then explained that Freud experts tended to be cagey because they are polarised between those who think Freud is unassailably great and those who think he took way too much drugs for his own good. Everyone was either for Freud or against Freud and there was no way of telling which side anyone was on. 'Which side are you on?' I asked. 'I'm not going to tell you,' he said, and hung up.

It got worse. I rang a professor at Cambridge University and asked him about Freud. He demanded to know what books I had read and whom I had spoken to. I told him. 'Well, then, there is no one else,' he said. I explained that I was still none the wiser and asked him about Thornton's book—was it true? 'Do *you* think it's true?' he asked. I didn't know. That was why I was ringing him. What about the facts—were they straight? 'Do *you* think they seem straight to *you*?' But the argument: Fliess, nasal reflex neurosis, Irma's injection. Did it stand up? 'Do *you* think it stands up?' he asked. Oh, Christ. I was talking to a machine that just scrambled the questions I was giving it and flung them back at me. Was this perhaps Freudian analysis in action? What about the Dream of Irma's Injection? What did it mean? What was the significance of trimethylamine? 'Do you know what trimethylamine is?' he asked. No—no, I had no idea at all. Finally he answered a question. 'Trimethylamine,' he said, 'is the chemical responsible for the smell of decomposing semen.' Then he hung up.

I didn't know whether to laugh or cry. Here was the dream that apparently demonstrated that the discovery of psychoanalysis lay in Freud's use of cocaine but no one wanted to explain why. Two experts had pretty much refused to talk to me altogether; one was no doubt composing a letter to me in blood even at this very moment; and all I could get from Cambridge was that trimethylamine was responsible for the smell of decomposing semen. I was rapidly going round in circles.

In desperation, I pulled out a piece of A3 paper and drew arrows and boxes all over it, attempting to summarise my findings. The facts, as I saw them, were fairly clear.

For at least twelve years, from 1884 to 1896, Sigmund Freud was a regular cocaine user. Although it is hard to ascertain the impact his cocaine use had on his work, we can be sure of one thing: it must have had *some* effect. Bearing in mind that he was laying down the groundwork for *The Interpretation of Dreams* at the time, it is reasonable to suppose that the drug played a role of some sort in his formulation of the theories in it. The true extent of this role, however, is disputed.

Two pieces of evidence point to a concrete relationship between Freud's use of cocaine and his discovery of psychoanalysis: Emma's case and Irma's dream. Both clearly indicate that Freud was using cocaine himself and that he was using it on his patients, that he had some weird ideas about medicine and that these were weighing heavily on his mind. But that's about all you can say. While Freud fans argue that there is no real evidence that cocaine played any significant role in his later thought, detractors say that the evidence clearly implies that it did. The thing is this: while it all seems possible, there isn't any hard proof. The key piece of evidence—the Dream of Irma's Injection—is unconvincing. For the last hundred years analysts have been reanalysing it in a desperate attempt to wring it out, to see if it contains anything else. But what if it doesn't contain anything else? Rereading the papers, it struck me that there was every possibility that these guys may be trying to decode something that was not, in fact, encrypted. Maybe—shock, horror!—the

Dream of Irma's Injection was just a dream. Looking at it baldly, I was forced to admit that nothing more had been proved than we already knew: namely that Freud was using cocaine and advising his patients to do the same and that this may have had some effect on his thinking at the time. Anything further was speculation—conspiracy theorising and trick cycling of the most heinous variety. After a number of weeks, the only thing I was really sure of was that tangling with Freudians was about as smart as sitting on an air hose, or hiding ice cream in your underpants. Which is to say: not smart at all.

I was trapped. Whatever I concluded about Freud I was bound to offend someone. If I said that cocaine had nothing to do with Freud's discovery of psychoanalysis, I'd have Swales and his gang after me. If, on the other hand, I concluded that cocaine was behind Freud's discovery of psychoanalysis, I'd have the entire Freudian community up in arms. The Freud–Fliess letters, Emma's near-death experience, Freud's cocaine use, Irma's dream . . . this was probably all stuff they didn't want aired again, anyway.

What if I knew too much already? Perhaps I should stop now: who knows what kind of strange things happen to people who ask too many questions in these psychoanalytical museums? I imagined myself tied to a chair in a secret vault beneath the Freud House, wrists bound with those green plastic ties psychoanalysts use to hold back their climbing creepers, heavy-duty psychoanalytical tape over my mouth. A faceless representative of the Freud family lurking in the shadows while some Viennese psychopath in a polo-neck sweater and wire-framed spectacles approached with a weird, tight-lipped expression and a large stainless-steel cylinder with a heavily insulated rubber handle, attached to a length of electrical flex: 'Ve do zis one ze same as ze uzzer one, jah?' the Austrian would ask. Freud would nod: 'Yes, Otto. Show Mr Streatfeild how we insert the Krauzfeld probe.' I would turn my head left and right and try to speak through the tape: 'No, please. Not the Krauzfeld probe . . .'

I had nightmares for a week. My housemate suggested I should get professional help. Unfortunately, it was professional help that I was afraid of.

6 Patent Cures, Snake Oils and Sex

Freud wasn't the only physician seduced by cocaine at the end of the nineteenth century. Despite growing awareness of the risk of addiction, its sales went through the roof. Cocaine was the only local anaesthetic available and new methods of application were being discovered all the time: in 1884 William Halsted perfected nerve-block anaesthesia; the next year J Leonard Corning discovered regional anaesthesia; in 1892 Carl Ludwig Schlein came up with the idea of infiltration anaesthesia; and in 1898 August Bier invented the most dangerous of all: spinal anaesthesia, in which cocaine was injected directly into the vertebral canal.

All of these techniques were dangerous, some extremely so. None is in common use any more, although if you have ever had an injection at the dentist you will be familiar with Halsted's nerve-block technique (today cocaine has been largely replaced with synthetic anaesthetics that produce the same numbing effect but none of the fun).

While the legitimate uses of cocaine were multiplying, the real money was being made in less valid, pseudotherapeutical patent medicines. The furore following Koller's discovery of local anaesthesia ensured that anything containing cocaine was in demand: punters had read about this new wonder drug and they wanted their medicines to contain it. The *New York Times* reported in 1885 that such was its reputation after the discovery of its anaesthetic properties, that, 'If a man exclaims that he has toothache as only a man who has toothache can exclaim, somebody at his elbow will shout "rub some cocaine on it".' Quack cure peddlers took note, adding it to their old formulas to give them more clout and cooking up all sorts of cocaine-based products to corner the new market. But with more and more coca and cocaine preparations available, they were forced to come up with harder-sell techniques to shift them. Regular marketing became aggressive marketing and it wasn't long before advertisers of these products resorted to the one factor guaranteed to sell anything: sex. In doing so they were perpetuating the oldest myth of all: that cocaine improves your sex life.

The idea of coca as an aphrodisiac was not new. The Incas had certainly regarded it as one, and reports of its racier qualities had hit the Old World with the journals of Don Hipolito Unanue in 1794, who reported sensationally, '*coqueros*, 80 years of age and over, and yet capable of such prowess as young men in the prime of life would be proud of'. As demonstrated by the explosion of Viagra on the world market in 1999, any drug that may conceivably cure impotence is guaranteed to find a vast market. Nothing is more likely to motivate the average Joe to get himself down to the pharmacy quicker than the prospect of a drug that may go some way towards improving his sexual performance. It was the same a hundred years ago. The more astutely marketed coca preparations, such as Metcalf's Coca Wine, had an added benefit: 'elderly people have found it a reliable aphrodisiac superior to any other drug'. Likewise Nyal's Compound Extract of Damiana, which was 'an aphrodisiac and for the restoration of virility in debility of the reproductive organs of both sexes'. Even Coca-Cola got in on the act, plugging itself as 'a most wonderful invigorator of the sexual organs'.[5]

There was so much talk about cocaine's abilities as an aphrodisiac that no one seemed to notice that much of it was self-contradictory. While coca drinks were touted as genital tonics, cocaine was also being lauded as having exactly the opposite effect, the *British Medical Journal* reporting:

> Professor Parvin has recently been exhibiting to his class, at the Jefferson Medical College, a case of profound nymphomania and masturbation, where the most satisfactory results have followed the application of a solution of cucaine into the clitoris and vagina. This is the first case, Dr Parvin thinks, where this drug has been so used.
>
> *BMJ*, 20 March 1886

---

[5] Coca-Cola has since maintained a strange relationship with sex. In a 1909 trial against the company in Tennessee, expert government witnesses did their best to convince the jury that Coke encouraged young boys to masturbate. Simultaneously the drink was undergoing a surge of popularity among certain categories of working women owing to the rumour that it was an effective spermicide. Used as a postcoital douche, it was said, Coca-Cola prevented conception.

The fact that the *BMJ* had previously cited coca as an aphrodisiac was not mentioned. Reports of coca's effects on sexual performance were similarly confused in America, where William Hammond was bemoaning the fact that cocaine did *not* cure such cases of masturbation, even when administered in ten per cent solutions to children as young as four or five. A US physician, Victor Vecki, brought attention to the confusion in his 1901 textbook on sexual impotence, noting that 'cocaine taken internally invariably produced sexual excitement in a man fifty-six years old...[but] this is diametrically opposite to the observations of Dr H Wells, of the United States Navy, who asserts that he has noticed in cocaine an anaphrodisiac effect'. We are perhaps lucky that Dr Wells ultimately realised that, whatever the effect of cocaine, it is not an *an*aphrodisiac—otherwise the US Navy might be navigating its way around the world's oceans to this day drinking tea laced with cocaine instead of bromine.

The dispute over cocaine's aphrodisiac properties lingers on. This is perhaps not surprising, as drugs and sex have always gone together: drugs make you feel great; sex makes you feel great; both are indulged only on special occasions; both are taboo to children. Sex is fun. Drugs are fun. You don't need to be an anthropologist to make a link between the two.

But was this just hearsay, or was there actually anything in it? There was a theory that cocaine, since it caused the pupils of the eyes to dilate, served to make the user more sexually attractive (pupil dilation has long been recognised as a sexual come-on; in the nineteenth century it was common for women to drop extracts of deadly nightshade into their eyes to enlarge their pupils. The plant's ability to make women more attractive like this resulted in its name, belladonna—'beautiful lady'). It was pretty tenuous stuff but it was better than nothing.

Then, in the British Library, references began to show up: in 1886 a German dentist by the name of Billeter reported cases of female patients becoming violently sexually aroused following doses of cocaine prior to oral surgery. A Swiss textbook on the drug likewise reported sexual arousal in females so violent that men were incapable of satisfying them, one exhausted male reporting:

After a night of sexual prowesses, compared to which the seven labours of Hercules were a mere nothing, I fell asleep, only to be immediately awakened by the renewed demands of my insatiable partner. I was able to verify on myself the degree to which cocaine renders women incapable of achieving sexual relation. Orgasm follows orgasm, each one further increasing the intensity of the desire. The most sexually potent man must eventually give up the hope of satisfying such a woman. There was nothing to do but flee in self-preservation.

Der Kokainismus, Hans Maier, 1926

Such was the effect on women, said the text, that all feelings of modesty would vanish and they would start making passes at any man in the room. Even 'young girls who have never had such feelings or needs before' would experience a terrible 'need for satisfaction'. If that satisfaction was not forthcoming, these unfortunate women would eventually resort to lesbianism. In America, likewise, young women became aroused on the drug. A dentist reported the case of a sixteen-year-old girl he had injected with cocaine prior to a tooth extraction, who:

gently closed her eyes and seemed to undergo an paroxysm of the most pleasurable excitement, accompanying her actions by words uttered in a half delirious manner, that fairly astounded me.

Medical Brief, 1891 *cit. Cocaine*, Spillane

Then there were the effects of cocaine on animals. Reports emerged testifying to male dogs which, upon dosing with cocaine, became uncontrollably priapic, of bitches suddenly becoming receptive to amorous advances from all comers. A PhD thesis from the University of Michigan in 1968 recorded the results of a student who had spent three years feeding commonly abused drugs to rats in the laboratory and monitoring their sexual antics. Cocaine, he concluded, enabled male rats to ejaculate more frequently than usual.

Perhaps there was something in cocaine as an aphrodisiac after all. But how could I be sure? The obvious way to find out was to try it. As journalistic assignments went, it would be a good one. Then I realised that my parents were likely to read the book and thought better of it. Who could I ask about cocaine and sex? Then I had a brainwave. I dug out my address book, and called Magic Eddie.

Allow me to explain. Magic Eddie is a drug dealer. But he's more than just a drug dealer. He is *the* drug dealer. Magic Eddie has forgotten more about narcotics than you or I will ever know. But then, to be honest, Magic Eddie has forgotten more about *everything* than you or I will ever know. This is not entirely surprising bearing in mind he has spent the best part of forty years taking drugs professionally. The first time he took drugs, he took them from Afghanistan to India. Now he takes drugs from the European mainland to Britain. As a self-employed man in the import business, Magic Eddie is perhaps the only person in Britain who actually thinks the Channel Tunnel is a good idea. 'It's like commuting,' he says, 'you know, on the underground.' Well, yes, Eddie—except people don't carry suitcases loaded with grass on the underground. 'I do,' he says with a shrug, and you know immediately that he's telling the truth.

Like all good drug dealers, Eddie lives in south London in a house so decrepit that it's actually held together by the undergrowth that's grown up all over the walls and windows. A visit to Magic Eddie is rather like a visit to a cosmic, surreal Miss Havisham—where Miss Havisham is permanently smoking a vast, loosely rolled cigarette with a pungent odour. I once asked him about his past and he told me that he had been a carpenter, then looked away and fumbled with a book of matches. 'Like Jesus,' he added as an afterthought.

Eddie had long been toying with the idea of writing a historical study of anarchist movements in fifteenth-century London. It would have been an amazing feat had he managed it because Eddie's memory had a half-life marginally shorter than that of a goldfish. It was quite common for him to stop a conversation in mid-sentence, look around, frown and then ask, 'Sorry—what was I just talking about?' This made Eddie's conversations somewhat hard to follow, as did the fact that he spoke a special language lodged somewhere between cockney rhyming slang and gibberish. Customers calling Eddie to enquire about availability invariably received a long monologue about meteorological conditions, the colour of the fields and the state of the 'farmer's daughter'. The object of this was to confuse the police, should they be listening in. Maybe it worked: it certainly confused the hell out of everyone else.

Eddie dealt only in marijuana, so I suspected he couldn't help me. I had once asked his opinion on cocaine and he had pulled a disgusted expression. 'Too expensive,' he had said. 'I mean, like a ball of snow. You know? This big—' he gestured. 'You throw a ball of snow up in the air—' here he mimed a throwing action '—and what happens?' He looked at me as if I ought to say something, so I did. 'I don't know, Eddie. What does happen?' There was a long pause. 'Sorry—what was I talking about?' he asked.

Eddie had repeatedly threatened to introduce me to a mate of his—a mysterious lighting technician by the name of Nigel—who was, Eddie assured me, the Rolling Stones' cocaine man. Nigel apparently accompanied them everywhere. His job was to carry the suitcase containing the coke and, doing so, he would follow the band around the world with a little satchel under his arm, like that guy that goes everywhere with the president, carrying the launch codes for the American nuclear arsenal.

Naturally, I was keen to meet Nigel, but whenever I asked after him he was mysteriously unavailable. One month he was suffering from shingles; the next he was away on tour. Then he was in the studio 'with The Manics'. 'I thought he was a lighting technician, Eddie,' I said, and he gave me a withering look. 'You think they don't need lights in studios, man?'[6]

Looking for the truth about cocaine and sex, I went to see Eddie again. Of course, Nigel wasn't available. Worse, Eddie was in the mood for a chat. He opened the refrigerator and removed a plastic carrier bag full of grass. 'Kerala,' he said, sniffing the bag like a connoisseur. 'Always keep it in the fridge.' Rolling a joint the size of the Hanger Lane gyratory system, he asked me what was on my mind. I explained that I needed to know about cocaine and he pulled a winsome face. Cocaine and *sex*, I added. Did he know anything about cocaine and sex?

Suddenly Eddie assumed a serious expression. He put down the unlit joint and looked up. 'I know where you're coming from,' he said. 'Now sex—sex is the one thing cocaine *is* good for.' Why? Eddie pulled up his forearm and clenched his fist. 'Feel that,' he said. I dutifully squeezed his wrist. 'Like a rock. A *rock*. Know what I mean?' But what did it actually do? I wanted to know. 'All night,' he said. 'All fucking *night*. Like a rock. Like a rabbit.' What about for women, I asked—was cocaine good for women? He raised an eyebrow, lit his joint and exhaled a plume of smoke. 'Women?' he said. 'Who cares?'

In fact cocaine, when eaten or snorted, does result in excitement but this need not be sexual; it depends as much on the individual as the drug. When applied topically as a feature of sex, however, the results are rather

---

[6] I never met Nigel and I suspect the reason I never met him was that he was fictitious. Our lawyers have asked me to point out that neither the Rolling Stones nor the Manic Street Preachers employ fictitious characters in any capacity.

different. As Koller discovered all those years ago, cocaine is a local anaesthetic—it deadens nerve endings. Thus, while it might provide staying power when applied topically, it is unlikely to heighten sensation—making this a very expensive numbing experience (ice is a lot cheaper). For women, results of its topical application are more impressive, as the vagina is a mucous membrane through which cocaine is readily absorbed. Thus it might be an ideal topical application for them apart from two key points: the first is that it is usually men, not women, who require this kind of anaesthetising prior to sex; the second is the fact that shoving cocaine into yourself can be extremely dangerous.

The quantity of cocaine absorbed by the body depends on the size of the membrane across which it has to travel: in terms of toxicity, snorting cocaine is comparatively safe because the surface area of the inside of the nose is relatively small. The vagina and anus, meanwhile, have considerably greater areas than the interior of the nose, so a dose that is safe when snorted may prove dangerous, and even lethal, when packed into another orifice. This was a fact not understood by early physicians, and because of it the majority of the deaths ascribed to cocaine in early medical papers were the result of genital surgery. Doctors had no idea that so much cocaine would be absorbed so fast, so they flooded the orifice they were operating on with high concentrations of the drug.

The most famous of these cases was the unfortunate surgeon, Kolomnin, who had administered 1,530 milligrams of cocaine (equivalent to some 30 'lines') to a female patient prior to cauterising a sore. The entire 1,530 milligrams had been absorbed into her body and she was dead within the hour. Even today in America, ER departments of major hospitals occasionally admit cases of women who have overdosed on cocaine taken internally during sex—women who have misjudged the amount of the drug they can take like this because they are used to snorting it. Every year, a number of them die because of it. Such is the attraction of a sex drug, however, that there is no shortage of new volunteers to try it out.

Ask any doctor and you'll be told that cocaine is not an aphrodisiac; speak to someone who's into the drug, however, and the chances are that they will tell you the exact opposite. One of the most commonly cited reasons for taking cocaine is 'sex', so there must be something in it. But what? Certainly an element relates to the very cost of the drug: like champagne, cocaine tastes better because it's extravagant. Of course, cocaine is also favoured by the very rich who, as we all know, have much more interesting sex lives than the rest of us. And better-looking partners. There is probably also an element of clandestine thrill involved: the presence of cocaine automatically makes a situation more exciting for the simple reason that it's illegal—as someone once remarked, 'Stolen sweets are always sweeter.' It is also a social drug: share a couple of lines with a stranger in a nightclub and you've automatically got something in common.

Then there is the fact that cocaine is a stimulant: when you're on it you're up, fast and running. You're feeling pretty much invincible and fear of embarrassment or failure simply does not feature. Aleister Crowley, the self-confessed 'most evil man in Britain', put it well in 1922, in a paragraph that also illustrates nicely the effect that the drug has on writing style:

> Until you've got a mouth full of cocaine, you don't know what kissing is. One kiss goes on from phase to phase like one of those novels by Balzac and Zola, Romain Rolland and DH Lawrence and those chaps. And you never get tired! You're on 4th speed all the time, and the engine purrs like a kitten with the stars in its whiskers. And it's always different and always the same, and it never stops, and you go insane, and you stay insane, and you probably don't know what I'm talking about, and I don't care a bit, and I'm awfully sorry for you, and you can find out any minute you like by the simple process of getting a girl like Lou and a lot of cocaine...
>
> *Diary of a Drug Fiend*, Crowley, 1922

Perhaps the best way to explain the confusion concerning cocaine's aphrodisiac qualities is to compare it to alcohol: is alcohol an aphrodisiac? It appears to be at office Christmas parties, doesn't it? I have a friend who invariably ends up naked in public when she drinks tequila; I have another who gags when she smells the stuff. Is tequila an aphrodisiac? You see the problem.

Although users and doctors disagree about the extent of cocaine's aphrodisiac qualities all agree that ultimately, given enough of it, the drug has a detrimental effect on performance. There are a number of reasons why this is the case but from the user's point of view the most important is simply a loss of interest in sex itself. Put simply, cocaine is more fun than sex and, although it's used in conjunction with sex initially, the urge to gratify the cocaine appetite eventually supersedes the urge to have sex. This has also been the result of every experiment ever conducted on animals in the laboratory. When wired up to apparatus that allows them to administer small doses of cocaine to themselves, all mammals ignore the availability of sex and stick with the cocaine. Repeated cocaine abuse, in humans as in animals, ultimately leads to sexual impotence.

None of this was known at the end of the last century. What was clear, however, was that cocaine made people feel great and appeared to cure a number of ailments that other drugs couldn't touch. A glut of new coca and cocaine products appeared on the market. After the arrival of the coca wines and tonics came household painkillers: cough drops, throat pastilles and toothache drops, all of which made use of cocaine's anaesthetic properties. A race ensued to come up with new and fancy ways of taking the drug. Chewing cocaine became possible with the arrival of Coca Bola ('a chewing paste which acts as a powerful tonic to the muscular and nervous system, relieving fatigue and exhaustion, and enabling the user to perform additional mental and physical labour without evil after-effects'). And as early as 1885 Parke, Davis was advertising coca cigarettes, guaranteed to soothe sore throats and lift bouts of depression—the first mention of the possibility of smoking the drug. In a handout for American physicians they cited the experience of a correspondent to the *Therapeutic Gazette*, a 'doctor M', of Wilmington, Delaware:

> At the time of the experiment which was tried upon himself he was feeling somewhat depressed—had the blues, in other words—owing to the absence of his family and the loneliness of his house without them. After dinner he smoked a couple of the cigars, with the effect that the 'blues' were expelled ...
>
> 'Coca Erythroxylon', Parke, Davis, 1885

The gazette went on to cite the success of their coca products in the treatment of dyspepsia, flatulence, colic, gastralgia, enteralgia, hysteria, hypochondria, spinal irritation, idiopathic convulsions, nervous erethism and the disability following severe acute infections. Although there was no truth in any of these claims, in coming up with the idea of smoking cocaine, Parke, Davis had hit upon a seriously good idea—and a seriously dangerous one. But, for reasons we shall come to later, smoking cocaine was a habit that was not to catch on for the best part of a century.

Patent-medicine makers started out cooking up elaborate coca-based preparations but it wasn't long before they realised that it wasn't necessary to deal with coca leaves at all. Far easier simply to dump a quantity of cocaine into your product. Particularly noteworthy for their high cocaine content were remedies for sinus and catarrh problems. Peddling cocaine to combat breathing disorders was a stroke of genius: as Freud was discovering, cocaine rapidly (but temporarily) dries sinuses and opens up breathing passages, making it appear ideal for the treatment of allergies and stuffy noses. Quack nostrums made the most of this, advertising themselves as cures for disorders ranging from asthma and hayfever to influenza; from coughs and colds to general breathlessness and even snoring. Dr Tucker's Specific, Agnew's Powder, Anglo-American Catarrh Powder, Dr Birney's Snuff, Ryno's Hay Fever and Catarrh Remedy and Az-ma-syde were just a few of the snuffs and sprays intended for these purposes.

Catarrh cures were usually sold with instructions to continue taking them until you were cured—advice pretty much guaranteed to lead to problems when their active constituent was an addictive stimulant that had no chance of curing anything. They could also be extremely strong: Dr Tucker's Specific was later analysed and discovered to contain 1.5 per cent cocaine; Nyal's Compound Extract of Damiana was stronger at 3.5 per cent, while Az-ma-syde took a large leap up, at 16 per cent. Agnew's Catarrh Powder weighed in at a hefty 35 per cent cocaine but the undisputed champion was Ryno's Hay Fever and Catarrh Remedy, manufactured by Dr EN Ryno of Michigan, which clocked in at well over 99 per cent pure pharmaceutical cocaine. These remedies sold for around 50 cents a packet. Not surprisingly, they sold well, fuelling a new cocaine industry whose sole aim was expansion.

Initially only two companies in the world manufactured cocaine: Merck of Darmstadt (Freud's source), and Parke, Davis of Detroit (who later paid him to endorse their product). As prices rocketed following Koller's discovery, both companies realised that there was now an almost unlimited market for cocaine and that if they wanted to make really big bucks they had to get their hands on a lot of it, fast. However, this was more difficult than it sounded. Because coca leaves tended to rot on their way over from Peru, even Parke, Davis and Merck found it impossible to guarantee reliable bulk coca supplies.

Meanwhile, every other drug company on the planet was trying to get into cocaine, and it rapidly became clear that whoever could control the coca trade—guaranteeing the delivery of good-quality coca leaves in bulk—would make a great deal of money. The first company to realise this was Parke, Davis. Clearly, they figured, someone would have to be sent to South America to sort things out.

Thus, when the SS *Acapulco* departed from New York harbour on 10 January 1885 in the direction of Arico, Chile, standing on the upper deck looking lost was a young man by the name of Henry Hurd Rusby. Although Rusby had only recently graduated from university, was not an expert in coca and had never been to South America before, he turned out to be the ideal choice of representative for Parke, Davis. It wasn't just that he was a qualified doctor and an accomplished botanist, but that he had another, more important quality: initiative.

When he eventually made it to Bolivia Rusby understood the nature of the problem immediately. He knew from his botanical research that coca would not grow in North America and yet its leaves when shipped were bulky and expensive and often went mouldy before they arrived. He put his mind to the problem. Then, in a dingy hotel in La Paz, he had a brainwave.

Rusby's idea was to process coca leaves into crude cocaine in Bolivia and then transport this product—which was much more robust—to the US for the last step of the refining process. It was a promising idea but there was one key drawback: the cocaine-extraction process was so complicated that it had to be done in a proper pharmaceutical plant, and there were no suitable facilities in Bolivia. Rusby thought again. What if there was a simpler way of extracting the cocaine from coca? That would make things easier. He was so excited about the idea of a new cocaine extraction process that he decided to find it himself.

Fired up by his idea, he started work on the project immediately, buying up a couple of sacks of coca leaves in the local market and experimenting on them in a spare room on the hotel's second floor. Predictably, a couple of days into the project, Rusby's fellow residents were shocked to hear a series of hysterical shouts followed by a huge explosion. He had been finalising an elaborate extraction process involving the distillation of a solution of coca leaves in pure alcohol. Not possessing the correct equipment, he had improvised, pouring the alcohol into a copper still, which he suspended over an open charcoal fire. The still, not made to take this kind of treatment, split, pouring the explosive mixture into the flames below. In a split second the whole thing was ablaze. Thinking quickly, Rusby grabbed the apparatus and flung it—flames, still, burning alcohol and all—directly out of the window. The fireball plummeted two storeys on to the street, where it set fire to the hotel veranda before eventually burning itself out on the cobblestones. Thankfully no one was walking in front of the building at the time.

Suitably chastened, Rusby started again and soon, by a combination of good chemistry and good luck, found what he was looking for: a new method of extracting the cocaine from coca leaves, leaving it in a form that was stable. Most importantly, the process was extremely simple. The technique he discovered is essentially the same one used by the drug industry today. Basically, it involves steeping the leaves in acid for a time to soak out the goodies and then scooping them out, leaving a murky brown soup. This is then shaken up with alcohol, which leaches the alkaloids out of the solution. The alcohol is then treated with a strong alkali such as sodium bicarbonate, upon which an off-white scummy substance precipitates out. This is known as *pasta basica* (basic paste) and, when filtered and dried out, contains 40–65 per cent cocaine.

In South America this is the standard unit of the cocaine trade, other than cocaine hydrochloride itself; cocaine barons seldom buy leaves— they buy paste. And they do this for exactly the same reason that Rusby invented the process by which they do it in the first place: because paste is stable and easily transportable. And, bearing in mind that 100 kilograms of coca leaves (enough to fill an average car) makes about 1 kilogram of paste (enough to fill a pint pot), the advantages are obvious.

Rusby's new technique was soon to lead to the collapse of the coca leaf trade: it was so much cheaper to trade in coca paste that it was simply not worth importing leaves any more. Small cocaine factories flourished around the coca-growing regions in Peru and Bolivia, and leaves became something of a scarcity anywhere except where they were grown. This was to have repercussions: because there were no longer any leaves around to experiment on, scientists simply assumed that coca was identical to cocaine itself—certainly as dangerous—and had no other intrinsic qualities. Thus, when cocaine's image was to change in the public consciousness and the drug was demonised, coca went with it. *Coqueros*, whose ancestors had chewed this harmless leaf for generations, found themselves categorised as addicts. Initially, however, the coca boom created great excitement in South America.

Peru did especially well out of the early cocaine trade. For a start, they had been growing coca here for centuries, so they not only had the plantations but they really knew what they were doing. Also, from the moment cocaine had been isolated by Niemann in 1860, they had been gearing up for a burst of international interest and here, 25 years later, it finally was.

Crude cocaine-processing factories sprang up around the Huánuco valley (home of the Incan coca industry five hundred years earlier and still the location of the trade today) and for the first time this rather backward country looked as if it might actually make some money out of the Old World. For a while it did: demand was such that the Peruvian coca industry took flight and by 1900 it was exporting 10,000 kilograms of cocaine paste—the product of over 1 million kilograms of coca—per year.

Unfortunately it was not to last. Peruvian and Bolivian experts had concluded that they were in the money for an indefinite period on the basis that coca could grow nowhere else apart from South America. They were wrong. Because, although Rusby had been the first drug company representative into South America after cocaine's arrival in medicine, other, more secretive visitors had already been exploring the potential of coca, hacking their way through the dense South American rainforests, thieving plant specimens as they went.

The leading experts in the field of horticultural theft were the British. Until the late 1800s, the most expensive drug in the world had been quinine—the only known cure for malaria, a veritable scourge in British India. Quinine comes from the bark of the cinchona tree, which, at the time, grew only in South America. Unsurprisingly, Kew Gardens was keen to get its hands on some, and sent a series of expeditions into the jungles of South America to procure seeds for transplantation.

Cinchona seeds and cuttings were shortly sent back to London, studied for a while and then dispatched to Ceylon and India. Once the new cinchona plantations came to fruition there the price of quinine plummeted. It was great news for the British—but not quite such good news for the South American quinine industry. The British were to repeat this performance with rubber (stolen from Brazil and transplanted to Ceylon) a few years later in 1876. And they had already done it with coca. In 1870 Kew Gardens sent coca seedlings to Ceylon, Jamaica, Malaya, Australia, British Guyana and India in the hope that they might grow well somewhere. In fact they grew well almost everywhere and British coca soon began to compete with Peruvian coca for the attention of the world market.

The uptake of coca as a commercial crop in Ceylon was assisted by an attack on the more staple crop, coffee, by a particularly virulent strain of fungus, which wiped out some 100,000 acres (40,470 hectares) in 15 years. Clearly, a new crop, resistant to the coffee blight, was needed. Coca became that crop. The British journal *New and Commercial Plants* remarked perceptively, 'In the course of a year or two, the European market will be supplied mostly from the East.' By 1912 Ceylon alone would boast nearly 4,000 acres (1,600 hectares) of coca. But, on a global scale, this was fairly small stuff: the British never really produced that much coca for the simple reason that other products were more profitable and easier to grow: opium, for example. While the Brits may have led the way with the theft of coca seeds from Peru, they weren't the ones to worry about. The ones who really shafted the Peruvians were the Dutch.

Just like the British, the Dutch had established coca plantations in the late 1860s—in Indonesia. Their initial plantation, the Lands Plantantuin ('Government Botanical Gardens') in Buitenzorg, southeast of Jakarta, experienced only limited success, however, until a Belgian company, Herman Linden and Co., sent out a new strain of coca in 1876. Planting of the new strain took place on Java, Sumatra and Madura islands. Significantly, this was a variety of *Coca novogranatense* distinguished not only by its very high alkaloid content (as high as 1.5 per cent by weight) but also by the fact that a special process was needed to extract its cocaine, a factor that made it less attractive on the coca leaf market in Europe.

Until the Germans stepped in, that is. In 1898 a German chemical company called Fabwercke came up with a sneaky new technique for getting the cocaine out of *novogranatense* coca. They immediately slapped a patent on the process, which was rumoured to be able to extract all of the cocaine from the Dutch plantations' now legendary '1.5 per cent plant'—a plant that happened also to produce four, rather than three, harvests a year. The Dutch leaf contained more than double the amount of cocaine in Peruvian and Bolivian leaf—making it all but unbeatable on the world market.

The only problem was that, owing to the tricky extraction process, *novogranatense* had to be sent to Europe in leaf form rather than as crude cocaine paste, a factor that made it slow to catch on—and bought the Peruvians some time. Once shipping problems were sorted out, however, it cornered the market—shipped in vast containers from Indonesia to Fabwerke for processing and then on around the world. But, just when the Germans thought they had the whole trade sewn up, the Dutch, who were apparently not bound by German patent laws, built their own *novogranatense*-processing plant on Java, started churning out their own cocaine and cut the Germans out of the loop entirely. Together with the coca plantation owners in Indonesia, the processors eventually formed a co-operative in 1900 called the Nederlansche Cocainfabriek (the Dutch Cocaine Factory). Javan cocaine flooded the world market.

International drug companies bought up crude cocaine, refined it and shipped it out—in increasingly ridiculous quantities. When the Germans' patent on their extraction process expired in 1903, moreover, the rest of Europe and America got in on the act, and Asian cocaine production went through the roof. By 1920, Java alone was producing 1,650 tons of coca leaf per year. Merck, the Darmstadt company that had supplied Freud with the cocaine that had started the craze in the first place, was to produce over 4 tons of the drug per year between 1906 and 1918.

All of these developments were to lead to a glut of cocaine on the European and American markets, resulting in a price collapse, increased availability—and increased addiction. As early as 1885 Freud's colleague Erlenmeyer had berated him for 'unleashing' the drug. He was soon joined by another outspoken doctor, Louis Lewin. Lewin went on to write the definitive account of narcotics of his time, *Phantastica*, in which he records the fate of the early cocaine addicts:

A cocainist who had sniffed 3.25gr of cocaine armed himself for protection against imaginary enemies; another in an attack of acute mania jumped overboard into the water; another broke the furniture and crockery to pieces and attacked a friend...These unfortunate beings lead a miserable life whose hours are measured by the imperative necessity for a new dose of the drug and with each such dose the tragedy of life and death takes a step further towards the inevitable end...a very small percentage of cocainists recover, the rest relapse.

Phantastica, Lewin, 1924

Most of these unfortunates were either doctors or morphine addicts attempting to kick their habit, and soon it became common knowledge that attempting to cure morphine withdrawal with cocaine was a serious mistake—Freud himself eventually admitting that it was like 'trying to cast out the Devil with Beelzebub'. By the end of 1887 the *New York Medical Record* concluded of this treatment that 'no medical technique with such a short history has claimed so many victims as cocaine. We fear that cocaine addiction has nothing but a dismal future.' This might have led to the drug's disappearance from the public consciousness but for one thing: everyone had noticed that cocaine was fun. While most of the early casualties had become addicted to the drug for 'medical reasons' (however misguided), a prescient piece in the *Medical Record* in November 1885 pointed the way forward:

> To some persons nothing is more fascinating than indulgence in cocaine. It relieves the sense of exhaustion, dispels mental depression and produces a delicious sense of exhilaration and well-being. The after effects are, at first, slight, almost imperceptible, but continual indulgence finally creates a craving which must be satisfied; the individual then becomes nervous, tremulous, sleepless, without appetite, and he is at last reduced to a condition of pitiable neurasthenia.
>
> *Medical Record*, editorial, 28 November 1885

By 1900, cases of death due to recreational cocaine abuse had overtaken those due to medical misadventure and it was clear that the world had a new addiction problem on its hands. In America, a Committee on the Acquirement of the Drug Habit was established, collating all information on drug addiction it could find from 1898 to 1902. The committee admitted that, while the population of the US had risen 10 per cent in the 4-year period, cocaine imports had gone up 40 per cent (this did not even begin to take account of cocaine produced inside the US by firms such as Parke, Davis). Meanwhile cocaine's use as an anaesthetic in surgery was dropping fast owing to the discovery of safer, synthetic anaesthetics such as procaine ('novocaine').

In 1890, following the initial boom, the US cocaine requirement was about one ton per year. Fifteen years later—when there should have been less, rather than more, demand—it was over seven tons. Yet the market was easily absorbing the excess. The commission sent out questionnaires to pharmacists across the country, which revealed that they had an average of 5 cocaine addicts each, leading to a total estimate of some 200,000 in the United States. The same year, the *British Medical Journal* reported that the city of Cincinnati alone contained some 10,000 cocaine addicts.

Although there was no federal legislation against cocaine, various states across the country began to take action on their own. Oregon started the ball rolling in 1887, banning the sale of cocaine without a prescription. Montana followed two years later and New York in 1893, and there was a flood of stateside bans leading up to 1900.

However, simply restricting cocaine sales didn't achieve a great deal since it was readily available in patent medicines. Penalties were lax, moreover, so pharmacists could easily be bribed to sell it. Also, since there was no conformity between the different states of the US on matters of drug regulation, cocaine would be illegal in one state but perfectly legal in the next. States where it was legal simply imported more and drove it across the border into a state where it wasn't. Local law-enforcement officers soon found it impossible to control supply as addiction continued to spread, and gave up. Only the medical community seemed to be paying attention.

For some time physicians had understood that sales of cocaine and opium needed regulation. Cocaine especially was viewed as pernicious, as the medical community had learned a hard lesson with it (as late as 1901, 30 per cent of the cocaine addicts in the US were dentists). Medical societies were especially angry about the continued sale of nostrum cures containing it—and their bogus advertising techniques. In the quest for higher and higher sales, anything was acceptable for these manufacturers. Testimonies were quoted from famous physicians who had never heard of the product they were endorsing; or physicians who had never existed. Patients who had been cured were likewise fictional. Even the medical profession itself was targeted by the pop-pharmaceutical industry: physicians who ridiculed patent medicines, it was said, did so because they had a vested interest in keeping people sick.

Various journalists had written pieces about cocaine and the dangers of patent medicines but no one wanted to listen. Until one exclusive series of articles blew the lid off the whole trade.

In the spring of 1905 the editor of *Colliers National Weekly* magazine, William Hapgood, decided that the time had come to fight back. After a long search through the ranks of American journalists, he hired the hardest-hitting hack he could find, a literary bruiser by the name of Samuel Hopkins Adams. He then put him on an expense account and told him to expose as many of these quack cures for what they really were as he possibly could. Adams targeted 264 of the most famous nostrum cures, buying up samples of each and sending them off to private laboratories to discover what they actually contained. As expected, they contained two main components: harmless colourants or flavourings designed to make them look or taste good, and doses of addictive narcotics. He asked scientists whether these products might actually be suitable for the treatment of whatever ailment the medicine was supposed to cure. The answer was invariably no.

It was immediately clear that Adams was not messing about here and that, if his reports made it into print, the people who made these medicines were likely to lose a great deal of money. Thus, fairly early on in his research he began to notice that he was being followed. There were bribery attempts, and a famous blackmail plot (it was suggested—fallaciously—that he was having an affair with a friend's wife). Adams wasn't cowed: he promptly hired his own private detectives and told them to follow the private detectives who were following him. He then discovered who they were working for, and counter-blackmailed *him* on the basis that he happened to be having an affair with someone else's wife. Adams was a man who meant business. When his reports appeared in *Colliers* in 1905, it became apparent that he didn't mince words, either:

THE GREAT AMERICAN FRAUD

Gullible America will spend this year some 75 millions of dollars in the purchase of patent medicines. In consideration of this sum it will swallow huge quantities of alcohol, an appalling amount of opiates, narcotics and a wide assortment of various drugs, ranging from powerful and dangerous heart depressants to insidious liver stimulants; and, far in excess of all other ingredients, undiluted fraud.

Colliers National Weekly, 7 October 1905

If Adams was angry about 'medicines' that contained nothing but coloured water and herbal extracts, he was positively incandescent about those containing narcotics. Not only would these not cure the ailments for which they were specifically advertised, but they were extremely dangerous, leading to possible overdose or addiction. One famous case cited in the *Boston Medical and Surgical Journal* in 1898 told of a man addicted to Birney's Catarrh Snuff, sniffing three to six bottles daily until he went bankrupt. (Birney's snuff was so popular that in some circles, cocaine taking was referred to as 'blowing the Birney's'.) Peddlers of these cures, said Adams, were participants in 'a shameful trade that stupefies harmless babies and makes criminals of our young men and harlots of our young women...Relentless greed sets the trap and death is partner in the enterprise.'

Adams's 'Great American Fraud' series was considered so important that the *Journal of the American Medical Association* reprinted half a million copies of it, reselling them at cost price as a public education service. Things began to look bad for the makers of patent medicines and nostrums. But, although they did not know it yet, they had an even greater enemy than Adams: a truly evangelical crusader by the name of Harvey Washington Wiley.

Wiley remains a something of a mystery to this day. Born on a farm in Indiana, he had fought in the Civil War and then taken up medicine but never actually practised as a doctor. In 1883 he had been appointed chief chemist to the Department of Agriculture and had swiftly developed a deep conviction that all edible products ought to be labelled with their contents so the public would know what it was buying. It was a reasonable idea—possibly the only one of his entire career.

Wiley was an atrocious scientist and far too highly opinionated to run any sort of public health department. To call his experiments 'amateurish' would be to heap lavish praise on them. Not only were they poorly planned and operated but hopelessly biased: so sure of his convictions as to the outcome of any given experiment was he that he employed only those experiments he knew would give the desired results. On occasions when even these experiments threw up results he didn't like, he simply disregarded them. As one chronicler noted in 1997, Wiley was to have a profound effect on US antidrug policy, being the first person to espouse a 'zero-tolerance' stance, and the first scientist to demonise drugs through 'bad science'.

However, Wiley's real speciality was not drugs, but food. He had started out 'proving' that benzoic acid (a natural preservative found in fruit) was poisonous (it wasn't) and had it banned. Elated by this triumph, he moved on to bigger targets with a series of increasingly harebrained and implausible schemes. Wiley's proficiency in the laboratory seems to have been entirely matched by his proficiency out of it: the third man in Washington ever to own a motor car, he soon became the first man in Washington ever to crash one.

Where he was effective, however, was in garnering public support. For the benzoic acid project Wiley had recruited twelve individuals as guinea pigs, referring to them as his 'poison squad' and feeding them all sorts of rubbish to see how they would react. Not having any idea just how shoddy his scientific method was, the public lapped it up. A Poison Squad! Brilliant! Wiley was America's Food Safety Guy and he was all over the papers and so, when it came to protecting the public from dangerous ingredients in their medicines, they wanted him, too.

Although Wiley was not a pharmacologist, he decided to tackle nostrum cures. From 1902 onwards, he worked on an act that would not ban drugs per se, but would force patent cure manufacturers to list the ingredients of their medicines on the bottle. If a medicine contained cocaine, it had to be clear that it contained cocaine. This was actually quite controversial: one of the key selling points of these medicines was often their 'secret formula'. Forcing them to reveal it might well drive them out of business (countless Coca-Cola imitations had sprung up within a year of its invention—and it had still maintained its secret formula). In February 1906 Wiley handed the Pure Food and Drug Act to the US Senate. They decided to debate it.

By chance, at exactly this point a book emerged that was to push the act through immediately. *The Jungle*, an exposé of the American meatpacking industry in Chicago, was written by a socialist reformer called Upton Sinclair. It revealed—in some detail—the truth about the meat eaten by the nation, revelling in such details as rats swarming all over abattoir floors, which, when caught, were simply thrown into the meat processors along with the beef. The public was outraged, and the Pure Food and Drug Act passed through the Senate without a hitch, to be signed by Theodore Roosevelt in June 1906.

The effect on the nostrum-cure industry was immediate. Many of the coca makers went out of business: people simply did not want to drink invigorating tonics when they had the word 'poison' written all over the bottle. Some sought to remove cocaine from their formulas and replace it with something else. Others tried to argue their point: by 1906 Angelo Mariani was claiming that Vin Mariani contained only 'an infinitesimal trace' of cocaine and so should be exempt from the law. He was later to argue that the cocaine in coca was no more representative of it than prussic acid was of peaches (a poison found in their pits). It was a pretty tenuous comparison but he actually had a point: lumping coca- and cocaine-based products together was unfair.

Unfortunately, the Pure Food and Drug Act did not discriminate between those patent medicines containing a lot of cocaine and those containing only traces of it. Wiley's real enemy was not the cocaine itself but the dishonest vendors who concealed its presence in their products. He said, 'We don't care about the amount—the amount makes absolutely no difference.' He was wrong. What the legislators did not understand was that coca leaves and tonics made from them were relatively harmless because it was possible to pick up only small amounts of cocaine by using them. Some of the patent cures, however, contained sizable quantities of pure cocaine and so were extremely dangerous: the key issue here was not the drug itself—but rather the dosage. Wiley never seems to have grasped this point.

Critically, the Pure Food and Drug Act also failed to legislate against the sale of cocaine itself: while the makers of coca wines and cordials went bankrupt, it was still possible to walk into a drug store in certain states of the US and buy pure cocaine hydrochloride for no other reason than that you wanted to.

The Pure Food and Drug Act was a success in that it removed roughly a third of all coca- and cocaine-based products from the market within a year. Yet it was a failure in that the products removed were not the ones that were doing the real damage. The first companies to go out of business were those peddling low-concentration coca tonics, who had two alternatives: remove the coca or ditch the product. Neither choice was especially attractive. Those with numerous other nostrum cures on their books soon gave up on cocaine: the publicity and effort were simply not worth the trouble. Those whose businesses relied entirely on coca found themselves in trouble. Angelo Mariani introduced a special cocaine-free Vin Mariani for the American market but it didn't sell. Meanwhile, cold and asthma cures were going great guns across the country. They slapped labels on their bottles warning that they contained cocaine and continued selling much as before.

While the act did remove a number of the cocaine-containing vehicles from the market, then, it did very little to curb actual addiction. Serious cocaine takers had not used the coca tonics anyway—they had used either high-concentration snuffs and sprays or pure cocaine. Clearly, more pressure was needed to remove the drug from the streets. But with Wiley out of the way focusing on his new project—that insidious drug, caffeine—where was this pressure to come from? The answer was not far away. Starting around the turn of the century, newspaper and radio reports began a movement that was ultimately to lead to the blanket ban of cocaine. They did this by whipping up the prejudices of Americans— and preying upon their deepest fears. They did it with racism.

7 Blacks, Chinks, Coolies and Brits

When reports of cocaine addiction first appeared in the press, they created a sensation. Not only did the drug have fascinating effects but the fact that addicts belonged to the middle and upper classes created a frisson of excitement among their contemporaries. Often doctors and professionals, these poor, sad individuals had had it all but lost everything. This riches-to-rags, people-like-us aspect gave the stories extra appeal. Addicts were portrayed as tragic figures, received sympathy and were referred to as 'unfortunates' or 'victims'.

However, as stories of cocaine addiction became increasingly common the reading public lost sympathy with them. Cocaine addiction was no longer sensational: it was just boring. As more cocaine flooded into the US, so the price dropped and more people could afford it—leading to an altogether less distinguished class of user. Reports began to feature not 'unfortunates' but 'addicts' and 'drunks'. These victims elicited even less sympathy because of the public perception that they had become addicted to cocaine not through legitimate medical afflictions but because they had taken it for *fun*. Thus the image of the addict evolved from the figure of the tragic yet respected gentleman (or lady) to the bad, selfish, dangerous—and quite possibly criminal—addict, or 'fiend'.

This move was to link cocaine with crime for the first time, establishing an apparently causal relationship which is still around today. As the drug became cheaper and more abundant the people who had started the craze distanced themselves from it, and eventually became afraid. It wasn't long before the association between cocaine and crime was deeply ingrained. In 1911 Dr Hamilton Wright—head of the US's anti-opium crusade, yet, ironically, himself an alcoholic—shocked readers of the *New York Times* with the revelation:

> It is the unanimous opinion of every state and municipal organisation having to do with the enforcement of state and municipal pharmacy laws that

the misuse of cocaine is a direct incentive to crime; that it is perhaps of all factors a singular one in augmenting the criminal ranks. The illicit use of the drug is most difficult to cope with, and the habitual use of it temporarily raises the power of the criminal to a point where in resisting arrest, there is no hesitation to murder.

New York Times, 12 March 1911

Not only did cocaine induce a propensity to violence and crime, it seemed, but also possibly violence towards the self. *Hampton's Magazine* ran a piece entitled 'Eight Years in a Cocaine Hell' about a female addict by the name of Annie Myers. Myers recalled how her need for cocaine had driven her to take desperate measures:

As the first effects of the drug were kleptomania, I was constantly in trouble... I deliberately took a pair of shears and pried loose a tooth that was filled with gold. I then extracted the tooth, smashed it up, and taking the gold went to the nearest pawnshop (the blood streaming down my face and drenching my clothes) where I sold it for 80c.

—cit. *Coca Exotica*, Kennedy, 1985

The author of this piece, one Cleveland Moffet—a man with the dubious distinction of having gone on the record prior to this report to predict that the motor vehicle would 'never catch on' in America—further linked cocaine to crime:

Let it be noted that crimes are committed by 'coke fiends' not only in their frenzy of desire to get the drug, but in the frenzy of exhilaration that follows taking it... only a few weeks ago the slayer of little Marie Smith at Asbury Park, New Jersey, confessed himself the victim of a cocaine habit, and no less than the assistant chief of the Chicago Police Department told me of an unsolved murder case where suspicion pointed to cocaine... This new vice, the cocaine vice, the most serious to be dealt with, has proved to be a creator of criminals and most unusual forms of violence.

—*Hampton's* 24, No. 1, 1911

Crime was scary but the real clincher, as it turned out, was race. If white people turned to crime under the effects of cocaine—well, what would black people do when they took it? Most people thought they were pretty crazy even without it. The answer to this question had been waiting in the wings since around 1900. It was so terrifying that it gained momentum fast, the *Journal of the American Medical Association* reporting that 'the Negroes in some parts of the South are reported as becoming addicted to a new vice—that of cocaine "snuffing" or "the coke habit"'. What would the effects of this be? It wasn't long before the public found out:

> The use of cocaine by Negroes in certain parts of the country is simply appalling...the police officers of questionable districts tell us that the habitués are made wild by cocaine, which they have no difficulty at all in obtaining.
>
> *American Pharmaceutical Journal*, 1901,
> cit. *The Cocaine Wars*, Eddy et al, 1988

But why were they taking cocaine anyway? The *British Medical Journal* explained all. It had all started, said the *BMJ*, down in New Orleans, where shift work, loading and unloading steamboats, went on for up to seventy hours nonstop. Black stevedores had discovered that cocaine enabled them to work harder, for longer, on less food and had in turn handed the habit down to the plantation workers, who had taken to the drug immediately. Before long, just as had happened to the Spanish supervisors at Potosi, the plantation owners discovered that cocaine had become necessary to maintain order:

> On many of the Yazoo plantations this year the Negroes refused to work unless they could be assured that there was some place in the neighbourhood where they could get cocaine, and it is said that some planters kept the drug in stock among the plantation supplies, and issued regular rations of cocaine just as they used to issue rations of whiskey.
>
> *BMJ*, 28 November 1902

Not only were the blacks taking cocaine but a lot of cocaine, reported Georgia's Colonel Watson—an avid anti-cocaine (and Coca-Cola) campaigner—in the *New York Tribune*: 'I have visited some of the Negro barrooms in Decatur Street, Atlanta, and the proprietors told me that the cocaine habit which had been acquired by the Negroes was simply driving them out of business.'

Reports of cocaine abuse by blacks across America were purpose-built to terrify middle-class Northern whites. They had read about the appalling effects of cocaine on educated white people such as doctors and lawyers—but Negroes! Goddamn! They couldn't even be trusted with liquor. It wasn't long before the paranoia of White America began to manifest itself in the newspapers. Colonel Watson continued:

> Unquestionably the drug rapidly affects the brain and the result has been that, in the South, the asylums for the insane are overflowing with the unfortunate victims. After a person has habitually used the drug for a certain length of time, he becomes mentally irresponsible. No man can use it long and retain his normal mental condition. It is a brain wrecker of the worst kind.
>
> New York Tribune, 21 June 1903

Watson's conclusion was resolute: 'Many of the horrible crimes committed in the Southern States by the coloured people,' he wrote, 'can be traced back directly to the cocaine habit.' Incidents of black cocaine-related crime accelerated throughout the early 1900s, stories of their antics becoming simultaneously more and more violent and less and less plausible. The most famous of all came from the New York Times, under the banner NEGRO COCAINE 'FIENDS' ARE A NEW SOUTHERN MENACE, by a true master of impartial reporting—Dr Edward H Williams, MD. It's the kind of article you read and burst out laughing—and then realise that it's actually not in the least bit funny at all. Williams is pictured in the middle of his text: an austere-looking chap with a neatly trimmed beard and wire-framed glasses. His expression says it all: a serious guy, a man of the world, a man concerned. And he certainly knows how to open a story:

> For some years there have been rumors about the increase in drug-taking in the South—vague, but always insistent rumors that the addiction to such drugs as morphine and cocaine was becoming a veritable curse to the colored race in certain regions. Some of these reports of alleged conditions read like the wildest flights of a sensational fiction writer. Stories of cocaine orgies and 'sniffing parties,' followed by wholesale murders, seem like lurid journalism of the yellowest variety. But in point of fact there was nothing 'yellow' about many of these reports. Nine men killed in Mississippi on one occasion by crazed cocaine takers, five in North Carolina, three in Tennessee—these are facts and need no imaginative coloring. And

since this gruesome evidence is supported by the printed records of insane hospitals, police courts, jails, and penitentiaries, there is no escaping the conviction that drug taking has become a race menace in certain regions south of the line.

New York Times, 8 February 1914

Yes, said Williams: there were five to fifteen times more drug addicts in the South than there were in the North. What were they taking? Cocaine. And what did cocaine do to you? Hallucinations and delusions, no less. And it caused the user to launch homicidal attacks on innocent passers-by. But cocaine had another, still more terrifying effect:

... the drug produces several other conditions that make the 'fiend' a peculiarly dangerous criminal. One of these conditions is a temporary immunity to shock—a resistance to the 'knock-down' effects of fatal wounds. Bullets fired into vital parts, that would stop a sane man in his tracks, fail to check the 'fiend'—fail to stop his rush or weaken his attack.

New York Times, 8 February 1914

As an example Williams cited a case related to him by a Southern law-enforcement officer, one Chief of Police Lyerly of Asheville, North Carolina. Lyerly had attempted to arrest a 'hitherto inoffensive Negro' who was 'running amok'. However, because of the cocaine, things hadn't gone according to plan. When the valiant Chief Lyerly informed this fiend that he was under arrest, he drew a knife and struck him, slashing him in the shoulder. Lyerly reacted immediately:

[Lyerly] drew his revolver, placed the muzzle over the Negro's heart and fired—'intending to kill him right quick'—but the shot did not even stagger the man. And a second shot that pierced the arm and entered the chest had just as little effect in stopping the Negro or checking his attack.

New York Times, 8 February 1914

Lyerly, realising he was getting nowhere, eventually gave up wasting precious ammo, holstered his revolver and bludgeoned the man to death with a club—apparently the only instrument powerful enough to have the effect he was looking for. Appalled by the superhuman strength of the 'Negro fiend' he had just killed, he promptly went home and did the only thing he could think of to guarantee his safety: he got himself a bigger gun. Across the South, law-enforcement officers did the same.

It was an appalling story but there was worse to come. Williams revealed a further, even more alarming, fact:

> Accuracy in shooting is not interfered with—is, indeed, probably improved—by cocaine...I believe that the record of the 'cocaine nigger' near Asheville, who dropped five men dead in their tracks, using only one cartridge for each, offers evidence that is suitably convincing. I doubt if this shooting record has been equalled in recent years...the deadly accuracy of the cocaine user has become axiomatic in Southern police circles.
>
> *New York Times*, 8 February 1914

Superhuman blacks, impervious to bullets? The word 'axiomatic' in a newspaper article? How could anyone have fallen for this rubbish? To get an idea of how easy it is to believe drug hype, it is necessary only to think back as far as PCP (phencyclidine, or 'angel dust'), an illicit drug that emerged in the 1960s. By the late 1970s stories abounded of PCP takers, crazed on the drug, performing such unlikely feats as picking up cars, throwing themselves through brick walls and—yes—refusing to die when shot. On the basis of such hearsay, PCP—a veterinary anaesthetic which tends to make people lie down and giggle—was categorised by the US House of Representatives in 1978 as 'one of the most dangerous and insidious drugs known to mankind'. A congressman actually stood up and declared PCP 'a threat to national security'. The result was pandemonium. Yet an ethnographic study the next year was baffled: even in mock setups where users, high on the drug, were invited to attack one another, nothing happened. Why?

> Even when the PCP user was designated to be the aggressor, the ability to fight was so seriously impaired by the anaesthetic effect of the drug that the outcome was seldom one in which serious injury was done to anyone. One user commented: 'I have a hard time walking down stairs, let alone fighting.'
>
> *Angel Dust*, HW Feldman (ed.), 1979

In fact, tales of addicts with superhuman, drug-induced strength are commonplace in the annals of drug mythology. Whenever an illicit drug attracts the attention of the law-enforcement community, you can pretty much guarantee that one of the first accusations to be levelled against it will be that it 'makes people violent'. Regardless of the existence of any evidence that this is the case, someone, somewhere, with some dubious experience in the field of drug rehabilitation or medicine, will claim that it leads to aggression. Consider this account, by the first US drug commissioner, Harry Anslinger:

> Those who are accustomed to habitual use of the drug are said eventually to develop a delirious rage after its administration, during which they are temporarily, at least, irresponsible and prone to commit violent crimes . . . a gang of boys tear the clothes from two schoolgirls and rape the screaming girls, one after the other. A sixteen year old kills his entire family of five in Florida; a man in Minnesota puts a bullet through the head of a stranger on the road; in Colorado a husband tries to shoot his wife, kills her grandmother instead and then kills himself. Every one of these crimes had been preceded by the smoking of one or two marijuana 'reefers'.
>
> *The Murderers*, Anslinger, 1961

Laughable, isn't it? Couldn't happen today, right? Think again: a 1997 high-profile debate into the legalisation of marijuana in England concluded that it should not be decriminalised because (you guessed it) it made people 'aggressive'. Where do these guys get their information from? Well, their own prejudices. If you are in law enforcement, it seems, it's a fact: drugs make people violent. Even marijuana. The notion that drugs are dangerous and cause violence is so ingrained that in 1999, when Charles Kennedy took over as leader of the Liberal Democrats in the UK and called for a Royal Commission to establish once and for all whether it was finally worth discussing the decriminalisation of marijuana, Ann Widdecombe, the shadow Home Secretary for the Conservative Party, lambasted him in the press for being 'irresponsible'. Apparently he was sending out 'the wrong message' about drug abuse: not only was decriminalising marijuana unthinkable—but the notion of even *discussing* its decriminalisation was unthinkable. While police chiefs and drug experts across the country called for an active dialogue, Widdecombe, for reasons best known to herself, had decided that it was never going to happen: a perfect example of a real-life 'Emperor's New Clothes' situation, if ever there was one. Such prejudiced and frankly Neanderthal attitudes towards the problem of drug abuse ensure that the fight against drugs and drug-based crime will never be won.

The fact is that sometimes, in their well-meaning attempts to save the public from the terrible scourge of drug addiction, law-enforcement communities play hard and fast with the truth. This is perhaps understandable: as with the Bible promising eternal damnation and hellfire, sometimes a truly appalling image is necessary in order to drive a message home to a frequently ill-educated and ambivalent public. The problem with demonising drugs like this, however, is that pretty soon people begin to realise that that they are not being told the whole truth and, once this happens, they start disregarding other things they are told on the basis that *they* may not be the truth, either.

Meanwhile, because of the exaggerated risks of drug abuse, including that of 'greater violence' from addicts, it is only reasonable to assume that the police, who have to deal with these offenders, are going to demand increased protection. Thus drug legislation to this day tends to revolve around two key points: banning illicit substances and buying more and bigger guns. This is exactly what happened with cocaine at the turn of the century.

But it didn't stop there. As well as playing the race card, the anticocaine lobby was smart enough to stir up another area that was bound to secure a response: sex. There was little doubt in anyone's mind that sexual perversion was a result of cocaine use—after all, didn't advertisers plug the stuff as an aphrodisiac? Dr Hamilton Wright, in his article on crime and cocaine in the *New York Times*, warned readers that cocaine consumption was currently running at a rate ten times the legitimate medical requirement—and we all knew what that meant...

> There is no doubt that this drug, perhaps more than any other, is used by those concerned in the white slave traffic to corrupt young girls, and that when the habit of using the drug has been established, it is but a short time before such girls fall to the ranks of prostitution.
>
> *New York Times*, 12 March 1911

From sex and cocaine it was only a short leap to the most explosive combination: sex, cocaine and blacks. Wright testified in front of a congressional committee in 1910 that 'cocaine is the direct incentive to the crime of rape by the Negroes of the South and other sections of the country'.

This scare story reached its logical conclusion:

Most of the attacks on white women of the South are the direct result of a
cocaine-crazed Negro brain.

Literary Digest, 1914, *cit. Cocaine*, Ashley, 1975

Black men having sex with white women? It was enough to make
every God-fearing American go out and trade up the calibre of his hand-
gun. Where did all this rubbish come from? Was there really an epidemic
of sexual assaults on white women by coke-crazed blacks?

Dr David Musto of Yale University, probably the world's foremost
authority on the history of drugs, says not. In fact, far from Colonel Watson's assertion that the insane asylums and prisons of the South were
'filling up', he quotes a survey of Georgia's penal institutions, which
revealed that, of 2,100 black detainees, a grand total of—wait for it—
two were cocaine users. Contrary to the reports of Williams and Wright,
there was no cocaine crime wave. In fact cocaine and drug addiction
were simply convenient ways of explaining high crime rates in the South.
Musto also points out that this particular period in cocaine's history happened to coincide neatly with a period of civil unrest in the South—
accompanied by a spate of racist crimes and lynchings. Cocaine was a
convenient scapegoat. In addition, as he pointed out to me when we met
in a hotel off Harvard Square in the summer of 2000, there was another,
more underhand reason for all this anticocaine polemic.

At the turn of the century the United States government was not
allowed to pass federal legislation for anything not specifically listed in
the constitution. This severely hampered its power. 'As a result the federal government was kept small and found itself unable to interfere in
Southern practices, such as taking the vote away from blacks,' says
Musto. 'In the South, people were very much opposed to a federal law
controlling the health professions locally. Because, if such a thing were
done and were constitutional, it would open the way to, let's say, voters'-
rights legislation.'

Government hawks were not at all happy with this situation. Thus it
was in their interests to create a scenario worrying enough to scare the
Southerners to ask them to step in. Once the South had *requested* the
North to act, the federal government would have a foot in the door—and
federal interference in the South's affairs would be plain sailing from then
on. 'So one of the techniques of government,' concludes Musto, 'was to
try to get the Southern people concerned about Northern pharmaceutical

companies supplying cocaine to Southern blacks, who were believed to turn violent against Southern whites. If they were concerned enough they would support a federal law to control the distribution of cocaine.'

Associating drug use with ethnic minorities was nothing new. Opium was already closely linked with the Orientals, who were especially reviled when rumours began spreading that Chinese men were using it to seduce white women. Marijuana would likewise be demonised, on the basis of reports that it was used by Mexicans. Not only were these sweaty Latinos smoking dope but—guess what?—they were messing with white women, too. By linking cocaine use with blacks and white women, antidrug campaigners were pulling out all the stops, as they knew that the image of racial minorities having congress with white women would strike at the heart of American society—the very bloodline of the country.

There's no denying the effectiveness of this ploy: just such an image—dirty foreigners seducing native women, contaminating the blood of future generations—was used to drum up hatred of the Jews in central Europe prior to World War Two. Anti-Semitism had its part in American cocaine legislation, too. A famous article in the *New York Times* in 1908 asked where all this cocaine was coming from. Which irresponsible person would sell a drug like this to Negroes? Well, who was known for buying and selling and double-dealing and making lots of money and having no morals whatsoever? You got it: 'there is little doubt that every Jew peddler in the South carries the stuff'. Perhaps fortunately, before the twisted tendencies of the drug legislators developed any further, a natural enemy emerged that everyone could agree that they hated: at the start of World War One, addiction was blamed on 'German' cocaine smugglers. There was nothing those Kraut bastards wouldn't stoop to.

The racist claptrap at the start of the last century mirrored the racist claptrap at the end of it. When cocaine eventually re-emerged in the 1960s it was available only (owing to its high price) to an elite, chosen few. As the price dropped, however, so it lost its exclusive image and more and more people began to use it. Suddenly it became a national problem and the people who had started using it—the rich, beautiful types—stopped. Correspondingly the drug dropped lower and lower down the social scale until it was produced in a form cheap and easy enough for everyone to be able to afford. That form was crack.

Today, crack is blamed for crime waves, all kinds of sexual offences and the disintegration of American inner cities generally. Yet at the root of the crack-cocaine problem lies a class problem. And at the root of that class problem lies a race problem. The fact is that cocaine, when used by rich, smiling white people with perfect teeth, great hair and good jobs, doesn't represent too much of a threat to society. Crack, however—used by unhappy, underprivileged, unemployed black people—does.

Thus, a hundred years ago the inflation of North America's endemic prejudices was used to generate the impetus to get the cocaine legislation wagon rolling. To some extent the same prejudices can be seen today, linking drugs and disease, drugs and crime, drugs and sex, drugs and violence and, ultimately, drugs and black people. As I was to discover again and again in the course of my research for this book, drugs are as much of a race issue today as they were a century ago. Don't believe it? Take a walk through Brixton until you come across a black man in a new BMW and ask the nearest white passer-by how he thinks that man made enough money to be able to afford it. Ten to one that, if he doesn't actually say 'dealing drugs', he'll be thinking it.

Drugs are dangerous and subversive; racial minorities are seen as dangerous and subversive. There must be a link. And crime? Over 50 per cent of all American crime over the last 75 years has been blamed on drugs, because drugs are the single most convenient scapegoat for a society that is unable to blame itself. When it comes to explaining the presence of those drugs themselves, blame is still not placed on American consumers, but on the foreign suppliers who grow the stuff. In America, there are no villains—only victims.

Not satisfied with stealing the virtues of the nation's women, cocaine was also apparently robbing American children of their innocence. *Hampton's Magazine* reported children as young as eight using cocaine. A *New York Times* of January 1907 reported BOY COCAINE SNUFFERS HUNTED BY POLICE, in which a sixteen-year-old lad was revealed to have become addicted to cocaine through one of the high-potency snuffs before realising that he could get the pure stuff cheaper from the pharmacy just across town. He bought it up an ounce at a time, took it to school and sold it to his friends to support his own habit. So seriously addicted was he that his mother reported that when he got home from school he didn't even know his own name and she had to 'roll him around on the floor' to get him to sober up.

Meanwhile, Harvey Wiley himself revealed cases of drug perversion so dastardly that only a 'Jew Peddler' could have conceived them: street vendors selling cocaine to children outside school playgrounds, allowing them the first few doses for free so that they would become addicted faster. Here again we have an illustration of an incident—of dubious authenticity—demonstrating to the public the utter, utter unspeakable evilness of drugs and those who use them. Here was cocaine again striking at the bloodline—the future of the country itself. And here, once again, is an image that lingers on to this day.

Wiley himself was largely left behind in the cocaine debate after the Pure Food and Drug Act. Convinced that caffeine ought to be removed from all products in the US, he was pursuing this notion with great gusto—especially when it came to his least favourite company: Coca-Cola. In fact, following an embarrassing court case in 1902 featuring witnesses testifying to children becoming addicted to the drink and adults drinking so much that they were unable to find their way home afterwards, Coca-Cola had already voluntarily removed all the cocaine from their beverage, but coca was still used for flavouring as part of the mysterious ingredient '7X'. Coca was shipped to the Schaeffer Alkaloidal Works in Maywood, New Jersey (of which more later), where the cocaine was removed, leaving the pulped leaves for their flavour. This was not good enough for Wiley: he wanted the drink banned outright. He launched a vendetta against the company and eventually managed to get the drink banned by the US Army in 1907, on the basis that it contained a vast amount of cocaine and as much alcohol as beer. When the military later realised that he was lying and reversed the ban, Wiley did not give up. In 1909 he confiscated forty barrels and twenty kegs of Coca-Cola syrup and attempted to prosecute the company on the basis that their product contained a poison (caffeine) and that it was falsely represented (it contained no cocaine). The case went to court in Chattanooga, Tennessee, in 1911, and a succession of government witnesses did their best to persuade the judge that Coca-Cola was a threat to society.

Wiley's pet scientists presented evidence, including the aforementioned report that the drink made boys masturbate, and the account of none other than Henry Hurd Rusby himself who (having changed his opinion on coca 180 degrees since his South American foray) testified that he knew Coca-Cola syrup was poisonous because he had flooded a rabbit's lungs with it and the rabbit had mysteriously dropped dead. The case never got very far but cost both sides a great deal of money.

By now Wiley was rapidly falling from favour on account of the fact that, as well as caffeine, he thought saccharine should be banned. He approached President Roosevelt about the matter and regaled him for some time about the need to ban this pernicious chemical. What he did not know was that Roosevelt was himself a big saccharine fan, using it every day to sweeten his coffee—'Anyone who says saccharine is injurious to health is a fool,' he said. Whoops. Wiley never really recovered and he was sacked in 1912. Predictably, he continued campaigning anyway.

Although Wiley's plaintive cries about food and drug additives were misguided, one thing was certain: something had to be done about the problem of cocaine addiction. The ensuing move to ban drugs outright was the start of a movement that was ultimately to lead to the 1919 Volstead Act—the dawn of the age of Prohibition. Because of this, it was also to lead to the emergence of the crime syndicates that would traffic first alcohol and then narcotics to circumvent it. Such syndicates would make and lose fortunes in drugs and alcohol and would eventually be responsible for the re-emergence of cocaine all those years later.

Meanwhile across the Atlantic, Britain was not nearly as concerned about cocaine. By 1900 cocaine was commonly viewed as a fairly harmless drug, one often associated with women. In fact cocaine has always had a strong feminine following for some reason, perhaps leading to its various street names today: *Lady, White Lady, Dama Blanca, Girl*, and so on. A hundred years ago its primary fans were actresses and prostitutes, who took it to help them get through their nightly performances. It was also, in the upper classes, associated with individuals 'of an artistic temperament'—those considered to be rather weak and emotional. This effete image of the drug was enhanced by a *Daily Mail* report in 1901, which referred to cocaine as having 'firmly established itself in London, not among the common people but among the cleverest people'. Cocaine, assured the article, remained 'an aristocratic vice'.

We can assume here that, as in the United States, cocaine had first hit society through the ranks of the doctors and dentists, who would have heard of it early on, had easy access to it and, more importantly, had the money to be able to afford it. And it was the doctors who had first paid the price: an article in *Chemist and Druggist* knew what it was talking about in 1901 when it stated that 'of all the horrors that have been created during the last twenty years, cocaine-taking is probably the worst'. Outside their ranks, however, it was a game: at this stage, although it was noted that cocaine was clearly a vice rather than simply a social habit, no one paid much attention at all.

One of the reasons Britain was not keen to legislate against addictive drugs was that it was making vast amounts of money by flogging opium to the Chinese. As much as 20 per cent of the entire financial output of the Indian Empire was made in this drug trade—a revenue so important that the Brits had actually gone to war with China in 1856 to protect it. Thus when the United States suggested a ban on opium trading, the British were not keen.

In 1909 America organised the first global antidrug conference in Shanghai in an attempt to persuade other nations to ban the Far Eastern opium trade. While the British had no intention of stopping their narcotic trading, they didn't want to look bad. Thus, after much wrangling, they agreed to show up but, when they did, ran circles all around the US delegates to ensure that nothing of any consequence could be agreed.

When everyone went home at the end of the conference the shell-shocked Americans thought they had secured an agreement from the thirteen other nations present to reduce and eventually cease opium trading with 'uncivilised races'. In fact they had got nothing of the sort. Nine resolutions, said the US, had been adopted unanimously. In fact none was adopted. However, it was clear even to the British that sooner or later they were going to have to face the music about opium. But how could they postpone such a decision? The Americans had decided that there should be another conference, this time in the Hague. The British sat down and cooked up some stalling tactics.

The Hague Conference took place in 1911 and, while the British managed to avoid making any cast-iron promises to reduce their opium trade, an agreement that this was probably necessary was extracted from them. In the conference that followed, Britain back-pedalled furiously. Initially they announced that the meeting should be postponed because Turkey and Peru were absent. Then they announced that the Hague Convention really ought to be more long-sighted, covering not only opium but also cocaine. To this day, no one is quite sure why they did this: perhaps they were being realistic about global drug traffic. On the other hand, it has been suggested that, knowing that Germany (America's ally in the matter of drugs talks) was at the time the world's number-one manufacturer of cocaine, they knew that this would create trouble. It did. For cocaine to be covered, all details of German cocaine production would have to be submitted to the meeting. But the Germans didn't want to reveal all their business interests in the global drug trade to their competitors. Again, everything was delayed. A British diplomat later recalled the Hague conference as 'face saving...to conceal a total failure'.

However, the Americans were not deterred and organised a further conference. And at this third meeting—again in the Hague—it was finally agreed that all attending nations would do their best to reduce trade in dangerous drugs with a view to eventually cutting it out altogether. All drugs were henceforth to be restricted to purely medical use. The Americans were delighted. All that remained was to get those countries not present at the conference to ratify the treaty. How difficult could that be?

The conference formally ended on 25 June 1914. Three days later Archduke Ferdinand was assassinated and World War One broke out. Suddenly everyone was concerned with killing, rather than saving, each other, and international antidrug efforts ground to a halt.

For the British, the war was the factor that really brought cocaine to the fore. London was the number-one spot to spend a long weekend's leave for soldiers back from the front, but soldiers back from the front weren't interested in the tourist sights. They wanted to drink. Not surprisingly, the West End's private clubs and bars came alive: here was an injection of money and action and an apparently unlimited number of young men who didn't see much point in saving their cash for later.

The authorities, realising what was going on in the heart of the West End, became concerned for the wellbeing of Britain's brave boys and decided that they were being corrupted. This was no way to treat our war heroes. Besides, when they went back to the front, they might be suffering from hangovers and unable to fight properly. Illegal clubs were raided and closed, prostitutes rounded up and arrested. A complete alcohol ban was mooted. A blanket ban was narrowly avoided but it was decided that bars and restaurants should be shut nightly at 9.30, and that they should remain closed in the afternoon to discourage drunkenness—a habit that continued across Britain until the late 1980s. The king announced that he and the royal family were going teetotal for the duration of the war.

There was no way that soldiers just back from the front were going to join him. They wanted alcohol, and lots of it. And they wanted to stay out later than 9.30 p.m. So they did—heading for the very same sleazy, underground establishments that the police were trying to close down. Alcohol was still expensive and there was cocaine around: and, since they were breaking the law just by being out anyway, what harm was there to be had in trying a little of the powder that made you stay up all night and feel great? The clandestine nature of the drinking clubs was tailor-made for the drug trade: secret, debauched, uninhibited and rich. The *Evening News* picked up on the new trend in 1916:

> I see that other people are turning their attention to the growing craze for opium smoking, to which I referred last week. West End bohemia is hearing some dark stories of what is going on. But still more prevalent is use of that exciting drug, cocaine. It is so easy to take—just snuffed up the nose...in the ladies cloakroom of a certain establishment two bucketfuls of thrown-away small circular cardboard boxes were discovered by the cleaners the other day—discarded cocaine boxes.
>
> 'Quex', *Evening News*, 3 January 1916

In 1916 Britain experienced its first drugs panic. 'There are signs that the cocaine habit is spreading in London,' warned the *Evening News*. Something had to be done. What if Our Boys were going back to France inebriated? Suddenly everyone was up in arms. The press lapped up the cocaine sensation. The *Daily Chronicle* reported that the cocaine situation had deteriorated in the last six months to a 'veritable mania'; the *Evening News* writing that cocaine use was 'spreading like wildfire in all classes of the community until, next to alcoholism, it is far and away the commonest form of drug taking'. Others were more sensational:

LONDON IN THE GRIP OF COCAINE CRAZE!
Secret 'coke' parties of 'snow snifters'

> With incredible swiftness, London has fallen victim to the drug habit... today London abounds with needle dancers (morphine fiends), dope fiends, coke fiends and others addicted to ether, herowin [sic] and numerous other drugs. Cocaine is the most popular, however...
>
> *Umpire*, 23 July 1916

The threat to our boys at the front was great: they must be protected from this terrible drug. *The Times* called cocaine a threat 'more deadly than bullets' (presumably a number of those returning to the front would rather have taken their chance with cocaine than the bullets: they would have stood better odds). There are reports of combatants at the front taking it to calm their nerves before going over the top. A French account relates that cocaine was a special favourite of early airmen:

> Cocaine infused into the few duellists of the air who made use of that cold and thoroughly lucid exaltation which—alone among drugs—it can produce... at the same time it left intact their control over their actions. It fortified them, one might say, by abolishing the idea of risk.
>
> *cit.* Woods, *Dangerous Drugs*, 1931

It seems unlikely that many airmen were taking cocaine in the conflict but other forces were certainly using it. The Australian Anzacs were especially partial to the drug: shell-shocked soldiers were treated by underqualified medics, and morphine and cocaine were simply handed out to one and all. One of the few qualified Australian pharmacists present at Gallipoli later recounted how he had been commanded, prior to a particularly severe attack, to distribute the battalion's cocaine supplies to the troops. The English were known to use cocaine on the battlefield, too: *The Times* of 20 December 1915 contains an advertisement from the pharmacists Savoy and Moore ('chemists to the King'), who were selling mail-order medical kits containing, among other medications, heroin and cocaine. 'A useful present for friends at the Front', crowed the advertisement. But what effect would cocaine have on the troops? *The Times* was in no doubt:

> THE COCAINE HABIT: RUINOUS RESULTS OF A DRUG
> To the soldier subjected to nervous strain and hard work cocaine, once used, must become a terrible temptation. It will, for the hour, charm away his trouble, his fatigue and his anxiety; it will give him fictitious strength and vigour. But it will also, in the end, render him worthless as a soldier and a man.
>
> *The Times*, 12 February 1916

The threat of cocaine on the army's efficiency was too much for the chiefs of staff. It was time to act. Cocaine had been covered under a 1908 act placing it in the category of a 'poison' and as such it was subject to certain regulations. It was decided to enforce these stringently. In early 1916 a number of chemists were prosecuted for selling it without due concern. Both Savoy and Moore (for their mail-order cocaine package) and a little-known London-based department store by the name of Harrods were prosecuted for selling cocaine without observing the correct regulations. But this was hardly going to stop the flow: the majority of it taken in the clubs was coming from the black market and the drug wasn't even illegal at the time.

Popular reports state that the real source of the cocaine habit among British troops was the Canadian army. Although the drug was available in the UK prior to the war, it was only when the Canadians—who had themselves picked up the habit from the Americans—really showed everyone how much fun it was that it was picked up. Francis Chester, an early addict, wrote in his autobiography that when he arrived from Canada with his battalion in 1915, cocaine was readily available all over central London—sold on Shaftesbury Avenue concealed between 'Views From London' postcards for five shillings (25p) a hit. The dealer told him when asked that she always sold more 'snow' than morphine. The fact that she called it 'snow' is a fair indication that she picked up the slang from Americans or Canadians—among whom this term was already in common use. Likewise, Cecil de Lenoir, another early addict, writes that the drug was easily available all over the West End in 1915. He knew, he said, at least a dozen chemists 'from Limehouse to Hammersmith' who would sell him up to a gram at a time—no questions asked.

The media portrayed cocaine and opium as part of a cunning Kraut plot to demoralise the British fighting man and finally, in May 1916, the army imposed a special deterrent for anyone caught supplying military personnel with narcotics: six months in jail. But it was clear that something more than this was going to be needed to ensure the safety of the British Army and so, on 28 July 1916, Defence of the Realm Act (DORA) regulation 40B was passed, banning the sale of cocaine- and opium-based products to military personnel without a prescription. This regulation was eventually to become the Dangerous Drugs Act in 1920—marking the start of British antidrug legislation.

Three months after DORA was passed, a committee converged at the Home Office to examine the problem of cocaine. Ostensibly the aim of the meeting was to discuss the problem of cocaine and unregistered dentists (there were some 7,000 unlicensed dentists in London; restricting the sale of cocaine to them would effectively put them out of business), but cocaine addiction turned out to be far more interesting. The committee, which included future Prime Minister Stanley Baldwin, discussed at some length the reasons why cocaine was taken, its possible aphrodisiac effects and the possibility of 'loose women' drugging and robbing British servicemen with it. Although there was a fair amount of exaggeration ('people who took it before would commit murder to get it,' reported a Canadian sergeant), it was generally agreed that the cocaine problem was not actually that serious and that DORA was a pretty effective piece of legislation.

The Americans had recently enacted a similar piece of legislation themselves. They were already some ten years ahead of Britain as regards cocaine addiction—Harry Anslinger, on his way to becoming the US's first narcotics commissioner, estimated that there were 200,000 cocaine addicts in the US. The *Canadian Pharmaceutical Journal* put the number much higher—at 6 million. Thus in 1914 the US had passed the Harrison Act, decreeing that all dangerous drugs must be handled only by qualified persons and that these persons had to keep accurate records of their use. The penalty for attempting to sell the drug without the correct documentation was up to five years in prison or a $2,000 fine. Sentences for selling cocaine would eventually be hiked up in 1922 to a $5,000 fine or ten years in prison—more than for heroin.

The end of the war saw the real beginning of an attempt to cut down on global cocaine consumption. Under the Versailles Treaty, Germany, then the world's largest single cocaine producer, was ordered to comply with the Hague Convention agreements. However, this did very little to curb the use of cocaine in Britain. Having taken off during the war, recreational cocaine use was very much in vogue. Of course, the place to find cocaine was London: the West End, where the partying never stopped, was the ideal place for a drug culture to form a toe-hold. Members of the young, smart set were more than happy to hang out in dingy, frequently illegal, private drinking clubs and here they were bound to come into contact with the London underworld. It was an environment ripe for drug experimentation. Although cocaine sales were now illegal without a prescription, the harder elements of the drinking clubs would be sure to have contacts who could procure some—if the price was right. For a great number of well-heeled young men and women, it frequently was. Perhaps because of its artificially high price, cocaine was still mostly taken by professional classes, the *Daily Mail* stating:

> Cocaine parties have long been a feature of the life followed by certain sections of professional classes in the West End of London. They existed

before the War and, notwithstanding legal restrictions, they still flourish...there are houses and flats in London where men and women, barris-
ters, politicians and actresses, music hall artists and others meet for a few
doses of cocaine and a night of revelry.

Daily Mail, 14 December 1918

Cocaine also maintained its image as a woman's drug. As such, it
made its way into the headlines following a series of sensational cases
involving the overdose of a number of famous actresses. The most
famous of these was Billie Carleton, a London showgirl, found dead in
her flat in November 1918. Cocaine was blamed and the trial of her supplier, a beau by the name of Reggie de Veulle, for manslaughter, kept the
public enthralled for most of December and January the next year.

The image of women as the chief victims of cocaine was to linger for
some time—eventually coupled with the American notion that 'foreign'
drug peddlers were to blame. Since there were very few blacks in Britain,
the blame was laid firmly at the feet of either Germans (they were the
world's number-one cocaine makers and, after all, we had just fought a
long and terrible war against them) or the Chinese. Chinese immigrants
were well-known drug users—after all, didn't they spend all their time
smoking opium in sordid dens? Soon the rumours became more elaborate:
the Chinese ran laundries and restaurants and enticed young girls into drug
use so that they could use them for their perverse Oriental sexual practices.
Once the girls were hooked on cocaine or opium they were unable to refuse
anything. When these evil Chinese had had enough of their recruits they
spirited them away across the sea, apparently to Buenos Aires (for no other
reason, it seems, than that it was a suitably godforsaken, faraway place),
where they were sold into slavery. Newspapers were outraged:

What sinister fascination is it that seems to draw so many girls and women
into the clutches of Chinamen...? It is by the seduction of the drugged
pipe that many and many a girl has been tempted into the dark rooms of
Chinatown to become the plaything, and often not even the wife, of Celes-
tials who have brought their Eastern vices with them.

Umpire, 6 August 1916

In the rush to find scapegoats for the drug problem, the fact that the
British had spent most of the last century peddling this 'Eastern vice' to

the Chinese was conveniently forgotten. The image of the Chinese drug and white-slave trade was to fuel countless second-rate novels and films, most notably Sax Rohmer's *Dr Fu Manchu* series. Rohmer was eventually to write a novel about cocaine abuse, *Dope*, featuring just such a cunning plot. A 1922 film, *Cocaine*, although it contained no Chinese cast members whatsoever, advertised itself with a picture of a Chinese woman.

Sure enough, in the next sensational cocaine case—the drug-related death of a showgirl, Freda Kempton, in 1922—a Chinese man was revealed to be at the foot of the problem. This unfortunate individual, who ran a restaurant on Regent Street, was dubbed 'Brilliant Chang' by the press ('an elusive, cunning Chinaman...the most devastating figure behind the scenes of illicit drug traffic, and a leader of Oriental vice'). In court, Brilliant Chang denied everything but it was no use: he was Chinese, he was rich and he had an evil-sounding name. His restaurant, like every other Chinese business venture in England, was a front for a sordid drugs and white-slave business. Chang was sentenced to fourteen months and deported.

Perhaps the most significant trafficker of the time was finally brought to justice in 1923. Once again, he was a foreigner. Edgar Manning, a 'smartly dressed Negro' from Jamaica, had come to the attention of London's CID in 1919 when it became apparent that he was shifting large amounts of cocaine and morphine through the capital. According to newspapers of the time, Manning had been the source of the drugs that eventually killed Billie Carleton. Although his confederate, Italian Carlo Ivaldi, was busted in fairly short order with thirteen packets of cocaine ('enough to have "doped" half London' said the *News of the World*), Manning 'led the police a merry dance', at one point even writing to the Chief Constable to accuse the CID of harassment. 'The fact is,' wrote Manning, 'I being by nature desine [sic]—Black, seems to make my persecution the more unbearable, it is now making my nerves a total wreck'. The letter didn't achieve much and the *News of the World* was delighted to announce his arrest in 1923:

EVIL NEGRO CAUGHT

King of London's dope traffic, a notorious West Indian, familiar in high places and low haunts, has gone to penal servitude at last. He was sentenced at the Old Bailey during the week to three years...and his conviction removes from the night life of the West End one of the most dangerous and disreputable characters Scotland Yard have ever had to book. This Negro was money mad, and he made it at the sacrifice of the souls of white women and white girls.

News of the World, 22 July 1923

In the meantime, British police staged a bold series of entrapment busts, undercover officers approaching likely looking individuals in Soho and attempting to buy cocaine from them. The cocaine, when they found it, mostly came from legitimate pharmacists taking under-the-counter payoffs. However, as these chemists were progressively arrested, supplies started to dwindle and enterprising smugglers began using new techniques to get cocaine into Britain. Cecil de Lenoir witnessed a cocaine-smuggling exercise himself: the drug was landed by boat off the secluded Essex estuaries, picked up by car and then driven directly to London. It came from Holland, he said, cunningly disguised in shipments of cigars. If the ship the drug was coming from was a big one, the drug would be sealed into watertight containers and heaved overboard before docking, to be picked up at night in fishing boats. In more elaborate cases the waterproof packages were tied to large blocks of sea salt so that they would sink, resurfacing only after the salt had dissolved, when customs and police officers were long gone.

While the British police's crackdown on cocaine was initially effective at removing the drug from the streets it raised its price, making smuggling more attractive. A German trafficker arrested in 1922 was asked why he had done it. He pointed out that the cocaine he had bought at home for £30 was worth over £3,000 in London. As police became more vigilant, so traffickers devised new techniques to circumvent customs. In a 1922 piece entitled AMAZING TRICKS OF THE COCAINE SMUGGLERS, the *Evening News* reported that recent busts had revealed cocaine concealed in fresh flowers and vegetables, German sausages, bottles of ink and even a stuffed dachshund (the woman concerned would have got away with it had she not been seen opening up the dachshund to retrieve some cocaine to fortify herself just before heading through customs). Meanwhile, bird keepers were smuggling carrier pigeons to the European mainland, tying cocaine to their legs and sending them home to England. The *Evening News* reported a case of smugglers shifting cocaine into Britain concealed inside wooden models of the cenotaph—a ploy so utterly tasteless that 'only the German mind' could have conceived of it.

The British were outraged. Voices were raised in the House: cocaine traffickers should be flogged, argued one MP, because 'these aliens are frightened by nothing else'. Courts were likewise unsympathetic: a Cypriot who had smuggled '6,000 doses' of cocaine into Britain in the same year had made the fundamental blunder of attempting to sell it to a pharmacist—one of the few people in the country who would have been able to buy the drug himself. 'Stupidity' was not a suitably mitigating circumstance, it seems: 'I wish we could shoot you, you blackguard,' ranted the magistrate, before sentencing him to the maximum possible jail term.

While the British were rounding up random Chinese immigrants in London, the cocaine scourge was sweeping across Europe. Cecil de Lenoir visited Paris in 1922, where he noted that 'cocaine was being used more extensively than anywhere I had yet been'. Ten years earlier medical journals had reported that over 50 per cent of Paris's prostitutes were using cocaine. The worst-hit districts were Montmartre and the surrounding night spots: the Halle district, the Latin quarter and a few trendy establishments on the Champs-Élysées. The French called cocaine 'dardo', a word emerging from the taking of the Dardanelles (*la prise des Dardanelles*—'*prise*' in French can also mean 'dosing' or 'sniffing'). Parisian police records for 1920 reveal that they confiscated 70 kilograms of pure cocaine in the city, yet as late as 1924 the drug squad for the entire country consisted of just eight men.

Spain was also hit, its police reporting exclusive 'cocaine addiction clubs' in Barcelona and Madrid. Likewise Belgium, where doctors reported four distinct classes of cocaine user: the intellectual, the physically ill, the mentally unstable and those involved in prostitution. In Italy the problem was even worse, the director of a leading insane asylum raising the alarm in 1920 following a huge increase in admissions presenting with paranoid delusions brought about by cocaine. This is perhaps not surprising: as he noted, at that point in Italy it was considered rather trendy to take up to five grams a day.

Germany was also in trouble. Throughout the war it had been stockpiling cocaine because there had been no guarantee that it would be able to maintain its coca supplies. It now emerged, broken and horribly in debt, with huge reparations to pay. Inside the country the black market exploded; financial and spiritual depression ensured that the population was looking for some light relief. Cocaine stockpiles mysteriously began to vanish—only to reappear on the street. One record tells that illicit cocaine was still sold in drug stores as late as 1920, without any sort of a prescription, in quantities of up to a kilogram at a time. Dealers bought up the drug in bulk, adulterated it heavily and resold it on the street at seven or eight times its retail value. Psychiatric clinics worked overtime as hitherto unknown quantities of young, apparently healthy Germans were admitted with paranoid delusions caused by cocaine. Inmate admissions to one German institute due to cocaine toxosis leapt nearly 1,000 per cent from 1916 to 1921.

Even Switzerland was in trouble. Troops evacuated here since 1916 had been swiftly followed by hangers-on—Parisian prostitutes, who brought the drug habit with them. In his classic 1926 study, *Der Kokainismus*, the Swiss psychiatrist Hans Maier explored the extent of cocaine addiction in the 1920s, writing up over a hundred cases of severe addiction (he witnessed one of his patients taking nineteen grams in a single night!). He noted all of the common features afflicting cocaine addicts today, including rhinitis, perforation of the septum between the nostrils (first recorded in 1904; 'snorting' cocaine probably started at the turn of the century among the poor, who could not afford the syringes with which the upper classes were so enamoured) and heart disturbances. He was intrigued to discover that, just as had been reported by the Indians all those years ago and by Mantegazza in 1859, cocaine did indeed have a sensational effect on muscular ability and staying power:

> Individuals under the effects of cocaine are capable of balancing and acrobatic prowesses requiring a level of muscular tension and dexterity of which they are incapable in the normal state. One of my patients, while fully hallucinating, was able to climb up the front of a multiple storey house with the facility of a cat.
>
> *Der Kokainismus*, Hans Maier, 1926

Maier was especially interested in one of cocaine's peculiar side effects: hallucinations. Freud's friend, Ernst von Fleischl-Marxow, had been the first to experience strange fantasies—feelings of snakes or insects crawling around beneath his skin. He was not alone. It soon became clear that this was a common trait of those suffering from cocaine toxosis and it was named Magnan's Syndrome—after a French physician who had studied it in 1889—though it has always been known more commonly by its street name: 'coke bugs'. German physician Louis

Lewin reported the extent that the deluded cocaine user could go to in his attempt to rid himself of these tactile hallucinations:

> Abnormal sensations in the peripheral nerves cause the patient to believe that there are animals under his skin. The result is frequently self-mutilation, and by a false application of subjective impressions, the mutilation of members of his own family, in order to remove the foreign substance from his body. A woman injured herself with needles in order to kill the 'cocaine bugs'. A man who suffered from twinges and pains in the arms and feet thought he was being forcibly electrocuted. He thought he could see electric wires leading to his body.
>
> *Phantastica*, Lewin, 1924

Magnan himself reported many cases of self-mutilation, including a businessman who suffered from

> visual hallucinations (all objects around the patient appeared to be in motion), auditory hallucinations (he would hear frightful knockings on his door every night), and tactile hallucinations (he had the sensation that his tongue was covered with black worms)... he could see dancing shadows, he felt surrounded by a swarm of bees and a turtle made gestures at him. All these objects, including horses and dogs, looked to him smaller than in reality. He claimed that he was forced to breathe a foul-smelling gas. He was constantly tapped on the shoulder, and foreign bodies crawled over his skin... he inserted needles, keys and a knife into his anus in order, as he put it, to breathe a bit, because his body was full of gas.
>
> Magnan, 1889, *cit. Der Kokainismus*, Maier, 1926

In the cases of less severely addicted individuals, cocaine-induced delusions were less serious: Maier notes that his more technically minded patients, when high on the drug, tended to spend their time inventing extraordinary mechanical machines and gadgets. One of his patients prepared elaborate plans for a machine capable of annihilating his enemies on the battlefield. A number of others repeatedly solved the problem of perpetual motion only to find, when the drug wore off, that they had simply scribbled reams of pages of gibberish. 'During the War,' Maier notes, 'the French Ministry of War received a large number of delusional projects from cocaine addicts.'

Cocaine was even taking its toll in the Soviet Union. The country had been a major cocaine consumer prior to the war—the Russian scientist Vassily von Anrepp was the unacknowledged discoverer of local anaesthesia by cocaine, and another, Sergei Kolomnin, had caused the first cocaine death by overdose. But cocaine was not only used professionally. An anonymous manuscript, 'Novel with Cocaine', appearing in a Parisian émigré journal called *Numbers* in the 1930s testified to the recreational abuse of the drug in middle-class circles in Moscow (it has since been alleged that this is a fake). Meanwhile, a survey of Moscow penal institutions shortly after the Revolution showed that they were riddled with addicts, mostly prostitutes. For some reason (perhaps scarcity during the Revolution, leading to an increasingly high 'cut' rate), a far higher percentage of them had perforated nasal septa than in the West. It was reported as being especially prevalent in the Russian army. However, it wasn't long before addiction levels in Soviet society dropped sharply. The reasons for cocaine's disappearance were pretty straightforward: violence, political intrigue and repression acted together to protect the emerging Soviet Union from the cocaine scourge. As the West would discover twenty years later, drug addiction—like unemployment, anarchy and religious apathy—is only really effectively cured by social upheaval on a grand scale. Since the arrival of illicit drug addiction in its modern sense, the only real low point in illegal drug abuse has been World War Two. Until then, cocaine taking was a familiar pastime throughout Europe and as far afield as Australia and Egypt. But such a huge world market for cocaine needed a correspondingly huge cocaine supply. Where was it coming from?

The main culprit was Germany. The German cocaine industry was made up of a group of around ten companies, all situated within 80 kilometres of Frankfurt. The most famous of these was, of course, Merck. As early as 1910 it had been churning out over 50 tons of pure cocaine a year—over 75 per cent of which was for export. With the postwar malaise and the rise in addiction, one might assume that the Germans slowed down cocaine production. In fact the opposite was the case. Cocaine was an extremely valuable commodity on the world market and as such was one of the few products capable of generating hard currency.

The Germans cranked up production. Illicit drug seizures again and again turned over containers of cocaine and heroin featuring the brand names and symbols of German pharmaceutical manufacturers. In the first four months of 1925 alone Germany was shown to have exported over 1,500 kilograms of morphine, 554 kilograms of heroin and 516 kilograms of cocaine to Switzerland. But these narcotics were clearly destined for markets further afield: this amount of heroin was enough to supply Switzerland's legitimate medical needs for the next 150 years.

Germany was playing a smart game. While all countries had been forced to ratify the Hague treaty, some had been slower than others. Switzerland had not yet got around to it—so it was not illegal to ship narcotics through there. Where they went after that was anyone's business—Germany had made its money. Switzerland was forced to comply with the new international drug laws and this loophole was shut. It wasn't long before others emerged.

In 1921 a new system had been introduced to monitor international shipments of dangerous drugs. This involved import and export certificates from countries involved in the world trade. Before importing cocaine a certificate stating that you were legally permitted to import dangerous drugs was submitted by the buyer to the seller. The seller country confirmed that the certificate was real and then issued their own export certificate to accompany the drug. Both sides of the deal had to maintain accurate records of their drug transactions. Thus by going through the records, it was hoped, international drug shipments could be tracked from country to country around the world without the risk of their going astray. Unfortunately, it didn't quite work like this.

For a start, drug treaties outlawed only a certain number of chemicals. Smart drug traffickers realised that by transforming their drugs into chemical variants of themselves they could relinquish the need for international certificates. Cocaine and heroin were doctored into forms that were not legislated against, shipped around the world openly and, on arrival at their destination, converted back into heroin and cocaine.

One famous Swiss drug company did a roaring trade in an apparently harmless chemical called acetyl-proprionyl-morphine until 1928, when it was pointed out that this was easily convertible back into morphine. The Swiss, knowing that this particular compound was not illegal, had simply been dispatching it to the market country by post. Another technique to circumvent international restrictions was to ship cocaine from the manufacturer not to the purchaser but to an international branch of the same manufacturer in the country of purchase. This way the cocaine would remain—technically—the property of the manufacturing country despite the fact that it was abroad. No import or export licence was necessary. Once it was in the foreign country, of course, it was simply dumped on to the black market. Sentences for this kind of smuggling were lax: a 1925 drug ring apprehended in Hamburg admitted that they had moved 'many hundreds' of kilos of cocaine around the world in the last two years. Only one member of the team received a custodial sentence: one month in prison.

Gradually, as international legislation and policing tightened up, such loopholes were closed. The largest, however, was to stay open for nearly ten years. In 1928 a 60-kilogram cocaine bust on board a container ship in Rotterdam was the first indication of a huge international smuggling operation that was to create all kinds of problems. When it was investigated, it emerged that various international pharmaceutical houses had discovered that the Netherlands had not yet ratified the international accords on import and export licences for narcotics. Effectively, trafficking dangerous drugs was legal, as long as they went via Holland. The 60 kilograms of cocaine was just the thin end of the wedge.

One particular Dutch company, Chemische Fabriek Naarden, in Bossum, near Rotterdam, was revealed to have shipped 850 kilograms of morphine, 3,000 kilograms of heroin and 90 kilograms of cocaine directly on to the black market in just eighteen months. In 1927 a single Swiss drug company, Roessler Fils, moved 4,349 kilograms of heroin through Chemische Fabriek Naarden. The licit world market for heroin that year was just 1,700 kilograms. Quantities of drug shipments were staggering: the Secretariat of the League of Nations concluded that, in the four years from 1924 to 1929 over 6 tons of cocaine had been shifted directly on to the black market via Naarden alone.

Most of Chemische Fabriek Naarden's illicit deals were routed through Japan via China. Archive research reveals that cocaine shipped out to Japan from Naarden—supposedly for different international distributors—was simply mailed to consecutively numbered PO Boxes in Shanghai for forwarding. All of the PO boxes were at the same address and owned by variants of the same company. But the Netherlands had been cunning. The country had completely tied itself up in red tape and, when the case came to court, managed to prove that Chemische Fabriek Naarden had violated no Dutch laws whatsoever. Holland eventually stopped this trade only after heavy pressure from the international community. By this time even the Dutch had realised that cocaine was bad news: testimony to the fact that they were sampling their own products, cocaine addicts began to spring up around the country and the Dutch government was appalled to read medical journals reporting that—shock, horror!—cocaine led to bisexuality in men. The final loophole in international legislation was closed.

But the biggest traffickers were only beginning to swing into action. Japan, although attending all the anticocaine meetings and conferences and signing all the accords, was pursuing its own agenda.

The Japanese had originally obtained their cocaine from Germany and England, but when World War One broke out the government became concerned that the empire might run out of this precious drug. To protect their supply lines they established their own coca plantations and refineries. Japan began to cultivate coca on Formosa (Taiwan) and looked into the prospects of buying into the Dutch plantations in Java. Following the enactment of international legislation, these plantations were rapidly losing their value: since anticoca legislation had come in, the licit market for cocaine was not big enough to sustain them. Javanese coca farmers began to lose money. They sold to the Japanese. The Dutch East Indies were capable of producing over 1,500 tons of coca a year— enough to make more than 15 tons of pure cocaine. The Japanese cranked them up to full tilt. In the meantime they also bought up land in South America (eventually their plantations would cover some 3,000 square kilometres in Peru alone) and seeded new plantations in Okinawa and Iwo Jima.

Yet again the name of the American pharmaceutical giant Parke, Davis crops up: Japanese expertise in coca farming and cocaine extraction came from a brilliant young scientist called Jokichi Takamine, who had been the first to isolate the hormone adrenaline, in 1901. After this he worked for Parke, Davis—the world's second biggest cocaine manufacturer— picking up all sorts of tips about industrial cocaine production. He took this knowledge with him when he returned to Japan to work as a consultant to a Japanese pharmaceutical company called Sankyo—which suddenly just happened to become one of Japan's largest cocaine producers. Unsurprisingly, following its massive investment in the cocaine trade, Japan leaped to the head of the international cocaine-production tables. It soon became clear to international authorities that Japan was both importing—and producing—far more cocaine than it could ever use.

Japanese-declared cocaine production in 1929 was 320 kilograms. In fact they had produced well over 100 tons of it. But where was it all going?

The Japanese had discovered, as had the British many years before them, that mainland China constituted an almost unlimited market for addictive drugs. As the British finally scaled down their opium trade with China, Japan stepped in and took over. They also began to peddle the Chinese a drug with which they were less familiar: cocaine. It has been suggested that the drug was introduced to China by missionaries who had heard rumours that it could be used to wean opium addicts away from the drug. If this is the case, then Chinese cocaine consumption can be blamed on the American drug company Parke, Davis, who, as we have seen, had first cooked up this myth in the *Therapeutic Gazette*. Either way, China soon joined the rest of the world as a consumer of the drug, with Japan more than happy to supply it. Many of the companies behind this trade were state owned. Mitsui and Mitsubishi were two of the biggest. They remain two of the largest corporations in the world today.

Money generated by the illicit trafficking of cocaine and opiates to China was more than simply an extra bonus. Japan had occupied large tracts of land in China in 1931, taking huge slices of Manchuria and creating the Japanese territory of Manchukuo. China was at this point undergoing a brutal civil war and Japanese property had to be protected, so large numbers of soldiers were stationed there. Maintaining an army in a foreign country like this cost a great deal of money. The world's stock markets had crashed in 1929 and there was a great shortage of foreign currency—so drug dealing seemed to be an ideal solution.

Soon the only real source of revenue for the Japanese territories in China was drugs. According to the Japanese after World War Two, drug trading in China was so prevalent by the time they arrived that there was no way they could have avoided it. Certainly many of the Chinese warlords were themselves making fortunes out of selling narcotics to their own troops, including Chang Kai Shek himself—leader of the Kuomintang and later president of Taiwan. As the Japanese government at home lost power to the military in the run-up to World War Two, so the army was placed in command of overseas stations and selling drugs to the Chinese became a military priority.

The full extent of Japan's dealings in the illicit cocaine trade will probably never be known. They were substantial enough, however, to shock Supreme Commander of the Southwest Pacific, General Douglas MacArthur, into asking in the US Federal Narcotics Commissioner, Harry Anslinger, to send a team out to China to deal with it following VJ-Day. Anslinger's boys were appalled at the scale of the operation, and narcotics trafficking was one of the charges Japan was to face at Nuremberg.

What is clear is that the government sanctioned the trade, and that cocaine was frequently shifted from production centres (sometimes even by warship) to China. Eventually a huge narcotics factory was built on the mainland to save the cost and time of shipping the drugs. At first, European and American drug legislators were simply puzzled by Japan's apparently large consumption of cocaine and opiates. Soon, however, confiscations of smuggled cocaine revealed the truth. The drug began showing up around Asia, packaged in Japanese boxes with the names of Japanese pharmaceutical companies printed on the side. Nowhere did the discovery of these packages create more panic than in the jewel of the British Empire—India.

India had been growing coca in the Nilgiri Hills since 1883, exporting some 1,800 kilograms of leaf per year from Madras to Britain for refining. Yet Indian cocaine was not the product of Indian coca—it was smuggled in, first from Germany, then from Japan. According to legend, cocaine abuse had first hit Bhagalpore in Bengal Province in 1886, when a rich landowner was prescribed some for toothache and discovered the drug's euphoric qualities. The habit had rabidly spread throughout the continent along the extensive railway network before hitting the slums of Bombay, Calcutta and Delhi. Benares (modern Varanasi) was also hit hard. Cocaine consumption in India was linked with the very same themes that had accompanied it in the rest of the world. First there was sex:

In India it is found that the majority of the victims labour under the false notion that it enhances the pleasure of sexual intercourse...

Then there was crime:

It would not be an exaggeration to say that the major portion of the crimes against property are committed by those who are habitually addicted to the use of cocaine...

And, once again, as in Britain, it was often taken by women:

In Saharanpur there are females who go into mandars (temples) to pay homage. They keep a secret pocket in their undergarment (langha) and in it they carry the 1/8th drachm phial of cocaine and sell it...

Cocaine and its Demoralising Effects, AP Bhargava, 1916

By 1902, according to a local doctor, Kailas Chunder Bose, the drug was decimating the population of Calcutta. Bose was concerned—there were so many cocaine addicts, he said, that pretty soon the government would have to set up inebriate asylums for them. He gave some examples from among his unfortunate patients:

> ...H, aged 29, cannot govern his own ideas, and loses the thread of his conversation. Dread of being chased by the police maddens him. Whilst loitering on the streets, if he should see any white powder he would carefully pick it up and put it on his tongue and then throw it down, saying it is not the thing he wanted. He plucks flowers from plants and puts them on his head. He now lives entirely upon the charity of others.
>
> *British Medical Journal*, 28 June 1902

The *British Medical Journal* picked up on this tragic report. 'Repressive measures' were called for, it said, 'if the evil is to be adequately dealt with'. The problem was especially hard to control because it was so widespread: cocaine was taken across the social spectrum all the way from the rich upper castes, who took it for kicks, to the lowest of the low, who used it to stave off their hunger, buying their fixes off the street in paper envelopes called *lifafas*. It was perhaps natural that the drug should spread so fast, as it was usually taken with betel—a weak stimulant commonly chewed across the country. Just a small pinch of cocaine made betel that extra bit more effective—without making the process of drug taking too unfamiliar. Cocaine was often sold to rich households as betel—and when the inhabitants discovered how good it made them feel, they soon ordered more. It was estimated that large cities contained five to ten addicts per thousand inhabitants, and that for Delhi the figure could be as high as twenty per thousand.

India was not the only country to feel the cocaine scourge: Burma was also affected. A superintendent in the Burma Excise Department explained why these pitiful human beings took the drug:

> The abject wretch who becomes possessed of a few coppers, realising that the amount will be insufficient for a square meal, buys an innocent-looking packet of cocaine, and mixing it with the small quantity of lime paste used by betel chewers in their quids, smears the mixture on his gums, and slowly swallows the saliva. Gone are the cravings for food; a feeling of

pleasant warmth suffuses his wasted body; he feels equal to any exertion... Cocaine has a greater power than either opium or morphia; the after distress is keener; and a slave to it is a slave indeed. And the harm it does, and the certainty with which it kills, is truly appalling.

Drug Smuggling in India and Burma, Anderson, 1922

The authorities became extremely concerned about the Eastern consumption of cocaine. Once again, racism played a role: if educated Western white men in England or America were incapable of regulating their consumption of the drug, what chance did these illiterate natives have? The *British Medical Journal* noted that 'oriental races are peculiarly addicted to nervines'. *The Times* agreed, warning that cocaine was capable of killing the average Indian in just three months. British authorities began actively hunting down cocaine dealers in the Raj, keeping detailed statistics of cocaine busts across the continent.

Copies of their original reports remain in the British Library's Oriental and India Office Collection today. In 1912–13 the records reveal that Bombay alone confiscated nearly 149 pounds (over 67 kilograms) of cocaine. Bengal Province busted a massive 373 pounds (169 kilograms)—Calcutta alone making up 339 pounds (154 kilograms) of this. Burma was next down the line, at 171 pounds (78 kilograms). As late as 1930, Indian authorities estimated that they were picking up less than 2.5 per cent of all the illicit cocaine heading into India. If this is accurate, we can surmise that Calcutta was getting through around 6,000 kilograms of cocaine a year—a stupendous figure, making the Indian cocaine epidemic one of the great unreported scourges of the last century. By the end of the 1920s it was estimated that between a quarter and a half a million Indians were regular cocaine users.

Statistics alone reveal very little. Even today, drug experts struggle to estimate how much cocaine is actually being used each year. Footnotes in the reports, however, reveal the concern of the authorities:

I regret to report that there is no sign of the diminution in the illicit trade of cocaine... there is no doubt that the cocaine habit exists, to a serious extent, in many of our large cities; and so long as there are habitués calling for supplies, so long will agents be found ready and willing to minister to their wants and the large profits afforded by an illicit trade. The traffic can, in my opinion, never be dealt with, root and branch, until the pressure of enlightened world public opinion enforces international control over manufacture and distribution of this dangerous drug. It is common knowledge that widespread smuggling, from its chief centre of production, Darmstadt [the home of Merck], to France, England and America and other countries, exists on a large scale.

United Provinces Report, 1921

By 1922 a note in the file indicates that the cocaine seized was no longer predominantly German but Japanese, and repeated footnotes testify to its vastly inflated price: licit cocaine was 30 rupees per ounce. On the black market it went for 150–200 rupees. Although cocaine hauls had dropped from 710 pounds (322 kilograms) in 1912 to just 130 pounds (59 kilograms) in 1936, this still represented a minute slice of the drug that was actually making it through to the illicit market intact.

Such was the extent of the Japanese–Indian cocaine trade that in 1930 the Home Office despatched a Mr J Slattery, OBE, to the Far East to find out what was going on. His secret report is in the Public Records Office at Kew. Slattery discovered that much of the cocaine being shifted bore the labels of Fujitsuru, Buddha, or Elephant brands, yet none of these was a recognised manufacturer. A couple of cocaine seizures had been found labelled with the names of known German pharmaceuticals houses such as Boehringer but these were fakes, easily identifiable because they were spelled incorrectly. Clearly of the impression that this cocaine all originated in Japan, Slattery could obtain no assistance from the Japanese authorities.

The Japanese Government...showed no great enthusiasm when the question of this visit to Japan was raised and expressed the hope that I would not extend the scope of my enquiry...in each case came the answer that nothing could be ascertained regarding the matter and that the particulars supplied were insufficient and did not afford a starting point for the investigation.

Report of Mr J Slattery, Central Board of Revenue, 1931

Even when details of specific trafficking operations were handed over to the Japanese, nothing was done. A 1926 seizure in Hong Kong led to the arrest of a Chinese trafficker whose cabin, when searched, was found to contain a series of telegraph cables to and from a guy in Kobe called Wai Kee. All of them concerned cocaine. When Wai Kee's details were handed over to the Japanese government, however, they mysteriously couldn't find him. Funny—his telegraphs were still getting through. Other investigative leads were likewise poleaxed: Slattery had the wrapping of a Fujitsuru cocaine package analysed to see who made the paper. He was informed, and it was later corroborated, that it was made by the Fuji Company of Japan, and the string that held the package together was also Japanese. He put this to the authorities who told him flat out that Fujitsuru had nothing to do with Japan, and that the paper could have come from anywhere. When they heard that the cocaine sold on the streets of India was heavily adulterated they told him seriously that it couldn't be Japanese, because in Japan they only made 100 per cent pure cocaine. Other evidence of Japanese cocaine trafficking, such as a Japanese rubber bag full of cocaine with a Sankyo seal was declared to be 'fake'.

He was then led on to visit a cocaine factory that turned out to be a couple of dingy rooms and a locked storeroom. The size of the place was supposed to indicate that the factory was only capable of manufacturing small amounts of the drug. Slattery was not impressed: 'I do not believe that the plant they showed me had anything to do with the manufacture of cocaine,' he wrote. When a press story broke concerning a huge Japanese drug bust of over £470,000 of narcotics in Dairen, he asked for more information. The head of the Dairen police told him that the bust had really been in Osaka but when he got there to check it out no one had heard of the bust at all—in fact, they said, it had been in Kobe. Of course, when he got to Kobe no one knew anything about it either. Eventually, worn out by the unending bureaucracy of the country, he gave up and went home.

> So far I had gathered little from my friends at the Home Department; but my welcome there was worn out. They pleaded pressure of work, enquired when I proposed to leave Japan; and on the occasion of my last meeting the interpreter was called away because he was said to be required elsewhere . . . as far as the voluntary supplying of information or other co-operation was concerned, my interviews with the police in Tokio, Kobe and Osaka proved a waste of time . . . [7]
>
> Report of Mr J Slattery, Central Board of Revenue, 1931

7 According to a recent paper by David Musto, Japan may have suffered its own problems with cocaine. From 1915 to 1935 the country's official statistics record 'intentional' deaths caused by the drug. Musto speculates that not all their unaccounted-for cocaine was going to India. If this is the case the country's current problem with amphetamines may well have predated the war by some years and cocaine may be to blame.

Back in India, despite the establishment of a special cocaine branch of the CID, the Indian authorities had problems apprehending the culprits behind this clandestine trade: serious traffickers were seldom caught because they concealed their trade among other—legitimate—businesses. As is the case today, those arrested for cocaine trading were generally low-level mules and middlemen. The real movers rarely broke cover and made sure that their hands were clean.

The Burmese Excise Department noted that large cocaine shipments were facilitated by means of bribery and that many cocaine confiscations were arranged by the traffickers themselves—small 'finds' to make it look as if the fight against cocaine was being won—so that law-enforcement efforts would not be stepped up. But cocaine was not smuggled only into India. One case in the archives, hidden in a secret Foreign and Political Department report of 1922, tells of an Indian national by the name of Sitaram Sampat Rao Gaekwar, caught smuggling 2 pounds (nearly a kilo) of pharmaceutical cocaine into Britain. Gaekwar, a victim of one of Scotland Yard's cocaine stings, had offered the drug to an undercover officer for £200 at Victoria Station.

The Foreign and Political Department was interested in this case not just because it involved an Indian national but because he was a VIP. The initial entry in the file contains a Reuters press cutting reporting the case followed by a single, handwritten enquiry: 'is this man any relation of the Gaekwar of B?' Someone has scrawled underneath that Gaekwar is not, in fact, a relation of 'Gaekwar of B' (they are referring to the Maharajah of Baroda). Twenty signatures testify to the fact that this is the case. The next page contains an update. After discussions with the maharajah, it appeared that Gaekwar was in fact his nephew, a barrister who had 'got into bad company'. Another twenty signatures acknowledge that this is the case.

No doubt Gaekwar's royal background accounted for his good manners on arrest—a contemporary newspaper report relates that, when it became clear he had been the victim of a sting operation, he had commented: 'Oh. You are police. What rotten luck. But still, I understand.' He got six months.

8 Down...But Not Out

With the exception of India and China, international efforts to stop the illicit cocaine trade were largely successful and by the early 1930s cocaine abuse had pretty much disappeared. While newspapers periodically crowed about another cocaine bust or the death of another drug fiend, their articles were mostly police PR efforts—news of drugs busts made them look good. And the police had done a good job: by 1928 one-third of all American federal prison inmates were inside for violations of the Harrison Act. The fact that these drug abusers were in jail proved, once and for all, that drugs drove people to crime. After all, if these people weren't criminals, what were they doing in jail? It was a de facto point, and it justified all further links between criminality and drug abuse.

But it wasn't simply police intervention that removed cocaine from the streets. The 1920s and 1930s saw the arrival of the amphetamines—cheap, legal and apparently safe stimulants which, to all intents and purposes, had exactly the same effect as cocaine. Amphetamines stepped in to take the place of cocaine and, since they were not against the law, the police found themselves something else to do. In America marijuana became their new target. By 1930 the Mayor's Committee of New York City concluded that 'cocaine as an addiction has ceased to be a problem'. The committee was right: cocaine addiction *had* pretty much disappeared as a problem—on both sides of the Atlantic. In England, cocaine abuse was reported to be 'on the wane' by 1924 and records show that, while there had been 239 cocaine-related convictions between 1921 and 1925, in the ensuing four years this dropped to just 27. With penalties so high, the little cocaine use there was was so clandestine that, seventy years on, the only real way we can track its use is in terms of references in the popular culture of the time. Even on the streets, word was that cocaine was bad news. Popular contemporary songs record public attitudes: the Memphis Jug Band's 1930 song 'Cocaine Habit Blues' reported '...cocaine habit's mighty bad—the worst ol' habit I ever had'. Leadbelly recorded a version of 'The Hop Song', whose original lyrics ran:

> *Cocaine is for horses and not for men;*
> *Doctors say it'll kill you but they don't tell you when;*
> *Singing honey baby, honey baby, won't you be mine?*
> *Take a sniff on me.*

Another traditional number, 'Cocaine Lil', recorded the fate of its eponymous heroine:

> *She went to a snow party one cold night*
> *And the way she sniffs, she was soon alight.*
> *There was hop-head Mag with Dopy Slim*
> *And Kanakee Liz and Yen-shi Jim.*

> *Along in the morning at half past three*
> *They're all lit up like a Christmas tree,*
> *So Lil went home and got into bed;*
> *She took another sniff and it knocked her dead.*

> *They laid her out in her cocaine clothes:*
> *She wore a snowbird hat with a crimson rose;*
> *And on her tombstone you'll find this refrain:*
> *'She died as she lived—sniffing cocaine'*

The Rev Gary Davis's 'Cocaine' ran: 'all you people ought to be like me—drink cold whisky and let the cocaine be'. (An alternative chorus to this track makes a knowing reference: 'cocaine: my mucous membranes is just a memory'. Soon we find songs not simply recording cocaine's dangers but its scarcity: 'Went to Mr Newman's in a lope, saw a sign on the door saying "no more dope",' sang the Memphis Jug Band. A number of other artists recorded this track, or variations of it, under titles ranging from 'Cocaine' to 'Furniture Man'. One verse concluded:

> *I call my Cora, hey-hey,*
> *She come sniffing with her nose all sore—*
> *Doctor swear he won't sell her no more.*

Cole Porter's 'I Get a Kick Out of You' (1934) originally featured the line 'Some get their kicks from cocaine'. This was hastily changed to 'Some get their perfume from Spain'. Others made fun of cocaine users: the 1938 classic 'Minnie the Moocher' features the eponymous character who 'fell in love with a bloke named Smokey/she loved him though he was cokey'. Clearly by this time cocaine use is not seen as an especially desirable trait in a partner.

Popular literature also played on cocaine's negative image: Proust reports its use by degenerates in a homosexual brothel in 1928 and describes one of his characters, the Vicomtesse de St Fiarcie, as having wrecked her appearance with cocaine. Nabokov writes lucidly about cocaine abuse in his short story *A Matter of Chance*, yet notes that the piece was rejected by his editor because 'we don't print stories about cocainists'. Agatha Christie occasionally mentions cocaine addicts in her thrillers: usually ageing rich women who have thrown everything away for the drug. Dorothy Sayers writes of an international cocaine conspiracy leading to tragedy and death in *Murder Must Advertise*. Leda Burke continues the trend in *Dope Darling*, in which the heroine, Claire, begs her boyfriend, Roy, 'Give me some dope, darling! Give me some cocaine!' before everyone becomes addicted and dies.

Such references served to reinforce the public's negative perception of the drug. In America the word 'dope', which had formerly meant simply a drug of any sort, assumed a new meaning. Soon 'dope addict' was a term of common abuse and eventually the word 'dope' itself would become synonymous with 'dimwit'—hence the character Dopey in *Snow White and the Seven Dwarfs*.

However, cocaine's dangerous side, coupled with its scarcity, added a certain perverse mystique to the drug. Cocaine—rare, dangerous and extremely exclusive—has always appealed to certain elements of society: not only the seriously drug-dependent but also the arty bohemian set, and disaffected higher classes with more money than sense. It was just this way in Europe. While we hear little about homeless degenerates on the streets of Berlin or Paris, rumours abound of decadent aristocratic balls and the bizarre sexual proclivities of the royal houses—including their supposed use of cocaine. Perhaps there is something in these rumours, but they may simply be part of the *Hello!* magazine syndrome so prevalent today: there has always been an impression that affluent, beautiful people with more money than they know what to do with must be up to something sordid.

* * *

One group of affluent people that really was up to something sordid was the Nazi Party. For the last thirty years there have been repeated allegations that the German high command was partial to cocaine. Herman Goering, it is said, was a full-time addict and Rudolf Hess was rumoured to have been on coke when he flew over to Britain in 1941. Use of the drug is supposed to have reached right through the ranks of the command structure. Is there any truth in this? Sort of.

There is no evidence that Goering took cocaine. He was, however, a morphine addict, so seriously addicted that by the time he stood trial at Nuremberg he was dosing himself with up to a hundred pills of paracodeine a day. While cocaine accusations are unconfirmed it seems likely that he used stimulants on his periodic crash diets (he was heavily overweight). Use of amphetamines or cocaine could well have been responsible, for example, for the 18 kilos he managed to shed in just two months at the start of 1939. Admittedly it is possible that he lost this weight through exercise and dieting but, knowing a little about Goering's personality, this seems unlikely. We will never know. The case of Hess is likewise unconvincing: there is no evidence whatsoever that he was on cocaine when he parachuted over Scotland that night in 1941.

So it seems that cases offered as evidence for Nazi drug taking are misguided. Except for one thing. While browsing through books on the Third Reich in an attempt to substantiate the rumours about Goering and Hess, I stumbled upon a study called *The Medical Casebook of Adolph Hitler*. And here was evidence not that the high levels of the Nazi command took cocaine, but that the highest of all—Adolph Hitler himself—was partial to it.

There is no doubt that Hitler used amphetamines. According to his valet, Heinz Linge (interrogated after the war), Hitler's personal physician, a Dr Theo Morell, would give him a 'vitamin' shot every morning. Before the injection Hitler would be lethargic; after it he was alert, active and eager to get out of bed. Clearly this was not in fact a vitamin shot but a 'pep' shot. As the war drew on and it became clear to the Führer that he was not winning it, he called for his doctor more and more frequently to give him further shots. Heinrich Himmler noted that these injections had an almost magical effect on Hitler, who became extremely energetic after them, and another member of his cabinet reported that he became 'cheerful, talkative and tended to stay awake long into the night' after them.

By the end of the war, Hitler was receiving two to five injections per day, alternating these with special pep tablets which, when analysed, were revealed to be Pervitin (a brand name for methamphetamine, or 'speed'). In fact he took so much of the stuff that he was unable to sleep at night, and had to be put to sleep with doses of sedatives. The result of these doses was that he was extremely hard to wake in the morning (the German response to the Allied landings on D-Day was delayed for precisely this reason: Hitler could not be woken). But there were other side effects. Towards the end of the war, Hitler began to experience signs of amphetamine toxosis: shaking, irritability and irrationality.

It is more than possible that Hitler alternated his doses of amphetamines with cocaine—a drug with almost identical properties. This seems more convincing bearing in mind that his doctor went to some lengths to wean him off amphetamines after 1944; one way of doing this might be to substitute them for cocaine. However, the real evidence for cocaine abuse comes from another of Hitler's doctors, Dr Erwin Giesing, who treated him for injuries following Claus von Stauffenberg's failed assassination attempt in July 1944. Giesing, an ENT specialist, dosed Hitler with cocaine in 10 per cent solutions when he complained of sore throats. Nothing unremarkable about this, apart from the fact that Giesing records in his notes that Hitler enjoyed the treatment so much that he asked for it to be continued even after his throat problems were gone. In fact, Hitler asked for cocaine so often that Giesing specifically had to warn him away from it lest he become addicted. Giesing eventually refused point-blank to dose Hitler with cocaine any more often. OK, said Hitler, the same number of doses. But what about increasing the strength of the cocaine solution?

Aside from the Third Reich, the one place where cocaine does seem to have remained, at least for a time, is Hollywood. Certainly there was a lot of cocaine here for a while: when Aleister Crowley arrived on a whistle-stop tour in 1916 he was shocked, reporting the locals as 'the cinema crowd of cocaine-crazed, sexual lunatics'. (Crowley, viewed by many of his contemporaries as the antichrist, was a tricky person to shock.) In truth, there was so much money in Hollywood, and so many people willing to do anything for a good time, that it would have been surprising had the drug not caught on there.

References to cocaine in early movies are none too subtle. A Douglas Fairbanks feature entitled *The Mystery of the Leaping Fish* (1912) is a

Sherlock Holmes parody, Fairbanks starring as the mind-frazzled detective, Coke Ennyday (geddit?). Another film the same year, *For His Son*, is clearly a take-off of the Coca-Cola story, telling of a pharmacological tycoon who invents a soft drink containing a mysterious, addictive stimulant. He names the beverage Dopokoke and proceeds to make a fortune with it—the terrible punchline being that his own son becomes addicted to the drink and eventually dies. A later film, *Cocaine Fiends* (rather like the marijuana classic *Reefer Madness*), portrays cocaine addiction in such ridiculous terms that commentators have suggested that it is a parody, to be appreciated only by cocaine aficionados.

By the 1930s cocaine would even be considered a suitable subject for humour: Charlie Chaplin, in *Modern Times* (1936), plays a down-on-his luck tramp who, on taking a few snorts from a container labelled 'nose powder', becomes a superman. *The Pace That Kills*, another silent feature, offered the caption: 'A bunch of "snowbirds" with their "happy dust", or "joy powder". But its slimy peddlers call it "Kid Catcher" because it is the first drug that starts on the downward path: on THE PACE THAT KILLS!'

However, at the start of the 1920s a series of scandals involving improprieties of leading Hollywood names led to a clampdown. The Fatty Arbuckle incident in 1920 led to the death of a young actress. The same year another murder charge linked one of the leading actresses in the Keystone comedies, Mabel Normand, to drug abuse: it was said she got through $2,000 worth of cocaine a month. The rumours ruined her career. Barbara La Marre, Douglas Fairbanks's co-star in *The Three Musketeers*, allegedly kept the cocaine that enabled her to survive on just two hours' sleep per night stashed inside her grand piano—until she overdosed on heroin. By 1923 the *New York Times* reported on the prevalence of drug abuse in Hollywood, citing it as evidence of the causal link between Prohibition and drugs.

The *Times* was right. Drug taking did go up in the 1920s following Prohibition. As Edward H Williams had noted in his article about bullet-proof Negroes on cocaine in the *New York Times* eleven years earlier, the excuse blacks gave for taking cocaine was "cause I couldn't git nothin' else, boss' (blacks were not allowed access to spirits in certain cities in the South at the time). Drugs were appealing simply because nothing else was available. Worse, bootleggers were stepping into the market to supply illicit alcohol. Profits from this trade were so great that they soon led to violence, and the origin of the organised-crime syndicates whose descendants still operate today. The main mobsters, such notables as Al Capone, Salvatore C Luciano ('Lucky Luciano') and Arnold Rothstein, initially shied away from narcotics on the basis that the penalties were extremely high, moving instead into alcohol, gaming and prostitution. But it wasn't long before they realised where the real money lay, and switched allegiance.

The authorities stepped down hard on Hollywood, successfully removing much of the drug abuse that had been rampant there, and after an initial salvo of arrests everything went quiet. Not only was cocaine increasingly hard to find, but the first wave of 'investigative/gossip' magazines arrived, dealing dirt on the rich and the famous. Selling cocaine to a screen star was just the sort of escapade that would make a cover story: the risk was no longer worth it, even in Hollywood.

Only a few die-hards continued to use the drug. Tallulah Bankhead was one such—reported in her biography as attending a meal in New York and placing two small glass bottles on the table before her. At the end of the meal she picked up her eyedrops and dropped a few beneath her eyelids before whispering the shocked revelation: 'I've put the wrong drops in my eyes'. Her companion suggested that she call a doctor, whereupon she shouted, 'I put the cocaine in my eyes and I don't tell that to doctors or anyone else!' and flounced out. Bankhead is supposedly also the source of the much-cited adage, 'Cocaine isn't habit-forming. I should know—I've been using it for years.'

She wasn't the only fan. Harry Anslinger writes in his memoirs about a 'swashbuckling' star, clearly identifiable as Errol Flynn, repeatedly reported to the police for trying to procure cocaine from doctors across Europe—for supposed symptoms ranging from 'inferiority complex' (!) to 'incurable haemorrhoids'. When pulled in and interrogated by Anslinger, Flynn denied being an addict before admitting that his real motivation for using cocaine was for sex.

Such cases, however, were few and far between. Cocaine was on the way out, a new generation emerging that had never even heard of the drug. The start of World War Two put the nails into the coffin. Not only were coca supplies and smuggling routes disrupted but, more importantly, America and Europe were so busy fighting the war that there was very little time for illicit drugs. One hundred per cent employment across Europe pretty much sorted out their drug problem (in England there were only three cocaine-related arrests from 1940 to 1943).

It was the war, however, that was to lead to an appreciation of just how much money there was to be made in the illicit drug trade, and thus the emergence of the first real narcotics syndicates. The blame for this emergence has been placed on Lucky Luciano, who had been co-operating with the US Office of Naval Intelligence since 1942 as part of the war effort, using his extensive underworld connections to hunt down 'spies' in the Brooklyn shipbuilding community, and helping to unite Italy's disparate crime societies—Mafia families—to assist the Allied invasion of Sicily in 1943. In return for his assistance, Luciano's 30–50-year sentence was conveniently forgotten on the condition that he return to Italy and never come back. His sentence was commuted on 3 January 1946 and he returned to Italy, where he swiftly made use of his links between Italian and American mobsters to revitalise the postwar heroin trade—a trade that was to find its zenith in the so-called French Connection in Marseilles in the 1950s. This organisation was to traffic 95 per cent of the world's heroin for the next twenty years.

By 1952 American heroin addicts numbered 300 per cent higher than they had before the war. As yet, cocaine was not on the menu but the profits generated from the global narcotics market were so great that they showed the way forward. Cocaine was down, but it was far from out.

The drug was indeed very rare at the end of the war: 'By 1948,' Harry Anslinger reports, 'we could scarcely find one cocaine seizure in all those that we made in this country.' The only real cases he can find to report are those of horse doping: in his 1961 book, *The Murderers*, he tells of a horse owner dosing up his steed with an injection called a 'Shotgun': 14 grains of cocaine, 3 grains of heroin and a mixture of various other stimulants. After the shot the horse was so agitated that it took five men to hold it down. Although in the end the horse won the race by a huge margin, it was so frantic that it had thrown its rider in the first ten lengths. When they discovered that the owner decided to teach the recalcitrant horse a lesson by beating it with a wooden bat, Anslinger's boys stepped in. They were too late. Before he had time to deliver the first stroke the owner was trampled to death by his paranoid horse.

There were periodic resurgences of cocaine taking, however. The drug was clearly still lurking in the bohemian underworld in small quantities in the 40s and 50s: jazz musician Milton Mezzrow, who played with Louis Armstrong, reports taking it in his autobiography, as does Anita O'Day in hers. Malcolm X writes in his autobiography that he became addicted to the drug in the 1940s (cocaine nearly got him into a great deal of trouble

when, after a binge, he noticed his white girlfriend and, fired up with
Dutch courage, wandered over to say hello—in front of her husband's
best friend). Likewise 1949 seems to have offered the possibility of a
revival. A *Time* magazine exclusive, THE WHITE GODDESS, reports a bust of
nearly a kilo, the cocaine nestled away snugly inside the diplomatic bag of
one Rafael Menacho Vicente—the Cuban consul to Peru. This was only a
minor trend, however. While New York police reported confiscating 400
ounces (15 kilograms) of cocaine in the city in just four months, once the
source was identified, the problem evaporated.

In fact cocaine prohibition was going so well that it was even beginning to look as if Peru and Bolivia might be persuaded to ban coca production altogether. The coca industry, originally a source of pride and a
great economic hope for both nations, began to wane. For a start, Peru's
majority role in the market had been swiftly taken over by the Dutch and
the Japanese in Indonesia. Meanwhile, as synthetic anaesthetics came in
and cocaine prohibition began to bite, there were fewer and fewer markets for the drug. At this point coca came under fire from a series of misguided 'reformers'.

Perhaps predictably, at the head of the anticoca brigade was the
Church. Christian authorities had been pissed off with coca ever since
they weren't allowed to ban it in 1552. Now finally, they saw their
chance. As Peru was progressively opened up in the late nineteenth century, so missionaries penetrated further and further into the interior, converting the natives as they went along. At the head of these were the
Seventh Day Adventists, who demanded total sobriety from their new
flocks and persuaded anyone willing to listen that it was about time
something was done about coca.

While the Seventh Day Adventists were never going to represent too
much of a threat to a 4,500-year-old industry, bigger guns soon moved
in. By the early 1900s a strong liberal wing had formed in Peru, all of the
opinion that it was time to improve the lot of the impoverished Indians.
In an attempt to discover what it was, exactly, that was keeping these
people so poor, they established a series of think tanks, all of which concluded that, if something was to be done about poverty, something
would first have to be done about coca.

What was really needed to persuade the government of this, however,
was some serious proof. They set out to find some. As with any number
of antidrug campaigns before and after, truth was not allowed to inter-

fere. If you're looking for misguided motives, Bad Science and lies, look no further. Because they were just plain wrong. Liberal campaigners had about as much chance of improving the Indians' lot by eradicating coca as Michael Jackson does of healing the world with his pain.

In the 1920s and 1930s, scientific investigators began to pop up all over Peru, conducting experiments into the addictive potential of coca. The godfather of them all was Carlos Ricketts. Ricketts had some serious clout: not only was he a qualified doctor but he had actually studied at Manchester University in England. He ran extensive investigations into coca, concluded that it was a Very Bad Thing and recruited as many of his medical colleagues as he could to agree with him. In 1929 he entered politics to promote the anticoca cause, suggesting a government monopoly on coca production as a means of controlling it. This was duly adopted. The anticoca bandwagon began to roll.

In 1936 at the University of Lima another scientist, Carlos Gutierrez-Noriega, began a further series of experiments to prove that coca was bad news. Pretty soon the results were incontrovertible. Well, they were to him, anyway.

To back up his preformed conclusions, Gutierrez-Noriega attempted to calculate the average dose of cocaine in a coca leaf and used some highly dodgy mathematics to conclude that Peruvian chewers were getting through 38,500 kilos of cocaine per year. In his quest to prove that coca was a national peril he pulled out all the stops, quoting early coca sources that rubbished the crop—such as Poeppig—but disregarding all of the positive accounts, ultimately concluding that prolonged use of coca led to insanity. It sounded impressive, but his reasoning was highly suspect. Take the following:

> It has recently been shown that a great percentage of illiteracy exists in the regions where coca is consumed in great quantities. A relationship was found between the percentage of illiterate people and the amount of coca leaves used annually... 80% of coca addicts have subnormal IQs.
>
> *Economic Botany*, 5 (2) 145–52, 1951

OK, so people who chew coca tend to be illiterate. But does that mean that coca is the cause? Couldn't lack of education in fact be to blame? Gutierrez-Noriega's arse-about-face logic accelerates as he moves on to IQ: how did he test these Indians' IQs if they were incapable of reading?

According to his own account, he applied the 'Binet–Simon criterion'—
a written test—which told him that the Indians 'intellectual coefficient is
very low'. This was not surprising: as he says, they were illiterate: they
couldn't read the questions. On this test it would be a shock if their intellectual coefficient (whatever that is) was anything other than zero.

At the end of his piece, Gutierrez-Noriega delivers an astonishing
coup de grâce:

> In general, coca chewers present emotional dullness or apathy, indifference,
> lack of will power and low capacity for attention. They are mistrustful, shy,
> unsociable and indecisive. In advanced stages many of them are vagabonds.
>
> *Economic Botany*, 5 (2) 145–52, 1951

At last, that old chestnut, the criminal connection: coca equals crime.
What Noriega does not reveal here—though he later admits elsewhere—
is that the source of his research subjects was in fact none other than the
central Lima jailhouse. By taking 100 per cent of his subjects from a
prison he was ensuring that they were all 'vagabonds' (it was later
revealed that the source of his 'insane' coca chewers had been the Central Lima asylum). On this criterion he could have produced a causal
relationship between people who drank water and crime. This did not
stop his work being taken seriously. Coca experts were few and far
between and the plant was about to hit the world stage.

In 1946 at a conference of the newly formed United Nations, the Soviet
Union accused a handful of American mining corporations operating in
Peru of exploiting the native Indians by paying them for their labour not
with money but coca. The United States delegates were highly embarrassed to discover that this was true: a number of businesses, the Cerro
de Pasco Copper Corporation amongst them, really were paying the Indians in coca. Of course, this was a tradition that went back to Inca times
and beyond—coca was a universal substance of value that could be
bartered for other products and the Indians often preferred it to cash.
The Russians, unimpressed at the Americans' explanations, drew unflat-
tering analogies between their mining trade in Peru and the British
opium trade in China: in both cases, they said, an advanced nation was
dominating a backwards one by feeding it stupifying drugs. It must stop.
It did, of course, but the damage was done: not only was coca all over the

news but Peru had been made to look seriously backward. The combination of the UN conference and the proselytising of Gutierrez-Noriega and his gang soon got results[8].

On 22 April 1947 the Peruvian representative to the UN delivered a proposal to the Narcotics Commission suggesting an international symposium to study the coca problem in Peru. The United Nations Commission of Enquiry on the Coca Leaf was rapidly established and, when Bolivia realised that Peru was about to get some expert help in, invited it to check out the situation there, too.

One might hope that a United Nations Commission would be at least vaguely impartial. One would be disappointed. The fact that it wasn't was made succinctly by the president of the newly established commission, Howard B Fonda (at the time vice-president of the pharmaceutical giant Burroughs Wellcome and a close personal friend of Harry Anslinger), upon his arrival at Lima. As he walked across the tarmac, Fonda was accosted by a journalist from *El Comercio*. Did *el presidente* have the time to answer a couple of questions about his new project? the journalist wanted to know. Sure he did. What did *El Comercio* want to know? Then it just fell out:

Q: Do you believe that the habit of chewing coca is harmful to the inhabitants of the Peruvian Sierra?

A: Absolutely.
    Comercio, 12 September 1949, *cit.* 'Coca Bonne, Cocaine Mauvais',
    R Romano, *Revue Européene des Sciences Sociales*, XXI, 64, 1983

It is hard not to question the impartiality of a UN Commission whose president is so openly prejudiced about his subject that he is willing to release the conclusion of his investigation to the press even before setting out on the preliminary fact-finding trip. It should come as no surprise, then, that, when the commission eventually produced its report in 1950, it was thumbs down for coca. Over a half of the rural population of Peru, stated the report—and a quarter of all inhabitants of Peru and

---

[8] Gutierrez-Noriega may have got his way but he was not to have much time to gloat over it: he was killed in Italy in the early 1950s when a car mounted the pavement and hit him. According to the friend who was with him at the time he had been receiving death threats for weeks before the accident and was very scared. It is postulated that his death was the result of his anti-coca stance.

Bolivia—were addicts. In no uncertain terms the United Nations Commission stressed that it was 'imperative to limit coca production' to improve the lifestyle of the Indians. In order to improve their economic status, it was concluded, they were to be taxed upon coca and, if they did not pay, criminal statutes were to be drawn up to take care of them.

Twenty-seven years before the report's publication, in 1923, the League of Nations had instructed the Andean nations to cease nonmedical coca production forthwith. At the time Peru had simply ignored the League of Nations and Bolivia had told them exactly where to get off. This time there would be no escape.

A few brave individuals raised their heads above the parapet to object to the commission's misguided conclusions. Two of the most famous were scientists, Carlos Monge (founder of the Institute of Andean Biology) and the father of Peruvian neurology, Fernando Cabieses. In protest they organised a follow-up coca conference, the Peruvian Commission, to re-examine the case of the coca leaf. The conclusions of the second commission were as balanced and well thought out as the conclusions of the first weren't, concluding that coca chewing was a harmless—and even sometimes beneficial—pastime.

It made no difference. The UN commission held international clout. Thus it was that Peru, which had thus far refused to sign international legislation committing it to the destruction of the coca trade, was forced to comply. In 1962 both Peru and Bolivia signed the Single Geneva Convention Against Drugs, committing themselves to the complete eradication of coca within the next 25 years. It was a pointless and impossible task that would have cost them millions of dollars to attempt, and one that, had it worked, would have put 200,000 Peruvians out of work. The eradication statute was generally ignored but the fact that it had been signed was to have important consequences.

These misguided attempts to mop up the coca trade exploited the long-standing confusion between the coca leaf and cocaine itself. When the Pure Food and Drug Act had been passed in 1906 the authorities were already confused, drafting a law that ensured that coca wines and other preparations containing the leaf were banned, while apparently forgetting that cocaine itself could be bought over the counter at any chemist in the United States. At the time no one outside the patent medicine business had paid much attention: such was the fear of cocaine addiction and the 'coke fiend' that no one ever stopped to question the left-field assertions of the drug legislators. Even such experts as Louis Lewin, one of the great pioneers of narcotic research, fell into this trap, writing scathingly of coca chewers:

> Physically and morally they behave like opium smokers. A cachetic state appears with extreme emaciation accompanied by a gradual change of demeanour. They are old men before they are adult. They are apathetic, useless for all the more serious purposes of life, subject to hallucinations, and solely governed by the one passionate desire for the drug, besides which everything else in life is of inferior value.
>
> *Phantastica*, Lewin, 1924

Meanwhile the true roots of Peru's internal persecution of coca lay in Germany, where a leading psychiatrist, Emil Kreperin, had written a landmark text in which he had—without any experience of coca whatsoever—concluded that coca was identical to cocaine. The piece was picked up in 1913 by a young Peruvian doctor on sabbatical in Italy, by the name of Herminio Valdisan. Thanks to Kreperin, Valdisan returned home convinced that coca equalled cocaine and, once there, proceeded to found the Peruvian Institute of Psychiatry—where students learned by rote that coca was dangerous. Both Carlos Ricketts and Gutierrez-Noriega were students of his.

The fact was that, by the 1940s, 'coca' was synonymous with 'cocaine'. Even open-minded thinkers such as Aldous Huxley—he of mescaline and *Doors of Perception* fame—were taken in. In 1958, in a letter to Albert Hoffman, inventor of LSD, congratulating him on his recent isolation of psilocybin, Huxley bemoaned the use of coca:

> I am writing now from Peru, the land of a most unsatisfactory and dangerous mind-changing drug—coca—still consumed in great quantities by the Indians...
>
> *Moksha—Writings on Psychedelics*, Huxley, 1977

It may appear that the confusion—coca = cocaine—was understandable and that, in the end, it can't have had terribly serious consequences anyway. In fact, neither assertion is true. In the first case, certain elements in the United States went out of their way to blur the distinction between coca and cocaine with the deliberate purpose of laying into both; in the second, this unnecessary demonisation of coca was to lead to all kinds of trouble later on.

As it happened, much of the impetus for this anticoca polemic came from the US, including funding for such 'scientists' as Gutierrez-Noriega and Ricketts. Americans were especially keen to stop the coca trade because they had been hit hardest by the wave of addiction at the turn of the century and—because they had no hand in the international trade in it—they had nothing to lose by its curtailment. Moreover, by the late 1940s drug legislation appeared to have been so successful that it looked as if this trade could really be stopped for ever. Looking at it more cynically, one could say that there was political capital to be gained by pushing the point: it gave Anslinger and his ilk something to do. This was a shame, because not only was it completely unnecessary (there was little or no cocaine around in the United States at the time) but, by attempting to drive the coca trade out of business, American legislators were laying the foundations of a far more dangerous trade in coca—just as they had with alcohol during Prohibition. Only, they didn't know that yet.

But there were more insidious forces at work within the world of coca legislation, as I was to discover when, in Washington, DC, I finally caught up with an American historian called Paul Gootenberg.

I had been looking forward to meeting Gootenberg for some time. In 1999 he had edited a compilation of essays on cocaine called *Global Histories*, which had been the first book to break new ground in ages. I was terribly excited to find it, and immediately gave him a call to ask if he had any more of this kind of material or knew of anyone else working in this field. The answer to both questions was an emphatic 'yes'. Gootenberg, it appeared, was one of only a couple of serious historians in the world currently researching cocaine. This made him a prime target for me. We exchanged emails for a couple of months, debating what I could trade him for access to some of this new, unpublished, research. We toyed with a few ideas, mostly revolving around second-hand copies of Mike Oldfield's *Tubular Bells*, and made vague arrangements to meet up when I got to Washington.

It was only when it emerged that the reason I was coming to Washington was to interview the drug tsar, General Barry McCaffrey, however (an interview that never took place in the end), that his attention was really piqued. The *New Yorker* had recently printed allegations by Seymour Hersh that McCaffrey had ordered the execution of 100,000 teenage Iraqi conscripts at the end of the Gulf War. Gootenberg wanted to know if it was true. I said I'd ask McCaffrey when I saw him. 'Christ—don't do that,' he urged. 'He might have you killed, too.' I doubted somehow whether Clinton's drug tsar would kill a British journalist just like that. 'I don't know,' said Gootenberg. 'He's killed before'. From that point on, our conversations revolved around McCaffrey and his relative merits both as a drug tsar and an alleged mass murderer and how pissed off he would be if I arranged an interview about US drug policy, but instead asked him about Iraq. Whenever I spoke to Gootenberg the first question he asked was, 'How's Barry?' It rapidly became clear through our repeated McCaffrey discussions that Gootenberg had very little time for conventional drug policy or its advocates and that he was of the opinion that, far from solving drug problems, it was American antidrug meddling that had created most of them in the first place. As I was shortly to learn, there was more than a little truth in this assertion.

We eventually met in his office in the Woodrow Wilson Center, off Pennsylvania Avenue, just behind the Reagan School of Government. 'How's Barry? Did you ask him about Iraq yet?' he asked. All around his office were piles of photocopied documents—Spanish, French, English: police reports, governmental statistics, think-tank notions, newspaper articles— all about cocaine and the origins of the trade in the 1950s and 1960s. He had spent six years collecting this stuff from public records offices all over the world, in many cases petitioning for documents to be declassified himself. Usually when you meet experts you discover that they have a few new points to make but that most of the stuff they talk about you sort of know already. Gootenberg was different: *everything* he had was new.

Naturally, he was wary of what I was going to do with all his research. Why should he give me his unpublished papers? What was this book really about, anyway? I explained the basic idea and he nodded. 'I get it,' he said. 'You're a gonzo journalist.' I denied it but the accusation stung. He then asked what he was going to get out of giving me a pile of research that he had yet to publish. I was a bit stumped. 'I mean, you are going to credit me for all this stuff, right?' he asked. Of course. What kind of credit did he want? He eventually concocted the right phrase. 'Say I am an intrepid and swashbuckling researcher cutting through the swathes of DEA [Drug Enforcement Administration] lies,' he said. 'Can you do that?' I couldn't see why not. After all, if I was a gonzo journalist I could probably write whatever I wanted. Well, if that was the case, '. . . can you say I look like Dustin Hoffman, too?' I was stretching my luck, even as a gonzo journalist, but I needed the information—and he did look like Dustin Hoffman. A bit. This agreed, we headed straight for the nearest bar, ordered a couple of beers and talked serious cocaine. Or rather, *he* talked serious cocaine. I tried to keep up.

Sure enough, Gootenberg was loaded with new and exciting cocaine information. He had looked into just about everything in exquisite detail, and spoken to literally everyone who mattered. He eventually sent me two unpublished papers, both of which turned everything I had heard about the early cocaine trade on its head.

The most intriguing revolved around the relationship between Peruvian anticoca legislation and the Coca-Cola company. Or rather, a subsidiary of the Coca-Cola company, Stepan Chemicals. Based in Chicago, Stepan (still operating today) is one of the unsung heroes of American industry— because in the heart of Building Number 2 of their Maywood, New Jersey, plant, protected by a series of armed guards and monitored by US federal authorities, a process takes place that fuels one of the most lucrative businesses in the world: Stepan is the company responsible for de-cocainising coca leaves before they are made into Coca-Cola. Stepan was recently estimated to import some 175,000 kilograms of *truxillense* coca a year, referring to it euphemistically as 'Merchandise Number 5' (this quantity of leaf would make about 1.75 tons of cocaine, worth around $200 million). Because of cocaine's bad image, however, Stepan is an extremely publicity-shy company. So publicity-shy, in fact, that as far as I can tell it has never provided assistance or interviews to a single journalist or historian looking into the Coca-Cola story. Coca-Cola has always been touchy about its association with coca—on occasion denying point-blank using coca in its recipe and even, in the mid-1980s, removing coca altogether (coca-less Coke turned out to be a marketing disaster and the company—brought to its senses with a jolt—swiftly rereleased 'Classic Coke', using its old recipe again and, sure enough, containing 'Merchandise Number 5'.)

No one gets co-operation from Coke or Stepan when they want to write about cocaine. Even Gootenberg had received short shrift when he wrote to them. This had not deterred him in the least. Through his examination of reams of recently declassified public documents, he had pieced together a fascinating portrait of the relationship between Coca-Cola, the global coca trade and twentieth-century narcotics legislation. In order to understand this relationship, however, it is necessary to go back a little in time, to the turn of the century.

* * *

American anticocaine legislation in the 1900s saw to it that production of the drug was limited, cutting down the number of companies that were allowed to manufacture it. American cocaine producers dwindled and by 1930 only two remained: the Rahway, New Jersey, branch of Merck Pharmaceuticals and another New Jersey firm called Maywood Chemical Works (bought out by the American pharmaceutical giants Stepan in the 1960s). Coca-Cola had done a deal with the fledgling Maywood company (then known as the Schaeffer Alkaloidal Works) in 1903 to remove the cocaine from their coca, whereupon the two companies had effectively merged. Maywood handled the potentially embarrassing cocaine side a safe distance away from Coca-Cola, who made and marketed the drink with the family image.

From the point of view of narcotics legislation, the fact that there were only two cocaine makers left made life simple. Instead of monitoring a myriad of tinpot pharmaceutical companies, federal authorities now had to deal with only two. All other requests to import coca or make cocaine were simply refused. Likewise, the arrangement was convenient for Maywood and Merck: as competition was effectively removed, they cornered the US market—protected against potential competition by the Federal Bureau of Narcotics under Harry Anslinger. The relationship between Maywood and Anslinger would prove to be particularly mutually beneficial.

From Anslinger's point of view Maywood and Coca-Cola were invaluable allies in the war against coca production in South America: because they had plantations there, they knew what was going on. They agreed to keep him informed of new developments, feeding him a constant stream of intelligence about the coca trade he so feared. Also, thanks to their buying power, they held a lot of clout in Peru and so were in a suitable position to lobby the government there whenever it was intransigent about narcotics enforcement. In return for this backup, Anslinger made sure that, whenever new international narcotics legislation was coming up, there would always be a couple of clauses in there to allow Coke the right to keep importing their leaves. Anslinger's protection of Coca-Cola went further than this, however, as he also discouraged other potential importers of coca (i.e. possible competitors) from attempting the trade. He also railed against the Peruvian government's plans to nationalise the coca industry—plans that would have increased the price of coca for Coca-Cola (he did this by means of a veiled threat to the Peruvian ambassador to Washington: basically, 'nationalise, and Coke will move all trade from Peru to Bolivia'. Coca was eventually nationalised but the price increase never took place).

Both Anslinger and Coca-Cola, meanwhile, kept a close eye on scientific studies of coca in Peru by Ricketts, Gutierrez-Noriega and Monge. Anslinger had especially good reasons for wanting coca not to be declared 'safe': if coca was not 'dangerous' he would have all kinds of trouble stopping its production. Coke, meanwhile, stood to lose because, if coca was vouched completely harmless, there would be no reason to ban its importation to the United States and the US would again be flooded with Coca-Cola impersonations—effectively destroying their monopoly on the market. There was, however, a caveat: while it was important that coca was deemed undesirable, it was crucial that it was not represented as too dangerous because, if it were, why were they putting it into a soft drink? What they really needed was a bit of negative press and a whole lot of confusion. Which, through their relationship with the Federal Bureau of Narcotics, is pretty much exactly what they got. Thus they supported Anslinger while at the same time diplomatically moderating his views so as not to shoot themselves in the foot. The relationship between Coca-Cola and Harry Anslinger was, says Gootenberg, 'intimate, institutionalised and ubiquitous'. It worked for so long because 'Coca-Cola and Maywood had much to offer the United States government in this sensitive area, and vice versa'.

There is no doubt that the mutually beneficial 'you-scratch-my-back' relationship between the FBN and Coca-Cola kept both sides happy for a long time. In fact, such was their mutual trust that in the 1960s, when it began to look as if coca might be eradicated altogether, the FBN allowed Coca-Cola to set up an experimental coca plantation in Hawaii so that they could attempt to breed a new strain of coca containing less cocaine (obviously, the complete destruction of the coca industry would be seriously bad news for Coca-Cola).

The experiment, codenamed the Alakea Project, ran from 1962 to 1966 at the University of Hawaii's Agricultural Experiment Research Station. So secret was it that even the governor of Hawaii was made to sign a nondisclosure contract. Despite the fact that Alakea failed to deliver a cocaine-free coca plant there is evidence that the project continued into the 1970s, when the research station's harvest was mysteriously attacked by a fungus called *Fusarium oxysporum*—of which more later.

Gootenberg readily admits that it is impossible to tell how far the collaboration between Coca-Cola and the Federal Bureau of Narcotics actually altered US drug policy. It was precisely such actions as those taken by the FBN and Coca-Cola to discourage the Peruvian coca industry, however, that were eventually to lead to the emergence of the illicit cocaine trade and thus the slow, steady rise of cocaine use in the 1960s.

The reason for this was pretty simple. When America began to shut down all the cocaine manufacturers in the US, Peruvian coca growers found themselves with nowhere to sell their product. The wonderful industry that looked like it was going to make Peru rich collapsed. Moreover, when the anticoca lobby—encouraged by such powerful organisations as the Federal Bureau of Narcotics and Coca-Cola—began to bite, pressure to ban coca became intolerable. Throughout Peru, crude-cocaine producers began desperately looking for new ways of making money out of coca. By the late 1940s, when the United Nations Commission of Enquiry on the Coca Leaf was setting out, things were desperate. Peru was the only source of cocaine in South America and it was pretty obvious to everyone that it was about to be forced to shut up shop. In 1949 the last real cocaine manufacturer, a Peruvian chemist by the name of Andres Avelino Soberon, finally called it a day. The UN came out with their report on the coca leaf and coca was promptly criminalised. Anslinger was delighted—but not for long. Because, while the eradication of the Peruvian cocaine industry marked the logical consequence of the anticocaine crusade that had started half a century before, it also marked the point where cocaine moved underground. As Gootenberg writes,

With no licit or political options left, throughout the 1950s and 60s aspiring cocaine-makers joined desperate peasants and eventually linked up with a new trans-national class of Latin American traffickers. The kerosine-drenched jungle *'pasta basica'* [i.e. raw, illicit coca paste, as made in the jungles today] of the 1960s looked suspiciously similar to Peru's old 'cocaina bruta' [what the Peruvian coca industry had exported to Europe before it became illegal] and peasant lore cites those origins.

Between Coca and Cocaine, Gootenberg, 2000

Peru's legitimate cocaine makers, driven out of business by international legislation, went underground and a new cocaine industry was born. It wasn't long before illicit cocaine began seeping out of the jungles of Peru. A number of the arrests of the 'Balerezo gang' (responsible for the 1949 cocaine resurgence in New York) turned out to be formerly respectable cocaine chemists who had been put out of work by the recent bans. Soberon himself was to prove a thorn in the side of US authorities, sending experts and recipes off to Bolivia to teach the locals there how to make cocaine, and stashing bricks of illicit product all over the country, ready for transportation to the US.

The threat of this new, illicit cocaine industry was far more insidious than that of the old, legal trade. Now that cocaine factories no longer worked above board, the FBN had no idea where cocaine was coming from, or who was making it. The illegal cocaine trade had begun and, while it was operating slowly at this stage, it was never to stop gathering speed. Thus when, in 1953, Anslinger reported that 'cocaine is scarce on the illicit market', he was not quite telling the truth. In fact, as Gootenberg puts it, by this stage there was a 'quiet panic' going on concerning the drug. Cocaine was coming back. So, Gootenberg told me as we finished our beers that night in Washington, 'there was a continual rise in cocaine production in Peru throughout the 1950s and 60s. The United States created the cocaine problem itself.' By the time I'd read his papers, I found it hard not to agree.

9 Comeback

It wasn't long before this new clandestine trade began extending its tentacles into other countries. What little cocaine there was in the United States in the 1950s and 1960s was coming from a country that was, one way or another, to remain the linchpin of the American cocaine industry for the next fifteen years.

The key to Cuba's role in the world cocaine trade was its position—less than an hour's flight from the US mainland. As Latin America curves around the southern rim of the Caribbean basin, Mexico, Honduras, Nicaragua, Costa Rica, Panama and Colombia stretch out along a semicircular arc—all within easy reach. In fact, if you wanted to design the perfect stop-off point for cocaine shipments on their way to the US from Latin America, you would be hard-pushed to invent somewhere more suitable than Cuba. But Cuba in the 1950s had more going for it than simply good geography.

In 1952 Cuba was taken over by Fulgencio Batista, who lost no time in doing deals with a number of leading American gangsters, the most famous of whom were Benjamin 'Bugsy' Siegel and Meyer Lansky. The island, a haven for Prohibition dodgers and card sharks since the 20s, became an illicit holiday paradise, a playground for the rich and beautiful where bars and clubs stayed open all night and gambling was legal. If you were rich and American—and you wanted wild nights—Cuba was the place for you.

At the head of the country's hotels and casinos, and thus the hub of tourist operations, were Siegel and Lansky. But Siegel and Lansky were astute businessmen and they were spreading their bets. Lansky, for example, was at the time shipping raw opium from Turkey through Lebanon to Sicily, where his boys were refining it into heroin: together with Lucky Luciano, he was the brains behind the French Connection. And, thanks to his excellent relationship with the Batista regime, heroin destined for the United States was routed through Cuba, where government officials could be relied upon not to be too nosy.

Heroin was never going to catch on in Cuba. The locals saw opiate addiction as an expensive, sordid affair. Cocaine, on the other hand, was much more their scene. The majority of Cubans regarded the drug as an indulgence rather than a threat. Meanwhile, wealthy Americans looking for fun had no prior knowledge of the drug other than its old, glamorous Hollywood image. It didn't require syringes or needles and it was supremely expensive, making it exclusive and thus desirable.

A market for cocaine began to develop, and for Lansky's organisation—capable of refining heroin and shipping it halfway around the world—it can't have been that hard to come up with a few ways of getting hold of the stuff. Cocaine was easy to make, its chief ingredient growing wild in any number of Latin American countries, all within easy reach of Cuba. All he needed was a source country.

Originally he settled on Chile—a country rumoured to have the best cocaine cooks in the world. Once out of the country the cocaine was flown or carried overland through Peru and Bolivia or Colombia, where, for a price, officials were happy to turn a blind eye. The Chilean government was more than willing to look the other way, too: at one point the Chilean army was even tasked to transport the American Mob's cocaine to Cuba.

While Anslinger was busy announcing that cocaine was gone, cocaine networks were spreading through the Andean nations. By the early 1960s, when 90 per cent of all illegal cocaine in the world was taken on the island, Cuba had found new suppliers. In 1959 a police sting operation traced Cuban cocaine back to its source, an illegal, Mafia-controlled laboratory just outside the second-largest city in Colombia: Medellín. Medellín was a city with an illustrious history of smuggling, and one that was to play a pivotal role in the cocaine epidemic of the 1970s and 1980s.

In its search for new sources of cocaine the Cuba-based Mafia also hit upon another country that was eventually to play a major role in the modern cocaine industry: Mexico. By 1960 Mexico was shipping cocaine under the watchful eye of a local gangster, George Asaf Bala—the 'Mexican Al Capone'. Bala originally brought his cocaine from Peru but a Mexican cocaine laboratory busted in June 1960 was testimony to the fact that he was more than capable of refining the stuff himself. The bust, which netted police 14 kilograms of cocaine and coca paste, was the result of a tip-off from a Cuban informant. Another clandestine laboratory was discovered later that year in Cuernavaca, when the cocaine cook got his maths wrong and the building exploded: as Henry Hurd

Rusby had discovered eighty years earlier, cocaine making is a dangerous pastime for those who don't know what they are doing. Six Cubans and a lone Mexican were revealed to be behind the factory.

But things were changing. In 1959 Fidel Castro took Cuba and chucked Batista out—along with his friends Siegel and Lansky. These upstanding traders, realising that a newly formed communist republic was probably not the best place to make a great deal of money, beat a hasty retreat to America, tails between their legs. Alongside them came waves of Cuban refugees, who swiftly established expat communities in Florida and vowed revenge on Castro. Just as Columbus had taken infectious diseases with him from the First World to the Third, so these travellers brought a present back with them on their journey to the First: cocaine.

For some time, the number-one drug in America had been heroin. Across the US and around the world, addiction rates were on the increase—a prospect that appalled narcotics legislators. What really shocked them, however, was the fact that the new drug users were not like the old ones at all. The addicts of the 1930s had been middle-aged, poorly educated and socially inadequate. The new ones were young, well-educated and fully capable of functioning in society. A new generation of narcotics users was emerging. The surge in heroin use in the 1950s was partly a result of increased availability thanks to the now clockwork mechanism of the French Connection. But it was also a result of another sociological factor: drug use was coming back.

While cocaine was winging its way through the decadent Cuban high life, social changes were under way in America that were to enable the drug to establish a firm foothold once it arrived. By the mid-1950s a new generation was reaching adulthood, youngsters who found themselves in the position of possessing enough intelligence, enough education and enough leisure time to question the system their parents had never had the opportunity to doubt. This generation, it seemed, delighted in breaking rules. In music, in literature and in poetry they rejected the conventional in favour of the chaotic, producing unpredictable, jerky works that entranced the young and outraged the old. Fed on a diet of popular music and the fast, unpunctuated writing of the Beat authors, they rejected the constraints that their parents had accepted before them and began living fast, unpunctuated lives themselves. The media soon picked up on this trend and before long screen heroes reflected the attitudes of the new, free-thinking generation. The popular image of the hero switched from that of the insider—the sheriff, the policeman or the politician—to that of the outsider, *fighting* the sheriff, the policeman or the politician. In 1955 James Dean showed how rebelling really ought to be done in *Rebel Without a Cause*.

Perhaps because the idea of rebellion was seen as romantic in itself, the image of the drug user began to change. While addicts at the turn of the century were seen as weak, spineless individuals, the 1950s users assumed rather a different mantle: that of the rebel. They broke federal laws with impunity and, more importantly, they wrote about it. Like James Dean, the new addicts, personified by inveterate drug taker William Burroughs, became symbols of American youth's disaffection with society, their peers, their parents and their own lives in general. The image was all the more potent because Burroughs and his entourage were intelligent, educated and informed. They were not incapable of participating in society: society was incapable of assimilating them. Such an uncompromising stance was terribly fashionable and it wasn't long before others began emulating their exploits, taking drugs themselves.

As yet, however, cocaine was pretty much unheard of. Burroughs himself, who seems to have had a ready supply of everything wherever he went, had trouble getting it, writing that, when a friend finally located him some in Mexico, it was a revelation because 'I had never used any good coke before'. For him the drug was of interest only as part of a speedball: a combination of heroin (or any suitably powerful narcotic) and amphetamine (or any suitably powerful stimulant) injected directly into the bloodstream. Despite its having been invented by Freud's friend, Fleischl-Marxow, in 1885, the fact that speedballing required intravenous injections of heroin meant that its appeal was strictly limited. Thus, at this stage, cocaine was used in America almost exclusively by heroin addicts. Burroughs tells it as it was in 1956:

> It is the standard practice for cocaine users to stay up all night shooting cocaine at one minute intervals, alternating with shots of heroin mixed in the same injection to form a 'speed ball' (I have never known an habitual cocaine user who was not a morphine addict).
>
> *Letter from a Master Addict*, 1956

For Burroughs the most worrying thing about speedballs was not that they tended to kill you but the fact that injections became more and more frequent, leading to a spiral that easily ended with that classic symptom of stimulant overuse—paranoia:

> One morning you wake up and take a speedball, and feel bugs under your skin. 1890 cops with black mustaches block the doors and lean in through the windows snarling their lips back from blue and bold embossed badges. Junkies march through the room singing the Moslem Funeral Song, bear the body of Bill Gains, stigmata of his needle wounds glow with a soft blue flame. Purposeful schizophrenic detectives sniff at your chamber pot.
>
> It's the coke horrors... Sit back and play it cool and shoot in plenty of that GI M [morphine].
>
> *Naked Lunch*, 1959

By the 1960s, the rebellious tendencies of the late 1950s were snow-balling. The Baby Boomers arrived and unprecedented numbers of affluent youths ended up at colleges around the world, providing perfect breeding grounds for drug abuse. Meanwhile, the arrival of airline travel for the masses facilitated the transport of narcotics from continent to continent and illicit drugs became readily available. The new teenagers were now two full generations away from the addiction epidemics of the early 1900s, so there was no first-hand information to warn them of the dangers of recreational drug use. While they received advice from their parents to steer clear of intoxicants, the 1960s generation chose, en masse, to ignore it.

The first drugs to catch on were the old ones: marijuana, morphine and heroin, but newer discoveries such as barbiturates and the hallucinogens were not far behind. Cocaine, however, was still in the wilderness. The UN Economic and Social Council reported in 1963 that 'cocaine seizures, mostly diversions from licit sources, are quantitatively not now significant'. Similarly in Asia, home of the most recent cocaine scourge, things were also quiet: 'cocaine seizures have been reported; the quantities involved are insignificant', reported the Council. The same year, under five kilograms were confiscated across the entire United States.

The increase in consumption of just about every other drug, however, prompted government action. In America in 1961 the first White House conference on drug abuse concluded that the nation had a serious prob-lem. LSD was banned. By 1965 the amphetamines and barbiturates were illegal, too. In 1966 the Katzenbach Commission recommended that illicit narcotics be stopped at both source and demand levels. Penalties for dealers were again increased but by now the wave was unstoppable. Soon marijuana smoking was such a common pastime that the image of the pot smoker as a killer or a violent felon simply collapsed, bringing down with it many of the drapes that made up contemporary federal narcotic legislation. Arrests for marijuana possession leapt over 1,000 per cent from 1965 to 1970, when a popular US poll revealed that 24 million citizens had deliberately broken the law by using the drug.

In 1968 Richard Nixon decided to do something about the 'rising sickness' of drug abuse. The first thing he did was to green-light a harebrained scheme to stop the vast influx of marijuana from Mexico. On the face of it, his plan, codenamed 'Operation Intercept', was as idiotic as it was ambitious: Nixon dispatched more than 2,000 customs agents to the border and instructed them to stop and search every single vehicle attempting to cross into the US. Operation Intercept stopped over 5.5 million travellers in three weeks, delaying the border crossing operation for each by half a day. Yet, despite being the largest peacetime search operation ever mounted, not a single sizable marijuana seizure was made. As an interdiction effort it was a complete failure. As a way of pressurising Mexico to do something about the marijuana trade, however, it was more effective. But there were unexpected side effects. Firstly, the Mexican marijuana industry moved to Colombia, a country that would soon realise the potential of cocaine over marijuana and create far more serious problems. Secondly, the initial lack of marijuana led illicit thrill-seekers to look elsewhere in their search for kicks. Finally, the cocaine that had been waiting in the wings began to arrive.

Conventional wisdom holds that cocaine really emerged into the mainstream again in 1967–68 in America, when references to it begin to appear in popular songs and literature, but in fact it surfaced some time earlier.

In England, Paul McCartney reports that he first tried the drug when he was writing *Sgt Pepper*, an album the Beatles started recording in late 1966. McCartney had first been introduced to cocaine by the London art gallery owner Robert Fraser, who was—perhaps crucially—also a heroin user. In this link we can see how the drug crossed the border between 'serious' addicts and occasional drug users.

Cocaine had been around in the UK prior to this but only in minute amounts: a 1951 bust in a Carnaby Street jazz club resulted in the arrest of three men, one of whom, a heroin addict, had a small amount of cocaine. The drug was still essentially known only in heroin circles, and even then not to many. A 1957 survey of heroin addicts revealed that, of the 359 in the country, 16 had tried cocaine. This exclusive club of cocaine abusers gradually began to recruit new members and, by 1959, 30 heroin addicts in the UK had tried cocaine.

The increase in cocaine use was partly due to the actions of the now notorious psychiatrist Lady Isabella Frankau—the leading light in cures for heroin addiction at the time. Frankau believed that only when addicts received the narcotics they craved from proper sources rather than disreputable dealers could they concentrate on freeing themselves from their addiction. Of course, she soon became famous among the addict community as the doctor who would write prescriptions, and addicts began queuing at her door. They always asked for more heroin than they actually needed and, when given it, proceeded to sell it on the street. But Lady Isabella did not prescribe only heroin. She also handed out cocaine. Although she seems to have appreciated the addictive nature of the drug, she was happy to give it out to those who said they needed it and soon began giving it even to heroin addicts who had never tried it before (here again we find the age-old myth that cocaine can be used in heroin withdrawal). Everyone enjoyed Lady Isabella's cocaine. They asked for more, and got it. By the mid-1960s the number of heroin addicts was up to 1,729. Of these, 413 had tried cocaine. Yet this was hardly a problem—according to Scotland Yard:

> There is some slight and casual traffic of heroin and cocaine by addicts, usually from their lawful supplies. In London there are approximately 400 such addicts but they do not present any special problem as far as the West End is concerned...no uniformed officers or officers in plain clothes are specially designated for the detection of offences connected with drugs.
>
> CID, New Scotland Yard—PRO HO 305/10—2 November 1965

At this point, however, as Burroughs had noted in America, the drug was used almost exclusively by opiate addicts. McCartney recalls that in 1966 cocaine was regarded by most acquaintances, including the other Beatles, as unknown and possibly dangerous, marking the borderline between 'soft', acceptable drugs and 'hard', addictive ones. While some of the Beatles' entourage were willing to have a tentative snort of Fraser's cocaine, most were unwilling to try the speedballs that he touted around in a test tube purloined from a chemistry set. Thus it would seem that, for at least one social

In June 1970 they would swoop, picking up over 150 Cuban syndicate leaders in a single morning. Seventy per cent of them were former Bay of Pigs operatives. It was only a small dent in the drug network, however. Cubans were to run the cocaine industry for the best part of another decade.

The Cubans were not only good at distributing cocaine: they were also no slouches when it came to tracking down new supplies. Originally, of course, they found them in Chile—yet no one in the United States had any idea that this was going on. Former DEA agent Jerry Strickler says, 'We knew that it was coming from Chile because almost all the couriers and their controllers were Chilean... [but] no one dreamed of there being clandestine labs in South America. It was seen as being beyond them.' When an informant reported the existence of an illicit cocaine factory capable of producing 13.5 kilos a month, he was laughed out of the office, one agent commenting, 'That's impossible!'

Chile seemed to have everyone guessing but the country's dominance in the cocaine market was not to last long. Soon the Cubans, intent on cutting out the middlemen between the coca plantations and the United States, began making their own contacts in the Andes. Simultaneously, the Chileans began trying to cut out the Cubans by finding their own distributors. For both groups of traffickers it was a terrible mistake. Because the people employed by both sides to assist were to prove the most voracious traffickers of all, and were eventually to take over the entire market. Of course, they were the Colombians.

Colombia was a country naturally suited to smuggling. It had a vast coastline, was largely undeveloped, and shared a border with Panama, offering it all the lucrative contacts of the canal free-trade zone. For all these reasons the country already enjoyed a reputation for trafficking—in electrical and luxury goods, coffee, alcohol and emeralds. While geography and experience were important, however, Colombia had another important asset in the fight for the world cocaine market: grass. Most importantly, good grass.

Throughout the 1960s, much of North America's marijuana came from Mexico but there were problems with Mexican grass. For a start, the quality was often not great. Then there were all the new problems with the border. And the risk of bumping into undercover drug agents. On top of all this there were the Mexicans themselves, who were so laid back as to be virtually horizontal. Allen Long, who smuggled over 400 tons of marijuana in the 1970s (and whose career is the subject of a new book by Robert Sabbag) told me, 'They didn't really give a shit about the business.

They might show up one day, they might not. You would never know.' This made transactions somewhat tricky. Generally, the further south into Mexico you went, the better quality the marijuana you would bring back—but the less likely you were to make any sort of deal whatsoever.

North American traffickers soon grew sick of substandard Tijuana grass and the Mexicans' coma-like business acumen and began searching for other sources. Colombia looked promising. Colombian grass was renowned for its potency and the Colombians themselves had tons of experience in smuggling. Compared with the Mexicans, they were a joy to do business with—showing up where they were supposed to be, when they were supposed to be there, with whatever it was they were supposed to be delivering. Admittedly, there was a guerrilla insurgency problem but even that could be dealt with if you were willing to be reasonable. Long recalls driving a truckload of Colombian grass into an ambush in the early 1970s. Realising that he was surrounded by a group of heavily armed Marxist insurgents, he began talking fast and offered them money. After settling on a sum for his life, he then realised that he had no cash on him. No problem, they said, these things can be arranged. After a brief chat, they all parted friends, he driving off into the sunset, truckload of grass and internal organs intact—the guerrillas heading back to their camp complete with a personal cheque from his account at the Chase Manhattan Bank. In Colombia, everyone was on the take. It was perfect.

Although cocaine was not produced there, Colombians had the savvy to know that this did not really matter. Electrical goods were not produced there either but this hadn't stopped them making money smuggling TVs and radios. They made contacts in Bolivia, Peru and Chile and set themselves up as the middlemen of the industry—somewhere between the Chileans and the Cubans. They then proceeded to expand in both directions simultaneously. Colombians began buying up coca paste or purified cocaine from Bolivia and Peru, shipping it to the US mainland themselves, and then distributing it themselves, too. So successful were they that, by 1970, Colombia was challenging Cuba for domination of the illicit cocaine market. And it was clearly a growing market.

Testimony to the fact that the Beatles and the Stones were not the only ones to pick up on the drug, in 1967–8 knowing references to cocaine began to pepper pop songs. These references, alluding to a drug that was largely unavailable except to a wealthy few, painted a picture of a product that was expensive, exclusive and unbelievably trendy. Obviously, it was going to catch on.

Most commentators date the first real year of cocaine as being 1969, the year of *Easy Rider*. Although the film, depicting Peter Fonda, Dennis Hopper and Jack Nicholson biking across the US, is famous for its portrayal of the use of marijuana and LSD, it was also a cocaine landmark: the packages they deliver to Phil Spector in the film's opening sequence contain cocaine or—as their Mexican connection calls it—'Pura vida!' (Pure Life). As Hopper recalled in a 1997 interview, he and Fonda had debated for some time what drug their characters should be carrying: marijuana was too bulky for a really valuable quantity to be carried on motorbikes while heroin had too bad a reputation. They had hit upon cocaine. 'I picked cocaine because it was the king of drugs,' said Hopper. 'I had gotten it from Benny Shapiro, the music promoter, who had gotten it from Duke Ellington.'

As opposed to the way the Beatles had come into contact with the drug—from the heroin underworld—Hollywood was now picking it up from that other bastion of clandestine cocaine use, the jazz scene. Hopper later credited himself with popularising cocaine in America through his film: 'The cocaine problem in the United States is really because of me... There was no cocaine before *Easy Rider* on the street. After *Easy Rider* it was everywhere.'

This is not quite true. As we have seen, there was cocaine around in the United States and Europe prior to the film. However, there is certainly some merit in it: *Easy Rider* took nearly $20 million at the box office, an astonishing amount for 1969, catapulting the drug back into mainstream popular culture for the first time in over fifty years.

But what was cocaine? Everyone knew that heroin was bad news and that 'speed kills', but cocaine's absence from the world scene meant that there was no real knowledge of its dangers any more. In addition, there was no need for a syringe—a factor that made the drug more acceptable. And then there were these rumours about its being an aphrodisiac...

As the 1960s marched into the 1970s, cocaine began coming back big time. Popular culture provided the advertising. A further rash of pop songs making sly references to the drug hit the charts from 1970 to 1972 by such notables as the Rolling Stones, the Grateful Dead, Steppenwolf and the Eagles, all of which enhanced its image. By 1972 it was clear that pretty much anything 'knowing' about cocaine would sell, and three items that year further enhanced this notion: the film *Superfly* (portrait of a fictional cocaine dealer), the book *Dealer* (portrait of a factual cocaine dealer) and an American manual wittily entitled *The Gourmet Cokebook*, which instructed users on everything from purity testing to how to flush your nose with water to avoid mucous-membrane damage. A popular T-shirt featured the word 'cocaine' as part of the Coca-Cola logo (Coke took the manufacturers to court and won). In 1970, *Rolling Stone* magazine dubbed cocaine 'drug of the year'.

The mainstream press was not far behind and it could be argued that it did as much damage. A 1971 piece in *Newsweek* entitled IT's THE REAL THING hardly painted a damning portrait of the drug, picking up on the two specific details guaranteed to ensure that readers would head right out there and find some: sex and money.

> ...the drug, made from the South American coca leaf, produces feelings of intense sexuality, psychic energy and self-confidence...'Speed kills, but coke heightens all your senses,' says a University of Tennessee co-ed. 'Orgasms go better with coke'.
>
> *Newsweek*, 27 September 1971

Blimey! I wish they had co-eds like that when I was in college. *Newsweek* then went on to estimate that a single pound (about half a kilo) of cut cocaine was selling in New York City for $125,000 before rounding off with a terribly misguided quote:

> 'So much publicity has gone out on heroin that people don't want to get started on it', says deputy director Irvine Swank of Chicago's Bureau of Narcotics, 'But you get a good high with coke and you don't get hooked'.
>
> *Newsweek*, 27 September 1971

Together, these assertions—that cocaine is fun but not dangerous, that it's worth $125,000 per pound, and that it makes co-ed students at the University of Tennessee have better orgasms—are pretty much enough to make me stop writing this moment, leap out of my house and score some right now. It would be hard to concoct a more positive piece without actually suggesting that you'll get paid for taking the drug while naked busty women feed you marshmallows, all the while rubbing you down with warm woolly oven mitts.

* * *

Just nine months later they did it again, giving the statistics this time so as
to make it quite clear how much money there was to be made by dabbling
in the cocaine trade. According to *Newsweek*, a kilo of pure coke was currently going in Peru for $3,500–4,000 while on the US mainland—if you
stepped on it enough—it was possible to make a clear $300,000 profit *per
kilo*. In case you didn't have enough money around, *Newsweek* even
advised on how to get smaller amounts of the drug through customs:
' "you can wrap a spoon of cocaine in aluminium foil and put it under your
tongue—and talk to the customs man as you go by" ' said 'a New Yorker'.
Here, once again, cocaine was described as 'not physically addictive'.
Another piece shortly afterwards reported a DEA agent as saying that:

> Right now anybody can go down there, turn a kilo for $4,000 and sell it
> back here for $20,000. And, as long as that is the case, we're in trouble.
>   'The VO5 caper', *Newsweek*, 7 December 1973

Newsweek was not the only one running pieces about cocaine and its
sensational effects, of course. Everyone was doing it. The *New York
Times* referred to it as 'the champagne of drugs'. Even the *Consumer's
Union Report* ran a positive piece about the drug, estimating that it was
sold on the streets at purities of between 9 per cent and 90 per cent (perhaps if *Which?* magazine ran more pieces like this today—advising how
to get hold of quality drugs and testing their purity—people would be
more likely to take out a subscription).

With all the classic ingredients—sex, money and exclusivity—
cocaine's champagne image was back. Periodic reports of traffickers'
downfalls were portrayed less in terms of the laws that these guys had
broken than in open-mouthed awe at the amount of money they had
managed to procure for themselves in the course of breaking them. As
early as 1970 American law-enforcement officials had seized more
cocaine than heroin for the first time. It was a trend that was to continue.
For the moment, however, to the American population at large cocaine
was still comparatively rare: its price was so high that its use was limited
to the extremely wealthy, and, to all intents and purposes, for this you
can read 'the entertainment industry'. This was a feature that was about
to change, however, thanks to a chance encounter between two strangers
that was to lower the price of illicit cocaine sufficiently to render it available to the man on the street. It was also ultimately to change everything.

10 George, Carlos and the Cocaine Explosion

There's someone you should meet. An unsung hero in the world of cocaine. His name is George. George is a decent guy who made millions of dollars (in his case, about 100 millions of dollars) by doing the one thing that came naturally to him. He's a laugh. A genuinely chatty, friendly guy. You'll like him.

I first heard about George Jung a month or so after arriving in the British Library. He sounded like exactly the sort of guy I ought to meet and I knew eventually I would have to give him a call. When I discovered that someone was making a feature film of his life, however, I realised I would have to move fast: if I waited until the film was released, every journalist on the planet would know about George and they'd all want to go over to the States to hang out with him, buy him drinks, laugh at his jokes and generally be his best mate—before heading home and dropping his name into conversations at parties to demonstrate what fascinating people they knew. He'd soon get sick of answering the same questions again and again, and I'd be left on the shelf. That would be a shame because George had a serious story to tell and I suspected that your average film reviewer might not do it justice.

I dropped him a line immediately, asking whether he would be willing to meet, and he wrote back to me straightaway. 'Let the British come forth!' said an almost unintelligible scrawl. 'I promise you lucidity, clarity and courage... but only if you bring Turkish cigarettes.' So it was that one fine June morning I stuffed a tape recorder, a notepad and a couple of packs of cigarettes into my shoulder bag, flung it on to the back seat of a hire car and headed north through upstate New York.

We met for lunch outside a small town called Otisville. I was a little late but he didn't seem too bothered: not much bothers George these days. I suspect not much ever bothered him anyway. He emerged from behind a pillar, comfortably attired in a loose-fitting khaki shirt and chinos, grinning. First impressions? Rangy, long hair, mid-50s. Huge grin.

And charisma. George is one of those people who are completely at ease in any circle: quite as capable of stealing your date at a nightclub as he would be of charming your granny over tea and cake. And a *serious* talker. George specialises in long, rambling anecdotes which continually meander into red herrings so that, by the time he has finished, you've quite forgotten what it was you asked him in the first place. He spins long elaborate yarns that have evolved through years of telling, interspersing them with his trademark phrase—'I mean, fucking *crazy!*'—and breaking into infectious laughter at his own antics. It's only natural. In a way, I figured, humour had been his living: he had been laughing at law-enforcement agencies for the last thirty years.

So we sat outside, that fine day in June, and drank Cokes and the sun shone and, over a period of hours, he told me his life story.

Although George was born in 1942, life really began for him—as it did for a million other American teenagers—in the 1960s. A high school football star, he attended a series of colleges until a sporting injury put him out of business. He then dropped out, went back home to Weymouth and tried to work out what to do with the rest of his life.

'I started listening to Bob Dylan,' he said, 'you know: "twenty years of school and they put you on the day shift"? I *believed* him. I said to my friends, "Listen to this fucking guy. Can you get this?"'

George went to the Golden Vanity Coffee House in Cambridge, Massachusetts, to hear Dylan play and decided that day shifts were not an option. Together with a friend, Tuna, he made a decision:

'I said, "This sucks, Tuna," and he said, "Yeah, it does suck" and I said, "Let's go to California" and he said, "When? Now?" and I said, "No, let's wait a couple of weeks." And then after Christmas the two of us were like "OK. Let's go *now!*"'

The pair drove right across the United States in a battered TR3 until they hit Long Beach, California. Pulling the car over to the side of the road, they shut off the engine and looked around. Their eyes were opened. 'It was like going to a fantasy world. Like "Holy shit! What's happening out here?" The women, the bathing suits—it was a make-believe world!'

George and Tuna embraced West Coast culture with a vengeance, growing their hair, smoking pot, dropping acid and, most importantly, sleeping with as many women as possible. When a friend from back home visited them in 1965, however, their lives changed.

'Frank stopped by and we had this punchbowl full of pot—everybody did. You could buy it for sixty dollars a kilo in southern LA. So he looked at it and he said, "Where'd you get that? How much did it cost?" I said sixty dollars. And he said, "The whole thing? Do you know how much we can get for that back at U Mass [University of Massachusetts]? Three hundred dollars!" And I said, "Let's go into business, Frank!" '

George began buying marijuana in bulk from a contact named Richard Barile, who ran a hairdressing salon on Manhattan Beach, then shipping it back to Massachusetts. At first he loaded it into suitcases, recruited a couple of airline stewardesses and gave it to them to take north when they flew. But the stewardesses could never carry enough. He decided to move up a level.

'We thought, This is fucking crazy! Let's just get some motor homes and start driving the stuff across the country! So we'd load up motor homes with a thousand pounds, two thousand pounds—stuff it in there—drive them across the country listening to Jimi Hendrix, smoking pot all the way... We started to see hundreds of thousands of dollars. And those days, if you had a job at twelve thousand five hundred dollars and a car, that was a big deal. And we had hundreds of thousands. It was crazy!'

George expanded again, buying a single-engined Cherokee 6 plane and flying his dope in directly from Puerta Vallarta in Mexico, where he could pick it up for just $8–10 per kilo. Now he was making an extra $50 per kilo, the money really started flooding in. By the age of 26, George had stopped carrying dope himself, having recruited a posse of pilots to do it for him. He and his girlfriend of the moment would supervise operations from the patio of a rented house overlooking the airstrip, drinking margaritas. Of course, things couldn't last. A couple of minor arrests later, George ended up skipping bail on a marijuana charge from Cook County Jail. He eluded the police for a couple of years before returning home to pay a visit to his parents—who promptly turned him in.

In 1974 he was sentenced to four years in the federal correctional unit at Danbury, Connecticut. Which, as it turned out, was the best thing that ever happened to him. Danbury was a white-collar jail, 'a crime school for upper-class criminals', says George. 'They had some big-time smugglers there. They were really good guys. It was great! And that was where I met Carlos.' *And that was where I met Carlos.*' An inauspicious description of one of the more auspicious meetings in the history of twentieth-century crime. In order to appreciate the significance of the moment, however, it is necessary to learn a little about this 'Carlos'.

Carlos Enrique Lehder Rivas was a young Colombian with a mixed background: his father was German, his mother a Colombian beauty queen. He had grown up in both Colombia and the United States and as a consequence spoke perfect English and Spanish. Seven years younger than George, Lehder cut a diminutive figure: just five foot six (1.7 metres) tall, he was distinctly handsome, if rather fragile-looking, and terribly bright. He had fallen foul of the law, however: one of his older brothers, Guillermo, ran an automobile dealership in Colombia and together they kept it in business, shipping cars there from the United States without paying import duties, then reselling them. Carlos's discovery that it was possible to make even more money out of this trade by stealing the cars in the first place marked the start of his problems with the law.

At the age of 22 he had been arrested in Mineola on Long Island for car theft and then, the next year, was again charged with shifting stolen cars in Detroit. Having made bail he did a runner to Miami, where he was caught, predictably, in another stolen car. This time, however, there was over 90 kilos of marijuana in the back. Lehder got four years. At Danbury.

George Jung recalls vividly the day in April that his life changed.

> You have two bunks. One was empty. I took the bottom one. You don't know who's gonna show up next, Rambo or Charles Manson, you know? I'd just got there. It was about the third day. Both beds were empty and I took the bottom one. A few hours later, in walks Carlos. Just a kid: young, handsome, well-mannered, polite—like he'd just walked out of fucking prep school. And I was like 'Wow! This is great! I got a nice guy!' I was glad: it could have been some asshole, you know—it was a relief. He introduced himself: 'Carlos.' And I said, 'Hi, how are you?'

At this point in the story George pauses to take a drag on his cigarette. He exhales deeply and shakes his head: 'The gods brought him to me. They brought him to my bunk.'

Gods or no gods, the Jung charm was soon working its magic and he began interrogating Lehder about his past. At least, that's the way he tells it. In fact it's more likely that George, who really does love to talk, broke the ice with one of his anecdotes. Either way, it wasn't long before the two men struck up a conversation, and it wasn't much longer before that conversation turned to what they were in for. Carlos told George how he was shipping cars to Colombia for resale. George recalled:

> I begin to get more interested, you know this guy isn't just a fucking car thief. He's smart. So I'm like, 'OK, let's hear some more.' So he says, 'What are you in for?' And I say, 'Flying pot out of Mexico.' He says, 'You must know a lot about airplanes and have a lot of people in the United States who buy drugs?' And I said, 'Yeah.' So he says, 'Do you know anything about cocaine?' I said, 'No—tell me about it.'... He said, 'You know, it sells in the United States for fifty, sixty thousand dollars for one kilo.' And I said, 'Well, how much do you get it for, Carlos?' And he said, 'Like—five thousand dollars.'

Here George, always the storyteller, pauses for another drag on the cigarette. He raises his eyebrows and leans forward intently: 'I said, "Tell me everything you know about cocaine, Carlos. *Everything*."'

For the next sixteen months Lehder and Jung discussed cocaine and how they would go about distributing it across the United States once they got out. Lehder said that he had a friend who could procure unlimited amounts of the drug. Jung, meanwhile, promised that he could transport and then sell whatever he was given. They made plans to go into business together when they were released. In the meantime, Lehder spent his sentence interrogating other inmates to see what he could learn from them. Various white-collar criminals taught him about aeroplanes, offshore banking and money laundering. While everyone else was goofing off in their bunks, Lehder was taking notes.

George was eventually released before Carlos, in spring 1975, and sent back home to serve out his parole. His parents were delighted to see him at first, then began laying a vast guilt trip on him for ever having been inside. So he was delighted when, in 1976, a telex arrived from Colombia. Carlos was out. 'Weather beautiful. Please come down. Your friend, Carlos.' Unable to break his parole, Jung sent a friend down to Colombia to check things out. They shortly arranged a 15-kilogram move, the cocaine to be handed over as part of a simple suitcase switch in Antigua.

George purchased two new Samsonites and gave them to a couple of girlfriends, who took off on an 'all-expenses-paid' holiday. Of course, the cases they returned with two weeks later were not the ones they had left with. George, who had never seen cocaine up to this point, recalls how impressed he was when he first got his hands on his new commodity:

I tried it the minute I got my hands on it. When it came in from Antigua I split the suitcases open and started snorting it and I said, 'This shit's *great*! This is fucking wonderful!' And I just never stopped...I thought it was magnificent. Like, energy that never stops. It's like the Energiser Bunny, you know? To be honest with you I didn't think it was an evil drug. I thought it was OK then.

George's share of the deal was 5 kilograms, 4 kilos of which he sold for a total of $180,000. After that single run it was obvious that he was about to start making ridiculous amounts of money.

Lehder and Jung now set up a cocaine-transportation business together. The Colombians arranged to get the cocaine to the United States and told them how to get hold of it, and the pair delivered it to the distributors, taking a cut of the profit. Then, crucially, things changed again. In February 1977 Jung picked up 50 kilograms in Miami and carried it to Boston, where he was supposed to meet up with Lehder. Lehder didn't show—he had nearly been arrested crossing over from Canada and was on the run. Not sure what to do now, Jung took the coke to California, where he contacted his old pot dealer, Richard Barile. Barile immediately saw the possibilities here: one of the few places in the country where people were rich enough to shift this amount of coke was Hollywood. He sprang into action and sold the entire load in a fortnight, grossing $2.5 million in cash. Hollywood had not seen cocaine of this quality for a long time. Finally, a week later, Carlos tracked him down.

'I received a phone call from my mother,' says George. 'She informed me that a nice young Latin man and his pretty wife were sitting in the living room and they were anxious to speak with me.'

George's mother handed the phone over to Carlos. He was distraught: where was the coke? The two men met up in Cambridge and George showed him the cash. Carlos was so relieved that his friend hadn't absconded with the money that he immediately went out and bought a brand-new BMW—with cash.

Shortly afterwards, when news hit Colombia that Carlos's partner, George, had not only shifted 50 kilograms in under a fortnight but had actually *come back* with the cash, George and Carlos became hot property. The Colombians had had trouble with gringos before, taking the coke—or the money—and simply vanishing. They didn't trust them. They didn't know anyone in the States with a really good, dependable network. Not until now, anyway. George was a godsend.

George and Carlos now moved into a flat in Ocean Pavilion Apartments on Collins Avenue overlooking Miami Beach and started distributing cocaine in quantities hitherto unheard of. Every week George would collect up to 40 kilograms of cocaine in Miami, board a flight for LA and hand them over to Barile, who would give him suitcases full of cash in return. Soon George and Carlos had more money than they knew what to do with. George alone was taking $10,000 per kilo, so that if he ran two 25-kilo trips a week, he would be making a clean half-million dollars, tax free, a week. What do you do with that kind of money? Build a house, call in the carpenters and have them install hollow heating ducts, is what you do. You then stuff all the money into the hollow heating ducts and hope it doesn't show. Unfortunately, the other thing you do—if you are George— is start taking vast amounts of your own product.

George started to get a bit messed up in the head, not caring whether he got caught or not. He tells of one close call:

> One time Barile and I were coming back and we came to LAX with camera cases loaded with cash and at the X-ray machine the woman went, 'Wow! What a lot of bread!' And we took off on the plane to Boston and Barile's like, 'We can hide it in the men's room, we can go in and take the panels out and hide it!' And I said, 'Fuck it, Richard. You do what you wanna do. I'm going upstairs to get shitfaced because if they're there, waiting for us, I want to be drunk. Whatever is gonna happen is gonna happen and I'm gonna be drunk when it does.' Nothing happened.

As word of their successes began to spread in Colombia, the loads got larger. By the summer of 1977 George was shifting 100 kilograms a week—trailing back with $5 million in cash each time. He decided to hire a Learjet to do it. Then the arguments started.

For a start, Carlos didn't think either of them should be using drugs. George countered that this was easy for him to say, bearing in mind that he wasn't the one carrying all the coke and the cash around every week. It was a high-stress occupation. This meant nothing to Carlos: money was everything. (At one point, according to legend, Carlos even sent his own mother to LA with a load. 'Everybody has to work,' he said, 'and, besides, she wanted to go to Disneyland.') Then there was the matter of George's contact. Carlos pestered George to introduce him to the man in California who was shifting all this cocaine. George realised that, if he did, Carlos would go straight to Barile without him, and refused to tell. In Los Angeles, Barile also wanted to meet Carlos. George was being squeezed from both sides.

There was also another matter, more important in hindsight, concerning a new route that George and Carlos had been planning for cocaine. Back in Danbury, George had suggested that they should fly coke into the US in light aircraft—the way he had flown marijuana in the late 1960s. They had agreed that this was an excellent idea and gone looking for a pilot. When they found one, however, he had told them that small planes didn't hold enough fuel to fly from Colombia to the US. He had a better idea. Why not fly to the Bahamas from Miami, pretend to stop there for the weekend but actually head on to Colombia, pick up the coke, take it back to the Bahamas, leave the plane and the coke on the airstrip until Sunday night, and take it back then? One small plane coming back among the end-of-weekend traffic would be virtually invisible. It seemed a great plan. It *was* a great plan.

The first shipment, in August 1977, flown by the guy who had come up with the plan, Barry Kane, ran like clockwork, Kane returning untouched with 250 kilograms. Lehder and Jung split a million dollars between them. George and Carlos had seen the future of cocaine trafficking, and it lay in the Bahamas. But the Caribbean connection was where everything started to unravel, and where George began to lose control.

Ever since Danbury, Carlos had fostered the notion of creating a criminal haven somewhere idyllic. He had learned from one of his fellow inmates (a doctor serving time for fraud) that Belize had no extradition laws, and decided that he wanted to live somewhere like that. Somewhere where he could break every law he wanted to and no one could touch him. He decided to create such a place. Having discovered that the Bahamas was an ideal transhipment point, he decided to do it there. George was dead against it.

He wanted to set up a transhipment point and haven for criminals, you know, no extradition treaties with any governments...But I just shined it on because I thought it was just crazy kid talk...I said, 'Look, Carlos, the only way to do this business is to hit and run. Keep changing our smuggling routes, never stay in one place. Then we don't have to be under anybody's thumbs. We make ourselves a hundred million apiece, or whatever. You go your way, I go mine.' But he had [this idea] in his mind. I didn't pay much attention to it—I guess I should have. I felt I could control him and as long as I did it would be OK. I believed that and that was my own stupidity.

Underlying the disagreement was a fundamental difference in temperament. George was content to move relatively small shipments, to keep moving about. He'd been happy flying grass from Mexico and had already come further than he had ever dreamed. He'd married into a Colombian network and his brother-in-law could keep him with a regular supply. He was happy. Carlos, meanwhile, had set his sights higher. He wanted to change the world with cocaine, and nothing was going to get in the way. This difference in personality was evident even at the beginning of their relationship. George was in the business, as were most of the original marijuana traffickers, partly for the thrill. Lehder wanted more.

He was an industrious little bastard. Even after he got married I had to go and live with them in Miami and he had, like, the briefcase and everything. I had everything in my head—I didn't get into smuggling to go walking around with a fucking briefcase! I wanted to be a pirate, you know, and he was a fucking little businessman. He should have gone to work for IBM.

One weekend when George was away in Los Angeles, Carlos linked up with one of his girlfriends, whose sister had a boat. They began scouting locations. Pretty soon he found one, an isolated Bahamian island called Norman's Cay. Unbeknown to George, Carlos decided that this was the place to launch his cocaine revolution. And, again unbeknown to George, he decided that George was not going to be a part of it. By now he had managed to wrangle the identity of the LA contact out of him and George had become superfluous. Carlos uprooted and moved to Norman's Cay. When George visited him to ask what was going on, why he was being frozen out, Carlos gave him his marching orders:

I went to see him. He said, you know, 'It's over. You have your brother-in-law and this and that, and you can do your own operation, but this is my island. I own it.' I became known as the guy who made Carlos.

Almost as suddenly as it had begun, it was over. Only it *wasn't* over. The repercussions of the relationship between Jung and Lehder were to be so immense that, even when their relationship was dead, it wasn't dead. Not really. It's still not dead today. But we'll come to that.

George and I talked through the afternoon. Then I glanced at my watch and realised that four hours had passed and I probably ought to be getting home. I had a long drive back to New York ahead of me. I also realised that, if I wanted to find out what happened next, I'd probably have to get out to Norman's Cay to check it out. A trip to the Bahamas. What a bummer.

Before I left, we chatted about George's film and my book. He wanted to know who else I was interviewing and suggested that I get in touch with a friend of his, a guy named Garcia. Who's he, a smuggler? I asked. It turned out that Garcia was acting head of the FBI. 'A great guy' was George's verdict. 'We're, like, best friends.' He gave me the number of Garcia's private line. 'Tell him that George told you to call and he'll speak to you. Who are you speaking to at the DEA?' I gave him the name of my lead contact. 'You're joking!' he said. Why? Did he know him? 'Oh, man!' he said, his face crumpling into a huge grin. 'He's the guy that busted me back in '84! Say hi to him from me!' This struck me as rather strange—after all, people who break the law usually have very little time for those who catch them— especially when the result is a jail sentence (in George's case, twelve years). Wasn't there any animosity between them? George was having none of it. 'Nah!' he said, grinning. 'A great guy. Really. Give him my regards.'

You could see why the Colombians had found him easy to deal with: he likes everybody. Johnny Depp, who was playing him in the movie, had bonded with him so thoroughly that he had invited him to live with him in the South of France. 'He's like a son to me now,' said George.

And then the interview was over. We shook hands and he leaned forward. 'Man, you're all right,' he said. Then he gave me a hug. It appeared that George liked even me.

As I headed off he called, 'Hey! See you on the publicity tour, when the film gets to England.' I imagined that any publicity tour involving George was in danger of becoming a serious Event. I assured him that, when he did make it to England, the beers would be on me. 'Beers?' he exclaimed. 'Fuck that! Scotch! Fucking Scotch!' OK, George—I said— Scotch it is, and walked away.

As I passed back through the corridors of the Otisville Federal Correctional Institute, I asked my escort about George's plans to visit England. He smiled sadly and shook his head. 'I don't think so,' he said. 'Not till 2014, anyway.' 2014! George would be 72 by then. What about an early release? Good Behaviour? An appeal? What about the publicity tour for the film? He pulled a sour face: 'Everyone in here thinks they're going to be out by the end of the year. If you're in here for twenty years, all you have is dreams.' I guess the Scotch will have to wait, George. But it's ready. Whenever you are.

I walked back past the razor-wire fence, was checked in a bulletproof lobby under a black light that caused the stamp on my left wrist to fluoresce, and allowed back to the bank of metal detectors. I shook hands with the warden ('A great guy,' George had called him), reclaimed my camera, bag, driving licence and car keys and, thinking of George—and still smiling—drove away.

There was nothing new about what Carlos was planning. The Bahamas had been a smuggling centre ever since the seventeenth century, when Henry Morgan and his mates launched periodic forays towards South America, plundering Spanish galleons heading home loaded with Potosi's silver. The lawless tradition of the place continued through the 1920s, when locals made their living rum-running during Prohibition, and continues today. Comprising some seven hundred islands spread out over 100,000 square miles, the Bahamas island chain is so vast that it's impossible to police thoroughly even with modern technology—a large wedge of the narcotics coming into the United States still makes its way through the Caribbean for just this reason. Back in the early 1970s drugs were already coming through here but Carlos's arrival marked something of a turning point. He was determined to be more than simply another trafficker: he wanted to be The Trafficker. His exploits, together with those of his Colombian colleagues, were to flood North America with cocaine. It was only a question of where to start.

I had tried to find out about Norman's Cay before setting out to meet George. Not entirely sure how to go about it, I rang the Bahamian Tourist Board. 'Norman's Cay?' said the woman on the phone 'No one goes there. No one lives there. Not any more.' 'Why?' I asked. 'Isn't it nice?' 'Well...' she mumbled, 'it's the place's reputation.' There was a long pause. I felt like the posh idiot in all those 1960s Hammer films who stops by the local pub to ask the way to Dracula's castle. All of a sudden everything goes quiet and the locals all stare and people stop playing darts and the barmaid with the bulgy eyes and the cleavage whispers, 'You'll not be goin'...up thar—will ye?'

I had more luck when I got to the Bahamas. A few enquiries at Nassau airport and I was well in: 'Norman's Cay? No problem,' said the guy at the counter. No problem unless you don't have the cash to charter your own plane, that is. Clearly it was going to cost. But then, I figured, how often do you get the opportunity to visit Norman's Cay? Not that often.

While George and Carlos had started the ball rolling, distributing large amounts of cocaine in the United States, it was Norman's Cay that really made the difference: cocaine-wise, the place was Ground Zero. It had to be worth it. I handed over a credit card and was introduced to my pilot, a genial guy in shorts and a polo shirt called David. He looked pretty young to me. 'How long have you been a pilot, David?' I asked as we walked across the tarmac towards the aeroplane. 'Got my licence last week,' he replied, 'and I haven't even crashed once yet!' Aaah, the famous Bahamian sense of humour. At least, I *hoped* it was the famous Bahamian sense of humour. By the time we reached the plane we had struck a deal: David would endeavour to get me to Norman's Cay without stoving his plane into any islands or mountains or seas, and in return I would endeavour not to throw up in the cockpit. As an arrangement, it seemed to work.

Situated 70 kilometres southeast of Nassau, Norman's Cay is an 8-kilometre-long island at the northern tip of the Exuma chain. Various books describe it as being the shape of a fish hook or an umbrella handle. If you look at it the other way up, it rather resembles a £ sign. As you approach from the air, however, the first thing you notice is not the shape of the island but rather the water that surrounds it. More specifically the *colour* of the water that surrounds it. A perfect, shallow lagoon in the crook of the island is so clear as to be opalescent. It's the sort of colour you see in photographs and assume that the photographer has used some clever filter to make it look that way. Only they haven't. The water around Norman's Cay really *is* that blue—so clear and perfect that it acts as a magnet not only for yachts and dive boats but also for wildlife. The lagoon here has an as yet unexplained property that draws sharks from all over the Caribbean to breed. The sharks are born here and, like salmon, return in droves to spawn every year. You can't blame them: the place is paradise. Truly. Which is pretty much what Carlos Lehder thought when he arrived here in the summer of 1977.

Once Carlos had realised that this was the place for him, he was eager to get started. But first there was the question of privacy. There were only ten or so houses on the island: he'd need to buy them up. Lehder showed up on the doorstep of the biggest with a suitcase full of cash, showed it to the owner and asked if he had ever considered selling. He picked up the rights to the island's guesthouse, the bar and the airstrip. He then painted a large yellow X at the foot of the runway (international pilotspeak for 'do not land here') and refused to allow any of the other residents to use it. The bar and small diving school were closed. Things were about to get seriously wacky down on Norman's Cay. One resident at the time was Floyd Thayer. I had tracked Floyd down in Martha's Vineyard and asked what he recalled of Lehder's arrival. He said that the first he knew that something was going down was when he bumped into his new next-door neighbour, a drug pilot associate of Lehder's called Jack Reed:

> I met him downtown one day and I said, 'I'm your neighbour. I'm Floyd and I live just down the road.' 'Oh,' he says. 'I'm Jack Reed.' So I say, 'How long are you planning to stay?' because I figure that they usually come in the fall and go back in the spring. 'Oh,' he says, 'the rest of my life.' I didn't know anything about him but that was kind of a fascinating comment.

Residents were intrigued to meet their new neighbour, the handsome young man who introduced himself as 'Joe Lehder' and flashed a lot of money around.

> It was a strange situation because he was good to his men, he had savoir-faire. He was very gentle with the ladies and everyone who lived there—before he kicked them off, anyway. When I first met him it was on his thirtieth birthday. And I said, 'Joe, how much are you worth?' And he said, 'Oh, about twenty-five million dollars.'

Intrigue soon turned to apprehension and then fear. Carlos set about buying everybody's house so that he could have the place to himself. But not everyone wanted to sell. Lehder, however, was not the sort of person who took no for an answer. As he became increasingly focused, he imported all sorts of unsavoury characters—bodyguards, traffickers, drug pilots—and began pressuring the residents to move out. Eventually he would forcibly evict them all. One resident was told, 'In case I didn't make myself clear, if you're not off this island today, your wife and children will die.' Another was hustled into his plane at gunpoint, the radio was shot out and he was ordered to take off. Only when he was airborne did he realise that Carlos's boys had siphoned the fuel out of his tank: without enough gas to get him to the nearest alternative airstrip, he was forced to crash land on the beach of a neighbouring island.

Now things got seriously weird. Carlos, who had always had a penchant for German militaria, imported forty German bodyguards, complete with automatic weapons and Doberman pinschers. Visiting yachts were waved away from the marina—including, famously, one containing Walter Cronkite. Yachters who came too close to the island were surprised to see jeeps laden with armed paramilitaries following their every move along the shore.

Floyd, a skilled handyman who had built his own house on Norman's Cay, was the last to leave. He was allowed to stay longer than the others because he served a purpose. Carlos had bought a couple of prefabricated aeroplane hangars in which to keep planes and coke, but when they arrived it turned out that no one knew how to assemble them. He asked Floyd to put them up. One day when Floyd was working, a plane landed and everything became clear.

> I saw a plane come in and unload. Some men with automatic rifles jumped out and a truck came by and they unloaded suitcases into the plane and off they went. I was building the hangar at the time, that's why I happened to be there. A Mitsubishi came in just skimming the water and it unloaded and it just took right off.

When the hangars were finished, Floyd was aware that his usefulness had run out but still refused to leave:

> At the very end, when things got so bad I was forced off the island, I told his superintendent that I would be interested in selling [the house] and I was told, 'He doesn't have to buy it. He's just going to take it.' ...His foreman came by and said, 'Look, he's coming by and he has some pretty rough men there and they probably won't kill you but they could certainly knife you up pretty bad.'

Floyd beat a hasty retreat. He was not to return to the island for over two years, by which time Carlos's boys had wrecked everything, taking his house to pieces and scattering his furniture and possessions all over the island. Floyd wasn't getting special treatment. Everything was wrecked by the time Carlos left.

With Norman's Cay to himself, Carlos now went completely off the rails. There were wild parties, women flown in for long periods, violence. Lehder himself began using coke heavily and ended up seriously paranoid, as did everyone else on the island—a dangerous scenario, bearing in mind that they were all armed to the teeth. Through drugs, violence, alcohol and debauchery, life on Norman's Cay turned into a sort of real-life *Lord of the Flies* scenario—in which everybody would end up crazy in the end.

No one really knows how much cocaine Carlos moved through Norman's Cay in the five years or so he was there, but there was none of this suitcase-switching-25-kilo-a-time nonsense he had been working with George. Generally the pilots flew 300–500-kilogram shipments at a time. One pilot later admitted to shifting 3,000 kilograms himself, worth an estimated $150 million wholesale. The logbook from another listed a total of just under 1,500 kilos. Not only did Lehder have an army of these guys but he made the Norman's Cay airstrip available to other traffickers. Soon it wasn't only cocaine that was moving but marijuana, amphetamines, Quaaludes. You name it. At his trial it would be estimated that he had personally made a $300 million profit from 1979–80 alone. There is a chance that this was only a fraction of the true amount: one investigative journalist cited Lehder as having moved up to thirty planeloads of cocaine *per day*. If this is true, $300 million is a serious underestimate. Whatever the total was, it was more cocaine than the world had ever seen before. And it was all heading into the United States.

Twenty years on, Norman's Cay still bore the scars. As I approached the island from the air nothing appeared amiss but every now and then there was a sign that something seriously strange had been going on. Protruding from the foliage at the top of the island's only hill was, for some reason, a houseboat. Some say it was put there as a lookout post; others see it as a wanton act of anarchy—hauled up by Lehder's mercenary buddies when they had nothing better to do. It's easy to imagine how sticking a boat this size on top of a hill might be a bit of a laugh—if you've taken enough coke. Then there was the large X at the foot of the runway, faded now but still clearly visible twenty years after Carlos had his boys paint it there. Finally there was the most famous landmark of all: the crashed DC-3 in the lagoon, slowly rusting away. Depending on whom you believe, this was either the result of a cocaine pilot so wrecked on his own cargo that he missed the runway altogether and landed his plane, complete with a full load of coke, in the water by mistake, or a command decision that it was just in the way so—what the hell!—let's chuck it in the sea. Still clearly recognisable, the wreck lay the right way up in 3 metres of water, its tailplane breaking the surface like a giant mechanical shark's fin.

On the ground Dale Harshbarger, who runs the island's only guesthouse today, emerged in shorts and a T-shirt, smoking a cigar. We shook hands. I felt a wet nose on the back of my leg and jumped, startled, only to realise that this was the island's dog introducing himself. 'That's Carlos,' said someone. 'Named after . . .' But they didn't need to complete the sentence. Everybody knew whom Carlos was named after.

We climbed into Dale's pickup and went for a spin. On the southern side of the island were the old hotel, jetty and a series of houses, all fallen to pieces. Cracked conch shells lined the beach. The place had rather an eerie feel to it. Or, rather, it would have had rather an eerie feel to it had not a thousand visiting day trippers pulled most of the buildings apart in a hopeful search for souvenirs, cash and lost stashes of cocaine. The old clubhouse and restaurant, where diners used to drink the night away, were covered with graffiti and the ceilings had long since collapsed. Beer cans and broken bottles littered the interiors; in one room an ancient filing cabinet had been pulled to pieces, in others old newspapers, cardboard boxes, rotting carpets and miscellaneous detritus that might have been something once but weren't any more lay in piles. An air-conditioning unit—or was it a safe of some sort?—sat on its side, rusting in the room next to the bar. Every wall was covered with scrapings, writings and scribblings. In what was presumably once the restaurant's office, I picked up a filing card and a baby hermit crab scuttled out from beneath it into the corner of the room.

Instead of leaving a mark on the island, something tangible that might last, Lehder seemed to have done the opposite: like antimatter or a black hole, he had *removed* what was there, leaving nothing in its place. The only traces of the 1970s were not the things he had created but the remnants of those he had destroyed: houses beyond repair, the clubhouse, the old customs building. These remains seemed a fitting testimony to a man who broke laws for a living. In his heyday, it seems, Lehder not only violated legal boundaries but also physical ones: boats on hills rather than in the water; planes in the water rather than the air. But the havoc he wreaked on Norman's Cay was nothing compared with the havoc his merchandise was about to wreak on the United States.

As the Colombians steadily took over the trade, others were edged out. The first to go were the Chileans. For years everybody had known that Chile was behind most of the coke that made it to the US. According to former DEA agent Jerry Strickler, it was common knowledge at the time that Salvador Allende's election campaign was funded with cocaine profits. 'When he got in,' he told me, 'the country became a safe haven for traffickers. We had numerous indictments we couldn't do anything about—because they were in Chile. All the major traffickers there were protected.' Things changed dramatically when Pinochet became head of state in 1973. Our *generalisimo*, who had received CIA backing for his coup (Allende was a socialist), demonstrated his gratitude by rounding up cocaine traffickers and chemists as fast as he could go. Extradition of Chilean nationals was illegal at the time so suspected traffickers were first stripped of their nationality before being herded onto planes and dispatched to the US. Strickler recalled one passenger jet full of Chilean traffickers, all of whom, when debriefed on arrival, revealed that they had been working in cahoots with the Chilean military. Some of them had been using the air force to fly loads into Andrews Air Force base.

With the Chileans out of the way, the Colombians held free reign in South America. Colombia had always represented a major outlet for the drug but in the late 1960s and early 1970s the trade was disparate and, once the US had appreciated its value, often led by North Americans. One such was Zachary Swann, hero of Robert Sabbag's biography *Snowblind*—still probably the best book about drug trafficking ever written. Swann, like George Jung and any number of other American traffickers, originally got into smuggling marijuana, trading up when he realised just how lucrative the cocaine trade was. At the time drug smuggling—and especially marijuana smuggling—was considered a bit of a laugh. The early 1970s thus saw a vast number of inexperienced amateurs trekking down to Colombia and trying their luck with a couple of kilograms. The cowboy image of the early cocaine trafficker was further enhanced by numerous accounts of close shaves and derring-do. A Jerry Hopkins anecdote in *Rolling Stone* in 1970 illustrates nicely the image that the early cocaine trafficker liked to maintain: that of a trafficker, carrying a couple of kilograms, approaching the customs booth coolly and handing over a note to the officer. The note read: 'I am a federal narcotics agent. I am travelling without ID. I am following the brunette with the big purse. Please expedite my crossing and hers. There could be violence.' For a while, like the marijuana trade, the cocaine industry was a laugh. Just not for long.

The Colombians had way too much smuggling savvy to let dumb gringos take all the money. They began edging non-Colombians out—using violence if necessary. Colombia had only recently emerged from a protracted state of civil war called La Violencia and there were plenty of guns and people around willing to use them. Trapped in a country they did not know, Americans needed only a warning—and perhaps the experience of being relieved of a load at gunpoint—to get the message and head for home. By 1972, the free-for-all was over. Once Colombian traffickers had seen off the foreign competition they began jockeying among themselves for priority. And they got smart.

The first thing they did was to buy up all the local police forces. Police officers were extremely badly paid and cocaine traffickers had more money than they knew what to do with, so this was hardly a surprise. But one has to admire the thoroughness with which they went about it. So effective were they in recruiting the police that by 1971 it was widely known that General Ordonez Valderrama, head of narcotics in the main law-enforcement agency in Colombia, DAS, was one of the main cocaine dealers in the country. For the next few years, no one really got busted at all. For those unfortunate few who were actually caught, charge sheets were mislaid and witness statements suddenly became incoherent. Moreover, throughout the early 1970s confiscated cocaine had an unfortunate habit of vanishing mysteriously from police storehouses. One of the first DEA agents into Colombia, David Knight, recalls that by the time he arrived, DAS had been taken over by a new general, Matallana, renowned as being 'clean'. Matallana had fired a huge swathe of the DAS officers en masse and replaced them with uncorrupted staff. It hadn't achieved much:

> It had a horrible reputation. They were absolutely considered the most corrupt law enforcement entity in Colombia—including the head of narcotics (who was gone by the time I got there). So Matallana put some military folk in charge and they really tried to recruit some honest, upstanding people and they made an attempt to clean it up. It probably lasted a year.

Cocaine trafficking, which had started in Colombia as a cottage industry, was evolving fast. In the beginning the drug was carried across borders in bags and body pouches, often by pickpockets and petty criminals on their way to the United States anyway. Even in San Diego—right on the Mexican border—a couple of ounces (almost 60 grams) was a real find. By the mid-1970s things had gone upmarket. Knight, a junior agent at the time, was eventually tasked to assemble intelligence dossiers on the emerging cocaine traffickers. He recalls the speed with which it caught on:

[By the mid 1970s] they were moving hundreds of kilograms...after a couple of years, when a new informant came in, I didn't want to talk to him unless we could do a hundred kilograms. At one point my partner sent two informants around, gave them a little money and said 'I want you to see if you can set up any 500-kilo deals' and they came back and they had several. The point was to see if they could put that kind of a deal together. The fact was that it was amazingly easy.

As cocaine movers competed, so market forces prevailed and the bigger ones drove the smaller ones out of business, becoming more powerful in the process. DEA agents became aware of the names of the bigger fish and noted an intriguing quirk: that, far from competing, the major players sometimes actually helped each other out. Often if someone had a move coming up and there was free space that they couldn't fill, cocaine would be drafted in from any number of apparently competing traffickers. If the load made it through, the profits were shared. If not, the loss was shared—and no one would go out of business. Knight, setting up his intelligence network, also became aware of the fact that the majority of the bigger players were centred in two cities: Medellín and Cali. While traffickers—and even factories—were busted in Bogotá, for some reason cocaine hit big in these two cities. Names of the lead players in each city began to show up in his filing system with alarming regularity.

Interestingly, from Medellín, the most notorious was a woman: Griselda Blanco de Trujillo. Although she would soon be overtaken by her more voracious colleagues, she had a fierce reputation—and a series of salacious nicknames to match (it was said that she had killed three husbands in a row—hence 'Black Widow'; in the US, where she also ran distribution rings, she would later be dubbed the 'Ma Barker of cocaine'). From the early 1970s Blanco ran cocaine to the US, increasing her loads each time. In 1974 she was indicted for importing 150-kilogram shipments—extremely large loads for the time. From our point of view Blanco is interesting chiefly because her organisation, known as Los Pistoleros, is credited with the invention of an assassination technique so effective that it was to feature prominently in Colombian life for the next 25 years. The standard Pistolero hit involved two men—a driver and a gunman—and a motorcycle. In rush-hour traffic the motorbike would weave up to the car containing the target and, as it drove past, the pillion passenger would open fire at point-blank range through the rear windscreen with a machine gun. The job done, the bike would simply vanish back into the gridlocked traffic, leaving bodyguards unable to give chase. The entire process lasted no longer than it took for the machine gun (usually a MAC-10 machine pistol) to empty its own magazine, which is to say, no time at all. Blanco's technique was so effective that it was to become the pre-eminent assassination technique in South America, but I wasn't sure about her: everything I'd read about her sounded a bit like comic-book crime reporting. Knight knew her well, however: she took out a contract on him in 1975, something he wasn't too chuffed about at the time. (Blanco was eventually caught in California and sentenced to 35 years.)

Other names began to show up. In Medellín, a wealthy horse-breeding family called Ochoa was up to its neck in cocaine. The three brothers, Juan David, Fabio and Jorge, would go on to create much of the empire that fuelled Medellín through the 1980s. A former cab driver, Jose Antonio Ocampo, was even bigger than they were. Another local, Jose Gonzalo Rodriguez Gacha, known as 'the Mexican', was an emerald smuggler who had crossed over into cocaine. Gacha, renowned for his penchant for extreme violence, would eventually handle the Ochoas' enforcement for them and the group, together with their transportation guru, Carlos Lehder in the Caribbean, would attain worldwide notoriety as the 'Medellín Cartel'.

Two hundred and fifty miles to the south, meanwhile, another cluster of names came up repeatedly and these marked the bedrock of Medellín's nemesis, Cali. Helmer 'Pacho' Herrera, Jose Santacruz Londoño and a family by the name of Rodriguez-Orejuela all appeared on the list.

The most famous name, however, was missing. Whether due to the fact that he was not big enough to merit inclusion on the DEA's hit list at this point, or because he just hadn't been noticed, is unknown. He was the Medellín man who would eclipse them all to become perhaps the most successful criminal of all time: Pablo Escobar Gaviria.

The definitive biography of Pablo Escobar has yet to be written and thus the information we have about his early days is largely apocryphal. Born in a suburb of Medellín called Envigado in 1950, he dropped out of school at the age of sixteen and launched himself into a life of petty crime. From the start, legend has it, he was involved with death: his first business was stealing gravestones, grinding the inscriptions off and then reselling them. This story is probably not true but it is perpetuated because it's the kind of story that *ought* to be true: revealing a great deal about the kind of man he was. It is more likely that he moved straight into street crime: muggings, car thefts and, like his hero Al Capone, protection rackets. From here he moved sideways into kidnapping (a national industry in Colombia and one that would become something of an obsession for him) and cocaine. Escobar was the ultimate predatory capitalist. There was nothing he wouldn't do for money.

September 1974 finds him in jail for stealing a Renault, indicating that he may have been little more than a petty thief at the time. Yet the fact that he was released just a couple of months later, that all records of the arrest vanished into thin air, and that the only two eyewitnesses would end up respectively shot dead and beaten to death with an iron bar indicate that this man was a cut above your average hoodlum.

Just eighteen months later he would be picked up by the police again, this time with 39 kilograms of cocaine on him. By now he was a force to be reckoned with. The judge received a death threat. The director of DAS received a death threat. The two arresting officers were murdered. Their regional boss was murdered. The judge who signed Escobar's arrest warrant was murdered. The journalist who published an account of this arrest eight years later was murdered. The newspaper that he edited was bombed. Pablo Escobar was just getting started.

As yet, however, he had not made an appearance on DEA radar. They had more pressing problems, anyway. Why, for example, despite working their behinds off to make arrests, were they making no impact on the cocaine trade in Colombia? Knight recalls how the system operated:

> My unit with the DAS, our first year or so, we were kicking butt. We were making cases, making arrests right and left, making nice seizures—I mean, major, good seizures—and I thought 'this is great!' Then about two years later as the cases come to trial we see that the major players are all released... by the time that case got to court, they would be released for lack of evidence—even if they had dope in their hands when they got busted.

The extent to which the Colombian authorities had been subverted became clear in 1975 when the DEA, following up a potentially huge cocaine bust, found themselves in a shootout—facing none other than their colleagues, DAS. That November they received a further shock. A 600-kilo bust in Cali revealed not only the size of the shipments moving through the city but also the anger busts like this could generate among the traffickers: the weekend after the bust forty people were murdered in reprisals in

Medellín alone. The amount of money that these guys were making was on a completely different level from that of drug traffickers in the United States. Knight recalls an incident in the mid-1970s that opened his eyes to this:

> We had one case where the cops were doing a wiretap in Medellín and one of their couriers got taken off with a million dollars in cash—or nine hundred and some-odd thousand. And the conversation over the wiretap was like, 'Oh, man! Damn!' And that was it. Then they moved onto the next topic.

To Knight and his colleagues the solution was clear: if something was going to be done about the cocaine trade in Colombia they needed more funds and more men. Cocaine had to be given a higher priority. Unfortunately, exactly the opposite was about to happen.

By 1975, when 27 per cent of all American high school seniors admitted to smoking pot in the last month (6 per cent of them to smoking it every day!), it was clear that simply ploughing money into the fight against drugs was not achieving anything. On top of this there was the notion, held by many DEA agents outside Colombia, that marijuana and cocaine were not really worth worrying about anyway. Heroin was where the resources should be spent; everything else was 'kiddie dope'. At least one bureau head in North America refused point-blank to allow his men time or resources to prosecute cocaine cases. The stuff wasn't dangerous, it didn't kill people. What was the point?

Medical opinion appeared to back them up. A textbook, *Cocaine, a Drug and its Social Evolution*, by Harvard lecturers Lester Grinspoon and James Bakalar commented that 'sniffing (or drinking in small doses, as in Freud's case) usually produces no more serious psychological problems than irritability, nervousness, and insomnia, with occasional depression and fatigue on coming down. Physiologically, the most common problem is rhinitis'. Likewise, a leading Yale psychiatrist, Dr Robert Byck—who had edited Freud's cocaine papers—was quoted (actually *mis*quoted) in the *Scientific American* as saying that cocaine was about as harmful as 'potato chips'. He was later widely cited to the effect that the drug was less dangerous than chicken soup on the basis that 'you can drown in chicken soup'. In May 1974 Dr Peter Bourne, who would go on to become the White House adviser on drugs under President Carter, echoed this opinion:

Cocaine...is probably the most benign of illicit drugs currently in widespread use. At least as strong a case for legalising it can be made as for legalising marijuana. Short-acting—about fifteen minutes—not physically addicting and acutely pleasurable, cocaine has found increasing favour at all socioeconomic levels in the past year.

'The Great Cocaine Myth', *Drugs and Drug Abuse Newsletter*, 5:5, 1974

In April 1975 the White House established a task force to examine the future of American drug policy. Five months later their completed 100-page document was submitted to President Ford. The gist of the White Paper was that drug intervention was costing a great deal of money and that, to reduce spending, it made sense to use the country's sparse resources on the drugs that really mattered. 'All drugs are not equally dangerous and all drug use is not equally destructive,' said the paper before prioritising commonly abused drugs in order of precedence, the most dangerous at the top. At the very bottom of the list came marijuana and, next to it, cocaine. Although the paper noted that cocaine use had increased dramatically since the 1960s and that the DEA was making vastly increased seizures, it was concluded that this was not such a serious development on the basis that the drug 'is not physically addictive'. Moreover,

The data observed from treatment programs and surveys generally reflect the fact that cocaine, as currently used, usually does not result in serious social consequences such as crime, hospital emergency room admissions or death.

White Paper on Drug Abuse, 1975

The paper received presidential approval and was released to the press in October. Cocaine was officially downgraded as a risk.

The White Paper on Drug Abuse was a well-meaning piece of work but its producers had made a mistake. They had concluded that the reason cocaine had not resulted in any 'serious social consequences' was that it was not dangerous. They were wrong. In fact, the reason that there had not been any problems yet was that it was so expensive that no one could afford enough to screw themselves up on it. As Robert Byck was later to comment, 'Tell me the last alcoholic you saw with cirrhosis of the liver when cirrhosis was caused by Dom Perignon. You almost never see it.' What the White House staff could not predict was that, when the price dropped, cocaine would produce a vast number of serious social consequences—just as it had seventy-odd years before. Not everyone agreed with the White Paper. One of the few people to realise that America was heading into trouble with its new cocaine policy was historian David Musto. Musto had heard all this stuff about cocaine's being 'not physically addictive' and 'acutely physically pleasurable' before.

> I knew about the first cocaine epidemic. I wrote about the first cocaine epidemic and I told people about the first cocaine epidemic. And I didn't see any effect. People saw it their way and that was that.

Even experts who should have known better dismissed the risks of cocaine: those who had read Musto's work assumed that the first cocaine scourge had been due to racism, or stupidity. There was something about the fact that it had happened a long time ago that meant it was old and, as such, no longer threatening. For others, modern science was assumed to have rendered the drug impotent in some vague way. This sort of thing didn't happen these days, did it? After all, this was the 1970s.

The fact that cocaine was downgraded as a threat, that efforts to halt its arrival were underfunded and that it was widely held to be nonaddictive meant that the United States was laid open to the arrival of the drug at the exact time when its production was on the verge of going ballistic. As North America failed to prepare itself for the arrival of cocaine, developments were under way in South America that were to ensure that the problem, when it hit, would be a big one. Cocaine was about to gain a serious foothold in North America, drug traffickers were about to become drug lords in South America and people were about to start dying. The world wasn't watching.

To understand how all this took place in such a short period of time it is necessary to take a brief glance back into the history of the cocaine-producing countries.

In Colombia, the textiles industry had collapsed in the late 1960s, putting thousands of manual labourers out of work. Many of them applied for green cards and fled the country, joining relatives in North America. Once there, however, they found that their situation was not improved, as manual labour was being farmed out to Thailand, Indonesia and Taiwan. The result was a large number of unemployed ethnic Colombians in cities across the country, notably New York and Miami. These close-knit Colombian communities knew the language, all the customs, maintained close links with relatives back at home and—most importantly—were desperate for money. They were to provide a perfect 'in' for the emerging cocaine industry. Colombians had never been very good at organising drug distribution in North America for lack of reliable contacts, which was why they had dealt marijuana and cocaine through Americans such as George Jung. This was about to change.

As Colombia geared up for cocaine distribution, so more was needed. To make more cocaine, more coca was essential. Representatives were sent to Peru and Bolivia to deal with it.

Things weren't going too well in Bolivia, either. The second poorest nation in the western hemisphere after Haiti had been in trouble for some time. Since the revolution of 1952, land had been redistributed and for the first time peasants had been allowed to choose where they wanted to live. Many upped sticks and headed out into the dense interior to make their fortunes in farming—after all, about the only thing there wasn't a shortage of was land. A common destination was the Chapare district, to the east of La Paz. Once they got there, however, they found that things were a bit trickier than they had imagined. Originally there had been great plans to make fortunes in mining, sugar and coffee, but these soon fell by the wayside: sugar didn't do well, coffee crops failed and the region lacked the infrastructure for distributing other products such as fruit. About the only thing that looked really promising was cotton. In 1974 the Banco Agricola invested 52 per cent of its reserves in the cotton industry. The next year the world cotton market collapsed. Just when things looked as if they couldn't get worse, they did. A series of droughts ruined all the maize crops. Then the tin market collapsed, leaving 27,000 workers unemployed. Still the migrants came. Fed by such rural migration, the Chapare's population more than quadrupled in just ten years.

The only crop that did do really well in the Chapare was coca. Soil that was too weak to sustain other crops would support it, it required very little farming know-how, grew on even the most unsuitable-looking land and yielded four harvests a year. And when waves of wealthy Colombians arrived, offering to buy up as much coca as anyone could grow, it didn't take a genius to work out where the future of the area lay. From 1978 to 1988 cocaine production in the Chapare alone was to leap 1,500 per cent.

The regions above and below the Chapare—Santa Cruz and Beni— were the country's centres of production for agricultural products and beef. Controlling the regions were a series of extremely wealthy plantation owners whose families owned great swathes of land. These people had the kind of facilities and organisational ability to manage coca growing on a commercial scale and they owned huge tracts of land that was conveniently remote. Many of them already had a number of airstrips. And now, thanks to the recent migration, they had tons of manpower. So, when Colombian 'businessmen' arrived to buy up coca, they, too, were ready.

Meanwhile, Peru had similar problems. Faced with terrible overcrowding in the country's major cities, in the mid-1960s President Fernando Belaúnde Terry had initiated a grand-scale project for rural development. Vast tracts of land between Huánuco and San Martín were deemed suitable for settlement and the Peruvian interior became a free-for-all. An immense construction project was born and roads were carved into the jungle. Now the way there was open, thousands of Peruvians relocated to the 'New Frontier'.

They fared no better than their Bolivian counterparts. Since most of the migrants were not skilled farmers and there was no other industry, they rapidly ran into trouble. People began starving. By the early 1970s the experiment was obviously not working and was abandoned, leaving tens of thousands of peasants stranded in the wilderness. They, too, were approached by Colombians looking for coca. Since coca was about the only thing that grew readily in weak soils such as those found in the Huallaga Valley, it seemed like a reasonable proposition.

A combination of all these factors meant that the Colombians were soon in a position to produce vast amounts of cocaine. They now resolved to expand their operations further.

Having managed to gain control of both cocaine production and transportation, they decided to take over the lucrative field of distribution in the United States—attacking the Cubans, and each other, with ruthless savagery. The first thing that anyone noticed was the violence. In scenes reminiscent of Chicago in the 1920s, Colombians fought vicious battles for territorial rights on the US mainland, usually in Florida. (The Sunshine State was the perfect place for the cocaine trade to establish itself: it was loaded with Latinos so everyone spoke Spanish; it was about as close to Colombia as you could get in the US; and it had over 8,000 miles of coastline, making it almost impossible to police.)

The most famous incident involved a white armoured van that pulled up outside a shopping precinct in Dadeland, Miami, in July 1979. HAPPY TIME COMPLETE PARTY SUPPLY, read the legend on the side. Out stepped a couple of Colombians, who followed their mark, a gangster named Jiminez Pannesso, into an off-licence before opening fire on him with sub-machine-guns. Having emptied the best part of a hundred rounds into Pannesso and his bodyguard, the gunmen ran back out into the parking lot, spraying the shopping mall with bursts of automatic fire for good measure. A number of passers-by were injured; Pannesso and his bodyguard, needless to say, were dead. Police later recovered the van (dubbed a 'War Wagon' by the press), together with a pile of bulletproof vests and a total of eleven firearms used in the raid. The doctor responsible for the autopsies on Pannesso and the bodyguard commented that they were like 'Swiss cheese'. Griselda Blanco was later revealed to have been behind the hit.

The Colombians were capable of inflicting incredible amounts of violence on one another—and anyone unfortunate enough to be in the way at the time. The DEA was appalled at the escalation. Former head of DEA operations, John Coleman recalled:

> With the heroin trade there was never that degree of violence. If there was a killing it was a mob killing—it was, in a way, justified by their rules. It was not indiscriminate, it was never against a family member. If Lucky Luciano didn't like Carlo Gambino he wouldn't kill Gambino's wife or mother or child. He would go after Carlo and if he couldn't get him he'd leave him alone. This was the way crime operated and all of a sudden we were visited by this alien variety of brutality and violence.

Soon, statistics began to reveal the extent of the carnage. When the FBI rated US cities according to criminal activity, three of the top ten turned out to be in Florida. Miami, the 41st largest city in the country, repeatedly topped the murder poll for the United States, boasting more than twice as many killings as New York—which had a population twenty times greater. From 1979 to 1981 the murder rate doubled. Soon, corpses were showing up all over the place. A special task force, Redrum, was established specifically to handle drug-related homicides, but they were fighting a losing battle: so many bodies were there—cite authorities on the subject—that at one point Dade County (in which Miami is situated) was forced to hire in refrigerated trucks to handle the excess. A quarter of all the bodies turned out to have been shot with machine guns.

By 1980 it was estimated that eighty planes per night were air-dropping drugs on to the Florida mainland and it was widely accepted that trafficking was the largest single source of income for the state. Marijuana alone generated considerably more than the tourist industry. So much grass was confiscated that authorities stopped destroying it in incinerators and gave it to the Florida Power and Light Company to burn in their ovens to generate electricity. In 1978 alone, cocaine entering the state was estimated at $7 billion.

It wasn't only Miami's crime statistics that were doing somersaults. As illicit cash poured in, the state's finances went haywire: in 1979 the Miami Federal Reserve Bank reported a mysterious cash surplus of $5.5 *billion*— more than that of all the other twelve Federal Reserve banks in the country put together. The Miami state bank, built to supply a city with a population of under 350,000, began supplying cash to the other twelve federal banks. It soon became obvious where all this money was coming from: in the banks, traffickers and their assistants showed up regularly with boxes, sports bags and even supermarket trolleys full of cash to deposit.

When they were finally rumbled and the Bank Secrecy Act was invoked (instructing banks to report cash deposits of more than $10,000 at a time) a new industry emerged. Traffickers employed runners to drive around the city's banks, making repeated deposits of just under ten grand. On occasions DEA agents would follow them—only to discover that they were being driven around in buses from bank to bank like tour groups, queues of them shuffling out with shoulder bags full of cash at each stop before re-embarking and moving on to the next one. So comedic was their appearance, all permanently queuing to get off the bus or into the bank, that the DEA named them after cartoon characters, the Smurfs.

Of course, once in the banks, the money had to be transferred and laundered before it could be moved back to Colombia. The easiest way to do this was to invest it in real estate. The result was that Florida property prices went through the roof. One economist estimated that 40 per cent of all properties valued over $300,000 were owned by offshore corporations and that, were they to pull out, a real-estate recession would ensue.

The result of all this activity was a rapid increase in the availability of cocaine across the United States. Through the late 1970s the drug made its way across the continent so that, while a national household survey revealed that 5.4 million Americans had tried it in 1974, by 1982 this number would be up to nearly 22 million. The drug, which was still exorbitantly expensive anywhere outside Florida, became a great status symbol: if you used cocaine, you were wealthy and in America, if you're wealthy, you're *somebody*. As Paul Gootenberg comments dryly, 'Cocaine entered the mainstream. The relationship of cocaine to seventies disco culture cannot be stressed enough: among other things, no one could have danced to that music, let alone listened to it.' Disco or no disco, cocaine was well and truly back.

Added to its champagne image was the fact that cocaine was still not regarded as dangerous. *Time* magazine ran a cover story on the drug in 1981 featuring a cocktail glass full of coke: THE ALL-AMERICAN DRUG, it read. The magazine would later be ridiculed for this headline but it had a point—the effects brought on by cocaine were exactly those appreciated by a fast moving metropolitan society such as the United States: speed, energy, confidence. The blooming yuppie generation, which famously didn't 'do' lunch, needed a little something to sustain it and cocaine was the answer. Across the country, paraphernalia stores and mail-order services did a roaring trade in cocaine gimmicks: gold-plated razor blades, gold straws, gold coke spoons made into necklaces or pendants (at one point McDonald's stopped issuing plastic coffee spoons because they were used so commonly for measuring cocaine). Men smirked openly when their girlfriends commented that they were going to 'powder their nose' and the 'powder room' assumed an entirely new meaning. At the 1981 Oscars ceremony the host, Johnny Carson, quipped that most of the Oscars came thanks to Columbia but 'not the studio—the *country*!' Not since Woody Allen sneezed over the coke in 1977's *Annie Hall* had there been such hilarity about a drug.

By 1982 John DeLorean was filmed by the FBI taking delivery of 20 kilograms of cocaine, holding it up and commenting that it was 'more valuable than gold'. The American public was left in no doubt as to just how desirable this stuff was. But the American public hadn't seen nothing yet.

When news of what was going on in Florida hit Washington, government watchdogs began to take note. Clearly something was going to have to be done. A spring 1980 Senatorial Committee drew a line in the sand, noting ungrammatically:

> The violence and corruption that are integral parts of organised criminal drug trafficking takes the lives of American and foreign officials and private citizens, undermines drug control efforts and threatens entire governments to the extent that the stability of friendly nations is threatened, particularly in this hemisphere. Our national security is jeopardised.
>
> President's Commission: 'America's Drug Habit', 1980

Declaring drugs a 'national security threat' was a major escalation in a battle that was eventually to become defined by as much by its very escalation as by its failure. With the arrival of Ronald Reagan in January 1981 the White House was all set to fire the opening shots in the longest war in American history: the War on Drugs. Although the idea of a 'war' on drugs had been around since Nixon's time (he had declared 'total war' on heroin in 1972), it was only under Reagan and Bush that federal efforts against narcotics really began to look like one.

In Florida the DEA launched Greenback, a sophisticated operation with the goal of tracking and confiscating traffickers' assets around the world via their elaborately laundered financial paper trails. An estimated $3 billion in cocaine cash was passing through US banks per year and, the way they saw it, the best way to hit the traffickers was in their wallets. Within a year Greenback had traced the best part of $2 billion and actually recovered $20 million. Clearly, this was a result, but by now a couple of million was not enough to make much of a dent in the traffickers' balances. Miami residents were not content with it, either. Sick of cocaine cowboys and shopping-mall shootouts, they petitioned the White House to step in. In December an elite force, CENTAC (Central Tactical Force) 26, was established to combat trafficking in Florida. CENTAC, as explained by its architect, Raol Diaz, was more like what Florida's residents were looking for:

> CENTAC 26 was created to kick ass. We were to target particular people and to make their lives a misery, and continue doing that until we caught them doing something illegal and put their asses in jail or until we killed them...they were going to die or go to jail or leave Florida.
>
> *cit. The Cocaine Wars*, Eddy et al

White House chiefs soon realised that fighting talk like this gained them considerable credibility. When Reagan had been elected he had promised that he would do something about the drug problem. Here was his chance. On 28 January 1982 he announced the establishment of the South Florida Task Force. He dispatched an army of federal agents— DEA, customs, lawyers and police—down to Florida to sort the problem out. Things were about to get serious.

In retrospect, the most significant move Reagan made, just ten months after assuming office, was to task the FBI with conducting antidrug operations inside the US. Ever since its inception the FBI had steered clear of drugs at the insistence of its long-time director, J Edgar Hoover, who had seen the kind of money that the narcotics trade generated and realised that this kind of cash had the ability to corrupt the agency. So the decision to employ the Feds in the War on Drugs was a bold turnaround. But Reagan was just getting started. At the same time as instructing the FBI to get involved he had also told the United States' intelligence community to stand to. When Reagan announced that he wanted the military to join the fray as well, it was pointed out that an old law, *Posse Comitatus*, dating back to the American Civil War, disallowed the US military from interfering in civil affairs. Reagan swiftly suspended the law and told the military to dig in.

Now the War on Drugs began to look like a real war, with military personnel, military technology and all the information-gathering apparatus of the US intelligence agencies. Weird gizmos that might be helpful in some way began to show up in South Florida: E2C surveillance planes from the navy, helicopter gunships from the army, and a series of aerostat balloons that hung, tethered to the ground, at 3,000 metres monitoring activity along the Caribbean's air corridors. In charge of all this, at least nominally, was Vice President George Bush.

It wasn't long before all this new manpower and technology began to reap results. In the first eight months of the operation, over 680,400 kilos of marijuana and 3,000 kilograms of cocaine was confiscated. More than eight hundred arrests were made and $13 million in assets was seized. On 9 March 1982, customs really hit the jackpot when an agent at Miami International Airport shoved a screwdriver into a cardboard box containing jeans from Medellín. When he withdrew it, white powder began to pour out. By the time all the white powder had come out, the US Customs Service found itself in proud possession of 1,800 kilos of pure cocaine. It was four times bigger than the largest cocaine seizure ever made.

Reagan and Bush were delighted. Both took to jetting off to Florida and sitting on bales of confiscated drugs for photo calls. November 1982 found Reagan declaring that:

> there is no question that the South Florida Task Force has been a clear and unqualified success. Since its inception drug arrests in the area covered by the task force are up 27%. Drug seizures are up about 50%. The amount of marijuana seized has increased by 35%, the amount of cocaine by 56%.
>
> cit. *The Fix*, Brian Freemantle, 1987

The way the White House saw it, more bales of drugs in police store-houses meant fewer bales of drugs on the street. Likewise, more traffick-ers in jail meant fewer traffickers on the street. Unfortunately, the argument didn't really hold true: in fact the cocaine trade was accelerat-ing so fast that even large seizures had very little effect. Similarly, the traffickers had such a large pool of manpower available that a few arrests—or even a few thousand arrests—made little difference. Despite all the good work of the combined agencies (and there is no doubt that they were doing good work), increased seizures did little to dent Amer-ica's emerging cocaine supply networks.

In 1983, 6 tons of cocaine would be seized. In 1985 this went up to 25 tons. By 1986 it was over 30 tons. Yet throughout this period the avail-ability of cocaine on the streets of the United States never wavered. Worse, its price dropped consistently. While Reagan and Bush thought they were winning the war against drugs they were digging themselves into a hole.

Meanwhile, seasoned agents got the distinct impression that the South Florida Task Force was high on rhetoric but low on credibility, that its real goal was not law enforcement but press management. One problem was that while Florida did initially receive a lot of extra manpower, because there was little extra funding, it was always at the expense of other areas. A number of commentators noted that the South Florida Task Force was unlikely to solve the cocaine problem because shuffling drug agents into Miami simply meant fewer drug agents elsewhere. It was far more likely simply to shift the cocaine traffic to other states—where there was less chance of getting caught.

This was exactly what happened. Within a year of the arrival of the 'US Cavalry' (as one newspaper put it), cocaine shipments began to show up elsewhere. In fact, they began to show up *everywhere*. By 1983 the Miami Federal Bank's cash surplus was down but the California Fed-eral Bank was registering a $3 billion surplus—indicating that cocaine was coming in via Mexico. Reports began surfacing of cocaine drops in other states, too. In October 1982 Reagan countered these threats by creating another twelve federal task forces. The next year he established the National Border Interdiction System, an effort to expand the Florida operation to other states at risk. The federal drug budget began to spiral.

There were other problems. So many agencies had been tasked to con-trol the war on cocaine that no one was quite sure who was actually in charge any more. The idea was that all the agencies would work together as a team, but this didn't quite happen. In fact, each individual agency was fiercely protective of its own staff, contacts and intelligence. There were disputes over which agency should claim responsibility for which drug bust. It eventually became clear that the wonderful statistics for drug seizures in South Florida were not all they seemed: in fact, totals were inaccurate because different law-enforcement organisations were claiming the same bust. As Elaine Shannon notes in her book *Desperados*, George Bush himself, on the way home from a fishing trip in the Florida Keys in 1984, took an afternoon off to pose in front of a couple of bales of confiscated marijuana before telling the press that his task force had been responsible for the seizure of 5 million pounds (2,268,000 kilograms) of marijuana and 28,000 pounds (12,700 kilograms) of cocaine. The DEA begged to differ: his figures, they said, were out by approximately a factor of 3. In fact seizures had been 2 million pounds (907,000 kilograms) of marijuana and 8,000 pounds (3,630 kilograms) of cocaine.

Most worrying, it was noted that—even though huge cocaine seizures were being made—the price of the drug was still dropping. This was counter to every law-enforcement theory in the book: the idea of seizing cocaine was to reduce its availability and thus increase its price. When the drug became extremely rare, fewer people would be able to afford it. It would be less worthwhile and the market for it would diminish. In fact the exact opposite was happening: despite the sterling efforts of the South Florida Task Force, so much cocaine was coming in that their seizures were having a negligible effect on the trade and thus its price was dropping.

White House strategists chose not to see it this way. According to one, when asked why the price of cocaine on the street was still plummeting, he explained that the president's antidrug agenda had been so successful that it had completely obliterated the cocaine market and thus demand had crashed—leading to a collapse in prices. This was utter twaddle. But politicians talking crap about drugs was something the world would have to get used to.

While drug abuse is a 'hot' issue politically, it is one that is fraught with problems. In America, public declarations of 'war' on drugs are potent images and garner politicians considerable mileage: frankly, calling for all-out 'war' makes the indecisive look decisive, the timid look fierce and even the most feeble bureaucrat look like a serious kicker of arses. It is exactly the sort of rhetoric that impresses voters. But it is a terrible mistake.

The very notion of a 'war' implies that one side will win and the other lose. The drug problem, however, is not a situation like this. While drug abuse may be *minimised*, even the most hopelessly optimistic government officials admit that it will never be eradicated. Thus there will never be a clear 'winner'.

By portraying the fight against drug addiction as a 'war' then, US politicians are painting themselves into a corner because it is, by its very nature, unwinnable. Once it is labelled a 'war', however, one thing is certain: 'we' don't want to lose. As Nixon had said in 1971, 'If we cannot destroy the drug menace, then it will destroy us.' By declaring a war on drugs, Reagan and Bush were committing themselves to an ever-escalating series of financial policies that would cost them a great deal but ultimately lead nowhere. Once the public had got it into its collective mind that this was a war, there was no way back.

America wasn't the only place where cocaine trafficking was beginning to resemble a war. Some 3,500 miles to the south, things had taken a serious turn for the worse.

11 Pablo, Roberto and the Fiancés of Death

In Bolivia the process of government is pretty much the same as it is everywhere else—only quicker. Bolivian democracy is like the rest of the world's democracy on fast forward: the government changes *all* the time. The presidents change *all* the time. Politics in Bolivia is like a weird amphetamine-fuelled game of musical chairs where the only qualities you need to win are money, guns and a couple of pairs of dodgy sunglasses.

Since independence in 1825 there have been over 189 coups d'état; 189—in 176 years! That's an average of 1.07 coups every year. Now, admittedly, there wasn't a coup every year. Some were dry. But then some were bonanzas. Between 1840 and 1849, for example, there were 65—that's over seven every year. This makes everything reassuringly democratic: in Bolivia, truly, anyone can have a go at being president. At one point or another, it seems most of them do.

Of all these coups d'état the single most impressive was the one that took place in 1980 at the hands of a chap by the name of Roberto Suárez Gomez. This is relevant here because Suárez just happened to be the country's most powerful cocaine trafficker. In fact, it wasn't really Suárez that brought down the government. It was cocaine. And the story of how it happened is so completely outrageous that you're never going to believe it. Truly.

Roberto Suárez was born in 1932 in the Beni district—to the north of La Paz. His family, which had dominated the rubber trade at the end of the nineteenth century, was loaded: one of his ancestors had been the first Bolivian ambassador to London and his Uncle Nicolas was known as the Rockefeller of Rubber (which perhaps sounds a bit more seedy today than it did back then). Reportedly, by the turn of the century, the Suárez family owned over 15 million acres of land in Bolivia. That's roughly equivalent to owning a farm the size of Denmark.

However, when the rubber trade moved to Malaysia, business levelled out and the Suárez clan began looking for other things to do. Roberto came up with the idea of growing coca and swiftly established himself as the country's largest coca paste merchant—at the exact moment when the Colombians were buying up all the paste they could get their hands on. Together with a couple of wealthy friends, José Roberto Gasser and Guillermo Banzer Ojopi, he decided that this was an opportunity too good to miss. With ready-made access to airstrips and planes, he began shipping paste in bulk to Colombia, where he had made contact with the emerging Medellín cartel. It was a lucrative business.

In his spare time Suárez liked nothing better to hobnob with General Hugo Banzer, a military despot who had seized the Bolivian presidency in 1971. Their friendship was to prove mutually beneficial: while the president kept Suárez's cocaine operations safe from prosecution, Suárez—an extremely influential businessman—watched his back, warning him of possible counter-coups. Banzer's presidency was a flourishing time for the cocaine industry: by the time he left office his secretary, son-in-law, nephew and wife had all been arrested for, or were suspected of, cocaine trafficking in the United States. One of Banzer's cousins, moreover, was Guillermo Banzer Ojopi, Suárez's business partner (at one point Banzer actually attempted to appoint him Bolivian consul to Miami—after vociferous complaints from the DEA this never came off). When Banzer came into office the DEA estimated that Bolivia was producing 11,800 tons of coca per year. Within a year this had leapt to 35,000 tons. So that was the way *he* saw the drug trade.

One day in 1977 Suárez visited President Banzer and told him that he was in trouble: the Colombians, increasingly confident about their role in the cocaine trade, were giving him gyp: sometimes they wouldn't show up to buy paste; sometimes they would show up to buy but pay less than the agreed fee; sometimes they would simply show up with a bunch of guns and steal the paste outright. Suárez was pissed off. Banzer commiserated and suggested that he needed a little help. He knew just the man.

He then introduced Suárez to a mate of his called Klaus Altmann who had helped him seize power in 1971. Altmann, who spoke Spanish with a strong German accent, had been living in Bolivia since 1951, working in the Ministry of the Interior's department of 'Psychological Operations'— which was exactly as sinister as it sounded. In reality 'Klaus Altmann' was none other than Klaus Barbie—the Nazi war criminal known as 'The Butcher of Lyons'. Recognising that Barbie was a man who knew how to get things done, Suárez hired him to protect his business from the Colombians.

Barbie recruited an army of Argentine-trained mercenaries, who rejoiced in the glorious name Los Novios de la Muerte ('the Fiancés of Death'). The Fiancés soon proved their worth, according to one former member, teaching the Colombians a lesson by shooting one of their trafficking planes out of the sky with a bazooka. Once they had shown the Colombians that they meant business, the cocaine trade returned to normal and they found themselves with time on their hands. The Fiancés took to hanging out in the bars and clubs of Santa Cruz drinking beer, watching TV documentaries about the war and singing Nazi battle songs. But they were about to be given another little job.

In July 1978 President Banzer resigned. Suárez, however, was not worried. By now he was being protected by another influential figure: a pot-bellied distant cousin by the name of Luis Arce Gomez. Gomez was a military official of some distinction: having been booted out of the army for allegedly raping the daughter of a superior officer, he had been rehabilitated and placed in charge of military intelligence. Ironic, really, because intelligence was one of the many qualities that he appeared to lack, hence his nickname, Opa Luis (Simple Luis). But Arce Gomez was not as dumb as he seemed. His first action on becoming head of military intelligence was to lead a raid on the headquarters of the Bolivian Secret Police, stealing all their files. In possession of such material he was, in effect, in control of all clandestine operations in Bolivia, and very capable of protecting his friend Roberto Suárez.

Despite his protection, Suárez was worried. Banzer's resignation had left a gulf: what would happen if a strong president came into office and sacked Gomez? Two years, four coups, two general elections and five presidents later, just such a character emerged. He was a hero of the revolution called Hernán Siles Zuazo. Not only was he democratically elected but he was anticocaine. Siles was due to take office in August 1980. Clearly something would have to be done. And fast.

Suárez convened a meeting of fellow traffickers, the Fiancés of Death, Klaus Barbie, Arce Gomez and a number of other notables—apparently in a bar called the Club Bavaria in Santa Cruz. Together, they decided to bring down the Siles government before it reached office. Realising that they would need a military figure of suitable standing to lead a successful coup, they put their heads together to come up with such a man, eventually settling on another military despot by the name of General Garcia Meza. Meza had as much to lose as anyone if Siles assumed office: he had been busily exterminating all sorts of innocent peasants for various reasons and was afraid that he might get into trouble if news leaked out.

Arce Gomez was dispatched to ask Meza if he was up for it. In return for leading the coup, he assured him, Meza would receive $1.3 million in advance—with the promise of more when the fighting was over. There was one condition: Arce Gomez wanted to be Minister of the Interior. Meza took the cash and agreed to lead the coup.

On 17 July 1980 the team sprang into action. The sixth army division started the ball rolling, announcing that Bolivia was under threat from 'Communist extremists' and demanding that Meza take charge to save the country. They then rejected the results of the general election, declared the Bolivian Congress unconstitutional and went on the rampage. Resistance was not tolerated. When a group of trade union leaders tried to organise a national strike the Fiancés of Death stormed their headquarters, shot a couple of representatives and abducted the rest. Those who survived were tortured, some of them to death. Virtually all of the female union leaders were gang-raped. Five hundred representatives were executed in the first fortnight. Another 2,500 were chucked into jail and tortured.

Of the 189 coups d'état in Bolivia's chequered history, this was by far the most violent. Meza went on national television to calm the nation: 'I will stay as long as I have to to eliminate the Marxist cancer,' he said. 'be it five years, ten or twenty.' Suárez's operation rapidly became known as the Cocaine Coup.

Before long Suárez, Meza and Gomez found themselves in proud possession of their own country. As agreed, Meza became president and Gomez Minister of the Interior. Suárez, in his own inimitable way, now decided to nationalise Bolivia's cocaine industry. Using Gomez's intelligence, he started his own brand of antinarcotics operations, exterminating competitors until the market was his. The Fiancés of Death handled the details, killing the cocaine merchants, confiscating their paste and handing it over to him. So much cocaine was there that at one point Suárez hired the Bolivian air force to move it all for him (he paid them $150,000 per week for this service). For safekeeping, he lodged all the coke in the vaults of the state bank.

Suárez had created the world's first 'narcocracy'. Within six months, cocaine production was up 500 per cent and everyone was on the pay-roll. Gomez did especially well, telling a friend, 'We are going to inun-date the gringos with cocaine.' A CBS *60 Minutes* special broadcast in the United States estimated that he was personally making $200,000 a week and dubbed him 'Minister of Cocaine'.

Human rights abuses continued unabated. In charge of the intelligence services was placed one Faustino Rico Toro—nicknamed 'the Magician' for his uncanny ability to make people disappear. Even the military was appalled. Clare Hargreaves, in her excellent study of the Bolivian cocaine industry, *Snowfields*, reports that troops eventually refused to carry out any more atrocities on Bolivian civilians and began deserting en masse. So fast did the army haemorrhage staff, she says, that remaining forces took to kidnapping new recruits from the terraces of football matches.

Still the cash rolled in. How much, exactly, is anyone's guess: 'It is impossible to calculate the money they made,' an analyst told the jour-nalist Brian Freemantle. 'Think of a preposterous figure, double it and know damn well that you've made a gross underestimate.' Suárez would later brag that his antics were the inspiration for Brian de Palma's 1983 film *Scarface*. He rejoiced in his title: Bolivia's King of Cocaine.

In some ways Bolivia's cocaine coup mirrored events that had taken place in Honduras two years earlier. Here the main offenders had been a marijuana and cocaine trafficker by the name of Juan Ramón Matta Ballesteros and a Mexican friend of his, Felix Gallardo. Together the two had helped to bankroll a successful plot to overthrow President Juan Alberto Melgar Castro and replace him with Policarpo Paz Garcia. Garcia's regime had then conveniently overlooked—and in some cases actually assisted—Ballesteros's cocaine and marijuana trafficking, creat-ing a significant new conduit for Colombian cocaine through Honduras. Delighted, Ballesteros set up his own air freight business, SETCO, which he used to fly his coke around. SETCO was to create all sorts of problems ten years on, as we shall see later. But on with the story.

Roberto Suárez really pissed the DEA off. Far from hiding his wealth, he flaunted it for all to see, knowing he was protected at the highest lev-els. He owned a series of lavish houses around Bolivia and held court in an armoured palace in a remote farming town called Santa Ana de Yacuma. From here he would dole out cash magnanimously, like a king, for suitably worthy causes. He rebuilt churches, surfaced roads and built schools. He handed out college scholarships to talented youths who couldn't otherwise afford to attend. At one point he even bought up a satellite TV system for the entire town so the inhabitants could watch foreign soap operas and live soccer matches. The locals loved him for it, referring to him affectionately as 'Papito' (Daddy).

It wasn't just his bragging that annoyed the DEA. They were especially angry with Suárez for the simple reason that they had nearly caught him in 1979 but that, through a combination of bad luck and poor planning, they had let him slip through their fingers.

Suárez, sick of dealing with the Colombians, had decided to cut them out of his empire by dealing cocaine directly to the United States. He had the technology to refine the cocaine in Bolivia and planes capable of flying it; all he needed was a distributor. In early 1980 his partner, Marcelo Ibañez, reported that he had bumped into just the guy in a nightclub in Buenos Aires. Unfortunately for the pair, the buyer was an undercover DEA agent called Mike Levine. Levine told Ibañez that he could buy up unlimited amounts of cocaine, that he could get it into the US easily and that he had paid off all the relevant American authorities so the operation would be safe. Levine suggested that Suárez and Ibañez fly out to his pad in Miami to meet the members of his operation and hammer out the details. When Suárez stepped foot on American soil, of course, he would be arrested and, once in custody, there was a very good chance he would never, ever, be set free. Suárez fell right into the trap and offered to supply Levine with over 900 kilograms of cocaine a month.

In Florida, preparations for the visit proceeded apace. A palatial house in Miami was borrowed and decorated in a style appropriate to a drug lord of Levine's supposed standing. Bugs and cameras were installed in every room, ready to record the historic arrest for posterity. Close on $10 million was borrowed and stuffed into suitcases to make the deal look authentic. But then it all went wrong. First, Suárez decided he didn't want to visit Miami after all—he wanted to make the entire trade in Bolivia. Then, when the deal went down, he didn't actually show up in person, instead sending his son, Robbie, to handle negotiations. In the end neither Robbie nor his father was arrested, but Levine picked up the bag men. The paste was destroyed and the money never reached Bolivia.

Despite the fact that Suárez remained safe, it was a considerable triumph for the DEA. But then even this turned sour. One of the defendants was simply sent home to Bolivia; the other was offered bail, took it, skipped it and was never heard of again. 'Amazingly,' wrote Levine later, 'the biggest sting operation in law enforcement history was suddenly without any defendants.' In his books *Deep Cover* and *The Big White Lie*, Levine suggests that the reason this sting never worked was that it had been sabotaged from the beginning. Levine holds that Suárez was in fact working with the tacit approval of the CIA; that the agency was protecting him because it was all in favour of Meza's 'cocaine coup' (the elected Bolivian president, Siles Zuazo, was a socialist). He claims that a tape recording of the original meeting held by Suárez at the Club Bavaria in which he, Barbie and Arce Gomez had discussed who should lead the coup, was in fact in possession of the CIA well before the event: they knew everything, he said, but did nothing. It was not to be the last time that a DEA agent was to accuse the CIA of sabotaging a cocaine operation—as we shall see.

The DEA was unlucky once again with regard to Suárez. In January 1981 Robbie Suárez was arrested in Switzerland carrying a load of hot cheques that his father had instructed him to pay into various bank accounts. He was rapidly extradited to the United States. Finally it began to look as if a real drug lord was about to go down. The matter was all the more amusing to the DEA because Robbie was Suárez's favourite son and was being groomed to take over the family business. They couldn't wait to hear what Suárez senior would have to say about this. They didn't have to. He went ballistic. Supposedly he hired a gang of hit men to kidnap a couple of Florida state judges (the judges' security was increased; no one ever touched them). Then he took a measure that was to propel him into the legends of drug traffickers: Suárez wrote a personal letter to President Ronald Reagan offering a straight deal—if Reagan released Robbie, Suárez would pay off the entire Bolivian national debt (at the time standing somewhere in the league of $4,000,000,000). It was a gesture that was to be repeated by a number of other traffickers in Peru and Colombia in the years to come. Perhaps none of these offers was real but, like the story about Pablo Escobar stealing gravestones, they just sounded as if they ought to be true. Who knows? Suárez's letter was never answered but, by some amazing judicial cock-up, Robbie was acquitted and sent home anyway. His coming-home party took place in March 1983 in Santa Ana. Suárez laid on food and drink for five thousand. The revelry lasted over a week, planes being dispatched to La Paz for replenishments when the alcohol ran out.

Not unnaturally, the DEA was extremely concerned. It looked like a catastrophe. In fact even worse developments were taking place 1,500 miles to the north in Colombia.

* * *

Prior to the mid-1980s, Colombians were not too worried about traffickers at all. There was such a history of smuggling in the country that there was no real stigma attached to it. Thus when the new generation of cocaine cowboys emerged, flashing their money and jewellery, no one paid much attention. The traffickers made good use of this ambivalence, worming their way into as many legitimate areas as possible to protect their interests. Pablo Escobar came up with a technique for recruiting established figures into his network, setting up an insurance scheme called *apuntada*, which enabled those without the necessary cocaine-based contacts to invest in shipments. The scheme was as simple as it was effective: for a few thousand dollars businessmen could buy shares in a load of cocaine on its way to the United States. When it arrived safely they would receive a windfall payment.

What made the system really smart was that it provided built-in insurance, guaranteeing investors that—even if the load of coke was interdicted—they would be reimbursed their initial investment. Escobar would take 10 per cent of the cost of the price of the cocaine *in America* as an insurance premium—provided the shipment arrived safely. If the load was confiscated, he would return the cost of the initial investment (at the Colombian end) to his new partners.

The price of cocaine in the United States was so high that, by taking 10 per cent cuts off numerous investors, he would make a healthy profit even allowing for the fact that an (estimated) one in ten shipments didn't make it through. So effective was this technique that at one point Escobar even offered to lend the initial cash payment to potential investors who couldn't afford it themselves. They could pay him back at the end of the deal. From the investment point of view, *apuntada* was a sure thing: if you hit you made it big (even allowing for your donation of 10 per cent of the profits to Escobar). If you lost, he gave you back your original investment. Businessmen with otherwise clean records got in on the act, and Escobar found himself running with the rich and the beautiful.

Soon Escobar and his pals were making so much money that they had trouble spending it all. Escobar, who was later estimated to have been making a clear half-million-dollar profit every day by 1982 (by the mid-1980s he would be on $1 million per day), ended up building himself a palatial ranch in Puerto Triunfo, 100 miles to the east of Medellín. The ranch, called Los Napoles, covered over 2,800 hectares (7,000 acres) and was reputed to have cost him over $50 million to build. It had its own airstrip, a number of separate swimming pools protected by mortar emplacements and slept a hundred. Above the main entrance was suspended a Piper Cub aeroplane—supposedly the first plane he ever flew to the United States full of coke. He bought a vintage American car, told everyone that it had once belonged to Al Capone, and posed for pictures in front of it. He bought up a menagerie of animals and turned them loose in the grounds, opening the place as a public zoo.

Meanwhile he set about improving living conditions for the poor: repairing churches, putting up street lights, resurfacing roads and eventually establishing his own political movement, Civismo en Marcha (Good Citizenship on the March). He built five hundred two-bedroom houses in Medellín and handed out the keys to the poor. The estate was known as Barrio Pablo Escobar. Just in case its new inhabitants were still hard up, he had a truck full of supplies sent up every fortnight to dole out free food. He dispatched doctors and dentists into poor areas and paid them to stay there until they had treated everyone who needed treatment. Anything that appealed to him, he did: he donated a church to the town of Doradal, 190 kilometres outside Medellín. He started soccer matches and gave rousing speeches, always ensuring that his own press agents were around when he did it. He distributed 5,000 toys every Christmas to poor street children. The poor adored him. By 1983 Colombia's leading news magazine, *Semana*, appeared to join them, dubbing him 'a *paisa* Robin Hood'.

Other traffickers were just as flash: Gonzalo Rodríguez Gacha donated countless thousands to civic projects in his home town of Pacho and established his own political party, as did Carlos Lehder, when he popped back from Norman's Cay. All of the key players in Medellín ended up building themselves vast estates and copying Escobar's idea of letting wild animals run loose there. The Ochoas apparently planned to release lions and tigers on to an island in the middle of one of their lakes. Everyone bought up their favourite sporting teams and began playing Fantasy Football for real.

In 1982 Escobar managed to get himself elected into the Colombian parliament as running partner to a character called Jairo Ortega, whose election campaign he had funded. This seemed like a smart move, as members of congress were immune to prosecution. He had been pulling strings behind the stage, too, ploughing huge amounts of money into political campaigns—usually betting on both candidates to ensure that the winner would be indebted to him. (In 1981 Escobar and the Ochoas donated substantial amounts of cash plus cars and transport to both presidential candidates.) When Escobar spoke to the press there was always a suitably genial front. The true source of his money was never revealed. According to one interview he had started up in the bicycle rental business before making his fortune in property. To another journalist he joked that he was just a normal guy on the basis that 'I always sing in the shower'. Escobar's and his colleagues' desire for public recognition was ultimately to be their undoing, however. Apart from anything else, it alerted everyone in the country to the existence of this group of super-rich individuals—all of whom now became targets.

The first to realise this was Carlos Lehder—shot in the back as he evaded a kidnap attempt by the Colombian guerrilla movement, M-19, in late 1981. He ordered up a bunch of bodyguards and refused to leave home without them. Rodríguez Gacha was likewise held up by another terrorist group, FARC. Just a month later, on 12 November, M-19 struck again, successfully lifting Marta Nieves Ochoa—one of the five Ochoa sisters—from outside Antioquia University in Medellín. The kidnap was to affect the future of the cocaine industry, and of Colombia itself.

On the face of it, kidnapping a member of an extremely wealthy family might seem like a good idea—especially in Colombia, where kidnapping is pretty much a way of life. One has to question the judgement, though, of a Marxist group—numbering only 2,500—that kidnaps anyone so closely related to as much money and power as was Nieves. The month after she disappeared a meeting of all the major cocaine-trafficking clans was called and it was suggested that it was time to do something about the kidnapping threat. Everyone agreed.

Three weeks after Nieves' abduction, a light aircraft circled over the main football stadium in Cali, dropping leaflets on to the crowd. As the leaflets fluttered down like snow, supporters grasped at them and read them, with wide eyes. The leaflets declared that an 'emergency meeting' had been held 'a few days ago' to discuss the problem of kidnapping in Colombia; '223 businessmen' had attended, and they had agreed to co-operate to stamp out the 'common criminals and subversive elements' responsible for such acts. To this end, the 223 businessmen had formed a vigilante group, MAS (Muerte a Secuestradores—'Death to Kidnappers'), each donating $20,000 and his ten best men to fight the kidnapping curse. There was no doubt about how the antikidnap squads were to behave:

> As from this date, these individuals will be carrying out the executions of all those associated with the practice of kidnapping...kidnappers will be executed in public. They will be hanged from trees in public places or shot by firing squads. They will be duly marked with the small cross which is the symbol of our organisation—MAS.
>
> cit. *The Cocaine Wars*, Eddy et al, 1988

MAS offered a 20-million-peso ($200,000) reward to anyone giving information leading to the apprehension of a kidnapper. Such information could be handed in to any number of 'mafia bosses', all of whom, said the leaflet, were 'widely known in this country'. The leaflets made it clear that there was to be no quarter in this new conflict:

> ...those kidnappers who are arrested by police will be executed in prison; if their whereabouts cannot be established, our people will act on their colleagues or nearest relatives instead.
>
> cit. *The Cocaine Wars*, Eddy et al, 1988

MAS was as good as its word and it wasn't long before bodies began to show up all over Colombia. The nation's guerrilla groups suffered atrocious casualties. Sometimes terrorists were handed over to the police; at other times they were simply shot. In some cases it made little difference: it was rumoured that the army stood by while the Marxists were eliminated anyway. In the first six weeks over a hundred members of M-19 were rounded up—a success rate the Colombian army had never even approached since the group's foundation in 1974. M-19 might be taking prisoners; the Medellín cartel was not.

It would seem that M-19 knew what was good for them; Marta Nieves was released. According to legend, no ransom was ever paid. Certainly, old Fabio Ochoa—father of the clan—made a public statement to this effect by buying a half-million dollar thoroughbred horse, naming it 'Ransom' and displaying it in public as often as possible. In fact, the truth is more complex.

It has been alleged that the release of Marta Nieves was not the result of the MAS persecutions at all but rather was negotiated by one of the traffickers' influential new friends, Manuel Noriega (at the time head of military intelligence in Panama). According to this account, Noriega interceded between the kidnappers and the Medellín boys via another intermediary: Fidel Castro. Instead of paying a ransom, the Ochoas agreed to transport weapons from Cuba to Colombia's two main terrorist groups, M-19 and FARC, in return for amnesty from kidnapping, assistance in guarding remote jungle laboratories and permission to traffic cocaine through Cuban territory (inaccessible to American lawmen).

This account may be untrue but the fact is that from this point on we find numerous examples of the guerrillas working hand in hand with traffickers—to devastating effect. On a number of occasions caches of weapons meant for Colombia's terror organisations were discovered on ships belonging to the Medellín cartel and the cartel was later alleged to have paid M-19 to pull off their boldest and most violent gesture yet, the storming of the Colombian Palace of Justice, in 1985. Whether the Noriega–Castro connection is true or not, the formation of MAS was to scare the hell out of the United States, which became convinced that there was a new threat to democracy in South America—that of the 'narco-terrorist'. The idea of heavily armed communist insurgents busily helping themselves to wads of cocaine cash was more than most American analysts could stomach and they were to do their best to persuade the Colombian government that they constituted a threat to their national security. There was always some doubt, however, as to exactly how closely the guerrillas and the cartels were working together. In fact MAS would eventually give birth to a new paramilitary organisation called ACDEGAM that would spend the next twenty years exterminating guerrillas, sympathisers, people who looked like sympathisers—and anyone unfortunate enough to get in its way.

In terms of the cocaine trade, MAS brought together disparate groups of cocaine traffickers to iron out their differences and to work out—together—how to streamline trafficking operations. Thus 1981 is the year when crime watchers date the arrival of the Medellín 'cartel': after this point there were regular meetings between the leaders as they put their heads together to solve various problems, to fill loads, move loads, distribute them, and protect the group's interests from competitors. It has been suggested that an earlier meeting, in April 1981, was really the occasion when the traffickers decided to work together; perhaps this is correct. Frankly, we should be grateful for the report of the MAS meeting, when we bear in mind the fate of the informant who reported it to the DEA:

Before he was killed, with his hands tied behind his back with barbed wire, the man who gave us all the details [of this meeting] had his tongue cut out.

The Fix, Brian Freemantle, 1987

Whether the meeting that cemented the relationships between cartel members took place in April or November is largely academic. The end result is the same: it made Colombia's cocaine-trafficking operations considerably more efficient. According to Guy Gugliotta and Jeff Leen— authors of the definitive book on the organised cocaine trade, *Kings of Cocaine*—the syndicate shifted a total of nineteen tons of the drug in the few months either side of it.

Having tamed the terrorist movement in Colombia, confounded American law-enforcement agencies, set up their own political parties, bought up local and national elections and—in Escobar's case—been elected to parliament themselves, it seemed there was nothing these new traffickers could not do. But there was trouble on the horizon, both for the cartels and for Colombia itself.

In March 1982 a new president, Belisario Betancur, was elected. Betancur himself did not represent too much of a threat to Escobar and his boys: his main priority was making peace with the terrorist organisations and drugs didn't really feature. Unfortunately for Medellín, however, he appointed a man in his cabinet who was soon to present them with a considerable threat, and whose struggle with the cartel was to affect Colombia for years to come. His name was Rodrigo Lara Bonilla.

Then Lara Bonilla was a brilliant young politician from Neiva, 100 miles to the east of Cali. Having graduated from the University of Bogotá, he had returned home to become mayor of his hometown at the grand old age of just 23 before helping to set up a breakaway faction of the Liberal Party. When he was elected, President Betancur was compelled to select some of his cabinet from opposition parties. In August 1983 his gaze settled on the idealistic young congressman and he chose Lara Bonilla as Minister of Justice. No sooner had Bonilla assumed office than he began a campaign against government corruption, looking under all sorts of stones to see what he might find there. Lara Bonilla was ahead of his time in that, unlike most Colombians, he recognised the damage that all the behind-the-scenes-payments were doing. The way he saw it, they were undermining the very democracy of the country. He was right. Many of his colleagues didn't see it this way, however, and they were keen that this ambitious young minister stop his investigations before he discovered anything too embarrassing.

At this point Pablo Escobar's congressional partner, Jairo Ortega, agreed that there was indeed a lot of drug money knocking about: why, only the other day—he told Congress—he had come across a case involving the transfer of a large sum of money to the election campaign of a minister by the name of Rodrigo Lara Bonilla. According to Ortega, Lara had received a cheque for a million pesos from a known trafficker. Ortega then played Congress a tape recording of Lara apparently thanking the trafficker on the telephone. It looked like Lara Bonilla was about to become the youngest former Minister of Justice in Colombian history. He had been in office just a fortnight.

He was built of sterner stuff, however. 'Ah,' he is supposed to have said. 'So now the birds are shooting at the guns.' He rallied to protect himself, pronouncing the tape a fake. But the accusation rankled. To clear his name he now began a crusade against the traffickers. It was eventually to bring the traffickers—and Lara himself—to their knees, and Colombia to the verge of civil war.

Lara Bonilla started off by investigating the backgrounds of the people he saw as being his accusers: instead of looking at who might have received narco-money, he suggested, perhaps the Colombian people would be interested to know where all this money had come from in the first place? What about Ortega's congressional partner, Pablo Escobar, for example? Conveniently, at just this point a television documentary, made by ABC News, with DEA assistance, was broadcast in the United States. In it some of Colombia's biggest traffickers were named, including Pablo Escobar. Lara Bonilla had tapes made and showed it to his fellow congressmen. The tapes shocked Colombia: prior to the film traffickers had been seen as rough, wild outlaws, yet here was one who happened to be a member of Congress. Lara revealed that Escobar was in fact a major cocaine trafficker and that he had been a leading light behind the MAS persecutions. Escobar threatened to take him to court and demanded proof. Lara went in search of it and, having found it, began publicly naming names. In August the country's leading newspaper, *El Espectador*, conveniently rediscovered all the papers pertaining to Escobar's 1976 arrest and stuck them on the front page. Escobar was so concerned that he dispatched an army of his boys at daybreak in an attempt to buy up every copy of the paper before anyone else could read it. It didn't make much difference: the damage was done.

In the meantime Lara looked into air transportation: why did all these

Medellín businessmen need so many aeroplanes, anyway? He revoked the permits of a number of traffickers' aircraft. In September, Escobar's 1976 cocaine arrest case was reopened. It soon emerged that the witnesses and arresting officers had been killed and that nine separate Medellín judges had refused to take the case following death threats. The judge assigned to reopen it was then murdered. Then the 1974 car-theft case resurfaced and that, too, was published in the newspapers. Escobar, disgraced, was forced to resign his seat in congress. It became clear to Colombia that, far from being a '*paisa* Robin Hood', Escobar was just a hood—full stop.

The next month Lara announced that six of the leading fourteen Colombian soccer teams were owned by drug traffickers, naming three in particular: Bogotá Millionarios (owned by the Rodríguez Gacha family), Medellín Atletico Nacional (owned by Hernán Botero Moreno) and Cali America (owned by the Rodríguez Orejuela family). The shock this news generated around football-mad Colombia was considerable: imagine if the Home Office announced that Manchester United, Liverpool and Aston Villa were all owned by East End crime syndicates. Lara also announced that a number of other sports, including cycling, boxing and motor racing, were pretty much owned by the cartels, too.

Lara Bonilla got personal. He began looking into Escobar's ranch, discovering that there were irregularities in the documents he had used to import his exotic animals, then took the animals away and slapped a law suit on him. For good measure, he filed a suit against the Ochoas for illegally importing thoroughbred bulls. Lara was convinced that the more legal problems he could lay into the laps of the traffickers, the less likely they were to be able to fight them. He was right.

At this stage Lara Bonilla was against the one thing the traffickers feared most: extradition. When the question of Escobar's extradition to the United States was raised, he argued against it. The way he saw it, Escobar was a matter for Colombian, not American, justice. When a leading politician lobbying for Escobar's extradition was murdered, however, he changed his tune:

> The more I learn, the more I know of the damage that the narcos are causing this country. I will never again refuse the extradition of one of these dogs. So long as Colombian judges fear drug traffickers, the narcos will only fear judges in the United States.

> *cit. Whitewash*, Simon Strong, 1995

While Lara looked as if he had the upper hand, Escobar was watching him closely. It soon became clear to the minister that he was being shadowed. On occasion he would pick up the telephone to hear recordings of his own conversations played back to him: not only were his phones being tapped but Escobar wanted him to know that they were tapped. Lara received first offers of money to stop his investigations, then death threats. He was having none of it, however, and authorised the chief of police, an upright officer by the name of Jaime Ramirez Gomez, to hit cocaine laboratories all over the country as hard as possible.

It was this move that was ultimately to prove the undoing of Rodrigo Lara Bonilla. And Jaime Ramirez, for that matter. Because deep in the Colombian jungle, 480 kilometres to the south of Bogotá, lay a trafficking secret so momentous that Lara and Ramirez's discovery of it was to prove the signature on their death warrants. The story behind the discovery of this secret, however, begins not in Colombia but 3,000 miles to the north, in Chicago.

In September 1983 a Colombian businessman by the name of Francisco Torres approached the JT Baker Chemical Supply Company in Phillipsburg, New Jersey, to place an order. What he wanted, he said, was 1,300 drums of anhydrous ethyl ether. Officials at JT Baker were intrigued: not only was this an extraordinary amount of the chemical (legitimate orders were usually in the region of five drums) but Torres insisted on paying the $280,000 transaction in cash. JT Baker smelled a rat, refused to supply Torres and sent him packing. A fortnight later, however, Torres received a call from another chemicals company called North Central Industrial Chemicals (NCIC) based in Chicago. North Central had heard on the grapevine that he was looking for a large quantity of ethyl ether, no questions asked. This was the kind of thing they did all the time. Torres travelled up to meet the men at North Central, two budding chemists named Mel Schabilion and Harry Fullett, and the deal was done. Within a month the first shipment—a container-load of 55-gallon drums incorrectly labelled 'ethyl formate'—was on its way down to Colombia.

Of course, Frank Torres was not a legitimate chemicals trader. He was a representative of the Medellín cartel and the ether was going to be used for cocaine production. The NCIC chemists might have been pissed off at this but then they, too, had not been entirely honest in the transaction: they weren't chemicals traders, either. They were undercover DEA agents. Not only that but in an inspired move, before they had dispatched the barrels to Colombia, they had concealed satellite beacons inside two of them that would enable the DEA—via their friends at the National Security Agency (NSA)—to pinpoint exactly where the ether was going, and thus where the cocaine was being manufactured. Torres's shipment was a Trojan horse.

Over the next two months NSA officials watched with bated breath as the ether shipment snaked its way down to South America—to the Ochoas' ranch outside Medellín—then continued into the jungle until it came to a stop deep in Caquetá province. The NSA now used a few sneaky bits of kit to see what was going on there. Whatever was going on in the jungle, they concluded, couldn't possibly be legitimate. For a start, satellite pictures revealed an immaculate 1,000-metre airstrip servicing no towns, in the middle of nowhere. Their Signals Intelligence kit picked up huge amounts of radio traffic emanating from the jungle—240 kilometres away from the nearest road.

When Justice Minister Lara Bonilla was informed of this development, he authorised Jaime Ramirez to pay the jungle site a little visit. Ramirez knew that an undercover operation of this size was bound to be compromised, so he made sure that no one on the raid itself knew what was happening, where they were going or when—until they were all safely in helicopters and airborne. Despite these efforts the traffickers managed to get wind of the fact that something was going down—but they weren't sure exactly what.

The day before the raid departed, Ramirez's brother was visited by a group of mysterious businessmen who told him that there was $3 million in cash in it for him if he could get his brother to call off whatever he was planning. (After the raid Ramirez located the source of the leak and sacked him; the informant was found a fortnight later burned, mutilated and very dead.)

On 10 March 1984 two helicopters, a Colombian SWAT team and a fixed-wing aircraft containing another forty-plus men from the antinarcotics branch of the Colombian National Police touched down on the clandestine airstrip. They exchanged fire with a number of men who were later revealed to have been members of the guerrilla group, FARC, before the guards ran off into the jungle. Then, left alone to the place, they began to look around. It was immediately clear that they had hit the jackpot. Named Tranquilandia, the site was pretty similar to other clandestine cocaine laboratories, except in scale. No one had ever seen anything quite like this before: there were separate dormitories for pilots, guards and chemists. There was a fully equipped kitchen capable of cooking for thirty people at a time. There were showers, flushing toilets and mains electricity. There were thousands of drums of chemicals needed to purify cocaine and an industrial sized cocaine-drying apparatus. An abandoned logbook indicated that the first two months of 1984 had seen over 15 tons of cocaine paste pass through Tranquilandia, much of it, according to a separate pile of receipts, from Roberto Suárez in Bolivia.

Most intriguingly, there was a pilot's notebook containing a hand-sketched diagram covered with numbers. It turned out to be a map of other cocaine laboratories in the region, and the radio frequencies on which they could be contacted. Ramirez's team hopped back into their helicopters and began to explore.

The next day they discovered another lab, named Cocalandia. Just outside the camp was a ton of cocaine in watertight containers. Then they found Cocalandia 2—with 500 kilos. On 14 March they came across Tranquilandia 2—complete with 4 tons. The next day they hit El Diamante, with half a ton. The raids went on and on as the Colombian police hit lab after lab, uncovering hidden stashes of guns, chemicals, planes and all sorts of other goodies. Everything was burned. Within a fortnight five airstrips, seven planes, nine conversion laboratories, 12,000 drums of chemicals, 1,500 kilograms of cocaine base and 8,500 kilograms of pure cocaine—with an estimated value of well over a billion US dollars—were gone. It was the biggest cocaine bust in the history of the world.

And someone was going to have to pay for it.

The assassination of Rodrigo Lara Bonilla was planned at the house of Escobar's brother-in-law, Gustavo Restropo. The hit, which was later revealed to have cost in the region of $500,000, was picked up by one of Escobar's private armies, Los Quesitos, and it was rumoured that a number of traffickers had paid for it—so that all would be equally implicated in the crime. Time was running out for Colombia's crusading Minister of Justice.

Lara was well aware of the fact that there was a contract out on his life but thought that his personal security team could handle it. 'I am a dangerous minister for those who act outside the law!' he joked. 'I only hope that they don't take me by surprise.'

As time went by, however, it became clear that the Colombian security forces could not guarantee his safety. On 30 April he telephoned the US ambassador to Colombia, Lewis Tambs, and told him that he had decided to leave the country to take up the position of ambassador to Czechoslovakia.

Behind the Iron Curtain, he figured, he would be safe. But he was worried: the hit men were so close, he said, that he might not last until his departure. He asked Tambs if he could be protected in the United States. Tambs agreed and it was decided to send Lara to a safe house in Texas used for snitches in the federal witness-protection programme. But it was already too late. Lara's friend, journalist Fabio Castillo, recalled that last weekend:

> [Lara] called me and asked me to write an article 'about what I am really doing here at the Ministry of Justice. I don't want to say anything about trafficking but about the real things we are doing here.' So I said OK. The article went out on Saturday the 28th and he called me the next Monday, the 30th. 'Thanks a lot, Fabio, that's great!' he said. 'I am going to be killed today but that article can be my will for the Justice Department.' Then he played me over the phone a tape of one of the fifty death threats he had received that morning. It was only 10 a.m. 'Listen to this,' he said: 'Aaah, you son of a bitch, we're going to kill you today...!' Then he gave me the private number of the phone in his car. He said 'If I don't answer this phone it will be because I am dead.'

That afternoon two young Envigado boys, Ivan Dario Guisado and Byron Velasquez, psyched each other up. They were about to make $20,000 each—more money than they had ever seen before—for just a few seconds' work. Like most of Escobar's *sicarios*, they were profoundly religious and had visited the shrine of Maria Auxiliadora in Sabaneta, just outside Medellín to say a quick prayer before leaving. Then they hopped on to a new Yamaha and set off to track down Lara Bonilla.

They found his white Mercedes stuck in traffic to the north of Bogotá. After Guisado, riding pillion, had signalled that he was ready, Velasquez accelerated towards the car and pulled the bike up until it was parallel with the right rear wing. He then held it steady as Guisado pulled out a MAC-10 machine pistol from beneath his jacket and emptied the magazine into the back seat. Lara's bodyguards opened fire on the motorcycle as it sped away, hitting Velasquez in the arm and killing Guisado outright. The bike collapsed from beneath them and they slid along the road. The security contingent had reacted as fast as they could but it wasn't fast enough: in the back of the Mercedes Lara Bonilla had been hit seven times, in the arm, neck, chest and head. Fabio Castillo recalls:

So after that [phonecall] I worked for a while in the Supreme Court and there was a little cafeteria there and I was having a coffee there with four or five friends and the owner of the café ran up and said, 'There has been an attempt on the life of Rodrigo Lara!' I'm like, '*What*?' I ran straight to the telephone and I dialled the number he had given me. No one answered.

The greatest antidrug crusader Colombia had ever known was gone. Examination of the dead killer later revealed that he had tucked a picture of the Virgin Mary into his underpants for good luck.

News of Lara Bonilla's death was greeted with a stunned silence from the Colombian people. At 3 a.m., however, President Betancur addressed the country on national radio. He announced that drugs were 'the most serious problem that Colombia has had in its history', and that the country was now involved in a 'war without quarter' against drug traffickers. He did not state, exactly, what form this war was going to take.

Lara Bonilla's memorial service was held at the National Cathedral in the Plaza Bolivar. The square outside the building thronged with mourners who wept for the young minister, proclaiming, 'Rodrigo! We love you!' President Betancur made a eulogy for the young minister, before dropping a bombshell into the proceedings:

Stop! Enemies of humanity! Colombia will hand over criminals...wanted in other countries so that they may be punished as an example.

cit. Desperados, Shannon, 1988

At the announcement of the reinstitution of extradition, the congregation rose to its feet and applauded.

The idea of extraditing criminals to the United States had been anathema to most Colombians. The way they saw it, not only was cocaine fundamentally an American problem, but the Americans spent far too much time meddling in South American politics. And what was so wrong with the Colombian legal system anyway? Was it really so inadequate? Thus the reaction to Betancur's announcement at Lara's memorial service marked a turning point in Colombian consciousness: the moment when people realised that cocaine was not simply a gringo problem but everyone's problem. If the cartels were capable of assassinating the Minister of Justice, what *weren't* they capable of?

For the traffickers, meanwhile, it also marked a turning point. Extradition was the one thing that they genuinely feared. The idea of a jail in Colombia wasn't so bad: guards could be bribed, judges could be intimidated, anything could be arranged to go wrong. They were safe in Colombia. But in the United States things were different. No one had yet managed to bribe their way out of jail there. And the sentences were barbaric. Thus Betancur's reintroduction of extradition was a very important event for everyone concerned with cocaine because the traffickers were willing to fight—with everything they had—against it. While Colombia thought it had declared 'war without quarter' on the cocaine bosses, in fact the cartels were about to declare war on Colombia itself. The results would be tragic.

It wasn't only in Colombia that eyes were beginning to open about the true extent of the cocaine problem. In America, eyes were opening wide, too. Just 220 miles from the Florida coast, events had been taking place that revealed that it was not only tinpot Latin American countries that could be corrupted by cocaine. At the heart of these events was our old friend Carlos Lehder.

Lehder had been having a ball on Norman's Cay. When he had first moved in, Escobar had flown out to inspect his operation, given it the thumbs-up and decided that he was the right kind of man to handle his transportation arrangements. Carlos had become the transportation guru of the Medellín cartel. From his hideaway in the Bahamas he had been shifting more cocaine into the United States than anyone had ever managed. But he hadn't been doing it quietly. It wasn't long before law-enforcement officials got wind of the strange goings-on in the island. DEA agent, Gene Francar, recalls:

> He was trying to run people off Norman's Cay. The problem was that anyone who's got a house there is usually fairly wealthy and there were a couple that had connections—in the US government and so forth—that they could call. So we start getting these phonecalls: 'there's something wrong over there. So-and-so, who is a friend of so-and so, has said that he is being threatened by guys with M16s and told that he has to get off the island. There's something going on'. That got everybody kind of interested.

By the spring of 1979 the Bahamian police were under no illusions about what was going on there. Assistant Police Commissioner Lawrence Major was keen to raid the island, warning the government that the drug-smuggling problem was so serious in the Bahamas that 'if present and efficient action is not taken now the security of our nation will be at stake'.

In June 1979 one of the last inhabitants to leave, Richard Novak, had paid a visit to the US embassy in Nassau and showed them photographs of Lehder and his boys. The embassy had passed them on to the DEA. Now people really began asking questions: what was going on at Norman's Cay?

The next month the leader of the Bahamas' opposition party, Normon Solomon, paid Norman's Cay a visit, only to be muscled off the island by a group of Lehder's heavies. He returned to Nassau, reported that there was some seriously strange stuff going on and suggested that the government do something about it. For his efforts, his house and his car were bombed. After further prodding, the Bahamian police lumbered into action and decided to launch a raid. Codenamed Operation Raccoon, it was a farce. The Bahamian police arrived on the morning of 14 September, only to find Lehder on his boat, calmly steering it into the shallowest part of the lagoon where he knew they could not follow him and watched, aghast, as he proceeded to empty a number of sacks of white powder into the water. He then waved at them and came over to introduce himself. Not surprisingly, after this performance, when the police searched the place, it was clean of cocaine. There was a small arsenal of weapons, however, which was confiscated. All together, thirty inhabitants were taken back to Nassau and locked up for the night. Lehder was not one of them. In fact, he was the only one *not* taken in.

He may have got away with it this time but the Bahamians were none too pleased with Lehder. In December, three months after the failure of Operation Raccoon, he was officially told to get off the island. He didn't. Again, nothing was done and the cocaine pipeline continued to flow. In July the next year he created another stir when a pleasure yacht, *Kalia III*, was spotted, apparently in trouble, in the vicinity of Norman's Cay. On inspection *Kalia III* turned out to be abandoned, the decks of the boat awash with blood, the bulkheads ripped to pieces by shotgun blasts. Bobbing along in the painter behind the yacht lay a mangled corpse. The discoverers of this macabre scene steamed off to Nassau, where they called the police. By the time they arrived to check it out, however, the body was gone. The boat was later revealed to have belonged to a retired Florida couple who were never heard of again. Although nothing was ever proved, it was pretty obvious that this unfortunate couple had strayed too close to the island and seen something Lehder didn't want them to see.

Four months later another raid, Operation David, was launched against Norman's Cay. This time, however, Lehder had been tipped off in advance and the place was clean as a whistle. The cocaine continued to flow.

The next year, under increasing pressure to do something about this, the Bahamian police stationed a permanent detail of policemen on Norman's Cay. When one of the island's former inhabitants heard about this he figured that the place was probably safe again and returned, only to find the police assisting Lehder's boys unloading a cocaine shipment before pushing the planes into one of the hangars for them.

By 1982, however, when the DEA filed for extradition, even Lehder began to feel the heat: he was way too close to the United States for his liking. In a typically brazen move, he contacted the agency and offered to sell the island to them at the knock-down price of $5 million—on the condition that they drop all charges. When his offer was not accepted, he pulled a schoolboyish act of defiance: on 10 July, the Bahamas' ninth anniversary of independence, there was a huge street party in Nassau. As the crowds partied in the streets, they were disturbed by the hum of a light aircraft. The plane circled over the carnival, dropping leaflets on to the crowd. The leaflets read DEA GO HOME. No one would have paid much attention but for the fact that stapled to the back of many of them were pristine $100 bills.

Lehder was eventually driven out of Norman's Cay in August 1984. He had been there for seven years, shipping cocaine more or less continuously. The question now arose: how could he have got away with this? The answer was simple—Lehder had bought his way into the government. George Jung's first pilot, Barry Kane, was an attorney. He had introduced Carlos to a crooked Bahamian lawyer called Nigel Bowe, who had offered his services as a middleman, making payoffs to high-ranking Bahamian officials to ensure that the Norman's Cay operation was not touched. He had also introduced Carlos to a notorious financial swindler called Robert Vesco. Vesco was interested in getting into the cocaine business; Lehder was interested in getting into the world of finance. They traded. Vesco bought an island a couple of miles away from Norman's Cay and Carlos showed him the ropes. In return, Vesco introduced Carlos to a number of crooked Bahamian civil servants who could make sure that the police never got too close to him. When George Jung had first flown to Norman's Cay in 1977, Lehder had introduced him to Vesco, commenting, 'This guy is getting us the prime minister of the Bahamas.'

The prime minister of the Bahamas at the time was Sir Lynden Oscar

Pindling, a British-educated lawyer. Pindling had been in office since 1967, and had been responsible for Bahamian independence in 1973. Although he denied it vociferously, as the Bahamian police repeatedly failed to apprehend Lehder, it began to look as if Pindling was crooked. In 1984 a Royal Commission of Enquiry was launched to establish the truth. Its findings were disturbing.

For a start there were the two failed raids on Norman's Cay, Operation Raccoon and Operation David. In the second Lehder had clearly been tipped off and given time to clean the place up, but nothing could be proved. In the first, circumstances were much more fishy. The raid had been postponed until the man who had called it—Assistant Police Commissioner Lawrence Major—was not available to take part. It was led by another assistant commissioner, Howard Smith. Under questioning, Smith stated rather implausibly that the reason he had not apprehended Lehder was that he had been unaware that he was the target of the raid. But, even assuming that this was true (and it certainly sounded as if it wasn't), how could Smith, leader of a hundred-man-strong police raid, watch Lehder methodically dump what must surely have been cocaine into the sea, then manage to pick up every single person on the island apart from him? It later turned out that the reason Smith had not touched Lehder was that he had been taken aside and handed a black plastic bin liner containing over $80,000 in cash.

It got worse. Not only had Smith failed to pick up Lehder but he had also failed to take into custody a notebook one of his men had found detailing protection bribes to 'top government ministers'. He later said that he had not bothered to take it in because he didn't think it was 'relevant'. The commission concluded that,

> Lehder did bribe the police to ensure his freedom, and we find that there must have been complicity on the part of Assistant Commissioner Smith and other senior police officers.
>
> *cit. Kings of Cocaine*, Gugliotta and Leen, 1989

But the corruption went higher than Smith. A total of twelve traffickers testified to the effect that top officials in Pindling's cabinet received payoffs to make sure the police looked the other way whenever Lehder's name came up. One trafficker alleged that he had specifically made repeated payoffs to the Bahamas' Minister for Agriculture, George Smith. When asked where the money was going, Smith allegedly said, 'I'm taking it to the PM.' The Commission did not manage to verify this but did prove that Smith had received a new BMW as a present from Lehder at the time when this exchange was alleged to have taken place. Smith resigned.

The accusations went further. One trafficker, Timothy Minnig, told the commission that he had seen Prime Minister Pindling and Lehder talking together on Norman's Cay. Pindling denied this but did admit that he had visited the island at about this time to check out the situation—because he had noticed a lot of aerials and fancy radio equipment there and been suspicious. When he got back to Nassau, he said, he had reported the strange things he had seen to Assistant Commissioner Major. Only, he said, Major had not done anything about it. This was also somewhat unlikely—after all, Major was the very man who had, three months earlier, warned that Norman's Cay was occupied by 'armed foreign criminals'. It was alleged that Lehder paid Pindling, through Bowe, between $80,000 and $100,000 per month to ensure his immunity. Another informant testified that he had seen Pindling on Norman's Cay numerous times, partying as if there were no tomorrow. He was challenged to prove this and is supposed to have come up with three photographs of the prime minister, surrounded by scantily clad women, piles of white powder on the table in front of him. No sooner had these pictures emerged than they vanished off the face of the earth. At least one DEA agent has gone on record to the effect that he saw them.

The Royal Commission found that Pindling's outgoings far exceeded his legitimate income, and that the PM had received well over $2.5 million in undisclosed 'gifts' in the exact period when Lehder was in residence at Norman's Cay. Because there were no receipts for most of these 'gifts', however, it was forced to conclude that there was no evidence that he had directly taken any drug money. Opposition politicians chose to see it the other way around: that Pindling had received a vast amount of cash from *somewhere* and that he had no receipts to prove that it had *not* come from drug money. The investigation launched a million smear campaigns. 'Wanted' posters sprang up all over the Bahamas. THE CHIEF IS A THIEF, ran the slogan. Allegations that Pindling had been involved with Lehder continued to dog his administration until he left office in 1992. At one point he was so concerned that he took out full-page advertisements in US newspapers 'to set the record straight'. No one believed him.

Twenty years on, Bahamians are keen to point out that 'nothing was proved'. When pushed, however, most agree that Pindling took bungs from Lehder. On my way back through Nassau after flying out to Norman's Cay my taxi driver took a route along Skyline Drive, the wealthiest residential street in Nassau. He then pulled over and pointed out Pindling's former residence—a vast Caribbean hideaway set in lush gardens with 125 rooms. The house had recently been sold for somewhere in the region of $2.5 million: not bad for a civil servant's salary. Pindling himself had moved upmarket, to Lyford Cay, the most exclusive private island in the Bahamas and home of, among others, Sean Connery. His new home, my driver assured me, was worth $4 million: again, not bad for a civil servant's salary. I asked the driver whether it concerned him that this house may have been bought with cocaine money. He clunked the car back into gear: 'Look around you!' he said. '*All* these houses were made with cocaine money!' Then, laughing, he dumped the handbrake and pulled out into the traffic.

Back in the United States a former (senior) DEA agent who had been stationed in the Bahamas later explained the situation to me: 'Pindling was a—yeah. He *should* be in jail. I think the Bahamians know it but he is also the father of Bahamian independence. And he's an old man. So what can you do?'

Lehder was not the only trafficker operating in the Bahamas. He was simply the most brazen. In fact the islands had been a transshipment point for South American marijuana ever since independence in 1973. Within a decade there was tons of it around. In 1980 Assistant Commissioner Lawrence Major found a pile of marijuana so large on the island of Black Rock that he decided that it was unfeasible to weigh it and instead paced it out. The stash stood nearly 2 metres high and, when he had finished pacing out its length, turned out to be about 3 kilometres long.

The vast increase in drugs in the Caribbean was to lead to a decrease in their price, and thus a corresponding increase in their consumption by locals. In the case of marijuana, the results were not too serious. In the case of cocaine, however, they were to prove extremely serious. In the late 1970s this was to have an effect that no one had predicted and was to lead to the greatest drug hype the world had ever seen.

12 Crack (Man Bites Dog)

I was sitting in the lobby of my hotel in Nassau when Doctor Humblestone ambled in. Watching him cross the road, I wasn't sure whether this was actually him or some lost windsurfing instructor: clad in pedal pushers, a baggy cream-coloured shirt, sandals and 1960s goggle shades, he looked far too laid back to be a real doctor. But it was him all right. Originally I had suggested that we meet in a local restaurant for dinner but this proved impossible—he played the bongos in a local band and tonight they were gigging at the Marriott on Coral Beach. For a doctor, I concluded, Humblestone was way cool.

We shook hands and I proposed that we grab a coffee in the hotel restaurant, but he was having none of it. He wanted to go to the beach. We repaired there for the interview instead, and, perched on a sun lounger in the shade, Humblestone told me about drug abuse in the Bahamas.

In the 1960s, he said, there was very little drug taking in the Caribbean. In 1967 Nassau's psychiatric clinic, Sandilands, where he was the head of psychiatry, was the first place in the Bahamas to establish an inpatient substance abuse unit: twenty beds for chronic alcoholics. While alcoholism was a worry, however, no other drugs were available: 'There was a little grass going around,' he told me, 'but nothing serious. Certainly no intravenous drug use. No heroin. No cocaine—or, if there was any, we didn't see it.' However, in the late 1970s, thanks to the efforts of Lehder and his cohorts, drugs began to show up in the most unexpected places.

'The Bahamas became a major transshipment point,' he told me. 'Cocaine was being moved in bulk. It was all over the place—in some cases it was literally dropping from the skies. Every now and then shipments would wash up on the beach. The locals would have huge cocaine parties until it ran out.'

It sounded unbelievable—mislaid cocaine shipments being shared out among the laid-back Nassau population—but it was true. Even today, bales of illicit drugs still wash up on the beach from time to time and fishermen catch them in their nets so often that they name them after a local fish: if you snag a bale, they say, you have caught yourself a 'square grouper'. While the occasional package of lost cocaine wasn't really a serious problem, however, by the end of the 1970s there was so much cocaine about that locals handling it for the traffickers would either steal or buy small amounts—and sell it to their mates on the street. Bahamians started getting into trouble with the drug and Humblestone began having patients referred to him for treatment. These individuals, admitted to Sandilands as psychotic, were obviously using something pretty powerful.

'They had a distinctive look to them: just as an alcoholic had a certain look to him, you could recognise these guys easily. Their skin had a dull, greyish hue. Frequently they were terribly underweight. Soon we started seeing people. A lot of people.' When asked what they were taking, Humblestone's patients admitted to using cocaine. 'Only they weren't snorting it,' he says. 'They were *smoking* it.'

Humblestone put me in touch with his successor at Sandilands, another psychiatrist called Nelson Clarke. Clarke told me about his first brush with cocaine smoking:

> The first case of cocaine I saw was in 1979. It was a taxi driver admitted with some sort of psychosis. Very paranoid. And he admitted that it was cocaine. The only reason I remember it is that it was a novelty: cocaine and psychosis. I had never seen a patient addicted to cocaine at this point. Shortly after that, perhaps two to three months, there was another case. I don't remember what he did for a living. I think he was unemployed. Maybe he was a dealer. He came in with intense hallucinations: bugs under the skin, scratching. We admitted him and he told us what had done this: cocaine smoking. When I saw this guy I thought, This is really going to take off.

Although they didn't know it at the time, Humblestone and Clarke were the first to notice the arrival of cocaine smoking in the Bahamas. And the Bahamas was the first place to experience an epidemic of what would later be termed 'crack'.

The idea of smoking cocaine was not new: as far back as 1886, Parke, Davis had marketed coca cigars. It had never caught on, however, owing to a quirk of the drug's chemistry. Cocaine hydrochloride—the form in which it is usually taken—is highly sensitive to heat. In fact, when burned, it destabilises completely, so placing a line of coke into a cigarette paper and attempting to smoke it pretty much ensures that you are simply burning money. In order to smoke it, the cocaine must be chemically changed into a form that vaporises rather than degrades when heated. Clearly, noted Humblestone and Clarke in 1979, such a form had been discovered.

Actually the discovery was not new. People had been smoking cocaine for years in South America. An early stage in the extraction of the drug from coca leaves involves its transformation into a paste called *pasta basica*, commonly known as *pasta*, *bazuko* or *basé*. This off-white sludgy substance is the standard currency of the cocaine trade: as Henry Hurd Rusby had discovered, it is easy to make, easy to transport, and just a couple of steps away from pure cocaine hydrochloride. What Rusby had not noted, however, was that *basé* could be smoked. It could be smoked because, prior to refining, *basé* vaporises nicely when heated. South Americans in the cocaine industry took to scraping up small amounts of *basé* and stuffing it into cigarettes. The result was a fast, intense rush. At this stage, however, no one smoked paste except those involved in cocaine production. It was a habit of the trade. But, with a high this intense, it was bound to catch on sooner or later.

At some point in the early 1970s someone in North America realised the potential of smoking cocaine. Although no one has ever managed to track down the guy responsible, the sequence of events that took place has been reconstructed by a professor at the University of California, Los Angeles (UCLA), Ron Siegel. Siegel, the world's foremost expert on the history of the science of cocaine, spent many years logging the evolution of crack way back before anyone had even heard the word 'crack'. In 1982 he published the definitive account in *The Journal of Psychedelic Drugs*. It has yet to be bettered.

The way Siegel tells it, at some point in the early 1970s, possibly 1970 itself, an American cocaine trafficker visited Peru to check up on production. While down there he noticed that some of the workers were smoking something they called 'basé'. He tried some and was bowled over by the results. Once back in the United States, he tried smoking cocaine the way he had seen it done in Peru. But there was a problem. Cocaine hydrochloride didn't smoke right.

Siegel speculates that this guy called a friend who knew something about chemistry to ask why it didn't smoke right, telling him that he was looking for a cocaine derivative that the Peruvians had called 'basé'.

Could the chemist help him to make some? Together they looked up the word 'base' in a chemistry encyclopedia and realised that cocaine hydrochloride was a salt but that it could be converted into a basic—or 'base'—form quite easily by removing the hydrochloride molecule. Presumably, they figured, that form was what the traffickers in South America had been smoking—hence their name for it, '*basé*'. In order to convert the cocaine salt into a base it was only necessary to add a strong alkali, dissolve the result in a powerful solvent such as ether and allow the cocaine to crystallise out. They tried it. It worked. Because the process involved releasing the cocaine base from cocaine hydrochloride, they called it 'freeing the base'—or 'freebasing'.

In fact these guys had got it all wrong. The growers in South America had been smoking a crude mixture of cocaine compounds that included cocaine sulphate. '*Basé*' was just their name for it. Instead of crude, contaminated cocaine sulphate, the Americans found themselves smoking pure cocaine base. As Siegel says, 'They were smoking something that no one on the planet had ever smoked before.' It was extraordinarily powerful. At the time, of course, cocaine was so rare and expensive that freebasing was slow to catch on. Even regular cocaine was rare in the early 1970s. But, once the market had picked up and the price began to drop, more and more people tried it.

Initially, freebasing was a great secret. It required a fair amount of good-quality cocaine—which precluded most of the population from trying it—and also some knowledge of chemistry and a few pieces of apparatus (beakers, measuring flasks and solvents). Also, it was in the interests of those who knew how to convert cocaine into freebase not to spread it around too much. Dealers who knew the secret went into the freebase business, hiring themselves out as 'chemists', showing up at the kind of parties where there would be a lot of coke (in the early stages, these were exclusively the preserve of pop stars and traffickers) and offering to cook up freebase in return for their own personal use of it. Marijuana trafficker Allen Long recalled how he was accosted by one of these characters in New York. Because he was making regular flights to Colombia, he always picked up a little cocaine to bring back for his own personal use.

It was at a party in New York and I had the coke—because I was picking it up for two dollars a gram, you know. So I had some and I just dumped it on to the table and I was doing this line and some guy said to me, 'You know, you're wasting that coke.' And I'm, like, 'Huh?' And he said, 'You should do

Above The pre-cocaine coca industry: Bolivian women gathering the leaves of *Erythroxylum coca* in 1867 (The Wellcome Library, London) and (*inset*) an early botanical study of the plant (Mary Evans Picture Library)
Below Bolivia, one hundred years later. Not much has changed, has it? (Carlos Reyes-Manzo/Andes Picture Library)

Left Freud and Martha on their engagement, 1884 (Mary Evans Picture Library)

Below The first cocaine addict? Freud's friend, Ernst von Fleischl-Marxow. (Mary Evans Picture Library)

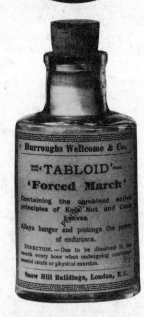

Above One of a myriad of Vin Mariani imitations, as advertised in the *British Medical Journal* (The Wellcome Library, London)

Above As used by Ernest Shackleton in 1909: Forced March cocaine tablets — manufactured, appropriately, in 'Snow Hill Buildings' (The Wellcome Library, London)

Right Testament to the European cocaine problem, a 1933 edition of *Police* magazine warns against *'Les Pourvoyeurs de Coco.'* Bizarrely, the woman on the cover appears to be smoking the drug. (Mary Evans Picture Library)

Left In Germany cocaine use was seen as a joke as late as 1922. (Mary Evans Picture Library)

Above 'I mean, fucking crazy!' George Jung at home, Otisville, 2000.

Above Carlos Lehder on a bad day. (Rex Features)

Above The remains of the customs building, Norman's Cay, 2000

Above 'What did you expect? Fangs?' Jorge and Juan David Ochoa, Medellín, 2000

Right Pablo Escobar in 1984. At this stage he was making over a million dollars per day. (Associated Press)

Left A miner chewing coca at Potosi (Carlos Reyes-Manzo/Andes Picture Library)

Right Peru 2000: the villagers of San Jorge with their crops. Moises kneels, centre, with a bale of dead coca.

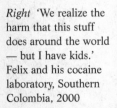

Right 'We realize the harm that this stuff does around the world — but I have kids.' Felix and his cocaine laboratory, Southern Colombia, 2000

Above The locals call it seca-seca ('dry-dry'). Scientists have another name for it: *Fusarium oxysporum.* Tingo Maria, Peru, 2000

Right Villains or victims? Inmates at the UMOPAR jail, Villa Tunari, Bolivia, 2000. The little girl is five years old.

Left White October? The cocaine submarine, Colombia, 2000. 'There is little doubt,' wrote the *Independent,* 'that it would have carried torpedoes.'

Below In Mexico, even when you win, you lose. Ten tons of cocaine awaiting destruction in 1997. (Associated Press)

Bottom 'The war goes on.' Colombia, 2000 (Associated Press)

this'—and he just took the cocaine to the kitchen and he made some base and we started to smoke it...He just did it in the kitchen. He called it freebase.

Soon it became obvious that there wasn't much of a secret to making freebase after all. The process required no understanding of chemistry whatsoever: it could be learned by rote. Pretty soon, alternative handbooks to cocaine began to appear in head shops across the United States describing how wonderful freebasing made you feel. Some of them instructed the reader how to make freebase. One 1979 manual I found in the Drugscope library in London, called *Attention Coke Lovers! Freebase = the best thing since sex!*, talked the reader through the process step by step, concluding that freebase is 'considerably less harmful, physically, than regular cocaine in any quantity'. This was a common misconception: at this point it was thought that the only risk of cocaine abuse was damage to the mucous membranes. Smoking seemed to be a way of avoiding even that. By the late 1970s, head shops across the States were selling all sorts of paraphernalia for making, and taking, freebase, from special pipes in which to smoke it to extraction kits that came complete with instructions and all the correct solvents. Siegel estimates that 300,000 freebase kits had been sold by 1980.

There was a problem with freebasing. The rush induced by smoking cocaine was extremely intense but it was matched by the brevity of the high. This served to make it considerably more addictive. Freebasers began behaving strangely, erratically, as they tried to get hold of more of the drug. Long explains:

> One of the habits of freebasers is that they start looking at the floor all the time, looking for spare little bits of freebase. Even if they're talking to you, all the time they're looking at the floor. It's strange but everyone does it. I once slapped a friend because of it. I was talking and he was looking around and I said, 'Stop that. Look at me,' and he went, 'Yeah, yeah,' and I said, 'If you don't look at me, I'm going to slap you.' And he went, 'Yeah' and was just looking all around the floor for these pieces of base. And so I slapped him. Didn't make any difference. I've seen people crawling around on their hands and knees under the table, convinced that there is some little bit somewhere on the floor.

All over the country cocaine users found themselves bickering like children. Whose cocaine was it? Who made the freebase? Whose pipe was it? And, most importantly, whose turn was it with the pipe? This was the problem with freebase: it was so pleasurable that, once you started, it was impossible to stop.

The medical community was well aware that cocaine smoking was catching on. In 1976 Siegel had published a paper indicating that monkeys in the laboratory could be taught to smoke freebase. This was an extraordinary revelation: trying to get mammals to smoke anything is hard because they have a natural aversion to smoke. Thus, in smoking experiments with other drugs, Siegel had had to coerce monkeys into inhaling by offering them a reward when they did it. Unlike any other drug he had tried, however, he found that monkeys would smoke cocaine with no other motivating factor. They actually enjoyed it. In his book *Intoxication* he describes the bizarre spectacle of one of his research subjects, a monkey called Phoebe, inhaling freebase deeply, then exhaling, and trying desperately to lick the smoke as it wafted away. He was impressed: 'We could never find a drug that monkeys would choose to smoke without a further enhancement, like a treat after they smoked a cigarette,' he told *High Times*, 'but cocaine freebase they would.'

For some years Siegel had been monitoring a group of cocaine users to see how the drug affected their lives. The number of those using freebase had been going up consistently. In 1977, 14 per cent of his study had tried it. A year later this was up to 39 per cent. This was not a good thing: the habit was dangerous in his view because, once they started, freebasers appeared to have no control over their intake. They would smoke and smoke for as long as they had more freebase. There were cases of freebasers smoking cocaine nonstop for 96 hours before simply passing out through exhaustion. And it wasn't only the humans: animals had just as much trouble: 'Of a sample of three monkeys, two did manage to control their intake. The third just kept smoking permanently,' he noted. Because freebase users ended up ingesting vast quantities of the drug, he concluded that the habit was considerably more dangerous than snorting. Realising that people should be warned about the risks of this hazardous new trend, he fired off a letter to the *New England Journal of Medicine*. It was published in February 1979.

To the Editor:

The nonmedical intranasal use of cocaine has resulted in remarkably few problems demanding clinical attention. Recently I have detected a growing

trend towards increased use of cocaine by smoking, a practice associated
with considerable dependency and toxicity...

New England Journal of Medicine, 300 (7), 1979

No one paid any attention. Because freebasing was comparatively rare
in the United States, there were few reports of its dangerous effects. As
it caught on, however, so hospital admissions began to rise. But the first
real indication of how dangerous smoking cocaine could be were to
come from further away.

While freebasing was creeping across North America, something very
strange was going on in South America. A Peruvian doctor, Raol Jeri, was
the first to notice it. In 1976 he published a paper about cocaine abuse in a
Peruvian medical journal. The habit of smoking coca paste, he wrote, had
caught on because of the explosion of the world cocaine market: more people were making cocaine, so more people were coming into contact with
coca paste. Once established in the rural communities, paste smoking had
then moved into the cities. Peruvians who had previously had no contact
with drugs were trying it—and becoming addicted. It was spreading fast.

The first city to be hit was Lima in 1974. From there it had spread across
Peru and into Bolivia, Ecuador and Colombia. Jeri noted that, while smoking coca paste initially made users feel good, it soon led to paranoia, anxiety and the need to continue smoking, whatever the cost. His patients
hallucinated, seeing lights, clouds and dots. They thought there were animals crawling around beneath their skin. They heard threatening voices.
Despite these weird side effects, they would continue smoking for two to
three days at a time, at the end of which they would lapse into uncon-
sciousness. Sometimes they would attempt to harm themselves: one of his
patients was found, intensely paranoid, repeatedly stabbing himself in the
chest with a kitchen knife. 'Coca paste dependency is now the main cause
of admissions to sections of addiction in the psychiatric hospitals in Lima,'
he wrote. 'We are facing a new epidemic which should be thoroughly controlled and investigated by all available resources in this country.'

In 1978 Jeri published a second paper, in which he wrote that paste
smoking was so compulsive that some of his patients had smoked up to
50 grams of it in a single sitting. Patients presented pathetic figures:

very thin, unkempt, pale and looking suspiciously from one side to the
other... [with] visual hallucinations (shadows, lights, human figures)...

On physical examination many had dilated pupils, rapid pulse, psychomotor excitement (instability, tremors, marked anxiety). A good proportion had scratch marks on the skin...three patients died in this series, two by acute intoxication and one by suicide.

El Syndrome de la Pasta de la Coca, Jeri, 1978

In Bolivia the story was picked up by another physician, Nils Noya, who reported that paste smoking was spreading like wildfire there, too. Bolivian paste smokers also went through terrible changes.

They live in a psychotic world, devoid of human relationships, affection or expressions of love and tenderness...the person becomes apathetic with no sensibility for the human problems around him...the sense of responsibility and the instinct to fight for life disappear completely. According to the police it is very common for users to be found smoking coca paste practically naked or with a minimum of clothing to protect them from the cold. The only thing the user can think of is the drug, how to get it, and where and when to smoke it.

Coca Paste Effects in Bolivia, Noya, 1978

Jeri's and Noya's papers went unnoticed in America partly because they were published only in Spanish, but also because at the time cocaine was not considered dangerous: everyone knew that cocaine didn't produce these kinds of effects. Either these two doctors were exaggerating, or they were just plain wrong. One man of this opinion was Yale's Robert Byck. It was Byck, remember, who had been quoted to the effect that cocaine was about as dangerous as 'potato chips'. Byck had a research student, David Paly, who was heading down to South America to look into levels of cocaine in the blood of coca leaf chewers. When he arrived in Peru in the summer of 1977 he realised immediately that something strange was afoot:

I was aware of it from the moment I arrived there because—I mean—you could smell it. The first day I got there I was staying in a middle class area in Lima and you could smell the stuff in the street and people were smoking it...it's got a very strong kind of sweet smell—a very characteristic smell. There's no missing it...I knew what it was very quickly. Everybody knew what it was. I developed a group of Peruvian friends down there. A lot of them were from aristocratic or upper-middle class families and they all had friends who were strung out on the stuff.

Although Paly was primarily interested in the levels of cocaine in the blood of coca chewers, he became interested in these smokers as well. Because he spoke Spanish he had been able to read the Jeri paper on coca-paste smoking—he had translated it for Byck—but, like Byck, thought that it was overblown. When he eventually met Jeri himself, however, he was persuaded:

> My initial reaction to the Jeri work was that it was exaggerated. I eventually went with him to the sanatorium, this private mental hospital, and interviewed some of the patients...they described how they couldn't stop using it and they were stealing money from their grandmothers and they were paranoid and they thought people were out to kill them. I heard the stories and I spoke fluent enough Spanish to understand them and they weren't being coached through this...I was pretty convinced that they weren't exaggerating.

Recruiting a handful of addicts from the streets, Paly led them to a laboratory, wired them up to a series of machines and gave them paste to smoke. He then took blood samples. When he returned to the United States he dispatched the samples for analysis of their cocaine content. Both Paly and Byck were intrigued to determine just how much cocaine it had taken to drive these Peruvians over the edge. They suspected that the cocaine blood plasma levels might be high—but they were surprised to discover just how high:

> They were the highest plasma levels that had ever been recorded in people that were still alive. There were higher levels that had been taken post-mortem from people that had overdosed—usually smugglers whose balloons had burst. But these were the highest that Byck had seen, that had been published at that time. He was pretty impressed with them, how high they were...

Not only did smoking cocaine allow the body to absorb a dose of cocaine faster but it also meant that repeat doses could be absorbed as fast as they could be taken: by chain-smoking paste cigarettes, addicts could place almost unlimited amounts of the drug into their bodies. Moreover, the spread of paste smoking was a natural result of the increase in illicit cocaine production—itself driven by the North American demand for the drug. And in the late 1970s North America's market was expanding exponentially. More cocaine production meant more paste and more paste meant more smokers. Byck and Paly were in no doubt that this could have serious consequences:

> I immediately recognised—and Byck and I talked about this—that if this stuff ever gets to the United States, there's going to be an explosion.

In July 1979, a Senatorial Committee on Narcotics Abuse and Control in Washington was convened under Senator Tennyson Guyer. Robert Byck was asked to testify as an expert witness. The committee was really interested in the dangers of cocaine snorting but Byck didn't have much time for that. He started off his testimony by readily admitting that he regarded the occasional line or two of cocaine as less than deadly but stressed that there was another threat—much more dangerous—to the drug: that of smoking it. Byck warned the committee that smoking had reached near-epidemic levels in South America in the form of paste, and that it was rapidly catching on in the United States in the form of freebase. He was adamant that something had to be done to stop this new trend taking off the way it had in Peru and Bolivia.

> We do not yet have an epidemic of freebase or coca paste smoking in the United States. The possibility is strong that this might occur. I have reports from California, from Chicago and from New York about people who are learning to smoke the substance and I hear there are numbers now in San Francisco smoking the substance. Here is a chance for the federal government to engage in an educational campaign to prevent a drug abuse epidemic.
>
> *cit. Dark Alliance*, Gary Webb, 1998

To stop the freebase trend before it became widespread, Byck suggested banning the sale of freebase paraphernalia, a broad range of public drug education policies and a lot of scientific investigation into the freebase phenomenon. However, just as no one had paid any attention to Siegel's warning in the *New England Journal of Medicine*, so the 1979 Senatorial Committee on cocaine ignored Byck's. In fact, the first time most Americans heard of freebasing was when the comedian Richard Pryor blew himself up doing it.

On 9 June 1980 Pryor was just winding up a freebase binge at his home in Northridge, California, when things went wrong. Having finished all his cocaine, Pryor decided to drink the high-percentage-proof rum from his water pipe. Unfortunately he had been smoking freebase for five days and was not entirely up to speed: he spilled it down his front. Also unfortunately, he then decided to light a cigarette. Finally unfortunately, he was wearing a nylon shirt at the time. Whoops. The moment he lit the match the alcohol, the shirt and Pryor himself exploded into flames. As he was later to report in a stand-up performance (after months of burns treatment) 'I did the one-hundred-yard dash in 4.3!' Prior's mishap provided great copy for the papers, propelling freebasing into the public consciousness. WHEN COCAINE CAN KILL ran the *Newsweek* headline.

Some time earlier than this the drug press had been half-heartedly warning readers about freebasing. In April, *Rolling Stone* had published a piece entitled FREEBASE: A TREACHEROUS OBSESSION. Even *High Times*, bible of the recreational drug abuser, ran a piece entitled CAN YOU SMOKE WITHOUT GETTING BURNED? concluding that 'it's a real nice high but it has no sustaining power. You get right up there but then you're back down two minutes later, and the next day you can feel really sick.' This kind of publicity should have discouraged the use of freebase in the United States. Perhaps it did. What it also did, however, was to introduce new recruits to the technique: if Richard Pryor was doing it—well, it *had* to be pretty good, right? As one crack addict I interviewed in the Bahamas pointed out to me, 'I first heard about cocaine smoking through Richard Pryor. That was what made it interesting to me.'

On the street it was widely assumed that the main danger of freebase was that of explosions: after Pryor, no one was really comfortable with all those chemicals around any more. So everyone was delighted when it was discovered that fancy chemicals and equipment were not really necessary. In fact making cocaine freebase was so simple that any number of chemicals could be used, the only key element being that you mix your coke with an alkali strong enough to leach off the hydrochloride.

For a while, freebasers experimented with a number of chemicals—the most popular of which was ammonia. Then they discovered a perfect alkali which just happened to be available in every corner store: baking soda. Making freebase with baking soda was so easy that even a child could do it. No dangerous chemicals, no expensive conversion kits. Nothing. In fact the baking soda recipe was not new: it had been around since the mid-1970s, even gaining a mention at Tennyson Guyer's hearings in

1979. However, it had not been widespread. Now it began gaining converts: the 1980 *Rolling Stone* piece on freebasing reported cryptically on 'an even simpler technique [for making freebase] that involved dissolving street cocaine in a solution of water and baking soda and letting the solution dry out'. In 1981 the secret was out, as a freebase journal, *The Natural Process: Base-ic Instructions and Baking Soda Recipe*, went into print. Although one new way of making freebase might have appeared insignificant at the time, the 'base-ic' technique was to create havoc. It was this form of freebase that hit the Caribbean in 1978 and 1979.

Early reports of baking soda freebase are sporadic: one researcher heard of a drug called 'roxanne', or 'baking soda base' from the Dutch Antilles, made by mixing cocaine with water, rum and baking soda. Another recalled hearing about a drug in the Turks and Caicos Islands that 'looked like a pebble and people would smoke it and go crazy'. The recipes may have varied somewhat but the idea was the same: this was the old freebase technique in a new, easy-to-use incarnation. With the amounts of cocaine that were passing through the Bahamas it was perhaps no surprise that there were people willing to experiment with it. According to David, one of the original crack users in Nassau, who started in 1979:

Cocaine was going for fifty dollars an ounce [at the time]. It was washing up on the beach for free, you know? One woman who picked up a consignment didn't know what it was and used it as washing powder. My friends and I would smoke it in a *komoke*—a sort of pipe made out of a glass and some tinfoil and some water. We always cooked it with baking soda, never ammonia or anything else. We didn't call it crack. It was 'freebase'. And then we called it 'rock'. I didn't appreciate it at first. But I was soon into it. And so was everyone else.

Michael, another cocaine smoker in the late 1970s, reported that the reason he tried freebasing was that there was so much cocaine in the Bahamas at the time that 'people were bored with it'. Smoking cocaine was something new. Baking-soda freebase, or 'rock', soon became the drug of choice in the Bahamas. And that's where the trouble started. Because the problem with freebasing was not that it was explosive on occasions but that it was terribly addictive. There was a good reason for this and it had to do with the chemistry of the drug in the brain.

When you take a drug, how high you get depends not only on the drug's ability to increase your brain's dopamine count, but on the speed that it does it. If dopamine levels in the brain rise slowly, you don't experience an intense high; if they leap up, you get a rush. Cocaine has a high addictive potential because of the speed with which it blocks the dopamine transporters. This accounts for both the intensity of the high (which leads to a greater motivation to repeat the dose later), and its brevity (which decreases the length of time between doses). However, there is another key variable: the speed with which cocaine hits your brain is also controlled by the method you choose to take it. Swallow a couple of lines and you'll wait for a while before it hits; shoot it into a vein and the result will be considerably faster. As Nora Volkow had told me at Brookhaven:

> The route of administration significantly affects the addictive liability of a drug. The faster the route of administration, the more powerful its effects. The speed at which dopamine is changed appears to be very important in enabling the reinforcing effects of cocaine, or other drugs. It's not just that dopamine increases. It's the *speed* of the dopamine release that is really important.

Volkow had also made a comparison between cocaine and the drug methylphenidate (Ritalin), which is remarkably similar in its actions to cocaine in that it, too, blocks the dopamine transporters. Yet Ritalin does not lead to a high when given orally and is thus nonaddictive. It is absorbed too slowly to lead to a rush, so children given the drug (it is prescribed for attention-deficit disorder) will not become addicted. Were the children to inject Ritalin, however, it would make them high and the story would be different. In the process of addiction the *speed* of administration is key. This is the reason why nicotine patches are not addictive while cigarettes, which contain the same quantity of nicotine, are.

The same trait had been noted in Peru by David Paly. One of the first things he noticed about coca leaf chewers was that their blood plasma levels of cocaine were surprisingly high—certainly as high as that recorded in American cocaine snorters. So why weren't the Peruvians getting high when they chewed the leaves? He designed a series of experiments to compare the same amount of cocaine chewed, snorted and smoked. The results were as he predicted:

> Euphoria was related to the rate of change of plasma level more than it was to absolute plasma level. It's something that's intuitively obvious if you think

about it. If you want to get a good buzz on alcohol, you don't drink a couple of beers all evening. You down two tequilas and you'll be flying. The amount of alcohol in two tequilas is probably no more than that in the beers but you'll absorb it very, very quickly and thus it gives you this destabilising euphoria. If you look at recreational drugs, as they are purified further and further and delivered by more and more rapid routes of administration, they become both more euphorogenic and more destructive.

Scientists are not the only ones to have realised that the faster the drug gets to the brain, the more pronounced its effects will be: drug users have noticed it, too. Traditionally, mainlining drugs was the fastest way of getting them into the brain. In fact, however, smoking them turned out to be even faster: the surface area inside the lungs is so vast that it has an almost unlimited capacity for getting stuff into your bloodstream. Because of the speed—and thus the intensity—of the onset of the rush, smoking is the most addictive mode of delivery for illicit drugs. Because the rush will be better, the user will experience more incentive to repeat the dose, the crash will be similarly increased and the duration of the rush will be shorter.

Smoked amphetamine, smoked heroin and smoked cocaine have all created serious problems for just this reason. Injecting cocaine ensures that it will hit your brain in about four seconds. Smoking it takes about three. Thus the high that freebasers were receiving was many times more pleasurable than regular cocaine. And many times more addictive.

Looking for the source of freebase and the roots of crack in the United States, I gave Ron Siegel a call. The biography inside the jacket of his book said that he 'probably knows more about how drugs work than anyone else alive'. It was an impressive boast: if this was true, he was way up there with Magic Eddie.

Although I was looking forward to meeting Siegel I suspected that the feeling was not mutual: '*Another* book on cocaine!' he had sighed on the phone when I called him. 'Aren't there enough already?' This was perhaps natural. He had performed John Belushi's autopsy, done the original experiments on freebasing and, when the CIA was accused of complicity in the crack trade, written a secret report for them on the true origins of the drug. He was America's Recognised Expert on cocaine and thus, every time the drug reappeared in the news, television crews descended on him looking for comments. He was bored of it but agreed to meet me anyway.

In *Intoxication*, Siegel had referred to cocaine as 'simply the best chemical the brain can receive'. I asked him about this and he explained that no other drugs known to man 'produce the kind of uniformity of ecstatic experience that cocaine does'. His appreciation of this point had led him to conclude that the drug had a high addictive potential way back in the early 1970s—when everyone else was yakking on about how harmless it was. But, if sniffing cocaine was dangerously addictive, smoked cocaine was much worse. Freebasers told Siegel that the habit was so pleasurable that they couldn't even begin to explain *how* pleasurable it was. Predictably, they compared it to sex: 'It feels like my brain and my lungs are coming,' said one. Sex came up again and again: when Siegel set up trials to witness the results for himself, they surprised even him:

> We had men who had never smoked cocaine before smoke it in the labs here, and the result was that they spontaneously ejaculated through flaccid penises...and when you see *that* kind of euphoric effect, well, it doesn't take a scientist to work out that someone might want to repeat this kind of experience...We knew it was going to be big when we first heard about it. Bob Byck and I were so concerned that we were unwilling to put out information on it in case it got out. We didn't want anyone to know about it.

I told Siegel that I was interested in tracing the freebase habit back as far as I could go and that I had been interested to read the account of its origins in his 1982 article. How much of the article, I asked him, had been speculation? Siegel admitted that, while his explanation of the naming of freebase (i.e. the base–*basé* mistranslation) was an assumption, he had, in fact, had an informant in 1970—a dealer—who had discovered smoking cocaine in South America and told him that he was determined to find a way of doing it in the United States:

> He was bringing in large amounts—for 1970—from Peru and Colombia into California, and he told me that he didn't want to tell anyone. It was like a secret. And he disseminated the information. He had undoubtedly been smoking *pasta basica* down in Peru and somehow it became known as 'base'...He was impressed. He said, 'Don't tell anyone about this'—but he didn't really know how to do it. He was aware that it was an extraction of cocaine...

This guy seemed like the real thing: 1970 was extremely early for an American to be smoking cocaine. Perhaps he really was the first to discover freebasing. He must have been one of the first. I asked Siegel if he could put me in touch with him. It turned out that he himself had been trying to find him recently but that no one knew where he was. 'Perhaps in jail,' said Siegel. The trail stopped there. It was as close to the 'inventor' of crack as I was ever going to get.

Instead, I chose another tack. As far as I could see the main thing about crack, when it hit the Bahamas and followed on to the United States, was not that it was 'new' (it had been around for years): it was its marketing. The key difference between crack and freebase was that crack became rapidly available at a price cheap enough to ensure that people who could not otherwise have afforded cocaine could have a go. Crack was a feat of *marketing*, not chemistry. But who had done this marketing? I may not have found the chemist but I could certainly have a go at the marketer. I thanked Siegel for his time, got into my car and headed south, down Interstate 5 to San Diego.

San Diego's Metropolitan Correctional Center is a 24-storey monolith at the corner of Union and F Streets in the heart of downtown. The first high-rise prison in the United States, its function explains its location: the penitentiary is one of twelve United States jailhouses for prisoners whose cases are being heard in federal court. In the case of San Diego, inmates are frogmarched to and from the federal hall of justice, half a mile away on 1st and Broadway, through a heavily guarded underground tunnel. As I looked up at it I came to the conclusion that it was the perfect setting for a big-budget feature film about an elaborate jailbreak—but that was not why I was there. I was there to meet 'Freeway' Ricky Ross. Prodigy. Capitalist. Millionaire. Crack lord. Kingpin. Killer. Depending on whom you believe, of course.

I had first read about Ross in the *LA Times*. A series on the origins of the crack scourge pointed its finger firmly at him:

> If there was an eye of the storm, if there was a criminal mastermind behind crack's decade-long reign, if there was one outlaw capitalist most responsible for flooding LA's streets with mass-marketed cocaine, his name was Freeway Rick...[he was] South Central's first millionaire crack lord, an illiterate high school dropout whose single-minded obsession was to become the biggest dope dealer in history.
>
> *Los Angeles Times*, 20 December 1994

The article, by one Jesse Katz, reported that Ross had single-handedly transformed California's drug trade in the early 1980s, converting everybody to crack rather than cocaine, making himself preposterously rich in the process. In a world of drug-related knock-on effects, Ross was the *primum mobile*, the first mover. If crack was an earthquake, he was the epicentre. When the *LA Times* eventually ran out of metaphors, they let him speak for himself:

> 'You know how some people feel that God put them down here to be a preacher?' asked Ricky. 'I felt that he had put me down to be the cocaine man.'
>
> *Los Angeles Times*, 20 December 1994

Clearly, if I was looking for the roots of crack, Ross was my man. I had a few problems tracking him down. He was on appeal, so no one was quite sure who, exactly, I should contact to get permission for a visit. However, after a frenzy of faxes, emails and letters, eventually someone in the US federal prison system threw up their hands and gave up. OK, they said, I could see him. So, one Friday afternoon, I parked opposite Café 222 on 2nd and Island, grabbed my shoulder bag and walked into the prison. I negotiated my way through the usual barrage of metal detectors, entry forms, luggage lockers and ultraviolet wrist stamps—with which, by now, I was all too familiar. Then I was herded into a stainless-steel elevator.

On the twelfth floor I was ushered out of the elevator into a brilliant-white room furnished with brilliant-white plastic picnic tables and brilliant-white plastic picnic chairs. It was a bit like one of those films where someone dies young and goes up to heaven to bargain with God for a couple more years of life. Only more scary. I had been told that, once the interview began, neither Ross nor I would be permitted to leave the room except to terminate it. I immediately regretted the litre of orange juice I had downed in the car park five minutes earlier.

Behind the bulletproof glass of the prison door, a face appeared. As I waited for the electronic lock to release the bolts in the door, I wondered what to expect of such a heinous villain. When the lock flew open with a *ker-chunk* and the door swung open, an ominous clanking emanated from the corridor behind it and I prayed that he wasn't going to be manacled. And then, suddenly, there he was. Ricky Ross. We shook hands and sat down.

What to say about Freeway Ricky? He doesn't look like his photographs.

Press pictures of Ross show a dangerous-looking dude with dreadlocks and a shifty look in his eye. In fact he has had all his hair shaven, is slightly built and short—certainly no more than five foot eight or nine. He smiles frequently and breaks into infectious laughter without provocation. He has the most amazingly delicate hands. Hardly what you would expect of the most evil man in America. But the greatest surprise is to come. Because, the moment he starts talking, one thing becomes abundantly clear: this guy is smart. *Seriously* smart. Of all the interviewees I contacted in the course of researching this book—including a Nobel Laureate and a number of extremely serious scientists—Ross came across as the brightest. By far.

We chatted about his appeal for a while and he told me how he had got into this mess. It was the story of crack cocaine in America.

Ricky Donnell Ross was born in Texas but his family moved to South Central Los Angeles in the 1960s. Their house was situated right by the main LA freeway so, since there were a number of other Ross families in the neighbourhood, Ricky became known as 'Ricky from the freeway', and eventually 'Freeway Ricky'. Like everyone else in his neighbourhood he went to school and, like everyone else in his neighbourhood, he couldn't see the point of it:

School wasn't for me. It wasn't something that I saw I could use. I'm looking for stuff that I can use. And if I can't use it, I don't want it. So school, now that I look back on it—nobody ever explained school to me. They never showed me why I should learn to read, why I should learn to write. Why I should learn mathematics . . . when it came to reading and writing, I didn't never catch on.

Ricky's lack of prowess in the classroom did not seem to matter, however, because he had something else going for him: he was a natural sportsman. Picked up by a talent scout in a local park, he soon found himself playing tennis. When his friends began competing in local competitions and winning, he started taking it seriously and by the time he was approaching the end of high school, he was considering going professional. What he needed first, however, was a sports scholarship to university. His friends were offered places at various colleges in California and Ricky felt that it was only a matter of time: he was a good player and he knew it. Then everything fell apart.

I wanted to go to Long Beach State but academically I just couldn't cut it. My coach asked me how my grades were. Found out I couldn't read. I was eighteen then. I was still in school... by nineteen my opportunities just started slipping away from me. People started finding out I couldn't read.

Ross's college hopes collapsed. He dropped out of school just months before graduation, gave up playing tennis and took to hanging out in a friend's garage, watching TV. Until this point, because of tennis, he had never had any contact with drugs: he was too busy and was aware that rumours of drug abuse had the potential to wreck a tennis career. Now, however, there was no reason not to. When a friend approached him at Christmas 1979 and gave him $50 worth of cocaine, he was intrigued:

One of my partners went to college to play football and somebody had turned him on to it there. He came back and showed it to me. He said, 'This is worth fifty dollars.' I looked at it and said it wasn't worth no fifty dollars. I said, 'What is it?' and he said, 'It's cocaine.' I didn't believe it. That's how I got introduced. I didn't try it. It took me a while. Maybe a couple of months. It was too expensive.

Ross took the cocaine and showed it to a few friends, one of whom immediately offered him $100 for it. He was impressed. A couple of hours later the friend rang him and asked if he could get his hands on any more. Now he was really impressed. Ricky Ross was about to become a cocaine dealer. At the time, cocaine was still a very expensive drug and most of the residents in Ross's neighbourhood couldn't afford it. There was a real lack of suppliers. Ross now found himself with a serious contact and a large circle of acquaintances willing to pay him money to supply them with cocaine. It was child's play:

The next thing I know, I'm making a hundred, two hundred dollars a day, sitting in the garage, listening to the radio and watching TV. People would just walk up. 'Hey man, I need a fifty-dollar.' 'I'll go and phone my boy.' 'Hey man, I need a fifty-dollar.' It just kept on going like that. And me and my boy, Arl—he had just got out of jail—so when he got out I said to him, 'Man, this stuff is rolling! This shit is cracking. It's *on*!'

As yet, Ross and his friend were selling other people's cocaine for them, taking a cut of the profit. Having realised the value of the market, however, they now decided to go into business for themselves. First they needed to buy a substantial amount of coke: $300 worth. They stole a car, stripped it down, sold the parts and came up with the cash. They then invested it in 3 grams of cocaine and started their own little supply business. Soon they found themselves plugged into all the wealthy homes in the neighbourhood. People would finish their jobs on Friday, collect their pay cheques and look for a way to celebrate. Ross helped them. Through a fortuitous meeting with a girlfriend's father—who had a lot of friends who were into cocaine—Ross found himself with a safe, exclusive client base capable of coming up with a lot of money every Friday. By now it was early 1980 and he had been dealing cocaine for just six months.

Ross had not yet encountered freebase. Although the friend to whom he had sold the first $50 rock of cocaine had cooked it up and smoked it in front of him, it didn't occur to him that there might be a market for it. As freebasing spread in the more affluent black neighbourhoods, however, so he began to deal more and more and people opened up to him. They were buying cocaine but they were not happy. 'Once we got to maybe two or three ounces [a week], people started coming all the time,' he said, 'early in the mornings and stuff like that, and they started saying, "Man! I got to go home and cook this stuff up! Shit! Why ain't you got this stuff ready?" And I was, like, "Huh?"'

Ross decided to cook up a little cocaine freebase and offer it to his customers ready to smoke so that they wouldn't have to bother when they got home. Although he didn't know how to make freebase, he had a friend called Stephan who did. He offered him $50 to make the first batch. Since cocaine chunks were known as 'rocks' and he was offering it ready to smoke, he called the result 'Ready Rock'.

We started selling Ready Rock. 'Oh, we got Ready Rock.' It was kind of like filling a gap, you know? When they come early in the morning, they got to go to work, you know, six o'clock, and then they got to go home and cook it up and they don't want to go through all that. So we just started saying, 'You want Ready Rock or powder? Whichever way you want it.'

Initially Ross's customers were suspicious of this new product: even freebasers didn't trust it. But the more astute soon cottoned on and people started asking specifically for Ready Rock. People who had never heard of freebasing began to try it. Of course, they liked it. The market expanded. Within a couple of months Ross's friend Stephan was cooking up multi-ounce quantities of cocaine three or four times a week. Ross paid him $300–400 a time. Then he got sick of paying.

> They wouldn't teach you how to cook cocaine in the early days. Because it was money. If you could cook, you could charge... I'd hire people to cook for me, and, after I'd watched them for a while—I was sitting there with them and I keep looking—and pretty soon I had enough dope and I was, like, well, if I fuck it up I'll lose, you know, but if *he* can do it, I can do it. So I tried it. And it worked. That's how I learned. From him. I fired him! He had to get him another job! And after that I started teaching all the guys how to do it.

Originally Ross and Arl had got into the cocaine business to make $5,000 so that they could buy a car. Three months after they had started trading they went into the bedroom where they kept their savings and counted all the cash. It came to $20,000. They caught each other's eye: 'We looked at each other. "Quit?" "Not a chance!" "Let's get a hundred!"'

Ross surrounded himself with homeboys and set about revolutionising South Central's cocaine scene. Each time he traded he buried his profits in more and more cocaine. The more cocaine he bought, the lower the price dropped. He passed on this discount to his clients. This brought in more customers—enabling him to buy more cocaine at still lower wholesale prices. Street prices of cocaine began to plummet in California. Ready Rock was a massive hit with everyone who came into contact with it. As he moved up the drug-dealing ladder, so he moved away from the street sellers and personal users and began supplying other dealers instead. He eventually established a hierarchy for the South Central cocaine industry, buying up houses, gutting the interiors and making Ready Rock industrially. Houses would deal in different denominations: small-time dealers would go to House A, where they had to spend $100 at a time. Bigger dealers might go to House B, where they would spent $1,000. At the top of the scale he established a main house where wholesalers would come to buy multi-kilo quantities.

In setting up houses like this, he says, he wanted to help small dealers become big dealers, to give them the opportunity to get into the cocaine trade and make some real money. The more they managed to sell, the higher the house they could visit and the lower the price of the cocaine. According to Ross many of his early customers went on to become millionaires.

As demand for Ready Rock began to outstrip that for powder cocaine, production had to be scaled up. Initially Ross had made freebase in small medicine vials, one gram at a time. When his house began filling up with vials he had moved on to pill bottles, then mayonnaise jars and baby-food bottles. Then he decided that it was just too time-consuming to fill all these bottles. By now he was selling Rock in quantities too big for any of them anyway. He industrialised the process.

In the end I was using big pots, industrial pots. Like...forty or fifty gallons [150–190 litres]. Two guys would have to pick it up. And we'd put in thirty, forty, fifty keys [kilograms of coke] at a time. I had two little guys and they'd be cutting and dumping in the cocaine. And another guy, he'd have a big box of baking soda...he'd dump in the baking soda and we pour the water in there and get a spoon, a big spoon—my partner said it looked like a boat oar—and start stirring. And you put a mask on, or you get high when you do it.

Since Ross had now hit the top of the cocaine food chain, he was buying in his supply directly from the people who were trafficking it. Not only was it cheap but it was pure. One kilogram of cocaine would produce one kilogram—possibly a little bit more if it picked up some baking soda—of Ready Rock. Thus Ross's technique would yield him, after a good couple of hours heating the mixture over one of his industrial stoves, one solid lump of crack weighing 30–50 kilograms. Sometimes it was white, sometimes yellow, sometimes pea-coloured. No one was concerned about the colour. They were worrying about the next stage: how to cut up this manhole-cover sized chunk of freebase.

They used to hit it with an axe. Ross laughed:

Yeah! An axe! Cut it into chunks—*bang*!—and when you cut it it just splits, like that, *ching*! And then you got another guy with a scale and he's, like, 'Such-and-such wants ten keys'—put it in a plastic bag. We had sports bags, Nike bags and stuff. Put it in there with their initials on it. Drop it in the car. Next morning, everybody meet at the breakfast spot, pick the money up and tell them where to pick the drugs up at.

Ross had a firm grasp of market economics. Not only did he build around himself a hierarchy that enabled him to supply others lower down the chain, but he also established an inspired technique to deal with competitors.

If I heard somebody [I didn't know] was selling it, I would go out and recruit them. Because they weren't getting it as cheap as me: they didn't have the buying power I had. It was always cheaper around me. I would go out and recruit... I would go out to different gang members and show them how to do it and maybe give them a start. I might give them eight ounces, ten ounces [225–280 grams]: 'Here.' So they went out and sold it. And then they *loved* me.

New recruits would invariably end up coming back for more supplies. By dealing with Ross they were getting the cheapest Rock around. Of course, as he got new recruits, he needed more cocaine and had the money to buy increasing quantities—further lowering the price. By 1982 Ross was the largest cocaine dealer in South Central, shifting 15 kilos a week. By 1983, the market for cocaine powder had collapsed completely: everybody wanted Ready Rock. Ross cooked it up for them. By 1984 he was getting through 50 kilos a week. When he had started up, a kilo of cocaine went at the wholesale price of $25,000. At his peak, Ross was buying in such bulk that he was getting it for $9,500. Even allowing for the fact that he was supplying the suppliers rather than dealing on the street, he could make $100,000–200,000 profit per day. Some days he would go through 1 or 2 million dollars' worth of cocaine.

As had happened in the Bahamas a couple of years earlier, the amount of cocaine available led to a plummet in its price, rendering it more accessible to people who had previously not been able to afford it. 'When I started getting involved with cocaine,' he says, 'no blacks were involved with it. It was still a white-echelon drug. They felt they couldn't afford it. Black people couldn't afford it. One of the things that I felt I did was I made it affordable for minorities—blacks, mostly—in my neighbourhood.'

The demographic of cocaine use changed. From being a rich man's drug, it became everyone's drug. In this way freebase cocaine spread up the West Coast.

Of course, it wasn't long before Ross's activities reached the ears of the police. Which was why I was talking to him in this weird white room with the electronically controlled, bulletproof doors. Ross's story was doubly tragic: while he was busy making his fortune and his product was wrecking the lives of countless Americans, he was also writing his own arrest warrant. It was sad, really, because, if he had worked in almost any other commodity with even half the success that he had enjoyed in the cocaine industry, he would be an all-American hero by now. The way I saw it, the fact that he was dealing in cocaine did not detract from the fact that he was a capitalist, a trader, in an already busy market, who happened to have the vision to see the way things could be and the nerve to go out there and act on it.

It was exactly the same vision that had made other Americans—Nelson Rockefeller, Asa Griggs Candler and Bill Gates—rich establishment figures. But the industry in which he chose to immerse himself was illegal and, as such, he was just another black drug dealer in jail.

I asked Ross how he felt about selling crack. Didn't he feel guilty?

Not at the time. I sold to my own kid's mother. I gave it to her. She was addicted but there was no physical—nothing was wrong. When she got high she just went and got high, went to sit in the corner on the couch and watch TV like everybody else. There wasn't no effects like I would have associated with PCP. With PCP people might take their clothes off, go and sit in a tree, run down the street naked. But with cocaine none of this stuff happened. So to me cocaine was just a thing where people had fun and spent their money.

As he talked, I tried to work out what to make of him. I'd interviewed a few criminals in my time, including some of the more famous ones. I'd also been warned that Ross was seriously charismatic. But he really took the biscuit. I had never seen a better example of the American Dream in action. I'll admit it: although I didn't approve of what Ross had done, I had to admire it. By the end of the interview, I was won over. I completely forgot to take any photographs. We shook hands and I was ushered back into the stainless-steel lift and passed back through the metal detectors. As Ross was marched back to his cell I signed myself out in the visitor logbook and wandered back out into the sunshine.

When I got back to England I took a recording of the interview home and played it to my parents. Despite the occasional expletive, they were won over, too. 'What a nice man,' said my mother. My father thought it was terrible that Ross could have been a tennis pro—if only he had been taught to read: 'Tragic, the way things like that happen to people.' My aunt, who had popped by on the off chance that there might be a cup of tea going and then become embroiled in Ross's story, thought that we should invite him over to tea. 'Do you think he'd come?' she asked. I explained that he was serving a long jail sentence in the United States. 'Perhaps when he's released?' she said. Perhaps. Perhaps.

I wasn't surprised that they fell for him. Frankly, if he ran for office, I'd *vote* for him.

While Ross was busy turning the West Coast cocaine market on its head, Ready Rock was spreading on the East Coast, too: it made the leap from the Bahamas to the Caribbean communities in Florida, and then to other states, notably New York. Initially, police and DEA agents were baffled. They found weird bits of evidence obviously involved in drug taking: broken glass pipes, wire meshes. Coke cans with holes poked in them. They didn't know what they were, or what they were for. Dealers stopped on the street would turn out to be empty-handed: it was easy to drop a couple of rocks of freebase when you saw the police arriving, and it was virtually indistinguishable from bits of stone on the road.

In 1983 the LA press began picking up scraps of information about 'rock houses' in South Central, but columns covering them were buried deep inside the papers and no one paid much attention. At the end of 1984 the drug made its debut in a national US newspaper when the *Los Angeles Times* reported: SOUTH CENTRAL COCAINE SALES EXPLODE INTO $25 ROCKS. The *Washington Post* picked this story up but noted that 'Rock' was a Californian drug: the story was dropped.

Then, one Sunday in November 1985 the *New York Times* printed an article that was to change everything. The piece, by a journalist called Donna Boundy, covered a cocaine-abuse treatment centre:

PROGRAMME FOR COCAINE ABUSE UNDERWAY

Three teenagers have sought treatment already this year ... for cocaine dependence resulting from the use of a new form of the drug called 'crack', or rock-like pieces of prepared freebase (concentrated) cocaine.

New York Times, 17 November 1985

There it was: the magic name, 'crack'. Following Richard Pryor's accident, freebase cocaine was no longer news. 'Crack' sounded like a new drug altogether. It was much more newsworthy. Two weeks later the story was picked up again. This time it was judged sufficiently interesting to merit a place on the front page. A NEW, PURIFIED, FORM OF COCAINE CAUSES ALARM AS ABUSE INCREASES, ran the headline. The article reported on the prevalence of 'crack houses' in Harlem, estimating that they were generating $500,000 per day. It quoted a Dr Arnold Washton of Regent Hospital on East 61st Street, who predicted an epidemic of crack use, and another healthcare worker who referred to 'crack' as 'the most powerful drug we've ever seen'.

Despite the fact that the only new thing about 'crack' was its name, the *New York Times* thought it was a sensation. It was new. It was dangerous. Its name sounded Bad. The drug story of the century started to roll.

By May 1986 crack was all over America's front pages. It hit television the same month, when CBS's Harold Dow interviewed a senior DEA agent:

Dow: This is it! This drug is so powerful that it will empty the money from your pockets, make you sell the watch off your wrist, the clothes off your back...

DEA agent (Robert Stutman): ... or kill your mother!

> *cit. Cracked Coverage*, Reeves and Campbell, 1994

Hype surrounding the drug was sensational. In June *Newsweek* ran a cover story on crack entitled AN INFERNO OF CRAVING, DEALING AND DESPAIR. Inside, in an open letter to readers, editor, Richard Smith, warned that 'an epidemic is abroad in America, as pervasive and dangerous in its way as the plagues of medieval times', and pledged that the magazine would cover the crack scourge as aggressively as 'the struggle for civil rights, the war in Vietnam and the fall of the Nixon presidency'. It was, he wrote, 'an authentic national crisis'. *Time* magazine called crack 'the issue of the year'. By the end of 1986, *Time* and *Newsweek* had run five cover stories on the drug each. But the biggest media event involving cocaine was to take place just two days after *Newsweek* hit the stands.

On 17 June 1986, Len Bias was one of the most fêted men in America. The 22-year-old University of Maryland sports star was selected as the National Basketball Association's second overall draft pick. He was going to play for the Boston Celtics—the previous year's NBA champions. The night of the 18th, after a whistle-stop publicity tour to pose for the press, he returned to his college to celebrate with friends. By the next morning he was dead. 'Cocaine poisoning', recorded the coroner. American sports fans were appalled. That a young, healthy athlete could die as a result of cocaine use sent shock waves through American society. In the time it took the news to break, cocaine's champagne image was gone. 'The lesson of Bias' death,' reported *Newsweek* 'is that cocaine kills.' The article was titled COCAINE IS A LOADED GUN. 'In life,' writes Dan Baum in his study of the War on Drugs, *Smoke and Mirrors*, 'Len Bias was a terrific basketball player. In death he would become the Archduke Ferdinand of the Total War on Drugs.'

Bias's death coincided perfectly with the arrival of the 'new' drug, crack. Although there was no evidence of it, the public immediately decided that it was crack that had killed him. By the end of the month, concerned parents and civic leaders were organising 'take back the streets' marches across the country. In July, ABC News broke new ground by sending a cameraman to accompany a police raid on a crack house. The footage was so exciting that camera crews from all over the world began asking whether they, too, could accompany crack busts. Federal authorities acquiesced and the result was a swathe of news reports consisting of jerky footage of heavily armed action men in bulletproof jackets and balaclavas battering their way through armour-plated doors.

Two months after the first crack-house footage aired, another TV landmark took place. On 2 September 1986, viewers tuned into CBS to hear a sombre Dan Rather (CBS's news anchor) announce: 'Tonight, CBS takes you to the streets, to the war zone, for an unusual two hours of hands-on horror.' The programme was *48 Hours on Crack Street*, and, with a plug like that it attracted a total of 15 million viewers—one of the highest viewing figures for any documentary in US history. Three days after *48 Hours* aired, NBC followed with its own version, *Cocaine Country*, and this, too, did well. It rapidly became clear that crack led to increased ratings. Three years after *48 Hours*, when CBS commissioners noticed a slump in documentary ratings, they would commission a sequel, *Return to Crack Street*, to boost them.

By September *Time* was running another crack cover story: a picture of a death's head bearing the legend: DRUGS: THE ENEMY WITHIN. Many made fun of the journal's apparent change of heart, contrasting this cover with one they had run just five years earlier—at the height of cocaine's glamorous phase—referring to it as 'the all-American drug' and warning that it made you 'alert, witty and with it. No hangover. No physical addiction. No lung cancer...instead, drive, sparkle, energy.'

The day before *Time* hit the newsstands, Ronald and Nancy Reagan made an unprecedented appeal to the American public, exhorting them to take part in a 'national crusade' against narcotics abuse. 'Our country needs you to be clear-eyed and clear-minded,' said Nancy. 'Say yes to your life. And, when it comes to alcohol and drugs, just say no.' As a piece of PR it was wonderful. As a means of stopping anyone from taking cocaine it was a waste of time. The 'Just Say No' campaign, derived from a phrase in a NIDA educational film when an elementary schoolchild was asked what he would do if he was offered drugs, was perhaps useful for young children. It was not suitable for cocaine users. Yet it was to become one of the best-recalled features of the Reagan presidency.

In the midst of all the crack hype, those closest to the drug, the DEA, realised that the press were going overboard. OK, there was crack around, they admitted, but there wasn't that much of it. In fact, outside certain regions of Miami, Los Angeles and New York, there wasn't any at all. The rest was hype. In August they tried to pour water on the flames:

> Crack is currently the subject of considerable media attention. The result has been a distortion of the public perception of the extent of crack use as compared to other drugs...crack presently appears to be a secondary rather than primary problem in most areas.
>
> *cit.* 'Beyond Cocaine, Basuco, Crack and Other Products',
> James A Inciardi, *Contemporary Drug Problems*, Fall 1987

As early as the summer of 1986 the DEA had been concerned about the over-hyping of crack. Special Agent Robert O'Leary told *Newsweek*, 'We are very concerned about a market being developed because of all the publicity. We feel it's being accelerated by media hype.' These warnings were studiously ignored: crack as a 'secondary problem' wasn't particularly exciting. A crack deluge, meanwhile, was much more promising. No one wanted to believe the truth: that crack was simply regular cocaine that could be smoked; that it had been around for at least a decade. The story continued to run.

The DEA were not the only ones to realise that the 'crack epidemic' sensation was not all it seemed. Back at UCLA, Professor Ron Siegel was appalled at the coverage. The press reported crack as a 'new' drug that had taken over in record time. Siegel, who had been researching freebase for over thirteen years, knew that it was anything but new. He recalled for me his reaction to the first crack broadcasts:

> Dan Rather's researcher rang me up and asked, 'Have you heard about crack?' I said no, because I never had. 'What is it?' She said, 'It's a new form of cocaine that you smoke.' And I said, 'Well, this sounds like free-base and we've been researching that for a long time. We've logged about a hundred and twenty street names for it—perhaps "crack" is a new one.' She just said, 'It's obvious that you've never heard of it'—and hung up. That night on the news, there was Dan Rather, saying crack was a new form of cocaine and it was smokable. I couldn't fucking believe it.

Ricky Ross, at the time South Central's largest dealer, was likewise baffled: 'When I first heard of crack, I was, like, "Man, I wonder what they got in that stuff." And then I get down to the courtroom and they're, like, "That was crack cocaine you had." "No it wasn't! It was cocaine! I didn't put no crack in there …"'

In their efforts to portray the drug as a larger-than-life scourge, the media adopted a number of tactics. The first was the straight lie. The most famous crack myth emerged in *Newsweek*:

> 'There is no such thing as recreational use of crack,' said Arnold Washton (director of the 1-800-COCAINE hotline)—'it is almost instantaneous addiction.'
>
> *Newsweek*, 17 March 1986

This was a bit of a porky. Cocaine is an extremely dangerous drug. It has a high potential for addiction, especially when smoked. But no one could ever argue—reasonably—that it is instantly addictive. *Nothing* is instantly addictive. Yet this story would emerge again and again. A 1987 poster advertising the dangers of crack cited the example of a young female addict:

> A sixteen year-old girl told doctors that her entire life was focused on crack. She was interviewed on a Friday and had used crack for the first

time the previous Monday. Within five days the drug had completely taken over her life.

US Department of Health, 'Crack', 1987

Another tactic used to demonise crack was to remind the public that it was new. Here was a drug, it seemed, that had emerged only very recently but was already wreaking havoc: if it could do this much damage in a couple of years, what could it do in the next five? In this way the crack scare was similar to the other great health scare of the mid-1980s—AIDS. Both were deadly, both apparently incurable. The way both were portrayed initially, it seemed as if they were going to wipe out most of creation. In the case of crack, both of the assumptions that fed this notion were false: as the DEA had already admitted, crack was not actually widely available in 1986 at all—except in certain specific areas. And, as scientists such as Siegel and Byck had testified, it was not nearly as new as it seemed. As early as 1979, if we recall, Tennyson Guyer's Senatorial Committee had been told how to make it.

To some extent the crack scare may be blamed on ignorance. Following the 1979 Senate hearings, no money had been ploughed into the problems of freebase and paste smoking. When reports of crack began hitting the papers and the phones began to ring at NIDA, no one really knew what to say. Robert Byck, who had warned the 1979 committee that freebase was coming, was livid, telling a senatorial committee:

> In 1979 in testimony before the House Select Committee on Narcotic Abuse and Control I warned of the dangers of freebase cocaine and described it as 'extremely dangerous'. I pleaded at that time 'for the federal government to engage in an educational campaign to prevent a drug abuse epidemic'. I emphasised that it was critical to find out about this form of abuse and to use media to illustrate the disastrous effects of cocaine smoking in order to forestall epidemic use. This advice went unheeded. We are not significantly more knowledgeable about cocaine smoking. No educational campaign was mounted...Today we are in the midst of the predicted epidemic.
>
> US Senate Permanent Subcommittee on Investigations, 15 July 1986

Because no one had conducted any research on crack, when journalists rang for assistance with their stories, there were no experts and no statistics to give them. Left to their own measures, they found their own sources.

Many of the stereotypes that had been applied to cocaine when it hit the United States in the 1880s were reapplied to it in the 1980s. The most disturbing was the threat the drug represented to children. *Newsweek's* article promised that 'there is no question that cocaine in all its forms is seeping into the nation's schools'. The edition, which featured a cover photo of a teenager snorting cocaine beneath the banner: KIDS AND COCAINE: A NEW EPIDEMIC STRIKES MIDDLE AMERICA, sold 15 per cent more than the average for that year. Worse even than hitting schoolchildren, however, were reports of the damage that crack did to unborn babies. The issue of the 'crack baby' was to prove an emotive one. As with much of the rhetoric surrounding the drug, however, all was not as it seemed.

Stories of the damage done by cocaine to prenatal children surfaced somewhat earlier than the crack scare. In September 1985 the *New England Journal of Medicine* published an article that indicated that cocaine use harmed babies *in utero*. This was immediately picked up by CBS, which broadcast a piece about 'cocaine babies' on the evening news. The report featured footage of premature babies apparently in distress, citing them as evidence of the link between cocaine abuse and any number of possible birth defects. Across the United States doctors began fielding calls from news networks. Where were the cocaine babies? Could they come and film them? Further news reports featured more damaged babies crying.

In the summer of 1986 the two stories—'cocaine babies' and the new killer drug, crack—merged. Thus when CBS broadcast a follow-up to their original piece they weren't 'cocaine babies' any more. They were 'crack babies'. They shook, cried and flinched from human contact. While the camera lingered on one child, viewers were informed that she would probably end up growing into a 'twenty-one-year-old with an IQ of perhaps fifty, barely able to dress herself and probably unable to live alone'. It was heartrending.

It was also untrue. The children filmed were not damaged by cocaine abuse. They were damaged by polydrug abuse: their mothers had used all sorts of drugs (of the patients monitored in the original medical paper, 100 per cent had used marijuana, tobacco and alcohol as well as cocaine throughout their pregnancy). When doctors tried to explain this to journalists looking for 'crack babies' they were ignored. Crack babies they wanted, crack babies they got. In some cases, reports Dan Baum, they actually filmed the children of heroin-addicted mothers—which really *were* born addicted—and used that footage for the cocaine-babies story instead: they looked sadder.

This is not to say, of course, that taking cocaine when pregnant is a good idea. Far from it. But the plague of permanently damaged, educationally subnormal crack children as predicted by the media simply failed to materialise. While there *is* evidence that children born to crack-using parents suffer neglect, this is perhaps not surprising: children born to drug-using parents tend to be neglected, anyway. In fact, the most common cause of problems afflicting the children in the news reports, agreed many of the doctors, was poverty. Children whose parents could not afford visits to the doctor tended to end up in trouble. As a summary of the crack babies' situation concluded in 1989, 'In the end it is safer for the baby to be born to a drug using, anaemic or diabetic mother who visits the doctor throughout her pregnancy than to be born to a woman who does not.' This never made the headlines.

After children, all the other scare tactics designed to make people pay attention to drugs emerged. Firstly came crime.

There was little doubt in anyone's mind that criminal activity was the result of crack use. A 1987 US Health Service anticrack poster told of a newspaper copy editor who, after just two weeks use of crack, took to 'robbing banks' to finance his habit. Violence could not be far behind. You had only to look at the footage of crack-house busts: why did the police need all those guns if the guys inside weren't violent? Added to this was the fact that, because the price of cocaine was dropping and crack could be sold in smaller quantities, you no longer had to be rich to use it. The main customers were poor: these were the people who committed violent crimes, anyway. Everyone had always suspected that they were villains.

In fact evidence is scant that crack use leads to violent criminal behaviour in those who were not formerly violent. Analysis since the crack scare reveals that crack users are 'only slightly more likely' to commit violent crimes than non crack users. What *does* lead to violence is the injection into depressed areas such as South Central LA, of an illicit industry that generates vast amounts of cash. As Professor Bruce Johnson of the National Development and Research Institute (NDRI) in New York—one of America's largest independent think tanks on narcotic abuse—concluded in 1995, 'the violence associated with the inner-city crack culture probably was not due to any pharmacological effect but rather to the systemic violence associated with drug sales'.

In other words, crack per se was not the cause of the violence: it was the money it generated that caused the violence. But that would seem to be a result of the people who were using it rather than the 'horrific' nature of the drug itself. Powder cocaine was used by nicely spoken rich white people, and when they got into trouble with it they had support networks to help them. They could afford to go into rehab clinics. Families, money in the bank and jobs to return to gave these people an incentive to kick the habit and snap out of it. They didn't carry out drive-by shootings and ram raids. They weren't visible. Unemployed ethnic minorities in the inner cities, however, had none of these backups. They were extremely visible.

Linked to the demographic change in cocaine use was the age-old issue of race. Because the new cocaine users were underprivileged and unemployed, there was statistically a higher chance that they would be non-Caucasian. Whites did use crack, but it was the ghettos that were hit hardest, and this was where the nonwhite folk lived. The image of the black—or at least ethnic-minority—crack user was perpetuated by almost every TV report. Crack-house busts showed decrepit houses in black neighbourhoods containing black people: it just made better TV than a group of white college students having a toke in the college dorm. While CBS's initial report on cocaine babies had featured white children, the second—on crack—featured exclusively black ones.

All of these factors: children, crime, violence and race—together with a dose of journalists' heady rhetoric—did a good job of scaring the public silly. But was this just another media frenzy? Some authors have asserted that it wasn't: that the crack hype was orchestrated on purpose at the hands of certain agencies to further their own interests.

There may be some truth in this. The 1992 autobiography of a senior DEA agent revealed how he had deliberately set about manipulating the media:

> There was no doubt in my mind that crack was on its way to becoming a national problem. But, to speed up the process of convincing Washington, I needed to make it a national issue and quickly. I began a lobbying effort and I used the media. Reporters were only too willing to co-operate because as far as the New York media was concerned, crack was the hottest reporting to come along since the end of the Vietnam War...
>
> *Dead on Delivery*, Robert Stutman

Robert Stutman, the man who had told NBC's Harold Dow that crack would make you 'kill your mother', revealed how he released statements to reporters and arranged for them to be taken along on crack busts. Within the first two months of Stutman's initiative, more than two hundred articles had been published on crack in New York alone. '1986 was the year of crack,' he wrote. 'From my perspective, Len Bias had not died in vain.' But was this a genuine, or a cynical concern? Just as various medical research establishments such as the Centers for Disease Control in Atlanta benefited from the panic surrounding AIDS and viruses such as Ebola, so US federal organisations involved in drug enforcement stood to gain from the arrival of a new, deadly drug. As did the legal profession. One DEA agent told me:

> I was sitting with a US attorney who's now a federal judge in —, and he was complaining that his arrest statistics were down and he was going to lose positions. And I said, '—, we're starting to see this stuff called crack here...and I think we need to go out and make some arrests...if you'll prosecute them, we'll give you a bunch of arrest stats that will help stabilise your office.' I think that was November of 1986, and sure enough after that we just—It was nonstop crack cases.

This is perhaps unfair on organisations such as the DEA. There is no doubt that they were doing their damnedest to stop the arrival of cocaine and it would take a true cynic to believe that they were rubbing their hands in glee at the arrival of crack. Equally, it was the DEA who had tried to cool the story by issuing a press release saying that crack was not as widespread as people were being led to believe. But the issue of US governmental agencies benefiting from increased funding as a result of scares generated by drug addiction is one that comes up again and again. As Reeves and Campbell say in their study *Cracked Coverage*, agencies involved in the control of narcotics 'have an interest in maintaining a perpetual state of urgency, even a state of hysteria, about cocaine'.

In the UK, Philip Bean, of the University of Loughborough, agrees with them. According to his study *Cocaine and Crack, the Promotion of an Epidemic*, the crack scare was imported to Britain by 'a small number of American evangelicals who saw the opportunity to justify American policies'. The European crack scare, which was to prove more intense but shorter-lasting, was, he says, largely media-led, supported by a number of 'self-seeking publicists'.

It all started for the UK in late 1986, when newspapers began writing about the new form of cocaine that was creating problems in America. By the start of 1987 the drug seemed to have arrived here: in February the *Observer* reported a case of a man found dead in London who 'might have' died of a crack overdose. Crack, the piece reported, was a new form of cocaine 'said to be so potent that a single dose can lead to addiction'. The problem for the media was that there didn't seem to be any crack around: there was nothing to write about. The papers toyed with the idea of crack for a while, then gave up. It took a real kick to get the story into gear. That kick took place the next spring.

In April 1988 a senior DEA agent gave a lecture on crack at the Ninth Annual Drugs Conference of Assistant Chief Police Officers in Wales. The speech was so spectacular that it propelled crack on to the front pages of the nation's newspapers. The speaker was none other than Robert Stutman—the very same man who had first started the crack scare in America. And yet, as Bean notes of the speech, '[Stutman's] information was largely incorrect, his evidence uncorroborated, and his views simpleminded'. Statistics he quoted were often bogus, framed in such flowery speech as 'one figure that will be released next week' or 'a study that will be released in the next two to three weeks'.

A copy of Stutman's speech is lodged in the Drugscope library. A brief flick through is all it takes to reveal that Stutman, in his zeal to persuade the audience of the dangers of crack, had reverted to all the standard stereotypes used to demonise cocaine in the past.

First there was the idea that crack was instantly addictive:

Numbers are meaningless compared to crack. A study that will be released in the next two to three weeks will probably say the following: that of all those people who tried crack three times or more, 75% will become physically addicted at the end of the third time.

Then there was the speed with which it had caught on:

In the past three years crack has gone from a drug which was largely unheard of in the largest city in the United States to now becoming 'the' drug of abuse in the United States...There is no other drug trend in history that comes close to spreading that quickly across that great of a piece of society.

There was the idea of children and drugs:

If I were to retire today and decide that instead of being in the drug enforcement business I wanted to design a drug that's aimed for kids, I couldn't improve on crack. I simply couldn't improve on it.

Then there was violence:

To show you how the times have changed, every DEA agent is issued a 9mm sidearm. We used to use .38s, then the .357. Now we have 9mm, 17-shot Austrian weapons and every DEA agent—all 3000 agents—are now issued sub-machine guns. THAT is what has happened in one country basically because of crack.

Finally there was race:

Right now crack is controlled by a fairly large number of organisations, basically because of its background: Dominicans and Jamaicans...now again, I don't have to tell any of you gentlemen this, but you have a large number of Jamaicans in this country.

Stutman summed up snappily:

I will make you a prediction...I will personally guarantee you that two years from now you will have a serious crack problem...I see by my watch, Mr Chairman, that I have about three minutes left. Is there anyone who has a question? An argument? A debate?

Heady stuff. While Stutman was clearly doing his best to help the UK avoid a crack epidemic, the veracity of his claims left a great deal to be desired. In the case of crack's addictiveness, the report 'which will be released' revealing a 75 per cent addiction rate was never released—for the simple reason that it never existed. The speed with which crack spread, meanwhile, was indeed fast but, as we have seen, it had actually been available since 1979—not, as he implies, 1985. In the case of children and guns, we can see his point, but don't they sound a bit too reminiscent of the sort of things legislators were saying at the turn of the century? Remember the case of Chief Lyerly of Asheville, North Carolina, who traded up the calibre of his gun because cocaine had made a 'Negro fiend' bulletproof?

The question of race is perhaps best ignored: while there are a lot of Jamaicans in England, there are a lot more in Jamaica and, as far as I can tell, Stutman did not bother to lecture there. The personal guarantee at the end of his speech speaks for itself.

The fact that the speech was not entirely true did not stop it from being extremely disturbing. The then Home Secretary, Douglas Hurd, told the *Daily Mail* that Stutman 'made a deep impression on me . . . scaring the hell out of the rest of the audience'. Two home secretaries in a row would visit Washington to witness raids on crack houses, only to return shocked (it was later alleged that, during the raids, federal law-enforcement officers were employed to fire guns into the ground a couple of blocks away to provide a more 'warry' atmosphere for the Brits). Hurd needed no more convincing. Not wanting to be the one who did not heed the warning about crack and left the country open to its arrival, he hastily convened a group of European ministers to spread the word about this dangerous drug and authorised the police to establish a national task force to take care of the epidemic.

The newspapers went bananas, reporting all sorts of stories about crack, often incorrect, largely because there was no one around who knew enough about the drug to contradict them. After all, there was little or no crack in the UK at the time. The one fact that everyone picked up on was Stutman's figure of a 75 per cent addiction rate for people who tried crack three times. It led to a swathe of headlines about 'three strikes'. These three strikes were then whittled down until it was reported that crack was addictive the first time. The story eventually prevailed that ruthless crack dealers were giving the first dose of crack to children for free. Since it was instantly addictive, they would soon be begging for more. It was rubbish.

And yet. And yet. Whenever I bumped into people in London and they discovered that I was writing about cocaine they invariably guffawed before asking, with a wink, whether I needed a 'research assistant'. These offers of assistance, I discovered, would be immediately withdrawn when I suggested that we head back to my place to smoke some crack. The excuses just fell out: 'You get addicted the first time'; 'It's a hundred times more addictive than smack'; 'You can die the first go.' Coke, it seemed, was a laugh. Crack was not. In terms of drug education, the idea that crack is instantly addictive is just terrible. But the fear generated by the 'instantly addictive' line had stopped even the most pharmacologically experienced people I knew from trying it. Perhaps it achieved something after all.

As Bean notes the scare was not promoted by reasoned arguments but by moral indignation and fear. There was no epidemic. In 1989 just 58 grams of crack were seized in London. In 1990, the entire seizure for the UK was still less than a kilogram. In May 1991, according to Clare Hargreaves, police seized their biggest haul yet—just under a kilo, worth, they estimated, more than £500,000. How a kilogram of cocaine (worth around £50,000 at the time)—could be worth £500,000 even if it had been cooked up into crack—was not explained.

The fact is that crack has never created much of a problem in the UK. There are a number of reasons why this is the case. For a start, there is nowhere near as much cocaine here as there is in the United States. Shipping cocaine from Colombia to Europe is a tricky business. It's a lot further away. There are no shared borders with countries that maintain good relations with Colombian traffickers—such as Mexico. There are few Colombian expat communities here to organise distribution and Colombians who don't speak English stand out, making easy targets for British police. Also, European customs agents are widely perceived as incorruptible and jail sentences meted out to traffickers are high.

Because there is less cocaine the price is higher—making it less available to the kind of people who might find crack appealing. Equally, it has been pointed out that in America there is an ingrained 'underclass' for whom a drug like crack is an escape. These people are unemployed and often unemployable. Their situations are desperate. While Britain does have unemployment and poverty, it is not on the same scale as that in the US. We have a good, free healthcare system. We just don't have the kind of 'ghettos' that our cousins across the Pond do. Other drugs such as amphetamines are widely available and cheaper. So there is less of a market for it. The British National Task Force was quietly wound down in August 1990.

This is not to say that there will never be a crack problem in Britain. Most of the DEA agents I interviewed admitted that crack had never hit the UK the way they had predicted, but rounded off with a warning that—at some point—it would. Perhaps they are right. Bruce Johnson at NDRI told me:

No one in Europe wants a crack problem like the one we have in the States. So anyone who laughs and says, 'We will never have a crack problem' should not be too complacent... all it takes is the underground economy to make a decision that they're going to start smoking crack—and you've got cocaine over there—and you could have a crack epidemic real easy.

After the initial flurry of sensational coverage the crack story died down in America, too. This was perhaps not surprising: the media had hyped it so much that there was nowhere left for it to go. Looking back on the scare today it is clear that, while there was an important shift in the use patterns of cocaine across the country, the statistics simply did not bear out the shock-horror headlines of the early news coverage. In 1985, while Stutman and the media were doing their best to scare the American public silly, there were 1,092 cocaine-related deaths in the United States. In the vast majority of these cases, the drug had not been smoked, so could not have been 'crack'. The next year, for every death in which cocaine played a part there were 100 alcohol-related deaths, and 300 tobacco-related deaths. But, as Reinarman and Levine note in their study *Crack in Context: Politics and the Media in the Making of a Drug Scare*, no one went on TV calling alcohol or tobacco use epidemics.

Statistics for children's use of crack were less impressive: by the time *Newsweek* got around to reporting 'a new epidemic' of children using cocaine in 1986, teenage use of the drug had been dropping consistently for four years. It would continue to drop throughout the crack scare. This did not stop the drug being portrayed as a scourge of youth. As Reinarman and Levine note, from 1985 to 1988—the very peak of the hype—cocaine use among high school seniors plunged 37 per cent. When asked how they were taking cocaine, just 1.3 per cent of the remaining users said they had been smoking it. So much for the 'new epidemic' of crack among children.

Where was the press's information coming from? Surveys of media reports on crack reveal that the vast majority of experts cited in news reports on the drug were taken from law-enforcement communities and politicians, followed by interviews with punters on the street. The single *least*-cited sources were academics—the people who had actually studied the drug. The reason? Academics tend to be less sensational and more circumspect. They don't launch into vitriolic condemnations of crack the way the police and politicians do. In short, their sound bites aren't as good.

Why was everyone making so much noise about crack? Analysis of media coverage compared with public attitudes towards drugs reveals the answer. In 1985, before 'crack' hit the headlines, just 1 per cent of Americans considered 'drugs' the most important issue facing the nation. The next year—after it hit—'drugs' was the number-one issue. In 1987, crack stories inexplicably dried up. As a consequence just 3–5 per cent considered drugs the most important issue. By 1988, however, crack was back in the press and over 50 per cent polled for drugs again. It would seem, therefore, that the American public's attitude to crack mirrored the amount of press coverage it received during this period. But was the press coverage the result of public hysteria, or was it the cause of it? More to the point, why would the American press suddenly start running stories about crack in 1986, stop in 1987, then start again in 1988?

Perhaps because the stories were politically driven: 1986 and 1988 were election years. As Reinarman and Levine note: 'the prominence of the drug issue dropped sharply in both political speeches and media coverage after the 1986 election, only to return during the 1988 Primaries'.

As we have already seen, 'drugs' is a good political issue to make a lot of noise about. Jumping up and down and being vitriolic about narcotics is guaranteed to gain votes because no one in their right mind is going to argue that drugs are a good thing. Instead of arguing against, say, abortion or handguns—both of which can be real vote losers—American politicians found that, if they stood up and raged against narcotics, *no one* would stop voting for them. By leaping on all the old stereotyped arguments about drug abuse (it's killing our children; it's done by foreigners; it causes violent crime and so on), moreover, it was possible to come out violently in favour of all the things that middle-class voters were in favour of—while making a seriously kick-arse speech at the same time. In fact, the more noise they made about drugs, the more assertive they looked and, well, the more *American* they looked. Drug use was un-American, goddammit. You wouldn't catch Abraham Lincoln smoking crack. Politicians realised pretty fast that standing up against drugs was interpreted by the public as pretty much identical to saying 'I love America'. Parents and those at risk from any of the spectral figures that used drugs were especially keen to vote for more punitive measures. And so the crack story rolled on.

Fear of crack led to incredible scenes in Congress. 'Drugs' was an issue that any politician could leap on and be guaranteed a good press. As the story gained momentum, soon those who advocated a little more consideration came a cropper. Senators and congressmen began challenging each other to take urine tests to prove that they were clean. Ronald Reagan took a test, as did George Bush. Bill Clinton pre-empted a strike from a political opponent by volunteering to take a test and passing; his opponent promptly went one higher, announcing not only that he would take a test but so would his wife, too. Clinton made Hillary take one in retaliation. In the 1986 Democrat Primaries in Georgia, underdog John Lewis challenged his opponent to an on-the-spot urine analysis test: 'we can go outside and go to the men's room and take the test right now!'. His opponent suggested that this sounded like McCarthyism and refused. He lost.

Now, it might be argued that a little bit of antidrug hysteria is no bad thing. After all, scaring people about drugs will stop them experimenting, right? There is certainly some truth in this but the tactic can backfire. By demonising drugs so seriously the media may actually be encouraging, rather than discouraging, experimentation. Consider media descriptions of crack. The papers quoted users who reported it as being 'the most powerful drug' they had ever encountered. 'Whole-body orgasm' was a commonly used phrase to describe the sensation of smoking it. Papers reported that it was equivalent to 'playing Russian roulette'. This kind of coverage can actually serve to make the drug *more* attractive to certain elements of society. As my interviewee in Nassau had told me, the reason he tried rock was because Richard Pryor had nearly killed himself doing it. The coverage produced by the media in such scares is so all-pervasive that it can act as a form of advertising.

In addition, portraying crack as the source of all the ills of the American ghettos was doing a disservice because it led the public to ignore the root source of the problem. Yes, poor people ended up in trouble when they took crack but *why* did they take crack in the first place? Perhaps as an escape. Legislators argued that they were poor because they took drugs. Liberals, meanwhile, held that they took drugs because they were poor. There is no denying that crack was—and is—a serious problem, but it was not the cause of all the violence and misery of inner-city America. It was portrayed as the cause because it was easier to blame an evil drug and come out guns blazing against the dealers than it was to handle the real causes: unemployment, poverty, underfunding, cuts in welfare and so on.

The other danger of overhyping crack was that it accelerated the fight against drugs, which soon assumed a life of its own. Politicians who advocated tolerance and understanding of the crack problem rather than simply hiking the penalties for possession were labelled 'soft on drugs'—and fell from favour. Pretty soon no one was willing to stick their head above the parapet for fear of losing their seat, and the Drug War became unstoppable.

Questioning antidrug policy today is still considered the most rank heresy. Politicians who ask awkward questions such as 'What is the war on drugs achieving?' are ostracised and find themselves in deep trouble. As Dan Baum notes in the introduction to his book *Smoke and Mirrors*, 'Even the mildest questioning of prohibition is the closest thing this country has to forbidden speech. For the moment, all paths away from excess are booby-trapped. We're stuck.'

The anticrack rhetoric was to have other costly consequences. Congress, swept up in its own polemic, was the scene of heated debates about what to do with these heinous drug dealers who were enslaving the youth of the country. Federal penalties for drug dealing went up and up. In 1988 Senator Jesse Helms (Republican, North Carolina) lobbied for a law dictating that, since crack was a hundred times more addictive than cocaine (no one knows where this statistic came from), possession of it should merit a penalty a hundred times greater. Unbelievably, it was passed. Today the penalty for possession of 5 grams of crack (worth about $350) is a mandatory five years in jail—equivalent to that for possession of half a kilogram of cocaine (worth about $10,000). And yet, as anyone who knows anything about cocaine will tell you, 500 grams of cocaine, when cooked up, will yield 500 grams—possibly even more—of crack.

The net result was that those found in possession of crack were sentenced to disproportionately heavy custodial sentences compared with those found with powder cocaine. This was to have profound effects, owing to the class of people who used crack versus the class of those who used cocaine. As Bruce Johnson explained to me at NDRI:

It is very clear that crack, more than any other substance, is primarily an African American low-income substance. And its sale in public places is very much dominated by African Americans (although there are some Latinos involved in it, as well). Cocaine powder tends to be more controlled and proportionally in the populations is more evenly distributed among the people who use illegal drugs. It's just that whites don't get involved that often in crack.

By 1989, 46 per cent of all arrests in New York City were for crack possession or dealing. Since powder-cocaine traffickers and users tended to be white (they could afford to buy cocaine in bulk) and crack users black (it was sold in small quantities cheaply), federal courts found themselves banging up blacks and members of other ethnic minorities as if there were no tomorrow. As prison numbers spiralled (doubling in the 1980s alone), so more and more blacks ended up in jail for possession or low-level dealing. At the time of writing, the US prison population has just hit 2 million—up from 300,000 in 1970—of whom 500,000 are in for drug offences. Currently African Americans, who make up just 12 per cent of the US population, constitute 50 per cent of the US prison population. Blacks are arrested for drugs offences at six times the rate of whites, so one-third of the black US population is under criminal supervision of one form or another. Crack is to blame for much of this. The 100:1 ratio crack law amounts to a form of institutionalised racism. This has been demonstrated by numerous academics and experts (recently even the US Drug Tsar, General Barry McCaffrey, lobbied for cocaine–crack sentencing parity) but Congress repeatedly votes against repealing it: no one wants to appear soft on drugs. Besides, banging up black crack users can hardly do that much harm, can it? It keeps them off the streets, after all. Once again, cocaine becomes a race issue.

I know what you're thinking. The crack problem in America is not simply a media fantasy. Crack isn't harmless. Crack can't be good for babies in the womb. Crack addicts who have no money end up breaking the law to sustain their habit. You're right, of course. Crack and cocaine have terrible effects on people and anyone who says they don't is just plain wrong. But the point is that the hype was out of all proportion to the original crack phenomenon. Crack has polarised academics in the US like no other drug. In his account of the history of the War on Drugs, *The Fix*, Michael Massing examines both sides of the coin, terming those who created the hype 'alarmists' and those who denied it 'revisionists'. But where is the truth?

The problem for the alarmists is that evidence really does indicate that many of the problems associated with crack are generated purely by the fact that it is illegal. Much of the violence brought about by crack dealing was the result of cocaine's high price—itself a result of repressive measures taken against it. Equally, as sentences went up, so crack dealers were more likely to shoot at policemen trying to arrest them rather than come quietly. So there was increased violence—but it was partly a result of prohibition. Alarmists don't like to admit this.

The problem for revisionists, meanwhile, is that no matter how much they harp on about the media or the politicians or the DEA deliberately creating a hype, there really was and is a serious crack problem in the United States. The drug really is dangerous and a lot of people have died because of it. How, then, can they reconcile the assertion that the 'epidemic' was only a media scare?

It's strange: in their zeal to try to solve the drug problem, both groups end up going too far, and seem to forget that they are actually on the same side. I interviewed a few law-enforcement officers who were utterly unwilling even to discuss such issues as decriminalisation of cannabis. Equally, I bumped into some liberals who talked as if the DEA were the enemy. That's the thing about crack, cocaine and the War on Drugs: the consequences of getting it wrong are so momentous that it's hard to be impartial. And television brings such explicit images into our homes that it's impossible not to have an opinion.

Of all the images of crack use in the 1980s none was as widespread as the crack house. Television reports showed inner-city buildings with security systems like Fort Knox: heavy steel doors, grilles over the windows and wire netting built into the walls to resist police battering rams. Often they were simply urban pillboxes, dispatching crack through a hole in the wall or on a pulley system operated from above—put your money in a cup and it would disappear into the loft, only to return again on the string containing your crack. Other houses were more like opium dens. Crack would be sold, pipes could be bought or hired and you could hang out in there—as long as you could afford to buy.

Goings-on inside these fortresses were reported by a series of intrepid ethnographers. These guys were interested in traits of drug use among underprivileged populations, getting into shooting galleries and interviewing heroin users. As crack took over in the 1980s they found the galleries were changing: because of the nature of the high induced by crack, people tended not to lie on the floor comatose after taking it as they did with heroin. They were active. Since a high percentage of users were women, houses often became dens of prostitution—of a degree of squalor not previously witnessed in America. One of the most respected ethnographers, Professor James Inciardi of the University of Delaware, reported:

Upon entering a room in the rear of the crack house...I observed what appeared to be the gang-rape of an unconscious child. Emaciated, seemingly comatose and likely no more than 14 or 15 years of age, she was lying spread-eagled on a filthy mattress while four men in succession had vaginal sex with her. After they finished and left the room, however, it became clear that, because of her age, it was indeed rape but it had not been 'forcible' rape in any legal sense of the term. She opened her eyes and looked about to see if anyone was waiting. When she realised that our purpose there was not for sex, she wiped her groin with a ragged beach towel...and rolled over in an attempt to sleep.

Women and Crack Cocaine, Inciardi et al

There have always been links between drug addiction and prostitution but something about crack made the relationship far more sordid. The short, intense nature of the high, coupled with the availability of more crack in the house, led women to agree to anything for more drugs. In many cases, such as the one above, women were kept in the house and supplied with as much crack as they could smoke on the condition that they were on call for all customers, 24-hours a day. Visitors who bought crack were offered complimentary access to the house woman. They were hideously exploited: such was their craving for the drug that women would virtually give themselves away for more of it. One user explained her pricing system to Inciardi:

If you're really looking good, haven't lost your good looks and you're out there just prancin' like some foxy bitch, sure, you can hold up your price. But when I need the money I'm bad up, I'm gonna go for $5.

Women and Crack Cocaine, Inciardi et al

Non-crack-using prostitutes were appalled at the antics of their drug-using colleagues: they would do anything, no matter how degrading, and they would do it for next to no money. Inciardi witnessed women performing oral sex on strangers for a single hit on a crack pipe—worth as little as 25 cents. Being completely off their faces, no one gave any thought to protection, and sexually transmitted diseases soon went hand in hand with the crack-house populations. This was right at the peak of the AIDS scare.

Having read reports of the goings-on inside inner-city crack dens, I decided that I had better check one out for myself. After a few phone calls I was put in touch with NDRI in New York. The head of NDRI, Professor Bruce Johnson, explained that getting me into a house might prove tricky—not because I was a complete stranger from another country but because crack had been falling from favour in New York since 1990: kids had seen the effect it had had on their older siblings and parents and stopped using it. Meanwhile, thanks to increasingly harsh sentencing laws, many of the original users were in jail. Others simply dropped dead. In the drug-taking community, crack users held the lowest social status of all, renowned as untrustworthy, wired people who would do anything for money. No one wanted to hang out with them. 'Crackhead' became a general term of abuse just as 'dope head' and eventually 'dope' had at the start of the century. Thus the phenomenon of the 'crack house', as experienced in the 1980s, was largely gone.

Johnson told me he would try to arrange a visit but that he couldn't promise anything. So I was surprised when, the day we met, he introduced me to a colleague, Elouise Dunlap, who offered to take me to a house that afternoon. Elouise told me that, if I wanted to get in, I had to be willing to pay. Crack users don't like strangers coming in to observe them like visitors in a zoo. Money might persuade them to open up. I headed off to the nearest ATM, pulled out a pile of cash and folded it into $25 wads. We got on to the subway and headed north into the heart of the South Bronx.

A couple of stops north of Yankee Stadium we got off the subway, boarded a bus and headed west. The neighbourhoods deteriorated noticeably as the bus chugged on and pretty soon I was the only white guy around. When we got off the bus and began walking, there was no doubt that I didn't belong here. But then, looking around, I realised that no one belonged here. Not really. A series of vast, identical, bland, red-brick high-rise flats loomed ahead. 'Projects,' said Elouise: New York's State housing projects. They were dismal. I was wondering how many people lived in each one when we took a sudden left and arrived at a front door. A black guy sat on the steps swigging beer from a fast-food-chain cup. After a few words, he got up and walked us in.

The woman who owned the house was called Ma. It was hard to tell her age. Perhaps fifty. As she showed me around, it became clear that Elouise had told Ma I was coming and that she had done a good job of cleaning the place up before I arrived. Everything smelled of bleach; piles of just-tidied-up junk lay everywhere. I counted at least three electric typewriters in addition to an old broken word processor, stacked up in a corner. A complete set of *Encyclopaedia Britannica* sat in the book-shelf. The house cat, Razor, wandered in and out from time to time, pay-ing no attention to anyone. After a brief tour we all adjourned to the bedroom. It was hot, and there was a fan in there.

As she prepared her paraphernalia, Ma began to talk. Crack houses had changed since the old days, she said. No one visits the armour-plated buildings with the guns and the wire windows any more: they are too obvious and get raided by the police. These days users visit friends' houses, places they can trust, low-key places. Most houses don't offer crack for sale any more, either: it raises the stakes if the police stage a bust. Instead, local dealers have pagers and are telephoned when sup-plies run low. About the only real requirements for a modern crack house, it seems, are a roof and somewhere to sit.

Having gathered together all her bits and pieces and settled herself on the bed, Ma stopped talking and started smoking. Watching her was about as exciting as watching someone smoke a joint: the only shocking thing about it was that it wasn't shocking at all. The crack itself, when it arrived, was prepackaged in green plastic wraps so that each $5 rock, or 'nickel' (about the size and colour of a saccharine sweetener) had to be opened with a pair of scissors or a penknife. When it burned it released a distinctive odour that I couldn't quite place: a dusty, musty smell that reminded me of old plumbing. It wasn't aromatic, like marijuana. If you didn't know what you were looking for you could walk through a room that had been used for smoking and think it just needed a good airing.

There was a long-running debate about how good this particular prod-uct was. Most agreed that it rated about seven out of ten but said that it had been cut quite heavily. At one point a nickel contained 'so much chemicals' that it had to be recooked: placed on a tabletop, heated with a lighter until it liquefied and allowed to cool. It was then scraped off the table with a razor blade. I asked what this achieved. 'Gets rid of the soda,' someone said. The older users all commented that crack wasn't what it used to be in the old days.

Like some weird, drugged-up TV chef, Ma explained what she was doing step by step as she went along. Smoking crack turned out to be pretty simple. First you need a 'stem'—a short length of Pyrex glass tub-ing which will act as your pipe. 'We get these from the Arab stores,' she said. 'A dollar a time.' An inch into the stem you poke a wad of wire gauze. Holding the stem like a cigarette, you now place the rock of crack into the gauze and heat it with a lighter, inhaling steadily as it vaporises. The whole process lasts as long as it takes to draw a lungful of air. You hold your breath for a while, then exhale. And that's it.

At one point Ma showed me how to make a pipe out of an empty miniature Malibu bottle, a length of tinfoil and a straw. After demonstrating how it worked she handed it to me. 'You can take that home with you, if you like,' she said. I felt like the kid at the birthday party who gets to keep the twisty-balloon dog.

Having read Ron Seigel's accounts of freebasing, I assumed that the effects would be pretty serious and pretty immediate. They weren't. Immediately after a smoke, certainly, there was a fair amount of slurred speech. Most tended to become incoherent and start ranting a bit. (To be fair, many of them were pretty incoherent before they started smoking, anyway.) But then, as Siegel had explained to me, crack is not the same as freebase. Real freebase is pure cocaine base and generates startling results. Crack, meanwhile, is its bastard brother, loaded with cuts and impurities. There was no competition between the two. But crack seemed to have a few effects of its own. There was no real conversation. Instead there was a series of people shouting out their opinions on random subjects. No one really listened to a word anyone else was saying.

Ma held forth much of the time. As people came and went through the flat it was always obvious that it was her place and that they were either paying to be there, or offering her some of their crack. As she talked, her voice grew quieter and quieter until we could no longer hear her, whereupon we had to give her a prod and ask her to speak up a bit. It didn't do much good. Her monologues were long and rambling, jumping from subject to subject. I asked her how long a $5 nickel would last:

> The idea is to still be in control of your mind. Me, I become more creative, like writing a book. Creativity, you know? I may feel tight and beat up and need a lift. Then I step to my business. It's motivation, mental recall, problem solving. People commit felonies because they got a good scheme but they lack the motivation... Anyway, what's that got to do with anything, whether I got skinny legs? I had to find my true beauty that was inside of me.

You see the problem. She then launched into an impenetrable anecdote about a fight she had had with a woman in the grocery store around the corner. As far as I could gather, Ma had won. How did she start using crack? I asked. 'King George introduced us to the cooking of small amounts of coke,' she said before her voice disappeared again.

Throughout the afternoon users traipsed in and out of the house. Sometimes they mooched into the bedroom and introduced themselves; other times they wandered up, sat opposite me and asked who the fuck I was. Occasionally a new face would appear around the door, see me and beat a hasty retreat. When they were happy to talk I asked them about their habits, watched them smoke and paid them money for their time. The phone was used frequently and the doorbell rang more or less constantly. No sooner had I paid one interviewee for their time than more orders were placed. A long line of ramshackle figures appeared, taking turns to sit down, light up a rock or two, and tell their stories.

David, a 36-year-old Hispanic truck driver, was the most coherent. He had been introduced to cocaine by a cousin and had been selling it since he was at school. By the age of fifteen, he was shifting 85 grams (3 ounces) a week. This was back in 1978. Drawing heavily on his stem and exhaling a plume of smoke, he recalled the first time he had smoked:

It was like—wow! I felt like I was floating. I was light-headed. I was racing. No—I wasn't racing: I felt elated. I felt good. I felt strong. I felt— wow! Like a fucking mummy. Stuck. Just stuck. And my head, just—floating. And it felt good, like it numbed my senses. I didn't feel pain, I didn't feel happiness, I didn't feel joy, sadness, depression, nothing. Just straight fucking numb.

It wasn't long before his habit led him to crime:

I stole from my mother, I stole TVs, I stole brand-new quilts, gold rings, gold watches—yep, from my mother—Let me look around. [Here he started pointing to things around the room that he had stolen.] I stole one of those, and one of those. And them. What's *that* thing? Oh, yeah—I stole one of them before. I've stolen fucking electric can openers, so much shit. Tools. I've sold brand-new clothes, new shoes. I've even sold used clothes of mine that were still looking presentable.

He was under no illusions about the drug:

Fucking evil. It speeds up your heart, it speeds up your fucking mind. It alters your mind to the point of not wanting to eat, not wanting to drink anything, not wanting to take a bath, not wanting to sleep. All you want to do is get more, get more, get more. So that you don't give a fuck what you got to do to get more.

David had a number of children, including a new daughter he had never seen—because on the way back from work to meet her for the first time the week before he had stopped by a friend's house and been offered some crack. He had been smoking, living down and out, ever since and had not yet got around to going home. 'I'm so fucking ashamed,' he would wail from time to time before lighting up another nickel.

Jane was another intelligible interviewee. When she walked in I assumed that she was someone's daughter, here to pick them up or run an errand, but it turned out that she was just a couple of years younger than I was. She was beautiful, with a ringing laugh, clear skin, dimples and eyes like a Disney cartoon character. She should have been a model. Instead she had been using crack since the age of thirteen, had two children (both living with relatives), was with her second husband and was facing time for dealing. Her best friend had been raped and stabbed to death as a result of a bad crack deal. One brother was in jail for murder, another had died in jail and another was educationally subnormal. When she talked about her friends and her brothers she said that she 'was the lucky one'. Although she saw no problem with her own crack consumption ('it don't bother me'), she was adamant that she didn't want her thirteen-year-old son to try it. Why? 'It's no good. It's no good for your body. It's no good, period. I don't want to see him get killed.'

Mike insisted on shaking my hand, which took me by surprise because he used his left hand to do it. When I saw his right hand I realised why: a deep 10-centimetre cut reached across the length of his palm, the result of an accident with a razor blade and a shrink-wrapped nickel of crack the night before. He laughed. 'I smoke so much, look what happened! Didn't even go to the doctor. Didn't feel nothing!' He told me all about his ten children, almost all of whom had different mothers. He had three grandchildren. 'I'm a very powerful man like that,' he said. He was just 37. Although it transpired that he was getting his crack for free from Ma (he was providing her with sexual favours), he was concerned that she was ripping him off. When Ma said she would bring him two nickels but they didn't arrive he became agitated: 'Tell her I want my shit, man! To get my shit, man, 'cos I came up here, I really want my shit. My two nickels—can I smoke it here while I'm talking to you?'

Eventually I got up and fetched two nickels for him myself. Once he had smoked he calmed down and, after a long monologue about his various criminal exploits ('Stealin' everything that moves: I stole out of my house, got stabbed, threatened, beat down, got holes in my head, in a coma thirty days'), I asked him whether he considered himself an addict. 'It doesn't control me. I'm in charge right now,' he said, then commented wistfully, 'I can go without it for a couple of days on my good days. But I'm not so happy and it's the only thing that makes me happy. But when it's gone I'm sad.'

As soon as one interviewee had finished talking I handed over $25 and another arrived, lit up and began talking. After nine or so crack users I began to notice certain common traits: all of them had been smoking for over ten years. All of them had an apparently unlimited capacity for crack. 'How much do you use?' I asked of one guy. 'As much as possible,' he replied, 'all day, every day if I can.' All of them had a lot of children, most of them more than five. Three had more than ten—most by different partners. All of them had been through detox, often many times. When asked why they had relapsed they all recited the same mantra: 'people-places-things' in a singsong voice—the standard detox line on cue-conditioned cocaine craving. It rolled off their tongues like some pointless advertising slogan. Most of them said that they were just about to do something about their crack problem, one that she was leaving for the clinic first thing the next morning. She then promptly burst into tears and took another hit. Bizarrely, all of them agreed that the crack problem was the fault of 'immigrants' (yet every single interviewee belonged to an ethnic minority)—Puerto Ricans or South Americans.

They all had horror stories. One told me of a friend who stole his mother's heart medication and withheld it from her until she agreed to tell him where her money was. When she eventually buckled and told him he tossed her the pill bottle, retrieved the cash and headed straight out to get high, leaving her in the middle of a seizure on the kitchen floor. Another admitted to having gay sex although he wasn't gay—because he wanted crack. Another reported that he had sat in a crowded crack house while a woman fellated a dog as a bet to earn more crack. She had already slept with everyone else in the building that afternoon.

This character assured me repeatedly that he was about to quit but said it was hard:

> I lost my family. I robbed my kids. I sold clothes that I bought for them. Stole from my wife, my mother, my brother and myself. I keep going away to get help. I stay clean for a little while and then I come back and start using again. It's sad, man...the depression is a motherfucker.

He put down the pipe and leaned towards me, intent: 'I'm gonna tell you something that no one has ever told you on this interview. Don't *ever* try it. One drag will get you hooked. Don't try it.'

Outside, children were screaming and playing and crying on the sidewalk and police sirens passed every few minutes. Inside, we were in our own little world. We soon established a rhythm: they smoked, I asked questions, they answered them and I handed over the cash. Someone would make a call, and the doorbell would ring and the dealer delivered the crack, right to the front door, like a pizza delivery man. Then the smoking would begin again. It was like a weird, screwed-up arcade game where you have to keep feeding in change to keep playing. But it was real and it wasn't change.

Only later did I realise how false the picture I was getting was. When I eventually listened to the recording of the afternoon I came across a conversation I did not recall. It turned out that it had taken place when I had left the room for a private moment with an interviewee, leaving the recorder playing. They whispered to each other while I was out of the room:

'How much we gettin' for this?'

'Twenty-five dollars.'

'How long we got to stay here?'

'You got to tell him what he wants. Let him know what you feel.'

'She told me to come at four.'

Listening to this conversation and thinking back over the way things had happened, I realised that I had been set up. The visit wasn't ethnography—it was choreography: nothing was spontaneous. The house was empty when I got there, new users arrived at half-hourly intervals, talked for a while, took their $25 then left. In a quieter moment, Elouise said that if I really wanted to know what crack houses were all about we would have to stay all night. She suggested, however, that it might be a good idea to get out before it got dark. There was another reason for leaving. I was out of cash.

Looking back on the visit, I realise that I was close to what was going on in one sense only: geographically. Although I kidded myself that I was fairly clued up, I had no idea who these guys were or what they were going through. I was just a dumb white guy handing out cash: cheque-book journalism at the bottom of the food chain. At the end of the day I was $250 worse off. I had, however, learned a lesson. Drugs reporting, except when done by the real experts (and Elouise was clearly one) is largely bogus. How could any outsider understand what it was like to be caught in this trap? I was a middle-class white guy with a tape recorder deep in the heart of a lower-class black neighbourhood, a spectator, trying to learn something. Without a clue.

I took the subway back to my friend's flat on the Upper East Side, plonked myself down in a bar on the street, and ordered a beer. I'd had enough of being indoors for a while. Behind me, two well-heeled yuppies in chinos and polo shirts whinged about their lives. 'I mean, sure, I have a five-figure salary,' said Yuppie A, 'but so what? So *what*?' Yuppie B chimed in: 'I shot a forty-one last week. I mean, *plee-eaase*.' 'Yeah,' commiserated Yuppie A. 'It's nothing to be proud of.'

Partly listening to these guys, partly watching the passers-by and partly making notes about crack, I sat and drank more beers. I wondered what was going on back in the house. Presumably Ma and her friends were still smoking, spending the money I had given them for their time; perhaps they were laughing about the dumb white guy who had come by to visit; perhaps they had forgotten me already. The more I thought about it, the more I drank and the more I drank the more the two yuppies behind me droned on about the misery of their situation and the more depressed I became.

By the time it began to drizzle, I was drunk. Just as the bar was about to close a dishevelled guy shambled up asking for loose change. 'Can you help me out?' he asked no one in particular. 'I got nowhere to go.' Like everyone else, I looked at my feet.

I picked up the bill, paid it, threw a couple of dollars on to the table as a tip, then staggered home and threw up.

13 Sandinista!

On 18 August 1996 a California-based American newspaper called the *San Jose Mercury News* ran the first section of a three-part feature called 'Dark Alliance'. The story, written by a veteran *Mercury News* reporter, Gary Webb, concerned the conduct of various US intelligence agencies during the Nicaraguan Contra war, more than a decade earlier. It was to create a sensation.

According to Webb, the Contras—whom Ronald Reagan had described as 'the moral equivalent of the Founding Fathers'—had funded their war against the Sandinistas by trafficking cocaine. This cocaine trafficking, he said, had been allowed to continue because it would not have been politically expedient to stop it: in effect, the CIA had deliberately looked the other way. Webb went on to demonstrate that the Contras' cocaine had ended up in Los Angeles, where, distributed through a tight marketing network in South Central, it had assisted the transformation of the powder cocaine market to crack cocaine in the early 1980s.

With remarkable prescience, Webb made sure that the *San Jose Mercury News* had posted the articles, a large number of the incriminating documents and all sorts of other goodies he hadn't had room to print, on the Internet. This transformed the story. Within a week the *Mercury News* site was receiving 500,000 hits a day. When National Public Radio broadcast a piece about the story a week later, this went up to 800,000. Suddenly national TV networks began calling and requesting interviews. The site soon registered over 1.3 million hits a day. The story appeared to have acquired a life of its own. Webb had created a monster.

It was the kind of scoop every journalist dreams of. But was it true?

For over fifty years Nicaragua had been controlled by a family dictatorship under Anastasio Somoza, an American-backed despot of whom Roosevelt had once commented, 'He's a son of a bitch. But he's *our* son of a bitch.' Somoza and his family ran the country into the ground, accruing fabulous wealth for themselves in the process. Human-rights abuses were terrible. In the 1960s an anti-Somoza faction was born, the Sandinista National Liberation Front (named after a nationalist fighter called August Sandino, who had been murdered—on Somoza's orders—in 1933). By 1979 the Sandinistas had brought the country to the verge of civil war. When an American TV journalist was murdered by Somoza's National Guard—in front of his own cameraman, who happened to be filming at the time—America decided that enough was enough. President Jimmy Carter cut all aid to the Somoza regime and it was clear that the US was going to let its former allies get what was coming to them. Somoza fled for his life to Paraguay, where he was eventually murdered by Argentine paramilitaries. A number of his henchmen, meanwhile, fled to America, where they formed close relationships with exiled Cubans, especially members of the failed Bay of Pigs operation, Brigade 2506. The two groups had a lot in common: both had been chucked out of their countries, both hated communists, both were entirely unscrupulous and both wanted revenge.

A number of anti-Sandinista factions sprang up, which would eventually be unified under the umbrella term 'Contras'. In 1981 America's ever-benevolent intelligence system decided to help them out, requesting $19 million from Congress to establish secret Contra training camps in Costa Rica and Honduras. Once trained, the Contras were to be infiltrated across the border into Nicaragua to bring down the Sandinista regime. Preparations were terribly hush-hush: even for the CIA, overthrowing a legitimate foreign government was a bit naughty. So the $19 million was represented to Congress as money to be used to interdict arms shipments to El Salvador—another country that looked as if it might go communist. For fear of discovery, the CIA agreed not to become involved itself: by deploying only 'UCLAs' (Unilaterally Controlled Latino Assets—i.e. foreigners), everything would remain deniable. Well, that was the idea, anyway.

In November 1982 *Newsweek* blew the whistle on the operation, running a cover story AMERICA'S SECRET WAR—TARGET: NICARAGUA. Despite Reagan's protests that the Contras were like 'the brave men and women of the French Resistance' (they weren't) and his assurance that 'the struggle here is not right versus left but right versus wrong' (it wasn't), Congress began a series of moves to stop funding for the Contra army. When it was revealed in 1984 that the CIA had placed magnetic mines in three Nicaraguan harbours, blowing up ships belonging to six different countries, including a Soviet tanker, funding was finally cut off.

Reagan, desperate to help the Contras, was distraught. By now, however, the CIA wanted out of the whole thing: none of their analysts thought that the Contras had a chance of winning this war; it was costing a lot of money and it had the potential to be extremely embarrassing. They managed to pass responsibility to the National Security Council. In charge of Contra operations was placed one Lieutenant Colonel Oliver North. Faced with the question of how to fund an army in Central America when Congress would not give him any money, North came up with the 'neat idea' of linking the Contra struggle with another underhand operation: the illegal sale of arms to Iran. TOW antitank missiles were shipped to Iran and the profits siphoned back to the Contras in South America. Now everybody had enough money. Of course, it had to go wrong.

On 5 October 1986 the Sandinistas shot down a C-123 cargo plane over Costa Rica. Inside were seventy automatic rifles, 100,000 rounds of ammunition, seven grenade launchers and two dead aircrewmen who hadn't bothered to put on parachutes that morning. Outside it, meanwhile, was one very alive aircrewman who had. Two days later US audiences were shocked to see TV reports featuring an American in Nicaraguan custody. 'My name is Eugene Hasenfus,' said the prisoner. 'I come from Marinette, Wisconsin. I was captured yesterday in Southern Nicaragua.'

Not only had the Sandinistas managed to take Hasenfus alive but the two dead crew members were found to be carrying American identification. Meanwhile, the aeroplane was full of incriminating evidence that the US was funding the Contra war effort, including address books, flight logs and contact telephone numbers. Back in Washington, North began shredding documents. The next month, when the Iranians spilled the beans on their side of the operation, it was all over. North's 'neat idea' became the least covert covert operation in history.

When the Irangate hearings began, the American public soon grew used to the spectacle of Ollie North repeating that he had 'no recollection' of a large number of illegal activities. In the midst of these hearings, however, other allegations surfaced. At one hearing in July 1987 a couple of Baltimore men staged a protest outside the courthouse, jostling to get themselves in front of the cameras. Once they got there, they held up a banner: ASK ABOUT THE COCAINE SMUGGLING, it read. After shouting a number of slogans, they were led away from the courtroom.

Allegations about the Contras and drugs were not new. Two years earlier, reports of their cocaine-trafficking antics had surfaced at the hands of two Associated Press reporters, Robert Parry and Brian Barger:

> Nicaraguan rebels operating in Costa Rica have engaged in cocaine traf-
> ficking in the past to help finance their war against Nicaragua's leftist gov-
> ernment...the smuggling activity has involved refuelling planes at
> clandestine airstrips and sometimes helping transport cocaine to other
> Costa Rican points for shipment to the United States...
>
> Associated Press, 20 December 1985

Perhaps because the Contra allegations were so sensational anyway no one paid much attention: the main priority for the American public was to determine how much the president had known about the Contra operation. Drugs were a side issue. One person whose attention was piqued, however, was Senator John Kerry (Democrat, Massachusetts). In June 1986 Kerry established a Senate Foreign Relations Subcommittee to look into the allegations. As special counsel he appointed a Washington attorney by the name of Jack Blum. Blum was an experienced investigator, having worked on senatorial subcommittees for over ten years. He and his team began the laborious task of tracking down and interviewing traffickers and Contra leaders, trying to ascertain whether there really were links between the two. It didn't take long before it became clear that the CIA had not been too scrupulous in their recruitment of people to supply the Contras. Blum told me:

> Some of the things we pieced together were utterly astonishing. For exam-
> ple, there was this one pilot who was simultaneously flying drugs, doing
> covert operations for the Drug Enforcement Administration, doing covert
> operations for the Customs Service, delivering arms to the Contras *and* fly-
> ing drugs for his own account. You know, it's like '*What!?*' And nobody
> seemed to know about any of the other operations. It was just so amazing.

This chap was not the only unsuitable character working for the government. A number of the companies that the CIA had used to transport aid to Contra factions in Costa Rica and Honduras turned out to be owned by drug traffickers. The Kerry Committee focused on the activities of four it felt to be particularly dodgy:

1 Costa Rican company, Frigorifico de Puntarenas, was run by Paco Chanes and Luis Rodrigues—both well-known cocaine smugglers. Word

on the street was that they were shipping a ton of cocaine into the US every week. In 1984 the Internal Revenue Service (IRS) had specifically told the FBI that Frigorificos was a front company for cocaine cash, but nothing had been done. Despite all these facts, Frigorificos received $231,587 of US 'aid' to take to the Contras from January to May 1986.

2 DIACSA—a Miami aviation company—was run by a Bay of Pigs veteran, Alfredo Caballero. Caballero and his partner, Floyd Carlton, were under indictment in the US for attempting to import 900 pounds (410 kilograms) of cocaine. Despite this, DIACSA received $41,000 of 'human aid' for the Contras.

3 Vortex Aviation was run by one Michael Palmer, at the time under investigation by the FBI in three separate jurisdictions. Palmer was under indictment for trafficking 136,000 kilograms (300,000 pounds) of marijuana to the US in 1982. Vortex won more than $317,000 of US government money.

4 SETCO AIR was owned by one Juan Ramón Matta Ballesteros—a DEA Class 1 violator. It was Matta Ballesteros who, together with a Mexican trafficker, Angel Felix Gallardo, had funded Honduras's cocaine coup in 1978, then tasked the military to assist their cocaine operations. The two men were the heads of Mexico's leading drugs cartel, based in Guadalajara. Matta's line of work was no great secret: in 1985 *Newsweek* declared that he was responsible for a third of all the cocaine reaching the US. From 1983 to 1985, SETCO was paid to carry over a million rounds of ammunition, as well as food, supplies and uniforms, for the Contras and, as late as 1986, received $185,924 for ferrying supplies that year alone.

It might have been the case that these companies won their US government contracts by some sort of terrible bureaucratic cock-up, but the fact remains that at least four of the companies employed by the State Department to run guns to the Contras—companies that had handled the best part of a million dollars of government funds between them—were run by major drug traffickers. It didn't stop there. One of Kerry's main informants was a guy called Jorge Morales. Morales, a wealthy playboy who held the world New York–Miami powerboat record, was a big-time cocaine smuggler. Under oath, he testified that he had been indicted for drug trafficking in 1984 but had been approached by a couple of men who said they worked for the CIA. If he agreed to pay $250,000 every three months to the Contras, he was told, he would remain a free man. Sure enough, once he started making these payments, law-enforcement officials stopped hassling him. By the end of the Contra operation, he said, he had personally donated $3 million to the Contra cause. In an attempt to verify Morales's assertions, Kerry's investigators contacted the head of one of the main Contra factions, Eden Pastora, who admitted that he had indeed received large amounts of cash from Morales—as well as a C-47 aeroplane and two helicopters. Two of Morales's drug pilots, Gary Betzner (who had flown the mines that caused all the trouble in 1984 down to Latin America) and Fabio Ernesto Carrasco, admitted to flying guns to the Contras in South America and cocaine back to North America. Betzner estimated that the Contras probably made in the region of $40 million out of drug sales back home.

Kerry's detractors (and there were many) accused Morales and Betzner of lying in a desperate attempt to reduce their sentences, but the fact was that they stood to gain nothing by admitting to further offences. In fact, neither was offered a sentence reduction—until it was discovered that they were assisting the Kerry investigators, whereupon they were both suddenly offered deals on the condition that they *stop* co-operating.

The rubbishing of Morales and Betzner was nothing new for Kerry's team: the administration took cheap shots at every witness—on the grounds that they were felons and thus disreputable. Blum recalled:

> They said, 'These witnesses are criminals, right?' So my response to this was, 'Well, when I find a boy scout troop leader who was there when the cocaine was being delivered, I'll use him as a witness. But, in the meantime, I'll use the people that were there.' It's pretty rare to find a boy scout troop leader who was around for the delivery of cocaine.

Blum soon discovered more uncomfortable facts. The list of the Contra supply operators read like a who's who of mercenary double-dealing. One of the main Nicaraguan Contra organisers, for example, was a Cuban, Rafael Quinto, who had been involved in a bungled plot to assassinate Fidel Castro for the CIA. Another lead player was Luis Posada Carillos—long suspected of bombing a Cuban airliner in 1976, killing 73 civilians, including the Cuban national fencing team. Yet another was Frank Fiorini, who had, under another name, been one of the original Watergate burglars. It appeared that the CIA, in their rush to get someone to help the Contras, had assembled a team of extremely disreputable characters.

Of all the CIA assets, however, the most impressive was Felix Rodríguez. Rodríguez, who had served under Ollie North in Vietnam, had also botched an attempt to assassinate Fidel Castro but had got more lucky in Bolivia, where he was present at the execution of Che Guevara (throughout his Contra operations, he wore Che's wristwatch). Rodríguez certainly got around: not only was he in charge of the Contra resupply operations at Ilopango air force base in El Salvador but he was also the man whom Eugene Hasenfus had named as his contact when he was shot down over Costa Rica. He had his finger in a number of other pies, too: in the middle of the Contra operation, his business partner was arrested and charged with smuggling $10.3 million worth of cocaine to finance another coup in Honduras. At one point, Blum was told, Rodríguez had flown 12 tons of cocaine directly into Homestead air force base in Florida.

How could the CIA have employed these people? Blum had no doubts how this had come about:

> Classic bureaucratic stupidity. Your job is to find somebody who's going to airdrop stuff to the Contras in Central America, or going to do X and Y. You are paid as a spy and you are told to keep it secret. You find someone and you tell them to do it—you don't exactly go out and vet him to see if he's a bad guy because by definition what you want done is criminal and he's a criminal so he's going to do what you want. It doesn't occur to you that the next morning you're going to wake up and find out that you were working with a major cocaine trafficker because you—as a spy—are stupid. You don't bother reading the newspaper and you don't have any political sense whatsoever. *That's* how this stuff happens.

For sheer jaw-dropping, bowel-flushing stupidity, however, Kerry's team was hard pushed to beat the case of Barry Seal. Seal was perhaps the best pilot of his generation, a man who would fly anything, anywhere, for money. A natural pilot, he had flown for Special Forces in Vietnam before being demobbed and moving on to more lucrative employment, transporting first guns, then marijuana and finally cocaine. His arrogance was astonishing: at one point, according to legend, he spotted a law-enforcement officer tailing him and, instead of trying to hide, walked up and introduced himself: 'You dumb sonofabitch,' he said, 'you'll never catch me!'

Seal was, simply, the best. Because he was so good, the Medellín cartel employed him to fly their cocaine. He was estimated to have transported more than 30 tons of the drug for the cartel.

Seal was eventually turned in by an informant and busted and in spring 1983 he agreed to turn informant himself. Since he was the only American who had a really good relationship with the cartel heads, the DEA leapt at the chance. Seal headed down to Colombia to set up an elaborate sting operation. Once there he was informed by Pablo Escobar that the Medellín cartel had established relations with the Sandinista regime and that the next shipment would be flown via Nicaragua. He was introduced to a government official named Federico Vaughan, who took him into Nicaragua and showed him a military airstrip called Los Brasiles where he was to land. Seal then flew back to the United States to buy himself a bigger plane and to report to his DEA controllers—who instructed him to go ahead with the shipment. He bought a suitably large plane, a vast C-123 Provider he nicknamed 'the Fat Lady' and the DEA, with a little help from the CIA, installed hidden cameras all over it. Seal was told to take pictures of everyone who showed up at Los Brasiles.

In June 1984 Seal touched down at Los Brasiles in his new plane, and took photos of Escobar and Vaughan loading 25-kilo sacks of cocaine into the back. He then flew it all to the US, where it was busted by the DEA. When the secret film was processed, his controllers were ecstatic: here was real footage of the cartel in action. Inside the DEA, plans were hatched to snare all the Medellín cartel kingpins in one go. With Seal's help, a huge sting operation could be arranged for the next trip.

Only there was no next trip. The pictures were leaked to the press and Seal's cover was blown. His snapshots would eventually be paraded on television by Ronald Reagan, who intoned: 'I know that every American parent concerned about the drug problem will be outraged to learn that top Nicaraguan officials are deeply involved in drug trafficking.'

US parents concerned about the drug problem may well have been outraged at the photos, but they weren't as outraged as Seal. His cover blown, he was assassinated in February 1986.

Who had leaked the pictures? One of the only non-DEA agents to know of their existence was Oliver North, who had been following the investigation closely. In fact, in a meeting to discuss Seal's operation, when it emerged that he was carrying $1.5 million worth of the Medellín cartel's cash, North specifically asked if he could have it to give to the

Contras. He was told that drug busts didn't work that way—officials couldn't simply *keep* the proceeds. Disappointed, he appears to have cooked up another scheme to make some money. As Blum told me:

> The whole thing stank. What we think happened was that Barry Seal was compromised so that Ollie [North] could get a vote from the House in favour of the Contras. He released information about what Barry Seal had done in a way that broke Barry's cover as an undercover informant in order to convince various members of the House that they should vote in favour of the administration on some vote regarding funding the Contras. It was just grotesque because it was that release of information that allowed the killers to work out where he was and to kill him.

Thus it was that Oliver North torpedoed perhaps the most promising anticocaine operation in history—as a publicity stunt. His leaking of the photographs not only shafted the entire investigation but led directly to the death of Barry Seal.[9] I told Blum that I found this shocking but he was not surprised:

> The guy [Ollie North] had a one-track mind. He's a marine. Somebody says, 'Storm the hill'—he storms the hill. He just doesn't have the capacity to sort out whether storming the hill is really what he should be concerned with. Nothing should surprise you because this guy was single-minded in his mission: 'The president wants me to save the Contras! By God, I'm going to save the Contras! Screw everything else.'

This, it seemed to me, was a pretty accurate summary of the Contra operation itself: an ill-fated, ill-considered, illegal, immoral undertaking so myopic in its goals that nothing else—ethics, funding, morals or drugs—was allowed to get in its way. The president wanted to storm the hill and the hill was duly stormed. Only later would the ramifications of this particular storming operation become known—and would the American public realise that, in reality, neither the end nor the means had been justifiable.

---

[9] North's antics in the Barry Seal case would return to haunt him. After the botched sting operation, Seal's C-123 supply plane, the Fat Lady, was sold to a company called Southern Air Transport, which—by a freak coincidence—happened to be one of the companies contracted to resupply the Contra army in Costa Rica. It was used to fly guns and supplies a number of times before being shot down in October 1986, revealing American complicity in the Contra operation and leading to the Iran–Contra scandal.

The Kerry Committee report, which was finally published in April 1989, included extensive indexes listing contacts, interviewees and sources. It also contained an appendix listing all the steps that various governmental agencies had taken to interfere with the investigation. Its verdict was damning.

> There was substantial evidence of drug smuggling through war zones on the part of individual Contras, Contra suppliers, Contra pilots, mercenaries who worked with the Contras, and Contra supporters throughout the region...US officials in Central America failed to address this drug issue for fear of jeopardising the war efforts against Nicaragua...and senior US policymakers were not immune to the idea that drug money was a perfect solution to the Contras' funding problems.

The committee concluded:

> In the name of helping the Contras, we abandoned the responsibility our government has for protecting our citizens from all threats to their security and well being...the credibility of governmental institutions has been jeopardised by the administration's decision to turn a blind eye to domestic and foreign corruption associated with the international narcotics trade.

It's worth noting at this point that this is not what Gary Webb wrote in the *San Jose Mercury News*. These are not the accusations of a journalist or CIA-basher. They are the conclusions of a US government investigation, whose witnesses were interrogated (and videotaped) under oath in the presence of a US senator. As such they carry weight. Despite this, no one paid any attention to them at all. Today, Blum explains why:

> We began to get this stuff out on the public record and of course the people in the administration just dumped all over us. They said we were crazy, wrong, they attacked Kerry, they attacked me, they attacked the investigation. They said our witnesses were bad. It was a concerted assault...I had been subjected to some of this back in the days of the Nixon period—but nothing remotely resembling this. It was an all-out assault. It was really quite severe.

As a result of governmental spin (in one memorable piece in *Newsweek*, Senator John Kerry himself was dubbed a 'randy conspiracy buff')—and perhaps the fact that the public was largely bored with the Iran–Contra story anyway—the Kerry Committee's findings were not picked up by the press. Allegations of Contra cocaine dealing remained, for most of the American public, rumours.

Until Gary Webb emerged on the scene.

I arranged to meet Webb in San Francisco. I was interviewing a couple of other people in the city anyway and he and his girlfriend, Rebecca, fancied a wander around town, so they offered to drive in from Sacramento, an hour and a half away. We decided to meet up for Sunday lunch. This, it emerged, was something of a tactical error: the weekend we had arranged to meet turned out to be Gay Pride weekend and Sunday lunchtime was the focus of the celebrations—culminating in a massive parade of floats and brightly outfitted marching bands through the city. For twenty minutes we fought our way through the backstreets looking for somewhere to sit while weird, overdressed transvestites and shrieking Village People lookalikes scampered past towards the parade. Eventually we found somewhere that was open, sat down by the window and ordered drinks. A giant brontosaurus surrounded by bodybuilders in loincloths wielding polystyrene clubs sailed past the window, followed by another, covered in prancing queens in cut-off hot pants waving wooden bats. ALL-AMERICAN GAY SOFTBALL LEAGUE, proclaimed the banner. Hmmn. We looked out of the window, then at each other and then at the menu. It was kind of a weird setting. But then, it was kind of a weird story.

When the drinks arrived, Webb explained how it had all started.

One day in July 1995, Webb said, he was contacted by a woman who said she had a hot story. Her boyfriend, a young Nicaraguan by the name of Rafael Corñejo, was in jail awaiting trial. He was deeply connected with cocaine—and the main witness against him was a former CIA operative who had sold cocaine for the Contras. Webb was less than enthusiastic: to his mind, CIA stories were the domain of conspiracy theorists and paranoiacs. He usually covered state issues, asset forfeiture, crooked judges, that sort of thing. And, besides, hadn't some investigation or other proved that there had been nothing in this? When the woman produced court transcripts of federal grand jury hearings in which the cocaine–Contra link was quite specific, Webb became more interested. He went to the library and looked for references on cocaine and Contras and it wasn't long before he came across a copy of the Kerry Subcommittee report:

I was stunned. I was sitting there reading the report every day, thinking, Why have I never heard of this stuff? I mean, they were talking about Manuel Noriega, the BCCI scandal—all this great stuff, years before it became public knowledge. When I finished reading the hearings I rang Jack Blum and asked him why there had never been any stories about this, and he expressed surprise, too, that the Washington press had just blown this off as some wide-eyed crazy theory and had never paid any attention.

Webb contacted Robert Parry, the journalist who had first run the cocaine–Contra story for Associated Press back in 1985. Parry left him in no doubt that the story was a career killer. His writing partner, Brian Barger, was accused of being a communist and found his house under surveillance. Together the pair were accused of poisoning Oliver North's dog (both were later cleared of this heinous crime; in fact it had died of natural causes). Less than a year before Hasenfus's plane was shot down over Costa Rica, kicking off the whole Iran–Contra investigation, they were instructed by their bureau chief to stop reporting on the Contra war because 'it's not a story any more'. Parry suggested that Webb leave the cocaine allegations well alone. Webb ignored the advice.

Webb's line of investigation was diametrically opposite to Blum's: while Blum had started out with all the big players in South America, Webb's story started on the street and led back to them. He didn't go into the big-time launderers and drug pilots: Kerry had already done this. He wanted to know where the cocaine they had brought in had ended up.

His story revolved around the activities of a couple of early Contra supporters, Norwin Meneses and Danilo Blandón, both exiled Nicaraguans. Of the two, Meneses was the more important. Known back home as 'el Rey de la Droga' (the King of Drugs), he was determined to raise money for the Contras on the US mainland through cocaine sales. He recruited Blandón. While Meneses took the East Coast, Blandón headed for the West, where, much to the delight of Meneses, he soon hooked up with a black cocaine dealer in Los Angeles, who had an apparently unlimited capacity to shift the drug. The pair began importing more and more cocaine to keep pace with the incredible demand in LA. The year was now 1981. And the black dealer who was shifting so much coke?
'Freeway' Ricky Ross.
The upshot of the story was that the Contra war had occurred at

exactly the time when crack was getting started in the US. Blandón and Meneses imported increasing amounts of cocaine for Ross who, pioneering the new trade, cooked it up and shifted it as Ready Rock. As we have already seen from Ross's interview, his impact on the LA cocaine scene was considerable: he was, by the end of his career, shifting some 700 kilos of crack a month. Thus Webb's contention was that the Contra effort had been a main cause of the crack explosion. As he told me:

> It was sort of a collision. Crack was coming up anyway, and it ran smack out into these planeloads of cheap cocaine that the Contras were bringing in and you have an explosion, a crack cocaine explosion. And that's essentially what my story is about. This collision of events.

Webb's story ran over 18, 19 and 20 August 1986. Initially the response was quite favourable. Then, all of a sudden, it wasn't.

More or less simultaneously, everyone launched a broadside on Webb's story. Perhaps this was professional jealousy, or because they were advised by contacts within the establishment who appeared to be in a situation to be able to deny the allegations. It has been suggested, however, that their real motivation was embarrassment. Most of them had gone on the record after the Kerry Report denying that there had been any links between cocaine and the Contras: they had missed the story. Anything other than a series of further denials would seem like a turnaround. Blum said:

> Here are all the newspapers who are in this thing and all they care about is saving their own reputations because they had previously not paid any attention to our report, so they go all out to trash Webb instead of asking the question: 'Is there anything in this story that is accurate that we overlooked last time around?' The answer is that there was plenty but they didn't bother covering that. All they did was trash Webb at the *San Jose Mercury News*.

A number of accusations were made to belittle Webb's story: it was said that Blandón and Meneses had not shifted much cocaine at all—certainly not enough to start a crack epidemic; that they had not made much money for the Contras; or that they didn't give it to the Contras but kept it for themselves. Everyone Webb interviewed, it was alleged, was a liar, on the basis that they were criminals, mercenaries and traffickers. Yet when America's national papers bothered to look for people to deny

Webb's allegation, they themselves were forced to accept the testimonies of other criminals, mercenaries and traffickers.

All sorts of other denials were thrown about: that the Nicaraguans were not important cocaine dealers; that they had been trafficking either too early, or too late, to have had any effect on Los Angeles' crack scene. Many of the newspapers wrote that they knew Webb's story to be incorrect because they had been told so by CIA contacts. These contacts were mysteriously unwilling to go on the record to make these denials, however.

Of all the papers attempting to discredit the story, perhaps the most virulent was the *Los Angeles Times*. This was, after all, their turf: why had they missed this story when an out-of-towner had picked it up? Webb had made them look bad. It seemed that they wanted revenge: according to an article in the *Columbia Journalism Review*, the team of reporters assigned to the cocaine–Contra story called themselves the 'Get Gary Webb Team' and delighted in the notion that they were about to stop him being awarded a Pulitzer prize. In its attempt to discredit the story the *LA Times* outdid itself in its assertion that Webb's story was rubbish because this crack dealer he was writing about, Ricky Ross, was a nobody, a nothing, who had never shifted a significant amount of cocaine in the first place.

> The explosion of cheap, smokable cocaine in the 1980s was a uniquely egalitarian phenomenon, one that lent itself more to mom and pop organisations than to the sinister hand of a government sanctioned plot...How the epidemic reached that extreme, on some level, had nothing to do with Ross.
>
> *Los Angeles Times*, 20 October 1996,
> cit. *Whiteout*, Cockburn and St Clair

There was some truth in this: Ross was not the only crack merchant at the time and it would be inaccurate to blame the crack epidemic entirely on him: as we have seen, by the time Ross began selling it, crack had already hit the Bahamas, and would have emerged with or without him. But to say that South Central's crack explosion had nothing to do with him was a bit ripe. At the peak of his career Ross, as he later testified, was selling $1–2 million worth of crack per day. That the effect of this could have been anything but significant beggars belief. The piece is all the more impressive when you consider that its author was a journalist by the name of Jesse Katz. Could this, perchance, have been the same

Jesse Katz who had written two years earlier of Ross as 'the criminal mastermind behind crack's decade-long reign'? Possibly. Just possibly.

The most successful technique to stop the story, however, involved not rubbishing but rather *manipulating* it. In October 1996 newspaper reports began denying that the CIA had deliberately brought cocaine into the US, and that there had been a CIA 'plot'. Webb's story was portrayed in the papers as a theory that the CIA had deliberately brought crack cocaine into the inner cities to subvert the black population. This was emphatically denied. And not surprisingly: it wasn't true. Webb had never made this assertion. He had not said that the arrival of cocaine in the US had been deliberate, and certainly had not suggested that crack was a plot to subvert ethnic minorities. Someone *else* had said that. As he recalled over lunch:

> I never made that allegation. All we said about the CIA was that these fellows had met the CIA agents while they were doing it and that there is evidence that the CIA knew about their activities because the people who were telling them what to do were working with the CIA. But as far as motive went—we never got into it...the problem was that when the *Washington Post* did its first piece, they made the accusation that we had said that. And when the *Washington Post* says something, people believe it. So it was the *Washington Post* who first raised the suggestion that we were saying the CIA targeted black Americans for this. Because the story never said it.

Once the story had been transformed to the realm of conspiracy, it was easy to downplay. Soon the cocaine–Contra link was directly associated with such dastardly plots as the deliberate design of the AIDS virus to target homosexuals and the supposed poisoning of soft drinks to render black men sterile. The story was relegated whence it had come—to the Internet, along with accounts of the Kennedy assassination, Area 51 and the fact that Elvis was alive and well and living in a trailer park outside Reno. As a means of disproving what Webb had actually written, it didn't achieve a thing. But, as a means of making it go away, it was very successful.

Webb's story was complicated: there were a lot of bizarre characters in it, many of them with aliases and almost all of them with long-winded double-barrelled names. What the reading public wanted was a simple quote that would explain whether this had really happened or not. Thus no one noticed that newspapers and government men were busily denying allegations that had never been made. As Jack Blum told me:

If you ask, 'Did the CIA sell crack?' the answer is a categorical 'no'. But, if you ask whether the US government ignored the drug problem and subverted law enforcement to prevent embarrassment and reward our allies in the Contra war, the answer is 'yes'.

By May 1997 the attack was taking its toll. Under extreme pressure, the *Mercury News*'s editor, Jerry Ceppos, ran an editorial in which he said that, while he stood by the main assertions of the story, he agreed that there were problems with it: they had not given the CIA the chance to respond to the allegations; they had not estimated how much cocaine had come in through the Contra supply lines and they had oversimplified the origins of the crack epidemic. Webb was livid:

> They said, 'A lot of the criticism against you is unfair but it's still out there and we have to deal with it and this is the way we'll deal with it, by running this column.' I said, 'That's idiotic. The way to deal with it is to keep on going after the story and not backtrack.' The newspaper was sick of getting beat up on and, if you're talking about political expediency, that's the easiest way to go, to say, 'The reporter fucked up, we're sorry.'

Despite his assurances that this was a clarification rather than an apology, Ceppos's editorial was taken as a retraction of the entire story. EXPOSÉ ON CRACK WAS FLAWED, PAPER SAYS, ran the *New York Times*. The *Washington Post* ran a column praising Ceppos, quoting him to the effect that the article was 'poorly written' (never once in his editorial had he used the phrase 'poorly written'). The story was then cut off. Although there was plenty of new material to justify more articles, these were never run. By the summer, Webb had been pulled off the story and shipped off to a district bureau out of harm's way. He resigned in disgust shortly afterwards. His departure from the *San Jose Mercury News* was taken as further proof that he had been wrong: one New York journalist asked me later, 'Why did he lose his job if he didn't screw up?'

As a result of the furore generated by Webb's story, however, the CIA agreed to an internal investigation under its Inspector General, Frederick Hitz. The investigation, said press releases, was to be 'the most comprehensive ever done'. It probably was. But it wasn't entirely free of underhand tactics. For a start, the night before the report was due to be released, there was a convenient 'leak'. In December 1997 the *LA Times* proclaimed, CIA CLEARS ITSELF IN CRACK INVESTIGATION. Other papers followed suit. At this stage, however, the report had not yet been released. Its release was then mysteriously delayed on the basis that it might damage ongoing investigations. The result of this was that the CIA got all the 'CIA is cleared' publicity without having to reveal anything of its internal investigation. And, because people tend to read headlines rather than columns, the general impression was that the CIA really had been cleared. As an exercise in media manipulation, it was a triumph.

When the report was eventually released in 1998, they tried the trick again. Jack Blum laughed:

> Man! Did they ever release that report at a wonderful time! Do you know when the report was released? Eight o'clock of the Friday night of the impeachment of William Jefferson Clinton. So the CIA's own Inspector General's report got virtually no press because everybody was busy with other stuff.

You had to hand it to the CIA: if they didn't want anyone to know what was in this report, they certainly did a good job of arranging it. But the spin was not yet over. Keen to get a look at the famous Hitz Report, I rang the CIA and asked where I could get a copy. I spoke to a charming young lady called Tanya, who told me that it was all available on the Internet. I asked her about it briefly and she told me that there had recently, in fact, been a third investigation, which had revealed that the first two investigations had been bang on in their assessment that 'the CIA was not complicit'. Funny: the understanding I had gained from everyone else was that the Hitz Report had been pretty damning and that it had vindicated the long-rubbished Kerry Report, together with large sections of Webb's 'Dark Alliance' series.

So here, reader, is a challenge. Get on to the Internet and go to www.cia.gov. Scroll down to the bottom of the page and look for the heading 'DCI and CIA Reports', click on to it and go to 'Overview of Report of Investigation'. There you will find two volumes of declassified summaries of the Hitz Reports on cocaine and the Contras: volume 1, 'The California Story', and volume 2, 'The Contra Story'. Have a look and decide for yourself: is the CIA guilty or not? Make sure you have the permission of the person who owns the phone line, because it's going to take you a while.

To nonexperts (i.e. normal people) the Hitz Reports are impenetrable. They are peppered with the names of Nicaraguan mercenaries, CIA contacts, agents, pilots, traffickers, smugglers and police and full of double-speak. As with *Peru—History of Coca: 'the Divine Plant' of the Incas* by William Golden Mortimer, you glance at them and then feel immediately unwell. Nowhere in the reports is there a handy conclusion saying 'Yes, we did it' or 'No, we didn't do it': that would make reading them far too easy. But is Hitz's report an admission or a denial? For those of you without either a computer or the inclination to spend a fortnight glued to a screen deciphering acronyms, here is the nub.

a) **Were the companies highlighted by the Kerry Committee really run by traffickers?** Yes. And they really did receive US State Department funds for their part in the contra war effort.

> **Sample admission**: Introduction, para 19: *CIA received drug trafficking allegations or information concerning 14 pilots and two other individuals who were associated with companies that provided support for the Contra program. CIA also learned of drug trafficking allegations or information concerning three companies that were used to support Contra activities from 1984 until at least 1988.*

b) **Were Kerry characters such as Jorge Morales really supplying money to the Contras?** Yes.

> **Sample admission**: Hitz I, para 195: *Pastora acknowledges that, while he led the Southern Front forces, he received funds and the use of a C-47 cargo aircraft, as well as another smaller aircraft, which had been donated by narcotics trafficker Jorge Morales.*

c) **Did any of the Contras traffic cocaine?** Yes. There is evidence that both the Southern and Northern Contra fronts were associated with active cocaine dealers.

> **Sample admission**: Introduction, para 16: *In addition to the five individuals associated with ARDE, CIA received drug trafficking allegations or information concerning 16 other individuals who supported Southern Front Contra operations based in Costa Rica.*

d) **Was any of the money generated by these traffickers used to fund the Contra war?** Yes.

> **Sample admissions**: Introduction, para 13: *CIA received information that one Contra-related organization—the ADREN '15th of September' group—engaged in drug trafficking for fund raising purposes.*

Hitz I, para 194: *Pastora states that he received money from several persons who later were arrested for, or convicted of, drug trafficking.*

e) **Was the CIA involved in this trafficking?** No. However, while no information was found to indicate that the CIA was ever directly involved in trafficking itself, in a number of cases CIA agents were aware of cocaine-trafficking activities by Contras but did nothing about them.

> **Sample admission:** Introduction, para 35: *CIA knowledge of allegations or information indicating that organizations or individuals had been involved in drug trafficking did not deter their use by CIA. In other cases, CIA did not act to verify drug trafficking allegations or information even when it had the opportunity to do so. In still other cases, CIA deemed the allegation or information to be unsubstantiated or not credible.*

f) **What about Gary Webb's allegations? Were they true?** Some of them. While there are endless disagreements about the relationship between Ricky Ross, Meneses and Blandón—how much they made, how much cocaine they shifted, when, and so forth—there is no doubt that some of Blandón and Meneses's money from cocaine sales went to the Contras. In addition, Eden Pastora (leader of the Contras' Southern Front in Costa Rica) admitted that Blandón had lent him his home in Honduras, rent free, from 1984–87.

> **Sample admissions:** Hitz I, para 179: *Bermudez told* [Blandón and Meneses] *of the trouble FDN was having in raising funds and equipment and asked him and Meneses to help, stating that 'the ends justify the means'.*
>
> Hitz I para 183 [Blandón] *estimates... that Meneses may have given the group* [of California Contras] *as much as $40,000 from drug profits during 1982–3.*

Whilst these are frank and alarming admissions, they are couched in clauses that appear to take them all back: in the case of donations to the Contras from cocaine traffickers, it is made quite clear that the traffickers never specifically informed the Contras that the money was the result of drug sales. The Contras, in return, never asked where the cash was coming from. Bermudez's comment that 'the ends justify the means', however, clearly implies that he knew money was coming from illicit sources. But, because this was never made explicit, Hitz can conclude that Bermudez never knew that Blandón was a trafficker. Equally, while it was quite clear that some of these traffickers were tasked to raise money for the cause, they were never explicitly told to do so by trafficking drugs. Hence Blandón's claim that 'Pastora never asked me to raise money by selling drugs' (Hitz I, paragraph 188) and thus the illusion that Pastora was unaware of the source of the money. This 'ask-no-questions-and-I'll-tell-no-lies' attitude ensures that the final impressions of these sections are those of wide-eyed innocence.

Is it not reasonable, however, to suppose that someone, somewhere, might have realised that convicted drug dealers, when asked to raise money, will do it by dealing drugs?

In the case of the crooked companies employed to supply the Contras, well, they weren't hired by the CIA but by NHAO (the Nicaraguan Humanitarian Aid Organisation—whatever that is). No blame on the CIA there, then. Equally, for summaries, it is always handy to conclude that the CIA did not deliberately engage in narcotics trafficking (no one ever alleged that it did), that it had no contact with Ross, Meneses or Blandón (no one ever claimed that it did), that Ross never gave any of his crack-generated profits to the Contras (no one ever claimed that he did) or that the CIA never tasked any Contra supporters to raise money by trafficking in drugs (no one ever claimed this, either). The result of all these denials is a report that reads like a nightmare script from the sitcom *Yes, Minister*: an admission heavily disguised as a denial. Perhaps this is not entirely surprising: after all, there's a world of difference between telling a lie and being 'economical with the *actualité*'. To the likes of you and me, that difference is called 'politics'.

So here's the nub: Webb was right.

Not in everything, certainly, but a lot. And yet even today, two years after the Hitz Report, there is still an aura of 'conspiracy theory' about his story. All of the DEA agents I asked about cocaine and the Contras denied that there was anything in the rumours. Professor Ron Siegel—the expert on the origins of cocaine smoking, among other things—told me that, despite his having given extensive interviews to Webb, his book, and the theory, were way out of line. Bruce Porter, author of *Blow*, George Jung's biography—and an adjunct professor at the Columbia Graduate School of Journalism—had likewise told me that the rumours were groundless. The BBC's man in Washington, Gavin Esler, in his book *The United*

States of Anger, also denied that it had happened, describing it as an 'appalling, unproven conspiracy'. Why did all these intelligent, informed people deny the veracity of Webb's claims? How could anyone still say that it 'hadn't happened'? Across the table Webb became animated:

What didn't happen? That's the part I don't get: what didn't happen? What they say is that this wasn't an organised conspiracy by the CIA— which no one ever accused them of in the first place. So I have never understood when people say, 'This didn't happen.' *What?* I mean, that these people didn't exist? That they didn't bring cocaine into this country? That the Contras didn't benefit from it? *What* didn't happen? And nobody can ever say, you know? It's the old story: once a story has been 'discredited', nobody has to pay any attention to the details because 'it's been discredited'... The propaganda has succeeded in throwing up such a cloud of doubt over this whole story that, even when the CIA came out and admitted it, nobody was prepared to believe it.

I paid the bill and Webb, Rebecca and I headed back out on to the street. The carnival was still in full swing. We all shook hands, I thanked them for their time and we wandered off in different directions.

Fighting my way through the crowds back towards my hotel, I bumped into a giant of a man in a T-shirt advertising FAT HAIRY HOMO SLUT. As I passed, he exchanged high fives with a six-foot-four transvestite in a micro-mini and fishnet tights. A bevy of Chinese women passed by, bare-breasted, drinking cappuccinos from Starbucks mugs and shrieking, 'Party!' The Gay and Bisexual American Latino Men's Association stall seemed to be doing a roaring trade and, as I was wondering where all these people came from, a cowboy dressed only in leather chaps, a Stetson and jockstrap gave me a hug. 'Love you, man,' he said, before strutting off purposefully into the crowd. Here they were, the fun-loving American public proudly asserting their rights and enjoying the wonderful freedom of America, all studiously ignoring the fact that their government was busily manipulating a truth so unsavoury that it had to be given to them diluted so that they could swallow it.

14 The Horsemen of Cocaine

While the Contra scandal was creating havoc in the USA, Colombia, the engine of the cocaine problem, was going down the toilet. The moment President Betancur re-introduced extradition after the assassination of Rodrigo Lara Bonilla everything fell apart.

For the traffickers, extradition represented a fate worse than death. 'Better a tomb in Colombia to a cell in the United States,' they said. To avert the living death of a life sentence in the US, they resorted to increasingly desperate measures: if the violence was cranked up enough, they figured, eventually the government would realise that extradition just wasn't worth it. However, while their increasingly violent reprisals gained them the clout that they needed to fight extradition, they were counterproductive, losing them public sympathy and making the government even more keen to deport them. Finding themselves in a vicious circle, the Medellín boys evolved from a bunch of bootleggers into a terror organisation so powerful that it threatened the democracy and the peace of the entire nation. The two groups—traffickers on one side and the Colombian government (heavily pushed by the United States) on the other—entered into a war of attrition in a terrifying game of chicken to see who would back down first. In the end, everyone lost.

From time to time in the swirl of bombings and killings that followed, the cartel offered the government an olive branch, offering to call a halt to the violence in return for immunity from extradition. For the period it took for the government to consider these offers, violence abated. Then the offer was either rejected or the cartel tried to push the government into making a decision by committing further atrocities, forcing the administration to stand up to it. Then the killing began again.

Sensing the public mood after the assassination of Rodrigo Lara Bonilla, Escobar and his mates high-tailed it out of Colombia, ending up in Panama under the protection of the country's controller, Manuel

Noriega. Safely ensconced in Panama City, it was clear that something would have to be done about the Lara situation. The cartel sent word to the Colombian government that the time had come to call a truce and arranged to meet two representatives of the Betancur administration, former President Alfredo Lopez Michelson and Attorney General Carlos Jiminez Gomez, in the Marriott Hotel on 4 May 1984. Escobar began the meeting by announcing that, while he regretted the death of Lara Bonilla greatly, he had had nothing to do with it. This was a truth couched in a lie. The cartel certainly regretted the killing; the Ochoa family in particular—which still denies complicity in the assassination—was livid with Escobar for killing someone with a profile as high as that of the Minister of Justice. Anyone with any common sense would have realised that this would lead to trouble. However, there was no doubt that Escobar had been responsible. A recent PBS interview with Carlos Lehder's personal pilot, Fernando Arenas, revealed that the cartel leaders were not the only ones in hiding out in Panama—a number of members of the crew responsible for Lara's death were there, too.

Having stated its position on the Lara assassination, the cartel then laid its cards on the table. The offer—which was later put down in a six-page memo so that President Betancur could read it for himself—was for Escobar and his boys to dismantle their trafficking networks, scuppering between 70 and 80 percent of Colombia's drug-trafficking capacity, and to transfer their money from international banks around the world back into Colombia, injecting an annual income of around $2 billion into the country's economy. In effect, it was a massive bribe. If it would put an end to the cocaine industry, however, it might just be worth it. After all, La Violencia, the state of civil war that had raged since the early 1950s had ended with a truce and a general amnesty. What was the difference?

It was not to be. News of the clandestine meeting was leaked to the press. The Colombian public (and the Americans—who were later alleged to have engineered the leak) was outraged: how could the government even consider doing a deal with the very traffickers who had killed the Minister of Justice just two months earlier? Reports of the meeting were swiftly denied ('There has not been, there is not now, nor will there ever be any kind of understanding between the government and the signers of the memorandum', said President Betancur) and the two sides withdrew to plan their mutual offensives. For the government, this involved rounding up the traffickers and posting them to the United States as fast as possible.

The cartel had other plans. If the government was not going to respond to reasonable offers, then it must be persuaded by other means.

A prime target in the killing spree that followed was the American embassy in Bogotá. Colombian traffickers would not be in this situation were it not for the meddling ways of the United States. A list of American targets was assembled: embassy officials, their wives and families, businessmen and foreign journalists were all legitimate quarry. A $350,000 contract was taken out on Francis Mullen, head of the DEA. In November 1984 a car bomb was detonated outside the US embassy, injuring six pedestrians and killing a female bystander. Security was hiked: the ambassador, Lewis Tambs, was followed everywhere by a five-car convoy, armed to the teeth. He was eventually provided with a body double to confuse assassination attempts. Everyone was driven around with bodyguards in bulletproof cars. Because families were deemed easier targets than embassy officials themselves, particular care was taken with their protection. Armed guards were placed on the homes of all staff; spouses were not permitted to go shopping alone but had to call the embassy car pool and arrange to be picked up by an armoured escort. Rotas were established so that different families would go shopping together, all under the watchful eye of a series of machine-gun-toting bodyguards. Mike Fredericks, who was stationed in Bogotá at the time, recalled the moment when he realised that this was no longer a game:

It sobered me up the day my four-year-old son came back from school. I was waiting on the street and he came up in one of the little vans that they had converted into a school bus—and it was armoured. It had thick armoured glass and so forth, and there was a chase car, three guys with machine guns and shotguns following it, and it pulled up in front of our apartment. And he got out of the van—four years old—and he said, 'Daddy, I know why we have thick glass on the school bus. Because there are bad men trying to kill us.' Out of the mouth of a four-year-old, that was a wake-up call. Until then I thought it was quite fun.

By the end of 1984 the situation had deteriorated so far that diplomats and DEA agents were instructed to send their families home. Nearly a third of the embassy staff left en masse. Such was the violence in Medellín that the DEA office there was shut down. The Cali office followed shortly afterwards. Staff remaining in the country were told to vary their working hours and the routes they took to work to deter assassination attempts. So many bombs were detonated outside the embassy that the concourse was redesigned with concrete-filled steel posts all around it so that car-bombers could not get close to the building. Not that this stopped the traffickers trying—at one point they took to firing anti-tank rockets into the walls. Ambassador Tambs was eventually evacuated to Costa Rica for his own safety.

Meanwhile Colombian judges began receiving death threats from a group calling itself the Extraditables. Those that refused to support the cartel were persuaded by other means: one received a promise that, rather than send him a 'wooden smoking jacket', the Extraditables would post him the remains of his family, quartered. Others received visits from mysterious businessmen who took out photograph albums and showed them pictures: their families; relatives; friends; their kids at school. Their kids' friends. Judges who might normally have stood up to personal threats buckled when their children were threatened. In the spring of 1985 the judge investigating the Lara Bonilla assassination, Supreme Court Justice Julio Manuel Castro Gil, revealed that Escobar was the 'intellectual author' of the hit. In July, five gunmen walked up to his car when he was stuck in traffic and opened fire through the windscreen. He was killed instantly.

The Betancur administration was not cowed and the first wave of extraditions began with the Medellín launderer Hernán Botero. Traffickers were appalled to see Botero's arrival in the United States, where he was paraded in chains in front of the TV cameras. He got thirty years. The message was obvious: if a mere launderer could get thirty years, the serious traffickers were in big trouble. It became imperative that they keep well clear of the law.

Jorge Ochoa, the leading light of the Ochoa family, beat a hasty retreat to Spain together with his wife and daughter. Once there, the family met up with a Venezuelan couple, Gladys Gonzalez Linares and her husband, Gilberto, who happened to be none other than Gilberto Rodríguez Orejuela—head of the emerging Cali cartel. Apropos of nothing, the Spanish police received a tip-off as to the real identities of these two families (in fact the tip came from doubled pilot Barry Seal) and they were arrested in November. The US immediately demanded their extradition. Quick-thinking Colombian lawyers simultaneously filed identical papers requesting extradition to Colombia.

Not that the legal system in Colombia was in any condition to handle them when they got back. In the aftermath of the Lara assassination, Colombia was having severe trouble finding anyone willing to be Minister of Justice. Lara's original successor, Enrique Parejo Gonzalez, had started well, explaining that extradition was the only way of dealing with the narcos and signing the first deportation orders. He was soon deemed to be in such danger that he was removed from office and dispatched abroad as Colombia's ambassador to Hungary. Ensconced in the embassy in Budapest—behind the Iron Curtain—he was considered safe. He wasn't. One night in January 1987 Parejo opened the door of his residence to find himself face to face with a young Colombian he did not recognise. The man drew a gun and shot him three times in the face. Amazingly, he lived. A three-man hit squad was eventually rounded up and sent back to Colombia where, for reasons no one could explain, they were all freed. Meanwhile, the hunt was on for Parejo's replacement; the office of Minister of Justice, it appeared, was pretty much tantamount to a death sentence. Colombia got through eight Ministers of Justice in just fourteen months, all of whom resigned after just a few months in fear for their lives.

On Wednesday 6 November 1985, a telecom truck pulled up outside Bogotá's Palace of Justice. Forty-two armed M-19 guerrillas leaped out and entered the building. Within fifteen minutes the Palace of Justice and all its occupants, including the Chief Justice of the Supreme Court, Alfonso Reyes Echandia, and the majority of the country's 24 associate judges, were held hostage. When the leader of the terrorist operation put Reyes on the phone to negotiate, his call was patched through to the local radio station and the entire process was broadcast live. Only, there was no negotiation process: President Betancur didn't feel like talking. As Colombian troops stormed the building (after attempting to drive a tank through the front door), the entire siege was broadcast across the capital. By the time the shootout was over, all but one of the terrorists were dead, as were eleven Colombian soldiers and police, and nearly a hundred of the building's inhabitants, including eleven of the twenty-four associate judges. Chief Justice Reyes was also dead.

One of M-19's demands, before the army went in, was the abolition of the extradition laws. Since no one was threatening to extradite M-19 guerrillas at the time, it was swiftly rumoured that M-19 had stormed the palace at the behest of the Medellín cartel. The building was the location of the country's extradition records, all of which were burned in the course of the siege. But were the Medellín boys behind it? The United

States was convinced that they were. The idea that Colombia's traffickers were in league with leftist terror organisations was immensely appealing from the point of view of fighting the drug menace: Peru and Colombia both appeared to be dragging their heels when it came to drug enforcement because they were busy fighting guerrilla insurgency movements. But if the guerrillas had merged with the traffickers, well, that might make them pay a little more attention. Ambassador Lewis Tambs coined a word for such a collaboration: 'narcoterrorism'. It stuck. Soon the allegation was more than simply that the narcos were doing business with the Marxists—but that they were doing so at the behest of the Nicaraguans. From the American point of view, all the pieces fitted together: a couple of Nicaraguan guns were found in the wreck of the Palace of Justice, the extradition records were all gone, and at just this point Barry Seal emerged with pictures of Escobar at Las Brasiles in Nicaragua. Since it was widely rumoured that Nicaragua's communists were in league with the Castro regime in Cuba, this all appeared to point to a grand-scale conspiracy originating in the Soviet Union. Reagan declared that, 'These twin evils—narcotics trafficking and terrorism—represent the most insidious and dangerous threats to the hemisphere today.'

No one has yet managed to prove a connection between the traffickers and the Palace of Justice incident. Although there clearly were occasional links between left-wing guerrilla groups and traffickers, at this stage in Colombia these were to prove the exception rather than the rule. In fact, while the narcos were waging war on the government, they were also going all-out against the communists. Traffickers had never liked the guerrillas since the MAS (Death to Kidnappers) affair. As time went by, MAS transformed itself into a series of right-wing death squads, often funded by traffickers, with the purpose of killing guerrillas and their supporters. Prime candidates were members of Colombia's Patriotic Union Party (PUP)—the public face of the FARC terrorist group. By 1987 over three hundred left-wing activists would be dead. Lower down the scale, the figures were even more shocking: from the start of 1988 until the end of 1989 Colombia's right-wing death squads would be responsible for the deaths of some 40,000 Colombians: homosexuals, prostitutes, beggars, street children and union activists.

Although the Palace of Justice raid did not further anyone's cause, the disappearance of most of the country's hard-line judges did. Most of the surviving judges refused to return to work after the siege as a protest against Betancur's handling of the situation. Others went on strike. All boycotted the memorial service for the lives of those killed in the M-19 action on the basis that Betancur was delivering the eulogy. This was not the first time the country had seen mass judicial resignations: in 1980 Medellín's entire 180-strong magistrates' court had resigned as a protest at the government's inability to guarantee their safety. New, younger judges appointed to replace them were easier to corrupt, and those who refused to take the money were swiftly dealt with. Reyes' successor as president of the Supreme Court, Fernandez Uribe Restropo, resigned after just five months following repeated death threats. His successor lasted less than a year, during which two further senior judges were assassinated and one died under extremely dubious circumstances.

Violent reprisals against the judiciary soon bore fruit for the traffickers. In a series of memorable cases, a single judge dropped charges against Gilberto Roriguez Orejuela and Jose Santa Cruz Londoño (Cali), Evaristo Porras (who had supposedly paid the bribe to Lara Bonilla) and Jorge Ochoa. Six months after the M-19 raid, the judge revising the US extradition treaty, Justice Hernando Borda, was assassinated. The same month, Jorge Ochoa's lawyers finally won his extradition battle and had him deported from Spain to Colombia. When the time came to go to court, however, no one wanted to convict. The judge pencilled to rule on his case was just 31 years old. Ochoa walked.

With the judges now keeping quiet about extradition it was time to silence the journalists. In July *El Espectador*'s Leticia correspondent, Luis Roberto Camancho, was assassinated after writing a series of columns about the coca paste trade. Five months later another correspondent, Echavarria Barrientos, publisher of *Diario Occidente*, was likewise killed, as was the editor of *El Espectador*, Guillermo Cano—one of the most respected men in the country. His crime? He had released the details of Escobar's 1976 arrest (the judge investigating Cano's assassination was himself later assassinated). The next day the country's journalists went on strike in protest against the government's inability to maintain law and order. In fear for their lives, a small elite group of journalists formed a syndicate dedicated to writing the truth about the traffickers. Seven of the country's top journalists met in secret to discuss events and write pieces about the drug trade. These were syndicated around the country with no indication as to who had actually written them: it was just too dangerous to write the truth.

Of all the journalists in danger, perhaps Fabio Castillo—the man who had tried to call Lara Bonilla just after the assassination—was in the most trouble. Following the death of Lara he had been handed some of his confidential files on drug traffickers in Colombia, and he decided to publish them in a book. Needless to say, Colombia's traffickers were not happy about this. Castillo, who worked for *El Espectador*, wrote the book in a series of friends' houses because he was not safe at home. He presented the first printed copy to one of the friends whose house he had visited. This friend had kindly mailed it to the Ochoa family:

> The next day I got the first death threat: 'You are not going to publish this book or you are going to die!' But the book was already printed. I never returned to *El Espectador*...At one point three guys with machine guns arrived at the downtown office, burst in, pointed the guns at the recep-tionist and demanded to know where I was. That night I flew to Quito. That was my first stop. From there to Miami...and then, to break the chain, I took a bus to New York. From New York I took a plane to Madrid under a false name. I had been living in Madrid for three weeks, living in a pensione when an envelope arrived for me—but addressed to my real name, not my new name. The owner of the pensione told me, 'Someone came by asking for a Colombian called Fabio Castillo,' and I said, 'Yes, we have a Colombian, but his name is not Fabio.' They just said, 'Give this to him.' Inside the envelope was a bullet. That same day I flew to Paris and stayed there and just thought, 'My God! What am I going to do?' I realised that I was not going to be able to go home to Colombia for a long time. In the end it was seven years.

Perhaps it was worth it. Castillo's book, when it hit the stands, became the bestselling nonfiction book in Colombian history. Titled *The Horsemen of Cocaine* in a reference to the Ochoa family, it was rapidly translated into English by the DEA and a single edition was run to be given to agents in Colombia, who had never seen an inside account of the cocaine business as comprehensive as this.

In 1987 a US magazine rated Escobar as the world's fourteenth rich-est man, and the next year both Jorge Ochoa and Rodriguez Gacha were among the 125 non-North American billionaires' list. It has since been estimated that the Medellín cartel was making five to six billion dollars per year and had around ten billion dollars' worth of fixed assets outside

South America by the end of the decade. Since it was illegal to pay hard currency into the country's banks without declaring it, the cartel paid in cash through the Central Bank's *Ventanilla Siniestra* (the sinister window), at which dollars were perfectly acceptable. So much US currency was floating around in Colombia in the mid 1980s that it was one of the few nations where dollars were sold on the black market below their actual price. A couple of Colombia's banks went bankrupt when traffickers showed up and asked to withdraw all their money.

By 1985 cocaine was estimated to be the sixth-largest private enterprise in the Fortune 500, grossing more than AT&T, Boeing and Proctor & Gamble. This kind of money bought the cartel a lot of military gear. In 1990 a clutch of French ground-to-air missiles was found in a Bogotá flat and, in April that year, it was narrowly stopped from buying up 120 Stinger missiles. Escobar alone employed a private army of 3,000. The sheer weight of the violence was not only to turn the government away from extradition but also to influence cocaine trafficking for years to come. Such was the revulsion at the quantity of death that, when the Cali cartel fell foul of the law in the 1990s, they did not even need to be that violent—just the *threat* of violence was sufficient to bring the government to the table.

Of all the assassinations that year none was as predictable as that of Colonel Jaime Ramirez, Colombia's former chief of antinarcotics operations. Ramirez had been the officer responsible for the Tranquilandia raid and the cartel boys had been itching to get their hands on him for some time. He had not stopped after Tranquilandia, either. Ramirez had personally overseen the confiscation of thirty tons of cocaine, a thousand cars, eighty boats and more than a hundred aircraft, and arrested nearly ten thousand traffickers. Ramirez knew that there were contracts out on his life but seemed to thrive on the pressure, monitoring their progress through a web of informants. However, when he was relieved as head of antinarcotics operations, his informants suddenly became someone else's informants. Cut out of the loop, he lost touch with the street and, when he was told that he was in the clear, believed that it was safe to emerge. He was shot at the wheel of his car, in front of his wife and children, on 17 November 1986.

Violence against the judiciary continued unabated. In December the Extraditables circulated a letter to members of the Supreme Court:

> We declare war against you. We declare war against the members of your family. As you may suppose, we know exactly where they are—we will do

away with your entire family. We have no compassion whatsoever—we are
capable of anything, absolutely anything.

El Espectador, 3 March 1988, cit *White Labyrinth*, Lee

As the violence escalated, people began to get the message: extradition was just not worth it. In 1986 the main cause of death for adult males in Colombia was 'murder'. Medellín had so many shootings that it passed the one thousand mark in the first six months of the year. By the end of the year, the total tally for the two-million-strong city was 3,500—nearly ten per day. Meanwhile, of the handful of traffickers sent to the US, none had been a major player. Nothing had been achieved and Colombia was digging itself into an increasingly violent conflict. A month after Ramirez's assassination the traffickers' lawyers found a weak link in the extradition law: it had not been signed by the president himself but by a delegate. Medellín lawyers argued that simply re-signing it now would be unconstitutional: either it must be debated again or scrapped completely and rewritten. By now the Colombian judiciary had had about as much as it could take. It was decided to vote on it. The vote, taken by 24 judges, came in at a 12–12 tie and it was ruled that an independent adjudicator should cast the deciding vote. Three separate judges managed to excuse themselves from the debate and the buck was finally passed to someone who couldn't come up with a good reason for not taking the work. This judge, Alfonso Suárez de Castro, knew that to decide for extradition would effectively sign his death warrant. He decided against it. The traffickers had won. For the moment.

As the risk of extradition faded, the multitude of charges that had accumulated around Colombia's narcos began to evaporate. Judges fell over each other to clear Escobar of his various misdemeanours. Lara Bonilla had slapped suits on him for the illegal importation of animals. These collapsed. Justice Castro Gil had named him as being responsible for the killing of Lara Bonilla. This finding was reversed. In 1984 Escobar had had five warrants out for his arrest. These all vanished. It looked like he was winning and he decided to lay off the killing for a while. Colombia fell into a quiet period. But not for long.

In February 1987 the Colombian police finally scored a hit when Carlos Lehder was picked up at a ranch in RioNegro. In fact this was a hollow victory: thanks to his increasingly erratic behaviour (he was fond of declaring to journalists that cocaine was Latin America's 'atomic bomb' and that he planned to drop it on the US), he had fallen foul of his Medellín colleagues and they had turned him in as a sacrifice, hoping to draw some of the heat from themselves. Although the extradition law was not in force at the time, Lehder's extradition papers had already been signed. There was no messing about: within 48 hours he was in American custody. When he came to trial in November, the US press was ecstatic: Jacksonville, Florida, where he was being held, was deemed to be under threat of a narcoterrorist attack and security was hiked. George Jung—who had never got over his treatment at the hands of his former friend—was called to testify. According to Jung, he sent a message down to Escobar in Colombia via his wife asking for permission to talk. The answer to George's question—'Can I take the stand against Lehder?'— was immediate and positive: 'Fuck him,' said Escobar. In Otisville, George recalled the meeting with Chief prosecutor Robert Merckle:

> He called me into his office and he said, 'I don't know if we can help you [with a sentence reduction].' And I said, 'Hey, I don't want any fucking help. I'm only here for one reason: for vengeance. All I want is to get that motherfucker and destroy him. And I'll probably end up destroying myself by destroying him but that's OK.' And he just said, 'I fucking *like* you.'

In court Lehder appeared shell-shocked by the whole experience. George recalls:

> Carlos was destroyed at the time. I don't know if he really believed what was happening to him. I don't know if he thought he could win the trial or what. I was the first witness and the whole place was packed. Merckle said, 'Why are you here today?' and I looked at Carlos and said, 'To relate the story of the friendship between Carlos Lehder and myself—and his betrayal of that friendship.'

Jung spent three full days relating the story of his relationship with Carlos. Partly on the basis of his testimony, Lehder was portrayed as the man responsible for the wholesale infusion of cocaine into the United States—at just the moment that crack was most visible. Merckle summed up his role in the narcotics trade, concluding that 'he was to cocaine what Henry Ford was to automobiles'. Lehder's lawyers, meanwhile, did not attempt to deny the accusations—and charged him the best part of $2 million for a summing-up to the effect that, while he was a serious cocaine trafficker, a disproportionally long sentence would not go any way towards stopping the cocaine scourge in the United States. It didn't achieve much: on 19 May 1987 Carlos Lehder was found guilty on all counts and sentenced to life without parole plus an additional 135 years.

At this point in Colombia a meeting occurred that was to change the face of the cocaine industry and, ultimately, bring about the downfall of the Medellín cartel. According to Fabio Castillo, Escobar called a conference of Colombia's major traffickers in late 1987 at one of his ranches in the Valle del Cauca. Escobar had recognised that while he was busy fighting the government, the Cali cartel was quietly stealing his business. He wanted to put a stop to this before it became too powerful. Thus he suggested that the two cartels merge to fight extradition together. However, by this stage, Cali was big enough not to need him and refused the merger. This is perhaps the origin of the split between the two groups— a falling out that was to cost hundreds, if not thousands, of lives—and would eventually cost Escobar his.

The first indication that something was afoot was the arrest of Jorge Ochoa on his way to this conference. In November 1987 he was pulled over at a roadblock for no apparent reason and arrested. This arrest was to start two wars: one between the two organisations (it was assumed that Ochoa had been turned in to the police by the Cali cartel) and the other between the traffickers and the government. The day after Ochoa was picked up a message was handed to the press:

In case citizen Jorge Luis Ochoa is extradited to the United States, we will declare absolute and total war against this country's political leaders. We will execute out of hand the principal chieftains...

cit. *Kings of Cocaine*, Gugliotta and Leen

The letter was signed 'The Extraditables'.

There now began another battle to extradite Ochoa. By December, however, the battle was lost and Ochoa was released. In charge of the investigation as to how this had happened was placed the Attorney General, Carlos Mauro Hoyos. He sacked two judges and five government officials and reaffirmed his position on extradition. A month later he was ambushed in his car on his way to Medellín airport and shot in the face eleven times. An

Extraditables press release declared that he had been 'executed because of his treason to the fatherland' and that 'the war goes on'.

Now, of course, Medellín was not only fighting the government but also Cali. The same month a 60-kilogram car bomb went off outside Escobar's apartment block, Monaco, in Medellín. Two innocent employees were killed but Escobar was not at home. His daughter, Manuela, however, suffered permanent hearing damage. Escobar launched a series of savage reprisals. He was now convinced that Cali's main scions, the Rodríguez Orejuela brothers, had cut a deal with the police, and since they laundered a fair whack of their money through Colombia's number-one drugstore, Drogas la Rebaja, he ordered branches of the chain to be firebombed. Meanwhile, possible conspirators were executed. Within ten months over eighty traffickers were dead, sixty of them in Cali. Although he was clearly slipping into paranoia, he would later be proved correct about Cali's relationship with the Colombian National Police. In reality, the two maintained a cordial, if clandestine, relationship in which Cali would provide intelligence on Medellín in return for a lenient hand on their operations: while the Medellín crew was busy fighting extradition, Cali was quietly forgotten. In 1988, when new warrants were issued for the arrest of Escobar, Gacha and the Ochoa brothers, none was issued for any of the Cali kingpins. The increasingly violent relationship between the two would eventually be responsible for the transformation of the world's cocaine supply lines.

In August 1988 President Barco called for 'peace talks' with Colombia's guerrilla groups. The Medellín cartel assumed that he meant them and got back in touch. This time the offer was less generous: while they offered to get out of the business, they did not offer to repatriate their wealth. After a year or so of dithering, the government had still not made up its mind what to do and Escobar got bored. He assumed that the dialogue was simply a stalling tactic. 'That man [Secretary of the Presidency, German Montoya, who was handling the government's negotiations] made a fool of us,' he told his lawyer. In retaliation for what he saw as Montoya's duplicity he bombed his office, kidnapped his son and eventually killed his daughter.

Meanwhile the death tally began to rise again: in March 1989 the secretary of the PUP was shot dead in the lobby of Bogotá airport; in July the governor of Antioquía was killed by a car bomb; and the next month Antioquía's police chief, Colonel Waldemar Franklin Quintero—who had made the fatal mistake of confiscating four tons of Escobar's cocaine—was murdered. Then on 18 August, the front runner in Colombia's 1990 presidential election, Luis Carlos Galan, was shot dead in front of a huge crowd of supporters. This marked the end of the peace initiative. Within 24 hours President Barco reintroduced extradition and began a clampdown on the traffickers. Restrictions were placed on the purchase of motorcycles (to deter bike-led assassinations) and a new witness protection scheme was enacted. Twenty traffickers would be extradited in the next four months and over $125 million worth of assets would be seized—including a total of nearly five hundred aeroplanes. The Extraditables lost no time in responding:

> We are declaring total and absolute war on the government, on the industrial and political oligarchy, on the journalists that have attacked and insulted us, on the judges that have sold themselves to the government, on the extraditing magistrates and on all those who have persecuted and attacked us. We will not respect the families of those who have not respected our families. We will burn and destroy the industries, properties and the mansions of the oligarchy.
>
> *cit. Whitewash*, Strong

The Extraditables now began blowing up everything in sight—notably the offices of *El Espectador* with a huge car bomb. By the end of the year two hundred bombs had been detonated across the country. They assassinated journalists, judges—everyone. The judges went on strike. The press went on strike. The Colombian public called for the extradition law to be refrozen. It was not. In retaliation Escobar bombed an Avianca commercial airliner. The bomb was apparently intended for Cesar Gaviria, the politician who had assumed Galan's mantle as potential future president of Colombia. Gaviria was not on board, but 107 innocent passengers were. They all died. The next month he nearly succeeded in killing the head of DAS, General Maza Márquez, placing a bomb on his car so large that it killed eighty civilians and injured seven hundred more. But Escobar was just getting warmed up. Infuriated at his failure to kill Maza, he put a $1.3 million bounty on his head and then offered a $1,000 reward for the head of any Colombian policeman. Meanwhile he hired a representative of the Basque terrorist group, ETA, to make him an 11,000-pound (5,000-kilo) truck bomb and detonate it outside the

DAS headquarters. He then teamed up with fellow kingpin Rodríguez Gacha to plan the assassination of America's vice-president, George Bush. The killing, which was to take place at the forthcoming Cartagena drugs conference, was apparently to have been achieved by a vast car bomb placed beside the road on the route that Bush would be taking to the conference centre. It was never attempted because of an unforeseen event: the killing of Gacha himself.

Gacha was not a popular man. The next most violent member of the cartel after Escobar himself, he had originally made his name in the emerald business but fallen foul of his co-workers when he had killed the emerald magnate Gilberto Molina, taking out another eighteen innocent bystanders at the time. Pursued by the emerald smugglers, the Colombian National Police and the military—and with intelligence as to his whereabouts being constantly fed to the authorities from mysterious sources in Cali—he found himself with nowhere to hide. He was shot to death, together with his son, Fredy, in a banana field in Sucre Province. It later emerged that Cali had not been the only invisible accomplices in the killing: an unnamed source alleged that European Special Forces were in on the act, too: 'Officially we say that the Colombians did it,' he said, 'but really it was us.'

Escobar himself was in great danger. In 1988 a team of former SAS mercenaries had been hired to kill him (the mission failed when its helicopter crashed). But Escobar's intelligence network was so efficient that he generally heard about raids before they even left the police precinct. Safe houses were guarded by two rings of guards—the outer ring half an hour's travel away. This meant that when the outer defences were breached he still had time to make a decent escape before anyone arrived. So many times did he escape at the very last minute that the police, incapable of understanding how he could elude them so often, coined the 'Underwear Theory': he always managed to get out so closely that he didn't have time to put on a pair of trousers.

His brashness was impressive: in one raid in 1988 he walked out of the house in plain view of the police, assuring an officer that he was part of the undercover surveillance team. In fact there was a more prosaic reason why he seemed to get away at the last minute: many of the houses he holed himself up in had hidden compartments. On a number of occasions police and military officers would be scouring the place discussing where their fugitive had gone when he was inches away from them, concealed in the walls.

While Escobar was clearly on the run his campaign of violence was eventually to bear fruit. In December 1989 he took twenty prominent hostages—journalists, editors and the families of politicians—and in mid January the government announced that it might be ready to make a deal for their release. The Extraditables offered again to turn in their laboratories and airstrips in return for immunity. They released a handful of hostages, together with a busload of dynamite and three cocaine laboratories. It looked like a serious peace offering. President Barco delayed the extradition of a number of traffickers to give himself time to think. But he thought too long: in March Escobar assassinated the Union Party's presidential candidate, Bernardo Jaranillo. Extraditions were rushed through and the killing started again.

On 25 March Escobar bombed Cali, Medellín and Bogotá simultaneously, killing twenty-six and injuring nearly two hundred more. He then increased the bounty on the Colombian police to $4,000 for any dead officer and added a bonus of $8,000 for any member of the Special Forces. Within three months a hundred and eighty policemen were dead. This was nothing compared to the total death toll in Medellín's civilian population, however, which, at its peak, would top 7,000 homicides per year.

Of course, Escobar wasn't only angry at the government—he was still pissed off at Cali and out to get their front men at any price. Later that year a group of his *sicarios* showed up at a soccer match and opened fire on the crowd with machine guns. Their mark was Cali bigwig Helmer 'Pacho' Herrera. They missed him, but managed to take out nineteen people who happened to be standing nearby at the time. Cali retaliated by killing Escobar's cousin and best friend, Gustavo Gaviria.

Escobar stepped up the violence again and took another eight influential hostages in August, including the daughter of former president, Julio Cesar Turbay. When the government eased up restrictions on traffickers and appeared to relax extradition, he responded by taking two more hostages—the sister of Secretary of the Presidency, Marina Montoya, and the editor of *El Tiempo*, Francisco Santos (the story of these kidnappings is told in Gabriel Garcia Marquez's *News of a Kidnapping*). Montoya and Turbay would both end up dead, one executed and the other caught in the crossfire when government troops stumbled upon her kidnappers' hideout by accident.

By September 1990, the government, exhausted with all the killing, cut a deal: decree 2047 offered no extradition and reduced sentences for all those who turned themselves in on the condition that they inform on their colleagues. The Medellín boys countered that, while they might surrender, they would never talk. It was good enough.

On 17 December 1990 Fabio Ochoa, youngest of the three brothers, turned himself in. 'I feel the same happiness entering jail as someone else feels when leaving it,' he was reported as saying. 'I only wanted to end the nightmare my life had become.' Within two months both of his brothers had joined him. Escobar wanted a cast-iron guarantee that he would not be deported either. At midday on 19 June 1991 he got one, when the Constitutional Assembly officially torpedoed the extradition treaty. He handed himself 'to justice' that afternoon.

'Terror won', reported *El Espectador*.

15 Mexico

There has always been an illicit trade between Mexico and the United States. Guns, money, cigarettes—you name it: if it's illegal or taxed in the US, someone, somewhere in Mexico will be trafficking it. The trade really picked up in the 20s with the onset of Prohibition, and many of the routes pioneered by liquor runners are still in use today. The Mexicans have a slang term for it: *fayuka*. Of course, these days the most important commodity is not alcohol but drugs.

While much of the marijuana trade moved to Colombia in the late 1960s and early 1970s, a fair amount stayed. Mexico also had a neat sideline in black tar heroin, a crude derivative of the poppies cultivated in the hills of Sinaloa. American efforts to combat this weren't terribly successful. In the late 1960s the US government put pressure on its southern neighbour to stop growing opium, whereupon the trade moved to Turkey. When Turkey was in turn leaned on, the trade moved again, to South-East Asia (the so-called Golden Triangle) and eventually began to trickle back into Mexico. A joint US-Mexican operation, code-named Condor, was eventually wound down in the early 1980s when it was revealed that herbicides given to the Mexican police for spraying on to drug crops were being flown out over the desert and dumped. When US operatives were present to supervise crop sprays, planes flew over the drug fields and let loose. Only later was it discovered that they were spraying not herbicides but fertilisers. Much of the money and equipment (76 aeroplanes and $150 million) given to the Mexican government for anti-drug operations as part of Condor was siphoned off and distributed to corrupt officials. Every now and then a few minor traffickers would be rounded up, but the big boys of the drug trade continued trafficking much as before. United States' law enforcers couldn't work out why they weren't having any success. They did not really understand the nature of the Mexican drug trade; while they thought it was run by groups of ill-educated *bandidos*, the truth was a lot more complicated.

The key to the Mexican narcotics industry, then as now, is state corruption. This corruption is so well established that it has its own name: *la plaza*.

In Spanish *plaza* actually means 'the square' or 'domain' but in Mexico it has a sinister alternative meaning. Policemen assigned different plazas have for decades sold the rights to criminals to traffic through them unhassled. Thus the question, 'Who has the plaza?' can yield two answers: the name of the policeman, or *commandante*, who is assigned that jurisdiction, and the name of the criminal who is paying him off for immunity there. Both operate above, and are protected by, the law.

Buying and selling plazas has gone on for as long as anyone can remember but in the 1960s—with the advent of wholesale drug taking in the United States—it became considerably more profitable. As the money to be made by policemen for the sale of plazas went up, so appointment to trafficking-friendly areas (such as border towns) became more lucrative. Mexican police began bribing their bosses to secure good plazas. To this day the best trafficking zones generate obscene amounts of money within the Mexican Police—because of the money that the new appointee can extract from traffickers there. Former DEA agent, Aaron Graham—an expert on the Mexican trafficking scene—told me:

> I had a *commandante* tell me that he had paid a significant amount of money for the plaza in Guadalajara. He had paid one point two million dollars to the Attorney General to have the plaza. And he had paid that money presumably because that was how much money he could make from the traffickers for protecting them. More interesting was that he told me he had paid six million dollars for the plaza in Tijuana—and got it...
> You have a couple of critical areas in Mexico: Guadalajara because the heavy traffickers live there, certain areas where the stuff lands, and the border cities where they stage the stuff before it enters the United States, and those are the most viable plazas.

The origins of the modern Mexican cocaine trade lie in the United States' efforts to stop the drug's passage through the Caribbean. With the arrival of the federal taskforces in Miami in 1981, things became too hot there for the Colombian narcos, who began scouting new routes.

Representatives were dispatched to the nerve centre of Mexican trafficking, Guadalajara, where they befriended various traffickers and found out who controlled the areas they needed.

One of the first major contacts they made was a guy named Pablo Acosta, who operated out of Ojinaga, on the Texas border. Acosta was busy making a fortune shipping marijuana to the US, where, as ever, there was an almost unlimited market for it. But the promise of cocaine—lucrative, easy to hide and compact—was not lost on him. Colombian planes began arriving at remote airstrips outside Ojinaga in 1984 or 1985. In many cases the drug was stashed in underground silos in the desert before being broken up into shipments and infiltrated across the border. Because Acosta held the plaza in Ojinaga, there was no danger of arrest. In fact, when he was transporting really large amounts of cocaine, the Mexican army would provide protection for him. In return for his delivery services, Acosta made somewhere between $1,000 and $1,500 per kilo. It was easy money: by 1986 it was estimated that up to five tons of cocaine was passing through his Ojinaga ranch every month.

The US–Mexico border straddles a distance of more than 2,000 miles (3,200 kilometres) through four separate US states. The Mexicans decided to hit all of them, starting with the biggest: Tijuana. Tijuana's cross-border traffic was so high as to make it a sure-fire bet for smuggling. Today, one of the main organisations shipping cocaine from Mexico is the Tijuana Cartel, run by two brothers, Benjamin and Ramón Arrellano Felix. While the Arrellano brothers are in hiding (they are on the FBI's ten-most-wanted list and the Mexican government has a $1 million bounty on their heads), they still control the Tijuana plaza and the cocaine continues to flow. Much of it crosses into the United States at a dusty spot half an hour south of San Diego, called San Ysidro.

San Ysidro is the busiest land border in the world: 15 million cars, containing nearly 35 million people, pass through it every year. Meanwhile over 20,000 pedestrians wander through every day. In total, nearly 41 million people crossed over from Mexico to California last year alone—just at this one border post. Traffic this size makes smuggling here extremely attractive: not only is stopping every visitor impossible but it's *obviously* impossible. Despite the sheer weight of traffic, last year US Customs seized nearly 3 tons of cocaine here, indicating that Tijuana, and San Ysidro in particular, is a hot spot.

I arrived at San Ysidro one Saturday morning in July and the US Customs Service press officer, Vince Bond, walked me across the border. It was an impressive operation, and it had to be: twenty-four lanes of traffic waiting to enter the US snaked all the way back into Mexico. This looked chaotic but was in fact deliberate: the moment cars enter US territory (20 metres before the booths, in the so-called Pre-Primary area) they are gridlocked, making it impossible for traffickers either to choose a particular lane or to bottle out, reverse and go home. Before they actually hit the inspection booths, they are inside US territory and can be arrested at any time. Although passengers think they are waiting to be inspected, the inspection has already begun: sniffer dogs wander around at random, checking out any interesting new scents.

As vehicles approach the immigration booths digital cameras photograph every single number plate—over 40,000 per day—simultaneously running the registrations through a US federal database of stolen and suspect cars. Anything dodgy alerts the officer inside the glass box. When they arrive at the booths, drivers are faced with a barrage of apparently random questions: 'Is this your vehicle?' is a typical opener ('It's my cousin's' may get you a pull; 'I borrowed it from a friend' will almost certainly get you a pull). 'Where is the car registered? Where did you buy it?' No one really cares too much about the answers: it's the hesitation that gives people away. One officer I spoke to had asked a driver to open the bonnet of his car just to see if he knew where the hood release was; he didn't. He's in jail now (not for not knowing where the release handle was—that would be a bit draconian, even for the US). One particularly memorable bust, Vince told me, involved a smooth-looking guy driving through Primary, answering all the questions perfectly and being told to proceed. His mistake? As soon as he was past the booth, he burst out laughing. An off-duty inspector passing by happened to notice and asked what the joke was. He wasn't sure. He's in jail now, too.

Vehicles pulled over at Primary are escorted to Secondary where the dogs make a reappearance, pinpointing the drugs before the cars are pulled apart to get them out. I was a bit sceptical of this at first: I'd read about narcotics being shrink-wrapped or packed in strong-smelling materials such as coffee or seafood. How could dogs identify concealed packages? Vince put me right: 'I've seen these dogs hit on loads that were vacuum-sealed, wrapped in grease or oil or detergent, resealed then sunk in a gas tank. They're low-tech but they work.'

Apparently these dogs were so sensitive that they had alerted on marijuana smokers who weren't carrying the drug but had wiped their hands on their jeans when smoking it the night before. Frankly, this gave me the willies: I tried to recall whether I had worn the same pair of jeans on my last visit to talk with Magic Eddie, but couldn't for the life of me remember. Clearly it would be a Bad Thing to be busted by a US Customs dog when interviewing the US Customs Service about drug interdiction. I resolved to steer clear of the dogs.

Sniffer dogs are not only effective but have the advantage that they cannot be bribed. Here at San Ysidro—as at any border post—corruption is clearly a risk. The ridiculous amounts of money generated by narcotics sales mean that traffickers have vast quantities of cash available to pay off willing accomplices. In one memorable case on the US border, a single officer was offered a $12 million bribe. To avoid situations like this staff are rotated, often and at random; no one knows where they will be working next week, tomorrow, or even in an hour and a half's time. Dogs are not given a set routine but wander according to their handlers' discretion. USCS and US Immigration Service officers are alternated according to no particular pattern.

In the early 1990s the Mexicans developed a new technique for avoiding inspection called 'port running'. The driver would edge up to the booth and, at the first sign of trouble, step on the gas and storm into US territory. The first few made it and the technique caught on. In 1994 there were 350 of them. Today all traffic is funnelled into a slow-moving system. Cars are controlled the whole way through with concrete Jersey Blocks on either side, so there is no way they can overtake each other. Meanwhile, when a port runner hits the gas, the booth attendant presses an alarm, which raises tire shredders 50 metres up the road. The first few runners to notice this change ignored the warning alarms and stop lights and barrelled off into the desert—their wheel rims leaving a cascade of sparks behind them. They didn't get far. Port running tailed off sharply after that.

It all seemed pretty impressive. But how much of the cocaine coming in were they actually picking up? I had read estimates that just 10 per cent of all drugs entering the US was interdicted but no one was quite sure where this statistic came from: traffickers don't file tax returns so it's impossible to know how much gets through. I was told, however, that about twelve walk-throughs were caught per day—which seemed impressive until I recalled that 20,000 pedestrians walked through every day. Could 19,988 Mexicans really be clean? I doubted it. Meanwhile, they had nabbed two carloads of drugs since 8.30 that morning. It was 11 a.m. Two cars every two and a half hours makes about twenty cars a day: again, pretty impressive. But what about the other 40,000? Were they clean? Recent cocaine seizures indicate that border crossing points such as San Ysidro are no longer used the way they were: in the old days the boot was filled to the brim with drugs in one, all-or-nothing effort (the boot of the average American car holds 200–250 kilos of cocaine, worth about $5 million). Today the traffickers play the odds and loads are broken up into small shipments of 50 kilos: it's less risky that way. Because, on the statistics I got that morning, for every single car picked up with drugs, another two thousand pass through.

There was no doubt about it: the US Customs Service was doing sterling work at San Ysidro, picking up drugs and other miscellaneous contraband (ranging, apparently, from human skulls to unlicensed cheese and Amazonian parrots). But I found it hard to believe that the Arrellano Felix brothers were having problems sleeping at night.

When you drive the Mexico–US border, there is pretty much nothing to see apart from sand, cacti and the occasional rattlesnake. As I headed east on Interstate 8 I began to see the problem with antidrug operations there. As Vince had told me, 'You could bring an army into the United States across that border and no one would even notice.' The further I drove, the more I realised that he was right. It's huge. Most of the way there isn't even a fence, just mile after mile of empty, godforsaken desert. Although the US government had done its best to minimise trafficking operations across the border by flying AWACS aircraft along it, looking for suspicious light aircraft and hanging tethered radar balloons at strategic intervals, they really had their work cut out for them. At one stage, according to authorities, twenty Mexican drug planes were crashing over the border every month. Not flying, mind, but *crashing*. Twenty! Imagine how many got through. These days most planes don't bother crossing the border at all. They simply fly up to it, land in the desert on the Mexican side and dump the cocaine at a prearranged spot. That night, the recipients drive landcruisers to the coke, pick it up and are well on the road north by daybreak. How do you stop people doing this when they can do it anywhere in a desert over two thousand miles wide? How indeed.

Cocaine is not the only commodity smuggled across the desert frontier like this. Immigrants come, too. It turns out that traffickers on the Mexican side make a healthy sideline of 'assisting' emigrants, taking a fee to guide them to the border and showing them which direction to walk in for America. They then abandon their charges, telling them that the US is just around the corner, just over that sand dune, or just past that cactus over there. In fact these poor bastards are nowhere near it. The traffickers, known as *coyotes* in this neck of the woods, then disappear in a cloud of dust. Periodically along the road there were signs displaying a running tally of the number of Mexicans who had died of thirst that year. The total was 242. It was July.

I drove and drove, keeping the border to my right, air conditioning on full, doing my best not to fall asleep. Above me, clouds too thin to provide any protection from the sun stretched across the sky like oil slicks and at either end of the car the road dissolved into a river of mercury. Every now and again I passed someone coming the other way but apart from that it was quiet. After a couple of hours I gave up looking to my right at the border. There was no indication that it was there at all. But they were out there, somewhere, the Mexicans—waiting till the time was right to move their people or their drugs across it.

The first night I stopped in a sleepy desert town called Yuma, just inside the Arizona state line. A thermometer on the side of a building read 115° but I suspected it was broken: it had to be hotter than that. It was like sitting inside a hairdryer: too hot to eat, to sleep, to move, to breathe. Not that the heat was stopping the Mexicans, it seemed: drug trafficking was clearly an issue in Yuma. On the back of my hotel door hung a warning that the police would be summoned, together with their 'canine unit' if visitors attempted to register into the hotel without parking in plain view of the office's surveillance camera. 'All walk-ins must be suspect,' proclaimed the note. Bearing in mind that this was a tourist joint in the middle of the desert, it struck me that everybody was a 'walk-in'. I eyed my fellow guests with suspicion, wondering which of them was a stooge for the Arrellano Felix brothers. Perhaps none of them. Perhaps all of them. It would be easy to become paranoid in a place like Yuma. It's just too hot to do anything else.

The next day I hit Tucson, Arizona, then I took Interstate 19 south back towards Mexico. Although I was heading for El Paso, I had a detour to make. I wanted to see Nogales.

Nogales represents an unusual threat to the US fight against cocaine.

Because, unlike San Ysidro in California—in which the border post is in the middle of nowhere—in Nogales the border divides the city neatly into two. Thirty thousand of Nogales's inhabitants live in the United States; four hundred thousand live in Mexico. This creates problems: how do you stop Mexicans crossing to the other side of their own town? You stick up a big fence, is what you do. The current fence is twenty feet high and floodlit at night. From the hills above the city, all you notice is this great steel wall, snaking its way over the precipitous hills into the distance, a bizarre Iron Curtain separating the First world from the Third. The existence of such a place, where all of six inches separates the provider of narcotics from the receiver, presents obvious problems: there is no no-man's land to pass the coke through. Heave the stuff over the fence and it's in America, ready for re-sale. This makes Nogales extremely attractive to traffickers, who have resorted to ridiculous lengths to facilitate the flow of drugs from south to north here. In other areas traffickers put cocaine into the boots of cars and drive them over the border, or wrap it around their bodies and walk it over the border or even—if they are rich (and name me a drug smuggler who isn't)—put it into a light aircraft and fly it over the border. In Nogales they think a bit more laterally. They take it *beneath* the border. Edward de Bono would be proud.

The most important aspect of Nogales's relationship with cocaine is not the fence, but the weather. Specifically, the rain. Because Nogales is built on a series of steep hills, it tends to rain here in summer—especially early July, the 'monsoon'. When the rains hit, water pours from the Mexican hills into the US, where it fills the streets, the drains, the houses and just about everything else. In order to combat this, thirty-odd years ago Nogales's town planners built a series of canals, called *arroyos*, beneath the city to handle the overflow. Instead of filling the city, rainwater was channelled into them and led away to the Santa Cruz river. It worked like a charm. However, there was a problem. Because the *arroyos* joined the Mexican and American sides of the border, by entering a storm drain on one side it was possible to make your way into the drainage system and then, if you knew what you were doing, to emerge on the other side. Nogales's *arroyos* soon became conduits for contraband.

To combat this the Americans installed giant steel doors in the *arroyos*. They didn't last long. Mexican traffickers took down oxyacetylene torches and cut their way through. Soon the US found itself having to send repair parties down into the *arroyos* twice a week to fix them. Once down there, they noticed something strange: extra tunnels that didn't feature in the original blueprints. They called in US Customs, who traced a tunnel all the way from Mexico into an old church next to Burger King on the American side. Two more popped up on Oak Street. Another emerged on Loma Street, half a mile away from the border.

Nogales's *arroyo* system, with some seventy storm-drain intakes on either side of the border, all linking up beneath the city, is tailor-made for smuggling. Padlocked grilles on the intakes don't deter the dedicated trafficker. The latest technique is to drive a false-bottomed van over an inlet, break the manhole cover with a hydraulic jack, and disappear through the floor of the truck into America. The week I arrived another tunnel had been discovered—the fifth in just eighteen months. This time they were smuggling marijuana, but it could have been people, cocaine, heroin, anything. Once you've opened a clandestine route to the United States, you don't hang around. No one knows how long the last tunnel was operational before it was busted. But suppose it was just a week: how much marijuana could you push through an *arroyo* wide enough to drive a car through in a week—if no one was watching? And then, if you were looking for a more profitable commodity, how much cocaine? The US–Mexico border, as I was beginning to discover, is a real opportunity for those with a little imagination.

The moment I arrived in Nogales there was a huge clap of thunder and the skies opened—the monsoon had arrived. It heaved with rain—and continued heaving with rain for the best part of twelve hours. I took a room as close to the border as possible. I wanted to be where the action was but it was impossible to tell where that might be: it was raining so hard that it was difficult to see more than three or four feet in front of you. Moreover, despite the *arroyo*, the streets immediately flooded and within half an hour the cars in the hotel car park were up to their axles in water. It was an impressive display.

That night I fell asleep, lulled by the sound of the rain drumming gently, incessantly, on the roof above my head. Beneath me the water sluiced silently through the *arroyos* into the Santa Cruz river somewhere out there in the dark, flooded desert. At four I awoke to the reassuring sound of raindrops dripping rhythmically on to the windowsill outside. Tap-tap-tap, they went. Tap-tap-tap. Tap-tap-*scrape*. In my sleep I raised an eyebrow.

What was that?

Tap-tap-tap. Tap-tap-tap. Tap-tap-*scrape*.

I sat up and listened, barely daring to breathe. The Mexicans! I imagined the Arrellano Felix brothers, twenty feet beneath me, in string vests and workmen's boots with lanterns on their miners' helmets, pickaxes poised in midair, entreating each other to be quiet. They were so close I could almost smell them: their unwashed miners' overalls, their fetid, Tabasco-laden breath. What if they got their calculations wrong and came up in my hotel room by accident? What if my hotel room was the target? Jesus Christ! The implications were terrible. I listened, rigid with fear, but there was nothing. It was nothing. Only the rain. I stuffed a pillow over my head and closed my eyes. Tap-tap-tap, went the rain. Tap-tap-tap. Tap-tap-*scrape*.

The next day the sun was shining again and I decided to pop over the border into Mexico to see what was going on. It turned out that nothing was going on apart from a grubby street lined with moneychangers and souvenir stalls selling sombreros, plastic kids' toys and bleached cow skulls. Moreover, no one I spoke to could tell me anything about the tunnels. However, as I passed the fourth pharmacy in under five minutes, something registered in the back of my mind: at San Ysidro Vince Bond had mentioned that Mexican chemists were frequently a source of contraband entering the US: pharmaceuticals requiring prescriptions in the US, including amphetamines, barbiturates and all kinds of weird stuff, are often sold over the counter in Mexico. Sure enough, this was the case in Nogales: within spitting distance of the border a chemist was advertising amoxycillin and ampicillin at 35 per cent discount. It wasn't quite the Tijuana Cartel but it was drug smuggling and I'd driven a long way, so I decided to check it out. It was a little too early in the day for amphetamines and I suspected that broad-spectrum antibiotics might interfere with my bowel movements. What could I buy? Then it hit me: ketamine.

Like phencyclidine, ketamine is a veterinary anaesthetic that occasionally emerges on the lists of abused drugs in Great Britain and the US. Known on the streets as 'Special K', it tends to provoke trancelike states in humans, its physiological effects including, bizarrely, an increase in the sense of smell: apparently in the 1960s ketamine users were easy to find, usually camped outside the local bakery, sniffing the air and grinning witlessly. This behaviour made them easy picking for narcotics police, who simply toured the better-smelling places in town picking up the users one by one. Consequently the species rapidly dwindled into extinction. From my point of view, ketamine was perfect; it was completely legal in Mexico yet very illegal in the US. I decided to try my luck.

Predictably, it was disaster. For a start, the pharmacist appeared to have no idea what I was asking for. 'Ketamine,' I repeated, waving a wad of dollar bills: '*Es muy importante!*' 'What are your symptoms?' he asked, in perfect English. This stumped me. Never having bought ketamine in a Mexican pharmacy before, I hadn't prepared a story. I blurted out the first thing that came into my head: 'It's for my friend. He's sick.' There was a pause as the pharmacist digested this and for a split second I thought he was actually about to sell me some ketamine. Instead he pulled a puzzled face. 'Ketamine—is for *animals*,' he said. I heaved a sigh: 'Well, yes,' I countered, 'but my friend is a dog.'

Oh Christ. Did I really say that? It was as if I had stumbled into some terrible British sitcom. 'I don't think so,' muttered the pharmacist, shaking his head, and I beat a hasty retreat. Just my luck: the only honest pharmacist in Mexico. I shambled back across the border and decided to get out of town before I embarrassed myself any further. I climbed into the car and headed east again towards real cocaine territory: El Paso.

El Paso really emerged on the cocaine scene in the late 1980s. Although it was clear that cocaine was passing through the border between the city and its Mexican twin, Ciudad Juárez, no one really had any idea how much there was until one day in 1989, when an informant told the DEA that they might like to have a look at a warehouse facility in a small place called Sylmar, on the outskirts of LA. The DEA and the LAPD checked it out together. The fact that neither of them expected much made the ensuing bust all the more exciting: inside the warehouse was a total of 21.38 tons of cocaine—with a street value of $6.5 billion—together with an additional $12 million in cash. The biggest cocaine seizure in US history: not bad for a day's work. Four men arrested at the time revealed that this cocaine had not come through San Ysidro but through Ciudad Juárez, to the east. No sooner had they said this, however, than a big-shot Colombian lawyer arrived, offered to handle their legal defence for free and instructed them to shut up. It was later revealed that the cocaine belonged to the Medellín cartel, who had contracted the Mexicans to ship their coke across the border and place it in storage until there was a sufficient quantity to distribute. Only, someone on the Colombian end forgot to do the distributing bit. This ring was eventually broken up, only to be replaced with an even more successful Juárez operation, headed up by an enigmatic Mexican who was shortly to become a legend: Amado Carillo Fuentes.

Almost everything anyone tells you about Carillo Fuentes is speculation. Depending on whom you believe, he was born in 1950, 1954 or 1955. He may have had eight brothers and sisters, or nine, or thirteen. It is said that he was a Mexican federal agent of some sort, that he was a street hoodlum, that he had a law degree, that he was illiterate. Apparently, he wore contact lenses to disguise his appearance, grew and shaved off beards and underwent repeated plastic surgery. The nephew of Guadalajara kingpin Ernesto Fonseca Carillo, El Coche Loco ('the mad pig'), he is rumoured to have murdered his cousin in a fit of rage at his own wedding. But what does anybody really know? The more press releases you read about Amado, the more you realise that journalists simply copy each others' articles. According to one DEA agent, Carillo was 'the filet mignon' of traffickers. Everyone else, however, referred to him as 'el Señor del Cielo'—'the Lord of the Skies'. For a long time the DEA had four mugshots of Carillo but no one was sure which, if any, was actually him.

The most authoritative source on Carillo Fuentes is Terence Poppa's book *Drug Lord*. This carries weight not only because it is clearly well researched but because, in the process of writing it, Poppa managed to acquire a $250,000 contract on his life, a sure sign that he was close to a nerve. According to Poppa, Carillo's uncle initiated him into the drug trade from his headquarters in Guadalajara—at exactly the time when Colombian businessmen began showing up. When they picked up on Pablo Acosta in Ojinaga, Amado was sent to work with him—to guarantee the safety of the investments. The two men worked successfully with the Colombians to move vast quantities of cocaine across the border: some 60 tons per year across the 400 kilometres that Acosta controlled. Every now and then, however, they would have a falling out. Usually these disagreements revolved around Amado's overreaction to something or other. DEA agent David Regela—one of the few agents ever actually to have met Amado—recalls a meeting in which Acosta was angry at him for having tortured six of his best men to death. Amado had suspected a snitch and figured that the end justified the means: 'It's better for six innocent men to die than for one guilty man to go unpunished,' he had said. This violent streak was to be a trademark of the Carillo Fuentes organisation until its demise in 1997.

Despite these occasional differences, Acosta and Fuentes got along well and business flourished until Acosta was shot dead by the Mexican Federal Police in April 1987. Luckily for Amado, he was not present that day (it has been suggested that Amado actually paid the police to kill Acosta so that he could inherit the Ojinaga plaza). He then appears to have vanished off the face of the earth. Perhaps he went to Colombia. Perhaps he stayed home. Either way, he laid low. When it was safe to emerge he came out of hiding and began killing traffickers. One paper estimated that in 1993 he was 'disappearing' 38 people per month.

It wasn't long before he was in control of the Mexican cocaine situation again. Amado maintained an especially close relationship with Miguel Rodríguez Orejuela, the nominal head of the Cali cartel in Colombia. As such he was the man to know. He began farming out Cali cocaine to other organisations along the border. From his new operations centre, Ciudad Juárez, he ran an international cocaine export business. And how.

American analysts peg the payoff budget between $500 million and $800 million a year flowing to his protectors in government. He was transporting eight tons of cocaine at a time in older, converted Boeing 727s or French Caravelles. Four hundred murders are attributed to him and his faction.

Drug Lord, Terence Poppa, 1998

Amado was smart. From the antics and treatment of the Medellín cartel in Colombia—and the death of the flamboyant Pablo Acosta—he realised that it was not a good idea to be in the public view. So anonymous was he that a 1994 assassination attempt in a restaurant in Mexico City failed because the gunmen couldn't work out which of the guys at the table was their mark. Hedging their bets, they opened fire with machine guns on everyone, taking out all of Amado's bodyguards. But Amado wasn't sitting at the table: he had seen the hit men walk in and was hiding beneath it. After the necessary reprisals, business in Ciudad Juárez continued much as normal.

One man who ran up against Amado Carillo Fuentes is former DEA agent Aaron Graham, who told me on the telephone about the way things operated in Mexico in the late 1980s and early 1990s. Although Graham had heard tales of Mexican corruption, nothing had prepared him for the way Carillo's cocaine operation had subverted the authorities:

> The Colombians would send anywhere between three to twelve aircraft [at a time]. One Colombian I debriefed in prison told me that at one point they had sent seventeen aircraft at a time. You can fit anywhere between five hundred and seven hundred kilos on each one, depending on the aircraft...They would schedule them. They had radio communications and they would pull them in just like an airport, they'd circle them and bring them in, one at a time, land them, unload them, refuel them and send them back out and they ran it like a commercial landing strip.

The reason that so many planes were sent in one go, of course, was that Carillo had paid for a window in Mexico's air-defence system: if he had, say, an hour and he'd paid a million dollars for that hour, it was in his interests to bring in as much coke as could possibly be brought in during that one hour. It was this attitude that led to his pioneering use of Boeing 727s to fly his cocaine. After all, a window is a window: why not use the biggest planes you can get? (It was just such antics that led to his nickname, 'Lord of the Skies'.) By 1997 it was estimated that Amado had transformed the Mexican drug industry into a $30-billion-a-year business. Government bribes alone, it was said, came to $500 million per year. He himself was shifting $200 million worth of cocaine every week, netting himself in the region of $10 billion per year. Thanks to his efforts, 70 per cent of the United States' cocaine was coming through Mexico (today it's down to just 60 per cent). If the narcotics industry collapsed there, it was suggested, it would destabilise the country's entire economy.

On occasions when the DEA received tip-offs about trafficking operations, they might follow the planes and bust one or two of them, but, as likely as not, they would find themselves mysteriously grounded for some reason: perhaps their planes needed servicing, or the weather conditions were not quite right. Other times the Mexican police simply made it clear that they were not welcome. Aaron Graham recalls the frustration:

> We were not allowed to be on the scene because of the Mansfield Agreement, which precluded us from participating in police action in a foreign

country, and that's what the Mexicans hid behind. In reality they wouldn't let us on the scene because that's where the negotiations took place to determine whether they would incarcerate somebody and seize the dope or take a million payoff and let the dope go. They would tell us in cases where they had taken the money, 'You guys gave us all the info but it was not valid and nobody landed there.' But we had informants who would tell us exactly what had happened: that two airplanes had landed and that a black car pulled up and a gentleman came out and gave the *commandante* a bag full of money and we all split some of the money and then we let them go. And that was routine.

On other occasions not only would the military and Mexican Police look the other way, they would be actively employed to oversee the cocaine shipments themselves. Often refuelling trucks at desert airstrips were discovered to belong to the Mexican Air Force, and instances of the army protecting and transporting shipments are legion. The most famous of such events still induces revulsion in those who were there when it took place. It involved an operation in 1991 in which a US AWACS aircraft tailed a trafficker's plane to a desert strip in eastern Mexico and directed a light aircraft containing Mexican drug agents on to it. The American AWACS then filmed what happened next: as the Mexican anti-narcotics agents landed, they were fired upon—by the Mexican army battalion that had been tasked to protect the drugs. From 35,000 feet the American AWACS pilot filmed seven Mexican drug agents being shot dead by their own military. John Coleman, former head of operations at the DEA, told me philosophically:

It was on VHS. In Chiapas, I believe. It didn't really surprise a lot of the folks who really knew Mexico because there are two Mexicos: there is the Mexico that is the friendly tourist country that people like to visit and have a good time, and then there's the other Mexico that has all the crime and corruption. Unfortunately, I think that ultimately the two Mexicos are incompatible with each other. I think right now the corrupt one is prevailing.

Daydreaming hopelessly about the problem of Mexican corruption—and trying desperately to stay awake—I headed on towards El Paso and Ciudad Juárez, home of Amado Carillo Fuentes. Half of me noted the names of the towns I was zipping by: Gunsight; Tombstone; Truth or

Consequences—this was cowboy country. Just past Las Cruces the road hooked sharply to the right and the radio stations all simultaneously started playing Stevie Ray Vaughan tracks. Interstate 10 turned bright red and a sign loomed up beside the road: WELCOME TO TEXAS, it read. DRIVE CAREFULLY—THE TEXAS WAY.

El Paso ('The Pass': this has been a border crossing for ever) is clean, well regulated and orderly. Seven hundred thousand people live there. Across the Rio Grande, however, Ciudad Juárez is the Third World writ large, containing 1.5 to 2 million inhabitants. Towering above the city in the desert hills is a huge message in white: LA BIBLIO ES VERDAD—LEEDA ('the Bible is the truth—read it'). Religion and poverty go hand in hand in Mexico. Together with cocaine. And violence. From the moment Amado Carillo Fuentes arrived in Ciudad Juárez, there was trouble. Killings, tortures, death everywhere. As he cranked up the city's cocaine quota, so he accumulated more and more money, and killed more and more people.

In El Paso I met up with another Customs Service agent, Roger Maier. Maier took me for a spin to the outskirts of town and we looked at Monte Cristo Rey (the Hill of Christ the King). From a couple of miles the problem became obvious: while there were fortified fences, floodlit at night, throughout the centre of the city, once the suburbs died out there was nothing. The fence that marked the border line snaked its way up the hill, then simply disappeared. We drove to a small town on the outskirts of El Paso, shunted up against the Mexican border, called Anapra. Here all that marked the border was a series of ancient metal obelisks and a chain-link fence—the sort of thing you might find around a tennis court. On the other side of the fence was a shantytown of houses constructed from old packing cases and forklift truck palettes. All there was stopping the inhabitants from making it into the US was this one chain-link fence. Even *I* could have scaled it. What was there to stop someone on the other side leaning a ladder against it and jumping over? I asked Maier. He asked me another question in return: 'What's to stop a car driving up on the US side and a couple of Mexicans heaving a bag of coke over the fence to them?' Well, as far as I could see, nothing. The entire operation would be over in a matter of seconds. 'You see the problem?' asked Maier. I did.

From Anapra we headed to the border crossing point itself. Although San Ysidro in California actually takes more people from Mexico into the US, El Paso carries more pedestrians. A huge bridge over the Rio Grande carries private vehicles and pedestrians alike. All of them are suspect. Inside the border post I was shown various techniques for searching cars. 'Buster' is a hand-held gadget that measures density—run along the side panels of a car, it reveals where spaces that should be hollow aren't. Fibre-optic cables are fed into petrol tanks to look for packages and dogs roam around from time to time. Meanwhile, agents look beneath the cars with mirrors, tapping anything that looks suspicious with converted golf clubs topped with copper hammers (copper is less likely to spark and start an explosion than steel). At the same time, agents watch the bridge for 'spotters'. Spotters like to hang around at the border to work out which customs lane is moving the fastest, or the slowest, or which looks to be the most lax—and direct their cars through that one. In the old days they used to lean against banks of payphones on the US side pretending to make calls, sending the signal to move only when the time was right (for example, when the sniffer dogs were taken inside for a rest). Customs solved this by moving the payphones around the corner, out of sight of the bridge itself. But by then mobile phones had arrived. 'They're probably watching us right now,' said one agent.

Inside the border post I was shown to the seizure room, a bare cell that smelled of disinfectant with a large set of scales and a blackboard in the corner. The blackboard had not been cleaned and still listed the total for the last bust: 822 pounds (about 370 kilos) of marijuana picked up the previous afternoon. How many busts had they had today? I asked. None. 'It's not yet midday,' someone pointed out. In a stainless-steel cupboard was a series of boxes full of chemical drug tests. I thought agents tested for cocaine by taste, like in the movies. 'Er, no, Dominic,' said one agent witheringly. 'We don't do that.' Today's test is a premeasured test tube containing copper thiocyanate. It's not hard to use: add the powder you have just confiscated, place the stopper on the top and shake. As with a pregnancy test, if it changes colour someone has some serious explaining to do.

When Customs pulls a vehicle the driver has two options: he can come quietly into US custody, or run. Mexico is so close—just 50 metres—that the latter option is often taken. It is almost always a mistake. Not because customs officials shoot the escaping fugitive but because of his reception when he gets home. Invariably when seizures are made in El Paso, bodies begin washing up in the Rio Grande. Most of them have their hands tied together with baling wire and a bullet in the back of the head. This is a throwback to the policy of Amado Carillo Fuentes, of course: the man who would rather kill six innocents than allow one guilty person to get through. Ciudad Juárez is a treacherous place. And all the more so for recent events.

In 1997 rumours began spreading that Carillo Fuentes was retiring. He started shuttling all over Latin America, shutting down bank accounts, buying up real estate in Chile. It was said that he was getting out of the trade for good. The stage was set for an impressive vanishing act.

On 3 July 1997, Amado Carillo Fuentes underwent an extensive series of plastic surgery operations to change his appearance. However, his heart, weakened by extensive use of freebase, could not take the anaesthetic and he died on the operating table. Now things got seriously weird. The three plastic surgeons who had treated him all ended up dead, their bodies stuffed into 55-gallon drums topped up with concrete. Then the real violence began. In the El Paso Customs HQ, Supervisory Customs Inspector Mitch Merriam talked me through it:

> Carillo died in 1997 and all hell broke loose over there…there was a battle—a war, if you will—between other drug lords in the area to take over the plaza. Several other organisations were trying to take over the area—and there was extreme violence. There were days, weeks here, pre-1998, when people were being gunned down in restaurants. On the road they would be stopped and killed. Cars were being machine-gunned. Extreme violence. There was a real battle going on. People were literally scared to go across into Mexico for fear that they might be eating in a good restaurant at the wrong time.

That summer, restaurant takes in Ciudad Juárez dropped 60 per cent because people were so scared of getting machine-gunned in them. It was just this fear that led to the world headlines concerning mass graves outside Ciudad Juárez in 1999. Six hundred policemen and 65 FBI agents, it was reported, were digging at a ranch outside the city where they had unearthed a series of bodies. Judging by the numbers of missing people in Juárez, they expected the dig to yield up to a hundred corpses. In fact, while more than this number had been killed by Carillo, the total was disappointing: fewer than ten. Of course, there are more out there, somewhere. Just not in the same grave. Today, according to authorities, the killing has subsided somewhat. The violence was finally over only when the Carillo organisation was reunited under Amado's baby brother, Vicente. Business as usual, then.

Such was the nature of Carillo's death, however, that it soon sparked controversy. It was said that he was still alive, that he was living like a king in Chile, or Mexico City. Admittedly, the DEA was allowed access to Carillo's body and did verify that it was indeed him, but there remains the question of how, exactly, they verified it: if his four mugshots were not actually him, who could say whether the corpse was Carillo's? And the body itself was in such a terrible state—having died in the course of extensive plastic surgery—that it would have been difficult to identify anyway.

Traditionally, drug lords are rumoured to be alive long after their deaths, so I was quite prepared to discount rumours of Carillo's survival until a couple of interviewees told me that they, too, had doubts. The first was James Nims, a senior DEA agent formerly based in Mexico. He told me that he had been convinced that Carillo was dead until a friend's wife, a doctor, bumped into a colleague at a conference of plastic surgeons:

> She was at a medical meeting in Culiacan and one of the doctors was laughing about the picture that always appeared in the papers of Carillo Fuentes before he died. It showed him with a beard, a good-looking guy. And he laughed and said, 'People say that's what Carillo Fuentes looks like but I've operated on him before and that's not him!' I guess that picture was his border-crossing card and that was the thumbprint that they used to verify that it was Carillo Fuentes when [his body] came to Mexico City. But what I think is that, if it was a fake picture, then obviously the thumbprint is going to be wrong, too. I thought the whole thing was fishy.

But what about the doctors? Wasn't the fact that the doctors had been killed evidence of a reprisal for his death?

> That just makes it even more fishy. Because, why kill all the doctors?... Maybe they knew too much. Maybe they knew that it wasn't him, you know? Word was that he wanted to get out, he had made so much money and was looking to get out of it and then, all of a sudden, this happens...

What gave this story some weight was that Nims was the agent sent to Mexico City to identify the body the day Carillo died. If he wasn't convinced that Carillo was dead, who was?

Another DEA agent shared his doubts with me. Aaron Graham told me that he, too had heard rumours:

> I met with an agent of Gobernación [the Mexican secret police] once I transferred to the corporate world who swore to me when we met a year ago that Amado Carillo Fuentes is still alive. I hate to even repeat it except that a guy who was secret police swore to it. There were many rumours that he was having plastic surgery, that the doctors killed him accidentally, or that they killed him on orders from somebody. It's quite an interesting mystery... I don't believe anybody has seen any autopsy photos of Amado that appear to be legitimate... it's easy to kill somebody else, mess up his face and say that it's him. Life is very cheap in Mexico. To sacrifice a human to protect Amado is clearly possible... I like to believe that he's dead, but in Mexico anything is possible.

Ultimately, no one can be sure that Amado Carillo Fuentes, Mexico's greatest drug lord, is really dead. Rumours smack of conspiracy theories but then, as Graham says, in Mexico anything is possible.

Regardless of the existential state of Amado Carillo Fuentes the cocaine trade continues unabated. The drug is so successful here partly because of a new technique the Mexicans pioneered in the 1980s. Former DEA Head of Operations, John Coleman, explained how it worked:

> When they first started their arrangements, rather than simply pay them, the Colombians would give them a percentage of the product. So if the Mexican transport organisations moved five hundred kilos of cocaine, for example, the Colombians might give them fifty. This gave the Mexicans the means to establish their own smuggling and distribution outlets and I think we ignored the significance of this barter. We thought that by going after the Colombians we would eventually collapse that Mexican infrastructure. Looking back now I think the weakness in the strategy was that we probably ignored the fact that this barter system was in effect offering a franchise to the Mexicans to operate their own sort of cartel.

Since they were doing such sterling work at the border, the cocaine accumulated and the Mexicans began setting up their own distribution networks in the United States, leading to a whole new echelon of organised gangs in the US—yet another problem for federal authorities to deal with.

Mexico is such a pain in the behind that US legislators are at a loss as to what to do with it. There are repeated calls for America to place sanctions on the country in the form of removing its 'co-operative ally in the War on Drugs' status. For various reasons this is never done. Unlike Colombia, Bolivia and Peru, it shares a 2,000-mile border with the US and America is wary of annoying its corrupt neighbour. The cocaine continues to flow—and the Mexican government continues to shield it. Following the torture and murder of a DEA agent, Kiki Camarena, in Guadalajara in 1986, the DEA broke all the rules and went out of its way to apprehend the killers: a doctor who had fed Camarena amphetamines throughout the interrogation to keep him awake was kidnapped and dumped in El Paso. Others were likewise forcibly extracted. This offensive has served to protect DEA agents in Latin America ever since: cartel bosses are aware that killing Americans leads to severe reprisals.

The Mexican Federal Police, however, didn't see it that way. In retaliation they published the names and addresses of all undercover DEA agents operating in Mexico in the national newspapers. And still they protect the traffickers. Aaron Graham recounted a typical case:

> There was a guy, Cleto Valle, and he was kind of a ghost. No one knew who he was but we were getting very good information on him. And we made a seizure of several hundred kilos near an army base and Cleto Valle was the source. He was a very quiet, low-key guy. We ultimately got seven tons, five airplanes, and arrested fifty people and the Mexfeds [Mexican Federal Judicial Police] kept telling us that he didn't exist, that we were just dreaming this stuff up. Well, at one point we ultimately proved that the Mexfeds were protecting him. We had communications between them and him and we proved it to them. Once we showed it to them he was arrested. Presumably he's still in jail.

The operation was a success but it took its toll. Graham was hastily evacuated from Mexico when it became apparent that there was a half-million-dollar contract on his head. In Mexico, even when you win, you lose. According to the DEA's intelligence branch, 60 per cent of the United States' cocaine still comes across the Mexican border. The figure has been stable for a number of years and shows no sign of changing.

It has been alleged that Mexico's drug kingpins are in fact puppets of the government: once they get too uppity, they lose their plaza and end up dead or extradited to the United States—token evidence of Mexico's 'successes' in its non-existent war on drugs. Meanwhile someone else is awarded the plaza and the trade continues. No one has any interest in stopping this: it's far too lucrative. Joint operations between the United States and Mexico are invariably compromised: a 1995 information-sharing exercise, for example, resulted in the US divulging the identities of a number of confidential informants operating in Mexico. Within two months, 60 of them were dead. Periodic purges achieve little: in 1996 Mexico's attorney-general fired a fifth of the entire federal police force— well over seven hundred agents—for corruption. In some jurisdictions the police force was deemed so corrupt that it was sacked en masse and replaced with the military. The drug trade continued untouched.

In 1997 US Drug Tsar Barry McCaffrey praised the new Mexican head of antidrugs operations, General Jesus Gutierrez Rebollo, as 'a guy of absolute, unquestionable integrity'. Two months later it was revealed that Rebollo was taking money from at least one major cocaine traf-ficker. All intelligence the US had shared with him on Mexican drug operations was immediately deemed compromised—giving it to Rebollo was pretty much akin to handing it over to the cartels themselves.

Meanwhile it was revealed that Mexican president, Carlos Salinas, architect of NAFTA and a man whom *The Economist* rated as 'one of the great men of the twentieth century', was linked to the trafficking syndi-cates. His brother, Raul, was later found to be in possession of banking details of a mysterious Swiss account that contained $120 million. Sali-nas's successor, Ernesto Zedillo, was likewise alleged to have been on the receiving end of narco-dollars; slush funds supporting his presidential campaign—fed by Mexican and Colombian syndicates—were estimated to have cleared the best part of three-quarters of a billion dollars. The Cali cartel alone donated $40 million: the election was bought. And the money that bought it was largely generated by cocaine.

I finished up my tour of the El Paso border and, finding myself with time to kill, decided to pop into Mexico to find the Juárez cartel to see if they felt like commenting on any of this.

Luckily, I didn't find them.

16 Bolivia

San Pedro jail is a horrific place. An intimidating building on Plaza Sucre in La Paz, Bolivia, it was built in the nineteenth century to house two hundred and fifty inmates but currently houses a thousand. Conditions inside are rough. Prisoners must buy their own cells or are forced to sleep on the kitchen floor—or in the open courtyards, exposed to the elements. In order to earn money to pay for food, many are forced to set up illicit businesses: inside there are shops, bars, counterfeiting operations, you name it.

In the 1980s a coca paste factory was uncovered inside the prison and there are rumours of a full-blown hydrochloride laboratory somewhere inside the walls. Meanwhile the more wealthy prisoners pay bribes to spend a night out on the town. Women are allowed in and inmates bring in their families either for visits or to live with them. The place's reputation for drugs and corruption led to a bizarre trade recently, when the guards used to arrange guided tours of the jail for backpackers. The main selling point of the tour was cocaine, which could be taken with impunity—because San Pedro was the only place in Bolivia where you were guaranteed not to be interrupted by the police.

So it was not entirely without trepidation that I walked in through a steel door on the side of the building and handed over my shoulder bag for inspection. A surly guard pulled out its contents and placed them on a table, shaking his head and muttering 'prohibido' (forbidden) after each one. At the end of the search, every single item in the bag was on the table—everything, it seemed, was prohibido apart from the bag itself. Then he had a thought. He turned the bag upside down and examined the underside closely. 'Prohibido,' he concluded and placed it on the table on top of its contents. I put everything back into the bag and handed it to another guard for safekeeping together with my passport. I was asked who I was visiting. 'Meco Domínguez,' I said. 'He's a friend of mine.' One of the guards looked up, raised an eyebrow, scribbled

'Domínguez' in the prison log and said, 'OK'. My forearm was stamped and someone signed their name on my wrist in ballpoint pen. He then nodded at a colleague who manned the cage door that separated the guards from the inmates, and the door swung open. I was in.

'Meco' Domínguez is a bit of a legend in these parts. In the 80s and early 90s he was a serious player—perhaps *the* serious player—in the Bolivian coke scene. When he was eventually caught and sent here, he installed himself in a private cell and immediately had a telephone fitted so that his business would not suffer. His business being cocaine, this phone was dubbed the *'narcotelefono'* (the drug phone) until it was eventually removed at the insistence of the DEA. Meco was a player all right. But would he talk? I had never met him before. Perhaps he hated journalists. Or English people. I didn't know.

Contrary to expectations, the interior of San Pedro was not squalid and overcrowded at all, but an open courtyard with plenty of space, nicely surfaced, with a basketball court. A number of well-dressed children ran around kicking footballs and shrieking while their parents watched from the bleachers beside the court, or sat at the Coca-Cola stand drinking coffees and chatting idly. It was actually a lot nicer than the street outside. Ah, explained my guide. This was because we were in *La Posta*, the exclusive area of the jail. People here get the star treatment because they can afford to pay for it. This is where the big boys live. We wandered around the courtyard for a couple of minutes waiting for someone to ask what we were doing here but no one seemed to notice us. Then, at random, we asked a passer-by if he knew where we might find Domínguez. He pointed at a clean-cut middle-aged man in a fashionable green shirt and slacks, watching the basketball. 'Meco!' he shouted. 'A gringo here to see you!' Meco looked up.

Suddenly a great beaming smile came over his face, he got up and bounded across the courtyard to meet us. 'Hi!' he said, shaking my hand. 'I'm Meco!' He led us into the recreation room, a whitewashed vault with a stereo and a pool table, and we sat down. I explained that I would like to know about his history in the drug business, what it was like in the 1980s and 1990s: his story. 'Sure,' he said. He could tell me about these things. But first there was something very important he had to know:

'Are you a Christian?'

Before I got a chance to answer, however, this amazing torrent of words poured out:

I have just been ordained as a pastor we have built a chapel in my old cell for the other inmates a house of prayer we have services and play together we have guitars people come here and they are converted and then they leave and they go out and preach when I came here I just begged for my soul I am not an educated man I didn't know that I wasn't a proper man until I knew Jesus Christ then I realised that everything I had been doing was wrong and now I want to preach.

Oh, no. Meco had become an evangelist. I was here to talk about weights and measures and this guy just wanted to break out the tambourines. All he wanted to discuss was God's love and God's way and how only prayer could save the world. Which, I have to admit, was pretty interesting—but not what I had come to Bolivia to hear. With some effort I managed to coax the conversation back to drugs and a couple of pieces of the story came out.

I used to be a professional footballer. A striker: number seven or number nine for the Guavidad [a national team] (when I was a dealer I later became vice-president of the club). Anyway, I was there and I had no money. They sacked me. So I had to work for a while as a taxi driver, but my wife was pregnant and I really needed money. That's why I got into drugs.

In 1980 Meco was approached by a friend who told him how much money there was to be made in cocaine paste and started him off in the production business, delivering paste in his taxi. Within a year he had his own Toyota, a top-of-the-range model, worth $20,000. It wasn't long before he made contact with the Colombians.

I didn't deal with the Colombians at first. I was making small amounts, like fifty kilos at a time. But when it picked up and I started making, selling, making, then I did. I used to deal with the Mexican [Rodriguez Gacha] and worked with Pablo Escobar. I once went to stay with the Mexican in Pacho near Bogotá. He was a simple guy. Never violent. Just simple.

This seemed a bit unlikely. Anyone describing Rodriguez Gacha as 'never violent' either didn't know him very well or was lying. I let it go. What happened next? I asked.

Nineteen eighty-six, -seven, -eight—that was when I really started making the big money. I was the biggest in Bolivia—I am lucky to be alive today. I'm happy because I'm alive. I thank God for that. I was using drugs—did you ever see that Al Pacino film [*Scarface*]? I was like that. Really. I had two helicopters and I don't know how many planes. The best cars, the best women in Bolivia. I said I had a life but I didn't really have a life at all.

I don't know, Meco—it sounds like you were doing all right to me. But he was off on a tangent: 'Are you a true Christian? Have you studied? Do you read the Bible?'

I wasn't really sure what to say at this point but it was clear that 'no' would be a bad option. I commented that I didn't read the Bible much these days but that I had studied a bit of theology in my time. Meco's eyes opened wide like saucers: 'Theology! We must pray together!'

He grabbed me by the hand and we were off to the prison chapel, which turned out to be his former cell, lined with stacking chairs, equipped with an electric organ, a couple of acoustic guitars and a series of diagrams on the wall that appeared to be graphs representing God's love and the world—but I didn't get much chance to have a closer look because Meco knelt me down, placed his hands on my head and told me to repeat after him: '*Nuestro Padre, que estas en el cielo santificado sea tu nombre...*'

At the end of the prayer Meco told me that he was very busy and I would have to leave now but that I could come back and pray with him any time I wanted. We exchanged telephone numbers (he gave me the number of his mother in Santa Cruz), shook hands a couple of times and hugged a lot. And then we left. I have to be honest: it was pretty weird. But then the story of what happened in Bolivia in the 1980s was pretty weird, too.

Following the cocaine coup in 1980 the US pulled out of the country and cut off all economic aid. Roberto Suárez, Bolivia's king of cocaine, whose income was at this stage in the region of $600 million per year, softened the blow by paying the shortfall out of his own pocket. Bolivia abandoned an IMF-backed project to repay its international debt and the country went into economic free fall. The García Meza regime was so busy filling its pockets that no one really cared.

However, Bolivia's new-found 'pariah nation' status was disturbing. Minister of the Interior, Luis Arce Gómez, who had been dubbed 'Minister of Cocaine' by CBS, flew to the United States in late 1980 to make amends, announcing to anyone willing to listen that he was personally going to do something about the problem of drug trafficking in Bolivia. In a way he kept his word. When he got home he set about arresting coca growers and paste manufacturers who refused to pay him sufficient tithes. Of course, friends of the regime were left untouched. The rest were chucked into jail and it was promptly announced that Bolivia was winning the war on drugs. Not only was the United States not convinced but the tactic had unexpected side effects: so many petty coca producers were locked up that there was a shortage of paste—just at the point when the Colombians were crying out for more. Suárez told Arce Gómez to stop mucking about and leave the trade alone. Gómez agreed to look the other way—for a one-off payment of $50 million. Blackmailing the man who had put him into office turned out to be a major error: in 1981 Suárez had Gómez sacked. But then, they were all sacked in 1981. Apart from Suárez himself, of course.

By April the country had just about had enough of the antics of García Meza, Klaus Barbie and Arce Gómez. The military, sensing the public mood, began booting out the Fiancés of Death. Many of the Fiancés, realising that it was better to jump before they were pushed, scooped up large stashes of cocaine and fled to Argentina, where, upon arrival, they were promptly arrested and thrown into jail for possession. Which was a fitting end, really.

Klaus Barbie, relieved of his henchmen, was effectively forced into retirement. He moved to La Paz and spent his days reminiscing and watching the world go by at the Café La Paz, just a couple of blocks away from the US embassy. In June 1981 his past finally caught up with him when an American magazine published his name, true identity and location in a world exclusive. He was arrested and extradited two years later. In 1987 the 73-year old Barbie was convicted of crimes against humanity and sentenced to life imprisonment. He died of cancer, in jail, in 1991.

The rest of the administration didn't fare much better. In August 1981 there was a quiet coup to remove García Meza from office. Suárez was one of its backers: somehow, things hadn't worked out quite the way he had planned them. García Meza himself was eventually tried for the atrocious civil-rights policies of his regime. Under interrogation he conveniently could not remember very much and it became clear that, thanks to numerous friends in high places, he was unlikely to receive a stiff sentence. He didn't. In 1988 however, when accused of selling Che Guevara's diaries to Sotheby's, the mood changed. He went into hiding, only to resurface in the 1990s to be arrested, tried and lobbed into jail for thirty years. He currently resides in his own separate unit in Chonchocoro High Security prison an hour to the north of La Paz.

Interior Minister, Luis Arce Gómez, also came to a sticky end. Following the removal of García Meza he fled to Argentina, where he went into the death squad business. He was eventually arrested in December 1989 and flown to Miami for trial. DEA agent James Nims, who accompanied him to the United States, recalls:

> We put him on a DEA plane at Cochabamba and all the time he's silent: sitting up straight, very proud. He thinks we're going to La Paz—where he'll presumably be able to get himself released. But after about an hour, he realises something's up and asks my colleague, Angel Perez, where we are going. And Angel tells him 'Miami.' Then later we hear this droning, whining kind of noise. Even the pilots can hear it up front through their headphones. We look around and there's Arce Gómez, just wailing, sobbing his heart out. It was pretty bizarre.

His lawyer portrayed Arce Gómez as a decent family man and to back this up it was arranged for his aged mother to be in court. Perhaps his 'family man' story might have held more water had he not repeatedly thrown tantrums in the courtroom. At one point he screamed at his own lawyer to shut up. He got thirty years.

Roberto Suárez continued trading. Thanks to the new government's tenuous hold on power, no one wanted to aggravate him. He was indicted, *in absentia*, in Miami for cocaine trafficking but was said to have laughed when he heard the news. Despite his cavalier attitude, however, he was in trouble. In 1984 the Colombians unilaterally decided to lower the price they were paying for coca paste by 25 per cent. Suárez wasn't having any of this and refused to sell. The bluff might have worked had not one of his relatives already agreed to supply paste at the new price. Suárez was eventually supplanted in the cocaine business by his own nephew, Jorge Roca Suárez—known as Techo de Paja ('Thatched Roof') on account of his blond hair. He struggled to reassert himself over the Bolivian market but nothing seemed to go right any more. Relatives were arrested, loads were interdicted. He lost money. The new Bolivian regime, under Hernán Siles Zuazo (whom Suárez had prevented from taking office in 1980) was antidrugs and began to step on his operations.

All was not yet lost, however: Roberto Suárez may have been down but he was far from out, as future events were to demonstrate.

Meanwhile the economy was well and truly shafted. In 1981 alone GDP dropped nearly 10 per cent while inflation rose over 100—and continued to climb. By the time the London Metals Exchange collapsed, annihilating Bolivia's tin market, inflation was running at a staggering 11,750 per cent. Fossil-fuel markets also slumped. In June 1983, Suárez decided to help out. The way he saw it, the government needed money—which he could give them. He, meanwhile, needed protection—which the government could give him. In a secret meeting with President Siles's narcotics adviser, Rafael Otazo, Suárez offered to cough up $2 billion in $500 million payments in return for immunity from prosecution. When this offer was rejected he held a press conference in which he bragged about his ability to take on the Bolivian state with his own private army. He had, he said, Libyan-trained ground forces, a number of Harrier Jump Jets and a fleet of Brazilian fighter planes—which he had every intention of using to overthrow the Siles government to install himself as president. Although this never happened, it turned out that he had already done enough damage to bring down the government anyway: when news of the Suárez–Otazo meeting leaked in August 1984 there was a public outcry and impeachment proceedings were begun against the president. To defuse the situation President Siles fired Otazo who, he said, had been working without his consent. No one believed this for a minute, especially when Otazo gave Congress a blow-by-blow account of the whole affair. The incident was dubbed the 'Bolivian Watergate' in the US press and Siles eventually resigned.

One of the first actions of the new president, Paz Estensorro, was to close down the state industries that were haemorrhaging money the fastest. Under a World Bank 'structural adjustment' programme, 22,000 miners were laid off. This was only to make the cocaine problem worse, as many of them packed up their things and headed off to grow coca. Traditionally, the two coca-growing areas in Bolivia, Yungas and Chapare, had produced the leaf for different markets: the Yungas leaf was small and pleasantly flavoured for chewing; the Chapare leaf meanwhile—large, high in alkaloid and no good for chewing at all—was excellent for processing into cocaine paste. Unemployed miners headed for the Chapare, where prices were highest. In this way the collapse of the Bolivian economy played into the hands of the cocaine traders: after all, the paste industry was the only one that was actually hiring.

The population of the Chapare more than doubled from 1984–89. In 1982 US satellite pictures of Bolivia's coca plantations revealed that they had the capacity to produce 90,000 tons of leaf per year. Still the price went up. By 1986 coca paste prices had reached an all-time high: the Colombians simply couldn't get enough of it. Such was the demand for leaf that even the Yungas crop was bought up in bulk for processing into cocaine: there may have been no coca to chew in Bolivia, but people were at least supporting themselves. By 1987 coca was generating the best part of $1.5 billion per year—a quarter of Bolivia's GNP. *The Economist* estimated that nearly one in three economically active Bolivians derived their income from the crop.

Coca growing was so ingrained that it was impossible to stop. Repressive measures by the authorities meant that growers were militantly antipolice. Intransigence by the farmers, meanwhile, meant that the police were militantly antigrowers. This led to conflicts: in October 1982 the Yungas reached flash point when the wife and daughter of a coca farmer were abducted and raped by police. Locals marched on the police station in the town of Chulumani. Having razed the building to the ground, they set about castrating and executing the police. Drug police were not to return to the region for another five years: no one wanted to mess with people this angry. Besides, the coca trade generated such wealth that traffickers could pay law-enforcement agencies vast amounts to stay away. If they wanted a fight they could try their luck, but the police were poorly equipped, unlike the traffickers, who had all the latest military gear. Drug-control efforts in Bolivia ran frantically to stand still. Meanwhile the US, now back in touch with the Bolivian establishment, wanted results: how hard could it be to stop people growing coca? Who was in charge of this country, anyway?

When it became clear that the Bolivian government was not achieving much in the field of drug interdiction, the US decided to act. In July 1986 the DEA arrived in force, together with six Black Hawk helicopters and two hundred personnel, to hit trafficking operations in the Beni department. This was Operation Blast Furnace. A number of clandestine labs were destroyed but no significant traffickers were apprehended: they had all been tipped off about the 'secret' operation weeks in advance. The US military soon discovered that it was hard to fight coca in regions where the locals didn't want to fight coca without coming to blows with them. In one operation a group of Blast Furnace operatives was forced to beat a hasty retreat when confronted by a rampaging mob armed with sticks and machetes, chanting 'Kill the Yankees!' How could you handle a problem like this? Not with force. Within four months most of Blast Furnace's resources had been sent home.

The US now tried another tack: perhaps these farmers could be coerced into getting rid of the stuff. It was clear that farmers would not stop growing coca until they were provided with a viable alternative. Efforts were made to find one. An aid programme was established to remove coca under the guise of a development deal by the United Nations Fund for Drug Abuse Control. The programme was known as AGROYUNGAS. In return for agreeing to grow something other than coca, Bolivian villages that signed up would receive various new facilities such as plumbing or electrical wiring. Bolivians were interested, but what could they grow that wasn't coca? The answer, said the UN, was coffee: it raised a high price on the international market and grew well in Bolivia. To compensate for the fact that it sold at lower prices than coca, the UN gave the Bolivians a new strain of coffee with an extra high yield. Locals agreed to try it. Unfortunately, while the coffee they were given was indeed more productive than regular Bolivian coffee, it required large amounts of fertiliser, which no one could afford. Then the international coffee market collapsed, leaving the *campesinos* with a crop that cost more to grow than it could possibly generate. Crops were left to rot in the fields: it just wasn't worth getting them in.

To add insult to injury, it turned out that the coffee they had been given by the UN had contained an insect infestation that ate the pulp inside the beans. Not only were the new strains of coffee destroyed, but the infection spread to strains that had been grown there for years, decimating them, too. Anywhere else, it might have been possible to spray the plants, but in the Andes the plantations were just too small, and situated on precipitous hills. There was nothing that anyone could do. It was eventually admitted by one and all that replacing coca with coffee was not going to work. Meanwhile, the peasants who had participated in the trial petitioned the government to have their debts written off. Some of them received compensation but many of them did not. All of them returned to the one crop that they knew would pay: coca.

Other forms of crop replacement were likewise unsuccessful. Mainstream fruit such as oranges sold so cheaply in Bolivia that they simply could not generate as much income as coca. More lucrative crops such as macadamia nuts and passion fruit were hard to transport and took many years of tending before they could be harvested. In addition, the country lacked the infrastructure to export these goods once they were grown. To combat this the UN set out to build new roads around the coca-growing regions to facilitate the export of all the fruit they were about to start producing. As with crop substitution, it was a nice idea that was doomed to failure. New roads encouraged more coca trading, as paste merchants simply landed their planes on the roads instead of building airstrips. The road-building programme was swiftly wound up.

The fact was that coca, which sold for about $2,600 per hectare, was a much more profitable crop than oranges or avocados, which made just $650. Meanwhile, the few successes that crop substitution had were often hijacked by other pressure groups: when it was revealed that thanks to crop substitution Bolivia was exporting 50,000 tons of soya beans per year, the American farm lobby was outraged. US soya farmers were, they said, being put out of business by their own administration. It was pointed out that Bolivia could not possibly represent that much of a threat to the US, which was at the time producing 17 million tons. The AGROYUNGAS project was eventually knocked on the head in 1990.

In April 1988 Roberto Suárez created another diversion, releasing a videotape of himself hobnobbing with a group of high-ranking Bolivian officials. It was revealed that these gentlemen had contacted him to ask for donations for the election fund of former president Hugo Banzer, who was running for office again. The scandal, dubbed 'Videogate', created a sensation and Banzer's election campaign was eventually suspended. However, in retaliation for the release of the tapes, the government finally decided to go after its number-one cocaine offender, and on Wednesday, 20 July 1988, the authorities finally caught up with Suárez, arresting him without a struggle at one of his ranches. It was later alleged that he had in fact turned himself in and cut a deal in return for a lenient sentence—on the condition that he stop releasing embarrassing videotapes. He himself agreed with this account: 'I knew what time they would come,' he said. 'I was ready with my things, dressed and smoking a cigarette.'

Upon his arrival at San Pedro he received a hero's welcome. He held a press conference at which he declared that he was not Roberto Suárez the drug trafficker but an innocent businessman with the same name, that he was a ruthless anticocaine campaigner, that he was innocent of all charges. He then announced that he would agree to be tried only by a grand jury overseen by the Pope. Notwithstanding this appeal, he was tried and sentenced to twelve years.

Clare Hargreaves, who interviewed him in jail in 1991, found him complete with wife, children and girlfriend in a large personal cell known as the 'Hotel San Pedro', watching TV and sipping Pepsi-Cola. He asked repeatedly after Margaret Thatcher (it appears that he was a fan), then suddenly instructed Hargreaves to leave when a government official arrived for a private conference. I had hoped to arrange an interview with him myself when I got to Bolivia but it was not to be: Roberto Suárez, Bolivia's grand old man of cocaine, died of a heart attack on 20 July 2000. *The Economist* ran a full-page obituary.

Of course, Suárez had not been the only major trafficker. The town of Santa Ana was home to some thirty major drug lords and would come to be dubbed 'the Medellín of Bolivia'. As had been the case with Suárez, traffickers outdid each other in their acts of munificence. If you visit Santa Ana today, pop into the Casa de Culture—a present to the town paid for with cocaine—or simply wander around safely at night thanks to the electric street lights: another cocaine bequest. Suárez had not been the only one to buy his way into the government, either. Everyone had been doing it.

The true extent of the Bolivian authorities' complicity in the cocaine trade of the 1980s and 1990s is only now beginning to emerge. What scraps of information there are, however, reveal that the rot went all the way to the top. When Meco Domínguez was picked up it emerged that he had been dealing with the MIR political party, starting with donations to their 1987 electoral campaign. On occasions he would personally collect the president, Jaime Paz Zamora, from the airport at Viru Viru and take him to his colleague Isaac Chavirria's house, where they would talk politics into the small hours.

Another trafficker I interviewed in Bolivia's highest-security prison, Chonchocoro, told me that he had made payments to a former vice-president of Bolivia called Nuflo Chaves Ortiz, who had given him security coverage in return. So close were the two that Chaves lent this trafficker his house in Santa Cruz, complete with bodyguards and car. This vehicle, which had diplomatic plates and was thus immune from police search, was then used to shift cocaine around the country.

Other payments were made to law-enforcement agencies to ensure that there were no unpleasant seizures. Between prayers, Meco told me that he used to arrange for a small quantity of paste to be discovered in one region while his boys were really shipping a huge amount through another area, safely out of the way. To turn a blind eye to operations like this, he said, UMOPAR (Bolivia's antinarcotics force) took $100,000 a time. Inside Chonchocoro prison, my trafficking friend told me that this was about right:

> Yes, I was paying for protection like that, too. It was like this: are they [the police] going to do something? Bust somewhere? We would pay them to find an excuse not to: 'Oh, we'll do it another day.' Also information: when the DEA really decided to do something we knew that they were going to do it because they would not take money. So we would be given the information in advance. The police knew the frequencies of our radios and that we listened to them twenty-four hours a day. They would have their own nickname, like a codeword, and when we got a call from that codename we would know something was up—and get out.

In 1989 corruption in the Bolivian antinarcotics forces was so bad that the US instructed the government to call in the military. This raised a few eyebrows. Everyone was aware that giving the army civilian powers was risky: the Bolivian army has a long and illustrious history of seizing power given half a chance. No one trusted them not to sneak in another quick coup. And what would happen if the army was corrupted by narco-dollars? The Bolivian navy had been tasked to stop the coca trade but this had ended in disaster: a random 1988 inspection of a convoy of naval 'food supplies' revealed that the navy was apparently subsisting on a diet of cocaine paste. The extent of the Bolivian navy's corruption became evident the next year, when the DEA and UMOPAR raided Santa Ana, only to find themselves under fire from the navy, which had been paid off to protect the place. The Bolivian air force was likewise riddled. One of Bolivia's main traffickers in the 1980s was Lieutenant Erwin Guzman, a retired air force officer who maintained close relationships with his former comrades: whenever the air force flew antinarcotics officers on raids, narcos were invariably tipped off in advance.

There were some who said that curtailing the cocaine trade could even be a bad idea. Rensselaer Lee wrote in 1989:

> If the cocaine industry disappeared tomorrow, the results could be catastrophic, at least in Peru and Bolivia: the evaporation of hard currency reserves, massive unemployment, and increase in crime and subversion in

rural areas, a flood of new migrants to the cities, and so on. Such a situation could only play into the hands of extremist groups on both the left and the right. For example, how long would democracy last in Bolivia if 200,000 dispossessed coca farmers decided to march on La Paz?

White Labyrinth, Lee, 1989

Not that this dampened the US's enthusiasm. In May 1990 America agreed to donate over $30 million in military gear if 1,500 soldiers were tasked to stop the coca trade. Bolivians were appalled. The way they saw it, sending in the army was pretty much guaranteed to increase the level of violence. Even the army themselves were appalled. Once they were sent in, they reckoned, if the fight against cocaine was not won, it would be their fault. And anyone could tell that the fight would not be won. This didn't stop them taking the money: the US had threatened to cut off economic aid if they didn't.

Bolivians do not like the US's anticocaine operations. For a start, there's the matter of national pride: why should Bolivia let the US tell it what to do? And cocaine is an American problem, anyway. The way Bolivians see it, if America has a problem, then America should pay to fix it instead of asking a poor South American republic to stop it. Bolivians love to point out that one of California's largest cash crops is marijuana. If the USA, with all its money and technology, can't even wipe out dope in one state, how can Bolivia—with no money and no technology—wipe out coca? Besides all this, there is a far more pressing danger: as was proved by Suárez in 1980, cocaine has the capability to jeopardise Bolivia's fragile democracy. Yet the money that makes it so dangerous is not generated in Bolivia: the market lies in the United States. Whose fault is this? Not Bolivia's.

There are others who see cocaine as actively beneficial to Bolivia. It's certainly true that the country saw a vast surge of hard currency in the 1980s due to cocaine. No other industry produced this kind of a spike. While the country was in the midst of a severe economic crisis, it has been argued, coca ensured that Bolivia's rural population was not left starving. Not only the coca growers and paste merchants made money out of coca, either. Wherever trading in coca and coca paste established itself, small economic zones would flourish. Every narco town that sprang up in the middle of nowhere had its own economy, which would never have existed without coca: builders, drivers, manual labourers, barmen and so on.

Amid all this chaos and corruption, however, the country was taking steps in the right direction. No sooner had Suárez been apprehended than Bolivia, under extreme US pressure (50 per cent of US aid was frozen until the Bolivian Congress agreed), drafted a surprisingly tough piece of legislation known as Law 1008, which directed that all coca should be eradicated in the Chapare, leaving an area of just 12,000 hectares (29,600 acres) in Yungas for legitimate production. This law led to all kinds of trouble: outraged that they were about to be put out of business, Bolivian coca growers' trades unions staged a 15,000-person roadblock around the city of Cochabamba, effectively bringing a large part of the country to a halt.

Such strikes have become regular fixtures in Bolivian life. In 1995, when the US again threatened to cut Bolivia's economic aid, the army was sent into the Chapare to measure coca plantations and start a new eradication project. Soldiers were barred from entering by the growers and another strike followed. Demands were the same: either stop the repression or provide a suitable alternative crop. Unfortunately, there were a couple of problems: the first was that most of the farmers weren't really farmers—but immigrants who flocked here in the 1980s—and so did not know how to grow anything other than coca; the second was that, even if they had been proper farmers, there was no suitable alternative, and coca was the only crop capable of supporting this many people in this area. The government declared a state of siege, rounding up and arresting over five hundred union leaders. All were detained under the new Law 1008.

Law 1008 still generates controversy today. Over coffee in a bar in La Paz, a Bolivian lawyer told me why:

Something very strange happened with this law. The accused is presumed to be guilty and has to demonstrate his innocence. It should be the other way around: the one who accuses should prove that the other is guilty. No one should have to prove their own innocence. This is known as inversion of proof. It ignores one's right to a fair defence. And there are abuses. For example: if you are my friend and I am connected with the drug traffic, even though you don't know it, when they arrest me they can arrest you too—because you are immediately an accomplice. Now you have to prove that you are innocent. And that's hard.

Regardless of its human-rights implications, Law 1008 got results. By 1990 it had been responsible for the destruction of over 400 hectares

(990 acres) of coca in Yungas and 320 hectares (790 acres) in Chapare and the incarceration of thousands of *cocaleros*. However, the application of the law was distinctly suspect: growers were compensated $2,000 for destroying their coca but eradicators charged them for inspections and verification that the coca was gone. This removed a fair whack of their cash. There were reports of coca farmers who had taken the money, destroyed their coca and then been visited by UMOPAR, who had searched their farms, found the compensation cash and confiscated it on the pretext that it might have come from the drug trade. Once again, coca growers were left penniless with no way of supporting themselves.

As had been the case with the repressive anticrack laws in the United States, Law 1008 largely failed to touch the real drug traffickers and instead hit the poor. Penniless farmers ended up in jail for producing coca. The huge increase in the prison population resulted in a backlog of prisoners awaiting trial. The average coca farmer incarcerated under Law 1008 ended up waiting two to four years in prison for his case to get to court, by which time he would have served more than the maximum penalty for his offence. And at the end of all this he might be proved innocent. There was no compensation for the victims of such cases. In 1999 more than 1,000 of the 1,400 prisoners in Colhabamba had never been sentenced. In April the inmates of five local jails went on hunger strike in protest, four women sewing their mouths shut with thread. Ten others crucified themselves.

Still the paste flowed. And the corruption was untouched. In 1991 President Jaime Paz Zamora appointed a known trafficker, Faustino ('the Magician') Rico Toro, as head of antinarcotics operations. Placing Rico Toro in charge of narcotics was, according to one US official, 'like asking a cat to look after a tin of sardines'. How could this have happened? It was rumoured that the president had a thing going for Rico's daughter, who had been a finalist in the Miss Universe competition, and a photograph of the two dancing together was printed in the press. In response, the US again froze Bolivia's economic aid package. Rico Toro was forced to resign and is currently serving a lengthy jail sentence in Cochabamba. Likewise, Minister of the Interior, Guillermo Capobianco, was forced into resignation when a convenient leak to the press detailed his involvement in the cocaine trade (Meco Domínguez admitted to supplying Capobianco cash). By 1994 such were the rumours surrounding the Paz Zamora administration that an investigation was launched into the president himself.

Coincidentally, despite corruption and the manifest failure of many of the antidrug operations in Bolivia, the trade began to diminish. This was not due to any particular eradication policy but to the only trend ultimately capable of denting the crop: market forces. Bolivia began to bow out of the coca market in the early 1990s when Colombia started growing its own. Since it was cheaper for the Colombians to use their own product rather than fly it in from abroad, the price of coca and coca paste dropped dramatically in Bolivia. Meanwhile the economy stabilised. From 23,000 per cent in 1985, inflation dropped to a more reasonable 11 per cent by 1995. There were also other jobs around. Estimates of coca workers in Bolivia indicated that there were between 100,000 and 200,000 in 1991–92. By 1995 this was down to fewer than 74,000.

This downsizing of the industry changed the nature of Bolivian trafficking. As the money coming into Bolivia for paste dropped, so the scale of operations went down and the status of the traffickers collapsed. There are no cocaine lords in Bolivia any more. General Tarifa, head of the FELCN antidrugs force, told me:

Before, there were people like Roberto Suárez or the others who ran huge organisations, but now everything has changed. There are no more big bosses like that any more. Everything is done in little groups, often family groups. In the old days we used to capture large amounts of drugs or a person who was the head of a group and when that happened you did some real damage to the drug traffic. But nowadays there are no visible heads. Everything is done in a network, a small trafficking group and in small amounts: fifty, forty, ten kilos. Not like before when they used to make tons.

This, in turn, has reduced the traffickers' ability to buy politicians. And yet talk of corruption still echoes in Bolivia's corridors of power, occasionally reaching up all the way to the current president, Hugo Banzer (yes, *that* Hugo Banzer), himself. Just eighteen months before I arrived, allegations concerning Banzer had hit the papers when a smuggling ring responsible for moving over eight tons of paste was broken up. This group was so well organised that it had tapped the telephones of FELCN to make sure that no one was on patrol when loads were being moved. One of the heads turned out to be Banzer's niece's husband, a guy called Diodato. Banzer denied having anything to do with him but this didn't explain why there was a picture of Diodato parachuting as a publicity stunt waving a BANZER FOR PRESIDENT banner. Equally, a host of rumours surrounded Bolivia's last big bust, in which Amado 'Barbaschocas' Pacheco had been fingered after an aeroplane containing seven tons of paste showed up in Venezuela. No one knew much about this but everyone agreed that moving this much paste was impossible without some sort of official assistance.

The downsizing of Bolivia's cocaine industry, however, made it easier to dismantle. So successful were antidrugs operations that in January 1998 President Banzer signed a multimillion-dollar agreement with the US called Plan Dignidad—the Dignity Plan. This plan committed Bolivia to eradicating all illegal coca from the country by 2002. He commented, 'We are not going to retreat one centimetre. Our firm commitment is to leave Bolivia without drugs by 2002, totally outside the drug circuit.' It has been suggested that Banzer's wholehearted backing of Plan Dignidad is an attempt to clear his name with the Americans to compensate for his not-quite-squeaky-clean past. But is this true? There are rumours that further evidence of corruption may be about to come out. My trafficker friend in Chonchocoro told me that he had bumped into the former president, Luis García Meza, a couple of days before I arrived. García Meza was not at all happy about his treatment at the hands of his old comrade:

> Banzer should do something about me here. He owes me. If he doesn't do anything I'm going to publish a book about him and he's going to come a cropper.

Banzer has more pressing concerns than whether García Meza will spill the beans, however, because, since its signing, Plan Dignidad has gone anything but smoothly. While eradication measures have taken the country from its position as the world's number-two producer of coca (after Colombia) to number three (after Peru), this has not come without a price. In April 1999 coca growers' unions protested against the plan by staging a series of roadblocks on the main road from Cochabamba to Santa Cruz. Banzer sent in the troops, who opened fire on the crowd with rifles. Five months later things had still not picked up: 15,000 workers marched on Cochabamba to demand Banzer's resignation. Again, troops went in, firing tear gas this time. Five protestors were killed, adding to the total of 29 peasants killed by police in one form or another since 1995 (four were babies killed by overexposure to tear gas). By spring 2000 things were still simmering. In April trades unions, led by coca growers, all went on strike together. Within a week so many roads were blocked that La Paz had run out of fresh fruit and dairy produce. Strikers' blockades along the roads to Chile cost Bolivia over $100 million in lost exports in the first ten days. The situation was so grave that it was debated whether Banzer's government could survive.

By the start of May the situation seemed to be more or less under control, but there was always the threat of violence. The month I arrived in the country four policemen had mysteriously gone missing in the Chapare. They had been found, tortured and dead, not long afterwards. Another policeman had been shot dead, supposedly by a sniper, while overseeing an eradication operation. President Banzer was under no illusions as to who was behind this: the unions. 'We will not surrender in our fight against cocaine trafficking,' he said, 'and those who believe we will are wrong. We will not tolerate any more violence and disorder.' Evo Morales, head of the peasant coca growers' unions (and member of parliament) was typically abrupt in response: 'President Banzer could do us all a great favour by retiring. Coca is a matter of life and death.'

Morales has a point. There is no doubt that eradicating coca destroys jobs in Chapare. Not everyone trusts his motives, however. General Tarifa, head of FELCN, assured me that the recent strikes in Chapare had been organised not out of fear of lost jobs but as a means of distracting the authorities so that more paste could be moved while they were held up elsewhere:

The blockade was used to move the cocaine that had been stockpiled... when they saw that one week was not enough they pushed it up to a month. We know this because at that time we captured large quantities—more than a hundred kilos in Santa Cruz, a hundred here, eighty there—all just leaving Chapare, right in the middle of the crisis. They made this big blockade, put up a lot of barriers to stop all the traffic and then they moved their drugs.

Tarifa went further and maintained that Morales himself was running an extortion operation to keep people in his union and stop them abandoning the coca cause. In effect, that he was operating not a coca union but a cocaine mafia:

There is an immigrant in Chapare who was ill and he was not able to take part in the strike activities. He was charged three to four thousand dollars as a penalty for not assisting. He said he didn't have the money and so they took his land from him. He [Morales] puts pressure on people and forces them to do things. Anyone who doesn't agree with him has everything taken away.

Evo Morales is not the only problem the Bolivian authorities have to deal with. One of the goals of Plan Dignidad is to deal with the problem of unemployment in the Chapare: as long as there are too many people and not enough jobs, then someone will grow coca. So the plan is to relocate 20,000 families from coca-growing regions to other parts of the country such as Potosi or Chuquisaca. Fair enough—but the thing is that most of these people came from Potosi and Chuquisaca anyway, in the 1980s, because there was no work there. Is sending them back really going to achieve anything? Or is it simply going to shift the poverty elsewhere? In addition, no one seems to know quite how close Bolivia actually is to achieving its goal of 'Coca Zero'. When I arrived I was informed that 95 per cent of all illicit coca had been eradicated, leaving just 2,000 hectares of illegal coca in the Chapare. It was estimated by hopeful officials that this 2,000 hectares could be eliminated by Christmas. However, the closer we got to Christmas the less likely this looked: not only did the numbers stop dropping but they actually started to go up again. By the time I left the country I picked up a newspaper at the airport that told me that Coca Zero had now been postponed until at least February. So much for the complete eradication of coca.

To gain an idea of what was going on, I took a bus to the Chapare's administrative headquarters, Villa Tunari. At a place called San Jacinto we hit traffic and everything ground to a halt. This, it turned out, was the inner circle of Bolivia's defence against trafficking. Armed UMOPAR soldiers wandered around eyeing travellers while their colleagues searched every vehicle that came through—in either direction—looking for chemicals going into or paste coming out of the trafficking zone.

Such efforts have transformed the paste industry in Bolivia. In the old days you used to be able to land planes and pick up huge loads. These days paste is made in small quantities in the jungle, then given to 'mules' (paid about $200–300 per trip) to carry through the forest in small amounts, 20 or 30 kilos at a time. These guys carry the paste on their backs for eight or nine days until they have crossed out of the central ring of defence and then meet up at a prearranged spot. Twenty or thirty mules converge at the rendezvous to hand over their loads. The paste is pooled and, when there is enough, flown on for processing. Because there are so many of these people carrying small amounts through unknown jungle paths it makes it very hard to stop the trade completely. You just can't catch them all.

Just outside Villa Tunari is the Chapare headquarters of UMOPAR. Inside the base the *commandante* was preparing to give a lecture to a group of visiting American senators but managed to spare the time for a quick chat. Chapare, he told me, covers 2 million hectares (5 million acres) and is covered by nine UMOPAR posts. This one had 250–300 people. 'We can't cover the entire area with that,' he said. 'It's just too big.'

The *commandante* was not sure how much coca there was left in Chapare but he thought it was around 5,000–7,000 hectares—at the time the official estimate was 2,000 hectares—and admitted that the idea of Coca Zero was not going to happen in December: 'Coca is going to continue because the peasants go on planting,' he said, concluding that there was probably always going to be the need for a military presence in the Chapare to stop them.

Behind the *commandante*'s office was a small prison used to incarcerate recently arrested traffickers before they are sentenced. I decided to pay it a visit.

The UMOPAR jail is probably a lot more cushy than a few other places traffickers could end up, but it seemed pretty dire to me. Measuring 30 metres by 10, it contained 150–200 people. It was cramped, hot and smelly. All internees were awaiting sentencing and many of them had brought their families in with them because they knew they would starve if left outside with no one to care for them. This made the jail more crowded and a lot noisier: wherever you looked there were young children crying, screaming, playing, whatever. I wandered through the jail nodding to people as I went, before finding a couple of inmates who were willing to share their experiences with me.

Edwin, who was just seventeen years old, was in serious trouble, having been caught the week before making cocaine paste. He explained what the problem entailed:

First you make a kind of box on the ground out of sticks. Then you line the box with plastic sheeting and put five or seven packages of coca in—about 350–450 pounds of leaves. You then add water and some acid, three or four people put on some boots and stomp up and down on it. It takes about six hours. When the water goes dark, almost black, it is taken out and put into another box and other people put acid into it and afterwards they get the drug...Several people I know do it but they only do it because they need the money. In my case I'm the oldest brother so I did it to help my family.

He was philosophical about his plight.

I guess it's fair [that I'm in jail]. But, on the other hand, the government doesn't help. If they would give us some other options—work on plantations or something—then we could do some real work...I don't think it's possible [to eradicate coca]. But if they do manage it, what are we going to do? If we grow fruit, it's not continual—it only pays three months a year. How are we supposed to live on that?

Beatriz was twenty-eight and had three children, two of whom (aged three and two) were incarcerated with her. She had been caught carrying coca paste in a taxi.

A man came up to me and gave me this bag and asked me to carry it from one town to another. It was two packages, both small, and another even smaller one. He said he would pay me 50 Bolivianos (under $8) to take it and that's what I did. My husband wasn't living with me—he works as a bus driver and doesn't send me enough money—so I had to earn some myself and that's how it happened. I was in a taxi and I passed through a police checkpoint and they caught me with it.

She and her children had been in the jail for a month, sleeping on the floor of a bare room with fifteen other inhabitants. She thought she might be leaving the UMOPAR jail in a week or so for another prison somewhere else but wasn't really sure; she couldn't afford a lawyer and the state defender hadn't told her anything. She had no idea where she was likely to be serving her sentence. The only thing she did know was that she would be taking her two daughters with her. Her third child, a son, was too young to go to jail so had been left with relatives. How long did she think she was going to be separated from him? Did she know what sentence she was likely to receive? 'I have no idea,' she said.

It is cases such as Edwin and Beatriz's that make Bolivia's coca growing unions so mad. These people are hardly the real villains of the drug trade—they are poor, illiterate peasants who can't find a way of earning themselves a decent living. Although they didn't know it (and I didn't tell them), under current Bolivian law the sentence for stomping coca is up to five years; for being caught with paste, it is eight to twelve. Beatriz wasn't going to see her son for a long time—and all for the sake of 50 Bolivianos.

This was the result of Law 1008. And it is this that has driven the *cocaleros* to violence.

To understand a bit more about their point of view I decided to pay a visit to Evo Morales, head of the growers' unions. Morales has a reputation for being none too keen on Europeans or Americans: the way he sees it, most of his constituents' problems are the results of *our* consumption of cocaine. Yet, whenever he points this out, he gets labelled a drug trafficker. Determined to get his point of view, I tracked him down to one of the farmers' co-operative offices in Cochabamba. Up a ramshackle flight of stairs I found the coca union office, signposted by a handwritten notice, COCA—PODER—TERRITORIO (Coca—Power—Territory). Pinned to the walls around the room were posters advertising socialist marches and rallies and, intriguingly, a newspaper clipping reporting that Morales had recently been given a special human rights award—by Colonel Gaddafi of Libya. I was trying to work out whether this was a good or a bad thing when Morales himself swept in. He gave a quick pep-talk to his boys and then came over to say hello.

Evo Morales proved to be the most difficult interviewee I came across in the course of researching this book. For a start he seemed to assume that I was attacking him—which wasn't true, but made his conversation extremely terse. When he did answer questions directly (which was rare), his answers were so heavily loaded with political rhetoric as to be almost impenetrable. He also had an unnerving habit of referring to himself in the third person. When I got back to the UK I gave a recording of the interview to two separate translators to make sure that I was reporting what he was saying accurately. Neither could work out what on earth he was going on about. Eventually, however, some real opinions did emerge. At least, I *think* they were real opinions.

For a start, I asked, how much coca was there in the Chapare? The press reported that almost all of it had been eradicated. Was this true? Morales took a deep breath:

In January the DEA said that there was around eight or nine thousand hectares of coca left but the very next day the CIA said there was more than twenty thousand. Today the government says that there is between six and eight thousand. Personally I think the CIA's figure is more accurate. But there will never be Coca Zero. The coca leaf is the backbone of Aymara and Quechua culture...there will always be coca. I'm sure that even in 2000, 2010 or 2050 there will be coca.

I was interested to know where Morales thought this problem came from. It seemed that the cocaine problem really picked up in the Banzer regime in the 1970s: wasn't it a bit hypocritical of him, now that he was back in power, to start repressing the very industry he had helped to create? Morales agreed.

My perception is that coca plantations increased in the time of his government and that he used the Banco Agricola's money to create even more...all the dictators are involved in the narcotraffic. For example, [Banzer's] son was caught with cocaine in Canada—when he was supposed to have been picked up by his mother-in-law in a Bolivian army aeroplane. It was the same with Chito Valle, the ex-prefect of La Paz, who was fired from parliament for corruption. Unfortunately the narcotraffic is part of the Bolivian government... The way I see it, Banzer has passed Plan Dignidad in order to clean up his image in front of the US government and the international community.

Morales said that Banzer was making a big show of cleaning up his act but the Plan Dignidad, which he called 'a plan for war', was an attack not on coca but on Bolivia's peasants, who were desperately defending their rights with 'an anti-neoliberal and anti-imperialist position'.

Wasn't it the case, though, I asked, that a large percentage of the Chapare region's coca was destined for the cocaine trade? Morales said that eighty per cent of Chapare's coca went to the licit market (this seemed highly dubious—official estimates put the figure at under five per cent). When asked whether this meant that twenty per cent went to the *illicit* market, he seemed unsure: 'I'd have to do some research into it,' he said.

But did he agree, I asked, that if this coca did go towards the illegal cocaine industry, the government had the right to eradicate it?

Not only the government. We ourselves have agreed to voluntary reduction of coca production as an effective support for the eradication of the drugs traffic but on the other hand we have requested the substitution of coca plantations and there has been none...in a legitimate way, bearing in mind the constitution, what harm can the coca plant do? If it were not for the precursor [chemicals]—the illegal market—no coca leaf would have been transformed into cocaine. Here there is aggression in order to divert coca to the illegal market. For us, for the Quechua–Aymara people, coca should not be reduced. It is just a plant, like this chair. What harm could this chair do?

So far Morales had disagreed with everything the government had said: there was a lot of coca left in the Chapare, Plan Dignidad wasn't working, the *campesinos* were eradicating their own coca, he himself was against the drug trade and very little of Chapare's coca went towards the narcotraffic anyway. Quite aside from the assertion that coca was a plant 'like this chair' (which had me confused for a minute or two), everything was contradictory. And here was the problem. Was he telling the truth? I pressed on. There had been reports of human rights violations in the quest to eradicate the Chapare's coca. Policemen had been killed. Could he talk a little about that?

Robbery of houses, torture of people, burning of houses. Even a child was burned, then a young student was killed. It's hard to believe but there are a lot of examples. With all these actions they are not only eradicating coca but bananas, oranges and several other fruits... they just want to satanise the *cocalero* movement in order to criminalise the coca leaf... this is just a matter of money.

Interesting: the police said the *campesinos* were killing them; the *campesinos* said they were being killed. By now Morales was beginning to fidget so I threw him a question I knew he would agree with. Did he think the war against coca was in fact an American battle being fought on Bolivian soil?

Behind this supposed fight there are international interests, mega-projects and geopolitical interests. The drug is just an excuse for the US to recover power and control over Latin American countries. The US dictates eradication and economical policies and when the sub-developed countries do not respond, then we have to pay with dead people and blood. Regretfully it is this way. Thank you very much.

And that, it seemed, was the end of the interview. Determined to try and salvage something out of this confrontation, however, I asked permission to pose one further question. Morales was widely portrayed in the press as deliberately trying to save the cocaine trade in Bolivia—riding piggyback on the cause of peasants' rights to chew coca. I suspected this was not true, that most of the bad press he had received was probably not justified. I told him that I would like to give him the opportunity to answer these accusations. It had been said, for example, that he was a trafficker, that he was operating a violent mafia, that he was in it for the money. Would he like to refute this on the record?

Unfortunately he took this completely the wrong way and assumed that I was accusing him of being a cocaine trafficker. His face changed colour and he began to bark. Who had said this? he wanted to know. I spluttered that I wasn't accusing him of anything but just trying to set the record straight. He wasn't having any of it.

If you are the ones who are investigating, then why don't you get all this proved? Go and ask—look for the proof. When it is said, 'the press says'— that means the government but they never prove anything. This is not the first time I have been attacked like this. Where is the proof? You are a bad researcher.

This really was the end of the interview. This bad researcher picked up his shoulder bag and slunk away sheepishly.

In a way the interview was a fitting end to my time in Bolivia because it raised more questions than it answered. How much coca is there? No one knows. How much of this coca goes into the cocaine trade? No one knows. Is Law 1008 an outrageous abuse of human rights or a justifiable measure to stop trafficking? No one knows. Is the Bolivian government or are the *cocaleros* behind the violence in the Chapare? No one knows. Is President Banzer the creator of the cocaine trade, or the destroyer? No one knows. Who are the good guys? No one knows.

That's the way it is with coca in Bolivia: after you've looked at it for long enough, what becomes amazing is not that they've had so many coups here, but so *few*. And so the situation goes on: coca growers striking and bringing the country to a halt, the authorities desperately trying to stop them but failing and everyone shouting at each other but no one listening—all accompanied by the slow, steady *sloosh* of money washing down the drain.

17 Peru

It was a good thing Fox Sanchez had a sense of humour because I was wasting his time. Third in charge of the Peruvian National Police headquarters in Tingo Maria, he had been volunteered to look after the visiting gringo writer. Normally this would have meant an hour, possibly two, of his time but, for some reason no one could quite understand, my arrival had been preceded by a fax from a general in Lima. This made things rather serious because, if you are a captain in the Peruvian National Police and you get a fax from a general in Lima telling you to take care of someone, you don't just have a cup of tea with them and wish them luck. You make damn sure that nothing bad happens to them. Sanchez was stuck with me.

I had arrived in Tingo Maria that morning after a nerve-jangling drive from Huánuco, home of Daniel Alomias Robles, composer of 'El Condor Pasa'—which was doing the rounds here a full half-century before Paul Simon hijacked it in 1969. The drive itself was an experience I would recommend you try—on the condition that you have adequate life insurance. You snake through Huánuco in your beaten-up taxi, skirting the city market where eight parakeets are sold in a cage the size of a shoe box and chickens are kept in string netting bags and lean, mangy, hungry, flea-ridden dogs slope around the place looking for shade. Shoeshine urchins surround the car like mosquitoes every time you slow down and everywhere you stop you are accosted by street vendors carrying trays around their necks like decrepit cinema ushers, hawking lollipops, sweets, electrical cables, hand-held fans, loose cigarettes and 'chicklets-chicklets-chicklets!' Departing the town, you head into the mountains, ignoring the road signs reminding drivers that here in Peru we drive on the right because, well, it's easier to take those sudden blind left hooks on the wrong side of the road and there's no one coming the other way. Probably. Likewise you ignore the 50 kilometre per hour speed-limit signs because there's no way your car is ever going to do 50 unless you drop it off a cliff and, besides, the speedometer broke years ago. So you plough your way into the mountains, burning low-grade gasoline with a smell as clean as singed rubber or hair, worming your way up the Andes.

At 3,000 metres you hit the Carpish Tunnel and pass *into* the Andes, only to emerge on the other side to find that you are deep in the clouds and the temperature has dropped 10 degrees in 500 metres. Suddenly you begin the descent, brakes whining for mercy, the whole car shuddering as you snake around the corners, still on the wrong side of the road, still praying that no one is coming the other way and wondering how long it would take you to reach 50 k.p.h. if the car were actually to drop off one of these cliffs. Every few minutes the temperature cranks up a couple more degrees. Families look up as you pass by, cleaning their clothes, their children and their teeth in the water run-off that cascades down from the mountains. Tiny villages along the way are covered with graffiti: FUJIMORI PRESIDENTE! PERU 2000—MARCA ASI! which seems pretty weird because the day before yesterday President Fujimori announced his resignation—just like that—refusing either to say why he was resigning or to leave Japan to come home to Peru and face the heat.

Eventually, you hit Tingo Maria and you meet a police captain who shakes your hand and introduces himself as Fox Sanchez. And you discover that you have been preceded by a fax from a general, and because of this fax you have to be escorted everywhere. Then you are introduced to a couple of uniformed goons with assault rifles and hand grenades and told that they are your escorts. Things are shaping up for a pretty weird day. Fox asks, 'What do you want to do?' And, because you weren't expecting any of this, you say, 'I don't know. What is there to do?' And at this point he laughs, shakes his head and his gun-toting pals all laugh, too, because he is the officer and they do what he does and you are glad that Fox Sanchez has a good sense of humour. Because if he didn't he might well just tell them to take you out the back and shoot you for being the stupidest fucker ever to set foot in the Upper Huallaga Valley, heart of Peru's cocaine industry.

My presence was all the more inappropriate because, the month I arrived in Tingo Maria, the valley's coca growers had staged the largest protest march the country had seen for ten years. It hadn't been long before things turned nasty. Enraged by the antidrugs operations of the police, which they saw as removing their only source of income, six thousand coca growers had smashed up all the phone boxes and tipped over a couple of cars. The police, realising that they were heavily outnumbered, had blockaded themselves inside their barracks, a move that was probably responsible for ensuring that no one was killed. Even on good days here they are targets.

As I walked into the base I noticed a landcruiser by the gate with a couple of smashed windows. Fox explained that people tended to lob bricks at them around town—that's how popular the Peruvian antidrugs police are here in the Huallaga Valley. My situation was perhaps worse because I was a gringo with blond hair, and thus immediately assumed to be with the DEA. It struck me that in a situation like this, where villagers threw stones at police cars simply because they were police cars, I might not get the chance to explain that I wasn't American, that I wasn't with the DEA, that I was only a writer. Bad things had happened to people like me here before. Former head of international DEA cocaine operations, Charles Gutensohn, had told me about one when we had met up in LA:

> There was a reporter, a young guy from a paper in Tampa, and he came out to Tingo Maria when we were there and he stopped in at the base and said he was going up into the hills to gather some information. We were like, 'Listen—don't do this,' and he said, 'Don't worry! I'm a reporter. People accept reporters.' He went about two hours away into some town and started asking questions. People thought he was a DEA agent. They killed him. Dumped his body on the airport runway.

It was this, perhaps, that had worried whatever general it was that had sent the fax.

Fox decided that the best thing to do would be to pay a visit to the state coca market, ENACO (Empresa Nacional de Coca), in the centre of town. Everyone slung their rifles over their shoulders and picked up a couple of tear-gas guns for good measure, then chucked them all on the floor of the landcruiser with the smashed windows and climbed in. 'We're going in this?' I asked Fox. 'Yeah,' he said, punching out the remains of the smashed passenger window. 'No windows. Nice and cool.' This worried me greatly. Christ—if people were chucking bricks at policemen the last place I wanted to be was in a car with a bunch of them. Sitting with these guys in this vehicle was about as smart as wandering around town in an I'M WITH THE DEA T-shirt with a large target painted on the back. If I'd been a coca grower, *I* would have lobbed a couple of bricks at me for good measure. Fox wasn't about to let me walk anywhere, however, and this was the only car available, so I climbed in and we headed off.

As we pulled out of the gate I noticed that beneath my feet was the largest machete I had ever seen. I picked it up and Fox grinned: 'That's what the villagers usually attack us with,' he said. 'Of course,' I said and put it back down. Bricks and machetes. Perfect—just perfect.

ENACO was established in 1978 to handle Peru's legal coca trade so that a clear differentiation could be made between coca used for chewing and drinking in tea and coca used to make cocaine. Today coca farmers register with ENACO and are given documentation stating that their coca is legal. After the 1 kilo of coca per week they are allowed to keep for their own personal consumption, all their produce must now be sold to ENACO, which then sells it on—with a licence so that everyone knows that it is legal. The problem is that ENACO pays just 44 soles ($12.50) per arroba. Traffickers, meanwhile, pay anywhere from $30–50 for the same amount, which is why of the estimated 18,000 coca farmers in the region, only 9,000 sell their coca to ENACO. And why, of the farmers who do register their coca, most grow more than they declare and sell the rest on the sly.

In the ENACO office I ran into a local farmer named Moises, who was declaring his coca. We chatted about the problems faced by *cocaleros* in the Upper Huallaga Valley before he revealed that he was in fact president of one of the coca growers' unions in a little village called San Jorge on the outskirts of Tingo Maria. Perhaps, he suggested, I might like to pay his village a visit to meet the growers to see what they had to say. I thought this was a great idea. Fox disagreed. It turned out that San Jorge had a dodgy reputation. 'Five years ago we wouldn't have gone in there unless we had at least fifteen men,' said Sanchez, 'and you wouldn't have gone in at all. Or, if you did, you wouldn't have come out.'

When we got back to the barracks, Fox's boss agreed: 'You're not going,' he said. Then Fox intervened: 'I could go with him,' he suggested, 'take some men.' This struck me as an extremely bad idea. I could think of nothing more likely to annoy a coca grower's union than to show up in a police van with a bunch of armed antinarcotics police. It showed very little trust and bad faith that I did not believe Moises when he had said that his village was safe. Fox thought it over. 'Don't worry,' he concluded, 'we'll be unobtrusive'.

The next morning Fox showed up with three soldiers, all armed to the teeth—but wearing jeans and T-shirts. He stuffed a pistol down the back of his jeans. 'See? I told you we'd be unobtrusive!' he said. By the time we were all assembled and the security contingent was in place there were nine of us. We eventually had to hire a minibus to get to San Jorge: this wasn't so much a courtesy call as an invasion.

On the way Moises, who had met us in town, explained that he had used the village's loudspeaker system to let the *cocaleros* know that a gringo investigator was coming to town and that they should be available at 9 a.m. if they wanted to air their grievances. The response had been enthusiastic until he had revealed that I was showing up with a bunch of policemen, whereupon many had flatly refused to meet me. He wasn't sure how many people would show up, he said, but there was bound to be a handful. When we arrived it looked like he had been a little overoptimistic. San Jorge was a one-street town half an hour outside Tingo Maria. And it was completely deserted.

Moises sprang into action, plugging in a battered amplifier and broadcasting to the village: 'The gringo investigator is here to talk about coca. Would the people waiting to speak with him please come to the co-operative office?' Nothing happened. From inside the van, where they had been told to remain with their guns out of sight until something went wrong, the police smirked. Fox grinned broadly. Clearly he thought the whole thing was fantastic. But then a couple of old ladies stopped by to take a look. A handful of children stuck their heads around the door, vanishing around the corner and giggling hysterically whenever I looked their way. As it began to drizzle, a few more people showed up and there was no longer enough room in the co-operative building. We moved a bench and a table outside and it suddenly became obvious that a lot of people were arriving. By the time Moises addressed the village again we were surrounded by a hundred inquisitive villagers, waiting patiently in the rain to see what this gringo was all about. In the van the police stopped smiling and fingered their weapons. This was a situation with the potential to turn nasty.

Moises made a little speech. 'We are honoured,' he said, 'to be the hosts for this gentleman—um—whose name I cannot pronounce, who wants to learn about coca. But first he would like to make a speech.' This was a downright lie. I didn't want to make a speech. I hate making speeches. What was I supposed to tell them? But Moises gestured for me to stand up and the crowd edged closer to hear what I was going to say.

For posterity, Moises recorded my little oration with a hand-held tape recorder. He needn't have bothered. In my battered Spanish I explained that I was English, that I was a journalist, that I was writing a book about coca to try to explain to the people in Britain what was going on in Peru. Then I screwed up. Racking my brain to come up with something else to say that might persuade these guys that I was a serious investigator, I tried to tell them that I was 31 years old and had been researching coca in England for two years. However, nerves, and the fact that my knowledge of Spanish is rudimentary at best, led to a fatal error: in Spanish the word 'años' has a very different meaning from the word 'anos'. I chose the wrong one. Thus the villagers of San Jorge were delighted to hear that I had 31 anuses and had been writing a book for two of them. A snigger ran through the crowd. It was probably the best thing I could have said. Clearly I was harmless: even the DEA wouldn't employ someone this stupid.

When I had finished my little talk a number of *cocaleros* came forward to tell me about their problems. They had all started, they said, in the 1980s.

Although the government had not been brought down by traffickers, the explosion of the cocaine economy was as disastrous here as it had been in Bolivia. Perhaps this was not surprising: both countries were economically shot; both had vast tracts of land suitable for coca plantations and swathes of unemployed manual labourers looking for work, and both countries' law-enforcement communities were easily corrupted. But, while the main obstacle to coca eradication in Bolivia was the growers' unions, Peru's problems were based around guerrillas. Specifically *Sendero Luminoso*: the Shining Path. When Peru began actively destroying coca—at US insistence—in 1982, attempts to stop coca cultivation in the Huallaga Valley led to pacts between coca farmers and terrorists. Both now had a common enemy: the state. The Shining Path agreed to protect coca plantations and villagers in turn agreed to protect the Shining Path.

The idea of a band of heavily armed Marxists with pockets full of narco-dollars (they were estimated to be making $20–30 million annually) was more than the government could stand. Because coca didn't represent too much of a threat to Peru itself it was thus resolved to fight not the coca trade but the guerrillas. Such was the risk of allegiances between terrorists and *campesinos* that when the military did stage antiterrorist operations they made sure that they did not tread on the coca growers' toes. After a few abortive attempts to send the police into the Upper Huallaga Valley led to violence, the antidrugs forces pretty much backed out. This left the valley's inhabitants free to grow as much coca as they liked and, with the Colombians paying top dollar for paste, they did.

In 1987 Peru was home to over 120,000 hectares (300,000 acres) of coca, producing 100,000–120,000 tons of leaf. Just a year later this was up to 190,000 tons. Peruvian coca made up over 50 per cent of the world market, worth around $1,000,000,000 per year.

A concerted effort to stamp out this trade was made with the arrival of President Alan García in 1985. García, who was convinced that cocaine represented a threat to national security, sacked 1,500 policemen on assuming office and despatched the army off into the jungle to bust laboratories. They were surprised by what they found: in eighteen months this operation, codenamed Condor, destroyed over 150 airstrips and 36 laboratories, confiscating 70 aircraft and over 30 tons of coca paste. The size and sophistication of some of the plants was incredible: one contained six dormitories, each capable of sleeping a hundred. Although airstrips and laboratories alike were destroyed, there was evidence that they were repaired shortly afterwards and went straight back into production. The police themselves had a hideous reputation both for human-rights abuses and corruption, and, when the military was brought in to stop traffickers' planes invading Peruvian airspace, it was soon bribed to leave windows in its cover by the Colombians. In 1984 the entire Huallaga Valley was declared to be in a state of emergency. The army was sent in but the paste never stopped flowing. In 1985 a fêted trafficker, Guillermo 'Mosca Loca' (Crazy Fly) Cardenas, offered—in a, by now, familiar gesture—to pay off the national debt. The bill came to $14 billion.

Meanwhile, the economy was collapsing. By 1988 the national debt was up to $18 billion and in 1989 inflation hit over 1,000 per cent. No one wanted to lend money to Peru any more: they knew they would never get it back. As in Bolivia, the collapse fuelled the cocaine economy as out-of-work labourers relocated in search of employment and found that coca cultivation was about as good a job as they could get. Over 100,000 families in the Huallaga Valley alone made their living out of coca. The money poured in, almost as if it were raining the stuff: in the town of Tocache, a four-hour drive to the north of Tingo Maria, the main street contained six banks, six telex machines, a long line of shops stocking expensive stereo gear and a number of flashy car salesrooms. Yet Tocache had no working sewage system or safe drinking water. Hand in hand with the narco-dollars came violence: an ENACO representative told me that he had been attacked there twice. On the second occasion his car had been surrounded by five hundred *cocaleros*, who had first tried to overturn it and then set it on fire. Private planes flew in from Lima every day to buy US dollars because the exchange rate in Tocache was so low: no one knew what to do with all the dollars. The place became a Mecca for anyone interested in making a quick buck. Peruvian popster, Mickey Gonzales, even released a hit, 'Vamos a Tocache!' ('Let's Go to Tocache!').

In the early 1980s crop substitution was presented as a possible solution. Various new crops were tried, from rice, cacao and palm trees to sugar and coffee. The US donated $18 million and the Peruvian government backed this up with another $8 million. This money was lent to farmers to enable them to bear the cost of uprooting one crop and buying and planting another. Yet with the loans came an extortionate interest rate of 106 per cent. Farmers who went for the money soon discovered that no crop other than coca was capable of generating enough income to repay a loan at this rate.

In 1983 a special agency, CORAH (Control y Reduccion de Coca), was established to enforce coca eradication. It was capable of sending out a task force of eighty people to uproot coca plantations by hand. These guys could get through nearly 50 hectares (120 acres) a day when they were really moving, but it was a dangerous job and wherever they went they were met by unhappy villagers. Often violence ensued. With the Shining Path out there in the valley somewhere, the government could not guarantee the safety of its workers. Meanwhile, farmers who agreed to allow CORAH to remove their coca were compensated with $1,000 per hectare. Many simply took the money and replanted coca: there was no way Peruvian farmers were going to eliminate their livelihoods by stopping growing coca even if they *were* given $1,000. The problem was that there was just no economic force capable of replacing coca. Meanwhile, USAID, the organisation behind many of the eradication and substitution efforts, grew so unpopular that trucks and motorbikes they had donated to the Peruvians had to be thrown away: it was too dangerous to ride around the Huallaga Valley in a vehicle with USAID stencilled on the side. From 1983 to 1987, CORAH eradicated 11,600 hectares (28,600 acres) of coca but, for every one, three or four new ones sprang up.

I asked the villagers of San Jorge about coca eradication and they became vociferous. Other crops produced fruit only once a year. Here in Huallaga coca could be harvested every two months and the plants lasted over 50 years. It wasn't hard to see why these guys stuck with coca.

The day before, I had visited Contradrogas, the organisation responsible for crop substitution in the Huallaga Valley. There I talked with a publicity officer who had assured me that seeds for cacao, coffee, maize and beans were distributed to villagers together with technical advice on how to grow them—all for free. But he had admitted that profits generated from the crops they were handing out were nowhere near those generated by coca. In fact the disparity was huge. As I later discovered, 1 hectare (2.5 acres) of land in the Monson Valley will generate $224 of cacao, $609 of coffee or $4,230 of coca. Small wonder that few people are willing to try their substitution policies. When I asked the villagers to raise their hands if they were engaged in crop-substitution activities with Contradrogas, no hands went up. But why didn't they at least take the seeds and try them? After all, they were free, weren't they? A woman came forward: 'That's a lie,' she said. 'The seeds are expensive. They sell them to us, they aren't free. They don't give us anything for free. We buy the seeds at two thousand five hundred soles (seven hundred and fifteen dollars) per kilo and when we sell the harvest they pay us just forty to sixty centimos per kilo.'

A guy came forward: 'If we plant maize, bananas, oranges, there is no market for these fruits. To get bananas you have to take care of the plants for a whole year. At the end when you get them to the market they will pay you four soles per kilo. Four soles for a year's work. We need markets to sell our products.'

A young man stepped up and interrupted: 'I sell my coca to ENACO but last month when I was at the market a helicopter landed in my field. CORAH cut down all my coca plants. They didn't care that I was selling to ENACO. They just destroyed everything. I wasn't even there and they took all my coca.'

It was hard to blame these people for being angry: their livelihoods were being taken away and they were receiving nothing in return. But what about all the development money that you are receiving for eradicating coca? I asked. Aren't you given facilities and training? Moises stepped up.

The government gave us two hundred and fifteen thousand dollars to build a new school. But the school only has six classrooms. So where did the rest of the money go? I didn't see a single sol! This road here was supposed to have been built all the way from the Marginal right to the end of town, but they only made a little bit of it and then went home. I don't know how much they got to build the road but it was a lot. So where is the rest of the money? They have used it for their offices, more secretaries, nice cars, administration expenses, publicity, a few beers. And why not a few nice blondes? Meanwhile the farmers here are starving.

The notion that development funds were going amiss was partly a result of changes in official policy. In the 1980s when money was delegated to be used for voluntary eradication, it was simply handed over to the farmers to spend as they chose. Unfortunately, it turned out that the farmers tended not to use the cash for its designated purpose but to buy themselves electronic goods and leave the coca where it was. Today money is given to villages in the form of development deals and, because the farmers no longer see the cash themselves, they are convinced that it is being skimmed. There is some evidence that they are right. Head of the secret police Vladimiro Montesinos, who apparently vanished off the face of the earth together with the details of various loaded private bank accounts in Switzerland, Miami and Panama in October 2000, was certainly up to something dodgy, as, it was rumoured—following his bizarre resignation in Japan—was the former president, Alberto Fujimori. A month after his resignation it was revealed that Fujimori's elections had been bankrolled by both Medellín and Cali cartels. Pablo Escobar's brother told a newspaper that he had himself been contacted by Montesinos a number of times and been asked to advance cash on Fujimori's behalf. Is it any surprise that Peru's *campesinos* don't trust their government?

The farmers of San Jorge may have been angry but, as far as the government was concerned, things were looking up. In 1992 the Peruvian air force had launched an offensive against traffickers' planes and regained control of the airspace over the Huallaga Valley. With US backing they installed radar sites in coca transporting regions to monitor traffickers' planes. A new aggressive policy was adopted, in which—with assistance from the US military—Peru would shoot down traffickers' planes if they refused to land on command. There are currently nine tracking posts and two radars staged in Peru and the shoot-down policy does seem to have had a deterrent effect. And so it should have: the radars cost somewhere in the region of $60 million.

More importantly, however, in the 1990s the economy began to pick up, growing an impressive 27 per cent between 1993 and 1995. Jobs began to reappear. Then the Shining Path, which had protected the cocaine trade, collapsed and all of a sudden illicit coca production began dropping. According to DEA estimates, coca cultivation in Peru has dropped from

214,800 hectares (530,000 acres) in 1995 to just 37,700 (93,000 acres) in 1999. Clear evidence, it seems, that eradication is working. But is this true?

In Lima I had run into a government official who said it wasn't. This official, who did not want to be named, told me that the figures for coca eradication in Peru—which made everyone look good—were hopelessly skewed:

> Coca production has gone down, yes, but this all depends on which year we compare it to. Unfortunately as a country we don't have an accurate figure because all the measurements are made by the Americans...who have to demonstrate that the figures are going down to justify their policies to Congress. They say it's only thirty-six thousand hectares [89,000 acres] but nobody believes that...I estimate that for Monson, Apurimac and Puno, these three regions alone could produce as much as the entire estimate. We don't have an accurate total but when we do it will be very different from the Americans'. Whether we will be able to release it when we do, I don't know.

There were serious problems with US-backed eradication policies, I was told. For a start, until recently CORAH's eradication technique was to chop coca plants down with machetes. But coca, when chopped down to the ground, doesn't die. It comes back after a relatively short period—and stronger than before. Although this was widely known (I had read about it in England in a book that had been published many years before), no one had thought to do much about it, and thus virtually all eradication prior to the late 1990s was a complete waste of time. Today CORAH has finally got wise to the fact that chopping down coca doesn't achieve much and uses a machine to dig the plants up from the roots, but this takes time.

> It doesn't pay to have people uprooting coca. You need a lot of men to take out the bushes plant by plant. It takes about five minutes to dig out a single plant, so for one hectare [2.5 acres] with a density of sixty thousand plants in Monson, it will take three hundred thousand minutes. We are talking about eighty-three hours per person for a sixty-man team. For a single hectare. It's too long. So they take out only the biggest and best plants and leave the rest.

Then there was the issue of the cocaine-production capacity of Peru's coca. US estimates on how much leaf can be produced per hectare of coca were, my economist told me, hopelessly underestimated. Better coca-growing technology has led to more dense planting, especially in the Rio Apurímac region, where coca plants can be successfully harvested at a density of not 60,000 plants per hectare—as in the Monson Valley—but 300,000. There is very little eradication activity going on in Rio Apurímac at the moment—CORAH is concentrating on Monson. Thus, claims linked to the assertion that 'we have eradicated X or Y areas of coca, therefore we have got rid of a potential cocaine production of Z' are inaccurate.

There is nothing new about this: underestimating world cocaine production is pretty much par for the course. In 1991 a series of Peruvian studies indicated that coca production was around 242,000 hectares. The same year the US estimated it was 120,800—under half that. In Bolivia from 1987–9 the US's estimate was 40 per cent lower than the Bolivians'. When it comes to yields, again the numbers are low. In 1996 the US estimated that one hectare of Bolivian coca produced 1.6 tons of dry leaf. The Bolivians begged to differ, calculating the yield as 2.7 tons per hectare—leading to a cocaine figure 38 per cent higher. Likewise the US estimate the cocaine yield in coca leaf at 2.5 grams per kilogram in Peru and 2.9 grams per kilogram in Bolivia. Peruvian estimates peg their figure at 3.1 grams—immediately hiking their cocaine yield by 25 per cent; Bolivia goes further, at 4.2 grams per kilogram—leading to an increase of 45 per cent. As the United Nations reported in 2000,

> While there are indications of 'some' underestimates of Bolivian and Peruvian cocaine production, there are indication of *'severe' underestimates of cocaine production in Colombia*. A review of available data suggests that the cocaine output per hectare in Colombia is probably at least three times higher [!] than reflected in US State Department estimates.
>
> 'UNDCP Estimate of the Value of Global Cocaine Retail Sales, 1995–98', 14 January 2000

But the shoot-down policy? That must have done something, surely? I had heard that the Peruvians had shot down nearly a hundred traffickers' aircraft and this was a great victory. Again my economist disagreed:

> In Peru? That's a lie. That was at the beginning of the 1990s. Drugs don't go by plane any more. From Monson they go out on foot and to the Ancash

zone on the north coast of Lima. From Puno they leave by river for Bolivia. From Aguatia, near Puculpa, they go to Iquitos and from there to the Putumayo frontier with Colombia. So it is very rare to get any aeroplanes containing drugs.

And yet, while the Americans' figures may well be flawed, there *has* been a significant reduction in coca production in Peru. As with Bolivia, this is largely to do with the increase in coca production in Colombia, but here in Peru there is another important factor at work. In the late 1980s rumours began emerging of a strange fungus destroying coca plantations across the country. With no known cure, it ran riot through Peru's *cocales*—turning the plants' leaves yellow and causing them to wilt and die. The locals called it *'seca-seca'* ('dry-dry'). Scientists had another name for it: *Fusarium oxysporum*.

There are so many worrying things about *Fusarium* that it's hard to know where to begin. For a start, there's the matter of its origins: where did this fungus come from? Well, actually, Hawaii. Since coca is not indigenous to Hawaii the next question is how a parasite supposedly specific to coca evolved on an island where there was none? The answer, of course, is that it didn't. *Fusarium oxysporum* emerged on the island of Kauai in the secret Coca-Cola plantations sometime in the 1970s. The United States government, immediately noting the practical applications of a fungus that killed coca, began investing in it and by 1995 had spent the best part of $15 million.

The next problem with *Fusarium* is one of distribution: how did a fungus isolated in Hawaii find its way to Peru? It's true that any number of mechanisms can spread the fungus or its spores but let's recall that Kauai is an island in the middle of the Pacific Ocean, 8,000 kilometres (5,000 miles) away. None of the more obvious natural methods for spore dispersal account for its voyage between the two countries.

So here, finally, is the big one: did the US take a fungus that had evolved (or been engineered) in a secret coca-growing station in Hawaii and deliberately drop it on Peru? They say no.

I had heard otherwise, and that was the real reason for my visit to San Jorge. I wanted to know what the villagers thought about *Fusarium*. It turned out that reports of helicopters or fixed-wing planes flying low over the *cocales* releasing brown sprays or white mists were so common that they had given the spray a name: *'lluvia blanca'*: white rain. And so, when we got to a lull in the conversation, I stood up and asked, 'Is there anyone here who has seen the white rain?' A young man emerged from the back and, with some encouragement from his mates, stepped forward into the open space.

> It was about two years ago. I was here on my land. I saw the *taka-taka* [helicopter] come down and start spraying something white, like water. The *taka-taka* came down really low over the plants on my uncle's field. I have seen it. I have seen the white rain.

This did not surprise me. In Lima the week before, a government official had told me for a fact that *Fusarium* had been deliberately deployed in Peru. I asked him how he could be sure.

> I was speaking with a Peruvian air force captain, a friend of mine who is not in the air force any more, and he told me, 'We are using helicopters to shoot cartridges into the ground. They shoot down into the coca plantations and the cartridges explode and release the spores. That's how we do it.'

If we accept these two accounts then the next question presents itself immediately: what does *Fusarium oxysporum* do? Is it completely specific to coca? This question has sparked quite some debate.

The scientist responsible for much of the work behind the use of *Fusarium* as a herbicide is Professor David Sands of Montana University. Sands, who just happens to run the company that owns the patent for the distribution mechanisms of *Fusarium oxysporum* (and thus presumably stands to make a great deal of money if it ever is used) was interviewed by the BBC just before I left for Peru. He waxed lyrical about the fungus:

> This fungus is the closest thing I have ever seen to a magic bullet...I have seen it take out ninety-nine per cent of the plants in the field. I think that's incredible and I think people should know that this kind of technology exists.
> *Panorama*, BBC, 2000

Ninety-nine per cent of the plants in a field? Impressive. But the thing is that dropping an atom bomb on to a coca plantation will take out all of them. The question is: how much damage is it going to do elsewhere? There are some 250 plants of the genus *Erythroxylum* that are not coca. Will *Fusarium* attack them, too? Could it possibly evolve into a new form that will attack something really important in Peru—such as coffee, or maize? There are more than a hundred species of *Fusarium* in the wild and many of them attack food crops. What stops this one from becoming like its cousins? Sands says this is impossible. In 1999 it was announced that *Fusarium oxysporum*, strain EN-4 (the coca strain), 'does not mutate'. And yet just a couple of months earlier, when it was suggested that another strain of *Fusarium*, adapted for use against marijuana, be deployed in Florida, this idea received short shrift. American environmentalists warned that *Fusarium* species tend to mutate extremely quickly and that, even if it was completely specific to marijuana when it was delivered, it might well adapt to attack another crop in the state. If it did, there would be no way of stopping it. Plans to use *Fusarium* in Florida were shelved.

It was too late for that in Peru, of course. *Fusarium* was already there.

To show me exactly what *Fusarium* did, the villagers of San Jorge brought along a barrowload of fruit for me to inspect. All were dead or dying. All, they said, were the result of *Fusarium* contamination. An old man came up to the desk: 'I have been growing coca since 1955,' he said. 'Before the 1970s there were never any problems with disease. I have always grown rice, too. But just last year I had a problem with this fungus. My fields are totally infested. I have tried many other crops, such as beans and yucca—but they just don't grow any more. In the past you could get large yields from just small pieces of land. Not any more. We work and work and get nothing.'

Another farmer agreed:

I grow coca and coffee and, when they sprayed my coca, the coffee was affected, too. Now I have disease all over the field. I grow two varieties of coffee. Both are sick—the leaves are all wilting. I've had this problem for three years and every year it's worse. I used to produce twelve to thirteen quintales [600 kilograms] of coffee before the fungus hit. Now I get less than one [50 kilograms] from the same area. I would like to know: who is responsible for all this? Because next year I probably won't get anything at all.

The president of one of San Jorge's subcommittees piped up: 'I have five hectares [12 acres] with coca, maize, cattle and pigs but it is not enough. Last year I planted a hectare of yucca. But now all the plants are dead. The same thing with my maize. There is nothing we can do. Even my orange trees, that were starting to do pretty well, are dying.'

At this point the villagers all crowded around, presenting me with examples of their produce that had gone wrong: pineapples rotten on the inside, undersized yucca, poma rosa and a huge bale of dead coca. A woman shouted out that *Fusarium* affected not just crops but people, too: 'There are a lot of sick people here.' 'And animals,' added a local wag. 'Look at the state of the dogs!' Everyone laughed. Another woman approached and showed me her hands: 'My family has skin infections—look at my fingernails, you can see the fungus here. We didn't have these infections before.'

Another old man asked to speak:

> Why have they done this? If we had coca, just a little coca, we could sell it—no matter what the price we sell it for. Then we could buy ourselves some rice. If we don't have coca they are going to kill us. We are farmers here. All we have are our plants. There are no other jobs. We need our land to be clean. We want our land to be cured so that we can go on living.

The problem is that, however the *Fusarium* arrived, the land simply cannot be cured. Because *Fusarium* is a living organism it is self-generating and merely stopping spraying (if they are spraying) will not achieve anything. It lives for up to forty years in the soil, and in the meantime it attacks coca, making no distinction between legal or illegal crop. Which is a problem if you make your living out of growing coca in San Jorge. Amid the general hubbub, Moises took me aside.

> Our land has been poisoned. This is not the result of nature: our land has been penetrated with a chemical disease prepared by man. And it's not just here but everywhere. We are desperate because our land is not producing. I want you to tell the president of the United States—and the presidents of other countries—that we need help here...In the name of all the farmers here, please go back to Europe and tell people what is going on, in newspapers, television, books, however you can. Everybody should be told about this so they can see the truth.

To this day I find it hard not to lose my temper when I discuss *Fusarium oxysporum*. Whether or not it was dumped on to Peru deliberately, there must surely be enough doubt concerning its safety to curtail its use elsewhere. And yet the United States is still trying to persuade Colombia to deploy it. The Colombian Minister of the Environment, Juan Mayr, told me in

Bogotá that there was no way the Colombian government was about to allow anyone to start firing *oxysporum* into its jungles. Yet recent press reports indicate that US scientists have started a series of experiments with the fungus in Ecuador, on Colombia's southern border. A release of *Fusarium* here would have a good chance of making its way into southern Colombia after a couple of years 'naturally'. No permission from the Colombian government would be necessary. These reports have been denied. We shall see.[10]

Back in Lima I popped in to see the chief of Contradrogas's alternative development section, Alfredo Mendevil, who was terribly keen to tell me about the new generation of crop-replacement policies. I told him what the villagers of San Jorge had told me—that they weren't interested in substitution at all—and he admitted that he could see why: most of the prior plans had been pretty crap. Admittedly, no other crop in Peru could compete with coca in terms of price, but he held that, if the price of coca could be driven down sufficiently by confiscating enough, *cocaleros* would eventually switch to other crops by choice. OK. But how could you drive the price of coca down?

Not only by eradication, destroying the coca crops, because that only increases the price. But if you combine that with the interdiction of [precursor] chemicals, of the traffic of coca leaves and so on, then you will create a very low price for coca leaves and in that way we can start with some advantages for alternative crops.

Mendevil told me that alternative development plans depended on the efficient operations of the police—because without effective interdiction the price of coca would be so high that no one would want to switch crops. How efficient was police interdiction at the moment? I asked.

'Fourteen months ago,' he said, 'the price of coca leaves was sixty cents per kilo. Now in some places it is almost three dollars per kilo.'

So let's get this right: in the last year interdiction, together with alternative development, has multiplied the price of coca by five? Bearing in

---

[10] I called David Sands to ask about *Fusarium* but he declined to be interviewed. He did, however, email an academic paper 'written by an anonymous scientist' that refuted all of the claims made by the villagers of San Jorge. The outbreak of *Fusarium* in Peru, it argued, was the result of nature, not man. *Fusarium* species, it continued, 'do not attack other plants and do not mutate to attack other plants'. The paper may be correct. I could, however, find no other scientists willing to verify the argument one way or the other. The paper, meanwhile, had not (as far as I could tell) been subjected to peer review or been published. There was no bibliography or indication as to where its information had originated.

mind your goal is to drive the price of coca down, this can hardly be perceived as a great success, can it?

'Not really,' he said. 'But a year ago the price was one dollar forty. One
dollar forty is a good price. We can compete with one dollar forty...'

Here is the root of the coca-eradication problem. Alternative development agencies say that only if law-enforcement agencies stop the trade
can they compete with alternative crops. Law-enforcement agencies,
meanwhile, say that they can't possibly stop the illicit trade unless there
are real alternatives for the *cocaleros* to grow. While both are busy blam-
ing each other, the trade continues. Mendevil admitted that coca production in Peru had probably gone up in the last year, rather than down, as
the US figured. So what was to be done?

The best answer anyone can come up with is to keep ploughing money
into both police and Contradrogas coffers in the hope that together they
may be able to do something. But the problem of coca, as any of the villagers of San Jorge can tell you, is one of poverty. Contradrogas may be
doing fine work in development but no sooner have they moved into one
area and provided running water or whatever than the *cocaleros* simply
move to a more remote region of the jungle and start again. There they
create an even more serious problem: environmental damage.

In the Peruvian Amazonia nearly 10 million hectares (24,700,000 acres)
of high jungle have been destroyed by ranchers and farmers. Of these, 2 million hectares—an area approximately the size of Israel—is the result of coca
cultivation over the last twenty years. Deforestation on this scale in turn
leads to a problem of soil erosion, which has now reached critical levels. At
the United Nations in Lima, Antonio Brack, an environmentalist, told me:

> Because of all this [erosion] there is high sediment coming down from the
> hills. So the rivers silt up with these sediments and destroy the best soils of
> Amazonia, the alluvial soils along the rivers. And it has an impact on other
> resources too: the fishes, for example, are all disappearing... For hundreds
> of kilometres you have the impact of this high sedimentation: the forest,
> fauna, wildlife, all disappear.

Untold damage is also caused by the wholesale dumping of used precursor chemicals in the jungle. A recent US State Department report estimated that every year 10 million litres of sulphuric acid, 16 million litres

of ethyl ether, 8 million litres of acetone and somewhere between 40 and 770 million litres of petrol are dumped into the Andes—by-products of the cocaine trade. What the impact of all these chemicals is when they hit the rivers of the Amazon basin, no one really knows. Meanwhile there are all sorts of other problems to worry about. Brack continued:

> The big problem in High Amazonia now is the migration of the Andes to the Amazon. This has happened for thirty years but in the last ten we have the highest rates...Thousands and thousands of families each year are coming to the high selva [jungle]. It has been promoted for the last seven years by the politicians.

As was the case with the migrations of the 1970s, the exodus is politically fuelled: there are few jobs in the Andes and there is lots of land in the jungle. Migrants are awarded up to 40 or 50 hectares at a time, which is burned and planted by people who don't really know anything about farming—only to find that the soil is not suitable for growing fruit or vegetables. There are a couple of other crops it might support, however. Said Brack:

> At the moment in these areas there is no coca cultivation. But they could grow opium. And if the production of coca goes down they will start growing coca immediately. Immediately. Because it is an income. To have nothing, or to have three, four thousand dollars per year? It's more than the minimum wage in Lima.

History repeats itself. In the 1960s and 1970s, both Bolivia and Peru deliberately moved tens of thousands of peasants from the cities out to the jungle to combat the overcrowding problem. This movement provided a willing workforce in an area where there was no employment other than coca, making the wholesale export of cocaine possible. In Bolivia the solution to this is currently to attempt to move everyone from the coca-growing regions back to the cities—where there are still no jobs. In Peru, meanwhile, they are still shovelling immigrants into coca-growing areas where there are *still* no jobs—and slapping them when they start growing coca. The real problem—poverty—is not solved but simply moved around. Meanwhile, other crops are emerging. Opium hit the big time in Colombia a while back and it has recently made an appearance in Peru.

I asked Antonio Brack if he didn't get depressed about all this. Was there really no solution? No, he said, there was a solution, and he proceeded to detail the only really sensible idea I have ever heard to combat the coca trade.

Supposing reforestation was an alternative to coca? In Quillabamba there is three hundred thousand hectares that needs reforesting. If you manage to do thirty thousand hectares per year, that's ten years' worth of labour. You would employ ten thousand people, working full time in reforestation and management of this new forest industry.

At this point he launched into all the trees that could be grown and harvested, at different intervals so as to protect the forest, that sold at high prices on the international market: *Barbasco cubae*—an Amazonian tree that produces the natural herbicide, rotenone—harvestable in under three years; Bolayne, a good wood for export, harvest time: seven years; balsa, harvestable in just four years. By planting and harvesting selectively, the *cocaleros* could be employed to re-create their own jungle. It's a great idea. But wouldn't it be expensive? Apparently not:

One hectare of reforestation: four hundred dollars. And that includes the care of the reforestation for two or three years. *Eucalyptus torealana* needs only two years of care before—*pffft!*—it shoots up! And in eight years you can harvest it—for six to eight thousand dollars per hectare if you sell the timber without processing. There is no bank in the world that will give you this return in eight years.

Brack grabbed a pencil and began scribbling sums:

Make the calculation: if one *cocalero* has, for example, twenty hectares (and many people have forty or fifty in Apurimac)—twenty hectares to be reforested each year—they can take two hectares of timber, reforest it, replant it, then the next year take the next two and replant that and they already have an annual income of five thousand dollars. That's a lot of money for rural people. It is possible. And it is *sustainable*.

It sounded like a real possibility to me. So why wasn't it happening?

Last week I had a meeting with Contradrogas and they were working on their strategic plan for 2001, working with pineapple, a little cacao, some coffee—the traditional things. And I said, 'Please! Reforestation of these areas costs only four hundred dollars per hectare—cheap! And employment—women working in the nurseries producing the seedlings and so on.'... There is a real possibility to export something that people really want here but this is never included in Contradrogas' projects.

Why? There were, he said, two reasons:

The first is that in Contradrogas there are a lot of army generals and police *commandantes—military people*!... They can't have military people there. They need technicians, people who know about the field, people with some sort of academic background... There was a UN project. Fifty million dollars for alternative development: coffee, cacao, whatever. And the person there who was promoting the cacao plantations had never in his life owned a cacao plantation. Terrible! And the same specialist for cacao the next year? The next year he was the specialist for coffee! And the next year pineapple! That's—well—that's the consultancy business for you.

The second problem is that in Peru no one will look beyond the next couple of years because the chances are that the government will change in that period and so whatever has been established will be forgotten. No one is accountable so no one tries reforestation—the one replacement policy that might actually repair the damage already done to the environment while providing a steady income that will eventually replace coca. Oh, well.

My time in Peru seemed to highlight only one thing: bureaucracy screws things up. From the American experts who won't estimate accurately the amount of coca in the country because they are afraid of telling the truth to their own government, to the Peruvian experts who won't tell the Americans that they know their estimations are incorrect for fear of losing their international support, to the Peruvian government, which is still pushing large amounts of the population into jungle that they will cut down and still be unable to support themselves, to Contradrogas and the police, who blame each other for being unable to stop the coca trade, to the fact that no one in Peru can set up a worthwhile long-term replacement policy, to the desperate and—in my view criminal—introduction of *Fusarium oxysporum* into the soil in the hope that it might do something when everything else failed.

And the end result? Well, it *looked* as if it was all working, but the truth was that coca was down because it had moved to Colombia. There was no sign that it would not come back. This had cost someone a great deal of money—and the villagers of San Jorge their livelihoods.

18 Colombia

How do you go about interviewing a drug lord?

From the moment I started reading about events in Colombia the one thing I knew was that I wanted to meet the Medellín cartel. Since Carlos Lehder refused to reply to my letters and Escobar and Gacha were dead, that meant the Ochoa family. I decided to get in touch. Everyone I knew told me that this was a bad idea: people who go to Colombia looking for cocaine connections invariably end up coming unstuck. Jack Blum, senior counsel for the Kerry Committee, had been appalled when I told him what I was hoping to do:

> God bless! I hope I get to talk to you again. I wouldn't go to Colombia to interview the Ochoa family on a variety of grounds, not least of which is unless I had a substantial amount of life insurance. Colombia is not a fun place, especially if you are asking questions about drug trafficking. I don't care who you're asking about or when you're asking. It's very, very dangerous. I hope to God you know what you're about.

From a guy like Blum, who's been around, this struck me as pretty serious advice. The way I saw it I had three options: a) get a substantial amount of life insurance; b) cancel my flight to Colombia; c) find out what to God I was about. Since the last option was likely to take a lot of time and my publisher kept repeating sentences involving the words 'Colombia', 'go' and 'now', I resolved on the former: insurance. Unfortunately it was not to be.

Having contacted a number of agents about high-risk insurance, I was soon forced to admit that I was in trouble. It wasn't that the premiums were high. It was that there appeared to be no one on the planet who would insure me—at any price. A typical response—from the leading Kidnap and Ransom underwriter in the City: 'I do not think that this is something I wish to get involved in from an underwriting point of view. I do however feel that Dominic's trip is fraught with danger…From an insurance perspective I do not feel I can charge an adequate premium to justify the risk.'

What made this more worrying was that I had deliberately not told them anything about plans to visit the Ochoas. I had just said I was going to Colombia to interview some 'former traffickers'. Without any sort of insurance, travel or otherwise, suddenly the trip seemed a lot more foolish. So the question arose again: how do you go about interviewing a drug lord?

Carefully. Very carefully.

By chance, four months earlier in New York I had bumped into a journalist with all the answers. Marcela had been writing about cocaine for the best part of ten years and she had better connections than most of the traffickers I'd met. We went out for lunch one day in August and she handed me a list of telephone numbers to call when I got to South America. The list included a string of Colombia's former presidents, the entire Ochoa family, most of the members of the Rodriguez Orejuela family and Pablo Escobar's mother. It was a seriously lucky break. The moment I got back to England I fortified myself with a couple of large drinks and dialled the Ochoas' home number. The phone was answered by a woman who asked what I wanted and I explained that I would like to speak to Juan David. She put me on hold (the Ochoas' phone plays an electronic version of *The Entertainer* when you are put on hold), then the line picked up and there he was. Juan David Ochoa. Hmm. I hadn't expected that. In my best confident journalist voice I explained that I was interested in arranging an interview and would like to write him a letter to explain who I was and what I was doing. Perhaps he had an email address? He did. Could he give it to me? He could. He did. I thanked him for his time, said goodbye, hung up and immediately sank a couple more drinks.

A week later I received an email from Medellín.

> Hi Dominic My name is Luis —. I am a close friend of the Ochoa family for many years, Juan D gave me the letter you sent him and ask me to respond it, they are willing to talk to you, and let you know whatever you need to know with no problem because they paid all their debts. The time to come depends the month of the year right now is a good time.

Well! This all sounded *very* promising. I exchanged a couple of emails with Luis and we decided that I should give him a call when I got to

Medellín. The day I arrived, I did. Luis kindly offered to pick me up at 7.45 the next morning so that we could grab some breakfast. What I didn't realise, however, was that when he said 'grab some breakfast', what he actually meant was 'grab some breakfast—*at Jorge's house with the entire Ochoa family*'. By the time I realised where we were going it was 7.50, I was in Luis's land cruiser—which for some reason had inconceivably heavy doors—and we were pulling up to a large metal gate in the Poblada district. Luis spoke into a CCTV surveillance camera, the gate slid sideways and, all of a sudden, we were in. It was that quick. Which is lucky, really, because if it had been any slower I might have realised what was going on and leaped out of the car.

What do you expect of a drug lord's house? Tanks? Dolly birds in skimpy bikinis? Shifty-looking Latinos with bulges beneath their jackets? You've been watching too many movies: there was none of that. Jorge's place was big, but not ostentatiously so. There was a pond, with a bridge leading across it to a large Disney-style Wendy house for the Ochoa children (it's a large family: Jorge has two brothers and five sisters; between them they have twenty-eight nephews and nieces). A couple of exotic-looking birds wandered around the pond aimlessly.

As we pulled up in front of the house and got out a face appeared at a balcony on the first floor and broke into a huge grin: 'Luis! Up here!' The guy on the balcony got up and waved enthusiastically. It was Jorge Ochoa. I suddenly remembered a poem I had read at school, *All there is to know about Adolph Eichmann,* which simply listed his physical description—height: normal, hair: normal, teeth: normal and so on until the last line when the poet asked, 'What did you expect: fangs?' What did I expect of Jorge Ochoa? Fangs? Perhaps I did. There were none, of course. Just this grinning, happy guy waving at me. Luis and I waved back, sat down on a couple of wicker chairs on the patio and waited for Jorge to descend. Noticing that all the doors and windows were open, I sneaked a quick look inside, only to be disappointed: there was a distinct lack of guns.

Jorge Ochoa has that kind of foot-tapping, nervous energy generally associated with extremely intelligent people and hyperactive children. He is genial, always laughing, fidgety and obsessed with answering telephones ('He's like a man who has been stung by a wasp, buzzing all the time,' said Luis. 'If *my* telephone rings, he'll answer it.'). This hyperactivity made him rather tricky to interview as he was constantly disappearing—often in mid-sentence—to do something more interesting.

Throughout the day he fidgeted ruthlessly with anything close to hand, usually the contents of my microphone box—jack plugs, extension leads, microphone clips. His attention wandered all the time. And yet, while he wasn't the easiest interviewee in the world, there was a certain ebullience to him that was hard not to find charming. At one point, when his wife said that she had a minidisc player just like the one I was using to record the interview, he commented that he had never heard conversation played through one. What was the sound quality like? We stopped recording, I passed over a pair of headphones and played Jorge our last conversation. The reaction was instantaneous: he burst into uproarious laughter at the sound of his own voice, beaming with delight like a child—'It's perfect!' he cried. 'Perfect!'—before handing the headphones to anyone else who might want to listen.

This natural charm, however, did not make the interview a great deal more simple. It was quite clear throughout our meeting that Jorge was not terribly interested in talking about cocaine. In fact, as we progressed, it seemed that the only thing that really interested him—and his family— was livestock, specifically horses and cattle. Thus, as we sat on his patio and began to talk, it was entirely appropriate that he should return to the family's origins—the ranching business.

Jorge's great-great grandfather, Abelardo, had been a businessman, signing a contract with the Colombian government to supply the country with railway sleepers in the 1920s.

> He made a lot of money with that. And he sailed back to Europe with his fourteen children and bought up a lot of different livestock—goats, don-keys, horses, cattle, pigs (different breeds)—and got a ship to bring all these animals back to Colombia. But one of his prize donkeys got sick on the way so he had to stop in New York. He had to stay there for two months while the donkey recovered, with all these animals still on the ship. Then he sailed on to Barranquilla, transferred the animals onto another ship and sailed up the Magdalena River. He arrived in a small port, Puerto Real...

A boat full of animals and immigrants? A mysterious tropical river? It sounded like the opening to a Gabriel Garcia Marquez novel—but that was where the story stopped. Suddenly a bevy of Colombian women arrived and I had to be introduced to all of them. It turned out that these were the Ochoa sisters, drafted in to meet the gringo writer. As I was introduced to them their names simultaneously ejected themselves from my head, apart from one: Marta. Could this by any chance be the same Marta who was kidnapped in 1981 and released following the intervention of MAS? I didn't have the courage to ask but, it later transpired, it was. We all shook hands and sat down again but just as Jorge looked as if he was about to resume the story, he changed the subject. 'Hmm,' he said, grinning, 'perhaps we need some *fuel*!' This was the cue for breakfast.

We trooped into the Ochoa family kitchen and the seven of us sat together around a large table which a couple of cooks piled high with traditional Colombian breakfast fare: arepas (corn bread), chorizo, unprocessed cheese, avocados, dark sausages and coffee. Throughout the meal Jorge was up and down, answering the telephone, speaking to visitors through the intercom system, eating breakfast and cracking jokes. Not for the first time in the research for this book, I found myself wondering what on earth I was doing here, having breakfast with one of the most wanted men on the planet. I couldn't really find any answer that made sense and, having made a couple of feeble attempts at conversation, shut up. It wasn't a terribly impressive performance. Still, it could have been worse. I could have wet myself.

No sooner had we finished eating than it was announced that we were moving. Where to? 'La Loma,' I was told—Ochoa Central. I was really getting the full tour. We headed for Luis's land cruiser with the incredibly heavy doors. Jorge, always the perfect host, insisted that I ride in the front while he sat in the back. No sooner had he slammed the door than, without prompting, he resumed the story he had curtailed half an hour earlier:

From the port, he transported all these animals into the southeast region. He had to build trails all the way. He brought in Holstein cattle, Hershey goats. Everything. He was awarded the greatest government distinction at the time, the Cruz de Boyacar. And since then it's been a family tradition, raising cattle, horses and farm animals. Every vacation we had from school we worked with horses at the farm. When I was thirteen and my older brother fourteen, we took a load of Paso Fino horses to the United States—Paso Fino is the endemic breed of horse from Colombia, a horse that walks so fast that the rider doesn't appear to move at all. It's like driving a Rolls Royce.

As we drove, Jorge continued talking. How was he at school? I asked. 'So-so,' he chuckled. 'Just so-so!' But it didn't seem to matter. This was a ranching family and that was where the Ochoa children were headed. Until the early 1970s.

> Nineteen seventy-three to four was when I realised the existence of the business—the marijuana business. It was run by people from the coast and another region, Los Llanos—a large extension of plains. The guys there were running the marijuana. There was no problem with drugs in Colombia at that time. There were a few people here and there who smoked pot but it wasn't usual to see people smoking—at that time people who smoked marijuana were known as *marijuaneros*, which was, like, junkies, like somebody who is lost. Cocaine was only used by people who were really 'in'. You never saw people doing it because it was a very high-class thing.

The Ochoa's first contact with cocaine, said Jorge, was innocent. In 1965 the family had started up a restaurant in Medellín, named Las Margaritas after great-grandpa Abelardo's ranch in Salgar. It was a good restaurant and, before long, it had become the high-class hangout in the city.

> [Las Margaritas] was one of the largest and best restaurants in the city. We used to see almost everyone there, from high-class executives to the early narcos. The first narcos were in the habit of going to get good meals and they were also getting into horses—Paso Fino horses. At that time, when someone came into money, the first thing they would do was to go out and get themselves a really good horse. Every social climber in the city would come to us to buy the best horses...Santiago Ocampo was one of the restaurant's best customers and he used to buy horses from us all the time.

Thus it was that this ranching family found itself plugged directly into the two main outlets for cocaine cash: food and horses. It was only a matter of time before the three Ochoa sons noticed the ridiculous amounts of money that were being made in the cocaine business, stopped bussing tables and moved on to greater things.

At this point, however, the interview stopped again. We pulled up to a large steel gate, which cranked open to accept us, and began to ascend a steep paved slope through the trees. Half a mile up the hill we emerged at the stables, a small car park and a large cobbled stableyard. A beautiful chestnut brown mare trotted past at triple speed, the rider utterly motionless. Jorge grinned: 'Paso Fino,' he said.

The ranch was beautiful and immaculately kept. All around us there were horses being trained, exercised, fed, cleaned. Riders and ranchers wandered past in chaps and stetsons. It was like the set for a Marlboro advertisement. We sat down, someone brought some coffees, and the talk continued.

At the time it [the cocaine trade] was not seen as a bad thing because it was something new and everyone in the country, even the highest social classes, were looking after these guys [the traffickers], trying to sell properties, houses, farms, to them. They got invited to all the parties and everything... it was not a large business like it is now... and so I happened to meet these people. There was a lot of money being made and we were very ambitious and very young. Nineteen seventy-five was the first time.

At this point Jorge vanished and Luis, who proved to be as inclined to talk about the cocaine business as Jorge was disinclined, filled in the gaps:

I can tell you about this. He was a commissionist. He went to the States to spend some time—like, tourist time—and, because of his relationship with the guys who were visiting the restaurant, he had friends in the States and he happened to cross by some guys who were looking to buy merchandise. So what he did was to make a couple of phone calls and get in touch with some guys who came to the restaurant and make a commission out of it.

Suddenly Jorge was back. How long was he in the States? I asked. 'A year,' he said, but Luis intervened: 'No. More!' 'A year,' repeated Jorge. There was a brief conference: 'We went in 1975 and came back in 1978—three years,' said Luis. 'Three years, back and forth,' repeated Jorge obediently.

This exchange turned out to be fairly typical of the interview. The more Luis talked, the less Jorge talked, and, even when Jorge did answer questions, Luis tended to contradict him and answer them himself. I thought this was a bit strange but listening to the recording of the interview afterwards it struck me that it was a pretty good way of fending off tricky questions without being abrupt. As the interview progressed it became obvious that, while the Ochoas were being extremely hospitable, they weren't especially interested in making any great revelations about their lives in the cocaine business. Luis was their safety valve, through whom tricky questions or unsavoury answers could be filtered without appearing discourteous. On occasion, Luis also added spin, downplaying quantities of cocaine moved and amounts of profits accrued: when asked about his first cocaine move, Jorge said that it had been 'a pound'; Luis translated this as 'half a pound, a third of a pound'.

Perhaps this was not surprising. The Ochoas stand to gain nothing by bragging about their trafficking exploits. So questions about how much cocaine they shifted or how much money they made were invariably answered with watery phrases such as 'whatever we moved it was nothing compared to the amounts they move today' or 'it was only small loads then, five hundred units [kilos] was the largest you could do—not like now'.

Equally, all the violence, without exception, was blamed on other members of the cartel—usually Pablo Escobar. The Ochoas don't want to do anything that might antagonise US authorities that are already pretty antagonised at them as it is. Gloating about how rich they all are would be sure to wind up the DEA, who are more than capable of making life extremely difficult for them. They had met up with a US TV crew the year before I arrived and Jorge and his older brother, Juan David, had both eulogised about America ('I think it's a great country . . . I really love the US,' said Juan David) and expressed regret for their part in the drug trade ('I only hope that the world will forgive me for it,' said Jorge). By portraying themselves as reformed sinners it seemed that the family was aiming to reintigrate itself into society.

There was a problem, however. In October 1999 their youngest brother, Fabio, was arrested on drugs charges, and it suddenly looked as though the Ochoas might still be involved in the cocaine trade. They were keen to deny this—and to get Fabio freed before the Americans got their hands on him. It was easy to see why—the head of the DEA's International intelligence section had made it quite clear to me when we met in Washington that there was a cell ready and waiting for Fabio in the US. Likewise the files were still open on the two older Ochoa brothers, who are understandably keen to make sure they don't annoy anyone who might have the power to come and get them, too. In addition, the way they saw it, almost everything that had ever appeared about them in print was inaccurate. No wonder they were a bit cagey.

Initially I found this disappointing. I had hoped for a candid meeting in which they would explain exactly how they had run their cocaine operations in the 1980s—much as Ricky Ross or George Jung had explained what they had been up to. This was a bit over-optimistic: the

Ochoas are not like Ricky Ross or George Jung. These guys are on a completely different level. And they are extremely wary of questions. How do you get people this cautious to open up? Simper? Give them the Paxman treatment? I don't think so. I ploughed on.

How much was cocaine going for in the mid 1970s? Again the spin machine was operating: 'Here, $2,000 a kilo, and the transport was $5,000,' said Jorge, before Luis leaped in, 'No, it was more like $7,000, and the transport was $5–8,000'.

Let's suppose that Luis's numbers are correct. $7,000 per kilo plus $5–8,000 for transportation and a sale price in the US of $28–30,000 means that the Ochoas were making, in the late 1970s, at least $13,000 per kilo. If an aeroplane carried 300 kilos (by Jorge's admission, loads went up to 500) and the Ochoas filled it themselves, that would make the family, even on these downplayed figures, $3,900,000 *per flight*. If we suppose that they were getting the coke at Jorge's figure of $2,000, which still seems high, we can estimate that they were making more like $6,000,000 per flight. Jorge didn't reveal how many flights he had sent to the US (one chronicler estimates—rather hopefully—that by 1984 he was capable of shipping out 2,000 kg per week) but frankly, at this rate, wouldn't one be enough? It's a great deal of money. While you can argue about the ethics of trafficking until you're blue in the face, if you put yourself in their shoes in the 1970s when cocaine trafficking was about as easy as walking under a bus and it was generating this kind of money, well—*wouldn't you*?

Throughout the late 1970s the business accelerated. Jorge said that while he had no idea how much he had expected to make when he got into the trade, once the ball started rolling it picked up speed fast: 'The business started growing up—and then it was just madness!' How did he account for his rapid success in the industry? Luis jumped in: 'The business grew very large [for the Ochoas] because of the way they are. They were always being used by people because they are very peaceful. People just liked to be around these guys.' Jorge was more rational:

There was no competition, because the most difficult part of any business is the sale. And in our case, the sale was the one thing that was guaranteed...We got to be well known because we were, by ignorance, very flashy. And because we were already well known in society. That's how we got to be so well known but that doesn't mean we were the biggest. There

were people around who were a lot bigger than we were that were not
nearly as well known...

OK, there were bigger people than you. But what about the violence?
Where did that come in? Of course, it came from Escobar. Surprisingly,
Jorge appeared to have little time for his former partner: 'We would
never have associated business with him. We were "friends"—in inverted
commas—with him but in a way it was respect rather than friendship...
he had led a very violent life—he had been robbing, holding up banks,
stealing cars and committing violent acts since he was very young.'
But they were partners, right? This was a cartel—or wasn't it?

No, no. There has never been a syndicate or a 'cartel'. That was just a name
given to us by the Americans in order to make things a little more flashy and
complicated. It was nothing like that...There used to be partnerships and
small groups that would get together to do business, for example Pablo had
his cousin, Gustavo, and they would call up people that they knew, for example, people that had something that was missing in the process. So someone
might have a contact that could get the merchandise from Haiti to the States,
and so on. That's the only way the groups would become associated.

And what was your speciality? Where did you come into the loop?
Jorge shrugged: 'We went all the way.'
Since meeting Marta that morning, I was intrigued to know if the stories
of her kidnap and release were true. Jorge admitted that, yes, she had been
kidnapped but had nothing but disdain for the stories of leaflets over football stadiums and MAS: 'That was just propaganda put out but it wasn't
true. The truth of the matter is that the army and the police helped us to get
her back. She survived. And we had to pay a ransom in the end.' So, for the
record: was MAS anything to do with you? 'No. Can we pause please?'
And he was off again. When he returned we tackled the American law
enforcement efforts in the early 1980s—the Special Florida taskforce.
Did it create problems? Not really: 'They [the American law enforcement agencies] go in and stay in one place and then forget about all the
others. That's when people start going other ways. It's simply a matter of
being ingenious and coming up with new routes.'
Had it really achieved that little? Jorge shook his head and chuckled.
No, he said, there was one thing it achieved: 'It drove the price up! The

more they fight the business, the better the business gets. All the merchandising and propaganda and advertising is done by them. And the price is kept high.'

There was a lot of truth in this. By their own admission, within three months of the start of the Florida operation, the Ochoas were getting $65,000 per kilo for their coke rather than just $30,000. Were all law enforcement efforts equally futile? What about Tranquilandia? Whilst Jorge admitted that the bust affected his operations for a while, he said that the Medellín boys had had information about the raid in advance and removed all the really valuable stuff. But what about the 8.5 tons of cocaine they confiscated? That, he said, was a lie. 'They didn't find anything,' he said, 'just lots of chemicals.'

We discussed the relationship between Pablo Escobar and Lara Bonilla, whose death, he said, the Ochoas had been powerless to avert: '[Pablo] wouldn't listen. Well, he would listen but he wouldn't pay any attention.' Jorge agreed that the real problems had started with the killing: 'The persecution started because of the death of Lara Bonilla... Everybody's reaction was the same. "Run! Let's get out of here."'

Were you surprised when the government brought back extradition after the killing? 'Yes...' But at this point Luis interjected:

> I wasn't surprised at all. It was an outrageous lack of respect to the whole state to do such a thing—and there wasn't any need for it. So when he [Jorge] says he was surprised, it doesn't mean he was surprised. It scared the shit out of him but I don't think anybody was surprised. Everybody knew that retaliation was going to come—in the worst fashion.

Obviously extradition was the fear. But what did it represent? Jorge was succinct: 'the worst' and his wife joined in, disgusted, 'People should be judged and tried in their own country'. Did the family think that perhaps the vehemence of the American response was related to the publicity surrounding the arrival of crack? 'Absolutely,' said Jorge's wife. Jorge agreed that crack was a far more dangerous threat than cocaine: 'A person snorting the powder—the most you can do is two, three, four, five grams. But someone who sits down to smoke base—they can go through kilos at a time.'

The violence of the reaction from the Colombian government following the assassination of Lara Bonilla led to the Medellín boys high-tailing it to Panama, where they made the famous peace offering. Why hadn't it worked?

The government never honours the deals it makes. When we made propos-
als they all started off very interested but in the end they didn't honour them.
That's why they'll never make peace with the FARC—because they have
shown a tendency not to honour deals made by previous administrations.

As he had with the US TV interview, Jorge denied any contacts with
the Contras or ever moving cocaine through Costa Rica or Nicaragua.
He did agree that Escobar must have had something going on there,
because he had seen the famous Seal photographs. Rumours of $10 mil-
lion payoffs to the Contra organisations to keep the US off their backs,
however, were dismissed as 'gossip'. We moved on to the subject of the
Extraditables—a group that, he said, had been entirely Pablo's creation.
Was he really not associated with them? No. Then how did it feel, being
accused of all these violent acts?

Bad. Very bad. We felt like any other Colombian family that was living
through the violence. But the fact was that every Colombian at that time
could have been subject to extradition for something or other...

And the surrender? How did that come about?

Fortunately at one point there was a strategy drawn up by the government.
There was no other solution for us: either die or be extradited, and it was a
lot easier at that point to get killed than it was to get caught and extradited.
So this law came about for surrendering and another guy and Fabio were
the first to submit themselves to justice. There were some conditions as
part of the deal. The first was that you would not get back into the business again and then the government would not extradite you. At this point,
however, the government is not honouring the deal, because they have my
brother in jail right now to be extradited. It's very unfair because he is not
guilty and has not been given the chance to prove that...we are hoping to
prove his innocence but [if he is sent to the US] he has no chance.

This last point I had to agree with: if Fabio was sent to America, he
would have no chance at all. Fabio is generally regarded in the US as the
man behind the contract on DEA informant, Barry Seal, and the US wants
him badly. If he goes to America, he won't be needing a return ticket.
We chatted briefly about the recently signed Plan Colombia—a deal by

which the USA was donating $1.3 billion in aid and military assistance to Colombia to fight the drugs problem. Jorge was not impressed: 'It will achieve nothing. The money will end up in the bank accounts of the politicians. It will increase corruption but won't decrease the trade at all.' And could it lead to an increase in violence? 'Absolutely.'

So what would it take to stop the trade?

Legalisation. It's the only way. Education and legalisation. There are historical examples of what should be done. If we talk about how good cocaine is, it's bad. I don't use it. But it's like many other things that are bad—alcohol and tobacco and so on... History has shown us how to stop this... What I want to say is this: controlling and legalising the trade will make the violence stop.

And do you really think this will happen? 'Absolutely. But it will take time.' At this point Jorge's older brother, Juan David, piped in: 'There's no way it [anti-drug legislation] can achieve anything in stopping the trade. As long as there is a demand for it there will always be someone ready to supply it. The only thing they can achieve is to maintain the high price.'

By this stage, Jorge was clearly bored. I had planned to interview Juan David too but when I started asking questions Luis told me that there wasn't much point: 'It's the same. The answers will be the same.' It was time to go. But, before that, would it be possible to take a couple of pictures? Sure, said Jorge, beaming again. Where do you want me? I suggested that he sat in a chair under the arch in the stables but he was suddenly adamant. 'No. Not here,' he said. I wondered why. 'The light is behind me. It won't come out,' he said. He sat against a wall and I took a couple of shots, then relocated Jorge and Juan David in front of a stable door for a shot of them together. I got three before they stopped me. 'That's enough,' said Jorge. 'I think those pictures are valuable enough, don't you?' Then it was over.

We shook hands, I climbed into Luis's land cruiser and we headed back down the hill.

Looking back on my morning with the Ochoa family, I still can't work out what to make of them. In the US these guys are public enemies just a couple of notches down from Nazi babykillers—but they seemed pretty normal to me. It did strike me, however, that the whole thing could be a fraud—a simple piece of media manipulation set up to fool the dumb gringo writer into producing something vaguely complimentary about a despicable family. If it was, it wasn't really necessary: I had no intention of writing anything nasty about them. I just wanted to get my facts straight. The way I see it, if people want to shove cocaine up their noses, they will probably find a way to do it and there will always be someone willing to supply them. The Ochoas sold cocaine. *Lots* of cocaine. Shit happens.

The violence, however, is another matter completely. While the Ochoas can be forgiven, in my books, for trafficking cocaine, if they were part of the extraordinary violence that hit Colombia in the 1980s, then they deserve all they get. But *were* they violent, or were they really the peaceful family men that their friends painted them out to be? I couldn't decide.

Then something happened that tilted me in favour of the 'peaceful' option. In order to understand it, however, it is necessary to drop back a decade in time, to the point where Pablo Escobar had 'submitted himself to justice'.

For Escobar, prison life was hardly arduous. As part of his surrender terms he had insisted that he be interned in his own personal prison—built on land he had himself sold to the government for the very purpose. Situated above his home town, Envigado, La Catedral—the cathedral—wasn't your average Colombian penitentiary. Inside the electrified perimeter fence (which he controlled) was a dirt bike track, a disco, a health club, a marijuana plantation, an underground bomb shelter and a couple of smaller chalets where women could be personally entertained. All of the inmates (his boys turned themselves in with him) had their own personal cells complete with video, TV and stereo. Escobar installed telephone and fax lines for his own personal use and continued his business as if nothing had happened. When he got bored, he left. On the anniversary of his 'capture' he took the night off and headed out to an Envigado night club to drink the night away, returning to prison at 4 a.m. When he wanted to attend a soccer match he was escorted to the stadium by a police entourage.

It couldn't last. Throughout the period running up to his imprisonment Escobar had funded his 'war' by taxing fellow traffickers, who paid him a percentage of their profits for the right to continue trading. He continued to extract these taxes from prison: the way he saw it, he had personally scuppered the extradition laws, making it safe for them to continue the business—and they owed him. Not all of them saw it that way.

When two former colleagues, Fernando Galleano and Kiki Moncada, showed up to argue against a tax increase (he had suggested that they pay him $1 million per month), Escobar had them tortured to death. This was about as much as the government could take and it was decided to move him to a proper prison.

Unfortunately, he got wind of the plan.

On 22 July 1992 Escobar walked out of La Catedral and went into hiding in Medellín. In response, the government launched the biggest manhunt in Colombian history, offering a $1 million reward for information on him. The DEA added another $2.5 million and the Moncada and Galleano families upped this by another million and a half. Suddenly everyone was looking for Escobar. To raise more money he kidnapped more and more people and raised his war taxes again, executing colleagues who refused to pay up. This had unexpected side effects.

As Bob Nieves, former DEA chief of International Operations, told me in Washington:

He calls in the Galleano brothers and he tortures them to death because these guys are witholding their war tax or something like that. Now the rest of the people in the organisation who are the earners—what message do they get from that? 'This guy has gone mad! He's killing his biggest earners! When is he going to kill me?' So there's a defection that takes place at this point and guys begin knocking on the Rodriguez brothers' door and Herrera's door [the Rodriguez Orejuela brothers and Pacho Herrera were the leading lights of the Cali cartel] and they say, 'Hey, we come in peace—this guy is a fucking maniac! It's only a matter of time before he kills me. Can you protect us?' And they say, 'Yeah—go back to Medellín, you're under our protection now. Keep tabs on this guy, let us know what's going on and we'll take care of the problem for you.'

The Cali cartel established a group called Los PEPES (People Persecuted by Pablo Escobar) dedicated to hunting him down. PEPES put up a $5 million reward for Escobar and began a ruthless programme dedicated to killing anyone who worked for him. As his lawyers, *sicarios*, colleagues and family members were either exterminated or defected, Escobar found himself isolated.

To the Colombian police, Los PEPES was a godsend: they were plugged into Escobar's movements and they were also willing to employ all sorts of nasty tactics that the police couldn't use (kidnappings, killings) to drive him out into the open. However, by accepting the help of this trafficker-led organisation they were creating problems for themselves further down the line. Joe Toft, special agent in charge of the DEA office in Colombia at the time, certainly heard warning bells:

> Initially I was not aware that Los PEPES were Cali. In fact, we applauded Los PEPES—we thought it was a great sign. But then little by little we put the pieces together and it became evident that Cali were pulling the strings. So at that point it became a very sensitive issue for us because we were working very closely with the Colombian Police trying to get Escobar and right in the middle they were working with Los PEPES. And we also came into contact with the PEPES from time to time because they were providing some very good information to the police. So it became a very sensitive issue for us...I certainly didn't want anyone to say that the DEA was cutting a deal with the Cali Cartel. I tell you, I had a lot of sleepless nights over that thing.

Another man who had a lot of sleepless nights over the hunt for Escobar was Hugo Martinez, who was running the police operation to find him. Martinez was in charge of a group of Colombian Special Forces troops known as Elite Force. When we met for a drink in Bogotá, Martinez recalled Escobar's reaction when he discovered the existence of this group:

> I got the first threat by radio because he knew I was listening to him. He just said that he was going to finish me and my family off. He said he would annihilate the Elite Force in a week. That first week he killed seventeen policemen with a bomb in a truck. The next week another carbomb killed fourteen more. He wanted the Elite Force out of Medellín. The government spoke with the heads of police in Bogota to see if we should perhaps get out, try something else. But to pull out the Elite corps—which was so visible— none of my officers, or I, wanted it. We wanted to continue. We were hurt and we wanted the chance to continue with our job until it was over.

Such was the pressure to get the man, and the notoriety that he had earned, that foreign governments began supplying the Elite Force with military kit that they thought might help. The British sent a team of SAS instructors; the French donated sophisticated triangulation equipment for tracking radio emissions; Germany chipped in with more mobile phone tracking kit; Italy sent counter-terrorist experts. Everyone wanted to get Pablo.

As Escobar ran, his former colleagues fed information on his where-abouts to the police and everyone around him was steadily eliminated by Los PEPES: it could only be a matter of time. However, first they had to find him. To disguise his location he made calls from the backs of moving cars—so that even if the Elite Force did manage to trace them, he would be gone by the time they got there. This kept them guessing for a while.

By the start of December, however, they were tracking Escobar effectively and had him located within an area of 200 square metres in Medellín. Unfortunately, that 200 square metres was in the heart of a heavily populated district and thus was impossible to surround. Martinez's superiors ordered him to move but he decided to wait for another call to see if he could get any closer. He sent his three signals-monitoring vans into the district where Escobar was known to be and told them to wait. As luck would have it, in charge of one of the mobile units was Martinez's own son, also called Hugo.

On the morning of 2 December, Escobar gave an interview to *Semana* magazine on the telephone via his own son, Juan Pablo, who relayed questions to him while he answered them in short phonecalls, changing phones or locations each time so that the calls could not be traced. Since the mobile units had been up all night, they were tired and were sleeping in their vans. Martinez senior recalled:

> That day the mobile units were resting because they had had no sleep at all. But I was awake and a call was made at 10 a.m. It was very short—after answering just two questions he hung up to change location. I called Hugo and I told him, 'Listen. Trace this call because he is about to make another one any second now.' He was on the street immediately, waiting for the next call. About an hour to an hour and a half later, the second call came. Hugo traced it. Escobar gave us the opportunity by speaking for more than five minutes. He spoke for six.

Escobar made another fatal mistake. Instead of talking from the back of a moving vehicle, he got bored and went inside to sit down. Not only was he on the phone for too long but he was now stationary. Here was the chance. 'Hugo circled around the building a few times to make sure this was really the right place,' Martinez recalled, 'then he called me and he just said, "I can see him at the window." So we were all sure. And he said, "send the Penetration Group".'

Escobar immediately realised that things were not right. 'Something is going on,' he told his son, 'I'm hanging up now.' But it was too late. Martinez recounted what happened next:

I was in my office and the head of the Penetration Group came on the radio, shouting 'Viva Colombia!' The feeling was just one of relief—that we hadn't failed again. This Passion I had been through was over—it was like having a piano lifted off me. I got a video camera, called the Police Director and gave him the news. He asked us to take his [Escobar's] fingerprints prints before giving it out . . . but we got in the car and turned on the radio and it was already on the news—all anyone was saying was that Escobar was dead . . . we listened to it the whole way. Steep [a DEA agent], the driver and my bodyguard were screaming and shouting, 'Viva!' and their joy was a bit infectious. I began to feel what I hadn't felt initially. Emotion. I wanted to get to the house to embrace my son.

Back in Bogotá, DEA boss Joe Toft was at his desk:

It was about three in the afternoon. General Vargas, who was the number two man in the police and was in charge of the hunt, called me up. 'Joey,' he said, 'we just got Pablo'. He was so excited. I hung up and I ran out into the hallway at the embassy where my office was and just yelled 'Pablo is dead!' I ran straight up to the ambassador's office and told him, 'We just got Pablo'.

The news spread across the country like wildfire and by the time Martinez arrived at the location, Escobar's mother was already there. Rushing into the garden she saw a crowd of people standing around a body and pushed through to get a closer look. It was not Pablo but his bodyguard, Alvaro de Jesus—known as 'Lemon'. She began to laugh, shouting, 'You're wrong! That's not my son!'

What she didn't know was that the shootout had taken place on the roof of the building and that de Jesus was on the ground because he had jumped at the last minute. Pablo had not made it as far as the edge.

When the news broke in Bogotá, cars began hooting their horns in celebration. The country's newspapers read THE KING IS DEAD! However, while the middle and upper classes celebrated, the lower classes were dumbstruck. To them, Pablo was a hero—a man who paid for their welfare and gave them all the things that the government did not. He was a martyr. When he was buried, 5,000 Medellín residents showed up and rushed the mortuary to try to touch his coffin. In the panic that followed, Pablo's wife was evacuated under escort for her own safety. The Colombian police had to place an armed guard on his grave for over a year.

Luis was not one of those who attended the funeral. On the drive home from La Loma, in his mysteriously heavy-doored car, he revealed that he had hated him. Escobar had killed Luis's best friend—Jorge's brother-in-law—Alonso Cardenas, and then tried to kidnap Luis's heavily pregnant wife. This had tipped the balance as far as he was concerned. He lost no time in taking his knowledge of Escobar straight to the people who wanted it most: the police. He told me that he had fed the DEA with a constant stream of information concerning Escobar's whereabouts throughout the hunt for him, right up till his death in 1993. And the source of the information?

> The Ochoas gave it to me. They fed me with information and I passed it on. They knew all the time that I was doing it, although I never specifically told them what I was up to. They knew that anything they said to me would go further—and they were prompt to hand over more information.

This was interesting. The Ochoas' assertion that they were not behind the violence committed in the name of the Extraditables held a lot more water when placed beside the fact that they themselves had turned informants against Escobar. But was it true?

Luis gave me the name of the DEA contact to whom he had fed his information and invited me to call him to verify the story. When I did, however, the agent concerned was reluctant to talk: 'I can't comment on that,' he said. This was understandable—revealing informants' identities jeopardises their safety. I argued that, since the informant concerned had volunteered this information to me, the story was different, but the agent wasn't having any of it: 'I still can't comment,' he said. So is Luis's story true?

Without any way of confirming it, it comes down to a matter of opinion. Call me naïve but I believe that it is. Perhaps I believe that because I want to, but it's my opinion that the Ochoas—Escobar's former partners-in-crime shopped him.[11]

---

[11] There *is* evidence that Luis was a member of PEPEs.

Good for them.

As we drove back to the hotel I asked about turning against Pablo: it must have been pretty risky, feeding information to the police. Weren't you scared? How did you protect yourself? Luis smiled. 'The first thing I did was to get myself this car.' All of a sudden the penny dropped and I realised why the doors were so heavy. I tapped the glass in the passenger window and noted for the first time how quiet it was inside the thing. The glass was an inch thick. I got out of Luis's bombproof car and wandered back into the hotel. But I wasn't quite finished in Medellín.

Before leaving La Loma, Jorge and Juan David had suggested that if I wanted to understand the violence that had swept through the city in the 1980s, I should take a visit to the communas to the north of town. Here, they told me, a combination of extreme poverty coupled with the injection of millions of dollars of cocaine cash had led to a new class of hired hands willing to do anything for money. It was this that had fuelled the violence, they said. Would I be interested to see them? Of course I would. That afternoon a taxi appeared at my hotel, manned by three of the Ochoas' employees who were to be my guides/guards. I hopped into the taxi and we headed north.

I've got to be honest: the communas don't *feel* that dangerous. They aren't slums. There is electricity, cafés, bars. OK, so everything is a bit run-down but it's not that bad. They could be state-owned housing projects somewhere around the Mediterranean—Turkey, perhaps. That's what I thought. Initially, anyway.

As we drove, the Ochoas' boys gave me a rundown of the streets we were driving through and it rapidly became obvious that this place was the real thing. Gunfire was common most nights. Suddenly I began to be a bit more worried but then I thought again. I was with the Ochoas' boys. This had to count for something. It did: the people we met were invariably wary of this gringo with the notepad—until one of the guides commented that I was a 'friend of Juan David' and then everyone relaxed. Suddenly we began to meet people who actually wanted to talk. In Medellín, the name 'Ochoa' opens doors.

Mike, in his late 30s, was more than happy to fill me in concerning his past. He had been recruited into the security business via his gang, Las Machacas, an organisation dedicated to 'stealing cars, motorbikes, killing people. Whatever. Business. You know—getting rid of people', and ended up as a bodyguard for the leader of one of Escobar's *sicario* gangs. The job had paid him $500 per month—a fortune for a young man who had never completed school. He explained how the *sicarios* worked: 'Let's say somebody stole something from Pablo. Pablo would call my boss and tell him what had happened. The boss would call us up. Send two or three of the boys round to take care of it.'

On work days Mike used to ride in one of two cars with a total of eleven other bodyguards. They followed their boss everywhere until Los PEPES came on the scene, when he told them that he needed to keep a lower profile and sent them home. One day a couple of guys walked up to him at a cattle fair and filled him full of lead.

Shortly after his boss's assassination Mike was himself shot down in the street. One of the bullets passed through his lower spine and he has never walked since. Today Mike makes a living selling Rivotril tablets (depressants—clonazepam) from the armchair in his front room. He gets the pills at 500 pesos and sells them at 1,000. In this way he supports a family of three, on $140 per month. Marijuana, he told me, was going on the street outside for 500 pesos per joint (about US 25c) and cocaine ('perico') is about 3,500 pesos per gram—under two dollars. Mike was not impressed by any of it.

This wouldn't have happened in his [Escobar's] time. Then there was work. Nobody took drugs. There was money. There was control; there were no thieves. People respected each other. *Sicarios* were paid. Today they kill each other for nothing. I really respected him. He was always good with us. He didn't let us use drugs—he wanted us to be healthy. We all loved him very much. Since he died, there's no work for anybody. He was an idol.

Perhaps. But did he think Escobar had been a good man?

In many ways, yes. He made some mistakes with all those bombs and stuff and a lot of innocent people were killed. But all the violence was not Escobar. He has been dead for years now and the violence has increased.

As an indication of just how low things had sunk, Mike told me that an assassination could be organised here for less than $500. Perhaps $250 would do. 'A friend might do it for free,' he said. And how would someone go about arranging a hit? I asked. One of my guides told me that hits were called in at 'La Oficina'—the office. And where was The Office? 'That's where we're going next,' said my driver.

The Office turned out to be a ramshackle one-room construction made of planks nailed together on the roof of a decrepit building just off Calle 98. There was a doorway but no door and the windows were covered with black cloth instead of glass. Inside, a group of youths aged between seventeen and thirty lounged around on stolen sofas smoking dope. As word of our arrival spread—and when we started buying beers—more and more gang members showed up to check us out.

What was this place? I asked. 'It's our place. Every gang has a parche—an area—where we can be because if we stand on the street corner, anyone can kill us. Even the police can kill us.' Do people try to kill you often? 'Sometimes. It can happen at night or during the day. Anytime. There are worse areas than this, though. That's why we like it here. It's safe.' And what, exactly, does your gang do? 'We're all unemployed. We leave our houses, we go out. If we see someone with a nice ring or something, we steal it.'

It turned out that a former resident of this area was a *sicario* named Dandeny Munoz Mosquera, aka: 'Tyson'. Tyson was shot dead in 1992 but remains famous for his violent exploits. Another local *sicario* was La Kika—responsible for bombing the Avianca airliner in 1989. These two guys had earned a lot of respect—and seemed to be something to aspire to. They were important. They had got there through extreme violence and doing what their employers told them. The message was the same for the guys who were sitting around me: do what you're told and screw the consequences and one day you might just end up being someone important, too.

Throughout the conversation they mentioned Escobar. Except here they didn't use his name. They called him The Man.

During The Man's time there was so much work that no one used to use drugs. Now there is no work and everyone uses drugs. There's nothing else to do. They shouldn't have killed him. When he died, all the money in Medellín disappeared. Now there is no more money, not in Medellín or in Colombia. And there is no work for us. There will never be anyone else like him.

Most of these guys were too young actually to have worked for Escobar, but I was intrigued by their attitude towards him. If he was around now, I asked, would you work for him? 'Yes.' And if that work involved killing people? 'That doesn't change the story. OK, he had a reputation for killing people. But just as many people are killed here today as they ever were. Everyone thought he was the problem and if we kill him the problem will go away. It hasn't. He was killed by the politicians.'

If I offered them $1,000 to kill someone, would they do it? At this there was a great debate: who was it? Where was he? Was he famous? Some agreed that they might do it for $1,000. All agreed to do it for $10,000. But what about guns? Where would they come from? There was a ripple of laughter: anywhere! One of the younger guys—who was probably just pushing eighteen years old—offered to go and get me a hand grenade for $20. You can get hand grenades here? I asked. Everyone laughed again, enjoying my naivity. Of course you could get hand grenades here. You could get anything here—if you had the money.

'Sometimes the police sell us the guns. They confiscate them from one person and then sell them to someone else. Because the police are paid so little, they take away your drugs and give them to someone else. They're as fucked up as we are.' At this point, in an act of bravado, the speaker pulled a box of pistol slugs out of his pocket: 'These are the pills that cure everything!'

One of the gang disappeared for a couple of minutes and returned with a folded piece of paper. He handed it to me. It contained about a gram and a half of cocaine. 'How much is this worth?' I asked. Under $2. Then a gun emerged and everyone encouraged me to check out how serious they were by verifying that it was real. This wasn't necessary: it was obviously real. One of the Ochoa's boys decided to demonstrate that these weren't really bad guys. 'How many of you rather be at university?' he asked. All hands shot up.

As a final detour we stopped off at Cancha la Tinajota—a football pitch a few blocks away that had been built by Escobar in the late 1980s. By now it was getting dark and nobody was playing football. Instead, groups of kids were hanging out behind the chain link fence beneath a small coppice of trees. Around the back we bumped into perhaps Medellín's smallest crime syndicate. Its leader, a 24-year-old male, was selling coke and marijuana through a network of three friends, all younger than him. Pooling all their income, they made 150,000 pesos per day—about $70. What did these guys think about Escobar? 'There has never been anyone else like him,' said one. 'He helped the poor, he helped the people. That's why when he died it was so painful for us' (and this from a youth who must have been nine years old when Escobar was killed). Would you have worked for him? 'Absolutely.' Even if it meant killing people? 'If he showed us the money in advance, yes.' If I was interested in buying some coke, could you arrange it? 'Of course.' What about if I wanted 50 kilos this evening? At this point they all became animated and began jostling: 'I can get it for you right now, Mister—and it'll be really good quality!'

Perhaps the Ochoas were right. If you want to see the cause of the violence that pervades the Colombian cocaine scene, you have to see the poverty. Because if you inject a couple of million dollars into these streets, surface a few football pitches and pay for some medical assistance, you can buy anything here—including the people. That's what Escobar did. He did it so effectively that they still worship him today. And that's what caused all the trouble. Perhaps it's worrying that the poverty is still as bad as it was in the 1980s but perhaps it's no great shock. Would it be a surprise if, at some point in the next few years, it all started again? Has it even stopped now? Who can tell?

Pablo Escobar's grave is situated in the Jardines Monte Sacro. I got there the next afternoon just as it was beginning to rain—somehow this seemed vaguely fitting but I couldn't really work out why. We managed to procure some umbrellas from somewhere and navigated our way gingerly through the sodden graveyard to the final resting place of the most famous man Medellín ever produced. It's a large grave, covered with a wire grille through which brilliant blue lilies grow. I didn't know this before I arrived, but Escobar is in fact buried in a double grave, beside Alvaro de Jesus—'Lemon'—a bodyguard so faithful that he had preceded his boss into the next world. Perhaps he is protecting him there.

At the head of the grave is a photograph of Escobar and his dates: 1949–1993. Beneath those, in marble, is an inscription:

MIENTAS EL CIELO EXISTA, EXISTIRAN TUS MONUMENTOS, Y TU NOMBRE SOBRE VIVIRÁ COMO EL FIRMAMENTO	While the sky exists, your monuments will also exist—and your name will survive as long as the heavens

The grave is beautifully situated overlooking the small town of Sabaneta. This is approriate because Sabaneta is home to the shrine of Santa Maria Auxilia Lidora—the favourite pilgrimage site for Escobar's *sicarios*. Before killings they would visit the shrine and pay the dour-looking woman behind the wooden gate a couple of pesos to light a candle for them—a candle that would perhaps still be burning as they climbed on to their motorcycles to hunt down whichever unlucky bastard they had been hired to take out that day. One former *sicario* told me later that, although he had never visited Santa Maria, his friends all swore by her: they thought that she improved their aim.

Testimony to the fact that *someone's* aim was pretty good, a couple of miles north of Escobar's grave is another cemetery called San Pedro. Here, without metal grilles or blue lilies, lie the bodies of the teenagers who killed for and were killed by Pablo—children plucked off the street, given a handful of dollars and a pile of guns they didn't need; children who never finished school, worshipped their mothers and went out to work with pictures of the Virgin Mary tucked into their trousers because they were so scared by what they were doing that they were willing to believe in anything that might help them out; children whose bodies were left at the gates of the cemetery anonymously because no one could afford to pay for their funerals. In the late 1980s so many teenage corpses accumulated at San Pedro that, even for those who could be identified, there was no room to log their names and dates of birth any more. The graves were numbered.

To initiate death and suffering on such a scale must surely be some sort of achievement. As I walked away from the cemetery the rain stopped and I thought that, while his grave may be a good place to remember him, perhaps San Pedro is Pablo Escobar's true monument. Perhaps it, too, will survive as long as the heavens.

Ultimately, while much celebrated, the death of Pablo Escobar did not reduce the flow of cocaine coming out of Colombia at all. Those closest to the operation realised this immediately—looking back on the hunt for Escobar, Hugo Martinez said:

> I have often asked myself, 'Was that effort worthwhile?' and the answer is no. I have always said that the orders we got to finish off the Medellín cartel were not going to stop drug trafficking in Medellín or anywhere. We knew that. Everyone knew that. The president knew it, the ministers knew it. We weren't going after drug trafficking. We were going after a guy who went crazy, killing people. We never thought that by ending the Medellín cartel—or the Cali cartel for that matter—we would stop drug trafficking. On the contrary, it went up.

It has even been suggested this increase in drug trafficking was specifically the result of the hunt for Escobar. Joe Toft recalls attending a Colombian police party to celebrate his death but feeling apprehensive:

> It was kind of an awkward situation because I was so glad—I was so focussed on getting Pablo that it was a tremendous feeling. But at the same time I knew we had won one battle but lost a huge war because of what had happened between Cali and the government. So I'm sitting there celebrating with these cops and I had a knot in my stomach knowing that some of the guys celebrating there had gotten very close to the Cali cartel and/or taken money from them during the hunt for Pablo. It was awful, just really awful.

Although officials deny making any deals with Los PEPES, the fact is that because of their complicity with senior members of the Cali cartel in the hunt for Escobar the police, and various higher levels of government, were tainted. In exchange for its information on Escobar, the cartel had also been more or less ignored throughout the period, giving it the opportunity to consolidate its position. By the time Escobar was dead the Cali cartel was in control of cocaine operations in Colombia and was all but unstoppable. In 1994 Gilberto Rodriguez Orejuela, who held what he called the *poder convocatorio* (the right to speak for Cali), wrote to President Gaviria that he thought he deserved special treatment because of all his help with catching Escobar.

Cali had learned from its predecessors' mistakes. Where Escobar and Lehder had run for office, the cartel stayed politically quiet; where Gacha and the Ochoas had become public figures, they remained in the shadows. An apocryphal story refers to one of the Rodriguez brothers chastising a colleague who had recently assassinated a government official: 'In Cali we don't kill people,' he said, 'we buy them.' Certainly they made a lot of noise about how they were not nearly as violent as Medellín, and with the fall of Escobar in 1993 Cali earned themselves the DEA joke nickname 'The kinder and gentler cartel'. But appearances can be deceptive. As Toft says:

> I think [Cali] were as violent as Medellín but they always covered up their murders. With Escobar, he would say to someone, 'I'll kill you,' then he'd kill you and leave his calling card there so the whole world would know that it was Escobar that had done it. Cali didn't operate like that...Escobar would go out there and put a bomb on the street and kill fifty people

that were walking about including nuns and children and everybody else. This was to intimidate the government. Cali never did that. Cali intimidated the government in a very personal way through bribery.

They did have their violent moments, however. Closely mirroring the kidnapping of Marta Nieves Ochoa, Cristina Santa Cruz (daughter of Jose Santa Cruz Londoño) was kidnapped by FARC in 1992. The ransom was $10 million. Cali responded by kidnapping twenty high-ranking leftist politicians and trades union leaders. Santa Cruz was released unharmed.

Not only was Cali more clandestine than Medellín, but a lot smarter, too. In the United States, under Cali head Pacho Herrera, the business of distribution was honed to perfection. DEA agents talk about modern distribution networks in terms of terrorist 'cells', small (ten to twenty people) self-sufficient groups insulated from the risk of informants by the fact that no one—apart from the boss—knows more than a couple of other people in the same cell. And the boss never, ever gets within a mile of the product or the money—making it almost impossible to break the organisation. As Bob Nieves explained to me in Washington, a typical bust might involve taking down a driver moving cocaine from point A to point B. The interrogation goes as follows:

'Who are you?' 'Mike.' 'Whose cocaine is this?' 'I don't have a clue. I take my orders from Jairo.' 'And who is Jairo?' 'I don't know. He calls me on a cell phone.' 'Well, how does he pay you?' 'He leaves the money in the car when I make pick ups.'...More often than not when we began to interview people like this we realised that they didn't freaking know anybody else. They had their singular job and that was it. They might meet one other person but he always had an alias and they never knew who he was except that he was Jairo, or Gerardo or Vicente or 'everybody calls him Boo-Boo'. Very compartmented. And they were *expert* at it.

In Los Angeles former chief of international cocaine operations Charles Gutensohn agreed that they were a lot smarter:

Cali invested in technology that made [tracking them] very difficult. They would buy cellphones by the hundred, use a phone for nine or ten days then throw it away. Because tracking the numbers—if you were going to do a wiretap you would have to show a pattern to get the court order—and there was never enough time to get the pattern. They would take a portable fax machine, hook it up [to a payphone] and call Colombia. Colombia would return the call from a different phone, hook up their fax machine and send the information. Unless you knew which phone they were going to use, you never knew what they were sending. And wiretapping a fax is difficult. You have to have special equipment. Yeah, they were very good.

In addition, arrested traffickers proved impossible to interrogate because Cali had made sure that they all had families remaining in Colombia—who were under threat of death if anyone chose to spill the beans. Working out what guys operating like this were up to was a nightmare. But periodic coups revealed that whatever they were up to, they were extremely good at it. Nieves said:

> In 1990–1 there was a big case made when the New York office seized two of Pacho Herrera's cells, arrested about twenty people and seized the computers, hard drives and floppy discs and were able to retrieve all of his transactional activity for 90 and 91. And it showed how efficient he was at record keeping, how he'd moved throughout the period and how he collected four hundred and something million dollars over the course of two years. And those were two cells—two cells only—and we knew that Herrera was busy in Miami, Los Angeles and Houston. So this is mathematics, right? Pacho Herrera alone doing a two billion dollar business probably. And there was every reason to believe that the Rodriguez brothers were doing the same level of business.

Cali's intelligence system in Colombia was even more impressive. In Cali itself, nothing could be done without coming to the attention of the Rodriguez brothers: in a smart move, they had bought up all the taxicabs in the city and instructed them to report on the locations of all foreigners and policemen. They also maintained computer links with airline checking offices, hotel reservation systems and credit card networks in the city, as well as paying bribes to a number of senior retired police officers, virtually all the airport police and nearly a third of the city's counsellors. When the Colombian National Police swooped on Jose Santa Cruz Londoño they took his computers in for analysis and discovered that he was running a telephone tracking system that enabled him to trace and monitor long-distance calls. The computer ran a relational analysis programme that warned him when his contacts rang certain 'hot' numbers. The DEA was appalled to discover that Santa Cruz was bugging the US embassy's confidential drug informant lines and had his computer rigged to alarm if anyone he knew rang any of their numbers. Sophistication such as this led to a scale of cocaine trafficking previously unknown and by 1994 former US ambassador Morris Busby would announce that Cali was the world's largest multinational business, with profits greater than those of Pepsi Cola.

More worrying than its trafficking successes was the extent the organisation bought its way into Colombian politics. By 1995 it was estimated that they had bought up over 35 per cent of the Colombian Congress. When allegations regarding their wholesale purchases of Colombian politicians emerged, it soon became obvious that the corruption went right to the top.

In 1995, leaked cassettes of taped phonecalls between President Ernesto Samper's campaign manager, Santiago Medina, and Gilberto Rodriguez Orejuela revealed that the cartel had donated $3.7 million to Samper's election campaign (the election was extremely close and it is likely that this donation swung the result). But had Samper himself known about it? Medina said yes. In 1996 the intermediary for the deal, Fernando Botero (the defence minister) commented, 'The president not only knew, he was the organiser. He was the prime mover.'

Both the campaign manager and the defence minister ended up in jail for their part in the operation but Samper received a vote of confidence and it was ruled that there was not enough evidence to pursue an inquiry. In February 1996 he was finally accused of illegal enrichment and electoral fraud but again exonerated. Two months later the US, bored with these allegations, decertified Colombia as an ally in the war on drugs, effectively withdrawing over $10 million in aid payments. *Time* magazine ran a front cover of Samper under the banner NARCO-CANDIDATE? This came as no surprise to DEA agents who knew Colombia. Joe Toft commented of the affair:

> I don't know how much money they contributed but it was many, many millions. When I left Colombia I went on TV and called Colombia a narcodemocracy and said that the evidence was that Cali had contributed millions of dollars to Samper's campaign and then I got on the plane and left... Samper was going to sue me. I would welcome him suing me because then I think I would have been able to get the evidence in front... In fact, at the end, even though he denied it when the evidence was overwhelming, he said, 'Well, I didn't know about it'—which was just a bunch of crap, if you'll excuse the expression.

Despite Samper's roasting in the international press—or perhaps because of it—it has to be said that his administration was singularly effective at rounding up the heads of the Cali cartel. Although a number of peace talks had been initiated by key members of the cartel, seven of them, including Jose Santa Cruz Londoño, the Rodriguez Orejuela brothers and Pacho Herrera, were arrested in 1995. However, the fact that none of them was extradited and they all received sentences of under ten years led to allegations that they had cut deals with the government. This could be an attempt to legitimise themselves, much as the Ochoas did in the early 1990s. The difference here is that while most people seem to accept that the Ochoas are not currently trafficking, word is that the Rodriguez Orejuela brothers, who have only a couple more years to serve, are still operating from prison. Thus claims that their capture was a triumph are misguided. Joe Toft says:

> To this day the Colombian government claims that the Cali cartel has been put behind bars. I disagree. I think their plan was to do this exactly... they spent years re-organising their operations, changing their modus operandi and their personnel so that it would appear that they were getting out of it but in reality the whole thing was still clicking. And the best evidence that I have—and I get into arguments with people in Washington about this, I mean, I can't believe that some of the people in Washington are so damn naïve—the best evidence I have that the Cali cartel is still in existence is that during a very short period of time all the Cali heads were put in jail. Less than a year: they were either arrested or turned themselves in or whatever. And the amount of cocaine coming to the United States or going out of Colombia never diminished during this period. Now, if the Cali cartel leadership was put out of commission there should have been a huge drop in cocaine—at least temporarily. But it never happened. This thing was already well greased and it was ready to go and it happened.

Whether the Cali cartel is still operating from inside prisons across Colombia is a moot point. The fact is that whether they are or not, the price and availability of cocaine outside Colombia has not been affected. *Someone* is still shifting coke.

According to the DEA, following the dismantling of Cali, the cocaine business fragmented. Instead of massive production operations and huge shipments, it downsized and spread out. This, it seems, has made the traffic even harder to fight—because no one is really sure who the villains are any more. As Mark Eissler, head of intelligence in Washington, told me:

> In essence, international drug law enforcement is a victim of its own success because we did know a lot about the major cartels. We had a target or... had

entire intelligence and operational units devoted to one organisation and had
half a dozen managers and agents devoted to one target. Today we really cannot do that because it's so much more diverse. So yeah, it's a problem.

Perhaps the fight against cocaine production in Colombia is a victim
of its own success. But, looking at use figures for the drug, we might
wonder what criteria we are actually using to measure that success? If
we talk about people in jail and confiscated loads, then it is clear that
there has been a great deal of success in the war on cocaine. If, however,
we define the goal of cocaine interdiction as aiming to remove cocaine
from the streets of Europe and North America, then it's rather hard to
see how this success has manifested itself. But things have certainly
become more complicated. The more you look at the current cocaine
trade, the more you have to admit that it's largely a mystery.

There are certain things that everyone agrees on, however. One of them
is that Colombia, which used simply to import coca paste from Peru and
Bolivia and then refine it, has become the largest producer of raw coca in
the world. Experts might tell you that this is a result of increasingly effective clampdowns on production in Peru and Bolivia but that's rubbish.

In fact, it's quite the other way around: coca production began in
Colombia because it was possible, and because it turned out to be cheaper
to buy in *pasta* from home than it was to send planes to pick the stuff up.
That's why coca production is dropping in Peru and Bolivia. As with
everything else to do with cocaine, it comes down to money. Colombia is
estimated to be home to some 122,500 hectares of coca, with an estimated
yield of 520 tons of cocaine. This is an increase of 140 per cent since 1995.

Keen to get a glimpse of some of this coca and cocaine, I headed south
towards the big coca areas and the places where, in Colombia, tourists
most definitely do not go.

In a dusty market town in southern Colombia, which I shall not name, I
hired a motor canoe to take me to the roots of the cocaine trade. After a
certain amount of haggling a deal was struck, the boatman cast off, started
his outboard engine and we began our journey up a silted-up tropical river.
A couple of miles upstream the canoe pulled over onto the right bank and
we trekked a short distance into the hills to meet my contact, a 25-year-old
cocalero called Felix. Felix's house was an open-plan affair consisting of a
concrete floor and a corrugated iron roof. He had chosen a seriously

remote spot to live: there was no electricity, no running water and no radio. In the centre of the building was the only enclosed space, a bedroom which Felix shared with his wife and two daughters, protected from the animals of the forest by a battered door held shut by a length of frayed string looped around a bent nail. Slung from the beams of the house swung a tiny hammock covered with cheesecloth containing Felix's youngest daughter, Maria. I never really met Maria: protected from the flies that plagued the rest of us, she slept silently through my entire visit.

We sat on rough wooden chairs and chatted while the house's other resident, a pet vulture named Spike, hopped around the floor making plaintive moaning noises until someone scratched his neck. Then, having recovered from our initial climb but still sweating profusely, we headed out behind the house into the hills until we came to a secluded ridge. There, out of sight of the river and concealed by dense jungle foliage, was the cottage industry that enabled Felix and his family to live in such luxury.

The paste factory consisted of a concrete floor of about ten square metres above which Felix had rigged a length of plastic sheeting to provide protection from the sun. To the right of the opening a tiny stream trickled down the hill. There were a couple of large drums full of dodgy-looking chemicals and a home-made coca press made out of a 55-gallon drum cut in half and peppered with holes. A spindle with a wooden handle protruded from the top.

Felix's *pasta*-making technique was a bit different to those practised in Bolivia or Peru but the basics were the same. First he spread his newly harvested coca leaves on the ground to dry. Then, after half a day or so, he went over them a couple of times with a strimmer to chop them into tiny pieces before sprinkling a small amount of powdered cement over them. I asked what this achieved but he wasn't sure. It was clearly important, however: he had tried it once without the cement and the result was a disaster: no *pasta*. To this day I am still not sure what the cement achieves but I didn't get much chance to ponder this because Felix was moving on apace:

I take all the broken leaves and put them into this big drum. Then I add gasoline and leave them to soak for a day. The gasoline sucks the alkaloid out of the leaves. The next morning I take out the gasoline with a siphon and transfer it into this other drum. Now it contains the alkaloid. But even when I have siphoned off all I can, there are still the leaves left and that's where the press comes in. I pour the leaves and the remaining gasoline

into the press and wind down the handle to extract any more liquid—
which I put into the drum with the other gasoline.

Now the cocaine was in the gasoline, the leaves were superfluous and
could be thrown away. But there was the question of what to do next:
50 gallons of cocaine-rich gasoline was pretty useless as it was—no one
could shove that much petrol up their nose and survive. It had to be
purified further. In order to get the cocaine out, Felix added a solution
of weak sulphuric acid—one bucket per arroba (25 kilos) of leaf.
Because the alkaloid was more soluble in acid than it was in petrol, once
the mixture was stirred, it moved into the water. And because water and
petrol don't mix, the two liquids separated nicely into layers.

Using a length of battered hosepipe Felix siphoned the cocaine-rich
acid into a bucket. Now instead of a couple of hundred pounds of leaves,
he had a couple of buckets of murky-looking smelly liquid. The next
stage was to get the cocaine out—a process that he achieved with powdered caustic soda: 'As soon as the soda hits the water, the alkaloid starts
to go solid. All I have to do now is filter it through a cloth and I have
pasta. Leave the pasta to dry in the sun for a while and push it through a
strainer and it becomes powder. And that's it.'

I thought this was all pretty neat. I had never seen a coca press like
Felix's. When I got back to the UK, however, I did a bit more reading and
found the following report, written in 1905, of the way cocaine paste
was prepared then. The process hasn't changed a bit:

> The leaves are mashed with a concentrated solution of sodium carbonate.
> The mixture is evaporated in the sun, and the powder is exhausted with
> benzin or petroleum ether, and is shaken with a solution of hydrochloric
> acid. Precipitation with sodium carbonate then liberates the crude
> cocaine, which is purified in Europe or the United States.
>
> *American Druggist*, April 1905, *cit. Cocaine*, Spillane

Instead of shipping boatloads of plantains or tangerines down river to
the local market, all Felix had to do now was take a river taxi with his kilo
of *pasta* in a backpack. Once in town it wasn't hard to sell: paste merchants came by every week to buy, regular as clockwork, announcing each
week the location of the next buy. The advantages of such a transaction
were obvious. A kilo of *pasta* could be carried in a shoulder bag and sold

in under an hour; 'proper' crops required serious transportation and took days to sell—if they sold at all. *Pasta* had the added advantage that it was the only thing that anyone was actually willing to buy:

> Here on this farm, I, and my father before me, used to grow plantains and yucca. We would sell them in the town of —— because there was a company there that used to buy them from us. But then the company disappeared. We kept harvesting the crops for a while but there was nowhere for us to sell them and in the end they all went off. You want to know why I grow coca, right? The answer is: because I can live on it.

Although Felix maintained just 2 hectares of coca, he managed an impressive 6 harvests per year, each one netting him 1,250 lbs of coca. Thus, each year, Felix—with the help of a couple of friends who were drafted in for the harvest—could produce 7,500 lbs of leaf, yielding 5 kilos of *pasta*. This *pasta*, containing 40 to 60 per cent cocaine, had to go through two more stages to become cocaine hydrochloride. The first involved dissolving it in solvents and resolidifying it out again until it was '*pasta lavada*' (washed *pasta*—approximately 90 per cent cocaine). It then had to be re-washed in a very pure solvent and crystallised out into cocaine hydrochloride.

These two final stages were conducted in special laboratories deep in the jungle—Felix didn't know where. At the end of the process, Felix's five kilos of *pasta* would yield approximately two and a quarter kilos of pure cocaine, worth about $45,000 in Miami, or $150,000 in London. The vast majority of this money, however, never made it to Felix: at the time I visited he was earning $5,000 per year. This, he told me, was because prices were high at the moment.

I had heard about attempts to stop the supply of the chemicals used to extract cocaine. What did he think of them? He laughed. 'What chemicals? Cement? Gasoline? Caustic soda? Are you kidding? It's easy! The acid is more difficult but at the moment we are all using battery acid because you can buy it anywhere. I don't know what it is but works the same as sulphuric acid.'

Felix had been growing coca for six or seven years and claimed that he had been one of the last in this valley to start. All of his neighbours were making *pasta* the same way. In fact, when they had wanted to get into the business they had all clubbed together to pay a chemist to come and show them how to do it. The only reason his plantation was so small was that if he started buying up gasoline and acid in greater quantities people in the town would become suspicious and he ran the risk of being caught. His friends further upstream, however, had much larger plantations: because they were so inaccessible the police never made it that far and they were safe. Felix's operation, closer to the town, was not nearly as secure and he had been busted twice. The first time the police set fire to all his paste-making stuff. The second they threw him into jail and he had to hire an expensive lawyer to get him out.

If you're caught with pasta it's pretty serious but if you are just growing coca and the army shows up they just tell you to get rid of it. They don't really make you do it. But if they see a laboratory, they'll torch it. If they find paste they will either burn it in front of you or just take it away and then they end up selling it themselves.

The next time he was caught, he told me, he faced a possible sentence of twelve years in jail. Why would anyone take such a risk? Why don't you grow something else? He sighed:

Let's say I decide to grow maize. Right now, two sacks go for about 50,000 pesos in the market. So in order to make the 1,000,000 pesos I am making with coca—well, how much corn will I have to grow? About 20 sacks. If I were to plant corn here I would have to clear the ground by burning it. Then I would have to plant the seeds and fertilize them. And corn is an annual harvest. It would produce about two tons. So I would have to take those two tons of corn down to the river to get them to the market—how many boat trips would that take? Who would load it for me? The entire operation would cost about 800,000 pesos. And the two tons would make me about 1,000,000 pesos. So I would have 200,000 pesos for the entire year (about $200). But a kilo of pasta—I can put it into my bag and just get on the nearest boat. And coca, once it's planted, will last 20 or 30 years.

But what about subsidies for coca replacement? Couldn't the government help?

Those are all lies. We were lent money at fourteen per cent interest. But then the interest rate went up to thirty per cent, thirty-five per cent, and we had to pay off the loan at the new rate—not the one we had originally negotiated. We had to sell everything we had and we were still in debt; we lost everything and we still owed the bank money.

Until I met Felix I had never really considered the fate of a drug-producing farmer. I had always assumed, perhaps as I had thought about drug traffickers until I actually met some, that these were evil bastards with no morals who were out to make a quick buck. Felix put me to shame. Not only did he have very few other options open to him but he also had a profound sense of morality about what he was doing:

> We've tried. We really have. We realise the harm that this stuff does around the world but I have kids. If I go to jail for twelve years, what are they going to do? How will they survive? I'd love to get out of it. I used to raise fish. I was able to sell them because there was a company that bought fish in town—I really made some good money out of it. But then my neighbour started putting in fish ponds—and what happened? There was too much fish and no one wanted to buy it any more. Unless the government can guarantee that someone is going to buy what we grow, we can't survive.

It was hard not to see the injustice of Felix's situation. What was he supposed to do? Starve? It was also hard not to be angry at the way the justice system worked. The maximum penalty for producing *pasta* is eighteen years in jail. The Ochoa brothers served five and a half. The Rodriguez Orejuela brothers meanwhile, are currently serving ten and nine (later bumped up to twenty-one), respectively. They are expected to be released after five and thirteen.

I was fascinated to meet Felix and honoured that he had decided to tell me—at some personal risk—all about *pasta* making. But Felix was only part of the problem. Because whilst anti-drugs legislators have to deal with thousands, and possibly tens of thousands, of Felixes if they want to stem the flow of cocaine, in Colombia they also have another problem.

Guerrillas.

Whomever you speak to, wherever you go, everyone agrees that the majority of the cocaine coming out of Colombia is handled, at one stage or another, by the Revolutionary Armed Forces of Colombia—FARC. FARC, a neo-Marxist guerrilla group formed in 1962, is dedicated to overthrowing the established Colombian order and replacing it with a new society in which the poor will receive the land and the rich will get what's coming to them. In their quest for power the group has proved itself willing to employ tactics such as extortion, kidnapping, bombing innocent villagers—and taxing the narcotics trade. Especially the cocaine trade. Because of its fearsome reputation, government troops do not venture into FARC-held territory, making it the perfect place to set up cocaine laboratories. They have proved willing accomplices in the drug trade, allowing traffickers into their land and protecting their operations for a slice of the pie. The agreement proves lucrative both for traffickers and the guerrillas themselves. The story of FARC's backing of Colombia's narcotics industry is hard to excavate. No one wants to talk too much about it and nobody knows how it all started. Off the record, however, no one is in any doubt: FARC is behind it.

Ever keen to get to the root of the cocaine trade, I flew into San Vicente del Caguan—centre of operations for the FARC and known as the capital of 'Farclandia'—to meet South America's most successful guerrilla army and ask them what was going on.

I wasn't at all sure how to approach an interview with FARC. What happens if you simply accuse them of being cocaine traffickers? Do they smile and agree that they are? Take you hostage to teach you a lesson? Or do they take offence, smack you about a bit, force you to your knees behind some old battered truck and stick a bullet in the back of your head? All of these options seemed possible. And when I actually started bumping into FARC guerrillas and realised that they all looked extremely professional and carried guns and what's more, usually more than one each, I made up my mind: these were people, I figured, that it would be good not to annoy.

As luck would have it, I arrived at the right time. In 1998 the Colombian government agreed to turn over 42,000 square kilometres of the country—an area bigger than the Netherlands—to FARC to use for 'peace negotiations' on the condition that they stopped killing and kidnapping people outside that area. Inside the demilitarised zone (DMZ), FARC was safe from persecution. This had apparently made cocaine even more lucrative for them, as handing over that size of area of prime cocaine-producing country to a guerrilla group not known for its scruples in fundraising activities was a pretty good way of ensuring that they were going to crank up production: if ever there was a license to make money—or make cocaine, which is probably more profitable, actually—this DMZ was one. But would anyone admit it? And how to go about getting them to admit it?

San Vicente is a dusty, dirty town to the west of the DMZ. Everyone I met assured me that I was perfectly safe there, though I do admit to having a few doubts when a couple of policemen were murdered by FARC in the next door village on my second night there. Apart from that, however, everything seemed fine. After a couple of calls and a long wait in FARC's main office, a meeting was arranged with one of FARC's five representatives at the Negotiating Table, an eloquent former banker called Simon Trinidad. Trinidad hung out at a place called Los Pozos, site of the government negotiations—and an hour and a half of extremely bumpy taxi riding away. There, over a couple of fruit juices, he began to talk.

FARC does not reveal its numbers but Trinidad told me that there were 60 guerrilla fronts spread out over 31 departments of Colombia. The only departments without FARC fronts, he said, were San Andres and Providence Islands. After a long introduction about the formation of the terror group, we chatted in a directionless fashion for a couple of minutes before he broached the subject I had been loath to bring up. 'OK,' he said. 'I want to talk about cocaine now.' Trinidad had something to say and, bearing in mind he was covered in guns, I wasn't about to stop him.

He launched into a brief but accurate synopsis of the evolution of Colombia's narcotics trade in the 1960s before moving on to the introduction of coca in Colombia. Illicit coca came here, he said, in the 1980s. The one thing that he was sure of—and he returned to this again and again—was that the *cocaleros* were not the real villains here.

> It is one thing to grow coca and another to make cocaine. Colombia has always grown coca, right back to the time of the pre-Columbian Indians, because they chew it. In the Amazon, in the southwest of Colombia, in the north, there are tribes that use coca and it's part of their culture. But coca is not cocaine. So the question is: who makes the coca into cocaine? The answer is: a global market, concentrated in the United States, in Europe and in Asia...The *campesinos* live in poverty, abandonment, without electricity, drinking water, education, health benefits. They are not even entitled to the legal rights to their land. And they are persecuted by the Colombian government, by the US, by the state. War is declared on them.

This was true: since meeting a number of *cocaleros*, their lot struck me as manifestly unfair. As had happened in the US with the anti-crack laws of the late 1980s, the ones who were really paying the price for this trade were not the guilty, but the poor. If this trade was so unfair, however (I countered), why was FARC participating in it? Wasn't it true that the guerrilla group taxed cocaine production? Yes. 'We tax the industrialists of Colombia: bankers, industrialists, businessmen,' Trinidad said. 'And in this group comes drug traffickers. Yes—it's true. We tax them. We tax the traffickers. But we don't tax the *campesinos*.'

How do you tax the traffickers? 'The traffickers themselves never come here. We make an agreement with their intermediaries. How much [paste] are they going to buy? The intermediary brings so much money to buy paste from the campesinos, so we say, OK, how much have you brought? And a percentage of that money will be for us.'

I was surprised by Trinidad's candour. I had expected a long meandering chat in which we would skirt the issue of drugs before perhaps extracting a couple of half-arsed confessions. FARC leader Manuel 'Tiro Fijo' ('sure-shot') Marulanda had announced 'Guerrillas and the narcotics traffic have nothing to do with one another, we are very different,' in 1984 and here was Trinidad, one of the five negotiators of FARC, admitting that the organisation made its money out of cocaine.

How much money? I had heard it was in the region of $500 million per year?

> That's not my branch. It does represent a part of our financing of our struggle but it is not all of it...in the figures of the DEA, the state, the Colombian authorities and the police—there are a lot of lies. If we really had all the money they say we have, we'd be in power by now—because we would have bought up all the weapons.

You are a Marxist group. Surely you can't think that Marx would have approved of this? (Long pause):

> It's a business. It's like the buying and selling of alcoholic drinks, or tobacco. The traffic in narcotics has existed since the nineteenth century. It is a business that remains illegal because that's what guarantees its immense profits. A question: is it moral to make money from a banking institution but immoral to take money from a capitalist business like drug dealing? ... It is a principle of war, a law: the guerrilla soldier must be well equipped, well maintained and well fed.

Throughout my conversation with Trinidad he returned again and again to the fate of the coca growers. He made it clear that FARC had no intention of taxing the growers—that FARC understood that they grew coca to survive. The government, he said, was the real villain, descending into the coca plantations, destroying the crops, flinging the *campesinos* into jail and leaving their families to starve. This was not simply unjust, it was downright inhumane. Wasn't the government supposed to care for its subjects? Why had it abandoned them? It was the government's responsibility, he said, to find the farmers a legitimate market for their crops—and if they couldn't do that then they could hardly blame them for growing coca.

How, I asked, was FARC helping the *campesinos* by getting them into drugs? FARC, he said, did not get the *campesinos* into growing drugs. In fact FARC specifically told them that if they had decided to grow coca they must also grow at least some food crops in case the cocaine market collapsed. FARC did not approve of cocaine.

> We are an enemy of the world drug trade. We are involved in a struggle to convert Colombia into an agricultural, business- and mineral-based economy...and we have a proposal for that: redistribute the land that is monopolised by the landowners. For example, give out good land near the cities to the farmers. We would like to give the farmer not only the land he needs but also the financial credit that he needs and the technical support he needs, the markets he needs—to enable him to get himself out of his miserable economic state.

Whatever you might think of the nature of his plan, Trinidad was right about one thing. People grow coca because they need money. Simple as that. But since there was no question of the FARC coming to power in Colombia in the near future, it seemed that the country was stuck with the next best option, which was the recently signed Plan Colombia—a deal in which the United States agreed to donate $1.3 billion in aid to fight drugs. This $1.3 billion was going to be used, among other things, to buy 63 helicopters and give them to 3 specially created battalions of the Colombian army to 'push into the coca-growing regions of southern Colombia'.

It struck me, as it had most people I spoke to in the country, that Plan Colombia was more likely to lead to increased violence than a cessation in the cocaine traffic. Trinidad agreed:

Plan Colombia is not a peace plan. A peace plan would be this: 'let's freeze the external debt and all its interest for, let's say, twenty years. That money could go into development—industrial, minerals, agriculture—to build up an infrastructure and resolve the problem of land democratisation. Instead of helicopters and trained troops, let's send tractors, technicians and scientists. Let's invest in natural resources like oil and gas, emeralds, gold, nickel—anything!' *That's* a peace plan. This is a war plan that will not resolve the economical and social problems. It's just going to make everything worse.

Everyone suspects that the Colombian government really wants the money not to spend on anti-cocaine operations but on anti-guerrilla operations—and especially anti-FARC operations. Since 60 per cent of the money is coming in the form of military aid, this seems quite possible. But even if this is not the planned intention of the Colombian government, the question remains: when US-trained, US-equipped Colombian soldiers come knocking at FARC's door asking for permission to come into FARC territory to destroy the cocaine laboratories that are currently earning FARC its bread and butter, will FARC let them in? Because if they won't, there is going to be trouble. The US wants results on cocaine. The cocaine labs are in FARC territory. So will the plan lead to violence? I asked Trinidad: will you stop the government troops?

We'll certainly try. There is going to be a very intense war—with all the technology that they have: planes, helicopters, radars, satellites. Yes, it's going to be a difficult war. We don't want it. We've told the US congress: 'Legalise the consumption of drugs and you will lower the price and terminate this business'.

But can't you see that this is going to lead to a lot of people getting killed? Because they *will* come. And there *will* be violence. Won't there?

Yes. That's the way it's going to be. Recently Marulanda [head of FARC] said to some of our commanders, 'We are going to have the privilege of confronting imperialism'. And that is the order of the Commandante. We will have that privilege.

I really enjoyed speaking with Trinidad and, while we disgreed on a number of points (I find it hard to believe that Marx would really have approved of any organisation trafficking drugs and kidnapping in his name), we had agreed on a key point—namely, that the need for a solution to the problem of poverty in Colombia must come before the search for a solution to the problem of cocaine.

I turned off the tape recorder and thanked him for his time but I was bothered: here I was, in the middle of nowhere, surrounded by FARC guerrillas, many of them considerably younger than me, and I was struck by the fact that in a couple of months they were going to be killing—and being killed—for these views. I suggested to Trinidad that, whatever happened with FARC, and the current government, and the peace talks—and the cocaine—I really, sincerely, hoped that no one was going to end up getting killed over this. 'Yes. That's what we all hope. But then dreams are one thing. Reality is different.'

We shook hands again and I had a thought. Because they had been very polite and didn't look like they were going to kidnap or kill me—and because I had nothing left to lose at this point—I suggested that I was keen to take a trip into FARC territory to view their cocaine laboratories. What would they think about that? It was a cheeky request but I thought it had to be worth a try. It was.

'You know, I think you would really learn a lot from seeing the laboratories,' said Trinidad. We chatted about this briefly and it appeared that he was willing to arrange for me to be accompanied by a platoon of FARC troops into the rainforest to inspect the laboratories that provided the world's illicit cocaine hydrochloride. He gave me his card and told me to email him. I didn't have a card, so I gave him my publisher's (if you are writing a dangerous book, always hand out your publisher's card, as everybody knows that publishers are immune to bullets) and we agreed to arrange a trip when I came back to Colombia in a month or so.

I emailed Trinidad at the first possible opportunity to thank him for his time and to remind him of our deal to see the labs. There was no reply: FARC had gone back into the jungle. Rumours said that they were in training, preparing for Plan Colombia to begin to bite. By the time you read this book, the fighting will have begun. How many people will have died by then? Perhaps Trinidad will be one of them?

Isn't cocaine a fun drug?

19 Cocaine

In September 2000 the Colombian National Police, intercepting traffickers' phone calls, picked up a number of references to 'something big' going on in a warehouse behind a Texaco station just outside Facatativa, 50 kilometres from Bogotá. Not believing that anything could possibly be happening out there in the middle of nowhere, they called the local police and told them to check it out.

The local police paid the warehouse a visit only to find that it contained a pile of expensive mechanical tools and a huge metal *thing*. Workers in the Texaco station said that the guys from the warehouse showed up every evening, worked through till dawn and then went home for the day. Testimony to their nocturnal activities were instructions written beside the warehouse door that whoever left last was to remember, please, to turn out the lights. Baffled, they summoned the Colombian National Police, who showed up, took a look, did a double-take and then pronounced that this big metal *thing* was in fact a submarine. Not only was this a submarine but the plans were in Russian.

They visited the Texaco people again, who suddenly realised that—oh, yeah—there had been some other guys who showed up from time to time: tall, blond-haired foreign men who were chauffeured in and out every couple of weeks. It was deduced that these were the Russian engineers and that this was evidence of a new and frightening alliance between the Colombian and Russian mafias.

Today the submarine is still behind the Texaco station. No one knows anything about it, and no one knows what to do with it. I arrived with a journalist from *El Tiempo* and the local police unlocked the door so we could take a look. The sub is in three pieces, each 10 metres long, double-hulled and, according to experts who know about these things, capable of carrying 200 tons of cocaine to the US mainland in a single trip. The mysterious Russian plans had gone missing but there, scrawled on a metal box outside the shed, was a Cyrillic word: OTVERDITEL: 'hardener'. We took a few pictures, climbed around inside the sub and then got back into our car—and argued all the way home.

'It's not a submarine,' said Mr *Tiempo*. 'How could it be?' I reckoned it was—and I had been on a submarine before. Twice. 'Hmph!' he said. 'Well, then, how did it get here?' Obviously, I argued, it had been built here by the Mafia, just as we had been told. 'My arse!' he said. 'Only the *Pastuso* mafia would be stupid enough to build a submarine here.' (People from Colombia's Pasto Department are universally regarded as the dumbest in the country.) He had a point: Facatativa is over 200 miles from the nearest ocean, the railway lines die out 100 metres up the track and there's no suitable waterway for the sub to navigate—not through the middle of the Andes, anyway, which is the route it would have to go to get to the Pacific. Why would anyone build a submarine here? There were no answers. No one had been apprehended, no cocaine had been confiscated. Nothing was known at all.

One would like to think that a cocaine submarine in the middle of a continent nowhere near the sea is one of the weirder things about this drug. But it's not. The more you look into cocaine the more you realise that everything about it is weird. Cocaine makes normal people do strange things, and strange people go completely off the wall. You don't even have to take the stuff, just hang around it for a while. When Alejandro Bernal-Madrigal, a.k.a. Juvenal, was taken down in October 1999, he boasted that he was capable of moving 30 tons of cocaine through Mexico per month. Thirty tons! How crazy is that? One of his Mexican compadres, Gulf cartel main man Juan Garcia Abrego received a sentence of 40 years in the US and a fine of $350 million. Or that?

Three months earlier in Miami I met up with a US Customs Service official, Zach Mann, who had taken me up the Miami river where the threat was 'Haiti, Bahamas, Jamaica, Mexico—in that order'. Old junk freighters registered to either Honduras or Belize would come in apparently empty, sit in the dock for a couple of months, load up with junk that had no value—old mattresses and broken bicycles mostly—and then steam off back home. How were they making money out of old mattresses? They weren't. They were making money out of the cocaine that they'd buried somewhere deep in the ships before they had arrived. Cocaine that US Customs had to find somehow.

Mann had taken me to meet the CET (Contraband Enforcement

Team), the guys whose job it is to check that these ships are clean of 'deep concealments'. CET is possibly the most unpleasant job in the world: it's 95 degrees at 90 per cent humidity outside and these guys have to wear full overalls and gas masks and crawl inside the fuel and waste-water tanks of Haitian steamers. Often they are women because they are smaller and so can crawl into more confined areas. Until recently one CET team included a midget—highly valued for wriggling into those places where even the smallest woman couldn't crawl. You get the picture: it's a nasty job. As you enter CET HQ a large sign above the door reads WELCOME TO THE HOUSE OF PAIN. Inside is a map of the Miami River, marked with snowflake stickers where they have found the coke. The map is *covered*. In the nine months before I arrived they had made eighteen seizures, totalling nearly four tons of cocaine. Meanwhile, offending crews were repatriated, their ships auctioned off and sold at low prices because they weren't really seaworthy. A couple of months later the same ships would show up again, renamed, resprayed—and full of coke. Three hundred thousand containers come into the Miami River every year. The CET team comprises just 39 people.

CET had a little museum displaying some of the more ingenious methods they had come across to ship cocaine: inside cement posts, alloy wheels, crates of wineglasses, hollow roofing tiles, tyres, electrical transformers (a good one, since the boxes contain carcinogenic chemicals), one-ton lead ingots, wooden pallets, hollowed-out planks, sacks of pumice stones. Inside the roller of a steam roller. Inside pressurised oxygen cylinders. But that was nothing compared with the live carriers: one guy turned up with cocaine stashed inside cavities hacked into his thighs and buttocks; another had a wooden leg full; and—my personal favourite—a crate arrived containing three hundred live boa constrictors all full of coke, their anuses stitched up to make sure they didn't pass any of the canisters (a later case repeated this with iguanas).

There were others, of course. Mann told me of the mules who hadn't made it—poor, wretched bastards whose cocaine packages had burst in their stomachs. If they didn't die in transit and get picked up by the authorities these guys' bodies were generally found in the middle of nowhere, hacked open so that their bosses could retrieve any unburst condoms in case there was any coke left. Cocaine makes people do weird things.

But if you are looking for weird you don't have to go much further than what happened in Panama in the 1980s.

* * *

The story of what happened in Panama in the 1980s can pretty much be told by looking at what happened to its leader, Manuel Noriega. Noriega, an illegitimate bully born in 1934, had been placed in a foster home at the age of five but somehow managed to win a scholarship to military school. From the start of his career, however, there was something different about this young officer. Not only was he imbued with a preternatural sense of cunning but a huge libido: he had twice been accused of rape—the second time of a thirteen-year-old girl. However, he had been protected from formal charges by a string-pulling pal of his, General Omar Torrijos, a military character who had seized power in 1968. Torrijos, sensing promise in the young Noriega, made sure that nothing bad happened to him. In return Noriega made sure that nothing bad happened to Torrijos—at one point foiling a coup attempt. As a reward for his loyalty Torrijos had Noriega promoted Lieutenant Colonel and put him in charge of G-2 military intelligence. This was a serious mistake. Noriega moved from strength to strength, gathering influence as he went. While Torrijos controlled the politicians and presidents, Noriega soon began controlling Torrijos. When Torrijos was killed in a mysterious plane crash in 1981, Noriega effectively assumed power, taking control of the Panamanian Defence Forces and making and breaking presidents according to his whim.

Noriega had an even darker side. Sometime in the late 1960s he struck a deal with the American intelligence community. In return for their looking the other way, Noriega guaranteed that the ten thousand American troops in Panama could stay there, along with the CIA, NSC and DIA signals intelligence stations—from which the Americans monitored Latin America's radio traffic. Most importantly, he guaranteed them access to the Panama Canal.

Panama had always been a centre for international money laundering. For just $1,000 it was possible to register a fictitious company in a bank, and such were the Panamanian bank secrecy laws that all money transferred through that company was untraceable. Colombian traffickers, sick of seeing their cash confiscated in the United States, began ploughing their money through Panama, and by 1980 foreign deposits were up to nearly $20 billion. Drug money was not the only thing that was passing through Panama, however: so were guns and military hardware to the Contras (which further endeared Noriega to the US intelligence community) and to various other Latin American groups who happened to need them—such as M-19 (which endeared him to the Cubans). Before you could say 'homicidal dictator bastard', Noriega had cut deals with the Medellín cartel, allowing them to ship coke through Panama for $1,000 per kilo.

Noriega was playing a smart game. Not only was he pitching various states' intelligence agencies against one another but he was also getting deeper into drugs. According to the standard party line he allowed the Medellín cartel to build a huge cocaine laboratory in the Darién jungle—just on the Panamanian side of the border—for between $2 and $5 million. He had also, of course, allowed the cartel sanctuary in Panama City following the Lara Bonilla assassination (he was reported to have taken $4–7 million for this). In fact it was estimated that he had made between $200 million and $1 billion from his illegal activities.

Then something went wrong. In May 1984 too many people heard about the Darién jungle laboratory and it was busted. The US portrayed the bust as evidence that Noriega was playing for the right team, but the Medellín boys didn't see it this way: where was their money? Noriega, according to legend, received a present from the Medellín cartel shortly after the bust—a gift-wrapped coffin. Terrified that he was about to be assassinated, he hightailed it to Cuba, where he prevailed upon Fidel Castro to mediate. The money was eventually returned and bygones were bygones.

As more and more reports accumulated detailing Noriega's complicity in the cocaine trade so the US found it increasingly difficult to ignore them. Things got especially tricky when his main political opponent, Dr Hugo Spadafora, decided to go to the press with details of the big man's drug deals. Unfortunately for Spadafora, news of his intentions leaked and he mysteriously disappeared in September 1985. His mutilated, headless body was later found in a post sack in Costa Rica. Eventually Noriega's number two, General Roberto Díaz, went public, announcing that Noriega had fudged all the elections, killed Spadafora and Torrijos and was running both drugs and guns for the Colombians.

By this time the US had had enough. In February 1988 Noriega was indicted in a Florida court for cocaine trafficking (US Senator Jesse Helms told NBC that he was 'the biggest head of the biggest drug-trafficking operation in the western hemisphere'). Something had to be done.

In the early hours of Wednesday 20 December 1989, Operation Just

Cause, the largest overt US military action since Vietnam, went into operation. Twenty-four thousand US troops hit Panama with the sole aim of bringing this drug-dealing tyrant to justice. Unfortunately, they couldn't find him. Such was the element of surprise that they had caught Noriega with his trousers down—literally: he was in a brothel in Tocumen. He eventually showed up at a Papal Nunciative in Panama City, demanding that the Catholic Church give him sanctuary. US Special Forces spent their Christmas blasting the building with pop music 24 hours a day in an attempt to break the inhabitants. Eventually the Clash's 'I Fought the Law (and the Law Won)' did the trick and on 3 January 1990 Noriega was ejected. He was taken to the US, tried on drug charges (Carlos Lehder was the star witness), found guilty and sent to jail for a very, very long time.

Well, that's the story, anyway. As with everything in the story of cocaine, however, the truth was more complicated. In fact everyone had known that Noriega was double-dealing the US for years but nothing was done about it: Noriega might be dirty—but he was on our side. Former DEA agent, Jerry Strickler, told me that Noriega was known to be up to his neck in narcotics trafficking since the early 1970s but that nothing was ever done. In fact, when someone did try to raise an indictment on him, his files all mysteriously went missing. (The absence of these files would make it much more difficult to convict Noriega under the Bush administration because the missing files made it impossible to show his continued involvement in narcotics trafficking from the early 1970s.) In response, reports Elaine Shannon in her book *Desperados*, a BNDD agent suggested that Noriega should be subjected to 'complete and total immobilisation'—or, put another way, assassination. Again, nothing was done: Noriega was a long-time friend of the US intelligence community and they were prepared to forgive him—for a while.

Following the murder of Spadafora however, Noriega began losing his grip on power. Not only that but it began to look as if he was turning anti-US. He refused to support the Contras overtly and began hassling American citizens in Panama, and it soon started to look as if he might be playing around with US access to the Canal. When the Panamanians began taking to the streets to persuade him to leave office and things turned increasingly violent it became clear his period of usefulness to the Americans had run out. Press reports concerning his cocaine-related activities provided the perfect excuse to get rid of him.

Suddenly it was open season on Noriega. Arrested traffickers realised that they could obtain reduced sentences in the US by testifying against him. But there were vested interests at work here. Fernando Arenas, Carlos Lehder's personal pilot, told PBS in 2000 that, far from protecting the cartel in Panama following the Lara Bonilla assassination, Noriega had originally planned to turn the Ochoas, Escobar and their entourage over to US authorities the moment they landed. Escobar had realised this in midair and rerouted to Nicaragua until things were sorted out. Likewise, Juan David Ochoa had said that no money had been paid to Noriega for protection. It appears that Noriega had indeed planned to arrest the cartel when they landed—to gain himself credibility with the DEA. 'As far as I know,' said Ochoa, 'he [Noriega] had nothing to do with the drug trade.' So why was everyone saying that he did?

> There was a saying out here that if any of us have problems with the US, Noriega is the best lawyer you could have—because if you declare against Noriega, you're free.
>
> Juan David Ochoa, *Frontline*, PBS, 2000

In Medellín I had asked the Ochoas about this. Were they paying Noriega for protection? 'No. That's not true,' said Jorge. Luis stepped in to elaborate:

> It's not true, and I am a very good witness of that because...I was a part of this. It's bullshit. Noriega had nothing to do with these guys [the Ochoas]. There was a colonel by the name of Melo who said that Noriega was in the middle. And Melo—yes, he did cut money not only from [the Ochoas] but from many people.

So there was *someone* in the Panamanian hierarchy who was protecting you? 'Yes, there was. But it was not Noriega.'

Well, well. So it would seem that the real reason for the invasion of Panama was not—as we were told—Noriega's cocaine trafficking, but the simple fact that he was losing power and was no longer useful to the US. Former head of international DEA cocaine operations, Charles Gutensohn, agreed that this was the case:

> The evidence kept building on what was going on in Panama. And Noriega became very anti-American and there were a lot of concerns about what he

was going to do. Would he all of a sudden turn around and say to the Russians and the Chinese, 'Why don't you come in? I don't want to deal with these people' or whatever?...It was all politics. The indictment of Noriega—and the arrest and prosecution—was just used as a tool to reach a political end.

So did the US invade Panama to stop this guy dealing cocaine?

No. No. There were other reasons...He's in jail now but that's not the primary reason. But it certainly was convenient. It was kind of like when Capone went down, he was put away for tax evasion, not for being a mobster. You do what you have to do to get rid of him. Had we just gone in: 'what is the US doing invading Panama!?' The reason wasn't drugs.

This is not to say, of course, that Noriega didn't have anything to do with drugs or that he shouldn't be in jail. He did, and he should. Just that cocaine is not the reason he's there. Such is the stigma attached to cocaine trafficking that a whiff of complicity is enough to create a furore—which can lead to immense political repercussions.

Noriega is not the only one. As any Latin American government falls from grace the first accusation levelled against it will be that it is related to the cocaine trade. As I was researching this book all kinds of allegations emerged about all kinds of governments in South America and the Caribbean. In March 1999 there were allegations that the son of Antigua's supremo, Vere Bird, was moving cocaine. The next month it emerged that the leader of Suriname, Desi Boutrese, was involved. Boutrese, who had seized power in 1980, had had a dozen political opponents executed, faced a guerrilla rebellion and single-handedly shafted the country's economy, was suddenly a villain. Not because of his atrocious human-rights record: it was the cocaine that people cared about. Accuse a crap political leader of being a crap political leader and you won't get anywhere. Accuse them of cocaine trafficking and people will sit up and listen. Cocaine gets headlines.

When I was halfway through the research for this book a sensational story broke in the news. Ninety-nine per cent of all UK banknotes, said the report, were tainted with cocaine. It sounded amazing: had all the banknotes in circulation really been used to snort the drug? No. When you examined it the truth was not quite like that. In fact a tiny percentage of banknotes had been used for snorting cocaine but, in the process of circulation, many other banknotes had rubbed up against these notes and thus been contaminated by them. The more I thought about this the more it seemed like a good analogy for cocaine corruption. It is not necessary for a political leader to have contact with cocaine. It is only necessary for him to have had contact with someone else who has had contact with cocaine—and suddenly he is filthy. Like a virus, cocaine contaminates everything it touches—and that in turn becomes infectious. Cocaine comes through Cuba—Castro is a trafficker! It comes through Haiti—the government is made up of traffickers! Everywhere cocaine turns up—and that's *everywhere* in Latin America and the Caribbean— democracy is corroded by simple dint of contact. Colombian police commander Colonel Orlando Pena commented wistfully in 1988, 'Drug money has contaminated the entire system. There isn't anything that is clean any more.' When it comes to cocaine, nothing is quite as it seems.

The War on Drugs is itself a casualty, falling into a morass of half-truths and almost-truths so that it is no longer possible to tell what is real and what is a distorted reflection. Historian David Musto gave me a great example of this when I met him in Harvard.

I wrote a piece for the *Wall Street Journal*, 'Lessons from the first cocaine epidemic', in 1986. I was surprised because it was quoted by President Reagan shortly afterwards at a press conference...I said, and this was just before the death of Len Bias, '[Cocaine] will decline and go away. But that isn't the issue. [The issue is] will we be socially destructive in the process of reducing this substance? Are we going to scapegoat minorities, write off the inner cities and do all these things which we did the first time in the process of decline?' So I said it wasn't an issue of whether it was going to decline but rather, would we be doing damage to ourselves in the process of trying to stop it? Well, President Reagan read the first part, the 'it's going to go away' bit, but then there was no reference to the second bit.

The War on Drugs is full of cases like this. Look at the statistics for Peru's coca eradication—or Bolivia's for that matter. Or the stories of crack babies, or cocaine-induced violence. Or the teen use of crack in the mid-1980s. Or the invasion of Panama. Nothing is quite as it seems. Here's a good example, from the *Bureau of Western Hemisphere Affairs Factsheet*:

Aggressive drug crop eradication, interdiction operations, and alternative economical development programmes in Peru and Bolivia have reduced coca cultivation in those countries by 66% and 55% respectively since 1995. In large part due to successful counter-narcotics programmes in Peru and Bolivia, coca cultivation in the Andean region has shifted to guerrilla and paramilitary-controlled territory in Colombia.

16 August 2000

This is true. But it's misleading in that it says that coca has moved to Colombia because of successful eradication in Peru and Bolivia—when the truth is more likely to be that eradication in Peru and Bolivia is successful *because* the crop has moved to Colombia. Equally, it gives the impression that there has been some kind of great victory in the war on cocaine (reductions of 66 and 55 per cent—terrific!) when in fact the price and availability of cocaine on the streets of America have been stable for the last six years. According to DAWN, the Drug Abuse Warning Network, cocaine-related emergency-room incidents have more than doubled from 80,355 in 1990 to 168,763 in 1999. Meanwhile, first-time users of cocaine in the US have increased 63 per cent over the last six years. Admittedly, they are nowhere near the peak, when 10.4 million Americans tried cocaine for the first time (note that this was in 1982—not the crack hype period of the mid-1980s) and it does seem as if cocaine use in the United States has stabilised to some extent. But, as the US National Drug Control Strategy 2001 Annual Report says, 'Despite the stabilization of domestic cocaine use between 1992 and 1999, improvements in the criminal distribution and production of cocaine and crack have increased their availability in suburban and rural communities ... in 1998 there were 934,000 new users of cocaine. This number represents a 37 per cent increase from 1990, when there were 683,000 new users.' According to the Monitoring the Future study, children using cocaine are up, too—from 2.3 per cent in 1992 to 4.7 per cent for 13 year olds, 3.3 per cent to 7.7 per cent for 15 year olds and 6.1 per cent to 9.8 per cent for 17 year olds.

In the UK the news is no better. Cocaine purity has increased from an average 51 per cent in 1998 to 63 per cent in 1999. Likewise the price of a gram on the street in London has dropped over the last 8 years from over £200 to under £60. Correspondingly the number of cocaine dealers caught has gone up by a factor of five and the number of deaths 'where cocaine was mentioned on the death certificate' has gone up by nearly as much. The number of 20–24 year olds using the drug more than doubled in 1998–1999 alone. We're not doing much better than America, are we?

According to the DEA, potential world cocaine production has dropped consistently from 1996 (950 tons) to 1999 (765 tons). Fantastic! But then why are the use statistics up? Why has the price not gone up? Why is street cocaine as pure as it has been for the last six years? How has this 185-ton drop manifested itself? And why did Interpol announce in September 2000 that world consumption of cocaine had doubled in the last five years? According to a US Department of State Office of the Spokesman press statement, on 19 December 2000:

> Bolivian President Hugo Banzer is today presiding over a ceremony to mark the elimination of all significant coca in the Chapare, which was [note the tense] Bolivia's principal coca-growing region.

Funny: I was in the Chapare in December and there was still significant coca there. Why was Banzer having a party to mark its elimination? It's official! We're winning the war on cocaine! Apparently.

One of the many myths surrounding the war on cocaine is that Science will somehow find a 'cure'. *Fusarium oxysporum* is the latest candidate but there have been others. Moth larvae dropped on to coca crops, drugs to reduce cocaine craving, cocaine vaccines—all appear to offer solutions to the problem of cocaine abuse. All sound credible and are pushed by serious, reputable scientists. Yet when it comes down to it all have caveats and none delivers the goods. Although they may offer assistance, there is, and will be, no 'cure' to this problem. Magic bullets are never quite as magic as they seem, are they?

In the midst of the misinformation and hype that cocoons the War on Drugs lie equally misguided accusations that the reason we haven't won this war yet is because we don't really want to. The DEA, say detractors, could beat cocaine if it really tried—but, if it did, there would be no need for a DEA any more and everyone would be out of a job. The US Customs Service, say critics, is one of the few US state departments that actually turns a profit. And it does: the Customs Service pays for itself and then some by confiscating traffickers' assets and auctioning them off. In Los Angeles I met up with Donna Warren, the lead plaintiff in a legal action taking the CIA to court for its complicity in the Contra affair, who told me:

> I don't think they are really trying to stop it. Do you? Do you really think the people who are making millions and billions of dollars really want to stop the drug trade? Nobody in this community [South Central LA] thinks that. You don't think they can go down to Bolivia and Colombia and offer them real alternatives to replace coca in their communities? I think they can.

Donna thinks that the reason the government doesn't want to win is that drugs keep the black population compliant. Is this true? No. But there *is* some evidence that the drug war is good for the government.

Traditionally the US military has always steered clear of drugs. Following the end of the Cold War however, it faced a dilemma: how do we justify our huge budget now there are no more Commies? Suddenly the military decided that fighting drugs was a pretty neat idea, much as the CIA had following the end of the Vietnam War. The FBI was the same. But the best example of this concerns the fight to control a new antidrugs unit called the National Drug Intelligence Center in Pennsylvania. It reads like a sitcom.

Under FBI head, William Webster, it was decided that the bureau wanted to get into drug enforcement. They lobbied the White House to get themselves 'concurrent jurisdiction' together with the DEA. They got it. US Customs saw that the FBI had just become more important and lobbied for concurrent jurisdiction, too. They also got it. Now DEA, FBI and Customs were all lead players in the War on Drugs.

At this point the Bureau of Alcohol, Tax and Firearms declared itself leader in the field of 'Drugs and Gangs' and everyone from the Park Rangers to the Department of Agriculture decided there were reasons why they should receive funds to fight drugs too. The DEA, which had originally been formed to eliminate infighting between its predecessor, the BNDD, and the US Customs Service, now found itself accompanied by 35 other US agencies—all tasked with fighting the drug menace. Then the CIA decided to put themselves in charge of drug intelligence—because they were an intelligence agency (makes sense, right?). The FBI liked the sound of this and, despite the fact that it is a domestic intelligence institution, began sending agents abroad (utilising DEA slots) to conduct investigations.

Meanwhile in Pennsylvania a town called Johnstown was suffering from high unemployment. Johnstown's congressman was a Republican called Murtha. Murtha, who was a bigwig on the military funding circuit, managed to raise $40 million to establish a drugs intelligence clearing house on the condition that it was in Johnstown. Only problem was— who would run it? The US military was not allowed to do this kind of thing in peacetime. Murtha managed to keep the military funding and passed control over to the Justice Department. Now the battle began to gain control of the new centre.

The FBI wanted in. If there was to be a national drug intelligence centre, they figured that they should be running it. The DEA objected: drug intelligence was their remit. 'OK,' said the FBI, 'you run tactical and operational intelligence and we'll run strategic intelligence.' It was eventually decided that the DEA and the FBI should run the new centre together. So far so good. The centre was built, in Johnstown, just as Murtha had wanted. The only problem was that not just any Tom, Dick or Harry can work in intelligence. It turned out that there was no one in Johnstown who was qualified to work there. A large group of staff was relocated from Washington to run the new centre. Charles Gutensohn, former head of cocaine for the DEA, was one of them. He thought it was a joke:

> It was a political pork barrel. The reason it was in Johnstown was that he [Murtha] wanted jobs in his district but we spent so much money travelling, just trying to get from place to place. We had people that would drive from DC—three and a half hours—just to catch a plane someplace. And you couldn't get the people you needed, the people to handle the computers and so on. You had to import them there and pay the housing... DEA was going to expand our existing intelligence operation and we were looking for more people—and it ended up being a whole separate centre which, as far as I know, still has no real good use. It was an absolute waste.

It gets better. Because the National Drug Intelligence Center had no intelligence-collecting capability (i.e. they didn't send agents out into the field) they had to rely on all the other organisations to get it for them. But, because the other organisations were all busy stabbing each other in the back, no one was willing to give them any good stuff. Said Gutensohn:

It was an absolute boondoggle. I was there from September to January right before I retired. I had gotten into a big argument with——and I guess he thought he could exile me or something. I went up to work there and he would say, 'Well, why can't we get this to work?' and I would say, 'Well, the FBI won't provide any information and your own intelligence centre won't provide any information'. It's like, 'What do we do?'

In 2000 the National Drug Intelligence Center announced that a certain prominent Mexican family was up to its neck in drugs. The family complained to the US government and the end result was that Attorney General Janet Reno had to apologise, declaring that the US government did not actually have any faith in the Drug Intelligence Center's intelligence.

When you read about something like this you can't help but gulp. Because, while it's not true that the US government is prolonging the War on Drugs for its own ends, this sort of thing makes you realise that sometimes the War on Drugs is not really about the War on Drugs at all—but politics. What's really tragic is that 56 DEA agents have died in the line of duty in the last 30 years: people get killed playing this game. While the politicians stay at home.

Meanwhile, the media are fed—and in turn feed the public—hype about drugs. When I got back from my first trip to Mexico I found myself in the middle of a swathe of cocaine headlines. In September the *Evening Standard* ran a front-page exclusive:

YARDIES FLY IN CRACK DEALERS

Jamaican Yardie gangsters are flying in small-time dealers to fuel a major crack cocaine epidemic in the heart of the West End. Crime 'godfathers' on the island are believed to be behind a sophisticated operation in which the dealers are sent to London to push crack cocaine on the streets in and around Soho.

Evening Standard, 26 September 2000

A *Standard* billboard ran: JUDGE WEEPS OVER CRACK DEALER, 12. Crime, blacks, children, cocaine—sound familiar? It was a good summer for coke hype generally: there was the submarine—of which the *Independent* reported, 'There is little doubt that it would have carried torpedoes' (where this information came from I have no idea), and a bit earlier, in June, the country had been shocked when a photograph of the former soap star Danniella Westbrook hit the front pages. Westbrook had succeeded, at the age of just 26, in completely destroying her nasal septum with cocaine. Everywhere I went, people who knew what I was writing about asked me about it. How much coke would you have to use to get to that state? Could your nose be repaired once you did? The one thing that the story manifestly failed to do was to convince anyone that cocaine was dangerous: everyone agreed that she must have done a vast quantity in a very short period of time and that they couldn't afford that much anyway. The fact that perforated nasal septa are not the most dangerous threat of cocaine was ignored.

Not long earlier, of course, had come the revelation that Camilla Parker Bowles's son, Tom—apparently a friend of Prince William—had used cocaine. As had Prince Charles's friend Tara Palmer-Tomkinson. Then there were the sportsmen: Lawrence Dallaglio and Robbie Fowler, who was fined a substantial amount of money after he scored a goal and then celebrated by getting down on his knees and pretending to snort a line in the penalty box. Meanwhile a survey of twenty-eight lavatory cisterns in the German Reichstag revealed that twenty-two carried traces of cocaine. Message? Cocaine is a drug for rich, famous, glamorous people and it can damage your nose if you take too much. Naughty, not dangerous.

In the midst of the autumn cocaine hype a bunch of misguided politicians again attempted to play the 'drugs' card. Behind the move was the shadow Home Secretary, Ann Widdecombe. 'Drugs are the cancer that threatens our very future,' she told the Conservative Party conference in October, before assuring an adoring audience: 'Zero tolerance of the biggest scourge of our society today—that's what's going to happen on my watch!' Her new policy announced the introduction of on-the-spot fines for cannabis possession, with repeat offenders going to court—for possession of even 'the smallest amount'. This sort of hard talk gained her a standing ovation. The party leader, William Hague, joined the fray, telling Channel 4 News, 'We are leading the way. At the moment efforts made to fight the drugs menace have been ineffective. So are we going to surrender or are we going to intensify the battle? I think we ought to intensify the battle.'

The images are always the same, aren't they? Widdecombe calls her period of office 'my watch', a specifically military term. Hague in turn refers to 'intensifying the battle'. This is all standard war on drugs stuff: the military images, the idea that fighting harder will solve the problem (at one point in the US, New York mayor Ed Koch suggested that the cocaine problem could be solved if the US bombed Medellín). Even the cancer image leads to notions of surgical intervention, as if anything in the War on Drugs so far has been surgical or even scientific. But it's good tub-thumping rhetoric: 'Surrender to the drugs menace?' crooned Widdecombe. 'We couldn't do that. We shouldn't do that. We won't do that.' Don't you just love it when politicians talk in threes?

When we met in Harvard, historian David Musto had drawn a good analogy concerning drug use and legislation:

> I call it the parental quandary. If your child comes to you and says, 'Can I try a line of cocaine—just once?' you first of all wish the child had never brought it up and [your response is] silence. And you are strongly tempted to exaggerate the danger. And if that doesn't work you might threaten bodily harm. And so you have it. The policies that we adopted in the 1930s were very parental. They were: (1) 'I don't want to hear about it'; (2) 'It will do something terrible to you if you try it'; (3) '*We'll* do something terrible to you if you try it.'

Currently we are stuck on Option 3: 'We'll do something terrible to you if you try it'. Because the harsher the penalties, the more likely it seems that people will be discouraged from trying it. Unfortunately for the Conservatives this time the hard line backfired, as police and community leaders railed against the plan. Even the *Daily Telegraph*, staunchly right wing, came out against the new policy, running a cartoon of Widdecombe floating in space with the caption 'Earth to Ann Widdecombe' and an editorial announcing that this 'zero tolerance' policy displayed 'zero common sense': 50,000 people were cautioned by the police for cannabis possession every year while a quarter of the adult population and half of all 16–29-year-olds had tried the drug. The way she was going, they would all end up with criminal records. How much would this cost? When it was pointed out that Widdecombe's proposal would have criminalised seven members of the Shadow Cabinet the policy was dropped.

Unfortunately, fed on a diet of sensation and propaganda, the public tends to vote for politicians who make increasingly strident speeches to prove how much they hate crime and love their country. The politicians then get into office and pass tough antidrugs policies that don't really achieve much in the long term but lead to impressive arrest and interdiction statistics, which are in turn fed to the press and...it just goes on and on. This combination of press and political hype tends to ensure that, while most people have heard a great deal of gossip about cocaine, they don't actually know much about it at all. So what's really going on? For anyone who is confused, here are some facts.

At the root of the cocaine problem lies the fact that people take drugs to mess with their brains because it's *fun*. Alcohol, nicotine, caffeine, marijuana, Ecstasy, cocaine: all drugs with specific neurological effects that people find pleasurable. This is not a new trait. As Aldous Huxley wrote:

> Everywhere and at all times, men and women have sought, and duly found, the means of taking a holiday from the reality of their generally dull and often acutely unpleasant existence. A holiday out of space, out of time, in the eternity of sleep or ecstasy, in the heaven or the limbo of visionary fantasy.
>
> *A Treatise on Drugs*, 1931

It's true: people like drugs. You can smoke cigarettes, live on espressos, shove down a couple of large whiskies or get jiggy with the oysters and champagne, but the end result is the same: you're taking drugs. People have always done this and probably always will. As Ricky Ross had told me when we met in San Diego: 'The money was so plentiful that there were [crack] houses in every neighbourhood. Some neighbourhoods had four or five. And you still can't get enough drugs. There's a drug craze in the United States! They can't get enough drugs! They want to be high—and they're *gonna* be high. And somebody's going to sell it to them.'

The problem is that, as man has advanced, so we have understood the nature of drugs better and managed to purify them. A couple of thousand years ago very few people drank themselves to death because no one knew how to distil alcohol and the weak brews they made were not really strong enough to kill anything. Today, however, 100-per-cent-proof alcohols of every flavour and colour are available, making it easy to drink yourself into oblivion. It's the same with almost everything we eat or drink. It's pretty hard to get overweight eating fruit or chewing sugar cane. Once the sugar has been refined, however, it will lead to obesity just as fast as you can shovel it down your gullet. Science has spent centuries distilling and purifying consumer products to enable us to wring the maximum amount of pleasure out of them, ways of giving us more, faster and more efficiently. It's the same with coca and cocaine. There is nothing dangerous about coca, chewed or in tea. The dose of cocaine in the leaf is so low that it's harmless. But, when you get into isolating the cocaine from the leaf and shoving it up your nose or into your veins, that's when the problems start. As people got better at getting high even cocaine was improved upon. In the search for bigger highs they began freebasing because the rush was even more intense. This in turn cranked up the danger level again.

So here's the first truth about cocaine: it's fun. And because it's fun people want to use it.

The second truth about cocaine is that it is not some evil spawn of Satan but simply a commodity. Admittedly, an illegal commodity but a commodity nevertheless. If you want to stop the trade in this commodity you have to find out what it is that drives the market. And what drives the cocaine market—as with any other market—is supply and demand.

I decided to see if it was possible to break the chain of supply and demand, but to do this I needed to find an economist. I looked on the Internet to locate a suitable candidate. One immediately presented himself:

MILTON FRIEDMAN ROCKS

Milton Friedman is the best economist ever. Milton Friedman won the Nobel Prize in 1976 for being the greatest economist ever to walk on the face of the earth. He is famous for disproving every word Lord Maynard Keynes ever said. He was an economic adviser to Ronald Reagan, Richard Nixon and Barry Goldwater ... He's up there with Thomas Jefferson. Milton Friedman is hard-core.

http://pw1.netcom.com/~garrrete/politics/friedman.html

Another website informed me that Friedman had won the Nobel Prize in 1976 'for his achievements in the field of consumption analysis, monetary history and theory and for his demonstration of the complexity of stabilisation policy'. I had no idea what this meant but it sounded impressive. At the bottom of the page was the news that a choir in Stock-

holm had named itself after him. That was all I needed to know. Friedman, clearly, was hard-core. I gave him a call and he was most friendly.
First off, I wanted to know if cocaine was in any way different from any
other commodity such as bread because of the fact that it was illegal:

No different whatsoever...For bread the sources of demand are consumers and the sources of supply are bakeries. For cocaine the sources of
demand are users who want to use cocaine. Suppliers are the people who
produce cocaine and manufacture it into drugs and are willing to provide
it to the buyers. The fundamental principle is the same...so it will behave
like any other commodity on the market.

I asked him who the suppliers were, and why they were doing it.

To make money. Why are you writing a book? These are people who want
to make money and this is the easiest way they could make money...and as
long as there are enormous profits to be made from dealing drugs, unless
you use really draconian measures, you're not going to stop them...Take a
place like Saudi Arabia, where the penalty for selling drugs is having your
arm cut off. I'm sure the price of cocaine is very high in Saudi Arabia
because very few people are willing to go into the business. But the fact of
the matter is that, so far as the other major countries like the United States
are concerned, they are not willing to go to that extreme.

I put it to Friedman that former President Gaviria of Colombia said
that American demand was the engine of the cocaine problem—not
Colombian supply.

He's absolutely right. What seems to me to be most immoral about drug
prohibition in the United States is that we impose in places like Colombia
the loss of thousands of lives because we cannot enforce our own laws.
Our laws make it illegal for people to consume cocaine. If we could
enforce those laws there would be no demand for cocaine.

So how do you go about getting rid of demand?

I do not think it is possible to eradicate demand. And after all, we've
had a lot of experience. The attempt to eradicate demand—there has

been an attempt to eradicate demand for years. Expenditures on drug prohibition have gone up steadily over time... The lesson we have failed to learn is that prohibition never works. It makes things worse rather than better.

These views agreed almost entirely with those of every drug trafficker I had interviewed. Jorge Ochoa had echoed Friedman when I asked him what effect law-enforcement efforts had on business: 'It drives the price up!' Crack dealer 'Freeway' Ricky Ross had a good take on the effect of law enforcement on supply and demand:

The first thing they do when they get more police is they gonna lock more people up, take 'em off the streets. But guess what happens with cocaine? It becomes harder to find. When it gets harder to find, guess what happens? Price goes up. Price goes up and guess what happens then? More people want to get involved: 'Oh, twenty thousand dollars a chance, huh? Was only five thousand yesterday. You got me now! I'm gonna take that chance!' So now it's back to the same thing, and the price goes down and you've got all these people and the police arrest them again and it's just going to keep on escalating... Like they say in LA, as soon as they take a guy off the corner there's another guy standing back just waiting to take over.

In 2000 the US prison population hit 2,000,000: the highest of any country in the world, including China. Five hundred thousand of these people were in for drugs offences. Back in Otisville, George Jung recalled, in his own inimitable way, what this meant:

We got fucking courts and prosecutors and fucking probation officers and— fucking armies of them! MCC San Diego, MCC New York, fucking five, ten thousand people all waiting to go to court and fucking buses and vans and trains and planes and airlifts and fucking—You ever seen 'Oklahoma'? It's like some kind of George Orwell trip. It's nuts! Moving people all over the country because they don't have a place to keep them. They just keep them in transit until they find somewhere with a bed for them. Federal Express trucks come here all day long, shipping cardboard boxes with people's toothbrushes and sneakers and fucking radios and shit. Man! And all day long this shit goes on:

boxes going in, boxes going out. How much do you think that fucking costs? All this stuff? They just ship it. FedEx. Fuck it. Who cares?

OK, you might think, traffickers are bound to disagree with current legalisation—after all, that's what put them in jail. But the problem, as Milton Friedman says, is that if there is a demand there will always be a supply. Currently the demand is so great that people are willing to take all the risks, health and legal, and pay £60 per gram to get this stuff even when it's adulterated by 50 per cent. When you have a situation like this supply is inevitable. Perhaps Bolivia is doing good work in the field of coca eradication and perhaps so is Peru. But there is the problem with Colombia. Give Colombia $1.3 billion. Then what happens?

There is a theory in drug interdiction called the Balloon Theory. Imagine a long thin balloon, half full of air and tied at one end. Try to squeeze the air out of it. Wherever you squeeze, the air will just bulge out somewhere else. Cocaine is like that. Push Peru, the bulge hits Bolivia. Push Bolivia and the crop moves to Colombia. Squeeze Colombia and it moves on again. Ninety-nine per cent of all land suitable for coca cultivation in the Andes is not being used for coca cultivation: there are a lot of places this drug can go. And let's suppose that the cocaine trade in South America were to fall apart completely. Coca has been grown commercially in India, Malaysia, Africa, Indonesia, Taiwan...

Not so long ago the first Thai coca showed up. At DEA headquarters in Washington, I asked about this and my expert laughed: it had contained 'a gnat's ass' of cocaine, he said, the implication being that therefore this did not represent a threat. But the fact that it was merely a 'gnat's ass' seemed unimportant; if coca had got there, there had to be a way to get more productive strains there. Already, it seems, the balloon is beginning to bulge somewhere else.

The only real solution is the legislation that dare not speak its name: legalisation. Ricky Ross figured that it was the only way out:

Some way they've got to take the value out. They got to make it so it's not worth so much money... Cocaine should be no more valuable than a bale of hay 'cos it don't cost nothing to grow and it don't cost nothing to process. But there's this artificial value that we place on it. We used to say that it was more valuable than gold. But it *becomes* valuable because of the value that we put on it, not because of what it's really worth. Like that tape recorder is valuable because of what it does, but cocaine is only valuable because of what society has put on it—so we have to take the value off it. Putting people in jail ain't the key because when you put people in jail that makes it more valuable—that's the number-one way of making it valuable! So eventually they're going to have to decriminalise it in some way because as long as it's criminal and the money is there, a kilo of cocaine at ten, fifteen, twenty thousand dollars, somebody is going to take that chance. And, as the price goes up, more people are going to be willing to take that chance.

George Jung agreed:

Legalise it. But educate people. Not just advertisements on TV. Education is the name of the game for this thing. It's idiotic. Somebody doesn't want it to happen. When you have the most intelligent people in the world saying 'do it' and they don't—why? Tell me why? A thirty-year war on drugs. What kind of fucking lunacy is that? The War on Drugs made drugs into a gigantic fucking monster.

Are we anywhere near legalisation? The Ochoas thought it was coming but they were the only ones. I asked Friedman if he thought cocaine would ever be legalised. 'Not in the foreseeable future,' he said. Until then we will continue to invest billions of dollars trying to stop a trade that is, in reality, unstoppable. In the last fifteen years America has spent over $300 billion—three times what it cost to put man on the moon—on stopping drugs entering the country. Last year alone the US federal drug budget was $18.8 billion, nearly four times what it was in the heyday of crack. Total US spending was $40 billion. 'It would be hard,' writes Michael Massing, author of *The Fix*, 'to think of an area of US social policy that has failed more completely than the War on Drugs.' Dan Baum, author of *Smoke and Mirrors*, writes: 'For sheer government absurdity, America's war on drugs is hard to beat.' He goes on:

After three decades of increasingly punitive policies, illicit drugs are more easily available, drug potencies are greater, and drug barons are richer than ever. The War on Drugs costs more than the Commerce, Interior and State departments combined—and a strangled court system, exploding prisons, and wasted lives push the cost beyond measure...costly, destructive and failing in its stated mission, the war on drugs is government lunacy...Yet we soldier on, speaking the language of war, writing the budgets of war, carrying the weapons of war, and suffering the casualties of war.

Smoke and Mirrors, 1996

Legalisation appears to be no nearer. In 1999 Washington DC voted on the issue of decriminalising marijuana for medical use. No sooner had the votes been counted, however, than the ballots were impounded and the result classified. 'Why?' asked the voters—but there was no answer. Some months later, when a professor of law petitioned to have the results declassified, they found out. It turned out that 60 per cent of the nation's capital had voted to decriminalise—but that the bureaucrats who counted the votes didn't want anyone to know about it. This is not the first time this sort of thing has happened. In March 1995 the World Health Organisation and the United Nations Crime and Justice Research Institute released the results of a global cocaine study. The study's press release contained the following contentious results:

- Generally cocaine users consume a range of other drugs as well. There appears to be very little 'pure' cocaine use. Overall, fewer people in participating countries have used cocaine than have used alcohol, tobacco or cannabis. Also, in most countries, cocaine is not the drug associated with the greatest problems.
- Responses to cocaine related health problems are poorly co-ordinated, inconsistent, often culturally inappropriate and generally ineffective.
- In many settings, educational and prevention programmes generally do not dispel myths but sensationalise, perpetuate stereotyping and misinformation.
- In most settings, people who have enough money to pay for cocaine—and who are familiar with a supplier—are able to obtain the drug despite its illegality.

The press pack for the WHO/UNCJRI Cocaine Project reported that it was the 'largest study on cocaine ever undertaken'. But it did not receive an appreciative reception. It was not, it seems, quite hard enough on the drug. At the 48th World Health Assembly in May, the US delegate, a Mr

Boyer, brought up the subject of this WHO report. The United States'
government, he said, had been

> surprised to note that the package seemed to make a case for the positive
> use of cocaine, claiming that the use of coca leaf did not lead to noticeable
> damage to mental or physical health, that the positive health effects of
> coca leaf chewing might be transferable from traditional settings to other
> countries and cultures, and that coca production provided financial bene-
> fits to peasants . . .

Meanwhile the Americans:

> took the view that the study on cocaine, evidence of WHO's support for
> harm-reduction programmes and previous WHO association with organi-
> sations that support the legalisation of drugs, indicated that its programme
> on substance abuse was headed in the wrong direction.

Then there was a thinly veiled threat:

> The United States government considered that, if WHO activities relating
> to drugs failed to reinforce proven drug-control approaches, funds for the
> relevant programmes should be curtailed.

Uh-oh. No more money. The WHO began back-pedalling. The report,
it said,

> Represented the views of the experts, and did not represent the stated
> policy position of WHO, and WHO's continuing policy, which was to
> uphold the scheduling under the convention. Consequently, WHO was
> making its position clear, and because of the wording of the study, which
> could lead to misunderstanding, it was now not the Organisation's pres-
> ent intention to publish the report as such. It would be looking into the
> matter carefully.

Mr Boyer took issue with the characterisation of the study as an
important and objective analysis. The way he saw it, the report was 'not
in conformity with WHO's basic and rigorous standards of analysis' and
there should be some sort of enquiry.

The WHO agreed.

Some members of the DEA admit that this is a battle we are not winning. Richard Hahner, who has served 29 years in drug enforcement, told me a story of a colleague's retirement party, when he found his friend sitting alone at a table with tears in his eyes. 'You know,' he was told, 'I've been in this for twenty years and I don't know if things are better now than they were when I started.' Hahner concluded that, 'Enforcement is not going to solve this problem. Period. I can keep putting people in jail until I'm ninety and I'll be the guy sitting at the table with tears in my eyes saying, "It's no better than it was before." '[12]

The Economist agrees. As the journal concluded in a scathing piece about Plan Colombia:

> Latin Americans pay a high price for the drugs trade: it corrupts their societies from top to bottom. If this price is ever to be reduced, Americans will have to look not just at the supply but also at the demand for drugs. This means they will have to consider alternative policies at home, even at decriminalisation. This is a war that will not be won with helicopters.
>
> 'A Muddle in the Jungle', *Economist*, 4 March 2000

Perhaps, however, there is another way out: time. David Musto told me,

> There are two ways of looking at drug use. One is that there is a steady demand amongst some people for drug use and you are going to have this steady demand no matter what. The other one is that you have big swings of drug use and, if you do the right things, these swings will go down. And these are incompatible positions. My studies have indicated that drug use does go down, that it is cyclical. Doesn't necessarily disappear but it comes down to a very low level...All my research indicates that the decline of drug use is very gradual. Even when it's going away it's very gradual, so you can hardly tell. You have to look over a three- to five-year period to see it's gone down. And if you take the length of the first cocaine epidemic as

---

[12] Before this book went to print I contacted Hahner again to let him know that I was planning to use this quote in case he felt that I was misrepresenting him. He replied, by email, immediately: 'I retired from DEA and government on 12.30.2000. My feelings and thoughts remain the same: there has to be a better way. We were and are valiant warriors in a battle that needs new strategies.' In the last ten years 19 DEA agents have been killed in the line of duty. I defy you to disagree with him.

a standard—I don't know if you should, but if you did—and try to apply it—you have forty-five years. And if you add forty-five years to 1970, it's 2015. So we have a way to go if we use the past as a guide.

Perhaps cocaine will fizzle out in the year 2015 the way it did in the early twentieth century. It deserves to. Seventy-seven years ago Louis Lewin wrote:

During recent years I have seen among men of science frightful symptoms due to the craving for cocaine. Those who believe they can enter the temple of happiness through the gate of pleasure purchase their momentary delights at the cost of body and soul. They speedily pass through the gate of unhappiness into the night of the abyss.

Phantastica, 1924

George Jung agreed. Only less poetically:

You need more to get up—when you're coming down, you need more to get up. I had a heart attack from it. It rips your system to pieces. It'll destroy your liver. It will destroy you. If it doesn't drive you nuts it'll kill you physically. It's really dangerous. Fucking evil.

Where is this drug going? Who can tell? Perhaps the only way to gain an idea is to look at where it's been. Unfortunately, we tend not to be very good at doing that. David Musto told me:

You know, I've been doing this now for thirty-three years, a historian of drugs, and I have no real sense that it has made much of a difference to anyone. I'd like to think it did but it didn't...I've discovered that people are interested in the history of things only after things haven't gone right. When they feel that they have caught the wave of the future they have no interest in history whatsoever. In fact history is very irritating because it tugs at their sleeves saying, 'You may be mistaken. Let's not go overboard.' It kind of ruins the party. But once the movement runs into difficulty then the public begins to ask: 'How did we get here? Why did we take this path?'

Perhaps the lesson to learn from history is that we should learn more lessons from history. Of course, while we are learning this lesson,

George, Ricky, Fabio, Meco, Edwin and Beatriz remain in prison. We chuck vast amounts of money at a problem that will not be solved with money, and law-enforcement agencies take casualties. And the crops in San Jorge are still failing.

In the two years I spent researching this book I travelled for three months in Peru, America, Mexico, the Bahamas, Bolivia and Colombia. As I came to the end of my travels in Peru I took an afternoon off. It was justifiable, I figured: I was tired. Besides, a cloud of mosquitoes had mangled my legs and the *palmito* salad I had eaten the night before had passed through my system like an Exocet, compelling me to spend a large part of the day perched on the lavatory. It was a beautiful afternoon. The sun was about to go down, and I had yet to check out the hammock at the end of the veranda. I eased myself in, slipped on a pair of headphones, plugged into a bit of music, turned up the volume and decided to try the coca again. I folded up a wad of leaves, added a small amount of *llipta* and stuffed it into my cheek. Nothing happened. Perhaps there was nothing in this chewing thing after all? But could forty centuries of South American Indians really be wrong?

I lay in the hammock thinking back over the last couple of years. Two years, dedicated entirely to cocaine. Freud, Coca-Cola, the Ochoas, Simon Trinidad and FARC, Ricky Ross, George Jung, William Golden Mortimer, The Contras, Magic Eddie, Kew Gardens. The girl in seat 2242. Those green plastic ties that people use to hold back their climbing creepers. At some point I was going to have to try to make sense of all this.

I was sitting in the hammock mulling all this over when, all of a sudden, something extraordinary happened. I grabbed my notepad and started to write:

It's going on 4.30pm and the alkaloid has just begun to bite...

Select Bibliography

If you are interested in learning more about coca and cocaine I would recommend:

Cocaine: from Medical Marvel to Modern Menace in the United States—Joseph Spillane, 2000
Cocaine Global Histories—Paul Gootenberg (ed), 1999
Dope Girls, the Birth of the British Drug Underground—Marek Kohn
Coca Exotica—Kennedy, 1985
Mama Coca—Anthony Henman/Santonil
Cocaine, its History, Uses and Effects—Richard Ashley, 1975
Cocaine: a Drug and its Social Evolution—Grinspoon and Bakalar
The Freudian Fallacy: Freud and Cocaine—EM Thornton
Snowblind: a Brief Career in the Cocaine Trade—Robert Sabbag, 1976
The Fruit Palace—Charles Nichol, 1985
Blow: How a Small-town Boy Made 100 million with the Medellin Cocaine Cartel and Lost it All—Bruce Porter, 1993
Kings of Cocaine—Guy Gugliotta and Jeff Leen, 1989
Snowfields—the War on Cocaine in the Andes—Clare Hargreaves, 1992
The Cocaine Wars—Paul Eddy, Hugo Sabogal and Sara Walden, 1988
Whitewash: Pablo Escobar and the Cocaine Wars—Simon Strong, 1995
The Man Who Made it Snow—Max Mermelstein, 1990
Drug Lord: the Life and Death of a Mexican Kingpin—Terence Poppa, 1998
Dark Alliance: the CIA, the Contras and the Crack Cocaine Explosion—Gary Webb, 1998
Lost History: Contras, Cocaine, the Press and Project Truth—Robert Parry, 1999
Women and Crack Cocaine—Inciardi, Lockwood and Pottieger
The Fit—Michael Massing, 1998

Smoke and Mirrors: the War on Drugs and the Politics of Failure—Dan
  Baum, 1996
The American Disease: Origins of Narcotic Control—David Musto, 1973
**Desperados: Latin Drug Lords, US Lawmen and the War America
  Can't Win**—Elaine Shannon, 1988

Of course no cocaine bibliography would be complete without a mention
of William Golden Mortimer's epic, **Peru—History of Coca: 'the Divine
Plant' of the Incas** (1901). Approach with caution!

For those of you into vicarious thrills, it is possible to make contact with
genuine Colombia traffickers at the Extraditables' web site: www.extra-
dition.org.

In September 2001, Fabio Ochoa, youngest of the three Ochoa brothers,
was finally extradited to the United States. Those interested in following
his long campaign for liberty can follow it up at www.fabioochoa.com.

Index